ANCESTRAL ROOTS OF
CERTAIN AMERICAN COLONISTS
Who Came to America before 1700

*Lineages from Alfred the Great, Charlemagne,
Malcolm of Scotland, Robert the Strong,
and other Historical Individuals*

CREATED by
FREDERICK LEWIS WEIS

CONTINUED by
WALTER LEE SHEPPARD, JR.

EIGHTH EDITION

Edited with Additions and Corrections by

WILLIAM R. BEALL

and

KALEEN E. BEALL

GENEALOGICAL PUBLISHING Co., Inc.

First Edition: Lancaster, MA, 1950
Second Edition: Lancaster, MA, 1951
Supplement to Ancestral Roots: Dublin, NH, 1952
Additions and Corrections: Peterborough, NH, 1956
Third Edition: Baltimore, 1964
Fourth Edition: Baltimore, 1969
Fifth Edition: Baltimore, 1976, 1979, 1982, 1985
Sixth Edition: Baltimore, 1988, 1990
Seventh Edition: Baltimore, 1992, 1993, 1995
Eighth Edition: Baltimore, 2004, 2006, 2008

Copyright © 1964, 1969, 1976, 1988, 1992
Genealogical Publishing Company
3600 Clipper Mill Rd., Suite 260
Baltimore, MD 21211-1953

Eighth Edition Copyright © 2004
by William R. Beall and Kaleen E. Beall
All Rights Reserved.
No part of this publication may be reproduced,
in any form or by any means, including electronic
reproduction or reproduction via the Internet,
except by permission of the authors.

Library of Congress Catalogue Card Number 2004108965
ISBN 978-0-8063-1752-6
Made in the United States of America

Dedicated to
Milton Rubincam, Herbert F. Seversmith
and John I. Coddington,
who started us in genealogy,
and especially to
Walter Lee Sheppard, Jr.,
who had faith in our ability to continue this work

TABLE OF CONTENTS

In Memoriam -- Frederick Lewis Weis... vi

In Memoriam -- Walter Lee Sheppard, Jr.. vii

Preface to the Eighth Edition.. viii

Preface to the Previous Edition... ix

Lines of Immigrants Discussed in This Volume... xi

List of References and Their Abbreviations.. xiii

Genealogical Terms and Their Abbreviations... xix

Ancestral Lines.. 1

Name Index... 267

IN MEMORIAM

Frederick Lewis Weis, Th.D., F.A.S.G.

Frederick Lewis Weis died 11 April 1966, in Brattleboro, Vt., after a long illness. He was born 22 August 1895, in Cranston, R.I., the son of John Peter Carl and Georgina (Lewis) Weis. He was survived by his wife, the former Elizabeth Williams Stone, a son, and a daughter. Dr. Weis attended Kimball Union Academy, Meriden, N.H., then moved to Hope Street High School and School of Design, Providence, R.I. He completed his secondary education at Wilmer and Chew's Preparatory School, Annapolis, Md., from which he was appointed to the United States Naval Academy. He graduated and was commissioned Ensign, U.S.N., 29 March 1917. He was assigned as Assistant Engineer Officer of the U.S.S. North Dakota and was promoted to Lieutenant (j.g.) on 1 July of the same year. Dr. Weis left the Navy to attend the Meadville Theological School, from which he graduated B.D. in 1922, and was Cruft Fellow at the University of Strasbourg, France, 1922-24. He was ordained minister of the Third Religious Society of Dorchester, Mass., 9 November 1924, and served there until 1929. During his incumbency he received his S.T.M. from Meadville Theological School. He received the degree of Doctor of Theology from the University of Strasbourg in 1930 and was installed as the twelfth minister of the First Church of Christ (Unitarian) of Lancaster, Mass., from which office he retired 28 October 1951. After retirement he made his home in Dublin, N.H. In 1957 Dr. Weis was elected a Fellow of the American Society of Genealogists.

Dr. Weis was the founder of the Society of the Descendants of the Colonial Clergy in 1930. He was Historian General and Editor of Publications for that society for thirty-three years. Among their publications (of which he was also the author) are the useful *Colonial Clergy of New England* (1936), *Colonial Clergy of Maryland, Delaware, and Georgia* (1950), *Colonial Clergy of Virginia, North Carolina, and South Carolina* (1955), and *Colonial Clergy of the Middle Colonies: New York, New Jersey, and Pennsylvania* (1957).

Dr. Weis was a member of more than fifty societies, for many of which he did historical studies. Author of numerous genealogical articles, he is perhaps best known for his *Ancestral Roots of Sixty Colonists* and for his *Magna Charta Sureties*. He compiled many manuscript genealogies, noteworthy being his "Phipps Genealogy" (1929-38) and "Genealogies of the Templeton Family" (1930) (1,000 pages) at the Narragansett Historical Society. He was deeply interested in church history, and made many contributions to the study of colonial congregations and their membership.

The bulk of his manuscripts, historical and genealogical, have been placed in the Library of the American Antiquarian Society, Worcester, Mass. His printed works, and additional manuscripts (including second copies of many of the items at Worcester), are in the Library of the New England Historic Genealogical Society, Boston, Mass. Earlier works will often be found in local repositories.

Walter Lee Sheppard, Jr.

IN MEMORIAM

Walter Lee Sheppard, Jr., FASG

Walter Lee Sheppard, Jr. died 6 September 2000, in Bryn Mawr, Pennsylvania. He had made his home in nearby Havertown for many years. He was born in Philadelphia, 23 June 1911, to Walter Lee Sheppard and Martha Houston (Evans) Sheppard. He received a Bachelor of Chemistry from the University of Pennsylvania in 1933. He was a member of Phi Kappa Psi national fraternity and Alpha Chi Sigma professional chemical fraternity. He was a professional engineer until his retirement in 1976, although he continued as a consultant.

He was married twice: first, from 1942 to 1947, to Dorothy Virginia (Cosby) Vanderslice; and second, from 1953 until her death in 1996, to Boudinot Atterbury (Oberge) Kendall.

His military career extended from 1932, when he became a reserve officer, through active duty from 1941 through 1945, and service with UNRRA after the war, until his retirement as a Lieutenant Colonel in 1950.

His interest in genealogy started early, and his first published article appeared in *TAG* in 1938. He continued to write and had more than 80 articles published in such major journals as *The American Genealogist, Genealogists' Magazine* (London), *New England Historical and Genealogical Register, National Genealogical Society Quarterly, The Genealogist, The Genealogical Journal, The New York Genealogical and Biographical Record,* and the *Pennsylvania Genealogical Magazine.*

He also published or edited a number of books, including books on the Evans and Fifield families; *The Ancestry of Edward Carlton and Ellen Newton, His Wife*; *Passengers and Ships Prior to 1684* (Welcome Society of PA); and from 1966 until his death, *Ancestral Roots of Certain American Colonists* and *Magna Charta Sureties, 1215.*

He was the founder of the Descendants of the Illegitimate Sons and Daughters of the Kings of Britain, one of the founders of Flagon and Trencher, a society of descendants of colonial tavern keepers, and the last of the original 50 Fellows of the American Society of Genealogists.

Among his other interests were Gilbert and Sullivan operettas and silent movies.

William R. Beall

PREFACE

to the Eighth Edition

As the fiftieth anniversary of *Ancestral Roots* was approaching, we were working with Lee on the fifth edition of *Magna Charta Sureties, 1215*. He commented that age was catching up to him, and he wanted someone he could count on to continue these publications. He was deeply concerned that the two books be continued in the same tradition that he had kept alive in Dr. Weis' honor, and we agreed with him. We were all aware, however, that it was time to extensively revise and update *Ancestral Roots*.

Therefore, over the last three years, as time permitted, we checked and verified all previously published Lines. As a result, 91 Lines have been extensively revised, although nearly every Line has had some minor corrections. A few Lines have been eliminated. We have added 60 new Lines of ascent, principally continental European ones. For this edition, we have not attempted to add significantly to the immigrant lines. The ancestry of many immigrants is being explored in contemporary journals. Some of these lines will connect to ones in this book.

Although there are only 275 Line numbers, there are actually 398 Lines. As in previous editions, we have used A, B. C., etc. to locate related lines next to each other where possible. It is noted at the beginning of a Line number if it has been revised. New Lines are also indicated. In addition, we have replaced the previous index with a new every-name index to make your search easier.

While we have checked every source available to us, there were some we were not able to locate. Many additional references have been used for this edition. The bibliography has been greatly expanded to include most citations used. This is an on-going project and, as much as we would like it to be, it is still not perfect. Please inform us of any errors or additions, and include detailed references.

This book should not be quoted as a primary source. One should go to the book or article noted, and to the sources indicated therein to verify the information.

We wish to acknowledge the kindness and generosity of the many people who have helped us. In particular, we would like to thank David E. Kelley, Norman W. Ingham, Don C. Stone, Dereka Smith, Ruth C. Bishop, James E. O'Dea, Lindsay Brook, Neil Thompson, and our son, Robert E. Beall.

William R. Beall
Kaleen E. Beall
PO Box 33918
Portland, OR 97292-2918

PREFACE

to the Previous Edition

It is certainly paradoxical that Dr. Weis should be best known for his *Ancestral Roots of Sixty Colonists*, the *Supplement* to it, and his *Magna Charta Sureties, 1215*. His reputation as a genealogist rests on a firm foundation of colonial studies (unfortunately mostly in manuscript) and his four books on the colonial clergy. He turned to compiling pre-colonial lineages for publications in the late 1940s, after he had become ill and was less able to travel, and had to rely more and more heavily on material sent to him by correspondents whom he trusted -- material that he did not or could not verify due to illness or unavailability of cited material.

The first edition of *Ancestral Roots*, in 1950, being his first effort in this type of compilation, contained many errors, and the year following Dr. Weis produced a second edition embodying a vast number of corrections. In the next year he brought out his *Supplement*. Unfortunately, only fifty copies of the second edition were printed, and the supply was quickly exhausted. The *Magna Charta Sureties* was published in 1955, and in the following year he published a sixteen-page *Additions and Corrections* covering such material as he had collected up to this time on all three volumes. Unfortunately, some of these *Additions and Corrections* also contained errors, and many were without cited evidences. Cross citations in a few cases made corrections in *Ancestral Roots* by reference in *Magna Charta*, so that the reader had to have both books to correct one. A further set of corrections for *The Magna Charta Sureties* was issued in 1957.

When supplies of Dr. Weis' original editions were exhausted, the Genealogical Publishing Co. decided to reprint them. Dr. and Mrs. Weis asked me to see what I could do to bring together as many of the known corrections as possible, and to try to make the books more accurate. Unfortunately, there was little time to do this, but I did what I could with corrections I had already noted and those sent to me by others <u>with cited evidence</u> which I could verify. Though some readers and reviewers have persisted in the belief that I was the editor of the third edition of *Ancestral Roots*, I had specifically disavowed responsibility for any of the material on which I had not myself worked. I did not see proofs of this reprinting prior to publication.

The 1964 edition (third for *Ancestral Roots*, second for the *Supplement*) was, in fact, merely a reprinting of the first edition, combined with the text of the Supplement, followed by the Errata page from the first edition, and then by the 1956 *Additions and Corrections*, just as these items were originally printed. The work includes a curious typographical error in the *Additions and Corrections*, where part of the last page was transferred in mid-sentence to the preceding page and grafted onto its text. My own typed corrections, having been received by the publisher after the book was in progress, were separately printed from a typed copy of my text, embodying a few typographical errors, and added to the copies as a slip-in. In the present edition, as in the sixth, all footnotes and corrections in earlier editions have been incorporated in the text, more recently discovered errors have been corrected, and many new lines added.

I want to make it absolutely clear to reviewer and public once more that I am not fulfilling the function of a true editor in this edition either. A true editor should verify all material offered. This I have not done, nor could I ever find time to do it. I have not checked the lines that I have not used. Where I have had occasion to use a line, I have verified those generations on which I worked. Some of the errors here corrected have been of long standing, and will be found in books long considered reliable, as well as in Wurts or Browning. Every one of my many correspondents has been asked to check anything he or she uses and to advise me of any errors found, <u>with cited evidence</u>, All these I have checked.

I have especially to thank Douglas Richardson, David Humiston Kelley, Milton Rubincam, John G. Hunt, Gary Boyd Roberts, and the late George Andrews Moriarty, Walter Goodwin Davis, John Insley Coddington, and Paul Prindle for extensive comments. Those others who have furnished data are too numerous to mention individually, but all have my gratitude; and when a new line has been included, if it is not one which I have myself prepared, I have identified the author.

Those interested in additional royal lines may wish to note the series of articles by me in the *New England Historical and Genealogical Register* on the illegitimate British royal children. The first article covering the period William I - Edward III appeared in volume 119, pages 94-102. Some corrections and additions to this appeared in volume 120, page 230, and in volume 121, pages 232-234. The second article, covering the period from Edward III through the end of the Stuart dynasty appeared in volume 121, pages 185-191. A third portion, covering the early Scots to James VI of Scotland and I of England, is in volume 122, p. 265. See also some notes and corrections published in that magazine.

Walter Lee Sheppard, Jr.

LINES OF IMMIGRANTS DISCUSSED IN THIS VOLUME

Herbert Pelham   Line 1
Nathaniel Littleton   Line 1A
Edward Carleton   Line 2
Maj. Richard Saltonstall   Line 3
Muriel Gurdon m. Richard Saltonstall   Line 4
Capt. Francis Champernoun   Line 6
Grace Chetwode m. Rev. Peter Bulkeley   Line 7
Capt. Jeremy Clark   Line 11
Gov. Roger Ludlow   Line 12
Sarah Ludlow m. Col. John Carter of Va.   Line 12
Mary Launce m. Rev. John Sherman   Line 13
Anne Marbury m. William Hutchinson   Line 14
Catherine Marbury m. Richard Scott   Line 14
Dr. Richard Palgrave   Line 15
James Claypoole   Line 15A
Elizabeth Marshall m. Thomas Lewis   Line 17
Govs. Francis and John West   Line 18
Rev. Peter Bulkeley   Line 31
Martha Bulkeley m. Abraham Mellowes   Line 31A
Frances Bulkeley m. Richard Welby   Line 31B
Elizabeth Bulkeley m. (1) Richard Whittingham, (2) Atherton Haugh   Line 31C
Obadiah Bruen   Line 33
Capt. George Curwen   Line 37
Rev. William Sargent   Line 43
Alice Freeman m. (1) John Tompson, (2) Robert Parke   Line 43A
Margaret Wyatt m. Mathew Allyn   Line 52
Robert Abell   Line 56A
Amy Wyllis m. Maj. John Pynchon   Line 57
Rev. Charles Chauncy   Line 69
Mabel Harlakenden m. (1) Col. John Haynes, (2) Samuel Eaton   Line 69A
Dannett Abney   Line 8IA
Mary Wolseley m. Roger Brooke   Line 81B
Alicia Arnold m. John Ross   Line 81C
Katharine Deighton m. (1) Samuel Hackburne, (2) Gov. Thomas Dudley   Line 84
Col. Thomas Lygon   Line 84C
Rev. Samuel Whiting   Line 85
Hon. Simon Lynde   Line 99
Ellen Newton m. Edward Carleton   Line 121D
Gov. Thomas Dudley   Line 143
Rosamond Lister m. Thomas Southworth   Line 170A
William Torrey   Line 197
Agnes Mackworth m. Col. William Crowne   Line 198
Elizabeth Coytemore m. (2) Capt. William Tyng   Line 199
Rev. George Burroughs   Line 200
Rev. John Oxenbridge   Line 201
Joseph Bolles (or Bowles)   Line 202
Rev. Thomas James   Line 203
John Throckmorton   Line 208

Henry Josselyn   Line 211
Oliver Mainwaring   Line 217A
Olive Welby m. Dea. Henry Farwell   Line 223
Katherine Hamby m. Edward Hutchinson   Line 224A
Susan Fiennes (d.s.p.) m. Maj. Gen. John Humphrey   Line 225
Arbella Fiennes (d.s.p.) m. Isaac Johnson   Line 225
Rev. Samuel Myles   Line 228
Nathaniel Browne   Line 230B
Margaret Tyndal m. Gov. John Winthrop   Line 232
Edward Rigby   Line 233
T'homas Gerard   Line 233A
Elizabeth St. John m. Rev. Samuel Whiting   Line 245
Wymond Bradbury   Line 246A
Agnes Harris m. (1) William Spencer, m. (2) William Edwards   Line 246E
Thomas Trowbridge   Line 246G
Ann Baynton m. Christopher Batt   Line 248
Christopher Batt   Line 248A
Samuel Appleton   Line 249
John Barclay   Line 252
Thomas Newberry   Line 253
Thomas Gordon   Line 256
Mary Gye m. Rev. Peter Maverick   Line 261

LIST OF REFERENCES

and Their Abbreviations

Altschul, Michael, *A Baronial Family in Medieval England: The Clares, 1217-1314* (1965).
Am. Antiq. Soc., Coll. - Collections of the American Antiquarian Society, Worcester, Mass.
(The) Ancestor (a journal).
Anselme, Père, *Histoire généalogique et chronologique de la maison royale de France*, 9 vols. (Paris 1726-1733, reprinted 1967).
(The) Armorial (a journal).
ASC - *The Anglo-Saxon Chronicle* (numbers given refer to dates).
Banks - *Baronia Anglica Concentrata (I), and Baronies in Fee (II)*.
Bartrum, Peter, *Welsh Genealogies,* two sets of volumes, the first "AD 300 to 1400," the second a supplementary set "1400-1500."
Baumgarten, N. de, "Généalogies et Mariages Occidentaux des Rurikides Russes, du X au XIII siècle," Orientalia Christiana, vol. No. 38, Rome.
Beard, Timothy, *Pedigrees of Some of the Emperor Charlemagne's Descendants,* vol. 2 (see v. Redlich).
Bede - *Ecclesiastical History of the English Nation.*
Beltz, George F., *Memorials of the Most Noble Order of the Garter...* (London, 1841).
Berry, William, *County Genealogies, Pedigrees of Families...* (various counties).
Brandenburg, Dr. Erick, *Die Nachkommen Karls des Grossen* (1935).
Brenner, S. Otto, *Nachkommen Gorms des Alten* (Kopenhagen, 1978).
Brook, Lindsay L., Editor, *Studies in Genealogy and Family History in Tribute to Charles Evans....* (APSG, 1989).
Burke's, *Extinct and Dormant Baronetcies* (not reliable, but more useful than Burke's *Dormant and Extinct Peerage).*
Burke's, *Peerage, Baronetage and Knightage* (1953) (1967).
Burke's, http://www.Burkes-peerage.net.
Burton, Wm., *Descr. of Leicester.*
CCN - *Century Cyclopedia of Names* (for handy reference only).
Chaume - The Abbé Chaume, author of numerous articles and books -- usually also cited by title in the text.
Chesnaye-Desbois, *Dictionnaire de la Noblesse* (19 vols. in 10) 1863-1876 (& CD-Rom version, Héraldique & Généalogie, 2003).
Clay, John W., *The Extinct and Dormant Peerages of the Northern Counties of England* (London, 1913).
Cleaveland, *The Family of Courtenay.*
CME - *Cambridge Mediaeval History.*
Coats of Arms (n.s.) (a journal).
Coll. Topo. et Gen. - *Collectanea Topographica et Genealogica.*
Collins, Arthur, *The Peerage of England*, 7 vols. (1768).
Collins' *Peerage of England* (Sir Egerton Brydges), 9 vols. (1812).
CP - G.E. Cokayne's (new revised) *Complete Peerage*, vols. I-XII pt. 2 (1910-1959), vol. XIV (1998).
Crispin, M. Jackson, *Falaise Roll* (London, 1938).
Cross, *A Shorter History of England and Great Britain* (1920).
Curwen, John F., *Curwens of Workington 1092-1904.*
DA - *Journal of the Devonshire Association of Art, Sciences, and Literature.*
Davis, Walter Goodwin, *The Ancestry of Mary Isaac...* (1955).
Davis, Walter Goodwin, *Massachusetts and Maine Families.*

Devon & Cornwall N. & Q. - *Devonshire and Cornwall Notes and Queries* (see note by N&Q below).
DNB - *Dictionary of National Biography* (English) (also Dict. Natl. Biog.).
Duchess of Cleveland, *Battle Abbey Roll, in 3 vols.* (1889).
Dudley Pedigree, Herald's College, 28 Jan. 1937, approved by A.T. Butler, Windsor Herald.
Dunbar, Archibald H., *Scottish Kings*, 2nd edition (1906).
DWB - *Dictionary of Welsh Biography* (also Dict. Welsh Biog.).
Dwnn - *Heraldic Visitations of Wales.*
Dworzaczek, Wlodzimierz, *Genealogia* (Inst. Hist. Polskiej Akad. Nauk, 1959).
Earwaker, *The Standish Family of Standish and Duxbury, County Lancaster, Charters and Deeds*
  (Manchester, 1898).
EB - *Encyclopedia Britannica* (for occasional reference).
Edwards, Steven, Editor, *Complete Works of Charles Evans. Genealogy and Related Topics* (Foundation for Medieval Genealogy, 2003).
Ellis, Clarence, *Hubert de Burgh* (1952).
English Chronicles, 1000-1300, including: Anglo-Saxon Chronicle, Bury St. Edmunds, Domesday Book, Gesta Stephani, Florence of Worcester, Henry of Huntingdon, Ingulf, Matthew of Westminster, Ordericus Vitalis, Roger of Hovenden, Roger of Wendover, and William of Malmsbury. For Scots and Irish Chronicles, see Line 170.
Eng. Hist. Rev. - *English Historical Review.*
ES - Detlev Schwennicke, *Europäische Stammtafeln.* Neue Folge, 21 vols. in 26.
Evergates, Theodore, *Feudal Society in the Bailliage of Troyes under the Counts of Champagne, 1152-1284* (1975).
EYC - Clay, Charles Travis, *Early Yorkshire Charters* (1952) (First three volumes by Farrer).
Farmer - Farmer's *Genealogical Dictionary of New England.*
Farrer, *Honours and Knights Fees.*
Fisher, G.P., *Outline of Universal History* (1885).
Fletcher, Geo. Dimock, *Leicester Pedigrees and Royal Descents* (1887).
Foster, Joseph, *Pedigrees of County Families of England Vol. I: Lancashire* (1873).
Foster, *Visitations of Yorkshire.*
Foundations - *Journal of the Foundation for Medieval Genealogy* (Online Edition at http://fmg.ac.).
Gardiner, Samuel R., *A Student's History of England* (1899), genealogical tables xxvii-xxxii, 216, 265, 286.
Garnier, Éd., *Tableaux Généalogiques des Souverains de la France et de ses Grand Feudataires.*
Gen.; *Genealogist* - (Marshall, editor) (the original magazine of this name).
The Genealogist (Neal Thompson, editor), a modern periodical (not abbreviated).
Gen. Mag. - *The Genealogists' Magazine* (pub. by Soc. of Genealogists, London, Eng.).
Handbook of British Chronology (2nd & 3rd Editions).
Harcourt-Bath, William, *A History of the Family of Harcourt.*
Harl. Soc. Pub. - Harleian Society Publications.
Hempstead's (Diary) - *Joshua Hempstead, Diary of … 1711-1758* (New London, 1901).
Her. & Gen. - *The Herald & Genealogist* (Journal).
Hête, Thierry Le, *Les Comtes Palatins de Bourgogne* (1995).
Hist. Cols. of Staffs - *Historical Collections of Staffordshire* (William Salt Society).
Hodgkin - Hodgkin's *History of England Before the Norman Conquest.*
Hutchinson - Hutchinson's *History of Cumberland.*
Isenburg, Prinz von, *Stammtafeln zur Geschichte der Europäischen Staaten*, v. 1-5.
Jackman, Donald C., *The Konradiner. A Study in Genealogical Methodology* (1990).
Jackman, Donald C., *Criticism and Critique. Sidelights on the Konradiner* (1997).
Jacobus, Donald Lines, *The Family of Rev. Peter Bulkeley.*

JAMS - *Journal of Ancient and Medieval Studies* (Octavian Society).
J. Med. Hist. - *Journal of Medieval History.*
Journal of the Sussex Archaeological Society.
Keats-Rohan, K.S.B., *Domesday People I. Domesday Book.* (Boydell, 1999).
Keats-Rohan, K.S.B., *Domesday Descendants* II. *Pipe Rolls to Cartae Baronum* (Boydell, 2002).
Keats-Rohan, K.S.B., Editor, *Family Trees and the Roots of Politics* (Boydell Press 1997)
Keats-Rohan, K.S.B. and C. Settipani, Editors, *Onomastique et Parente dans l'Occident Medieval* (Prosopographica et Genealogica, 2000).
Knetsch, Dr. Carl, *Das Haus Brabant* (1931).
Libby & Noyes - Davis, Libby & Noyes, *Genealogical Dictionary of Maine and New Hampshire.*
Lincolnshire Pedigrees, edited by A. R. Maddison, 4 vols.
Maddison('s Wills) - A.R. Maddison, *Lincolnshire Wills, 1500-1617,* 2 vols. (1888-1891).
MC - Adams and Weis, *Magna Charta Sureties 1215.*
Med. & Hum. - *Medievala et Humanistica* (a journal of medieval studies published by the University of Colorado).
Misc. Gen. Her. - *Miscellanea Genealogica et Heraldica.*
Moncrieffe, Sir Iain, *Royal Highness, Ancestor of the Royal Child* (1982).
Morant, *History of Essex* (1768).
Moriarity, George Andrews, *The Plantagenet Ancestry* (1985).
Moriarty Notebooks - 19 vols. ms. at New Eng. Hist. Gen. Soc., Boston.
Murray, Alan V., The Crusader Kingdom of Jerusalem (Prosopographica et Genealogica, 2002)
Muskett, *Suffolk Manorial Families.*
N. & Q. - *Notes & Queries* (England). There are also several separate Notes and Queries for individual counties.
N.G.S.Q. - *National Genealogical Society Quarterly* (Washington, D.C.).
NEHGR - *New England Historic Genealogical Register.*
Nichols, J., *Hist. of Leicester.*
Nichols, Thomas, Annals & Antiquities of the Counties and County Families of Wales, 2 vols. (1872).
Nicol, Donald M., *The Byzantine Family of Kantakouzenos* (1968).
Norfolk Arch. - *Journal of the Norfolk Archaeological Society.*
Nottingham Medieval Studies (a journal).
Noyes, Libby & Davis - Davis, Libby & Noyes, *Genealogical Dictionary of Maine and New Hampshire.*
NSE - *New Standard Encyclopedia.*
Old-CP - Former edition of Cokayne, *Complete Peerage.*
Onslow, Richard W.A., *The Dukes of Normandy and Their Origin* (1945).
Les Origines du Duché de Bourgogne (Chaume).
Ormerod, *History of the County Palatine and City of Chester,* 2nd ed., revised Helsby (Routledge, 1882).
Owen, Hugh, *The Lowther Family* (1990).
Page, Augustine, *Topographical and Genealogical History of Suffolk* (Ipswich, 1847).
Parkin, Rev. Chas., *An Essay ... History of Norfolk,* etc., 6 vols. (London, 1775).
Planché, J. R., *The Conqueror and His Companions,* vols. 1 & 2 (London, 1874).
Powley, Edward B., *The House of de la Pomerai...* (London, 1944).
Proc. Mass. Soc. - *Proceedings of the Massachusetts Historical Society.*
Reg. Mag. Sig. Reg. Scot. - Registrum magni sigilli regum Scotorum (Register of the great seal of Scotland).
Ritson, *Annals of the Caledonians, Picts and Scots of Strathclyde, Cumberland, Galloway and Murray,* 2 vols. (Edinburgh, 1828).
Rösch, Siegfried, *Caroli Magni Progenies* (1977).

Rogers, W. B. Hamilton, *Antient Sepulchral Effigies and Monumental and Memorial Sculptures of Devon* (Exeter, 1876).

Round, J. Horace, *Family Origins and Other Studies* (1970).

Round, J. Horace, *Feudal England* (London, 1909).

Round, J. Horace, *Geoffrey de Mandeville* (1891 rep. Burt Franklin, NY).

Round, J. Horace, *The King's Serjeants & Officers of State with Their Coronation Services.*

Round, J. Horace, *Peerage and Pedigree*, vols. 1 & 2 (1970).

Round, J. Horace, *Studies in Peerage and Family History* (1970).

Rye, Walter, *Calendar of the Freemen of Norwich 1317-1608.*

Saillot, *Le Sang de Charlemagne.*

Salisbury, E.M., *Family Histories and Genealogies.*

Saltonstall, Richard A., *Ancestors and Descendants of Sir Richard Saltonstall of New England* (1897).

Sanders, *English Baronies, a Study of Their Origin and Descent 1086-1327*, 203 pp. (1960).

Scottish Genealogist (a journal).

Searle, Wm. George, *Anglo-Saxon Bishops, Kings and Nobles* (Cambridge, 1899).

Settipani, Christian, *Les Ancêtres de Charlemagne* (1989) and Addenda (1990, 2000).

Settipani, Christian, *Nos Ancêtres de l'Antiquité* (1991).

Settipani, Christian, *Continuité gentilice et continuité familiale dans les familles séatoriales romaines à l'époque impériale* (2000).

Seversmith, Herbert Furman, *Colonial Families of Long Island, New York and Connecticut* (in five vols.) (1939-1958).

Shepherd, William R., *Historical Atlas*, 9th Edition (1964).

Sheppard, *Ancestry of Edward Carleton and Ellen Newton his Wife* (microfilm, c/r 1978).

Shrop. Parish Rec. Soc. - *Shropshire Parish Register Society* (various publications).

Sirjean, Gaston, *Encyclopédie Généalogique des Maisons Souveraines du Monde....* (should be used with care).

SP - James Balfour Paul, *The Scots Peerage*, 9 vols. (Edinburgh, 1904-1914).

Speculum (a journal).

Stokvis, A.M.H.J., *Manuel d'Histoire, de Généalogie et de Chronologie de tous les États du Globe...*, 3 vols. (1888-1893) (many lines are now updated in other sources).

Stone, Don Charles, *Some Ancient and Medieval Descents of Edward I of England* (Philadelphia, PA 2003).

Strange, Hamon Le, *Le Strange Records* (1916).

Sturdza, Mihail-Dimitri, *Dictionnaire Historique et Généalogique des Grandes Familles de Grèce, d'Albanie et de Constantinople* (1983).

Surtees Soc. (the original magazine of this name) - *Surtees Society* (Durham publications).

TAG - *The American Genealogist.*

Thatcher, Oliver J., *A Short History of Mediaeval Europe (New* York, 1897).

Thompson, Neil D. & Robert C. Anderson, Editors, *A Tribute to John Insley Coddington...* (APSG, 1980).

Topo. et Gen(eal). - *Collectanea Topographica et Genealogica.*

Trans. Shrop. Arch. Soc. - *Transactions of the Shropshire Archaeological Society.*

Turton - Lt. Col. W.H. Turton, *Plantagenet Ancestry* (1928) (not very reliable).

Vajay, Szabolcs de, *Annales de Bourgogne (1964); Der Eintritt des Ungarischen Stammesbundes in die Europäische Geschichte (862-933)* (1968).

VCH - *Victoria County Histories* (followed by the name of the county).

Vis. (or) Visit. - Visitations (of the various counties).

Vivian, Lt. Col., *Visitations of Devon* and *Visitations of Cornwall.*

v. Redlich, *Pedigrees of Some of the Emperor Charlemagne's Descendants*, vol. 1 (Chicago, 1941) (contains no references; some lines questionable) (subsequent volumes, other editors, also without references).

Wagner, Anthony, *Pedigree and Progress* (London, 1975).

(The) Wandesfords - H.B. McCall, *The Wandesfords of Kirklington and Castle Camer (1904).*

Warlop, E. (Dr. Hist.), *The Flemish Nobility before 1300*, in 4 vols. (1975).

Waters, *Genealogical Gleanings in England,* 2 vols. (1901).

Wedgewood - Author of various biographical studies of Members of Parliament.

Weever, *Ancient Funerall Monuments,* etc. (London, 1631).

Weis - Various volumes of *The Colonial Clergy.*

West Winter (H.M. West Winter), *Descendants of Charlemagne,* Part One (1987) and Part Two (1991) (at NEHGS).

Whitaker, Thomas Dunham, T*he History and Antiquities of the Deanery of Craven in the County of York* (London, 1805).

Wightman, W.E., *The Lacy Family in England and Normandy 1066-1194* (1966).

Winkhaus, Eberhard, *Ahnen zu Karl dem Grossen and Widukin* (1950), and *Supplement* (1953).

Wm. Salt Soc. - William Salt Society, *Historical Collections of Staffordshire.*

GENEALOGICAL TERMS

and Their Abbreviations

abt. - about
adm. - admitted
ae., aet. - aged
aft. - after
als. - alias
ante - before; by
app. or appt. - apparently
b. - born
bap., bapt., bp. - baptized
Bar. - Baron
bef. - before
bet. or betw. - between
Brg. - Burgrave
bur. - buried
ca. - about (circa)
Cal. - Calendar
cf. - compare
cit. - the work cited (citato)
Co. or co. - county
coh. - co-heir
Coll. - College
cr. - created (as a peer)
Ct. - Count
Cts. - Countess
d. - died
D. - Duke
d.c.e. - writ of diem clausit extremum ("he has closed his last day")
d.s.p. - died without issue (sine prole)
d.s.p. legit. - died without legitimate issue
d.s.p.m. or d.s.p.m.s. - died without male issue
d.s.p.s. - died without surviving issue
d.v.m. - died during mother's lifetime
d.v.p. - died during father's lifetime (vita patris)
d.y. - died young
dau. - daughter
dea. - deacon
disp. - dispensation
div. - divorced
Dss. - Duchess
dtd.- dated
Emp. - Emperor
fa. - father
ff. - following
fl. - flourished or living (only approximate date known)
frm. - freeman, a voter in a colony. The date following is the date he was admitted.
gen(s) - generation(s)
gent. - gentleman

gr. - granted
GS - gravestone
h. - heir (or heiress)
H.C. - Harvard College
husb. - husband
i. - issue
I.p.m.; Inq.p.m. - An inquest held to determine the deceased's land holding. (Inquisition post mortem, usually dated by "regnal year"; example: 3 Hen. 4; 3 Hen IV - Third year of the reign of Henry IV)
Ibid. - the same
J.P. - Justice of the Peace
j.u. - jure uxoris, right of wife
k.- killed
K. - King
K.B. - Knight of the Bath
K.G. - Knight of the Garter
K.T. - Knight of the Thistle (Scotland)
knt.; kt. - knight
L. - Lord
lic. - license
liv. - living
loc. cit. - place cited
m. - married
m. (1); m. (2); m. (3) - married first; married second; third; etc.
M.I. - monumental inscription
M.P. - Member of Parliament
matric. - matriculated (entered and recorded at college or university)
ment. - mentioned
Mich. - Michaelmas, the Feast of St. Michael (Christmas)
Mrg. - Margrave
Mrq. - Marquis
ms. - manuscript
N., N.N. - name not known
n.i. - no issue
N.S. or n.s. - new series
nr. - near
ob. - died
occ. - occurs
op. cit. - the work cited above (opere citato)
p.; pp. - page; pages
P.C. - Privy Council
PCC - Prerogative Court of Canterbury
perh. - perhaps
Pr. - Prince
pres. - presumed
pro. - probated or proved (will)
prob. - probably
psh. - parish
Pss. - Princess
pub. - published
purch. - purchased
Q. - Queen
q.v. - quod vide (refer to, which see)
ref(s). - reference(s)

regnal year - the date most often used in medieval documents referring to the number of the year of the reign of the monarch at the time the document was dated.

Rot. - Roll; Rolls (rotalus). A term used for many types of early records.

s. - son

sett. - settled

sh. - shortly

Sn. or sn. - Seigneur

suc. - succeeded

succ. - successively

summ. - summoned

suo juris - in his (or her) right

surv. - survived

ult. - ultimo (last)

unkn. - unknown

unm. - unmarried

Vcte - Viscount

Vcts. - Viscountess

vol. - volume

w. - wife

wid. - widow

y. - young

yr. - younger

yr(s). - year(s)

yst. - youngest

ANCESTRAL ROOTS OF
CERTAIN AMERICAN COLONISTS
Who Came to America before 1700

ANCESTRAL LINES

Line 1   Revised for 8th Edition

1. CERDIC, d. 534, King of the West Saxons, 519-534, was a Saxon earldorman who founded a settlement on the coast of Hampshire, England, in 495, assumed the title of King of the West Saxons in 519, and became the ancestor of the English royal line (*ASC*, Dorothy Whitelock, Editor, see dates 495, 519, 530, 534; *CCN*, 230; William G. Searle, *Anglo-Saxon Bishops, Kings, and Nobles* (1899), 330-351; *ES* II/77).

2. CYNRIC, d. 560, son [or grandson] of Cerdic, was king of the West Saxons, 534-560. (*ASC*, 534, 552, 556, 855; *ES* II/77).

3. CEAWLIN, d. 593, son of Cynric, King of Wessex, 560. (*ASC*, 560, 565, 568, 591, 592, 593; 855; *ES* II/77; *CCN*, 227).

4. CUTHWINE, killed in battle 584, (*ASC*, 577, 584, 685, 855). (See Trelawney D. Reed, *The Rise of Wessex*, 31).

5. CUTHA, son of Cuthwine and father of Ceolwald, did not rule. (*ASC*, 584, 568, 855).

6. CEOLWALD, did not rule, visited Rome, 688. (*ASC*, 584, 688; *The Chronicle of Florence of Worcester* (1856), 31; Searle, 330-334).

7. CENRED, d. 694, son of Ceolwald, and father of King Ina and Ingild, did not rule. (*ASC*, 688, 855; *ES* II/ 77).

8. INGILD, d. 718, son of Cenred and father of Eoppa, did not rule. (*ASC*, 688, 715, 718, 722, 728, 855; Searle, 330-335).

9. EOPPA, son of Ingild, father of Eafa, did not rule. (*ASC*, 855).

10. EAFA, son of Eoppa, did not rule. (*ASC*, 855).

11. EALHMUND, King in Kent 784, son of Eafa; m. perh. a dau. of Æthelberht II, King of Kent, 725-762. (Don Charles Stone, *Some Ancient and Medieval Descents of Edward I of England* (2003), Chart 10: "Descent from Cerdic and Alfred the Great;" *ASC*, 784, 855; *ES* II/77).

12. EGBERT, b. abt. 775, d. 837/9, son of Ealhmund, King in Kent. Egbert was King of Wessex, 802-827, and was the first king of all England, 827-836, m. Rædburga, of unknown origin. The male line of kings descends from him to Edward the Confessor and the female line to the present time. (*ASC*, 800, 823, 825, 827, 828, 836; Searle, 342-343; Moriarty, 16; *ES* II/77-78).

13. ÆTHELWULF (1B-14) b. abt. 795/800, King of Wessex, 839-855, d. 13 Jan. 858; m. (1) Osburga (Osburh), repudiated 853, d. aft. 876, dau. of Oslac, the royal cup-bearer; m. (2) 856, Judith, b. abt. 844, d. aft. 870, dau. of **CHARLES II**, "the Bald" (148-15), King of France and Ermentrude, dau. of Eudes, Count of Orléans. (*ASC*, 823, 836, 840, 853, 855; *ES* II/78; Paget I: 5). Note: Gens. 1-13: Dating descrepancies in printed sources exist. See Don Stone, *cit*, and esp. note 1.

14. ALFRED THE GREAT, by (1), King of England, 871-899, b. Wantage, Berkshire, 849; d. 26 Oct. 899; m. 869, Ealhswith, d. 904, dau. of Æthelred Mucill, ealdorman of the Gaini, by Edburga, his wife. (*ASC*, 853, 871, 891, 894, 897, 901; *DNB* 1: 153-162; Asser, *Life of Alfred; ES* II/78).

15. EDWARD I, "the Elder," King of England, 899-924; b. abt. 871/5; d. 17 July 924/5; m. (2) or (3) 919, Eadgifu, d. 25 Aug. 968, dau. of Sigehelm, Ealdorman of Kent. (*ASC* 924, 925; *DNB* 1: 157; *NSE* X: 193). (Note: Burke's *Peerage*, 1967 edition, "Kings of England, the Royal Lineage," calls Egwina, said by some to be 1st wife, his mistress.

Edward mar. (1) or (2) Elfreda, dau. of Ethelhelm, Lord of Meopham, Cooling & Lenham in co. Kent).

16. **EDMUND,** "the Magnificent," by (2) or (3), King of England, 939-946; b. 920/1; d. 946; m. (1) 940, St. Ælfgifu, d. 944. (*ASC,* 942, 946; Hodgkin;`DNB` 16: 401).

17. **EDGAR,** "the Peaceful," King of England, 959-975; b. 944; d. 975; m. (2) 965, Ælfthryth (Elfrida), b. 945; d. 1000, a nun at Wherwell; dau. of Ealdorman Ordgar of Devon. (*ASC,* 965; *NSE* X: 165-166; *DNB* 16: 365; *ES* II/78).

18. **ÆTHELRED II,** "the Redeless," King of England, 979/1013, 1014/1016; b. abt. 968; d. 23 Apr. 1016; m. (1) 985, Ælfgifu (Elgiva), d. 1002, dau. of Thored, Ealdorman of Northumbria; m. (2) abt. 1002, Emma, d. 1052, dau. of **RICHARD I** (121E-20), Duke of Normandy and his 2nd wife, Gunnora. Emma m. (2) 1017, Canute, King of Denmark and England. (*CP* V: 504; *CP* IX: 704. Gens. 13-31: Thatcher, 321; Gardiner, xxvii-xxix; *DNB* 18: 27; Gabriel Ronay, *The Lost King of England* (1989), 8, 20; David Douglas, *William the Conqueror,* 167; *ES* II/78, Burke, 1967).

19. **EDMUND II** "Ironside," King of England, 1016; b. abt. 989; d. 30 Nov. 1016; m 1015, Eldgyth, widow of Sigeferth, a Danish nobleman. (Burke, 1967 ed; *ES* II/78; *CCN,* 352; *DNB* 16: 403; Ronay, *cit.* 117-121; Allstrom, 132).

20. **EDWARD,** "the Atheling" called the "Exile," b. posthumously 1017; d. 1057; m. Agatha, b. 1020s, d. abt. 1068, probably dau. of **IAROSLAV I** (241-5), Grand Prince of Kiev, by his wife Irina (Ingigerd) of Sweden. This parentage for Agatha is now the most probable. See René Jetté, "Is the Mystery of the Origin of Agatha, Wife of Edward the Exile, Finally Solved?" *NEHGR* 150 (1996): 417-432; and Norman W. Ingham, "Has a Missing Daughter of Iaroslav Mudryi Been Found?" *Russian History/Histoire Russe* 25 (1998): 231-170 (with references to alternative theories).

21. **MARGARET** (St. Margaret of Scotland), b. Hungary, 1045, d. 16 Nov. 1093; canonized 1250; m. Dunfermline, 1067 or 1070 as 2nd wife, **MALCOLM III CANMORE** (170-21), King of Scots, 1058-1093; b. abt. 1031; d. 13 Nov. 1093. (*CP* V: 736 chart; *CP* VII: 641-642; *SP* I: 1-2; Dunbar, 25-34, 280-281; *DNB* ,36:132, 35:400; Ronay, *cit.* 175-182; Paget I: 8).

22. **MATILDA (MAUD)** of Scotland, b. Dermfermline, 1079, d. Westminster Palace, 1 May 1118; m. 11 Nov. 1100, **HENRY I** (121-25), Beauclerc, King of England, 1100-1135; b. 1068/70; d. 1 Dec. 1135. (He m. (2) 29 Feb. 1121, **ADELIZA (ADELA) OF LOUVAIN** (149-25), b. abt. 1103; d. 23 Apr. 1151 (s.p. by this marriage); she m. (2) 1138, William d'Aubigny, Earl of Arundel, d. 12 Oct. 1176). (*CP* I: 233-235; *CP* IV: 669 chart II; *CP* V: 736; *CP* VII: 737; *SP* I: 1-2; *CCN,* 494. Gens. 13-23: Cross, xv; *DNB* 37: 52; *DNB* 25: 436).

23. **MATILDA,** b. abt. 1102-1104; d. 10 Sept. 1167; m. (2) Le Mans, 3 Apr. 1127, **GEOFFREY V (PLANTAGENET)** (118-25), Count of Anjou, Duke of Normandy; b. 24 Aug. 1113; d. 7 Sept. 1151. (She m. (1) 1114, Henry V, Emperor of Germany, who d.s.p. Utrecht, 22 May 1125). (*CP* V: 683-5, 697; *SP* I: 1-2; *CCN,* 494; *DNB* 37: 54).

24. **HENRY II,** "Curtmantel," King of England, 25 Oct. 1154-1189; b. Le Mans, 5 Mar. 1132/3; d. 6 July 1189, bur. at Fontévrault; m. Bordeaux, 18 May 1152, **ELEANOR OF AQUITAINE** (110-26), b. 1123/5, d. 31 Mar. or 1 Apr.1204. (Divorced wife of **LOUIS VII** (102-25), King of France). (*CP* V: 736; *SP* I: 1-2; *CCN,* 494; *DNB* 26: 1; *DNB* 17: 175).

25. **JOHN,** "Lackland," King of England, 1199-1216; b. Oxford, 24 Dec. 1166/7; d. Newark, 19 Oct. 1216; m. (2) Bordeaux, 24 Aug. 1200, **ISABELLA OF ANGOULÊME** (117-27, 153-28); b. 1188; d. 31 May 1246. (*CP* V: 736; *CCN,* 547-548; *DNB* 29: 402; *DNB* 29:63).

2

26. HENRY III, King of England, 1216-1272; b. Winchester Castle, 1 Oct. 1207; d. 16 Nov. 1272; m. 24 or 25 Jan. 1236/7, **ELEANOR OF PROVENCE** (111-30), b. 1217; d. Amesbury, 24 or 25 June 1291. (*CP* V: 736; *CCN*, 356, 494; *DNB* 26: 12; *DNB* 17: 179).

27. EDWARD I, "Longshanks," King of England, 1272-1307; b. Westminster, 17-18 June 1239; d. 7 or 8 July 1307; crowned 19 Aug. 1274; m. (1) 18 Oct. 1254, (he age 15, she age 10) **ELEANOR OF CASTILE** (110-30), b. 1241, d. 1290; m. (2) 8 Sept. 1299, **MARGUERITE OF FRANCE** (155-30). (*CP* V: 698, 707, 736; Don Stone, *Some Ancient and Medieval Descents*...: Chart 11, note 4; *CCN*, 353; *DNB* 17: 14, 178).

28. EDWARD II, by (2), King of England, 1307-1327; b. Caernarvon, Wales, 25 Apr. 1284; d. near Gloucester, 21 Sept. 1327; m. **ISABELLA OF FRANCE** (101-31). (*CP* V: 736; *CCN*, 353; *DNB* 18: 38; *DNB* 29: 64).

29. EDWARD III, King of England, 1327-1377; b. Windsor Castle, 13 Nov. 1312; d. Sheen, Richmond, co. Surrey, 21 June 1377; m. York, 24/25 Jan. 1327/8, **PHILIPPA OF HAINAUT** (103-34), b. 24 June 1311, d. 15 Aug. 1369, dau. of William, Count of Hainaut and of Holland and Zeeland, by Joan, dau. of Charles of France, Count of Valois. (*CP* II: 153; *CP* V: 736; *The Genealogist* 1 (1980): 138-139; *CCN*, 353; *DNB* 17: 48; *DNB* 14: 164. Gens. 23-30: Cross, xv-xvi; Thatcher, 324; *CME* (in Two Volumes) 1: 600-601 chart).

30. JOHN OF GAUNT, b. Ghent, Mar. 1340; d. Leicester Castle, 3/4 Feb. 1398/9; Duke of Lancaster; m. (1) Reading, 19 May 1359, Blanche, d. 12 Sept. 1369, dau. of **HENRY** (72-33), Duke of Lancaster; son of **HENRY**, Earl of Lancaster (17-29); m. (2) Roquefort, Sept. 1371, Constance, b. 1354, d. 1394, eldest dau. and coh. Pedro I "The Cruel," King of Castile and Leon (see at 225-34); m. (3) Lincoln, 13 Jan. 1396, Catherine (Roet) Swynford, b. 1350, d. 10 May 1403, dau. of Sir Payn (Paon) de Roet, Guinne King of Arms, and widow of Sir Hugh Swynford. (*CP* V: 320, 736 chart; *CP* VII: 415; *DNB* 29: 417, *DNB* 55: 243; *The Genealogist* 12 (1998): 252; S. Armitage Smith, *John of Gaunt* (reprint 1964)).

31. JOHN BEAUFORT, by (3), Earl and Marquis of Somerset, b. abt. 1371/72 (in adultry by then mistress, Catherine; legitimated by statute, 1397); d. 21 Apr. 1410; m. abt. 1397/9, **MARGARET DE HOLAND** (47-33), d. 30 Dec. 1439. Margaret m. (2) Thomas, Duke of Clarence. (*CP* IV: 416; *CP* VII: 415; *CP* XII (1): 39-45 (see esp. p. 44 note *h*); Paget I: 23; *DNB* Suppl. i, 158; Gens. 1-32: Moriarty, *The Plantagenet Ancestry*).

32. EDMUND BEAUFORT, Duke of Somerset, Marquis of Dorset, Lieut.-General of France, Normandy and Guienne; b. abt. 1406; slain at 1ˢᵗ Battle of St. Albans, 22 May 1455; m. without license, abt. 1431/5, **ELEANOR (BEAUCHAMP) ROS** (87-34), b. Eddgenoch, co. Warwick, 1407; d. 6 Mar. 1467; widow of Thomas Ros, Lord Ros, and dau. of Richard Beauchamp, 5ᵗʰ Earl of Warwick, and Elizabeth Berkeley, dau. of Thomas Berkeley, Baron Berkeley; she m. (3) Walter Rokesley, Esq. (*CP* II: 131 note *c*, 145; *CP* IV: 417; Burke; *DNB* 4: 38).

33. ELEANOR BEAUFORT, d. 16 Aug. 1501, Countess of Wiltshire; m. (1) poss. Apr. 1458, James le Botillier (Butler), b. abt. 1420, beheaded 1 May 1461, 5ᵗʰ Earl of Ormond and Wiltshire, son of **JAMES LE BOTILLIER (BUTLER)** (7-33) 4ᵗʰ Earl of Ormond; m. (2) bef. 1470, Sir Robert Spencer, Knt., of Spencercombe, co. Devon, b. abt. 1435, living 1502. (*CP* IX: 720; *CP* X: 126-128).

34. MARGARET SPENCER, b. abt. 1472; m. abt. 1490, Thomas Cary of Chilton Foliot, co. Wilts, and Moulsford, co. Berks, M.P., b. 1455, d. 1500, son of Sir William Cary of Cockington, co. Devon, b. 1437, beheaded 1471, an eminent Lancastrian, by his wife, Alice, dau. Sir Baldwin Fulford. (*CP* IX: 720; *NEHGR* 104: 271).

35. WILLIAM CARY, b. abt. 1495; d. 22 June 1529; Gentleman of the Privy Chamber and Esquire of the Body of King Henry VIII; m. 31 Jan. 1520/1, **MARY BOLEYN** (22-37), sister of Queen Anne. (*CP* II: 146; *CP* IV: 159-160; *TAG* 18: 211-218).

36. KATHERINE CARY, d. 15 Jan. 1568/9; Chief Lady of the Bedchamber to Queen Elizabeth; m. abt. 1539, Sir Francis Knollys, K.G., b. abt. 1514; d. 19 July 1596, of Rotherfield Greys, co. Oxford. (*CP* IV: 159-160, XIV: 243; Collins, *Peerage* V: 170; Anthony Richard Wagner, *English Genealogy* (1960), 424, Table IV).

37. ANNE KNOLLYS (228-38), liv. 30 Aug. 1608; m. 19 Nov. 1571, **SIR THOMAS WEST** (18-38), 2nd Lord DeLaWarr. (*CP* IV: 159-160; *NEHGR* 33: 287-291).

38. PENELOPE WEST, b. 9 Sept. 1582; d. abt. 1619; m. abt. 1599, Herbert Pelham II, b. abt. 1580; d. Boston, co. Lincoln, 20 July 1624; of Hastings, co. Sussex, and Boston, co. Lincoln. (*CP* IV: 159-160; *NEHGR* 33: 287-291).

39. PENELOPE PELHAM, dau. of Herbert Pelham II and **PENELOPE WEST,** sister of **HERBERT PELHAM III** (1-39) fol., b. abt. 1619, d. 28 May 1702; m. 9 Nov. 1641, Richard Bellingham, Gent., b. Boston, co. Linc. abt. 1592, d. 1672, son of William Bellingham)and Frances Amcotts), of Manton and Bromby, co. Linc.; M.P. 1628-1629, came to Mass. 1634, Gov. of Mass. 1641, 1654, 1665-1672 (no issue by this marriage). (*CP* IV: 159-160; *TAG* 18:138; *NEHGR* 33: 289; *Linc. Pedigrees, Harl. Soc. Pub.* 50: 118).

39. HERBERT PELHAM III, ESQ., b. abt. 1600; bur. Bures, co. Suffolk, 1 July 1673; came to New England, 1639/40; first Treasurer of Harvard College, 1643; Commissioner of the United Colonies, 1645; m. (1) Jemima Waldegrave, dau. of Thomas Waldegrave and granddau. of Thomas Waldegrave; m. (2) 1638, Elizabeth Bosvile, wid. **of COL. ROGER HARLAKENDEN, ESQ.** (69A-41), and dau. of Geoffrey Bosvile. (*NEHGR* 33: 287-291). (*TAG* 18: 210).

40. PENELOPE PELHAM, dau. by (1), b. 1631, bapt. Bures, 1633, d. 7 Dec 1703; m. Gov. Josiah Winslow, b. 1628, d. 1680, Governor of Plymouth Colony. (Goodwin, *Pilgrim Republic,* 540-542. Ref. on Pelham see *TAG* 16: 129-132; 201-205, 14: 209-214).

40. CAPT. EDWARD PELHAM, GENT., son of Gen. 39 by (2), of Newport, R.I., b. abt. 1650/2, d. 20 Sept. 1730; m. 18 Apr. 1682, Freelove Arnold, b. 20 July 1661, d. 8 Sept. 1711, dau. of Gov. Benedict Arnold of Rhode Island. (Colket in *TAG* 18: 144-145; *NEHGR* 33: 291. For Gen. 31-40, see Meredith B. Colket, Jr. in *TAG* 18: 211-218; *TAG* 19: 197-202. Few early New England settlers may be traced so far down in the *Complete Peerage*).

Line 1A

31. JOHN OF GAUNT (1-30), Duke of Lancaster, b. 1340; d. 1398/9; m. (1) 19 May 1359, Blanche of Lancaster (his cousin), had (*DNB* 29: 417; *DNB* 26: 101).

32. HENRY IV, King of England, 1399-1413; b. Bolingbroke Castle, Lincs. 3 Apr. 1367; d. Westminster Palace, 20 Mar. 1412/13; m. Rochford, Essex, bet. 30 July 1380 and 10 Feb. 1380/1, Mary de Bohun, dau. and coh. of **HUMPHREY DE BOHUN** (97-33), Earl of Hereford, Essex, and Northampton. She b. abt. 1370; d. Peterborough, Northants, 4 July 1394. (*CP* VII: 417; *CP* VI: 473-477; *DNB* 26: 31).

33. HUMPHREY, Duke of Gloucester, b. 3 Oct. 1390; d.s.p. legit. Bury St. Edmunds, 23 Feb. 1446-7; m. (1) bef. 7 Mar. 1422/3, Jacqueline, Countess of Holland, Zealand and Hainault, dau. and h. William, Count of Holland, annulled 9 June. 1428; m. (2) 1428, Eleanor, dau. Sir Reginald Cobham, who had been his mistress, died a prisoner at Peel Castle, Isle of Man, 1454. It is often suggested, but without proof, that Eleanor was mother before mar. of Humphrey's 2 illegit. chn.: Arthur and Antigone. No proof of their maternity. (*CP* III: 354 note d; *CP* V: 730, 736; *DNB* 28: 241).

34. ANTIGONE, b. bef. 1428, perh. to Eleanor Cobham, raised by her father, Humphrey (she legitimated June 1451, by Charles VII, King of France); m. (1) 3 Jan. 1434/5 to **SIR HENRY GREY** (47D-35), Count of Tancarville (whose m. he had bought); b. abt. 1419; d. 13 Jan. 1449/50; m. (2) by June 1451, Jean d'Amancier. (*CP* V: 736 note *n; CP* VI: 138-139, 699; *Visit Salop.* (*1623*), 105, 295; *Coat of Arms* 8 (1964/5): 170).

35. ELIZABETH GREY by (1), b. abt. 1440; d. co. Salop aft. 1501; m. (2) 1465, Sir Roger Kynaston, Knt., b. abt. 1430; d. 1495/6. (*CP* I: 142-143 note *h; CP* VI: 143, App. C: 699; *Visit. Salop.* (1623), 105, 295, 459).

36. JANE KYNASTON, b. abt. 1470; m. Roger Thornes of Shelvock, Salop, d. 1531, bur. St. Mary's, Shrewsbury. (Blakeway, *Sheriffs of Shropshire*, 734; *Trans. Shrop. Arch. Soc* (2nd Ser.) VI, pt. II (1894): 211-213, 215, on Kynaston).

37. JOHN THORNES (s. & h.) of Shelvock, liv. 1535; m. Elizabeth Astley of Patishull, Staffs, dau. of Richard Astley. (*Trans. Shrop. Arch. Soc-, op. cit.*, 330; Bakewell I: 56; *Visit. Salop.*(1623), 459).

38. RICHARD THORNES (2nd s.) of Condover, Salop; m. a Margaret NN.; or a Joan, dau. of Evan Lloyd Vychan of Abertenent. (*Visit. Salop (1623)*, 460; *Trans. Shrop. Arch. Soc.* (4th Ser.) III, pt. II: 303, on Littletons of Munslow).

39. ALICE THORNES, b. abt. 1530; d. Rushbury, parish of Munslow, Salop, 21 Mar. 1596, will 5 Mar. 1596, pro. 12 Dec. 1597 Consis. of Hereford; m. abt. 1548, the Rev. John Littleton, vicar of Munslow (B.L. Oxford 1532), d. Munslow 30 Nov. 1560, will 12 Aug. 1560, pro. 10 June 1562 PCC. (*Visit. Salop (1623)*, 460; *Visit. Worcs.* (*1634*), 64; *Trans. Shrop. Arch. Soc.* (4th Ser.) III, pt. II: 302-333).

40. SIR EDWARD LITTLETON, KNT., of Henley, co. Salop., bapt. Munslow, 23 Mar. 1550; d. Llanfaire, co. Denbigh, 25 Sept. 1622, admin. 22 Nov. 1622 PCC; m. Ludlow, co. Salop., 9 Apr. 1588, Mary Walter, b. Ludlow, 1 Nov. 1565, bur. Ludlow, 23 Oct. 1633, dau. of Edmund Walter. (*Trans. Shrop., op. cit.*, and pp. 263-276, Walters at Ludlow; *Visit Worcs.* (*1634*), 64; *Visit. Salop.* (1623), 483; *Shrop. Parish Rec. Soc.* 15 (Reg. of Munslow): 8, 16, 60, 351).

41. NATHANIEL LITTLETON, bapt. 22 Dec. 1605, Hopton Castle, co. Salop; d. in Northampton, Va., Oct.-Dec. 1654; m. Northampton Co., Va., abt. 1638, Ann Southy, widow of Charles Harmar, b. in Somerset, Eng., abt. 1620; d. Northampton Co., Va., will pro. 28 Oct. 1656. (*Visit. Worcs.* (*1634*), 64; *Shrop. Parish Reg.* (parish of Hopton Castle) 9; *Deeds & Wills*, # 7 and # 8, Northampton Co., Va. 22, etc.).

Line 1B   Revised for 8th Edition

14. ÆTHELWULF (1-13), King of Wessex (England) 839-858, d. 13 Jan 858; m. (1) Osburga, dau. of Oslac.

15. ÆTHELRED I, King of Wessex (England) 868-872, d. 872.

16. ÆTHELHELM, d. abt. 898, Ealdorman of Wiltshire, was devised of Compton, in Sussex, & Crondall, in Hampshire, by King Alfred the Great.

17. ÆTHELFRITH, d. abt. 927, Ealdorman of Mercia, first holder of the bequest from King Alfred. (*JAMS* V (1986): 38).

18. EADRIC, abt. 946-47, d. abt. 949, Ealdorman, held Ogburn & Washington by devise; m. Aethelgifu.

19. ÆTHELWERD, "the historian," seen 965, d. abt. 998, Thegn in Sussex 973, Ealdorman in Wessex 974.

20. ÆTHELMAER CILD, "the Great," d. abt. 1015 having outlived his son Wufnoth by about a year, Thegn in Sussex abt. 1007, Ealdorman in Devonshire 1005.

5

21. WULFNOTH CILD, d. 1015, Thegn of Sussex abt. 1007; held Compton, revolted 1009. (*NEHGR* 111 (1957): 30-38 and chart).

22. GODWIN, d. 15 Apr. 1053, thegn in Sussex, Ealdorman of Wessex 1018; m. 1019/20 Githa, dau. Jarl Thorkill Sprakalaeg. (*ES* II/78, 97, 98).

Note: *ES* II/78, shows (without citing authority) Jarl Thorkill (or Thurkill) Sprakalaeg as son of Styr-Bjorn (son of Olaf Bjornson 985, King of Sweden) by Thyra, d. 18 Sept. 1000, dau. of Harold "Bluetooth," King of Denmark. This line is followed by Moriarty, (Harold was son of Gorm the old, King of Denmark d. 936 and Thyra "Danebod.") However, Brenner, in his *Nachkomen Gorm des Atlen* (1978), does not include Thorkill as a child of Thyra, and only gives a dau. Gunhild, and a son (by Thyra's 3rd husband) Harold Olavsson, who d. aged 1 yr. See also: *Royal Historical Society Transactions* (3rd Ser.) 7: 129-150; *JAMS* V: 35-46.

23. HAROLD II "Godwinson," b. abt. 1022, slain in Battle of Hastings 14 Oct. 1066, Ealdorman of East Anglia, succ. father 1053 Ealdorman of Wessex, King of England 1066 (succeeded Edward the Confessor); m., as 2nd husb., **EDITH** (176A-4), wid. of **GRUFFYDD I AP LLYWELYN** (176-2), Prince of North Wales. By Ealdgith (Edith) "Swansneck", his "handfast wife" (non-Christian mar.), before he m. Edith of Mercia, he had with others

24. GYTHA of Wessex; m. abt. 1070 **VLADIMIR II MONOMAKH** (242-7), b. 1053, d. 1125; Grand Prince of Kiev. (Moriarty). For Gens. 16-24 see *Royal Historical Society Transactions* (3rd ser) (1913) 7: 129-149, chart; *NEHGR* 111: 30-38, charts; TAG 33 (1957): 188; David H. Kelley, "The House of Aethelred," *Studies in Genealogy & Family History in Tribute to Charles Evans...* (1989), 63-93).

Line 2

31. JOHN OF GAUNT (1-30), Duke of Lancaster, son of **EDWARD III** (1-29), King of England; m. (3) 1396 Katherine Swynford, widow of Sir Hugh Swynford, dau. of Sir Paon Roet. (*CP* V: 320 chart; *CP* VII: 415; *CP* XIV: 101; *Ancestor* 12 (1905): 143-145).

32. JOAN BEAUFORT, d. Howden, 13 Nov. 1440; m. (1) by lic. 27 Sept. 1369, **SIR ROBERT DE FERRERS** (62-34), of Willisham,Wem, and Oversley, co. Warwick d. bef. 29 Nov. 1396 grandson of **SIR ROBERT DE FERRERS** (61-32), 3rd Lord Ferrers, of Chartley and Joan de la Mote; m. (2) bef. 3 Feb. 1396/7, **RALPH DE NEVILLE, K.G.** (207-34), cr. Earl of Westmorland, 1397, b. bef. 1364, d. Raby, 21 Oct. 1425, will made 18 Oct. 1424, pro. 14 Nov. 1425-7 Oct. 1426, son of John Neville, 3rd Lord Neville of Raby, and Maud de Percy. (*CP* V: 320 chart; *CP* VII: 415; *CP* IX: 502 ii-iii chart: *CP* XII (1): 39-40; *CP* XIV: 101).

33. MARY DE FERRERS, Lady of Oversley, b. bef. 1394, d. 25 Jan. 1457/8; m. **SIR RALPH NEVILLE**, ygr. son of **RALPH NEVILLE** (10-34), 1st Earl of Westmoreland, d. 26 Feb. 1457/8. (*CP* II: 232-233; *CP* V: 320; *CP* VII: 415-416 note *j*; *CP* XIV: 102).

34. JOHN NEVILLE, ESQ., d. 17 Mar. 1481/2, of Althorpe, co. Lincoln, *j.u.* (Inq.p.m.) M.P. for Lincolnshire, 1444, sheriff of Lincolnshire, 1439-1440,1452-1453; m. (1) Elizabeth Newmarch, dau. of Robert Newmarch of Wormesley. (*CP* II: 232-233, *CP* V: 320; *CP* VII: 415-416; *CP* IX: 504).

35. JANE (JOAN) NEVILLE, of Oversley and Wormesley; m. (1) abt. 1448/50, Sir William Gascoigne of Gawthorpe, co. York, d. 1463/4, son of William Gascoigne. (Gens. 34-36: Foster, *Visit. of Yorkshire, 1584/5*, 384-385; Clay, 157).

36. MARGARET GASCOIGNE, m. Sir Christopher Ward, d. 31 Dec. 1521, of Givendale, co. York. (Inq.p.m. 4 Feb. 1522/2; she was sister of Sir William Gascoigne, Knt., of Gawthorpe, who m. **MARGARET PERCY** (3-35), qv. (*CP* IX: 717).

37. ANNE WARD, d. 1522/3; m. (2) 1500/1, **RALPH NEVILLE, ESQ.** (204-39), of Thornton Bridge, co. York. (*CP* IX: 501 ff. for Neville of Raby; John Burke, *Hist.* of the *Commoners* I: 57).

38. KATHERINE NEVILLE, b. abt. 1500; m. (1) 1515, **SIR WALTER STRICKLAND** (41-36), of Sizergh, co. Westmorland, d. 9 Jan. 1527/8. (John Burke, *Commoners, op. cit.* Gens. 33-38: G. A. Moriarty in *TAG* 17: 105-109).

39. WALTER STRICKLAND, ESQ., of Sizergh, b. 5 Apr. 1516, d. 8 Apr. 1569; m. (1) Agnes (perhaps) Hammerton. (See *NEHGR* 114: 51-58; *NEHGR* 115: 316; will dated 23 Jan. 1568/9, left £ 200 to his dau. Ellen).

40. ELLEN STRICKLAND, liv. 1622; m. by 1592, John Carleton of Beeford, co. York, b. abt. 1550/5, bur. 27 Jan. 1622/3, son of Thomas Carleton and Jennet Wilson.

41. WALTER CARLETON, bapt. Beeford, 28 Dec. 1582, d. Horsea, 4 Oct. 1623; m. 1607 Jane Gibbon, liv. 1639.

42. EDWARD CARLETON, bapt. Beeford, 20 Oct. 1610, sett. Rowley, Mass., 1639; m. co. York, 3 Nov. 1636, **ELLEN NEWTON** (121D-41), bapt. Hedon, 24 Feb. 1614, dau. of Lancelot Newton and Mary Lee. (For Strickland of Sizergh, see John Burke, *History of the Commoners* I: 55-58. Gens. 38-42: Dr. Tracy Elliot Hazen in *NEHGR* 93: 10 chart opp.; S.H. Lee Washington in *NEHGR* 96: 106-107 chart; 314 chart opp.; v. Redlich, 151; Sheppard, "Ancestry of Edward Carleton and Ellen Newton his Wife" (c 1978, microfilm)).

Line 3

32. JOAN BEAUFORT (2-32), granddau. of **EDWARD III** (1-29), d. 13 Nov. 1440; m. (2) **RALPH DE NEVILLE, K.G.** (207-34). (*CP* V: 320 chart; *CP* IX: 502 ii-iii chart).

33. ELEANOR NEVILLE, d. 1463; m. sh. aft. Oct 1414, **SIR HENRY PERCY, K.G.** (19-33), 2nd Earl of Northumberland, b. 3 Feb. 1392/3, slain at St. Albans, 22 May 1455, Warden of the Marches of Scotland. (*CP* X: 464; Collins IV: 84-91, *Gen.* (n.s.) 3: 110).

34. SIR HENRY PERCY, KNT., 3rd Earl of Northumberland, b. 25 Jul 1421, slain at the battle of Towton Field, 29 Mar. 1461; m. abt. 25 June 1435, Eleanor de Poynings, b. abt. 1422, d. Feb. 1483/4, dau. of Richard de Poynings, d.v.p. 10 June 1429, son of Robert, Lord Poynings, d. 2 Oct. 1446. (*CP* IX: 716-717; *CP* X: 464, 663-665; Collins IV: 84, 92-97).

35. MARGARET PERCY, m. Sir William Gascoigne, Knt., d. 4 Mar. 1486, of Gawthorpe, co. York, son of Sir William Gascoigne and **JANE NEVILLE** (2-35). (*CP* IX: 717 note d).

36. DOROTHY GASCOIGNE, m. Sir Ninian Markenfield, of Markenfield Hall, Ripon, co. York. (*Misc. Gen. et Her.* (orig. ser.) 2 (1876): 75-76, 81).

37. ALICE MARKENFIELD; m. abt. 1 Dec 1524, Sir Robert Mauleverer, bur. 31 Jan 1540/1, son of William Mauleverer and Jane Conyers.

38. DOROTHY MAULEVERER; m. 21 Jan 1542/3, John Kaye, Esq., of Woodsome, co. York, Esq., 1585. (Gens. 35-38: Richard A. Saltonstall, *Ancestors and Descendants of Sir Richard Saltonstall of New England* (1897), 84).

39. ROBERT KAYE, ESQ., of Woodsome, 1612, J.P.; m. Anne Flower, dau. of John Flower of Whitewell, co. Rutland. (Waters II: 939-940).

40. GRACE KAYE; m. Sir Richard Saltonstall, b. 1586; d. abt. 1686; of Huntwick, one of the patentees of Massachusetts and Connecticut; sett. Watertown, Mass., 1630, J.P. (Waters II: 939-940, 969-970; *NEHGR* 95: 72).

41. MAJOR RICHARD SALTONSTALL, b. 1610, d. 1694, sett. Watertown, Mass., 1630, Ipswich, Mass., 1635; m. June 1633, **MURIEL GURDON** (4-41), dau. Brampton

Gurdon of Assington Hall, sheriff of Norfolk, 1625-1629. (Waters II: 939-940, 969-970; *NEHGR* 95: 72; Saltonstall, *cit.* Generations 35-41: see Flower, *Visit. of Yorkshire* (1563-1564), 196-197, Foster, *Visit of Yorkshire* (1584/5) and (1612), 220, 320, 384-385, 570).

Line 4

30. **EDWARD III** (1-29), King of England, 1327-1377; m. **PHILIPPA OF HAINAUT** (103-34). (*CP* II: 153).

31. **THOMAS OF WOODSTOCK, K.G.**, Duke of Gloucester, b. co. Oxford, 7 Jan. 1354/5, murdered at Calais 8 or 9 Sept. 1397; m. abt. 1376, **ELEANOR DE BOHUN** (97-34), d. 3 Oct. 1399. (*CP* II: 153; *CP* V: 136).

32. **ANNE**, Countess of Buckingham, Hereford and Northampton age 17+ in 1399/1400, d. 16 Oct. 1438; m. (2) Edmund de Stafford, Earl of Stafford, d. 1403; m. (3) 20 Nov. 1405, **SIR WILLIAM BOURCHIER** (155A-32), Count of Eu, in Normandy, d. Troyes, 28 May 1420. (*CP* II: 153; *CP* V: 176-179; *CP* VI: 475-6).

33. **SIR JOHN BOURCHIER, K.G.**, 1st Lord Berners, d. May 1474; Knt. 19 May 1426; M.P., 1455-1472; K.G., abt. 23 Apr. 1459; Constable of Windsor Castle, 1461-1474; m. Margery Berners, d. 18 Dec. 1475, dau. of Richard Berners and Philippe Dalyngridge, dau. of Sir Edward Dalyngridge. (*CP* II: 153, XIV: 89).

34. **SIR HUMPHREY BOURCHIER**, slain at the battle of Barnet, 14 Apr. 1471; m. **ELIZABETH TYLNEY** (136-34), d. 4 Apr. 1497, dau. of Sir Frederick Tylney of Boston, co. Lincoln. (*CP* II: 153, XIV: 89).

35. **SIR JOHN BOURCHIER, K.B.**, b. abt. 1467; d. Calais, abt. 19 Mar. 1532/3, K.B., 17 Jan. 1477/8, M.P., 1495-1529, Chancellor of the Exchequer, 1516-1527, 2nd Lord Berners; m. **KATHERINE HOWARD** (16-35), d. 12 Mar. 1535-6, dau. of **SIR JOHN HOWARD** (16-34), K.G., Duke of Norfolk, by 2nd wife, Margaret Chetwode. (*CP* II: 153-154, XIV: 89; Vivian, *Visit. of Devon*, 106; *CCN*, 175; Berry, *Berkshire Pedigrees*, 55).

36. **JANE** (or **JOAN**) **BOURCHIER** will made 8 Apr. 1560, pro. 9 Mar. 1561; d. 17 Feb. 1561/2; m. **SIR EDMUND KNYVET, ESQ.** (188-14), b. 1490, will dtd. 24 June 1537, pro. 1546, d. Apr. 1539, of Ashwellthorpe, co. Norfolk. (CP II: 155; Vivian, *op. cit.*, 106; Berry, *Berkshire Pedigrees*, 55).

37. **JOHN KNYVET, ESQ.**, of Plumstead, Norfolk, living 1543, but d. in his mother's lifetime; m. (settlement, 28 Feb. 1513), Agnes Harcourt, dau. of Sir John Harcourt, Knt., of Stanton-Harcourt, co. Oxen. (*CP* II: 155 note *b*; Berry, *Berkshire Pedigrees*, 55).

38. **ABIGAIL KNYVET**, m. Sir Martin Sedley, b. 1531, will made 12 May 1608, pro. 5 Mar. 1609, of Morley, co. Norfolk. (Waters II: 969-970; *NEHGR* 95: 72). See Beard, *Pedigrees of Some of the Emperor Charlemagne's Descendants* II (1974), p. xcviii & xcvix.

39. **MURIEL SEDLEY**; m. Brampton Gurdon, Esq., will dated 19 Oct. 1647, codicil 1 Feb. 1648, pro. 15 May 1650, d. 1649, of Assington Hall, Suffolk, sheriff of Suffolk, 1625-1629, son of John Gurdon of Assington, by Amy Brampton. (Waters II: 956-957; *NEHGR* 95: 72).

40. **MURIEL GURDON**; m. Jun. 1633, **MAJOR RICHARD SALTONSTALI, ESQ.**, (3-41), b. 1610; d. 1694, Ipswich, Mass. (*NEHGR* 95: 72; Harleian ms. 4630 (p. 512); Waters II: 956-957; v. Redlich 175; *Saltonstall Genealogy*, 84.) This is a long established pedigree.

Line 5

30. EDWARD III (1-29), King of England; m. **PHILIPPA OF HAINAUT** (103-34). (*CP* II: 153; *ES* II/84; *CCN*, 614).

31. LIONEL "OF ANTWERP", Earl of Ulster, Duke of Clarence, b. Antwerp, 29 Nov. 1338, d. Alba, Italy, 7 Oct. 1368; m. 9 Sept. 1342 (at age four), **ELIZABETH DE BURGH** (94A-34), dau. of **WILLIAM DE BURGH** (94A-33), 3rd Earl of Ulster, and Maud de Lancaster, dau. of **HENRY** (17-29), 3rd Earl of Lancaster. (*CP* VIII: 444-445, IX: 714, III: 257-258, XIV: 184; *The Genealogist* 2 (1981):124; *CCN* 614; DNB, "Lionel of Antwerp").

32. PHILIPPA, *suo jure* Countess of Ulster, b. 16 Aug. 1355, d. on or bef. Jan. 1377/8; m. abt. May 1368, **EDMUND DE MORTIMER** (29-34), b. 1351, d. 27 Dec. 1381, 3rd Earl of March. (*CP* VIII: 444-447, IX: 714, XII (2): 180; Thatcher, 324; Gardiner, 286).

33. ELIZABETH MORTIMER, b. Usk, 12 Feb 1370/1, d. 20 Apr 1417; m. bef. 10 Dec. 1379, **SIR HENRY PERCY, K.G.** (19-32), "Harry Hotspur," killed at Shrewsbury, 14 Aug. 1403. (*CP* IX: 714; *The Genealogist* 2 (1981):124-125; *CCN*, 794).

34. ELIZABETH PERCY, d. 26 Oct. 1437; m. 1404, **JOHN DE CLIFFORD** (26-34), 7th Lord Clifford, M.P. 1411-1421, sheriff of Westmorland, d. Meaux, France, 13 Mar. 1421/3. (*CP* III: 293, IX: 714 note f, XII (2): 180, 549-550, XIV: 188, I: 183 note c).

35. THOMAS DE CLIFFORD, 8th Lord Clifford, b. 25 Mar. 1414, Sheriff of Westmorland, M.P. 1436-1453, slain at St. Albans, 22 May 1455; m. aft. Mar. 1424, Joan Dacre, dau. of Thomas Dacre, d. 22 May 1455, Lord Dacre of Gillesland, by Philippe de Neville, dau. of **RALPH DE NEVILLE, K.G.** (207-34), 1st Earl of Westmorland, and **MARGARET STAFFORD** (10-33). (*CP* III: 293).

36. MATILDA CLIFFORD; m. (2) **SIR EDMUND SUTTON, KNT.** (81-37), d. aft. 6 July 1483, son of John Sutton, K.G., Lord Dudley. (*CP* IV: 479-480; George Adlard, *The Sutton-Dudleys*, etc., N.Y., 1862: Pedigree A, Pedigree C: *The Dudleys of Yeanwith, Cumberland*).

Line 6

28. EDWARD I (1-27), King of England, 1272-1307; m. **ELEANOR OF CASTILE** (110-30). (*CP* IV: 469, X: 118; *CCN*, 356).

29. ELIZABETH, Princess of England, Countess of Holland, b. 7 Aug. 1282, d. 5 May 1316; wid. of John, Count of Holland, d.s.p. 1299; m. (2) 14 Nov. 1302, **HUMPHREY DE BOHUN VIII** (97-31), b. 1276, d. 16 Mar. 1321/2, 4th Earl of Hereford and 1st Earl of Essex (*CP* V: 135, VI: 467-469, X: 118).

30. MARGARET DE BOHUN, d. 1391; m. 1325, **HUGH DE COURTENAY** (51-32), d. 1377, 2nd Earl of Devon. (*CP* III: 344, IV: 466, VI: 469 note j; Herbert Seversmith, *Colonial Families of Long Island*, 2,380-2,392).

31. SIR EDWARD COURTENAY, b. abt. 1331/2, d.v.p. betw. 2 Feb. 1368 & 1 Apr. 1371, of Godlington; m. in or bef. 1346 Emeline Dawney, d. 28 Feb. or 20 Mar. 1371, dau. of Sir John Dawney (Dauney), Knt., and Sybil Treverbin.

32. SIR HUGH COURTENAY, d. 15 Mar. 1425, of Haccombe, co. Devon, Knight of the Shire of Devon, 1395; m. (2) Philippa l'Arcedekne, dau. & coh. of Sir Warin l'Arcedekne, b. abt. 1354, d. 1400, Lord Arcedekne, by Elizabeth Talbot, d. 1407, dau. & coh. Sir John Talbot of Richard's Castle, co. Hereford. (*CP* I: 187-188; *Family of Courtenay* (1735), 238-239; Cal. Inq.p.m., 15: 292-294; *NEHGR* 124 (1970): 85-87; *ES* III.4/630).

33. JOAN COURTENAY, m. **SIR kl** (28-37), d. 1446/7, Baron Carew and Molesford (*Courtenay, cit*). She m. (2) Sir Robert de Vere.

34. SIR THOMAS CAREW, Baron Carew of Ashwater; m. Joan Carminow, dau. of Thomas Carminow and Jane Hill. (Vivian, *Visit. of Cornwall*, 68, 74).

35. SIR NICHOLAS CAREW, of Ottery-Mohun, d. 6 Dec. 1470, Baron Carew and Mulsford; m. Margaret Dinham, d. 13 Dec. 1470, dau. of **SIR JOHN DYNHAM** (214-35), Lord Dynham, d. 1458, and Joan (Jane) Arches, dau. of Sir Richard Arches. Margaret was the sister of John Dinham, Lord Dinham of Nutwell, Lord Treasurer of England. Sir Nicholas and Margaret were buried in Westminster Abbey.(Vivian, *Visit. of Cornwall*, 70).

36. SIR EDMUND CAREW, KNT., of Mohuns Ottery, d. 24 June 1513; m. Katherine Huddlesfield, b. abt. 1478, dau. & coh. of Sir William Huddlesfield, of Shilling Ford, co. Devon, Attorney General to King Edward IV, d. 22 Mar. 1499, by (1) wife Elizabeth Bosum, wid. of Sir Baldwin Fulford and dau. of John Bosum. (*Visit. of Devon* (1564), 139; *Gen. Mag.* 2 (1926): 77-78).

37. KATHERINE CAREW, m. **SIR PHILIP CHAMPERNOUN** (51-38), of Modbury, Kent, d. 1545. (Gens. 28-37: Waters, "Pedigree of Captain Francis Champernoun of York, Maine, 1665", in the *Proceedings of the Essex Institute*, 17: 16; *Devonshire Pedigrees* (1859), 123; Vivian, *Visit. of Cornwall*, 70 and note 1).

38. SIR ARTHUR CHAMPERNOUN, KNT., of Dartington, will pro. 19 Apr. 1578; m. Katherine Norris, sister of Lord Norris and dau. of Sir Henry Norris of Rycote (*Visit. of Devon* (1620), 53).

39. GAWINE CHAMPERNOUN, ESQ., of Dartington, will pro. 3 Apr. 1592; m. 19 May 1571, Roberte de Montgomery, dau. of Comte Gabriel de Montgomery and Isabel de la Touche. (B. G. de Montgomery, *Origin and History of the Montgomerys* (1948), 232, 244, 258, 274).

40. ARTHUR CHAMPERNOUN, ESQ., of Dartington, co. Devon, liv. 1620; m. Dunsford, 17 June 1598, Bridget Fulford, dau. of Sir Thomas Fulford, of Great Fulford, co. Devon, b. abt. 1553, d. 31 July 1610, by Ursula Bamfield, dau. Richard Bamfield of Poltimore, co. Devon, d. 1594. (Vivian, *Visit. of Devon*, 39, 379-380).

41. CAPTAIN FRANCIS CHAMPERNOUN, of York, Maine, 1665; will made 11 Nov. 1686, pro. 28 Dec. 1687. (Gens. 37-41: Vivian, *Visit of Devon*, 160, 162-163, 379-380; *Devon. & Cornwall N & Q.* XVII: 185, 234; Waters, *cit.*).

Line 7   Revised for 8th Edition

29. ELIZABETH, Princess of England (6-29), widow of John, count of Holland and Zealand, dau. of **EDWARD I** (1-27) and **ELEANOR OF CASTILE** (110-30), m. **HUMPHREY DE BOHUN VIII** (97-31), Earl of Hereford and Essex. (*CP* IV: 669, X: 118).

30. ELEANOR DE BOHUN, d. 7 Oct. 1363; m. 1327, **JAMES BUTLER (le BOTILLER)** (73-32), b. 1305, d. 6 Jan. 1337/8, cr. Earl of Ormond, Oct. 1328, son of **EDMUND BOTILLER (BUTLER)** (73-31) and **JOAN** (178A-8), dau. of **JOHN FITZ THOMAS FITZ GERALD** (178A-7), 1st Earl of Kildare. (*CP* X: 116-119).

31. JAMES BOTILLER (BUTLER), 2nd Earl of Ormond, b. Kilkenny 4 Oct. 1331, d. 1382; m. (disp. 15 May 1346) Elizabeth (Anne) Darcy, d. 24 Mar. 1389/90, dau. of Sir John Darcy of Knaith, prob. by (2) Joan de Burgh, wid. of Thomas Fitz John (Fitz Gerald), 2nd Earl of Kildare, dau. of Richard de Burgh, Earl of Ulster. (*CP* X: 119-121).

32. JAMES BOTILLER (BUTLER), 3rd Earl of Ormond, b. aft. 1361, d. Sept. 1405; m. bef. 17 June 1386, Anne Welles, d. bef. 13 Nov 1405, dau. of Sir John de Welles, by Maud de Ros, dau. of William de Ros. (*CP* X: 121-123; Miscl. Gen. et Her. (5th Ser.) VIII (1932/34): chart 229-231).

33. JAMES BOTILLER (BUTLER), 4th Earl of Ormond, b. 1391, d. 23 Aug. 1452; m. (1) abt. 28 Aug. 1413, **JOAN DE BEAUCHAMP** (120-36), d. Aug. 1430. (*CP* X: 123-126, XI: 705).

34. ELIZABETH BOTILLER (BUTLER), b. 1420, d. 8 Sept. 1473; m. bef. Mar. 1445, **SIR JOHN TALBOT, K.G.** (8-35), b. abt. 1413, d. 10 July 1460, 2nd Earl of Shrewsbury, Lord Treasurer of England. (*CP* XI: 705, 731 chart).

35. SIR GILBERT TALBOT, K.G., 2nd son, b. 1452, d. 16 Aug. 1517, of Grafton, co. Worcester; m. (2), as 3rd husb., Audrey Cotton, dau. of Sir William Cotton, of Landwade, co. Cambridge by wife Alice Abbott (identification discovered by Chas. Fitch-Northen). (*CP* XI: 706 note *a*, 717, 731; Paget II: 249).

36. SIR JOHN TALBOT, KNT., son by (2), b. 1485, d. 10 Sept. 1549, of Albrighton, co. Salop, and Grafton, co. Worcester, sheriff of Shropshire, 1527,1537, 1541; m. (1) **MARGARET TROUTBECK** (20-36), b. 1492, living 1521, dau. of Adam Troutbeck, Esq., of Mobberly, co. Chester, by Margaret Boteler, dau. of Sir John Boteler of Bewsey in Warrington, co. Lancaster. (*CP* XI: 717, 731).

37. ANNE TALBOT, b. 1515; m., as 2nd wife, Thomas Needham, d. 1556, of Shenton in Adderley, co. Salop, son of Sir Robert Needham and Agnes Mainwaring.

38. ROBERT NEEDHAM, b. 1535, d. 1603; m. Frances Aston, dau. of Sir Edward Aston, of Tixall, co. Stafford. (*CP* VII: 260, esp. note *a*).

39. DOROTHY NEEDHAM, b. 1570, d. after 1629; m., as 2nd wife, **SIR RICHARD CHETWODE, KNT.**, (150-42), b. abt. 1560, d. aft. 1631, Knt. 1602, son of Richard Chetwode and Agnes de Wahull, of Warkworth. (*Misc Gen Her* (2nd Ser.) I (1886): 75).

40. GRACE CHETWODE, b. 1602, d. New London, Conn., 21 Apr. 1669; m., as 2nd wife, Apr. 1635, the **REV. PETER BULKELEY, B.D.** (31-40), first minister at Concord, Mass. (Gens. 34-36: Collins III: 30-49; Gens. 36-40: Frank Bulkeley Smith, *The Chetwode Family of England (1910)*, 1945, pp. 76 ff. with charts, corrected by Donald Lines Jacobus, *Bulkeley Genealogy*, 69-83; *TAG* 21: 69-83, 9: 227. Gens. 32-40: *TAG* 70: 96-103, esp. chart p. 97).

Line 8

28. EDWARD I (1-27), King of England; m. **ELEANOR OF CASTILE** (110-30). (*CP* X: 118; *CCN* 356).

29. JOAN, of Acre, b. Acre, 1272; d. 23 Apr. 1307; m. (1) Westminster Abbey, abt. 30 Apr. 1290, **SIR GILBERT DE CLARE, KNT.**, (63-30), 6th Earl of Gloucester and Hertford, Earl of Clare. (*CP* I: 346, IV: 269, 670 chart iii, V: 702-710, 736).

30. ELEANOR (ALIANORE) DE CLARE, b. Oct. 1292; d. 30 June 1337; m. (1) 1306, aft. 14 June, **SIR HUGH LE DESPENSER, KNT.** (74-32), Baron Despenser, hanged and quartered at Hereford, 24 Nov. 1326; m. (2) 1327, Sir William la Zouche, d. 1337, formerly de Mortimer. (*CP* IV: 267-271, cf. 269, 670 chart iii, V: 736; *TAG* 49 (1973): 2).

31. ISABEL DESPENSER, m. 9 Feb. 1320/1, **SIR RICHARD FITZ ALAN** (60-32), Earl of Arundel, d. 1376. (*CP* I: 243-244).

32. ISABEL FITZ ALAN, d. 29 Aug. 1396; m. John le Strange, 4th Baron Strange of Blackmere, b. 1322, d. 12 May 1361, (son of John le Strange, 2nd Baron Strange of Blackmere, son of Fulk le Strange, I st Baron Strange of Blackmere and **ELEANOR GIFFORD** (29A-30)). (*CP* I: 346 note *b*, XII (1): 344, XIV: 596; Banks I: 421-422).

33. ANKARET, Baroness Strange of Blackmere, b. 1361, d. 1413; m. bef. 23 Aug. 1383, **RICHARD TALBOT** (14-32), b. abt. 1361, aged abt. 35 Sept. 1396, , Baron Talbot

11

de Blackmere; M.P., 1384. (*CP* XII (I): 616-7; *CP* XI: 698; Banks I: 422, 427-428; Hamon le Strange, *LeStrange Records*, 289-321).

34. SIR JOHN TALBOT, K.G., b. 1384, d. 17 July 1453, cr. I^st Earl of Shrewsbury, 1442, Lord Lieutenant of Ireland; m. bef. 5 Apr. 1406/7, Maude, b. abt. 1392, d. abt. 1423, Baroness Furnivalle, dau. of Sir Thomas Neville, Lord Furnivalle, by (1) Joan de Furnivalle, dau. and heir of William de Furnivalle, Lord Furnivalle. (*CP* XI: 698-704, 731 chart; Banks I: 428).

35. SIR JOHN TALBOT, K.G., 2nd Earl of Shrewsbury, b. abt. 1413, d. 10 July 1460, Lord Treasurer of England; m. bef. Mar. 1444/5, **ELIZABETH BOTELER (BUTLER)** (7-34), b. 1420, d. 8 Sept. 1473. (*CP* I: 242-244, IV: 267-272, XI: 704-705, 731 chart).

Line 8A   Original line prepared by Douglas Richardson. (Editorial additions to 8th Edition)

29. JOAN, of Acre (8-29), b. 1272, d. 1307, dau. of **EDWARD I** (1-27); m. (1) 1290, **SIR GILBERT DE CLARE** (63-30), 9th Earl of Clare, 6th Earl of Hertford & of Gloucester, b. 1243, d. 1295; m. (2) 1297, Ralph de Monthermer, b. 1262, d. 5 Apr. 1325, 1st Lord Monthermer, Keeper of Cardiff Castle, fought at Bannockburn, 1314. (*CP* IX: 140-142).

30. SIR THOMAS DE MONTHERMER, b. 4 Oct. 1301, slain at the battle of Sluys 24 June 1340, 2nd Lord Monthermer; m. Margaret, d. May 1349, prob. widow of Henry Teyes, Lord Teyes. (*CP* IX: 143).

31. MARGARET DE MONTHERMER, b. 14 Oct. 1329, d. 24 Mar. 1394/95, Baroness Monthermer, heiress of Stokenham, co. Devon; m. 1343 John de Montagu, of Wark-upon-Tweed d. 1390, Lord Montagu, s. of Sir William de Montagu, d. 1344, 1st Earl of Salisbury, Lord Montagu, by his wife, Katherine de Grandison, d. 1349, dau. & event. coh. of William de Grandison, d. 1335, 1st Lord Grandison, & Sibyl de Tregoz, d. 1334, dau. & coh. **SIR JOHN DE TREGOZ** (255A-30), Lord Tregoz. (*CP* IX: 86-88, 143-144 Appendix E: 36, XI: 385-388, 391-393).

32. JOHN DE MONTAGU, K.G., b. abt. 1350, beheaded 1400, 3rd Earl of Salisbury, Lord Montagu; m. bef. 4 May 1383, Maud Francis, d. 1424, wid. (successively) of John Aubrey & Sir Alan Buxhall, dau. of Sir Adam Franceys, Lord Mayor of London, 1352-1354. (*CP* IX: 89, XI: 391-393).

33. SIR THOMAS DE MONTAGU, K.G., b. abt. 1388, d. 1428, 4th Earl of Salisbury, Lt. Gen. of Normandy; m. (1) 1399 **ELEANOR DE HOLAND** (78-34), b. 1387, liv. 1413, dau. Sir Thomas de Holand, d. 1397, Earl of Kent; m. (2) bef. Nov. 1424 Alice Chaucer, d. 20 May 1475, wid. Sir John Philip, d. 1415, & dau. & h. of Thomas Chaucer, Chief Butler to Richard II & Henry IV, speaker of the House of Commons, prob. son of Geoffrey Chaucer, English poet, bro.-in-law **JOHN OF GAUNT** (1-30). (*CP* XI: 393-395; *DNB*; Dasent, *Speakers of the House of Commons*, 71-72; Roskell, *The Commons and Their Speakers*, 149-151).

Line 9

29. JOAN, of Acre (8-29), dau. of **EDWARD I** (1-27), and **ELEANOR OF CASTILE** (110-30); m. 1290, **SIR GILBERT DE CLARE, KNT.** (63-30). (*CP* I: 346, IV: 269, 670 chart III; V: 702-710, 736).

30. MARGARET DE CLARE, b. abt. 1292; d. 13 Apr. 1342; m. (1) 1 Nov. 1307, Piers de Gaveston, Earl of Cornwall, executed 19 June 1312 d.s.p.; m. (2) Windsor, 28 Apr. 1317, Hugh de Audley, d. 10 Nov. 1347, Lord Audley, 8th Earl of Gloucester, 16 Mar.

1336/7; Ambassador to France, 1341; son of Hugh de Audley, Lord Audley, and **ISOLDE DE MORTIMER** (207-31), dau. of Edmund de Mortimer of Wigmore, by 1st wife, whose name unkn. (*NEHGR* 116: 16-17; *CP* I: 346-347, III: 433-434, V: 736, XI: 101-102; Weaver, *op. cit.*. 323).

31. **MARGARET DE AUDLEY** (see also 10-31), only dau. and heir; d. 7 Sept. 1349; m. bef. 6 July 1336, **SIR RALPH DE STAFFORD, K.G.** (55-33), d. Tunbridge Castle, 31 Aug. 1372, M.P. 1337-1349, Baron of Tunbridge, Steward of the Royal Household, 1337, Seneschal of Aquitaine, 1345, fought at Crecy, cr. Earl of Stafford, 5 Mar. 1350/1, K.G., 23 Apr. 1349, son of Edmund de Stafford and **MARGARET BASSET** (55-31). (*CP* V: 736, XI: 101, XII (1): 174-177; Banks I: 408-411; *DNB*).

32. **BEATRICE STAFFORD**, widow of Maurice (FitzMaurice), Earl of Desmond; m. 1358, **THOMAS DE ROS** (89-32), 5th Baron de Ros, d. 8 June 1384, of Helmsley; M.P., 1362-1384. (*CP* V: 736, XI: 100-101; Banks I: 378).

33. **SIR WILLIAM DE ROS, K.G.**, 7th Baron de Ros, d. Belvoir, 1 Sept. 1414, of Belvoir, 1400, M.P. 1394-1413, Treasurer of England, 1403-1404, K.G., 1403; m. 9 Oct 1394, **MARGARET D'ARUNDEL** (21-32), d. 3 July 1438, dau. of **SIR JOHN D'ARUNDEL** (21-31), 1st Lord Arundel. (*CP* I: 341, XI: 101-103; Banks I: 378. Gens. 32-33: Robert Thornton, *The Antiquities of Nottinghamshire* (London, 1677), 115; John Nichols, *History of Leicestershire*, II Part I, 27 ff.).

34. **MARGARET DE ROS**, liv. 1423; m. abt. 1415, **JAMES TUCHET** (176B-36), 5th Lord Audley, b. abt. 1398, d. 23 Sept. 1459, M.P. 1421-1455. (*CP* I: 341, XI: 102-103; Banks I: 100-102).

35. **ANNE DE AUDLEY** (TUCHET), m. **SIR THOMAS DUTTON**, of Dutton (32-35), d. 23 Sept. 1459, son of Sir John Dutton and Margaret Savage. (*VCH Lanc.* VI: 305; Visit. of Cheshire (1580), 88).

36. **ISABEL DUTTON**, m. Sir Christopher de Southworth, Knt., b. 1443, d. 1487, Lord of Samlesbury; knighted in Scotland, 1482. (*VCH Lanc.* VI: 305. According to George Ormerod, *History of the County Palatine and Duchy of Chester* (London, 1819), 662, 712, and Christopher Townley, *Abstract of Inquisitions and Post Mortems from mss, at Townley* (Chetham Society) ⋯ Sir Christopher de Southworth m. Isabel Dutton, dau. of Sir Thomas Dutton of Dutton, co. Chester, by wife, Ann Audley, dau. of James Audley, Lord Audley; and Sir Thomas Dutton was son of John Dutton, Esq., by wife Margaret Savage, dau. of Sir John Savage, of Clifton).

37. **SIR JOHN DE SOUTHWORTH, KNT.**, b. 1478, d. 1517/8, Lord of Samlesbury, Sheriff of Lancashire, knighted 12 Feb. 1503/4; m. Helen de Langton, dau. of Sir Richard de Langton, d. 1500, Baron of Newton and Lord of Walton-le-Dale, by wife Isabel Gerard. (*VCH Lanc.* VI: 305.).

38. **SIR THOMAS SOUTHWORTH, KNT.**, of Samlesbury, b. 1497, d. 13 Jan. 1546, fought at Flodden Field, 9 Sept. 1513, high sheriff of Lancashire, 1542, enlarged Samlesbury Hall, 1542-1545; m. (2) abt. 9 Aug. 1518, **MARGERY BOTELER** (46-38), dau. of **THOMAS BOTELER, KNT.** (46-37), of Bewsey. (*VCH Lanc.* VI: 306).

39. **SIR JOHN SOUTHWORTH, KNT.**, d. 3 Nov. 1595, of Samlesbury Hall., co. Lancaster, knighted 1547, high sheriff of Lancashire 1562, M.P. 1566, commended for valor in Scottish wars 1557, owned vast estates but was land poor, imprisoned for harboring Catholic priests; m. St. Leonard's Middleton, 23 Jul 1547, Mary (Assheton) Gouland, of Offerton, co. Derby, dau. of Sir Richard Assheton of Middleton, co. Lancaster, Knt. (*VCH Lanc.* VI: 306; his will (published in James Croston, *History of the Ancient Hall of Samlesbury*) mentions Thomas, eldest son, and John, eldest son and heir of Thomas.).

40. **THOMAS SOUTHWORTH**, eldest son and heir, b. abt. 1548; d. 30 Nov. 1616; m. bet. 1563 and 1571, **ROSAMOND LISTER** (170A-39), dau. of, **SIR WILLIAM LISTER**

(170A-38). of Midhope and Thornton, co. York, d. 1582, by wife Bridget Pigot, of Midhope. (James Stowe, *Survey of London*, 1633). The will of William Lister, probated in 1582, desires that he "be buried according to the Church of England." The will mentions the testator's son-in-law, Thomas Southworth, as the son of Sir John Southworth. With Thomas Southworth, his son-in-law, the testator left annuities for his four children, including Sir Matthew Lister, physician to King Charles I. Thomas Southworth had become a Protestant by 1584, for which reason his father, Sir John, a moderate Catholic, threatened to disinherit him. (Letter of Sir Francis Walsingham, 1584, in Peck, *Desiderata Curiosa*, 1779). The son was liv. in London in 1584; both father and son had returned to Samlesbury in 1594. (Gens. 34-41, *VCH Lanc.* VI: 305-306; Crosby, *Visit. of Somersetshire*, 102; Dr. Samuel G. Webber, *Southworth Genealogy* (Boston, 1905), 425-442, cf. 425-426).

    41. EDWARD SOUTHWORTH, youngest son, b. London 1590, liv. 1602, but d. bef. 1622. (The only support for the connection between generations 41 and 42 is the coincidence of dates and names. Edward of Leyden may or may not be the same man as Edward of London.)

    The Line is inadequately supported at this point. Edward Southworth of Leyden was b. 1590, d. abt. 1621. Letter of Robert Cushman to Edward Southworth at Heneage House, London, 17 Aug. 1620, in Bradford's *History of Plimouth Plantation*, Boston, 1901, page 86. Edward's wife was a widow in July 1623. He m. Leyden, Holland, 28 May 1613, Alice Carpenter, b. abt. 1590; d. Plymouth, Mass., 26 Mar. 1670, dau. of Alexander Carpenter of Wrington, Somersetshire. She came to Plymouth, 1623; m. (2) Plymouth, 14 Aug. 1623, Gov. William Bradford. The sons, Constant and Thomas Southworth (see below), were brought up in the home of Gov. Bradford. (Goodwin, *Pilgrim Republic* (1920), 460-464; Col. Charles E. Banks, *The English Ancestry and Homes of the Pilgrim Fathers*; *Boston Evening Transcript* (I) 31 Aug. 1931; (II) 2 Sept. 1931. For probably the best recent discussion of what is known about the ancestry of Edward Southworth, see Robert L. French, *The Mayflower Quarterly* 88 (1992): 10-15).

    42. ENS. CONSTANT SOUTHWORTH, b. Leyden, 1614, d. Duxbury, 10 Mar. 1678/9; m. Duxbury, 2 Nov. 1637, Elizabeth Collier, dau. of William Collier.

    42. CAPT. THOMAS SOUTHWORTH, b. Leyden, 1616, d. Plymouth, Mass., 8 Dec. 1669; m. Sept. 1641, Elizabeth Raynor (Reyner), dau. of Rev. John Raynor.

Line 9A   Revised for 8th Edition

    34. WALTER CALVERLEY, alias **SCOT**, fl.1429, d. 1466; m. Elizabeth Markenfield, dau. of Sir Thomas Markenfield. (Foster, *cit.*).

    35. SIR WILLIAM CALVERLEY, of Caverley, Knt., d. 1488; m. 1441, **AGNES TEMPEST** (170A-34), dau. of Sir John Tempest, Knt., of Bracewell, Sheriff of Yorkshire 1440, 1459, and **ALICE SHERBURNE** (170A-33). (J. W. Clay, *Dugdale's Visitation of Yorkshire* I: 243-244; Thomas Dunham Whitaker, *The History and Antiquities of the Deanery of Craven in the County of York* (London, 1805), p. 35, "Lister of Gisburn-Park in Craven," p. 95, "Pedigree of Lister of Mydhope and Thomton").

    36. JOAN CALVERLEY (170A-35); m. 20 June 1467, Christopher Lister (or Lyster), of Midhope, co. Yorkshire, son and h. of Lawrence Lister, (son of John Lyster), and Ellen Banestre, dau. of Christopher Banestre. (Whitaker, *op. cit.*, 35, 95).

14

37. WILLAM LISTER (LYSTER) ESQ. (170A-36), of Midhope, d.1537; m. (disp. 1491) Elizabeth Banestre, dau. of Thurstone Banestre of Swindon, co. Wilts. (his cousin). (Whitaker 35, 95).

Line 10

31. MARGARET DE AUDLEY (9-31), m. bef. 6 Jul. 1335, **SIR RALPH DE STAFFORD, K.G.** (55-32),cr. Earl of Stafford. (*CP* V: 736, XI: 100-101; Banks I: 408-411; *DNB*).
32. SIR HUGH STAFFORD, K.G., 2nd Earl of Stafford, b. abt. 1342, M.P. 1371, d. 6 Oct. 1386,; m. bef. 1 Mar. 1350/1, Philippe Beauchamp, d. bef. 6 Apr. 1386, dau. of **THOMAS BEAUCHAMP** (87-31), 11th Earl of Warwick, and **CATHERINE DE MORTIMER** (120-34), dau. of **ROGER DE MORTIMER** (120-33, 176B-31), 1st Earl of March, by **JOAN DE GENEVILLE** (71-32). (*Warwick Castle and Its Earls*, 828; *CP* XII (1): 177-179).
33. MARGARET STAFFORD, d. 9 June 1396; m., as 1st wife, **SIR RALPH DE NEVILLE, K.G.** (207-34), 1st Earl of Westmorland. (*CP* IV: 502a-502b, Neville Chart, XII (2): 547; *Notes & Queries* (3rd Ser.) 9: 376; 152: 219; *VCH Worcester*).
34. SIR RALPH NEVILLE, of Oversley, co. Warwick, 2nd son; m. **MARY FERRERS** (2-33), dau. of **SIR ROBERT DE FERRERS** (62-34) and **JOAN BEAUFORT** (20-32). (*CP* V: 320, chart; VII: 415-416 note *j*; *Gen.* (n.s.) 3: 109; Clay, 146-147).

Line 11

29. JOAN OF ACRE (8-29), d. 1307, dau. of **EDWARD I** (1-27), King of England, and **ELEANOR OF CASTILE** (110-30); m. 1290, **SIR GILBERT DE CLARE, KNT.** (63-30), 6th Earl of Gloucester and Hertford, Earl of Clare. (*CP* I: 346, IV: 269, 670 chart III, V: 346, 702-710, 736).
30. ELIZABETH DE CLARE, (sis. and coh. of Gilbert de Clare, 7th Earl of Gloucester and Hertford), b. 16 Sept 1295, d. 4 Nov. 1360; m. (1) **JOHN DE BURGH** (94A-32), d.v.p. 18 June 1313; m. (2) as 2nd wife, **SIR THEOBALD DE VERDUN** (70-32), d.s.p.m. 27 July 1316, Lord of Weoberley, Baron 1308, of Alton, co. Stafford; m. (3) 1317, Roger Damory, 1st Lord Damory, d. 1321. (*CP* IV: 43-44, V: 346, XII (2): 250-251; Banks I: 445).
31. ISABEL DE VERDUN, by (2), b. Amesbury, co. Wilts., 21 Mar. 1316/7, d. 25 July 1349; m. bef. 20 Feb. 1330/1, **HENRY FERRERS** (58-32), 3rd Lord Ferrers of Groby, b. abt. 1294, d. Groby, co. Leicester, 15 Sept. 1343. (*CP* V: 333 chart, 344-347, XII (2): 251-252).
32. WILLLAM FERRERS, KNT., Lord Ferrers of Groby, bapt. Newbold Verdon, co. Leicester, 28 Feb. 1332/3, d. 8 Jan. 1370/1, knighted 6 May 1351, will pro. 19 July 1372; m. (1) bef. 25 Apr. 1354, Margaret d'Ufford, d. 25 Sept 1375, dau. of Robert d'Ufford, Earl of Suffolk, and Margaret de Norwich, dau. of Sir Walter de Norwich; m. (2) bef. 25 May 1368, Margaret Percy, wid. of Sir Robert d'Umfraville, dau. of **HENRY DE PERCY, K.G.** (161-29) Lord Percy, and **IDOINE DE CLIFFORD** (205-33). (See also 87-32, 232-32). (*CP* V: 333 chart, 348-351).
33. HENRY FERRERS (see 248-34), Lord Ferrers of Groby, b. 16 Feb. 1355/6, d. 3 Feb. 1387/8; m. bef. 27 Apr. 1371, Joan, d. 30 May 1393, perh. dau. of either Sir Thomas de Hoo of Luton Hoo, or of Luke Poynings. (*CP* V: chart 333, 351-354; XIV: 321; X: 665-666)).
34. WILLLIAM FERRERS (248-34), Lord Ferrers of Groby, bapt. Luton, co. Bedford, 25 Apr. 1372, d. 18 May, 1445; m. (1) aft. 10 Oct. 1388, Philippa de Clifford, dau. of **SIR**

ROGER DE CLIFFORD (26-32), Lord of Westmorland, sometimes called Lord of Clifford, and Maud de Beauchamp, liv. 4 July 1405, dau. of **THOMAS BEAUCHAMP** (87-31) and **CATHERINE DE MORTIMER** (120-34); m. (2) Margaret de Montagu, dau. John de Montagu, Earl of Salisbury, by Maud Franceys, dau. of Sir Adam Franceys, of London; m. (3) by 26 Oct. 1416, Elizabeth Standisshe, wid. (successively) of John de Wrottesley and of Sir William Botiller, dau. of Robert de Standisshe. (*CP* V: 333 chart, 354-357).

    35. THOMAS FERRERS, ESQ., (2nd son by (1)); d. 6 Jan. 1458/9; m. **ELIZABETH FREVILLE** (216-34), dau. of **SIR BALDWIN FREVILLE IV** (216-33), of Tamworth Castle, co. Warwick. (*CP* V: 333 chart, 357 note *a*).

    36. SIR HENRY FERRERS, KNT., d. 28 Dec. 1500; m. Margaret Heckstall, dau. of Sir William Heckstall; their male issue still continued at Baddesley Clinton, co. Warwick, 1925. (*CP* V: 333 chart, 357 note *a*; *Visit. of Warwick* (1619), 5).

    37. ELIZABETH FERRERS; m. abt. 1508, James Clerke, gent., of Forde Hall, d. 20 Sept. 1553, son of John Clerke, of Ford, Kent. (Will of Sir Edward Ferrers dated 10 July 1535, son of Sir Henry Ferrers and brother of Elizabeth (Ferrers) Clerke.) (*CP* V: 357 note *a*; *Visit. of Kent* (1574), 38; *Visit. of Warwick, ibid*).

    38. GEORGE CLERKE, GENT., b. 1510, d. 8 Mar. 1558; m. abt. 1533, Elizabeth Wilsford, dau. of Thomas Wilsford of Hartridge, par. of Cranbrook, co. Kent. (Will of Sir Edward Ferrers; Inq.p.m., 16 Oct. 1558).

    39. JAMES CLERKE, GENT., b. abt. 1540, d. 1614, of East Farleigh, Kent; will made 13 July 1614, pr. 1 Nov 1614; m. abt. 1565, Mary Saxby, dau. of Sir Edward Saxby, Baron of the Exchequer and (2) Elizabeth (Fisher) Woodliff, wid. of William Woodliff of Wormeley, co. Herts. (*Visit. of Kent* (1574), 38; *NEHGR* 74 (1920): 68-76, 130-140).

    40. WILLIAM CLERKE, GENT., of East Farleigh, co. Kent, and London, bur. East Farleigh 12 June 1610; m. London, (license) 10 Feb. 1598/9, Mary Weston, bapt. Roxwell, co. Essex, 26 Apr. 1579, d. prob. bef. 13 Jul 1614, dau. of Sir Jerome Weston, of Roxwell, co. Essex, and Mary Cave, dau. of Anthony Cave. (Parish Registers of East Farleigh and London; *NEHGR, cit.*).

    41. CAPTAIN JEREMY CLARKE (220-41), bapt. East Farleigh, co. Kent, 1 Dec. 1605; bur. Newport, R.I., Jan. 1651/2; m. 1637, Frances Latham, bapt. Kempston. co. Beds, 15 Feb 1609/10, d. Sept 1677, wid. of William Dungan, dau. of Lewis Latham, Gent.. Frances m. (3) by 18 Jan. 1656, Rev. William Vaughan. Jeremy had, among other ch., (Gens. 31 to 41: Justice, *Jeremy Clarke*, etc., 1922, pp. 34-35, *NEHGR, cit.*; *MC*: 100-16).

    42. GOV. WALTER CLARKE, b. Newport, Rhode Island, abt. 1640, d. 28 May 1714, Gov. of R.I. 1676-77, 1686, 1696-98; m. (1) 1660, Content Greenman, dau. of John Greenman, 3 ch.; m. (2) 1666/7, Hannah Scott, dau. of Richard Scott, 6 ch.; m. (3) 1682/3, Freeborn (Williams) Hart, dau. of Roger Williams; m. (4) 1711, Sarah (Prior) Gould, dau. of Matthew Prior. (*NEHGR* 74: 68-76, 130-40; *Gen. Dict. of RI*; *Dict. of Am. Biog.*; *Natl. Cyclopaedia of Am. Biog.*; *Hist. of R.I.*; *MC* 100-17).

    42. WESTON CLARKE, (son of Gen. 41), b. Newport, Rhode Island, 5 Apr 1648, d. aft. 1728; Atty Gen. and Treasurer of Rhode Island, 1681-1685; m. (1) 25 Dec. 1688, Mary Easton; m. (2) 21 Nov 1691, Rebecca (Thurston) Easton. (*MC* 100-17).

    42. MARY CLARKE (220-42), (dau. of Gen. 31), b. abt. 1641, d. Newport, Rhode Island, 7 Apr. 1711; m. (1) 3 June 1658, Gov. John Cranston, of Rhode Island, b. abt. 1626, d. 12 Mar. 1680; m. (2) Philip Jones, merchant of New York, Boston and Rhode Island; m. (3) John Stanton of Newport, Rhode Island. (*NEHGR, cit.*; Torrey, *New England Marriages*, ms. addendum to Stanton section; *MC* 100-17).

42. REV. JAMES CLARKE, (son of Gen. 41), b. Newport, Rhode Island, 1649, ord. Newport (2ⁿᵈ Bapt. Church) 1701, sett. Newport, 1700-1736, d. Newport, 1 Dec. 1736, ae. 87 years; m. Hopestill Power. (*MC* 100-17).

Line 12

30. MARGARET DE BOHUN (6-30), d. 16 Dec. 1391, granddau. of **EDWARD I** (1-27), King of England, and **ELEANOR OF CASTILE** (110-30); m. 1325, **HUGH DE COURTENAY** (51-32), d. 1377, Earl of Devon. (*CP* IV: 324, 335).

31. ELIZABETH DE COURTENAY, d. 7 Aug. 1395; m. 1359, Sir Andrew Luttrell (Lutterell) of Chilton, Devon, d. 1378/1381. (Seversmith, 2,345-2,346; Vivian (1895), 244, 537).

32. SIR HUGH LUTTRELL, of Dunster, co. Somerset, d. 24 Mar. 1428; Privy Councillor to King Henry V; m. Catherine de Beaumont, d. 28 Aug. 1435, wid. of John Streche, dau. of Sir John Beaumont. (Seversmith, 2,341-2,345; Vivian (1895), 537).

33. ELIZABETH LUTTRELL, liv. 1439; m. (1) abt. 1406, William Harleston, d. sh. aft. 18 Mar 1416; m. (2) aft. 1423, John Stratton, Esq., of Lye Hall, Weston, co. Norfolk, liv. 1459. (Gens. 30-33: Sir Henry Lyte, *History of Dunster, Mohun and Lutterell;* Bloomfield, *History of Norfolk; Boston Evening Transcript,* 19 Oct. 1926, 27 Feb. 1928, Note 4041, Ludlow-Brewster; Seversmith, 2,337-2,338, 2,341).

34. ELIZABETH STRATTON, will pr. 11 Dec 1474; m John Andrews (Andrewe), Esq., of Baylham, co. Suffolk, d. 1475, son of James Andrewe and Alice Weyland. (Old-*CP* VIII: 185; Banks I: 466; Seversmith, 2,335).

35. ELIZABETH ANDREWS, liv. 1485; m. (1) **SIR THOMAS WINDSOR** (12A-35), b. abt. 1440, d. 1485, of Stanwell, co. Middlesex, son of **MILES WINDSOR** (12A-34), d. 30 Sept. 1451, Italy. (*CP* XII (2): 792-794; Banks I: 466).

36. SIR ANDREWS WINDSOR, b. Manor of Stanwell, co. Middlesex, 1467, d. 30 Mar. 1543, 1ˢᵗ Baron Windsor of Stanwell; m. **ELIZABETH BLOUNT** (59-39). (*CP* IX: 337, note *d;* Old-*CP* VIII: 185; Banks I: 466; Waters I: 276; Berry, *Buckinghamshire Pedigrees;* Hoar, *History of Wiltshire; Boston Evening Transcript,* as above; Colket in *TAG* 15: 129-143; *CP* XI: 337 note *a;* Seversmith, 2,193, 2,204).

37. EDITH WINDSOR, d. bef. 25 May 1580, when husb. made his will; m. bef. 26 Mar. 1543, George Ludlow, Esq., will pro. 4 Feb. 1581, of Hill Deverill, co. Wilts; sheriff of Wiltshire, 1567, son of William Ludlow (Ludlowe) and Jane Moore, dau. of Nicholas Moore. (Waters I: 172-174, 275-276; Seversmith, 2,187, 2,193; *Harleian Ms.* 1544).

38. THOMAS LUDLOW, of Maiden Bradley, Dinton and Baycliffe, co. Wilts, bur. Dinton, 25 Nov. 1607, will pro. June 1608; m. 1582, Jane Pyle, dau. of Thomas Pyle and Elizabeth Langrich. (Waters I: 275-276; Seversmith, 2,095).

39. ROGER LUDLOW, (3ʳᵈ son of Thomas, Gen. 38), bapt. Dinton, 7 Mar. 1590, d. Dublin, Ireland, 1666, Balliol Coll. 1610, came to America 1630, Deputy-Governor of Mass., 1634, and of Conn.; m. by license Chard, co. Somerset, 18 Dec. 1624, Mary Cogan, bur. Dublin, Ireland 3 June 1664, dau. of Philobert Cogan, b. Chard 1563, will pr. 1641 (son of Thomas Cogan by Elizabeth Fisher), and Anne Marshall, dau. of Thomas Marshall and Mary Cotton. [Mary Cogan's sister, Elizabeth Cogan, b. 1607, m. (2) as his 2ⁿᵈ wife, Gov. John Endecott, of Mass.] (Seversmith, 595-597; Waters I: 275-276; *Pedigree of Ludlow of Hill Deverell* (1884);. Gens. 35-39: Colket: "The Royal Ancestry of the Ludlows," in *TAG* 25: 138-143; *Search for the Passengers of the Mary and John 1630,* Vol. 26: 49; *NGS Qrtrly* 51: 233; Seversmith, *ibid*).

17

40. SARAH LUDLOW, b. Fairfield, Conn., 1639; m. by 1662, as 2nd wife, Rev. Nathaniel Brewster of Brookhaven, L.I., son of Francis Brewster by Lucy, who m. (2) bef. 1 Feb. 1647/8 Thomas Pell of Fairfield, Conn. (Seversmith, 359-364, 389-390, 2,057). [Note: for Nathaniel Brewster and his ancestry see Seversmith, 359-410].

39. GABRIEL LUDLOW, (2nd son of Thomas, Gen. 38), bapt. Dinton co. Wilts, 10 Feb. 1587, d. shortly after 1639; m. Phyllis, whose will dtd. 12 Sept. 1657, pro. 18 Dec. 1657.
40. SARAH LUDLOW, b. abt. 1635; m. Col. John Carter, of Lancaster County, Virginia (parents of Robert Carter, "King Carter of Corotoman"). (Seversmith, 2,906-2,907).

39. THOMAS LUDLOW, (4th son of Gen. 38), bapt. Baverstock, co. Wilts, 3 Mar. 1593, d. Warminster, co. Wilts, 1646; m. 1624, Jane Bennett, bapt. Warminster, 15 Apr. 1604, d. 19 Dec. 1683, dau. of John Bennett of Steeple Ashton and Smallbrook.
40. GABRIEL LUDLOW, bapt. Warminster, co. Wilts, 27 Aug. 1634, res. of Frome, co. Somerset; m. Martha.
41. GABRIEL LUDLOW, b. Castle Cary, co. Somerset, 2 Nov. 1663, bapt. 1 Dec. 1663, d. 1736; to New York, 1694, clerk of New York House of Assembly, 1699-1733, merchant; m. 5 Apr. 1697, Sarah Hanmer, dau. of Rev. Joseph Hanmer, formerly of Iscoyd, co. Flint, chaplain to His Majesty's Forces, New York, and Martha Eddowes, formerly of Whitchurch, co. Salop, whose m. banns pub. Whitchurch, 27 Mar. 1659. (Seversmith, 2,097; NYGBR (1919) 50: 34-38).

Line 12A   New to 8th Edition

21. WALTER FITZ OTHER, b. abt. 1045/1050, d. sh. aft. 1100, keeper of the forest of Windsor, cr. castellan of Windsor Castle by William the Conqueror, son of Other, b. abt. 1020 by Beatrice. (Seversmith 2,247-2,248; Sanders, 116-117; Brydges, Collins, *Peerage* III: 638-641; *CP* X: 10; *Ancestor* 1 (Apr. 1902): 121-126, 2 (July 1902): 98 chart; Keats-Rohan, *Domesday People* I (1999): 455).
22. WILLIAM FITZ WALTER (DE WYNDESORE), of Eton, 1st of the name in succession, b. abt. 1075/80, d. 1161, appt. constable of Windsor Castle 1100. (Round, *Geoffrey de Mandeville* (1892): 169, note 4).
23. WILLIAM II DE WYNDESORE, b. abt. 1115, d. abt. 1190/1; m. Christina de Wiham? (Seversmith, 2,245-2,246).
24. WILLIAM III DE WYNDESORE, b. abt. 1137/8, d. sh. aft. 1176/1177; m. Hawisia. (Seversmith, 2,244-2,245, esp. notes on 2,243-2,244).
25. WILLIAM IV DE WYNDESORE, b. abt. 1167/8, d. bef. 1247, berh. by 1242; wife's name is unknown. (Seversmith, 2,239-2,244, see esp. notes on 2,243 and 2,244 which correct Round, *Ancestor* 1: 122-126 and 2: 97; *CP* XII (2): 874ff).
26. WILLIAM V DE WYNDESORE, d. 1279 Inq.p.m.
27. WILLIAM VI DE WYNDESORE, d.v.p. 1273; m. abt. 1255, Margaret de Drokensford, dau. of John de Drokensford. (Seversmith, 2,236-2,237, 2,249-2,250).
28. SIR RICHARD DE WYNDESORE, b., prob. at West Hakebourne, co. Berks, 1258, minor in 1273, [heir of his grandfather, William de Wyndesore V], d. 20 Jan. 1326; m. Johanna (Joan) Stapleton, d. 21 Jan. 1327/8, dau. of Sir Nicholas Stapleton and Margery Bassett, dau. of Sir Miles Bassett and Agnes Lascelles, dau. of John de Lascelles. (Seversmith, 2,232-2,236, 2,257-2,264; Clay, 210).

29. RICHARD DE WYNDESORE, b. 1296/1298. d. 3 or 6 Apr. 1367; m. (1) Johanna Moleyns, dau. of James Moleyns, d. bef. 1342, and Margaret de la Sale aka Bentworth, liv. 10 Feb. 1344; m. (2) Clarice Drokensford. (Seversmith, 2,227-2,231).

30. JAMES WYNDESORE, by (1), b. 1323, d.v.p. 2 Oct. 1360, aged 37; m. Elizabeth Streche, dau. of Sir John Streche, d. 29 Sept. 1355, and Elizabeth Reed, d. 27 Nov. 1355, dau. of Walter Reed by Joan Crispin, dau. of William Crispin. (Seversmith 2,227, 2,272-2,276).

31. SIR MILES WYNDESORE, bapt. Bentworth, co. Hampshire, 10 June 1353, d. 31 Mar. 1387; m. Alice de Wymondham, d. aft. Mar. 1387, dau. of Adam de Wymondham and Margaret Staundon.

32. BRYAN WYNDESORE, b. 1371, d. 30 Apr. 1399; m. abt. 1395, Alice Drew, dau. of Thomas Drew(e) and Emma (NN) Cary.

33. RICHARD WYNDSORE (WYNDESORE), d. London, 16 Apr. 1428, bur. at Stanwell, co. Middlesex, (succ. older bro., Miles (d. 1401), as lord of the manor of Stanwell, which was held during his minority by a maternal anc., Lawrence Drewe); m. Christian Faulkner, liv. Apr. 1428, dau. of Richard Faulkner, of Fauconer.

34. MILES WINDSOR (WYNDSORE), b. 1415, d. at and bur. in, the Monastery of St. Bartholomew, Ferrara, Italy, 30 Sept. 1451; m. Joane Greene. (Gens. 31-34: Seversmith, 2,217-2,226).

35. THOMAS WINDOR, b. Stanwell, co. Middlesex, 1441, d. Stanwell, 29 Sept. 1485; m. abt. 1483, **ELIZABETH ANDREWS** (12-35). (Seversmith, 2,209-2,217).

Line 13   Revised for 8th Edition

30. ELEANOR DE BOHUN (7-30), d. 7 Oct. 1363, granddau. of Edward I, King of England, and Eleanor of Castile; m. 1327, **JAMES BOTILLER (BUTLER)** (73-32), 1st Earl of Ormond. (*CP* X: 116-119).

31. PETRONILLA (PERNEL) BOTILLER (BUTLER) (73-33), liv. 28 May 1365, dead 1368; m. as (1) wife by 8 Sept. 1352, **GILBERT TALBOT** (95-32), b. abt. 1332, d. 24 Apr. 1387, Lord Talbot, of Eccleswall, co. Hereford; M.P. 1362. (*CP* IV: 63, 71, XII (1): 614-617).

Line 13A   Revised for 8th Edition

32. SIR HENRY DE GREY, aged 30 or more in 1370, Lord Grey of Wilton, son of Reynold de Grey and Maud Bourtetourt, said to have been dau. of Sir John de Bourtetourt m. bef. 3 Feb. 1379/80, Elizabeth Talbot, d. 10 Jan. 1401/2, said to be dau. of **GILBERT TALBOT** (95-32) Lord Talbot, and **PETRONILLA (PERNEL) BOTILLER (BUTLER)** (13-31, 73-33). (*CP* IV: 63-65,71; CP VI: 176-178, chart bet. 128-129; CP XIV: 235).

33. MARGARET DE GREY, d. 1 June 1454; m. **JOHN DARCY** (88-35), Lord Darcy of Knayth, b. abt. 1377, d. 9 Dec. 1411. (*CP* IV: 63-65, 71).

34. JOHN DARCY, b. abt. 1400; d. 1458, 2nd son, m. **JOAN GREYSTOKE** (62-36). (*CP* IV: 71).

35. RICHARD DARCY, b. abt. 1424, d.v.p. 1458; m. Eleanor Scrope, dau. of Sir John Scrope, Lord Scrope of Upsal, and Elizabeth Chaworth, dau. of Sir Thomas Chaworth of Wiverton, Notts. (*CP* IV: 71).

36. SIR WILLLIAM DARCY, b. abt. 1443, d. 30 May 1488; m., lic.. 23 Jan. 1460/1, Eupheme Langton, dau. of John Langton, Esq., of Farnley, co. York. (*CP* IV: 71, 73).

37. SIR THOMAS DARCY, K.G., b. abt. 1467, cr. 1st Lord Darcy, of Temple Hurst, beheaded 30 June 1537,attainted of high treason and his peerage forfeited; m. (1) Dowsabel Tempest, d. 1503/20, dau. of Sir Richard Tempest, of Giggleswick, co. York, and Mabel Strickland, dau. of **WALTER STRICKLAND** (41-33), of Sizergh. (*CP* IV: 71; Foster, *Visit. of Yorkshire* (1584/5), 47; Clay, *Extinct and Dormant Peerages of the Northern Counties*, 43.).

38. SIR ARTHUR DARCY, 3rd son, Lieut. of the Tower of London, b. abt. 1505, d. 3 Apr. 1561; m. Mary Carew, dau. of Sir Nicholas Carew of Beddington, co. Surrey. (*CP* IV: 71).

39. SIR EDWARD DARCY, KNT., of Dartford Place, co. Kent, b. abt. 1543, matric. Trinity Coll., Cambridge, 1561, M.P. 1584, knighted 1603, d. 28 Oct. 1612; m. Elizabeth Astley, dau. of Thomas Astley, of Writtle, co. Essex. (*TAG* 21: 174; Burkes *Peerage* (1953) "Darcy of Knyath"; *Visit. of Yorkshire* (1563/4), 92-93).

40. ISABELLA DARCY, b. abt. 1600, d. London, 1669, will made May 1668, pro. 4 Aug. 1669, mentions "my dau. Mary Sherman"; m. (1) abt. 1619, John Launce, b. abt. 1597, of Penare, St. Clement's Parish, Cornwall, son of Robert Launce and Susan Tubb, dau. of George Tubb. (Waters II: 1186-1187).

41. MARY LAUNCE, b. bef. 1625, d. Watertown, Mass., 9 Nov. 1710; m. abt. 1645, the Rev. John Sherman, b. Dedham, co. Essex, 26 Dec. 1613, ordained Watertown, 1647, d. Watertown, 8 Aug. 1685. (Gens. 32-41: Given briefly and with slight errors in *Your Family Tree* (1929), p. 184 which is not a reliable reference. This is a well-known line, the paternity of Mary Launce being mentioned by Cotton Mather. The best account, by Donald L. Jacobus, may be seen in *TAG* 21: 169-177. *TAG* 20: 129-135; Waters II: 1186-1187; Weis, *Colonial Clergy of N.E.*, 186).

Line 14

31. PETRONILLA (PERNEL) BUTLER (13-31), great-granddau. of **EDWARD I** (1-27), by **ELEANOR OF CASTILE** (110-30); m. bef. 8 Sept. 1352 as 1st wife, **SIR GILBERT TALBOT** (95-32), 3rd Lord Talbot, d. 24 Apr. 1387. (*CP* XII (1): 345, 614-617).

32. SIR RICHARD TALBOT, Lord Talbot, b. abt. 1361, d. 7-9 Sept. 1396; m. bef. 1383, **ANKARET LE STRANGE** (8-33), b. 1361, d. 1413, Baroness Strange. (*CP* XI: 698; *CP* XII (1): 616).

33. MARY TALBOT, d. 13 Apr. 1434; m. (1) Sir Thomas Greene, Knt., of Greene's Norton, co. Northampton, b. abt. 1368/9, d. 14 Dec. 1417, sheriff of Northamptonshire 1416, son of Sir Thomas Greene, b. 1342/3, d. 1391. (For Gens. 33 and 34 see: Neil D. Thompson, "The Sir Thomas Gre[e]nes of Greene's Norton," *The Genealogist* 13 (1999): 24-29).

34. SIR THOMAS GREENE, of Greene's Norton, b. Norton, 10 Feb. 1399/1400, d. 18 Jan. 1461/1462, sheriff of Northamptonshire 1454; m. (1) by 16 Dec. 1421, **PHILIPPA DE FERRERS** (61-35) and prob. had, evidence unverified, (*CP* V: 320 chart; *NEHGR* 123: 180-181).

35. ELIZABETH GREENE, m. abt. 1440, William Raleigh, Esq., of Farnborough, co. Warwick, d. 15 Oct. 1460, son of John Raleigh and his wife Idony Cotesford, dau. of Thomas Cotesford. (The fact of this marriage is stated in two later pedigrees, one Greene (British Library, P 13573 Harl. 1412) and one Raleigh (*Visit. of Warwick* (1619), 77), and supported by the Inq.p.m. of Elizabeth's brother, Sir Thomas Greene, recording that on 4 July 1452 William Ralegh (with other feoffees who were related to Thomas's wife Mathilda (Maud) Throckmorton) were seised of the Greene manor of Kegworth, co. Leicester, which they released to Thomas Greene and his wife Mathilda; but see note at end.) (Dugdale, *Warwickshire*, 382; *NEHGR* 123: 180-181, 145: 3-21).

36. **SIR EDWARD RALEIGH, KNT.**, of Farnborough, b. abt. 1441, sheriff of Warwickshire and Leicestershire, will pro. 20 June 1509; m. 1467, Margaret Verney, dau. of Sir Ralph Verney, Lord Mayor of London. (See 150-39). (Dugdale, *op. cit.*, 382; *NEHGR, cit.*).

37. **SIR EDWARD RALEIGH, KNT.**, of Farnborough, b. abt. 1470, d.v.p., will pro. 1508; m. bet. 1496 and 1505, **ANNE CHAMBERLAYNE** (238-13), dau. of Richard Chamberlayne, of Sherburne, co. Oxford, and his wife Sybil Fowler, dau. Richard Fowler, Chancellor of the Exchequer of King Edward IV. Anne m. (2) Ralph Fulshurst. (Dugdale, *op. cit.*, 382-383; *NEHGR, cit.*).

38. **BRIDGET RALEIGH**, m., as 1st wife, Sir John Cope, Knt., of Copes Ashby, co. Northampton, sheriff of Northamptonshire 1545, M.P. 1547, will dtd. 16 Aug. 1558, d. 22 Jan. 1558/9, son of William Cope and Jane Spencer. (*VCH Warwick* VI: 115f; *NEHGR, cit.*).

39. **ELIZABETH COPE**, m. John Dryden, Esq., of Copes Ashby, d. 30 Sept. 1584, monumental brass in parish church of Canons Ashby. (Mill Stephenson, *A List of Monumental Brasses in the British Isles* (1926): 420; *NEHGR, cit.*).

40. **BRIDGET DRYDEN**, b. abt. 1563; will made 12 Feb. 1644, adm. 2 Apr. 1645; m. abt. 1587, Rev. Francis Marbury, bapt. London 27 Oct. 1555, will proved 14 Feb. 1610/1611, son of William Marbury and Agnes Lenton, dau. of John Lenton. (*NEHGR, cit*; Lennam, *Francis Marbury 1555-1611* (Studies in Philology, lxv 2 Apr. 1968), pp. 207-222).

41. **CATHERINE MARBURY**, b. abt. 1610; d. Newport, R.I., 2 May 1687; m. Berkhampstead, co. Hertford, 7 June 1632, Richard Scott, d. Providence, R.I., bef. Mar. 1681. (*NEHGR* 80: 12 chart; *NEHGR, cit*).

41. **ANNE MARBURY**, (sis. of Catherine), bapt. Alford, co. Lincoln, 20 July 1591, killed by the Indians, in N.Y., Aug. 1643; m. London, 9 Aug. 1612, William Hutchinson, bapt. Alford, co. Lincoln, 14 Aug. 1586, d. Newport, R. I., 1642, son of Edward Hutchinson. (*The Genealogist* 14 (2000): 159; Generations 31-41: v. Redlich 257-258; Meredith B. Colket, Jr., *Marbury Genealogy* (1936). Gens. 39-41: White, *Ancestry of John Barber White* (1913), pp. 151-152, 155-156; *NEHGR* 20: 283-284, 363-367; 98: chart opp. p. 18; see also *Boston Evening Transcript*, Note 5930, 28 Sept. 1927 and Note 1072, 6 Nov. 1935).

Note: the 1585 King of Arms Greene pedigree, cited in gen. 35, states that Thomas and Philippa had three sons (Thomas, Anthony, and John) and four daughters (Elizabeth, wife of "Sir William Rowley of Co. Warwick," Joan, wife of John Reading, Isabel, wife of Edmund Cornwall, and Margaret, wife of Nicholas Haulte) (printed in *The Greene Family of England and America with Pedigree*s (Boston, 1901)). Search of published contemporary records has provided as yet the identification of only two children of Thomas and Philippa: Thomas and Isabel (*Cal. Close Rolls*, 33 Henry VI [1454], p. 36). Further research is needed.

29. ELIZABETH, Princess of England (6-29), dau. of **EDWARD I** (1-27) and **ELEANOR OF CASTILE** (110-30); m. 1302, **HUMPHREY VIII DE BOHUN** (97-31), 4th Earl of Hereford and 1st Earl of Essex. (*CP* IV: 669, X: 118).

30. SIR WILLIAM DE BOHUN, K.G., b. 1310/12, d. Sept. 1360, fought at Crecy, cr. 6th Earl of Northampton, 16 Mar. 1336/7; m., as 2nd husb., 1335/8, **ELIZABETH DE BADLESMERE** (65-34). (*CP* I: 245, 373 note c, IV: 669, IX: 664-667).

31. ELIZABETH DE BOHUN, d. 3 Apr. 1385; m. abt. 28 Sept. 1359, **RICHARD FITZ ALAN** (20-31, 60-33), b. 1346, beheaded 21 Sept. 1397, 15th Earl of Arundel and Surrey. (*CP* I: 244-245, IV: 669).

32. ELIZABETH FITZ ALAN, d. 8 July 1425; m. (1) Sir William de Montagu; m.(2) July 1384, **THOMAS DE MOWBRAY** (16-32), 1st Duke of Norfolk, b. 22 Mar. 1365/6, d. Venice, 22 Sept. 1399; m. (3) bef. 19 Aug. 1401, Sir Robert Goushill, of Haveringham, Notts.; m. (4) bef. 3 July 1414, Sir Gerard Usflete. (*CP* IX: 604, XII (1): 604).

33. ELIZABETH GOUSHILL, b. abt. 1402; m. **ROBERT WINGFIELD** (15A-33), b. 1403, of Letheringham, Suffolk, d. 1451. (*CP* IX: 604 n; G-A. Moriarty in *NEHGR* 103: 295.

34. ELIZABETH WINGFIELD, d. 1497, m. bef. 1462 Sir William Brandon, Knt., d. 1491. (*DNB* 6: 218-22; *NEHGR* 103: 102-107; TAG 47 (1971): 205).

35. ELEANOR BRANDON, aunt of Charles Brandon, Duke of Suffolk; m. John Glemham of Glemham, co. Suffolk. (*NEHGR* 102: 95).

36. ANNE GLEMHAM, m. Henry Palgrave (Pagrave), Esq., b. abt. 1470, will proved 14 Jan 1517/1518, of Little Pagrave and Thruxton, Norfolk, son of John Pagrave and Margaret Yelverton, dau. of Sir William Yelverton. Monumental brass for Henry Pagrave and Anne, his wife, in parish church of Barningham Northwood, Norfolk. (*Palgrave Memorials*, 16; *NEHGR* 102: 95; Mill Stephenson, *A List of Monumental Brasses in the British Isles* (1926): 321).

37. THOMAS PALGRAVE, GENT., b. 1505/10, of Thruxton; m. Alice Gunton, dau. of Robert Gunton of Thruxton. (*NEHGR* 102: 95).

38. REV. EDWARD PALGRAVE, bapt. Thruxton, 21 Jan. 1540/41, d. Dec. 1623, Rector of Barnham Broom, 1567-1623; name of wife unknown. (*Palgrave Memorials*, 140; *NEHGR* 102: 96).

39. DR. RICHARD PALGRAVE, b. abt. 1585, d. Oct. 1651, physician at Wymondham, Norfolk, and Charlestown, Mass., 1630; freeman 18 May 1631; m. Anna, maiden name unkn., d. Roxbury, 17 Feb. 1669. (*NEHGR* 102: 95-97; Moriarty Notebooks).

40. MARY PALGRAVE, b. abt. 1618/1619, m. abt. 1637, Roger Wellington of Watertown, Mass., ancestors of Roger Sherman, the Signer of the Declaration of Independence, 1776. (*NEHGR* 102: 97).

40. SARAH PALGRAVE, (dau. of Gen. 39), b. abt. 1620/1621, d. 1665, m. abt. 1648, John Alcock, of Roxbury, Mass. (Harvard Coll., 1646), physician at Roxbury.

40. ELIZABETH PALGRAVE, (dau. of Gen. 39), bapt. Wymondham, 10 Apr. 1626, d. Boston, Mass. abt. 1707, m. by 8 June 1651, John Edwards, Sr., of Green Bank, Stepney, London. (This line through John Glemham to Edward I was given in the *Boston Evening Transcript*, 12 Feb. 1930, Note 9665; and Jan. 1928, Note 6455; *TAG* 25: 24-26).

33. ROBERT WINGFIELD, b. 1403, of Letheringham, co. Suffolk, d. bet. 6 Oct. 1452 and 21 Nov. 1454; m. **ELIZABETH GOUSHILL** (15-33), b. abt. 1402, of Letheringham, Suffolk, liv. Oct. 1452. (*CP* IX: 604 n; G-A. Moriarty in *NEHGR* 103: 295; *TAG* 47 (1971): 205; Charles M. Hansen, "The Descent of James Claypoole of Philadelphia from Edward I," *TAG* 67 (1992): 100; *Visit. Suffolk* (1561): 212, 215).

34. SIR HENRY WINGFIELD, of Orford, co. Suffolk, b. abt. 1435/40, will pr. 6 May 1494; m. (2) Elizabeth Rokes, dau. of Thomas (or Robert) Rokes, of Fawley, co. Bucks. (*NEHGR, cit; Visit. of Northamptonshire, 1564, 1618/9*: 204; *TAG* 47: 205, 67: 101; *Visit. Suffolk* (1561): 212, 216).

35. ROBERT WINGFIELD, ESQ, of Upton, co. Northamptonshire, d. bet. 4 June. 1575 and 6 July 1576; m. abt. 1530 Margery Quarles, d. by 14 June 1574, dau. of John Quarles, of Ufford, co. Norfolk. (*TAG* 67: 101-102. Note: This corrects *AR* 7th edition and *TAG* 47: 205)

36. ROBERT WINGFIELD, ESQ., of Upton, co. Northampton, b. abt. 1532, d. 31 Mar. 1580, MP for Peterborough; m. Sept. 1555 Elizabeth Cecil, bur. Tinwell, co. Rutland 6 Dec. 1611, sis. of William Cecil, Lord Burghley, minister of state, and dau. of Richard Cecil, Esq., d. 19 Mar. 1552/3, of Burghley, near Stamford, co. Northamptonshire (son of David Cecil, d. Oct. 1535), and Jane Heckington, d. 10 Mar. 1587/8, dau. of William Heckington, of Bourne, co. Lincolnshire; Elizabeth m. (2) Hugh Allington. (*TAG* 47: 205, 67: 104; *CP* II: 428, XIV: 125; *DNB*).

37. DOROTHY WINGFIELD, bur. Northborough Nov. 1619; m. Stamford, co. Lincoln, 30 Sept. 1586, Adam Claypole, bapt. Northborough 20 June 1565, d. 2 Mar. 1631/2, son of James Claypole. (*TAG* 47: 205, 67: 105)

38. JOHN CLAYPOLE (CLAYPOOLE), bapt. 13 Apr. 1595, liv. in 1664; m. London 8 June 1622, Mary Angell, d. 10 Apr. 1661, dau. of William Angell, Esq., d. 1629. (TAG 67: 105-106).

39. JAMES CLAYPOOLE, b. Oct. 1634, d. Philadelphia, PA 6 Aug. 1687; m. Bremen, Germany 1657/8, Helen Mercer, d. 19 Aug. 1688. (*TAG* 47: 205, 67: 106-107).

39. NORTON CLAYPOOLE, (son of Gen. 38), d. Sussex Co., Delaware 1688/9; m. Rachel. (TAG 73 (1998): 131-134).

Line 16

28. EDWARD I (1-27), King of England; m. (2) 8 Sept. 1299, **MARGUERITE OF FRANCE** (155-30), dau. of **PHILIP III** (101-29), King of France and **MARIE OF BRABANT** (155-29). (*CP* V: 736; Burke (1967); *CCN*, 353; Weever, 775).

29. THOMAS, "of Brotherton," b. 1 June 1300, d. 1338, Earl of Norfolk by special charter 16 Nov 1312; m. (1) aft. 1316, Alice Hales, d. aft. 8 May, 1316, dau. of Sir Roger Hales (Hayles) of Harwich. (*CP* XI: 609; Weever, 775).

30. MARGARET, Duchess of Norfolk, d. 24 Mar. 1399; m. (1) John de Segrave, 4th Lord Segrave, d.s.p.m. 20 Mar. 1353; m. (2) aft. 30 May 1354, Walter Manny, 1st Lord Manny; issue by both. (*CP* XI: 609-610; Weever, 775).

31. ELIZABETH DE SEGRAVE, by (1), *suo jure* Baroness Segrave, b. Abbey of Croxton, co. Leics., 25 Oct. 1338, d. bef. 1368; m. by Papal disp. 25 Mar. 1349, her 3rd cousin, John de Mowbray, b. Bretby, co. Derby, 13 Sept. 1340, of Axholme, co. Lincs., Lord Mowbray, slain at Saracens, 1368, 4th Lord Mowbray, crusader, son of John de

Mowbray, 3rd Lord Mowbray, d. 1368, and **JOAN**, 'of Lancaster" (18-30), gr.·granddau. of HENRY III (1-26, 17-27), King of England. (*CP* XI: 610, IX: 384; Weever, 775).

32. **SIR THOMAS DE MOWBRAY, K.G.**, 1st Duke of Norfolk, b. 22 Mar. 1365/6, d. Venice, 22 Sept. 1399; m. 1384, **ELIZABETH FITZ ALAN** (15-32). (*CP* I: 253, IV: 670, IX: 601-604; Weever, 775, for above gens.).

33. **MARGARET DE MOWBRAY**; m. abt. 1420, Sir Robert Howard, K.G., b. abt. 1383, d. 1436, of Stoke-by-Nayland, Suffolk. (*CP* I: 253, IX: 610-612).

34. **SIR JOHN HOWARD, K.G.** Lord Howard, cr. 6th (1st) Duke of Norfolk, 28 June 1483, slain at Bosworth Field, 22 Aug. 1485; m. (1) Catherine Moleyns, d. 3 Nov. 1465, dau. of Sir William Moleyns; m. (2) Margaret Chetwode, d. 1494, wid. of (1) Nicholas Wyfold and (2) John Norreys, Esq., dau. of John Chetwode (Chedwode). (*CP* I: 253, IX: 610-612. VI: 583).

35. **KATHERINE HOWARD**, by (2), d. 12 Mar. 1535/6 (a half sister of Sir Thomas Howard, 7th (2nd) Duke of Norfolk); m. **SIR JOHN BOURCHIER, K.B.** (4-35), 2nd Lord Berners, d. 19 Mar. 1532, will made 3 Mar. 1532, translator of Froissart's Chronicles. (*CP* II: 154; *CCN*, 175; Berry, *Berkshire Pedigrees*, 55).

Line 16A   Revised for 8th Edition

28. **GARSIE DE GABASTON**, a desc. of Garsie-Arnaud, Lord of Gabaston, liv. abt. 1040, and Raimond-Garsie de Gabaston, liv. 1154.

29. **ARNAUD DE GABASTON**, a leading Baron of Béarn, liv. 1269, d. bef. 18 May 1302; m. Claramonde, d. 4 Feb. 1287, dau. of Arnaud-Guillaume de Marsan, d. 1272.

30. **PIERS DE GAVESTON**, b. Gascony, abt. 1284, cr. Earl of Cornwall, 1307, exec. Scarborough, 19 June 1312; m. 1309, **MARGARET DE CLARE** (9-30), not the mother of Amy. (Paul C. Reed, "'Proving' Illegitimacy: Amie the Daughter of the King's Favorite, Piers de Gaveston · Not That of His Wife," *NGSQ* 88 (2000): 32-49; J. S. Hamilton, *Piers Gaveston, Earl of Cornwall, 1307-1312:...*, (1988). 19-28; *TAG* 35: 100-106, 245; 37: 45-51; 40: 95-99, 253; *CP* III: 433-434, XIV: 208).

31.   **AMY DE GAVESTON**, by unknown mistress, (damsel of the Chamber to PHILIPPA OF HAINAUT (103-34) wife of EDWARD III (1-29) King of England), b. soon aft. 6 Jan. 1312, d. aft. 30 Nov. 1357; m. by 18 June 1338, John de Driby, d. aft. 30 Nov. 1357, son of Robert de Driby of Wokefield, co. Berks, d. aft. 30 Nov. 1357. (J. S. Hamilton, "Another Daughter for Piers Gaveston? Amie de Gaveston, Damsel of the Queen's Chamber," *Medieval Prosopography* 19 (1998): 177-186; J. S. Hamilton, *Piers Gaveston, Earl of Cornwall, 1307-1312:...*, (1988): 102).

32. **ALICE DE DRIBY**, b. abt. 1340, d. 12 Oct. 1412, will as Alicia Basset de Bytham, Apr. 1412, pro. 26 Oct. 1412, Inq.p.m. 1413 #15; m. (1) Sir Robert Tuchet, d. abt. 1367, no issue; m. (2) Sir Ralph Basset, Lord Basset of Sapcote, d. 17 July 1378, issue; m. (3) Sir Anketil Mallory, Knt., of Kirkby Mallory, co. Leics., d. 26 Mar. 1393 (4 chn.). (*TAG, op. cit*) (Order of first two mars. uncertain.) (See TAG 77: 57-65, esp. chart p. 58).

33. **SIR WILLIAM MALLORY** of Shawbury, 2nd son, by (3), b. abt. 1375, d. 1445, prob. at Shelton, Beds., or at Papworth; m. (1) unknown wife (perh. a Papworth desc.); m. (2) Margaret, who may have been a relative of Giles de Erdington. (*TAG, op. cit.*).

34. **MARGARET MALLORY**, b. abt. 1397, d. 1438 (Inq.p.m. 17 Hen. VI), dau. by unknown 1st wife; m. **ROBERT CORBET** (29B-33) of Moreton Corbet, d. 1440. (*TAG, op. cit.*).

24. **GILBERT DE SEGRAVE**, son of Hereward de Segrave, co. Leicester, who d. prob. bef. Michaelmas 1201. (*CP* XI: 596-597).
25. **STEPHEN DE SEGRAVE**, d. Leicester Abbey, 1241; m. (1) Rohese Despenser, dau. of Thomas Despenser and sister of Hugh Despenser; m. (2) Ida (Ella) de Hastings, d. sh. bef. 2 Mar. 1288/9, sister of Henry de Hastings; she m. (2) Hugh de Peche. (*CP* XI: 597, IV: 259, XIV: 576).
26. **GILBERT DE SEGRAVE**, 2nd son by (1), d. Pons de Poitous, bef. 8 Oct. 1254; m. 30 Sept. 1231, Amabil de Chaucombe, dau. and coh. of Robert de Chaucombe; she m. (2) **ROGER DE SOMERY** (55-29), Lord Dudley. (*CP* XI: 601-603; *DNB*).
27. **NICHOLAS DE SEGRAVE**, age 16 on 17 Dec. 1254, 1st Lord Segrave, d. 12 Nov. 1295; m. Maud (poss. de Lucy), d. 1337. (*CP*: XI: 603-605 esp note *d*; *DNB*).
28. **JOHN DE SEGRAVE**, 2nd Lord Segrave, b. abt. 1256, d. 1 Sept. 1325; m. Christian du Plessis, liv. 8 May 1331, sis. of 1st Lord Plescy, dau. of Hugh du Plessis. (*CP* XI: 605-608, XIV: 576, X: 545).
29. **STEPHEN DE SEGRAVE**, 3rd Lord Segrave, d. Thames, 1 Dec. 1325; m. Alice or Aline de Arundell, d. 7 Feb. 1340. (*CP* XI: 608-609).
30: **JOHN DE SEGRAVE**, 4th Lord Segrave, b. 4 May 1315, d. 26 Mar. 1353; m. **MARGARET** (16-30), Duchess of Norfolk. (*CP* XI: 609).

26. **WILLIAM D'AUBIGNY** (149-26), Earl of Arundel; m. **MABEL OF CHESTER** (126-29).
27. **MAUD D'AUBIGNY**, d. bet. 1238 and 1242; m. bef. 1222, Robert de Tateshal, minor in 1214, d. 16 July 1249, son of Walter de Tateshal and Iseult Pantuff, dau. of William Pantuff, of Breedon, co. Leics. (*CP* XII(1): 648-649, XI: 296 note *b*)
28. **ROBERT DE TATESHAL**, b. 1222, d. 22 July 1273; m. bef. 1249, Nichole, liv. 30 May 1277. (*CP* XII(1): 649-650).
29. **JOAN DE TATESHAL**, b. abt. 1250; m. Robert de Driby, d. 1279.
30. **JOHN DE DRIBY**, app. b. out of wedlock, d. 1334.
31. **JOHN DE DRIBY**, yeoman, d. aft. 30 Nov. 1357; m. by 1338, **AMY DE GAVESTON** (16A-31). (*TAG* 37: 50).
32. **ALICE DE DRIBY** (16A-32); m. (3) Sir Anketil Mallory, Knt.

27. **HENRY III** (1-26), King of England, b. 1 Oct. 1207, d. Westminster, 16 Nov. 1272; m. Canterbury, 14 Jan. 1236, **ELEANOR OF PROVENCE** (111-30), b. 1217, d. Amesbury, co. Wilts, 25 June 1291. (*CP* V: 736).
28. **EDMUND**, "Crouchback," b. London, 16 Jan. 1244/5, cr. Earl of Leicester, 1265, cr. Earl of Lancaster, 1267, d. Bayonne, 5 June 1296; m. (2) bet. 18 Dec. 1275 and 19 Jan 1275/1276, **BLANCHE OF ARTOIS** (45-30), b. abt. 1245/50, d. Paris, 2 May 1302, wid. of Henry I of Navarre. (*CP* I: 244, VII: 378, 386-387, XIV: 421).
29. **HENRY**, "of Lancaster," 3rd Earl of Lancaster and Leicester, b. 1281, d. 22 Sept. 1345, bur. Newark Abbey, co. Leics.; m. (1) bef. 2 Mar. 1297, **MAUD DE CHAWORTH** (72-32), b. 1282, d. bef. 3 Dec. 1322; m. (2) **ALIX DE GENEVILLE** (71A-31) d. 19 Apr. 1336,

wid. of Jean d'Arcis, d. 1307, dau. of **JOHN DE GENEVILLE** (71A-30), Sénéschal of Champagne, son of **SIMON DE JOINVILLE** (71A-29). (*CP* I: 244, II: 61, VII: 156, 396-401; *ES* VII/6).

30. ELEANOR, of Lancaster, by (1), b. abt. 1318, d. at Arundel Castle, 11 Jan. 1372; m. (1) bef. 23 Aug. 1337, **JOHN DE BEAUMONT** (114-31), b. 1318, d. bet. 24 Feb. 1342 and 25 May 1342, Earl of Buchan, Lord Beaumont, knighted 2 May 1338, M.P. 1342, son of Henry Beaumont, Lord Beaumont and **ALICE COMYN** (114A-29), of Buchan; m. (2) Ditton, 5 Feb. 1345, as his 2nd wife, **RICHARD (FITZ ALAN) D'ARUNDEL** (28-33, 60-32), 9th Earl of Arundel and Warenne. (*CP* I: 243-244, II: 60-61, IV: 670; *ES* III.4/685; Paget, 17).

31. HENRY BEAUMONT, Lord Beaumont, b. 1340, d. 17 June 1369; m. as 1st husb., **MARGARET DE VERE** (79-32), d. 15 June 1398, (bur. Gray Friars with 3rd husb.), dau. of John de Vere, 7th Earl of Oxford and Maud de Badlesmere; she m. (2) as his 2nd wife, Sir Nicholas Lovaine (Gov. Thomas Dudley is a descendant of this marriage. See Line 79.), she m. (3) 17 June 1379, Sir John Devereux, Lord Devereux, d. 22 Feb. 1392/3. (*CP* II: 60-61, IV: 296-9; *Gen. Mag.* 15: 251-255, 284-292; Maclagen, Michael, " The Ancestry of the English Beaumonts, " in *A Tribute to Charles Evans* (1989), 190-196 and chart VII).

32. JOHN BEAUMONT, K.G., Lord Beaumont, b. abt. 1361, d. Stirling, 9 Sept. 1396, knighted 23 Apr. 1377, Warden of the West Marches towards Scotland, 1389, Admiral of the North Sea, Constable of Dover Castle and Lord Warden of the Cinque Ports, 1392, K.G. 1393; m. Catherine Everingham, d. 1426, dau. of Thomas Everingham, of Laxton, co. Nottingham. (*CP* II: 61).

33. HENRY BEAUMONT, K.B., Lord Beaumont, b. abt. 1380, d. June 1413, cr. K.B. 13 Oct. 1399, commissioner for peace in France 1410-1411; m. bef. July 1405, Elizabeth Willoughby, d. sh. bef. 12 Nov. 1428, dau. of William Willoughby, Lord Willoughby of Eresby, and Lucy Strange, dau. of Roger, Lord Strange of Knokyn. (*CP* II: 61).

34. SIR HENRY BEAUMONT, b. 1411, d. 1446-7, of Thorpe-in-Balne, co. York; m. (2) Joan Heronville, liv. 1460, dau. & h. of Henry Heronville, of Wednesbury, co. Stafford. She m. (2) Charles Noel. (*The Genealogist* 5 (1984): 131-157, esp. chart 140; *CP* II: 62 note g).

35. SIR HENRY BEAUMONT, KNT., of Wednesbury, d. 16 Nov. 1471, sheriff of Staffordshire, 1471; m. **ELEANOR SUTTON** (221-37). (*The Genealogist* 5 (1984): 131-157, esp. chart, 140).

36. CONSTANCE BEAUMONT, b. abt. 1467; m. John Mitton (or Mytton), sheriff of Staffordshire, M.P., son of **JOHN MYTTON, ESQ.** (98-36) d. 16 Feb. 1532, and Anne Swinnerton. (*The Genealogist* 5 (1984): 131-157, esp. chart, 140).

37. JOYCE MITTON, b. abt. 1487; m. by 1505/6, John Harpersfield of London.

38. EDWARD HARPERSFIELD alias **MITTON, ESQ.**, of Weston-under-Lizard; m. 1530, Anne Skrimshire.

39. KATHERINE MITTON, m. Roger Marshall, merchant, of Shrewsbury, d. 4 Aug. 1612 (GS). (Libby & Noyes I: 340; *NEHGR* 101: 88-91).

40. ELIZABETH MARSHALL, d. bef. 1640; m. St. Chad's, Shrewsbury, 29 Aug. 1618, Thomas Lewis, b. Shrewsbury, abt. 1590, emigrated to New England, lived at Saco, Maine, by 1631, d. bef. 1640, son of Andrew Lewis, of Shrewsbury, co. Salop, and Mary Herring. (Libby & Noyes I: 430).

41. MARY LEWIS, bapt. 28 June 1619; m. Saco, Maine, aft. 10 May 1638, the Rev. Richard Gibson, A.M., of Portsmouth, N.H., ret. to Eng. (Libby & Noyes I: 259, 430; Weis, *Colonial Clergy of N.E.*, 91-92).

41. JUDITH LEWIS (sis. of Mary), bapt. 23 Oct. 1626; m. abt. 1646, James Gibbins of Saco, Maine. (Generations 34-38: Walter Goodwin Davis in *TAG* 19: 12-15. Generations 39-41: *NEHGR* 101: 16-23, 88-91. See also Walter Goodwin Davis, *The Ancestry of Nicholas Davis* (1956), 118-125, 137-188, includes many additional noble lines).

Line 18

29. HENRY "of Lancaster"; son of **EDMUND**, "Crouchback" (17-28), b. abt. 1281, d. 22 Sept. 1345; m. (1) bef. 2 Mar. 1296/7, **MAUD DE CHAWORTH** (72-32).
30. JOAN, of Lancaster b. abt. 1312, d. 7 July 1349; m. 28 Feb 1327, 1327, **JOHN DE MOWBRAY** (18A-30), 3rd Lord Mowbray, d. 1361, Magna Charta Surety, 1215. (*CP* VII: 401, note *b*).
31. ELEANOR (or **ALIANORE**) **MOWBRAY**, d. bef. 18 June 1387, m. as 3rd wife, bef. 23 July 1358, Roger la Warre, Baron de la Warre, b. 30 Nov. 1326, d. Gascony, 27 Aug. 1370, son of John la Warre, Knt., d.v.p. shortly bef. 24 June 1331, and **MARGARET DE HOLAND** (47B-31), d. Aug. 1349, dau. of Sir Robert de Holand, 1st Lord Holand. John la Warre (d. 1331) was the son of John, Baron de la Warre, d. 9 May 1347, and **JOAN DE GRELLE** (99-31), dau. of Sir Thomas de Grelle. (*CP* IV: 144-147, VII: 453-454, chart 452-453).
32. JOAN LA WARRE, d. 24 Apr. 1404; m. (2) by 2 or 24 May 1384, Sir Thomas West, 1st Lord West of Oakhanger, co. Hants, b. 1365, d. 19 Apr. 1405, son of Sir Thomas West b. abt. 1321, d. 3 Sept. 1386, and Alice, d. sh. bef. 1 Sept. 1395, dau. & h. of Sir Reynold Fitz Herbert, d. 1346. (*CP* I: 152, XII (2) 519-521; *VCH Beds*. II: 351-352).
33. SIR REYNOLD WEST, Lord de la Warre and Lord West, b. 7 Sept. 1395; d. 27 Aug. 1450; m. (1) bef. 17 Feb. 1428/9, Margaret Thorley, d. bef. 24 Nov. 1433, dau. of Robert Thorley, of co. Cornwall, and Anne (or Amy) de la Pole wid. of Gerald de Lisle, and dau. of Sir Michael de la Pole. (*CP* IV: 152-154, XII(2): 521, XIV: 243).
34. SIR RICHARD WEST, 2nd Lord de la Warre, b. 28 Oct. 1430; d. 10 Mar. 1475/6; m. bef. 10 June 1451, **KATHERINE HUNGERFORD** (51A-36), d. 12 May 1493, dau. of Sir Robert Hungerford and Margaret Botreaux, dau. Sir William Botreaux, M.P. 1455-1472. (*CP* IV: 154-155, XII(2): 522).
35. SIR THOMAS WEST, K.G., 3rd Lord de la Warre, b. abt. 1457, knighted 18 Jan. 1477/8, M.P. 1482-1523, K.G. 11 May 1510, d. 11 Oct. 1525; (1) Elizabeth Mortimer, h. of bro. John Mortimer, dau. of Hugh Mortimer and Eleanor Cornwall, dau. of John Cornwall; m. (2) Eleanor Copley, d. 1536, dau. of Sir Roger Copley of Roughway, Sussex, by Anne Hoo, dau. abt. 1447, dau. & coh. Sir Thomas Hoo, Lord Hoo and Hastings, d. 1455, by his 2nd wife Eleanor de Welles, dau. & h. of **SIR LIONEL DE WELLES** (202-35), Lord Welles. (*CP* IV: 155-156, VI: 561-565, XII(2): 443-444, 449-450, 522).
36. SIR GEORGE WEST, by (2), of Warbleton, co. Sussex, d. Sept. 1538; m. Elizabeth Morton, dau. of Sir Robert Morton of Lechlade, co. Gloucester. (*CP* IV: 158).
37. SIR WILLIAM WEST, Lord Delaware (de la Warre), b. abt. 1520, d. Wherwell, co. Northampton, 30 Dec. 1595; m. (1) 1555, Elizabeth Strange, dau. of Thomas Strange of Chesterton, co. Gloucester. (*CP* IV: 158-159).
38. SIR THOMAS WEST, 2nd Lord Delaware (De la Warre), b. abt. 1556, M.P. 1571-1593; knighted 7 Dec. 1587, d. 24 Mar. 1601/2; m. 19 Nov. 1571, **ANNE KNOLLYS** (1-38), dau. of Sir Francis Knollys, by **KATHERINE CARY** (1-37). (*CP* IV: 159-160, XIV: 243; *NEHGR* 33: 286-291; Chester, *Herbert Pelham, His Ancestors and Descendants*. Gens. 31-38: Baines, *History of Lancashire*, I: 276-277; *CP* VII: chart between pp. 452-453). They were par. of the six ch. fol.,

39. GOVERNOR THOMAS WEST, 3rd Lord Delaware (De la Warre) bapt. 9 July 1577, A.M., Queen's Coll., Oxford, 1605, M.P. 1597-8, Knight, first Lord Governor and Captain General of Virginia, 28 Feb. 1609/10, d. 1618, Port La Have, Nova Scotia, on a return trip from England to take up his post as governor of Virginia; m. London, 12 Nov 1602, Cecily Shirley, bur. Wherwell 31 July 1662, dau. of Thomas Shirley of Wiston, Sussex, by Anne Kemp, dau. of Sir Thomas Kemp. His descendants remained in England. (*CP* IV: 161, XIV: 243; *Gen. Mag.* 18 (1976): 289).

39. GOVERNOR FRANCIS WEST, (son of Gen. 38), b. 25 Oct. 1586, came to Virginia, 1608, Governor of Virginia, for two years from 14 Nov. 1627, and a member of the Council until his death, will dtd. 27 Dec. 1629, pro. 28 Apr. 1634; m. (1) Margaret, wid. of Edward Blayney; m. (2) Mar. 1628, Temperance Flowerdew, d. Dec. 1628, wid. of Sir George Yeardley, Governor and Captain-General of Virginia, m. (3) Jane Davye.

39. GOVERNOR JOHN WEST, (son of Gen. 38), b. 14 Dec. 1590, came to Virginia, 1618, member of the House of Burgesses, 1628-1630, member of the Governor's Council, 1631-59, Governor of Virginia, 1635-1637, d. abt. 1659; m. Ann.

39. NATHANIEL WEST, (son of Gen. 38), b. 30 Nov. 1592, came to Virginia, prob. in 1618, d. by Feb. 1623/4; m. in Virginia, 1621, Frances Greville. She m. (2) Abraham Peirsey, and (3) Capt. Samuel Mathews. (Gen. 39: Virginia M. Meyer and John Frederick Dorman, eds., *Adventurers of Purse and Person, Virginia 1607-1624/5* (1987), 655-656).

39. ELIZABETH WEST (228-39), (dau. of Gen. 38), b. 11 Sept. 1573, d. 15 Jan. 1632/3; m. Wherwell, co. Hants, 12 Feb. 1593/4, as 2nd wife, Herbert Pelham, the elder, of Fordingham, co. Dorset, and Hellingly, co. Sussex, b. abt. 12 Apr. 1564, d. 1620, (father, by his 1st wife, Catherine Thatcher, of Herbert Pelham, the younger, b. abt. 1580, d. 20 July 1624, husband of Elizabeth's sister, Penelope (fol.)). (*TAG* 16: 129-132, 201-205).

39. PENELOPE WEST (1-39), (dau. of Gen. 38), b. 9 Sept. 1582, d. abt. 1619; m. abt. 1599, Herbert Pelham, the younger (her sister's step-son), of Hastings, Sussex and Boston, co. Lincoln.

Line 18A   New to 8th Edition

21. ROGER D'AUBIGNY, Seigneur d'Aubigny, son of William d'Aubigny by the sis. of Grimald du Plessis; m. Amice. (*CP* IX: 366).

22. WILLIAM D'AUBIGNY, master butler of the royal household, m. Maud Bigod, dau. of Roger Bigod, Baron le Bigod, b. abt. 1150, d. bef. Aug. 1221. (*CP* IX: 366-367, 578 note c; Clay, 188).

23. NELE (NIGEL) D'AUBIGNY, yngr. son, and bro. of William d'Aubigny, 1st (4th) Earl of Arundel, d. Nov. 1129, held grant of Monbrai in Normandy forfeited by Robert Mowbray, Earl of Northumberland; m. (1) Maud de l'Aigle, former wife of said Robert de Mowbray, sister of Gilbert de l'Aigle (see also 113A-25) and dau. of Richer de l'Aigle by Judith, sister of Hugh, Earl of Chester; m. (2) June 1118, Gundred de Gournay, sister of Hugh de Gournay, dau. of Gerard de Gournay, d. abt. 1104, and Edith de Warenne, dau. of William de Warenne. (*CP* IX: 367-368; Hannay, James, *Three Hundred Years of the Norman House. The Barons of Gournay* (London, 1867), 197-198).

24. ROGER DE MOWBRAY, by (2), minor in 1129, d. 1188, m. abt. 1145, Alice (Adeliza) de Gaunt, widow of Ilbert de Lacy, d. abt. 1141, Lord of Pontefract, dau. of Walter de Gaunt (or Gant) and Maud of Brittany, dau. of **STEPHEN I** (214-24), Count of Brittany. (*CP* IX: 369-372; X: 780; Clay, 84; *DNB*).

25. NELE (NIGEL) DE MOWBRAY, of Thirsk, d. Acre, 1191; m. abt. 1170, Mabel, d. abt. 1203, of unkn. parentage (*CP* IX: 372-372; West Winter, XIII.319 ca, XIV.463d).

26. WILLIAM DE MOWBRAY, of Thirsk, d. Axholme, in or bef. March 1223/4, Magna Charter Baron (*MC* 63-1), m. Avice (or Agnes) whose parentage has not been satisfactorily proven. (*CP* IX: 373-374).

27. ROGER DE MOWBRAY, son of William (and heir of his bro., Nele de Mowbray), a minor 2 Oct. 1230, of age 1240, d. Axholme, abt. Nov. 1266, bur. Friars Preachers, Pontefract; m. Maud de Beauchamp, d. bef. Apr. 1273, sis. and coh. of Simon de Beauchamp, eldest dau. of William de Beauchamp, Baron of Bedford; she m. as 2nd husb., Roger le Strange of Ellesmere, d. 1311. (*CP* IX: 375-376, XIV: 492; Dugdale, *Baronetage* I: 125).

28. ROGER DE MOWBRAY, minor in 1266, cr. Lord Mowbray, 24 June 1295, d. Ghent, 21 Nov. 1297; m. 1270, Roese de Clare, aged 15 at mar. (not b. 17 Oct. 1252 as stated in some sources) liv. 1316, sis. of Gilbert de Clare, dau. of **RICHARD DE CLARE** (63-29), Earl of Gloucester and Hertford by **MAUD DE LACY** (54-30), dau. of Sir John de Lacy, Earl of Lincoln. (*CP* IX: 376-377, XIV: 340; Clay, 139-140).

29. SIR JOHN DE MOWBRAY, KNT, 2nd Lord Mowbray, said to have been born 4 Sept. 1286, d. York, 23 Mar. 1321/2; m. Swansea, 1298, Aline (Aliva) de Braose, d. by 20 July 1331, dau. and coh. of William de Braose (Lord Braose/Brewes), lord of Gower in Wales and Bramber in Sussex; she m. (2) Sir Robert de Peshale, liv. Nov. 1342. (*CP* IX: 377-380; Sanders, 146-147; *DNB*).

30. JOHN DE MOWBRAY, 3rd Lord Mowbray, b. Hovingham, co. Yorks, 29 Nov. 1310, d. 4 Oct. 1361, in the Scottish and French wars; m. (1) aft. 28 Feb 1327, **JOAN OF LANCASTER** (18-30), d. 7 July 1349, 6th and yngst dau. of **HENRY OF LANCASTER** (17-29); m. (2) Elizabeth de Vere, d. 16 Aug. 1375, wid. of Hugh de Courtenay, dau. of **JOHN DE VERE** (79-31), Earl of Oxford, by Maud or Margaret Badlesmere, wid. of Robert Fitz Payn, and dau. of Bartholomew Badlesmere, Lord Badlesmere by **MARGARET DE CLARE** (54-33). Elizabeth m. as 3rd husb., bef. 18 Jan. 1368/9, Sir William de Cosynton. (*CP* IX: 380-383; *DNB*).

31. JOHN DE MOWBRAY, by (1), 4th Lord Mowbray, b. Epworth, 25 June 1340, slain near Constantinople 9 Oct. 1368; m. 1349/53, **ELIZABETH DE SEGRAVE** (16-31, 223-33), b. Croxton Abbey, 25 Oct. 1338. (*CP* IX: 383-384).

32. SIR THOMAS DE MOWBRAY, K.G. (16-32). 6th Lord Mowbray, d. Venice 22 Sept. 1399, cr. Lord Segrave 12 Feb. 1382/3, Earl of Nottingham, Earl Marshal 30 June 1385; m. (1) Elizabeth Strange, d.s.p. 23 Aug. 1283, dau. of John Strange, Lord Strange of Blackmere; m. (2) 1384/5. as her 2nd husb., **ELIZABETH FITZ ALAN** (15-32), dau. of **RICHARD FITZ ALAN** (20-31, 60-33) Earl of Arundel, by **ELIZABETH DE BOHUN** (15-31). (*CP* IX: 385; Clay, 140).

33. THOMAS DE MOWBRAY, Earl of Nottingham, Lord Mowbray and Segrave, b. 1358, d.s.p. 1405; m. **CONSTANCE DE HOLAND** (47C-33), who. m. (2) **SIR JOHN GREY** (93B-33). (*CP* IX: 385)

33. ISABEL DE MOWBRAY, (dau. of Gen. 32), m. (1) Henry Ferrers, son of William Ferrers of Groby; m. (2) James, 5th Lord Berkeley. (Clay, 141).

33. MARGARET DE MOWBRAY (16-33), (dau. of Gen. 32); m. Sir Robert Howard, K.G.
34. SIR JOHN HOWARD, K.G. (16-34), slain at Battle of Bosworth 22 Aug. 1485; Duke of Norfolk by cr., 28 June 1483. (*CP* IX: 385, Append. G: 46-47).

Line 18B   New to 8th Edition

Line 18B   New to 8th Edition

32. SIR THOMAS DE MOWBRAY, K.G. (16-32; 18A-32), 6th Lord Mowbray; m. (2) 1384/5, as her 2nd husb., **ELIZABETH FITZ ALAN** (15-32).
33. JOHN DE MOWBRAY, (son of Gen. 32), Earl of Nottingham, Lord Mowbray and Segrave, son. of Gen. 32, (and heir of his bro., Thomas) d. 19 Oct. 1432; m. 12 Jan. 1411/12 Catherine Neville, dau. of Ralph de Neville, 1st Earl of Westmorland. Catherine m. (2) Sir Thomas Strangeways; m. (3) John Beaumont; m. (4) Jan. 1465, Sir John Woodville (he aged 20 at mar.), son of Richard Woodville (Wydvill), 1st Earl Rivers, and **JACQUETTA OF LUXEMBOURG** (234B-33). (Clay, 141; *CP* IX: 503; *DNB* 21: 887).
34. JOHN DE MOWBRAY, 3rd Duke of Norfolk, 9th Lord of Norfolk, b. 12 Sept. 1415, d. 6 Nov. 1461; m. 1444, Eleanor Bourchier, d. 1474, sister of Henry Bourchier, Earl of Essex and Count of Eu, dau. of **WILLIAM BOURCHIER** (155A-32), Earl of Eu in Normandy. (*CP* II: 248).
35. JOHN DE MOWBRAY, Earl of Nottingham, Duke of Norfolk, Lord Mowbray and Segrave, b. 18 Oct. 1444, d.s.p.m. 17 Jan. 1475/6; m. bef. 20 Oct. 1462, Elizabeth Talbot, dau. of John Talbot, 1st Earl of Shrewsbury. (*CP* IX: 385; Clay, 141).
36. ANN DE MOWBRAY, Countess of York, 11th Baroness Mowbray, 12th Baroness Segrave, d.s.p. 1481, aged 8 yrs, 11 mo. (reburied Westminster Abbey, 1966); m. (she age 5, he age 4) 15 Jan. 1477/1478, Richard, Duke of York, 2nd son of Edward IV., King of England. (*CP* IX: 385; *DNB*. Gens. 32-36: see also Burke, *Peerage and Baronetage*, 1967).

Line 19

29. HENRY, of Lancaster (17-29); m. bef. 2 Mar. 1296/7, **MAUD DE CHAWORTH** (72-32).
30. MARY, of Lancaster, b. 1320, d. 1 Sept. 1362; m. by Royal Assent 14 Aug. 1334, **HENRY DE PERCY** (161-30), Lord Percy, b. 1320, fought at Crecy, 26 Aug. 1346, d. abt. 18 May 1368. (*CP* I: 244, X: 462-463).
31. HENRY DE PERCY, K.G., b. 10 Nov. 1341, 4th Lord Percy, cr. 1st Earl of Northumberland, 6 July 1377, Lord Marshal of England, d. 19 Feb. 1407/8; m. (1) 12 July 1358, **MARGARET DE NEVILLE** (186-6), d. May 1372, wid. of William de Ros of Helmsley. (*CP* IX: 708-714, X: 464).
32. SIR HENRY PERCY, K.G., "Harry Hotspur," b. 20 May 1364, knighted Apr 1377, slain at Shrewsbury, 21 July 1403; m. bef. 10 Dec. 1379, **ELIZABETH MORTIMER** (5-33). (*CP* IX: 714, X: 464).
33. SIR HENRY PERCY, K.G., b. 3 Feb. 1392/3, Earl of Northumberland, Warden of the Marches of Scotland, slain at St. Albans, 22 May 1455; m. sh. aft. Oct. 1414, **ELEANOR NEVILLE** (3-33), d. 1463. (*CP* X: 464; Collins IV: 84-91).

Line 20

30. **ELEANOR,** of Lancaster (17·30), gr.·granddau. of **HENRY III** (1·26, 17·27), d. 1372; m. Ditton, 5 Feb. 1344/5, **SIR RICHARD FITZ ALAN** (60·32), b. abt. 1313, d. 24 Jan. 1375/6, Earl of Arundel and Warenne. (*CP* I: 243·244, IV: 670, XIV: 38).
31. **SIR RICHARD FITZ ALAN, K.G.**, b. 1346; beheaded in Cheapside 21 Sept 1397, 9th Earl of Arundel, 10th Earl of Surrey; m. 1359, **ELIZABETH DE BOHUN** (15·31), d. 1385 (*CP* I: 244·245, 253, IV: 670 chart, IX: 604).
32. **ELIZABETH FITZ ALAN,** d. 8 July 1425; m. (3) bef. 19 Aug. 1401, as his 4th wife, Sir Robert Goushill, of Hoveringham, Notts d. bef. 1414. (*CP* I: 253, IV 205, IX: 604; Banks I: 415; *DNB* 54: 75).
33. **JOAN GOUSHILL,** liv. 1460; m. **SIR THOMAS STANLEY, K.G.** (57·36), b. in or bef. 1405, Lord Stanley of Lathom and Knowsley, M.P. 1432; K.G. 1456; Lord Lieutenant of Ireland, d. 11 Feb 1458/9. (*CP* XII (1): 250·251; Collins III: 54·56; *DNB*; *VCH Lanc.* I: 345·349).
34. **MARGARET STANLEY,** m. (1) 1459, Sir William Troutbeck, Knt., b. abt. 1432, d. 1459, of Dunham-on-the-Hill, co. Chester; m. (2) 1460, as his 3rd wife, **SIR JOHN BOTELER** (46·36), of Bewsey in Warrington, d. 26 Feb. 1463; m. (3) Lord Grey of Codnor. (*CP* IV: 205; *VCH Lanc.* I: 345·349).
35. **ADAM TROUTBECK,** d. bef. 1510, of Mobberly, co. Chester; m. Margaret Boteler, of Warrington, co. Lanc.
36. **MARGARET TROUTBECK,** b. abt. 1492, d. aft. 1521; m. **SIR JOHN TALBOT** (7·36). (*CP* XI: 717, 731 chart; Old-*CP* VII: 147).

Line 21

30. **ELEANOR,** of England (17·30), great-granddau. of **HENRY III** (1·26, 17·30); m. **SIR RICHARD FITZ ALAN** (60·32). of Arundel. (*CP* I: 243·244, IV: 670).
31. **SIR JOHN D'ARUNDEL,** 1st Lord Arundel, Marshal of England, Lord Mautravers; M.P. 1377·1379, d. 1379; m. 17 Feb. 1358/9, **ELEANOR MAUTRAVERS** (59·34), b. 1345, d. 10 Jan. 1404/5. (*CP* I: 253, 259, VIII: 585, XI: 102·103).
32. **SIR JOHN FITZ ALAN (D'ARUNDEL),** b. 30 Nov. 1364, d. 14 Aug. 1390; m. bef. 1387, **ELIZABETH DESPENSER** (74·35). (*CP* I: 253,260, V: 736, XI: 102·103; Banks I: 378).

32. **MARGARET D'ARUNDEL,** (dau. of Gen. 31), d. 3 July 1439, (sis. of Sir John Fitz Alan); m. by license, 9 Apr. 1394, **SIR WILLIAM DE ROS, K.G.** (9·33), Baron Ros, d. 1414. (*CP* XI: 102·103; Banks I: 378).

Line 22

33. **MARGARET MOWBRAY** (16·33), descendant of **JOAN,** of Lancaster (18·30), gr.·granddau. of **HENRY III** (1·26, 17·30), and of **ELIZABETH DE SEGRAVE** (16·31), gr.·granddau. of **EDWARD I** (1·27), by **ELEANOR OF CASTILE** (110·30); m. abt. 1420, Sir Robert Howard, K.G., b. abt. 1383, d. 1436, of Stoke-by-Nayland, Suffolk. (*CP* I: 253, IX: 610·612).
34. **SIR JOHN HOWARD, K.G.** (16·34), Lord Howard; cr. Duke of Norfolk, 23 June 1483, Earl Marshal, slain at Bosworth Field, 22 Aug. 1485; m. (1) 1440, Catherine

Moleyns, d. Stoke-by-Nayland, co. Suffolk, 3 Nov. 1465, dau. of Sir William Moleyns of Stoke Poges, co. Buckingham, d. 1425. (CP IX: 610-612).

35. SIR THOMAS HOWARD, b. 1443, cr. Earl of Surrey, 28 June 1483; cr. Earl Marshal, 10 July 1510; 2nd Duke of Norfolk, 1 Feb. 1513/4, d. 21 May 1524; m. (1) 30 Apr. 1472, **ELIZABETH TYLNEY** (136-34), d. 4 Apr. 1497, wid. of Sir Humphrey Bourchier, and dau. and h. of Sir Frederick Tylney, of Ashwellthorpe, co. Norfolk, by Elizabeth Cheney, dau. of **LAURENCE CHENEY** (136-32) and Elizabeth Cokayne. (CP IX: 612-615; Banks I: 360).

36. ELIZABETH HOWARD, d. 3 Apr. 1537; m. by 1506, **SIR THOMAS BOLEYN, K.G.** (120-39), b. abt. 1477, d. 12 Mar. 1538/9, Earl of Wiltshire and Earl of Ormond. (CP II: 146, X: 137-140, XII (2): 739; Banks I: 360).

37. MARY BOLEYN (sister of Queen Anne, wife of King Henry VIII), d. 19 July 1543; m. 31 Jan. 1520/1, **WILLIAM CARY** (1-35). (CP II: 146; Banks I: 360 pedigree; see also Meredith B. Colket, Jr., in TAG 18: 211-218, for full details).

Line 23   Revised for 8th Edition

33. JOAN GOUSHILL (20-33), granddau. of **ELEANOR OF LANCASTER** (20-30); m. **SIR THOMAS STANLEY, K.B.** (57-36), Lord Stanley of Lathom. (CP IV: 205).

34. ELIZABETH STANLEY, sis. of Thomas Stanley, 1st Earl of Derby; m. bef. 1432, Sir Richard Molyneux of Sefton, co. Lancaster, d. Blore Heath, 23 Sept. 1459, Chief Forester of the forests and parks of West Derbyshire. (VCH Lanc. III: 69-70).

35. SIR THOMAS MOLYNEUX, KNT., eldest son, knight banneret, d. 12 July 1483; m. abt. 11 Jul 1463, **ANNE DUTTON** (176B-38), d. 22 Oct. 1520, dau. of Sir Thomas Dutton, of Dutton. (VCH Lanc. III: 69-70).

36. SIR WILLIAM MOLYNEUX, of Sefton, co. Lancaster, s. & h., b. 1481, d. 1548; m. (1) Jane Rugge (Rydge), dau. and h. of Sir Richard Rugge, co. Salop; m. (2) Elizabeth Clifton, dau. & h. of Cuthbert Clifton, Esq. Monumental brass for Sir William Molyneux and his two wives in parish church of Sefton. (VCH Lanc. III: 69-70; Mill Stephenson, A List of Monumental Brasses in the British Isles (1926), 272).

37. SIR RICHARD MOLYNEUX, KNT., of Sefton, son by (1), sheriff of Lancashire 1566-1568, d. 3 Jan. 1568/9; m. (1) **ELEANOR RADCLIFFE** (36-39), dau. of **SIR ALEXANDER RADCLIFFE** (36-38); m. (2) Eleanor Maghull, dau. of Robert Maghull, Esq., of Maghull. Monumental brass for Sir Richard Molyneux and his two wives in parish church of Sefton. (Gens. 33-37: VCH Lanc· III: 69-70; Baines, History of Lancashire II, 390; Mill Stephenson, A List of Monumental Brasses in the British Isles (1926), 272. Gens. 34-37: DNB).

38. ALICE MOLYNEUX, dau. by (1), d. 11 May 1581; m. James Prescott, gent. d. 1 Mar. 1583, eldest son of James Prescott and **ALICE STANDISH** (34-40), purchased the manors of Driby and Sutterby, co. Lincoln, 1579/80, transferred them to trustees. (Inq.p.m. James Prescott, gent., of Driby, 1583, No. 185 and "Pedigree of James Prescott, gent., and Alice Molyneux, John Prescott, Esq., and Elizabeth Manby, James Prescott, gent., and Mary Copeland," by the Rev. W.O. Massingberd, Rector of Ormsby with Driby, co. Lincoln, 21 Mar. 1901, in Frederick L. Weis, The Families of Standish of Standish and Prescott of Prescott of Standish Parish Lancashire, England (typed ms.) 1948, (at the American Antiquarian Society, Worcester, Mass.), pp. 58-60, 65-67; White, Ancestry of John Barber White (Haverhill, 1913), 123; brass effigies in Driby church with inscription and arms of Prescott and Molyneux; F.L. Weis, The Descent of John Prescott Founder of

Lancaster, Massachusetts, 1645, From Alfred the Great King of England, 870-901 (Clinton, 1948), Part III,. p. 8).

Line 24 Line cancelled

Line 25 Revised & expanded for the 6th Edition by Douglas Richardson

26. WILLIAM DE TRACY (222-26), b. aft. 1090, d. shortly aft. 1135, by unknown wife had

27. N.N. de TRACY (called Eva in Devon & Cornwall N&Q xix 194-201 but this is perhaps an error for her niece, Eva or Emma de Tracy, who mar. Warin de Bassingbourne); m. say 1165, Gervase de Courtenay who was probably closely related to **REGINALD DE COURTENAY** (138-25) as both families gave grants to Tor Abbey and Ford Abbey (the latter abbey having the Courtenay family as its chief patron). Gervase de Courtenay and his wife had two identifiable children, Hugh de Courtenay (who had control of his uncle Sir William de Tracy's barony of Bradninch, Devon, in the latter part of the 1190s) and William de Tracy (living 1198-1199). This 2nd son William de Tracy is perhaps identical with the William de Tracy who was holding the manor of Bradford Tracy, (East) Spreweye and Ivedon, Devon, in 1242-3. Besides these two sons there may have been a third son, Oliver (No. 28 below), but the evidence does not prove or disprove it. (*Book of Fees*, pt. II, pp. 759 & 792; George Oliver, *Monasticon Dioecesis Exoniensis*, pp. 183, 187, 338, 346, 347; *Devon & Cornwall N & Q* xix: 194-201; *Calendar of Documents Preserved in France*, ed. Round, I:194-195; *Curia Regis Rolls*, 12:440, 13:137-138, 247, 287, 364-385, 395).

28. OLIVER DE TRACY, possibly s. of the above couple, perhaps identical with the Oliver de Tracy who witnessed a charter dated about 1185-1191, granted by Hugh de Courtenay, who is mentioned above. In 1199 Oliver was granted the manor of Bremridge, Devon, which he held of the honour of Barnstaple. In 1242-3 he was also holding the manor of Wollacombe (later called Wollacombe Tracy), Devon, which fee he held of the honour of Bradninch, Devon. These two land holdings tend to suggest he was either closely related to the Tracy family who held the honour of Branstaple or else that he was closely related to the Tracy family who held the honour of Bradninch. Circumstantial evidence would lean toward the latter position as Oliver's descendants differenced their Tracy coat of arms with a label of azure which label is a remarkable feature of the Courtenay coat of arms. This heraldic evidence, such as it is, would suggest that Oliver was likely a son of Gervase de Courtenay and his wife (nee Tracy) above. (*Devon & Cornwall N & Q, cit.* xix: 194-201; *Calendar of Documents Preserved in France*, ed. Round, I: 194-195).

29. HENRY DE TRACY, held Wollacombe and Bremridge, Devon, in 1284. (*Devon & Cornwall Notes & Queries, cit.*)

30. ISABELLA DE TRACY, dau. & event. h., born say 1280-85; m. (1) by 1303 Simon de Roges (or Fitz Rogus) of Porlock, co. Somerset, held manor of Huntshaw, d. sh. bef. 22 July 1306 (Inq.p.m. Edw. I, IV 238-239); m. (2) by Nov. 1317 Herbert de Marisco (or Marsh), m. (3) Edmond Botiler (divorced); m. (4) Sir John Stowford, d. 1359, justice of Common Bench, Crackaway, co. Devon. (*Devon & Cornwall N&Q, cit.*; *Feudal Aids* I: 418; Cal. Inq.p.m., Edw. I, IV: 238-239; Pole's *Collections towards a Description of Devon*, pp. 420-421; Cal. Pat. Rolls 1358-1361, p. 283; *Somerset Rec. Soc.*-I, 172 (Cal. Reg. John de Drokensford, Bishop of Bath, 1309-1329); Cal. Close Rolls, 1327-1330, p. 24, 68, 70).

31. JOAN STOWFORD, dau. by (4), and event h. to Wollacombe Tracy; m. Sir William Fitz Warin of Brightleigh, Devon, living 1363. (*Devon & Cornwall N & Q, cit.*; *VCH Somerset* III 62-63 (manor of Aller, Somerset, a Stowford property); Pole, *ibid*).

32. SIR JOHN FITZ WARIN (also known as John de Brightley), d. 1407; m. by 12 Nov. 1375 Agnes de Merton, b. 1 Dec. 1359, d. by 29 Nov. 1412, dau. & coh. of Sir Richard de Merton by his first wife, Margaret. (*VCH Somerset, ibid*; Cal. Inq.p.m. Edw. III, XIII: 242-243, XIV: 175-176; *Register of Bishop Edmund Stafford*, p. 187; Pole, *op. cit.*, pp. 380, 420-421).

33. ISABEL (or Isabella) **DE BRIGHTLEY**, dau. & h., d. 21 Oct. 1466; m. (1) by 22 Nov. 1408, Robert Cornu, lord of Thornbury, Devon, son of Walter and Constance Cornu; m. (2) aft. 1420, John Cobleigh of Brightley in the parish of Chittlehampton, Devon. He m. (2) Joanna (perh. a Pyne), who d. 1480 (Harleian MS 1538 fo. 154b indicates that Isabel de Brightley had no issue by her marriage to Cobleigh but that she gave "all her inheritance of Brightly unto her husband and his heirs forever."). Isabel did have two sons by her marriage to Robert Cornu, namely Nicholas and William Cornu. At William Cornu's death in 1491, his heir was found to be his distant Cornu cousin John Speccot, and no mention is made of any Cobleigh relations. In the time period 1486-1493 a chancery court case was filed which involved William Cornu's heirs John Speccot, Richard Pollard, and William Willesford. Again, no Cobleigh is mentioned as being a party to this action. Therefore it would seem that Isabel did in fact have no issue by her Cobleigh marriage. That this is likely can be construed from Pole's statements that after Isabel's Cornu sons died without issue, her third share in the Merton estates passed on to her Stowell cousins. That such a transfer took place underscores that Isabel had issue only by her Cornu marriage. Although Isabel's memorial brass proves she married both Cornu and Cobleigh, Pole states that Cobleigh actually married Isabel's cousin, another Isabel de Brightley who was granddaughter or great-granddaughter of No. 31 above. If true, this could explain how only the Tracy, Stowford and Brightley lands came into the Cobleigh family and not the Merton lands. At the present time, there is no known corroborative evidence for this second Isabel de Brightley's existence except for the fact that the Brightley coat of arms was quartered by later Cobleigh descendants. The quartering would typically represent the marriage of a Cobleigh ancestor with a Brightley heiress; however, in this case, the Brightley arms might have been quartered on the basis of the Cobleighs being "representatives" of the Brightley family due to the transfer of the Brightley estates into the Cobleigh family. In any case, this line would appear to break at this point until further research sheds more light on this family. If two Isabel de Brightleys did exist, it is obviously possible that both could have married John Cobleigh. If this is the case, it would appear that the second Isabel was John Cobleigh's first wife followed by her cousin, Isabel, widow of Cornu. (Pole, *ibid*; *Register of Bishop Edmund Stafford*; *Devon N&Q* I: 210-214; DA 34: 689-695; *List of Early Chancery Proceedings* Vol. III (Lists & Indexes no. XX), p. 103; Cal. Inq.p.m. Henry VII, I: 289-290).

* * *

34. JOHN COBLEIGH, perhaps a son by the second Isabel de Brightley mentioned above, b. say 1445, d. 1492 per the Inq.p.m. held on his estates; m. by 1479 Alice Cockworthy, dau. of John Cockworthy of Yarnscombe, Devon, Escheator of Devon, by his w. Thomasine Chichester, dau. Sir John Chichester. Alice m. (2) John Fortescue of Spridleston in the parish of Brixton, Devon, d. 1537, by whom she had further issue. John Fortescue was uncle to Jane Fortescue below, who m. Alice's son, John Cobleigh (No. 35). (*Devon & Cornwall N&Q, ibid*, also XIII 42-44; Devonshire Association (hereafter

DA), *ibid*; Thomas (Fortescue), Lord Clermont, *History of the Family of Fortescue* (1886); Vivian, *Visit. of Devon*, p. 353).

35. JOHN COBLEIGH, b. abt. 1479 (age 13 in 1492); m. (1) by 1502, **JANE FORTESCUE** (246F-37), dau. of William Fortescue of Pruteston or Preston in Ermington, co. Devon, d. 1 Feb. 1519/20, & wife Elizabeth Champernoun, dau. & coh. Richard Champernoun of Inworthy, Cornwall (see Thomas Fortescue, *History of the Family of Fortescue* (1886) pp. 1-9.). Jane died by 12 May 1527, and he m. (2) Elizabeth Owpye, wid. He d. 24 Oct. 1540, Elizabeth surv., Inq.p.m. 33 Hen. VIII (1546) shows he held manors of Brightley, Stowford, Snape, Bremridge, Stowford Carder, & Nymet St. George. (DA 34: 619-692; Vivian, *Visit. of Devon*, pp. 353 & 357).

36. MARGARET COBLEIGH of Brightley, b. abt. 1502, d. 1547, Inq.p.m. 15 Oct. 1547, seized of the manors of Brightley, Stowford, Snape, Wollacombe Tracy, Bremridge, Nymet St. George; m. Sir Roger Giffard of Halsbury, d. 1547, of Brightley, par. of Chittlehampton, co. Devon, younger son of Thomas Giffard, b. abt. 1461, d. 1513, of Halsbury, co. Devon, by his second wife, Anne, living 1511, dau. John Coryton of Newton, Quethiock, Cornwall. (DA, *cit*. 34:679, 689, 692-693; *Wm. Salt Soc.* NS V: 29, 32, 34, Vivian, *Visit. of Devon*, p. 397).

37. JANE GIFFARD, d. 1596, will pro. 16 Apr. 1596; m. **AMYAS CHICHESTER** (52-43), b. 1527, d. 4 July 1577. (Chichester, *History of the Family of Chichester from 1086 to 1870*, pp. 32, 77-80; Vivian, *Visit. of Devon*, 397, 400; Bolton, *Ancestry of Margaret Wyatt*, chart; *NEHGR* 51: 214).

Line 26

26. JOHN "Lackland" (1-25), King of England, 1199-1216. (*CP* V: 736).

27. RICHARD FITZ ROY (natural son), d. bef. 24 June 1246; m. Rohese (Rose) de Douvres (Dover), d. bef. 11 Feb. 1261, d. & h. of Foubert (Fulbert) de Douvres (Dover), Lord of Chilham and Isabel de Briwere. (*CP* II: 127, XIV: 87; *Gen* (n.s..) 22 (1906): 107-108; *ES* III.2/356 b.).

28. ISABEL, d. 7 July 1276; m. bef. 12 July 1247, Maurice de Berkeley, b. 1218, d. 4 Apr. 1281, feudal Lord of Berkeley, son of Thomas de Berkeley, b. abt. 1170, d. 1243, lord of Berkeley, by Joan de Somery, dau. of **RALPH DE SOMERY** (81-28), Baron Dudley. (*CP* II: 126-127).

29. SIR THOMAS DE BERKELEY, b. Berkeley, 1245, d. 23 July 1321; m. 1267, **JOAN DE FERRERS** (59-30), d. 19 Mar. 1309/10. (*CP* II: 127-128).

30. SIR MAURICE DE BERKELEY, d. 31 May 1326, Lord Berkeley of Berkeley Castle; m. 1289, **EVE LA ZOUCHE** (39-30), d. 5 Dec. 1314, sis. of William La Zouche, dau. of Eon La Zouche. (*CP* II: 128-129, III: 291, XIV: 87).

31. ISABEL BERKELEY, d. 1362; m. June 1328, Robert de Clifford, b. 1305, d. 20 May 1344, son of **ROBERT DE CLIFFORD** (82-32), 1ˢᵗ Lord Cliiford. (*CP* III: 290-291).

32. ROGER DE CLIFFORD, bapt. Brougham, co. Westmorland, 20 July 1333, d. 13 July 1389, 5ᵗʰ Lord Clifford, sheriff of Cumberland, Governor of Carlisle Castle, 1377; m. Maud de Beauchamp, d. Jan./Feb. 1402/3, dau. of **THOMAS DE BEAUCHAMP** (87-31), Earl of Warwick, K.G., and **KATHERINE DE MORTIMER** (120-34). (*CP* III: 292, XIV: 188, 321).

33. THOMAS DE CLIFFORD, eldest son, d. 18 Aug. 1391, 6ᵗʰ Lord Clifford, sheriff of Westmorland, Governor of Carlisle Castle; m. **ELIZABETH DE ROS** (89-33), d. Mar. 1424 (*CP* III: 292, V: 736; Old-*CP* VI: 401; Banks I: 378).

34. JOHN DE CLIFFORD, K.G., 7th Lord Clifford, d. 13 Mar. 1421/2; m. **ELIZABETH PERCY** (5-34), d. 26 Oct. 1437. (*CP* III: 293).

Line 27

26. JOHN (1-25), King of England, 1199-1216. (*CP* IX: 276).
27. JOAN (29A-27) (natural dau. by unknown mistress) Princess of North Wales; m. **LLYWELYN AP IORWERTH** (176B-27), Prince of North Wales. (*CP* IX: 276).

Line 28

29. ROGER DE MORTIMER (176B-29), b. abt. 1231, d. Kingsland, 1282, 6th Baron Mortimer of Wigmore; m. 1247, **MAUD DE BRAOSE** (67-29). (*CP* IX: 276).
30. ISABELLA DE MORTIMER, d. sh. bef. 1 Apr. 1242; m. (1) **JOHN FITZ ALAN** (149-30), Lord of Clun and Oswestry, b. 14 Sept. 1246, d. 18 Mar. 1271/2,. (*CP* I: 240, 253, IV: 670 chart II).
31. SIR RICHARD FITZ ALAN, Earl of Arundel, b. 3 Feb. 1266/7, d. 9 Mar. 1301/2, Earl of Arundel, 1289; M.P. 1295; m. bef. 1285, Alasia di Saluzzo, d. 25 Sept. 1292, dau. of Thomas I di Saluzzo, Marquis of Saluzzo, and Luisa di Ceva, dau. of George di Ceva, Marquis of Ceva. Thomas I, di Saluzzo, was son of Manfredo III di Saluzzo, Marquis of Saluzzo d. 1244, by his wife, **BEATRIX** (274D-29) of Savoy, d. 1259, dau. of **AMADEUS IV** (247D-28), Count of Savoy, b. 1197, d. 1253, son of **THOMAS I** (247C-27), Count of Savoy, b. 1178, d. 1233, by his wife, **MARGARET (BEATRIX) OF GENEVA** (133-26). (*CP* I: 240-241, 253, IV: 670; *ES* II/190, XI/158).
32. SIR EDMUND FITZ ALAN (D'ARUNDEL), KNT., Earl of Arundel b. 1 May 1285, beheaded at Hereford, 17 Nov. 1326, knighted 22 May 1306; M.P. 1306; m. 1305, **ALICE DE WARENNE** (60-31, 83-30). (*CP* I: 241-242, 253, IV: 670).
33. RICHARD FITZ ALAN (D'ARUNDEL) (60-32), 9th Earl of Arundel, b. abt. 1313, d. 24 Jan. 1375/6; m. (1) 9 Feb. 1320/1, **ISABEL DESPENSER** (8-31); m. (2) **ELEANOR**, of Lancaster, (17-30). (*CP* I: 242-243).
34. SIR EDMUND FITZ ALAN (D'ARUNDEL), by (1), Knt. 1352; liv. 1377; m. bef. July 1349, Sibyl de Montagu, dau. of William de Montagu (Montacute), d. 30 Jan. 1343/4, Earl of Salisbury, Earl Marshal of England, and Katharine de Grandison, dau. of **WILLIAM DE GRANDISON** (263-30), Lord Grandison. (*CP* I: 244 note *b*).
35. ALICE D'ARUNDEL; m. Sir Leonard Carew, b. 1342, d. 1370, son of Sir John Carew and Margaret de Mohun. (*CP* I: 244 note *b*; *Gen.* (n.s.) 18 (1902): 31).
36. SIR THOMAS CAREW, b. abt. 1361/2, d. 1431; m. Elizabeth Bonville, dau. **SIR WILLIAM BONVILLE** (124A-35) of Shute, co. Devon, d. 1407/8, by 1st wife, Margaret Daumarle (or de Albemarle).
37. SIR NICHOLAS CAREW, d. 25 May 1447, Baron Carew of Molesford; m. **JOAN COURTENAY** (6-33). (Generations 32-37: Waters, Pedigree of Francis Champernoun in *Essex Institute Proceedings*, 17:16; *Devonshire Pedigrees* (1859), 121, 123).

Line 29

32. EDMUND DE MORTIMER, of Wigmore, d. 1331, (eldest son of **SIR ROGER DE MORTIMER** (176B-31), by **JOAN DE GENEVILLE** (71-31, 71A-31)); m. 27 June 1316

ELIZABETH DE BADLESMERE (65-34), d. 1356. (*CP* I: 373 note c, VIII: 442-3, IX: 284-285; Banks I: 112, 336).

33. SIR ROGER DE MORTIMER, K.G. (1349), b. Ludlow 11 Nov. 1328, d. 26 Feb. 1359/60, 2nd Earl of March; m. Philippa de Montagu, d. 5 Jan. 1381/2, dau. William de Montagu, Earl of Salisbury, by Katharine de Grandison, dau. of **WILLIAM DE GRANDISON** (263-30), & Sibyl de Tregoz, dau. of **JOHN DE TREGOZ** (255A-30). (*CP* I: 373 note c, VIII: 442-445, IX: 285).

34. EDMUND DE MORTIMER, b. 1 Feb. 1352, d. Cork, 26/27 Dec 1381, 3rd Earl of March, m. **PHILIPPA**, Countess of Ulster, (5-32), dau. of Lionel of Antwerp, Duke of Clarence, and granddau. of **EDWARD III** (1-29), King of England. (*CP* VIII: 442-447, IX: 714).

Line 29A   Revised for 8th Edition

26. JOHN "Lackland" (1-25, 27-26), King of England, 1199-1216, b. Oxford, 24 Dec. 1167, d. Newark, 19 Oct. 1216. (*DNB*; *TAG* 35:2932; Henry R. Luard, ed., *Annals of Tewksbury*, p. 101, published in Vol. I, *Annales Monastici* (London, 1864), being Part I, Vol. 36 in the series, Rerum Britannicarum Medii Aevi Scriptores; *Cal Patent Rolls, Henry III, 1225-1232*, p. 230).

27. JOAN, (nat. dau. by unknown mistress), Princess of North Wales, b. well bef. 1200, d. 30 Mar. 1236 or Feb. 1237; m. 1206, **LLYWELYN AP IORWERTH** (176B-27), Prince of North Wales, b. 1173, d. Aberconway, 11 Apr. 1240. (*DNB*; J.E. Lloyd, *History of Wales* II: 587, 616, 693, 766; *TAG* 35 (1959): 29-33, 62:180, 41: 99, 122). Joan's mother poss. Constance of Brittany, wid. of John's bro., Geoffrey, *TAG* 48 (1972): 176-178.

28. MARGARET, m. (1) abt. 1219, John de Braose, b. abt. 1197/8, d. 18 July 1232, of Bramber, Sussex, son of William de Braose, starved to death by King John 1210, by his wife, **MAUD DE CLARE** (63A-28); m. (2) aft. 1233, Walter de Clifford, of Clifford's Castle, Herefordshire, d. 1263, son of Walter de Clifford, son of Richard Fitz Ponz. (Lloyd, *op. cit.*; *TAG, op. cit*: .Burke, *Peerage & Baronetage*; *The Genealogist*, 6 (1985): 86, 92).

29. MAUD DE CLIFFORD, by (2), d. 1282-1285; m. (1) William III Longespee, Earl of Salisbury, d. 1257; m. (2) abt. 1257/8, Sir John Gifford, Lord Gifford of Brimsfield, b. abt. 1232, d. Boyton, Wilts., 29 May 1299. (*CP* XI: 384, V: 639-642; *TAG, op. cit.*).

30. ELEANOR GIFFORD, dead 1324/5; m. Fulk le Strange, b. abt. 1267; dead 23 Jan. 1324/5, 1st Baron Strange of Blackmere. (*CP* XII (1): 341; *TAG, op. cit.*). Fulk was the son of Robert le Strange of Wrockwarden, crusader abt. 1270, d. 1276 (4th son of John III le Strange of Knokyn, and **LUCY DE TREGOZ** (255-29) by Eleanor de Whitchurch, who m. (2) Bogo de Knovill, d. abt. 1304. (*Le Strange Records* 153, 170-175, 305).

31. ELIZABETH LE STRANGE, m. by Mar. 1323, Robert Corbet, b. 1304, d. 1375, of Moreton Corbet. (*TAG, op. cit.*) (See also Line 29B).

32. JOAN CORBET, m. Sir Robert I de Harley (Inq.p.m. 1359). (*Throckmorton Fam. in Eng. and the U.S.*, 33-48; A.E. Corbett, *The Family of Corbett* (1917) II: 47, 100-107.

Line Breaks here. Connection with No. 33 [Joan de Harley liv. 1341] in previous editions disproved. See: *The Genealogist*. 1 (1980): 27-39, 10 (1989): 35-72. Joan was dau. of another Sir Robert de Harley.

Line 29B

31. ELIZABETH LE STRANGE (29A-31); m. by Mar. 1323, Robert Corbet, of Moreton Corbet, b. 1304, d. 1375. (*TAG* 35: 29-32).

32. ROGER CORBET, d. abt. 1394, of Moreton Corbet; m. Margaret Erdington, d. 1395, dau. of Sir Giles de Erdington of Shrewsbury. (*TAG, op. cit.*)

33. ROBERT CORBET of Moreton Corbet, sheriff of Shropshire, 1419, d. 1440; m. **MARGARET MALLORY** (16A-34), dau. Sir William Mallory, Knt., of Shawbury.

34. MARY CORBET, m. **ROBERT CHARLTON** (31-35) of Apley, b. by 1430, d. 1471. (*TAG, op. cit.*).

Line 30

25. HENRY II (1-24), King of England, 1154-1189, b. 1133, d. 1189. (*CP* V: 736; *SP* I: 1-2).

26. WILLIAM LONGESPEE (natural son of Henry II by Ida (poss. de Toeni, dau. of Roger de Toeni, b. 1104, d. 1157/62) See *TAG* 77 (2002): 137-149, 279-281), b. prob. abt. 1176, d. 7 Mar. 1226, Earl of Salisbury, by right of his wife; m. 1198, **ELA** (108-28), Countess of Salisbury, b. abt. 1191, d. 24 Aug. 1261,. (Gens. 26-28: *ES* III.2/356 a; *CP* XI: 379-382, App. F 126; *VCH Lanc.* I: 312; *Dudley Pedigree; Gen. Mag.* 14: 361-368).

27. WILLIAM II LONGESPEE, Earl of Salisbury, d. 7 Feb. 1250; m. abt. Apr. 1216, Idonea de Camville, of age 1226, d. 1251/2, dau. of Richard de Camville, by Eustache Basset, dau. of Gilbert Basset.

28. IDA LONGESPEE, d. aft. 6 Aug. 1271, m. **WALTER FITZ ROBERT** (130-30), of Woodham-Walter, Burnham, Roydon, Dunmow, Henham, Wimbish and Tey, co. Essex; d. sh. bef. 10 Apr. 1258. (*CP* V: 472, XI: 382; *Dudley Pedigree;* Turton; D.L. Jacobus in *Boston Evening Transcript* (1 Feb. 1928) note 2257, Pt. XIII). (Walter Fitz Robert and Ida also had a son **ROBERT FITZ WALTER** (130-31), b. 1247).

29. ELA FITZ WALTER, d. abt. 1312; m. William de Odingsells (Odyngselles, Oddingeseles) of Maxtoke & Solihull, co. Warwick, Justiciar of Ireland, d. 1295, son of William de Odingsells, of Maxstoke & Solihull, co. Warwick, d. abt. 1268, by his wife Joan. (*CP* VI: 144-145, XIV: 354; Banks II: 108-109).

30. MARGARET DE ODINGSELLS, m. Sir John de Grey of Rotherfield, co. Oxford, d. 17 Oct. 1311, son of Sir Robert de Grey of Rotherfield, Somerton and Hardwick, co. Oxford, by his wife, Joan de Valognes d. 1312, dau. & h. Thomas de Valognes, of Shabbington, co. Buckingham, d. abt. 1275. (*CP* VI: 144-1455; Banks II: 108-109).

31. SIR JOHN DE GREY, K.G., of Rotherfield, bap. 1 Nov. 1300, d. 1 Sept. 1359, 1st Baron Grey of Rotherfield; K.G., 23 Apr. 1349; m. (1) bef. 27 Dec. 1317, Catharine Fitz Alan, d. bef. 7 Aug. 1328, dau. and coh. Sir Brian Fitz Alan, Lord Fitz Alan; m. (2) **AVICE MARMION** (219-31), dau. of **JOHN MARMION** (218-30), Lord Marmion. (*CP* V: 397-398, VI: 145-147; Banks II: 308; *Dudley Pedigree*).

32. MAUD DE GREY, by (2), m. (1) John de Botetourte, d.s.p. 1369; m. (2) abt. 1374, **SIR THOMAS DE HARCOURT, KNT.** (143-33). (*ES* X/139; *Dudley Pedigree*).

26. WILLIAM LONGESPEE (30-26), Earl of Salisbury, d. 7 Mar. 1226; m. 1198, **ELA** (108-28), Countess of Salisbury. (*CP* XI: 379-382 *ES* III.2/356 a; *VCH Lanc*. I: 312; *The Gen. Mag.* 14: 361-363).

27. STEPHEN LONGESPEE, d. 1260, of Sutton, co. Northampton, and Wanborough, co. Wilts, Justiciar of Ireland; m. 1243/4, **EMELINE DE RIDELISFORD** (33A-27), d. 1275/6, wid. of Hugh de Lacy, (*CP* X: 16 note c, XI: 382; *ES, cit.*).

28. ELA LONGESPEE, dau. and coh., d. aft. 1276; m. abt. 1267, **SIR ROGER LA ZOUCHE** (53-30), of Ashby and Brockley, d. sh. bef. 15 Oct. 1285, Baron Zouche of Ashby. (Old-*CP* VIII: 222, XII (2): 934-935; *ES, cit.*).

29. ALAN LA ZOUCHE, b. 9 Oct. 1267, d. sh. bef. 25 Mar. 1314, Baron Zouche of Ashby, 1299-1314, Governor of Rockingham Castle and Steward of Rockingham Forest; m. Eleanor de Segrave, dau. of Sir Nicholas de Segrave, d. sh. bef. 12 Nov. 1295, I[st] Lord Segrave, by his wife Maud. Eleanor's maritagium was the manor of Great Dalby, co. Leicester. (*CP* VI: 530; Old *CP* VIII: 222, XII (2): 935-936; Nichols, *Hist & Antiq. of the Co. of Leicester*, III, ii; Baker, *Hist. & Antiq. of the Co. of Northampton*, I, ii; *Eng. Historical Review*, 86: 449-472).

30. ELENA LA ZOUCHE, b. 1288; m. (2) abt. 1317, Alan de Charlton, d. 3 Dec. 1360, of Apley, co. Salop. (*CP* XII (2): note *l*).

31. ALAN DE CHARLTON, b. abt. 1318/9, d. 3 May 1349; m. Margery Fitz Aer, b. 4 Apr. 1314, d. 1349.

32. THOMAS DE CHARLTON, of Appleby, co. Salop, b. 1345, d. 6 Oct. 1387.

33. ANNA DE CHARLTON, b. bef. 1380, d. by 1399; m. William de Knightley, son of Richard Knightley of Fawesley, co. Northampton.

34. THOMAS DE KNIGHTLEY DE CHARLTON, b. 30 Mar. 1394, d. 4 Jan. 1460; m. Elizabeth Francis, dau. of Sir Robert Francis (Franceys) of Foremark, co. Derby. (See *TAG* 35: 62-63).

35. ROBERT CHARLTON, alias Knightley, b. bef. 1430, d. 1471; m. **MARY CORBET** (29B-34).

36. RICHARD CHARLTON, b. 1450, d. 1522; m. Anne Mainwaring, dau. of William Mainwaring of Ightfield, co. Salop. (Generations 31-36: *Visit. of Shropshire* (1623), 100-101; *Mis. Gen. Her.*, (orig. ser.) I (1868): 95, 97-98).

37. ANNE CHARLTON, b. abt. 1480; m. 1500, Randall Grosvenor, b. abt. 1480, d. 1559/60, of Bellaport, co. Salop.

38. ELIZABETH GROSVENOR, b. abt. 1515; m. Thomas Bulkeley, b. abt. 1515, d. 1591, of Woore, co. Salop.

39. REVEREND EDWARD BULKELEY, D.D., b. abt. 1540, buried 5 Jan. 1620/1; m. Olive Irby, b. ca, 1547, buried 10 Mar. 1614/5, dau. of John Irby, of co. Linc., d. 1579, by Rose Overton, dau. of Cutler Overton.

40. REVEREND PETER BULKELEY, B.D., b. Odell, co. Bedford, 31 Jan. 1582/3, d. Concord, Mass., 9 Mar. 1658/9; A.B., St. John's Coll., Camb., 1604/5, A.M., B.D.; Rector of Odell, succeeding his father, 1610-1635; Ord. Cambridge, Mass. (for Concord), Apr. 1637; sett. Concord, 1636-1659; m. (1) Goldington, co. Bedford, 12 Apr. 1613, Jane Allen, d. Odell, 8 Dec. 1626, dau. of Thomas Allen; m. (2) Apr. 1635, **GRACE CHETWODE** (7-40). (Generations 30-40: Jacobus, *Bulkeley Genealogy*, 11-17, 22-25, 34-36; *Misc. Gen. Her., cit.*; Frank Bulkeley Smith, *The Chetwode Family of England*, 76 ff. with charts, corrected by Donald Lines Jacobus; Weis, *Colonial Clergy of N.E.*, 45-46, 103; v.Redlich 134). For descendants through the Harris family, see *MC* 98.

Line 31A   Revised for 8th Edition

39. REVEREND EDWARD BULKELEY, D.D. (31-39), b. abt. 1540, buried 5 Jan. 1620/1; m. Olive Irby, b. ca, 1547, buried 10 Mar. 1614/5, dau. of John Irby, of co. Linc., d. 1579, by Rose Overton, dau. of Cutler Overton.
40. MARTHA BULKELEY, b. abt. 1572; m. Abraham Mellowes, d. Charlestown, Mass., 1639.

Line 31B   Revised for 8th Edition

39. REVEREND EDWARD BULKELEY, D.D. (31-39), b. abt. 1540, buried 5 Jan. 1620/1; m. Olive Irby, b. ca, 1547, buried 10 Mar. 1614/5, dau. of John Irby, of co. Linc., d. 1579, by Rose Overton, dau. of Cutler Overton.
40. FRANCES BULKELEY, b. abt. 1568, bur. Moulton, co. Lincoln, 1610; m. abt. 1595, Richard Welby, bapt. 1564, son of Thomas Welby, d. 1570, and Elizabeth Thimbleby, dau. of Richard Thimbleby. (*MC* 8-18).
41. OLIVE WELBY, bapt. Moulton, co. Lincoln, 1604, d. Chelmsford, Mass., 1 Mar. 1691/2; m. Boston, Linc., 1629, Dea. Henry Farwell, of Concord and Chelmsford, b. 1605, d.. 1670. (*TAG* 70: 100).

Line 31C   Revised for 8th Edition

39. REVEREND EDWARD BULKELEY, D.D. (31-39), b. abt. 1540, buried 5 Jan. 1620/1; m. Olive Irby, b. ca, 1547, buried 10 Mar. 1614/5.
40. ELIZABETH BULKELEY, b. abt. 1579, d. Boston, Mass., 14 Oct. 1643; m. (1) Richard Whittingham, gent., of Sutterton, co. Lincoln; m. (2) Atherton Haugh, gent., d. Boston, Mass., 11 Sept. 1650.
41. CAPTAIN JOHN WHITTINGHAM, by (1), bapt. Boston, co. Lincoln, 29 Sept. 1616, d. Ipswich, Mass., 1639; m. Martha Hubbard; ancestors of Rev. Samuel Mather, D.D.

41. REV. SAMUEL HAUGH, by (2), bapt. Boston, co. Lincoln, 23 Dec. 1621, d. Boston, Mass., 30 Mar. 1662, minister at Reading, now Wakefield, Mass; m. Sarah Symmes.

Line 31D   Revised for 8th Edition

39. REVEREND EDWARD BULKELEY, D.D. (31-39), b. abt. 1540, buried 5 Jan. 1620/1; m. Olive Irby
40. SARAH BULKELEY, (245-40) b. 1580, d. 1611; m. 1597 **SIR OLIVER ST. JOHN**, (85-40), Gent., of Keysoe, co. Bedford, b. abt. 1575, bur. Keysoe, 23 Mar. 1625/6.

39. REVEREND EDWARD BULKELEY, D.D. (31-39), b. abt. 1540, buried 5 Jan. 1620/1; m. Olive Irby.
    40. DORCAS BULKELEY, b. abt. 1577; m. by lic. 10 Dec. 1598, as his 2nd wife, Rev. Anthony Ingoldsby, d. Fishtoft, co. Lincoln, 1627.
    41. OLIVE INGOLDSBY (203-41), bapt. 1602; m. Rev. Thomas James.

Line 32

29. ALAN LA ZOUCHE (31-29); m. Eleanor de Segrave. (*CP* VI: 530).
    30. MAUD LA ZOUCHE, b. 1289, d. 31 May 1349; m. by 1309/10 Sir Robert de Holand, 1st Lord Holand, b. abt. 1270, d. 7 Oct. 1328, bur. at Preston, co. Lancs., M.P. 1314-1321, son of Sir Robert de Holand, of Upholland, co. Lancs. and Elizabeth Samlesbury, dau. of William Samlesbury. (*CP* VI: 528-531, XII (1): 558 note *c*; *NGSQ* 60: 25-26).
    31. MAUD DE HOLAND; m. Sir Thomas de Swynnerton, d. 1361, of Swynnerton, co. Stafford, son of Roger de Swynnerton and Matilda.   See note at end concerning this marriage. (*CP* VI: 530-531, cf. 530 note *i*, *CP* XII (1): 582; Banks I: 427; *Wm Salt Soc.* VII Pt. II: 24-46, n.s. vol. (1914), 4; *Visit. Cheshire* (1580) (Glover for Flower, *Harl. Soc. Pub.* 93), 203; *VCH* Lanc. III: 141, VI: 303-304; *English Historical Review* 86: 449-472).
    32. SIR ROBERT DE SWYNNERTON, KNT., d. abt. 1395, of Swynnerton, co. Stafford; m. Elizabeth Beke, dau. of Sir Nicholas Beke (Beck), Knt., and Jane (Joan) de Stafford, dau. **SIR RALPH DE STAFFORD** (55-32) and Katharine de Hastang (see also MC 136). (*CP* VI: 344, XII (I): 588, XIV: 606; Banks I: 427; *Wm Salt Soc.* VII pt. II, *cit.*, n.s. vol. (1914), 2-5; *Visit. Cheshire* (1580), 201).
    33. MAUD DE SWYNNERTON, only dau., b. abt. 1370; m. (3) Sir John Savage, Knt. (see 233-37), of Clifton, d. 1 Aug. 1450. (*CP* XII (I): 588 note *k*; Banks I: 427; *Wm. Salt, cit.*; *TAG* 26: 21; *Gen.* (n.s.) 31: 78).
    34. MARGARET SAVAGE, m. 1418, Sir John Dutton, d. 1445, son of Sir Piers Dutton of Dutton. (*TAG* 26: 21).
    35. SIR THOMAS DUTTON of Dutton, d. 23 Sept. 1459; m. **ANNE DE AUDLEY (TUCHET)** (176B-37) (9-35). (Gens. 30-35: *CP* VI: 528-531; Banks I: 427; Old-*CP* VIII: 222; *SP* III: 142; Ormerod, *History ... of Chester* (Helsby ed.), I: 662, 712-713; *VCH Lanc.* III: 141, VI: 303-305; John Burke, *History of the Commoners* II: 602).

Line 33

34. MARGARET SAVAGE (32-34), a descendant of **HENRY II** "Curtmantel" (1-24); m. Sir John Dutton of Dutton.
    35. MAUD DE DUTTON, m. Sir William Booth, Knt., of Dunham-Massie, co. Chester, sheriff of Cheshire, fl. 1476.
    36. SIR GEORGE BOOTH, of Dunham-Massie, d. 1483; m. **KATHARINE MONTFORT** (86-37).
    37. SIR WILLLAM BOOTH, KNT., of Dunham-Massie, d. 9 Nov. 1519; m. (2) Ellen Montgomery, dau. of Sir John Montgomery, of Throwley, co. Stafford. (*Ancestry of John Barber White*, 193, 200, corrected by v. Redlich 126-127, 130).

38. JANE BOOTH; m. (1) Hugh Dutton of Dutton; m. (2) Sir Thomas Holford, Esq., of Holford, co. Chester.

39. DOROTHY HOLFORD, m. John Bruen of Stapleford, co. Chester, d. 14 May 1587, son of John Bruen, Esq.

40. JOHN BRUEN, ESQ., of Stapleford, b. 1560, d. 18 Jan. 1625/6; m. (2) aft. 1596, Anne Fox, dau. of William Fox. (*TAG*: 26: 14-15, 24).

41. OBADIAH BRUEN, bapt. Tarvin, 25 Dec. 1606, d. Newark, New Jersey, bef. 1690; sett. Marshfield, Mass., 1640, Gloucester, 1642, New London, Conn., 1651; m. Sarah, d. abt. 25 Mar. 1684.

42. MARY BRUEN, d. Milford, Conn., 2 Sept. 1670; m. John Baldwin, Senior. (Gens. 34-41: *Ancestry of John Barber White*, 191-193, 200-204; v. Redlich 126-127. Gens. 35-42: *Boston Evening Transcript* 16 Apr. 1928, #5291 by Frank Bruen signed "Obadiah").

Line 33A

23. HENRY I, King of England (121-25), b. 1070, d. 1135, by **NEST** (178-2), dau. Rhys ap Tudor Mawr, Prince of Deheubarth, South Wales, father of (*NEHGR* 116: 278-279).

24. HENRY FITZ HENRY, of Narberth and Pebidiog, b. abt. 1105, d. 1157, by an unknown wife had, besides Meiler Fitz Henry, Justiciar of Ireland, a dau., (*NEHGR, op. cit.*; Orpen, *Ireland under the Normans* I, chart p. 18; *ES* III.2/354)

25. AMABILIS FITZ HENRY, m. Walter de Ridelisford of Carriebenan, in Kildare, d. aft. 1226. (*NEHGR, op. cit.*; Orpen, *Ireland under the Normans* I, chart p. 18; Cart. St. Mary's i.30).

26. WALTER DE RIDELISFORD, Lord of Bray, d. bef. 12 Dec. 1244; m. Annora. (*NEHGR, op. cit.*)

27. EMELINE DE RIDELISFORD, d. 1275/6; m. (1) as 2nd wife, Hugh de Lacy, Earl of Ulster, d.s.p. 1242; m. (2) abt. 1243/4, **STEPHEN LONGESPEE** (31-27), Justiciar of Ireland, d. 1260, 3rd son of **WILLIAM LONGESPEE** (30-26), Earl of Salisbury. (*NEHGR, op. cit.*; *CP* XI: 381-382 note *k*, XII (2): 171; *ES* III.2/356 a).

Line 34   Revised for 8th Edition

19. ÆTHELRED II (1-18), "the Redeless," King of England, 979-1016; m. (1) 985, Ælfgifu (Elgiva), dau. of Thored, Ealdorman of Northumbria. (*CP* IV: 504, IX: 704).

20. ÆLFGIFU (Elgiva); m. (3) Uchtred, Earl of Northumberland, murdered 1016, son of Waltheof, Earl of Northumbria. (*CP* IV: 504, IX: 704; *SP* III: 240-241).

21. EALDGYTH (Aldgitha); m. **MALDRED** (172-20), slain in battle, 1045, Lord of Carlisle and Allerdale (bro. of **DUNCAN I MAC CRINAN** (170-20), son of Crinan the Thane, Lay Abbot of Dunkeld, and **BETHOC** (**BEATRIX**) (170-19), dau. of **MALCOLM II** (170-18) King of Scots. (*CP* IV: 504, IX: 704; *SP* III: 239-241; Archibald H. Dunbar, *Scottish Kings*, 1005-1625, 2nd Edition (1906), 4-5).

22. GOSPATRIC I, b. abt. 1040, d. 1074/5, Earl of Northumberland, 1067-1072, 1st Earl of Dunbar, 1072-1075, Lord of Carlisle and Allerdale, visited Rome, 1061; name and parentage of wife unknown, but she had a bro., Edmund (or Eadmund). (*CP* IV: 504, IX: 704; *SP* III: 241-245; *Surtees Soc.*, vol. 51; Dunbar 5).

23. GUNNILDA, m. Orm, son of Ketel, Baron Kendal, son of Eldred, the Thane; held the manor of Seaton, also the towns of Camberton, Craysother and Flemingsby. (*SP* III: 245; Jackson, *Curwens of Workington Hall, 3).*

24. GOSPATRIC, d. 1179, of High Ireby, Lord of Workington in Coupland; exchanged his lands with his cousin, William I de Lancaster, Baron of Kendal, d. 1170 (son of Gilbert, a Norman Knt. and **GODITHA** (88-24), dau. of **ELDRED THE THANE** (88-23), Lord of Workington, and sister of Ketel, Baron Kendal. The Barony of Kendall prob. passed to William through his aunt, Christiana, wife of Ketel, 3rd Baron Ketel, prob. dau. of Ivo de Tailbois, Baron of Kendal) for the lands of William de Lancaster at Workington in Coupland; m. Egeline, perh. dau. of Ranulf Engaine. (*Trans. Cumberland. and Westmoreland Ant. and Arch. Soc.* 62 (1962): 95-100; Sanders, *English Baronies*, pp 56-57; Hinde, *Westmorland Pipe Rolls, 24 Henry II*, p. 167; *NEHGR* 96: 93; Pipe Roll, 24 Henry II).

25. THOMAS OF WORKINGTON, son and h., d. soon aft. 13 Nov. 1200; m. Grace, who m. (2) bef. 1209/10, Roger de Beauchamp. (*Register of St Bees*, 61-64, and charters numbers 35 to 37 and 61).

26. ADA, m. (1) William le Fleming, b. abt. 1150, d. 1203, of Aldingham, son of Michael le Fleming II, d. 1186, and Christian de Stainton, dau. of Gilbert de Lancaster, Lord of Stainton in Kendal d. bef. 1220, and illeg. son of **WILLIAM II DE LANCASTER** (88-26), Baron Kendal; she m. (2) William le Boteler, Lord of Warrington. (*NEHGR* 96: 314-315 chart, 317-319; Keats-Rohan, *Domesday Desc.* II: 539).

27. SIR MICHAEL LE FLEMING III, b. 1197; m. **AGATHA OF RAVENSWORTH** (226-29), dau. of Ranulf Fitz Henry, and granddau. of Henry Fitz Hervey, Lord of Ravensworth. (Gens. 24-33: *NEHGR* 96: 319-320, Clay, 73). (See 226-28).

28. WILLIAM LE FLEMING of Aldingham. (*VCH Lanc.* VIII: 324 note 28).

29. ALINE (ALICIA or **ELEANOR) LE FLEMING**, Lady of Aldingham; m. Sir Richard Cansfield, Knt., Lord of Cancefield and Farleton, co. Lancaster. (*CP* VI: 314; *VCH Lanc.* VIII: 324 note 29).

30. AGNES CANSFIELD, Lady of Aldingham, d. 1293; m. Sir Robert de Haverington, of Harrington, co. Cumberland, d. 1297. (*CP* VI: 314).

31. SIR JOHN DE HAVERINGTON (HARINGTON), KNT., b. abt. 1281, d. 2 July 1347, of Aldingham, Cancefield and Farleton, knighted 22 May 1306, 1st Lord Harington, M.P. 1326-1347; m. Joan (prob. a Dacre). He held the manors of Aldingham, Thurnham and Ulverston in co. Lancaster, Witherslack and Hutton Roof in Westmorland, and Austwick and Harrington in Cumberland. (*CP* VI: 315; *VCH Lanc.* VIII: 202; Cal. Inq.p.m. vol. IX: 30; Banks I: 244).

32. SIR JOHN HARINGTON, d. 1359, of Farleton, Melling Parish, co. Lancaster (younger bro. of Sir Robert Harington, Knt., *CP* VI: 316); m. Katherine Banastre, dau. of Sir Adam Banastre, Knt., beheaded 1314, and Margaret de Holand, sister of Sir Robert de Holand of Upholland, co. Lancaster, and widow of Sir John Blackburn; in Sept. 1352, Henry, Duke of Lancaster, granted to John de Harington of Farleton a lease of the manor of Hornby. He also held the manors of Bolton-le-Moors, Chorley and Aighton; 1358, went to London in the King's service. (*CP* VI: 315, note *j*; *VCH Lanc.* VII: 3, VIII: 202).

33. SIR NICHOLAS HARINGTON of Farleton, b. 1345, liv. 1397; m. Isabel English, dau. of Sir William English, of co. Cumberland. (*VCH Lanc.* VIII: 202).

34. SIR JAMES HARINGTON, KNT., of Blackrod, Justice of the Peace, and soldier at Agincourt, 1415; m. Ellen Urswick, dau. of Thomas Urswick, Esq., of Urswick. (*VCH Lanc.* III: 424, V: 300; Whitaker, *Richmondshire* II: 251 for the Harington pedigree; *Ancestry of John Barber White*, 107-112; Paget 2: 415).

35. SIR RICHARD HARINGTON of Blackrod in Westleigh, d. 1467; m. bef. 16 Aug. 1414, Elizabeth Bradshagh (or Bradshaw) of Blackrod in Westleigh, de jure suo jure

Baroness Verdon, age 13+ in 1416, dau. of Sir William Bradshagh, of Old Hall, Westby, co. Lancaster, minor in 1485, d.v.m. and d.s.p.m. 2 Oct 1415, son of Hugh de Bradshagh, of Old Hall, d. sh. bef. 20 Aug. 1383 and Margaret de Verdon, *de jure suo jure* Baroness Verdon, d. 24 Nov 1436, dau. of Edmund de Verdon of Brixworth, and granddau. of Sir John de Verdon, b. 24 June 1299, d. aft. 23 Oct. 1376. (Margaret de Verdon m. (2) Sir John Pilkington, Knt. (see below). Sir John Pilkington was son of Sir Roger de Pilkington, b. abt. 1291, d. 1343 and Alicia de Bury.). (*VCH Lanc.* III: 424, V: 330; Inq.p.m. 1449 (29 Henry VI); Sir Henry Chauncy, *The Historical Antiquities of Henfordshire*, II: 209-212; *CP* XII (2): 244-246; Old-*CP* VIII: 26 gives the father of Elizabeth as Robert Bradshagh).

36. SIR WILLIAM HARINGTON, of old Hall and Brixton, co. Lancs., *de jure* Lord Verdon, d. 12 Aug. 1487; m. 1442, Elizabeth Pilkington, dau. of Edmund Pilkington, of Pilkington and Elizabeth Booth, dau. of Sir Thomas Booth, Knt.; granddau. of Sir John Pilkington, Knt., and Margaret (Verdon) Bradshagh (Inq.p.m. 1449, as above), granddau. of Sir John Verdon, Knt. (son of Thomas de Verdon, bapt., Whiston, co. York., 10 Jan 1275/6, d. sh. bef. 10 Aug. 1315, age 39; m. bef. 1299 Margaret, dau. of Bewes de Knovill, 1st Lord Knovill, son of John de Verdon, b. 11 June 1256, d, sh. bef. 23 Apr. 1295; m. bef. 1276, (as 1st husb.) Eleanor de Furnivalle, dau. of Sir Thomas de Furnivalle, of Sheffield, co. York.) (Sir William Harington's sister, Margaret Harington, married Sir Thomas Pilkington, slain 1437.) (Old-*CP* VIII: 26; *VCH Lanc.* III: 242, V: 300; *Visit. of Lancashire* (1533),. 89 note; Burke, *Landed Gentry* (1847), II: 1042-1043. For the Pilkington pedigree from the Escheat Rolls in the Tower, see Chauncy, *op. cit.*, II: 209-212).

37. SIR JAMES HARINGTON, GENT., *de jure* Lord Verdun, b. 1447 (age 40 in 1487), d.s.p.m. 26 June 1497 (Inq.p.m. 14 Nov. 1498), of Old Hall and Brixworth; m. **ISABEL RADCLIFFE** (35-36), d. 20 June 1497, dau. of Sir Alexander Radcliffe of Ordsall, Knt. (*VCH Lanc.* III: 424, VI 194, VIII: 202; Inq.p.m., 14 Nov. 1498; Berry, *Hertfordshire Families*, 109-110; *NEHGR* 50: 31; Burke, *Landed Gentry* (1847) II: 1091; *Ancestry of John Barber White*, 111-112).

38. ALICE HARINGTON, dau. and coheir, b. abt. 1480, liv. 1537; m. abt. 16 Aug. 1497, **RALPH STANDISH ESQ.** (170-35), of Standish, b. abt. 1479 (age 28 in 1507), d. 1538, eldest son and h. of Sir Alexander Standish, Knt., of Standish, and Sibyl Bold, dau. of Sir Henry Bold, of Bold. (*VCH Lanc.* III: 424, VI: 194, VIII: 202; *Visit. of Lancashire* (1533); Inq.p.m., Sir James Harington, 14 Nov. 1498; *Publications of the Chetham Society*, vol. 98 (1876); J. P. Earwaker, *The Standish Family of Standish and Duxbury, co. Lancaster, Charters and Deeds* (Manchester, 1898), No. 182, p. 61; No. 218, p. 65; Frederick L. Weis: *The Families of Standish of Standish and Prescott of Prescott of Standish Parish; Lancashire, England* (1948) (typed ms.), 203 pp. cf. pp. 43-49, at the American Antiquarian Soc., Worcester, Mass.).

39. ROGER STANDISH, ESQ., of Standish, co. Lancaster, mentioned in Earwaker, *op. cit,* No. 218, p. 65, dated 24 Mar. 1513/4, as third son of Ralph Standish, Esq., of Standish. *The Visitation of Berkshire, A.D. 1566*, under "Standyshe of Wantage" gives the following: "Roger Standyshe of Standyshe, co. Lanc., Esq. had issue. ·· Rauffe, his eldest son and heir; and three daus., whereof one mar. __ Prescott, and another mar. to __ Barnes." (*Genealogist*, II: 106; pedigrees of Standish of Standish and Prescott of Prescott in the Lancaster Collection, Lancaster Town Library, Lancaster, Mass., compiled from records, deeds and wills by the Rev. John Holding, of Stotford, Baldock, co. Hertford, 1902).

40. ALICE STANDISH, bur. at Standish, 1564; m. James Prescott of Standish, Shevington and Coppull, co. Lancaster, b. 1508, d. 1568, son of William and Alice

Prescott. *The Visitation of Berkshire, A.D. 1566*, a contemporary record, explicitly states that she was the dau. of Roger Standish, Esq.

41. JAMES PRESCOTT, eldest son, d. 1583; m. **ALICE MOLYNEUX** (23-38).

Line 35

33. SIR NICHOLAS HARINGTON (34-33), of Farleton, b. 1345, liv. 1397; m. Isabel English, dau. of Sir William English, of co. Cumberland. (*VCH Lanc.* VIII: 202).

34. SIR WILLIAM HARINGTON, K.G., of Hornby Castle, d. 22 Feb. 1439/40; standard bearer at Agincourt, 1415; wounded at the siege of Rouen, 1419; m. **MARGARET DE NEVILLE** (247-31), d. bef. 1387. (*CP* V: 204 note *b*, IX: 490-491; Banks I: 245; *VCH Lanc.* VIII: 194, 202).

35. AGNES HARINGTON, d. 1490; m. Sir Alexander Radcliffe (Radclyffe), Knt., of Ordsall, b. abt. 1401, d. 20 July 1475, son of Sir John Radcliffe, Knt., of Ordsall, and Clemency Standish, dau. of Hugh Standish, of Duxbury, co. Lancs.. (*VCH Lanc.* IV: 211; Burke, *Landed Gentry* (1847), II 1091; *ibid* (1921), 1468-1469; http://www.Burkespeerage.net :Radclyffe of Lew).

36. ISABEL RADCLIFFE, d. 20 June 1497; m. **SIR JAMES HARINGTON** (34-37), d. 26 June 1479, of Wolfage and Brixworth. (*VCH Lanc.* VIII: 202; *Mis. Gen. Her.* (5th Ser.) v. 1 (1914/5): chart p. 281).

Line 36

35. AGNES HARINGTON (35-35), m. Sir Alexander Radcliffe, Knt., of Ordsall. (*VCH Lanc.* IV: 211).

36. WILLIAM RADCLIFFE, of Ordsall, Esq., b. 1435, d. 15 May 1497; m. 1443, Jane Trafford, ygst. dau. of Sir Edmund Trafford of Trafford, Knt., by Alice Venables, dau. of William Venables. (*VCH Lanc.* IV 211).

37. JOHN RADCLIFFE, of Ordsall, d. 12 Apr. 1497; m. Elizabeth Brereton, dau. of Sir William Brereton, Knt. (*VCH Lanc.* IV: 211).

38. SIR ALEXANDER RADCLIFFE, KNT., of Ordsall, b. 1457, Kt. Lillie 14 Oct. 1513, high sheriff of Lancashire 1547, d. 5 Feb. 1548; m. Alice Booth, dau. of Sir John Booth of Barton, Knt. (*VCH Lanc.* IV: 211).

39. ELEANOR RADCLIFFE, m. **SIR RICHARD MOLYNEUX** (23-37), of Sefton, Knt. (Baines, *History of Lancashire* II: 370; Gens. 36-39: http://www.Burkes-peerage.net; *ibid*).

Line 37   Revised for 8th Edition

25. THOMAS OF WORKINGTON (34-25), d. soon aft. 13 Nov. 1200; m. Grace NN. (Hutchinson, *History of Cumberland*, II: 143; Jackson, *Curwens of Workington Hall*, 1-21; *Transactions of the Cumberland and Westmorland Antiquarian and Archaeological Society*, vol. 13, extra series).

26. PATRIC DE CULWEN of Workington (younger son), liv. 1210-1237.

27. GILBERT I CULWEN of Workington, 2nd son, Sheriff of Cumberland 1276/82, d. 1325; m. Edith.

28. GILBERT II CULWEN of Workington, Sheriff of Cumberland 1308, d. 1329 (Inq.p.m. 3 Edward III); m. abt. 1295, Edith Harington, d. 1353. The arms of Harington also bear a fret, (frette), the famous Harington Knot. Both the Haringtons and the Curwens are descended from Thomas of Workington, whence, perh., the similarity of the arms. (Boutell, *Manual of Heraldry* (1930), 30 and plate xxviii, opp. 236).

29. SIR GILBERT III CULWEN, KNT., of Workington Hall, b. 1296, (age 33 in 1329), kt. 1346, d. 1370, m. (1) Avicia; m. (2) Margareta.

30. GILBERT IV CULWEN (CURWEN), by (2), of Workington Hall, of age by 1370, d. 1403 (Cal. Inq. p.m. 49 Edward III, v. 2, p. 352); m. (1) Alice Lowther of Lowther; m. (2) Isabel Derwentwater, wid. of Christopher Moresby.

31. WILLIAM CURWEN, by (1), of Workington Hall, of age 1376, summoned to Parl. 1379, 1392/4, 1397, Sheriff of Cumberland 1397, d. of the plague 1403; m. (1) Elyn de Brun, coh. of Sir Robert de Brun; m. (2) Margaret Croft, dau. of Sir John Croft. About 1433 the spelling of Culwen was changed to Curwen. (*VCH Cumb.* II: 218-219).

32. SIR CHRISTOPHER CURWEN, by (2), of age in 1398, lord of Workington 1404-1450, d. 17 July 1450; m. Elizabeth Hudleston, dau. of Sir John Hudleston of Millom. (*VCH Cumb.* II: 218-219).

33. SIR THOMAS CURWEN of Workington Hall, of age 1436, d. 1470; m. Anne Lowther, dau. of Sir Robert Lowther of Lowther. (*VCH Cumb.* II: 218-219).

34. SIR CHRISTOPHER CURWEN II of Workington Hall, d. 6 Apr. 1499; m. (1) Anne Pennington, dau. of Sir John Pennington. (*VCH Cumb.* II: 218-219; John F. Curwen: *Curwens of Workington*, pedigrees v, viii, ix, x; Jackson, *Curwens of Workington Hall*, p. 21; Hutchinson).

35. THOMAS CURWEN, b. 1469 (age 30 in 1499), d. 1522; m. (1) Anne Hudleston, dau. of John Hudleston of Millon Castle. (Thomas was bro. of Margaret Curwen, (Gen. 35 in previous editions) who m. William Curwen of Camerton).

36. SIR CHRISTOPHER CURWEN, Sheriff of Cumberland 1525, 1534, d. 1534; m. 1492, Margaret Bellingham, dau. of Sir Roger Bellingham.

37. SIR THOMAS CURWEN, b. abt. 1494, Sheriff of Cumberland 1537, d. 1544, will pr. 8 Nov. 1544; m. (1) Agnes Strickland, dau. of **SIR WALTER STRICKLAND** (41-36).

38. SIR HENRY CURWEN, a minor in 1544, d. 1597; m. by 1550, Mary Fairfax, dau. of Sir Nicholas Fairfax. (Gens. 26-38: John F. Curwen, *A Pedigree of the Family of Curwen of Workington and Kindred Branches 1092-1904*, 1-42, and chart 1, pts. 1 and 2; Gens. 33-38: *Visit. of Cumberland* (1615), 30). Note: William Bladen, b. 1673, bur, Annapolis, MD, 1718, is a descendant of Thomas Curwen, b. 1464, d. 1522. See: Robert W. Barnes, *British Roots of Maryland Families* (1999), pp 56-57.

Line 38   Revised for 8th Edition

22. GOSPATRIC I (34-22), b. abt. 1040, d. 1074/5, Earl of Northumberland, 1067-1072, 1st Earl of Dunbar, 1072-1075, Lord of Carlisle and Allerdale, visited Rome 1061; m. NN, parentage unknown, but had a bro., Edmund. (*CP* IV: 504, IX: 704; *SP* III: 241-245; *Surtees Soc*, vol. 51; Dunbar 5).

23. WALDEVE (WALTHEOF), Lord of Allerdale; m. Sigrid, living 1126. (*SP* III: IV: 137, 243-245; *CP* IV: 504 and note c).

24. GUNNILD OF DUNBAR, m. Uchtred, of Galloway, d. 22 Sept. 1174, son of Fergus, Lord of Galloway d. at Abbey of Holyrood, 1161, prob.by **ELIZABETH** (121B-26), yngst illeg. dau. of **HENRY I** (121-25). (*SP* III: 245, IV: 136-137).

25. ROLAND, Lord of Galloway, Constable of Scotland, 1189-1200; d. 19 Dec. 1200; m. Elena de Morville, d. 11 June 1217, sis. of William de Morville, d. 1196, dau. of Richard de Morville, d. 1189, of Lauder in Lauderdale, Constable of Scotland, by Avice de

Lancaster, dau. William I de Lancaster of Kendal (see 88-25). (*SP* IV: 138-139; K. J. Stringer, ed., *Essays on the Nobility of Medieval Scotland* (1985); *Bulletin of the Institute of Historical Research* 29 (1956):1-27).

26. ALAN, Lord of Galloway, named in the Magna Charta, Constable of Scotland, 1215-1234, d. 1234; m. (1) said to be a dau. of Reginald, Lord of the Isles; m. (2) 1209, **MARGARET OF HUNTINGDON** (94-27); m. (3) 1228, a dau. of Hugh de Lacy, Earl of Ulster (died 1243) by his 1st wife, Lesceline, dau. of Bertran de Verdun (Orpen, *Ireland under the Normans* III chart p. 286) or dau. or sister of Roger de Lacy of Pontefract (*Trans. of the Dumfrieshire & Galloway Nat. Hist. Soc.*, 49:49-55);. (*SP* IV: 138-143; *CP* IV: 670 chart; Jacobus, *Bulkeley, 12*).

27. HELEN OF GALLOWAY by (1); d. 21 Nov. 1245; m. as his 1st wife **ROGER DE QUINCY** (53-28), d. 25 Apr. 1264, 2nd Earl of Winchester, 1235, Constable of Scotland. (Old-*CP* VIII: 169-170, XII (2): 934; *SP* IV: 142; Banks I: 469; *N&Q* (3rd Ser.) II: 466 for Galloway).

28. HELEN (ELENA) DE QUINCY, of Brackley; d. sh. bef. 20 Aug. 1296; m. bef. 1242 Sir Alan la Zouche, d. 12 Aug. 1270, Baron Zouche of Ashby la Zouche, co. Leicester; Constable of the Tower of London, eldest son and h. of **ROGER LA ZOUCHE** (39-28). (*SP* IV: 142; Banks I: 469; *CP* XII (2): 931-934; *ES* III.4/708).

Line 39   Revised for 8th Edition. <u>See</u>: Line 119A

23. GUETHENOC, Viscount of Chateautro-en-Porhoët, liv. 1008-1021; m. Allarum, of unkn. parentage.

24. JOSSELIN, Viscount of Brittany and Viscount of Rennes, d. 1074; m. NN.

25. EUDON (EON) I, Viscount of Porhoët and of Rennes, liv. 1066-1092; m. (1) Emme (or Ann) de Leon, d. bef. 1092.

26. GEOFFREY, Viscount of Porhoët, d. 1141, m. Hawise (Havise), parentage unknown. (Gens. 23-26: *CP* XII (2): 930-931; *ES* X/13).

27. ALAN CEOCHE or LA COCHE, otherwise de **LA ZOUCHE**, d. 1190, in England by 1172, of North Molton, co. Devon, 1185; m. Alice de Belmeis, dau. and event. h. of Philip de Belmeis of Tong, co. Salop., and Ashley, co. Leics., by Maud la Meschin, dau. and coh. of **WILLIAM LE MESCHIN** (132B-26). (*CP* XII (2): 930-931; *Gen.* (n.s.) 20: 223).

28. ROGER LA ZOUCHE, younger son, h. to bro. William de Belmeis 1199, sheriff of Devonshire 1228-31, a witness to Henry III's confirmation of the Magna Charta, d. shortly bef. 14 May 1238; m. Margaret NN, liv. 1232. (*CP* XII (2): 931-932; *ES* X/13).

29. EUDO (EON or EUDES) LA ZOUCHE, of Ashby, younger bro. of Sir Alan la Zouche (see 38-28), of Haryngworth, d. 1279; m. bef. 13 Dec 1273, **MILICENT DE CANTELOU** (66-30), d. abt. 1299, wid. of John de Mohaut, sis. and coh. of her bro., George de Cauntelou, Lord of Abergavenny, dau. of William de Cantelou, Baron Abergavenny, of Calne, Co. Wilts and Aston Cantlow. co. Warwick, and **EVE DE BRAOSE** (66-29). (*CP* I: 22, XII (2): 932, note *i*, 937-938).

30. EVE LA ZOUCHE, d. 5 Dec. 1314; m. 1289, **SIR MAURICE DE BERKELEY** (26-30, 59-31), d. 1326, Lord Berkeley of Berkeley Castle. (*CP* II: 128-129, VIII: 584, XIV: 87).

31. THOMAS DE BERKELEY, Lord Berkeley, d. 27 Oct. 1361, Marshal of the English army in France 1340; Captain of the Scottish Marches 1342; m. (1) July 1320, Margaret de Mortimer, d. 5 May 1337, dau. of **ROGER DE MORTIMER** (176B-31, 120-33) and **JOAN DE GENEVILLE** (71-32, 71A-32); m. (2) 30 May 1347, at Charfield, co. Gloucester, Katherine de Clivedon, d. 13 Mar. 1385, widow of Sir Piers de Veel, of Tortworth, dau. of

Sir John de Clivedon (Clyvedon), b. abt. 1287, d. abt. 1373, of Aller, co. Somerset, Keeper of Bristol Castle, M.P., and his 2nd wife, Emma. (*CP* II: 129-130; XIV: 87).

32. MAURICE DE BERKELEY, Lord Berkeley, M.P. 1362-1368, wounded at the battle of Poitiers, 19 Sept. 1356; d. 8 June 1368; m. (age 8) Aug. 1338, Elizabeth Despenser, d. 13 July 1389, dau. of **HUGH LE DESPENSER** (74-32) and **ELEANOR (ALIANORE) DE CLARE** (8-30). (*CP* II: 130).

33. THOMAS DE BERKELEY, b. 5 Jan. 1352/3; d.s.p.m. 13 July 1417; Lord Berkeley, M.P. 1381-1415; served in the wars in France, Spain, Brittany and Scotland; m. (age 15) Nov. 1367, Margaret de Lisle, *de jure suo jure* Baroness Lisle and Tyes, b. 1360, d. May/Sept. 1392, dau. of Warin de Lisle, Lord Lisle, d. 1382, by Margaret Pipard, dau. of Sir William Pipard. (*CP* XIV: 87).

34. ELIZABETH DE BERKELEY, *suo jure* Baroness Lisle, Teyes, and Berkeley, Countess of Warwick, d. 28 Dec. 1422; m. (1) Sept. 1393 **RICHARD BEAUCHAMP** (87-33), 13th Earl of Warwick. (Gen. 31-34: *CP* II: 129-131 and 131 note c).

Line 39A   New to 8th Edition

29. EUDO (EON or EUDES) LA ZOUCHE (39-29, 253-29) of Haryngworth, d. 1279, a younger bro. of Sir Alan la Zouche (see 38-28 above); m. **MILICENT DE CANTELOU** (66-30), d. abt. 1299, wid. John de Mohaut, and dau. of William de Cantelou, Bar. Abergavenny. (*CP* I: 22, XII (2): 937-938).

30. ELEANOR (or ELLEN) LA ZOUCHE, received manor of Bingley, co. York, as maritagium; m., evidently as a child, by 1286, **SIR JOHN DE HARCOURT, KNT.** (93-30), b. abt., 1275 (ae. 11 in 1286), d. 1330, of Stanton Harcourt, co. Oxford, and Bosworth, co. Leicester, knight of the shire, Oxford, 1322. (*Feudal Aids* 6:21, 23 refers to "Elienora de Zuche" as holding the manor of Bingley of her mother "Milisenta de Monte Alto" in 1284-5; Rev. C. Moor, *Knights of Edward I* 2:183-184).

31. SIR WILLIAM DE HARCOURT, KNT., of Stanton-Harcourt, co. Oxford and Bosworth, co. Leicester, knight of the shire, Oxfordshire, 1322, b. abt. 1300, d. 6 June 1349; m. **JANE DE GREY** (143-32) of Codnor. (*CP* VI: 126 note *a*.). (Generations 27-30: Dudley Pedigree; Nichols, *Leicestershire*, IV Part II, 519a-520a for the pedigree of Harcourt; Banks I: 122; Collins IV: 240; Rev. C. Moor, *Knights of Edward I*, 2:183-184; *ES* X/139; *Wm Salt Soc*, n..s. 35 (1914): 195-196).

Line 40

22. GOSPATRIC I (34-22, 38-22), Earl of Dunbar and Northumberland; m. a sister of Edmund, par. unkn. (*CP* IV: 504, IX: 704; *SP* III: 241-245).

23. ATHELREDA OF DUNBAR, m. abt. 1094, **DUNCAN II** (171-22), King of Scots, her cousin. (*CP* VIII: 247; *SP* I: 2-3, III 245; Dunbar 282).

24. WILLIAM FITZ DUNCAN, d. bef. 1154; m prob. bef. 1138. Alice de Rumilly, d. 1187, dau. and coh. of **WILLLIAM LE MESCHIN** (132B-26), d. 1130, of Skipton-in-Craven, Egremont & Copeland, by his wife, Cecily de Rumilly, d. 1151/5, dau. and coh. of Robert de Rumilly, d. abt. 1096, lord of Skipton-in-Craven, co. York. (*CP* VIII: 247-248; *SP* I: 2-3; Dunbar 282; *NEHGR* 96: 93, Keats-Rohan, *Domesday Desc.* II: 880; Sanders, 142).

25. AMABEL FITZ WILLIAM, heiress of Copeland & Egremont, Cumberland, d. bef. 1201; m. Reginald (Reynold) de Lucy, d. abt. 11 Jan. 1198/9. (*CP* VIII: 247; Keats-Rohan, *Domesday Desc.* II: 880).

26. RICHARD DE LUCY, d.s.p.m. 1213, lord of Egremont & Copeland, Cumberland; m. abt. 1200, Ada de Morville, liv. 1230, dau. of Hugh de Morville, forester of co. Cumberland, and **HELEWISE DE STUTEVILLE** (270C-27). Ada m. (2) as 2nd wife, 10 Mar. 1217/18, Thomas de Multon, d. 1240, of Multon. (*CP* VIII: 248-249, IX: 397, 399-401, XIV: 456; *NEHGR* 96: 93).

27. AMABEL DE LUCY; m. 1213, Lambert de Multon, d. bef. 16 Nov. 1246, son of Thomas de Multon (see at Gen. 26, above) by 1st wife, Sarah de Flete dau. & h. of Richard de Flete. Lambert m. (2) Ida, died bef 16 Nov. 1246, wid. of Geoffrey d'Oyly) (*CP* VIII: 249, IX: 397, 401-402; *NEHGR* 96: 93).

28. THOMAS DE MULTON, b. 1225, d. sh. bef. 29 Apr 1294; m. (1) Ida, parantage unkn. (*CP* IX: 402-403).

29. SIR THOMAS DE MULTON, KNT., son & h. by (1), d. bef. 24 July 1287; m. Jan 1274/5, Emoine (or Edmunda) le Botiller, d. bet. Sept. 1284 and. 24 July 1287/7, d. & h. Sir John le Botiller, d. by 1275, tenant-in-chief in Ireland. (*CP* IX: 403).

30. THOMAS DE MULTON, 1st Lord Multon (of Egremont), b. 21 Feb. 1276; d. bef. 8 Feb. 1321/2; m. Ipswich, 3 Jan. 1297, **ELEANOR DE BURGH** (75-32). (*CP* V: 437, IX: 403-404).

31. ELIZABETH DE MULTON, dau. of Gen. 30, b. 1306, age 28 in 1334; m. (1) abt. 1327, Sir Robert Harington, Knt., d. Ireland, in or bef. 1334, of Aldingham, co. Lancaster, knighted 1331, son of **SIR JOHN DE HAVERINGTON** (34-31); She m. (2) Walter de Birmingham. (*CP* VI: 316, IX: 405, XIV: 368; Banks I: 244).

32. SIR JOHN HARINGTON, Lord Harington of Aldingham, b. abt. 1328, d. Gleaston Castle, 28 May 1363, M.P. 1347-1349; m. Joan, said to be dau. of Walter de Birmingham. (*CP* VI: 316).

33. SIR ROBERT HARINGTON, K.B., Lord Harington of Gleaston Castle, 28 Mar. 1356, d. Aldingham, 21 May 1406; m. (2) 1383, Isabel Loring, widow of Sir William Cogan of Huntsfield, d. 1382, dau. of Sir Nele Loring, K.G. 23 Apr. 1349, d. 1386. (*CP* XII (1): 250-251; Beltz, *Order of the Garter*, p. 68).

33. ISABEL HARINGTON, (dau. of Gen. 32), of Hornby, co. Lancaster, m. **SIR JOHN STANLEY** (57-35), d. 1437. (Collins III: 54-5).

Line 41

22. GOSPATRIC I (34-22), Earl of Dunbar and Northumberland.

23. GOSPATRIC II, slain at the battle of the Standard, 23 Aug. 1138, Earl of Dunbar, Baron of Beanley. The name of his wife is unknown. (Sybil Morel, dau. of Arkil Morel, d. 1095, was the wife of his son, Edward. See: *SP* III: 248, note 8). (*SP* III: 246-249; *CP* IV: 504-505).

24. EDGAR OF DUNBAR, liv. 1140; m. Alice de Greystoke, dau. of **IVO FITZ FORNE** (265A-24) Lord of Greystoke. (*SP* III: 249; *The Ancestor* 6 (1903): chart bet. 131-132).

25. AGNES OF DUNBAR, m. Anselm le Fleming (also styled de Furness & de Stainton), d. 1210/17, son of Michael II le Fleming (see also 34-26), d. 1186, by Christian de Stainton, dau. of Gilbert de Lancaster, Lord of Stainton, d. bef. 1220, illeg. son of William II de Lancaster (88-26).

26. ELEANOR LE FLEMING, m. Ralph d'Eyncourt, of Sizergh, co. Westmorland, d. 1228/33, son of Gervase d'Eyncourt, enfeoffed with Sizergh, 1175-1184. (*NEHGR* 107 (1953): 122-124).

27. SIR RALPH D'EYNCOURT of Sizergh, d. abt. 1251; m. Alice.

28. ELIZABETH D'EYNCOURT, heiress of Sizergh, d. 1272/4; m. June 1239, Sir William de Strickland, d. 1305/6, son of Sir Robert de Strickland, of Great Strickland, co. Westmorland. Their dau. Joan de Strickland, m. 1292, Robert de Washington of Carnforth in Wharton, co. Lanc., believed ancestors of Gen. George Washington. (*NEHGR* 96 (1942): 307-320).

29. SIR WALTER DE STRICKLAND, of Sizergh, d. abt. 1342; m. (1) abt. 1295/6 Eleanor de Goldington, dau. of William de Goldington (divorced 1298); m. (2) ?Maud. (NEHGR 96 (1942): 117).

30. SIR THOMAS DE STRICKLAND, maternity uncertain, d. 1376; m. Cecily de Welles, dau. of Sir Robert de Welles.

31. SIR WALTER DE STRICKLAND, d. 1407/8; m. Margaret de Lathom.

32. SIR THOMAS DE STRICKLAND, d. 1455; m. Mabel de Beethom.

33. WALTER STRICKLAND, ESQ., d. 1467, knight of the Shire of Westmorland, 1442; m. Douce Croft, dau. of Nicholas de Croft.

34. SIR THOMAS STRICKLAND, d. 1497; m. Agnes Parr, dau. of Sir Thomas Parr, by Alice Tunstall, dau. of Thomas Tunstall, co. Lancs. (*CP* III: 377; Clay 157; *Topo. et Gen.* III: 352-360).

35. SIR WALTER STRICKLAND, K.B., d. 1506; m. Elizabeth Pennington, dau. of John Pennington, Knt.

36. SIR WALTER STRICKLAND of Sizergh, d. 9 Jan 1527/8; m. (2) **KATHERINE NEVILLE** (2-38). They par. of **WALTER STRICKLAND, ESQ.** (2-39) (Generations 22-36: John Burke, *History of the Commoners* I: 55-58; S.H. Lee Washington in *NEHGR* 96 (1942): 99-126, 307-320).

Line 42

23. GOSPATRIC II (41-23), Earl of Dunbar, Baron of Beanley. (*SP* III: 246-249).

24. JULIANA OF DUNBAR, m. Ralph de Merlay, d. 1160, Lord of Morpeth, son of William de Merlay, (*SP* III: 249).

25. ROGER DE MERLAY, d. 1188; m. **ALICE DE STUTEVILLE** (270D-28), dau. of **ROGER DE STUTEVILLE** (270D-27) of Burton Agnes, d. 1202, Sheriff of Northumberland, 1169-1183. *NEHGR* 79 (1925): 372-378).

26. AGNES DE MERLAY, m. Richard Gobion, d. Gascony, bef. 29 Dec. 1230, son of Richard de Gobion,and Beatrice de Lucelles. (*NEHGR* 79: 359-364).

27. HUGH GOBION, succeeded his father, 1230, d. 1275 (Inq.p.m.); m. Matilda. (*NEHGR* 79: 363-364).

28. JOAN GOBION, liv. 1312; m. (1) John de Morteyn, d. 1296, of Tilsworth and Marston, co. Bedford, son of John de Morteyn, d. aft. 1265, and Constance de Merston, d. abt. 1293; m. (2) Henry Sewell. (*NEHGR* 79: 365-369).

29. SIR JOHN DE MORTEYN, of Merston and Tillesworth, co. Bedford, d. 1346; m. Joan de Rothwell, dau. of Richard de Rothwell. (*Gen.* (n.s.) 38: 194-203).

30. LUCY DE MORTEYN, liv. 8 Mar. 1361 (sis. of Edmund de Morteyn, D.C.L., canon of York and parson of Merston); m. as 1st wife, Sir John Giffard, b. 1301, d. 25 Jan. 1368/9, of Twyford, co. Bucks., and Somerston, Fringford and Cogges, co. Oxford, fought at the battle of Crécy (1346), son of Sir John Giffard le Boef, b. abt. 1270, liv. 30 Mar. 1328, of Twyford, Knt., by his wife Alexandra de Gardinis, d. by 1328, dau. & h. Sir Thomas de Gardinis, of Oxfordshire. (*NEHGR* 74: 232, 75: 57-63, 79: 368, 81: 156-178).

31. SIR THOMAS GIFFARD, KNT., of Twyford, b. abt/ 1345, d. 25 Sept. 1394; m. (1) abt. 1361, Elizabeth de Missenden, d. 1367; m. (2) 1367, Margery, liv. 1374; m. (3) bef. 6 July 1383, Sybil, d. 26 Feb. 1428/9.

32. ROGER GIFFARD, ESQ., of Twyford, son by (1), b. abt. 1367, d. 14 Apr. 1409; m. (1) bef. 6 July 1383, Joan de Bereford, dau. of Sir Baldwin de Bereford; m. (2) abt. 1399 Elizabeth, d. bef. 1407; m. (3) Isabel Stretele, who m. (2) by 1415, John Stokes.

33. KATHARINE GIFFARD, by (2), b. abt. 1399; m. Sir Thomas Billing, Knt., Lord Chief Justice of England, d. 1481, son of John Billing of Rowell and Rushenden, co. Northampton. (Gens. 30-33: *NEHGR* 75: 130-133).

Line 43

32. ROGER GIFFARD, ESQ. (42-32), of Twyford, co. Buckingham, d. 1409; m. (3) abt. 1407, Isabel Stretele.

33. THOMAS GIFFARD, by (3), of Twyford, b. Fringford, co. Oxford, 1408, d. 29 May 1469; m. Eleanor Vaux, daughter of William Vaux, Esq., of Bottisham and Northampton.

34. JOHN GIFFARD, ESQ., of Twyford, b. abt. 1431, d. bef. 23 Sept. 1506; m. Agnes Wynslow, dau. & coh. of Thomas Wynslow of Burton, co. Oxford, d. 1463, by Agnes Throckmorton, dau. of John Throckmorton, b. abt. 1380, d. 13 Apr. 1445, of Fladbury, co. Warwick and Eleanor Spinney, dau. of Sir Guy Spinney. (*The Genealogist* 1 (1980): 27-39; *NEHGR* 98: chart bet. pp 114-115).

35. ROGER GIFFARD, ESQ., of Middle Claydon, co. Buckingham, yngr. son, d. 23 Jan. 1542/3; m. abt. 1490, Mary Nanseglos, liv. 8 Feb. 1543/4, dau. of William Nanseglos (Nansicles), of Shaldeford, co. Essex. Monumental brass for Roger Giffard and his wife Mary in parish church of Middle Claydon. (Mill Stephenson, *A List of Monumental Brasses in the British Isles* (1926), p. 37, *NEHGR* 74: 269).

36. NICHOLAS GIFFARD, Gent., b. abt. 1508, d. 19 May 1546, of St. James, co. Northampton; m. bef. 1528, Agnes (Anne) Maister, d. 1581/4, dau. of John Maister (or Master), of Sandwich, co. Kent. (*NEHGR* 71 (1917): 171-172).

37. MARGARET GIFFARD, b. abt. 1535; m. abt. 1554, Hugh Sargent of Courteenhall, co. Northampton, b. 1530, d. 28 Feb. 1595/6.

38. ROGER SARGENT, b. abt 1560, bur. July 1649, par. All Saints, co. Northampton; m. 3 June 1589, Ellen (Eleanor) Makerness, bapt. Northampton, 24 Nov. 1564, bur. 20 Oct. 1645, dau. of William Makerness and Agnes Harrgat.

39. THE REVEREND WILLIAM SARGENT, bapt. Northampton, 20 June 1602, d. Barnstable, Mass., 16 Dec. 1682; emig. 1638, deacon and lay preacher at Malden, Mass. (F.L. Weis, *Colonial Clergy of N.E.*, p. 182. Gens. 32-39: *NEHGR* 75: 133-143; 79: 358-378).

Line 43A New to 8th Edition

34. JOHN GIFFARD, ESQ., (43-34); m. Agnes Wynslow (Winslowe).

35. THOMAS GIFFARD of Twyford, liv. 1472/3, d. 10 Oct. 1511; m. Jane Langston, d. 22 Mar. 1534/5, dau. of John Langston of Caversfield, co. Buckingham, by Amy Danvers, dau. John Danvers of Ipswell, co. Oxford. (*Misc. Gen. Her.* (5th ser.) 6 (1926/8): 138-139; *NEHGR, cit.*; *Burke's Landed Gentry*, 18th Edition (1972), p. 371; H.J. Young, *The Blackmans of Knight's Creek*, pp. 55-134, 138-158).

36. AMY GIFFARD, b. abt. 1485/90; m. bef. 1511, Richard Samwell, d. 3 May 1519, son of John Samwell, of Edgecote, co. Northampton,. (*Misc. Gen. Her.*, (5th ser.) 6 (1926/8): 138-139; *TAG* 29: 215-218).

37. SUSANNA SAMWELL, b. abt. 1510/15; m. abt. 1535, Peter Edwards, of Peterborough, co. Northampton, b. abt. 1490, d. abt. 1552, son of Peter Edwards. (*TAG, op. cit.*).

38. EDWARD EDWARDS, Gent., of Alwalton, co. Huntingdon, b. abt. 1537, d. 1591/2, will dtd. 25 Dec. 1591, pro. 16 Sept. 1592; m. Ursula Coles, bur. 2 Feb. 1606, dau. Richard Coles. (*TAG, op. cit.* and 13: 1-8).

39. MARGARET EDWARDS; m. by 25 Dec. 1591, Henry Freeman of Cranford, co. Northampton, b. 1560. (*TAG* 13: 1-8).

40. ALICE FREEMAN, d. New London, Conn., 11 Feb. 1664/5; m. (1) abt. 1615, John Tompson, Gent., of Little Preston, parish of Preston Capes, co. Northampton, b. abt. 1580/90, d. London 6 Nov. 1626; will dtd. 6 Nov. 1626, pro. 11 Apr. 1627. (The baptisms of their children are recorded at Preston Capes.); m. (2) Roxbury, Mass., bef. 30 May 1644, as his 2nd wife, Robert Parke. (*The Genealogist*, 4 (1983): 176-179, 184-185).

Line 44

15. ALFRED THE GREAT (1-14), King of England; m. 868, Ealhswith.

16. ALFTHRYTH (ETHELSWITH) of Wessex, d. 7 June 929; m. **BALDWIN II** (162-17), Count of Flanders, d. 917. (*ASC*; Ethelwerd, *Chronicle, 1-2*; *William of Malmsbury*, 121; *L'Art de Verifier Les Dates*; etc.) All descendants of Lines 162 to 169 belong to the posterity of King Alfred the Great.

Line 45

16. EDWARD "the Elder" (1-15); m. (1) Elfreda (Alfflaed), dau. of Ethelhelm, Lord of Meopham.

17. EDITH, d. 26 Jan. 946; m. as 1st wife, Sept. 929, **OTTO I**, the Great (147-19), b. 23 Nov. 912, d. 7 May 973, Holy Roman Emperor.

18. LUITGARDE, b. abt. 931, d. 18 Nov. 953; m. abt. 947, **CONRAD** (192-20) the Wise, d. 10 Aug. 955, Duke of Lorraine, Count in Wormsgau, son of Werner, d. abt. 920, Count in Nahegau, Speyergau and Wormsgau. (*ES* I.1/10, I.1/12).

19. OTTO, Duke of Carinthia, d. 1004; m. Judith, d. 991, prob. dau. of Henry, Count of Verdun.

20. HENRY, Count in Wormsgau, d. 28 Sept. 989/1000; m. Adelaide, d. 19 May 1039/1046, dau. of Gerard of Lower Alsace. (Henry's bro. was Bruno of Carinthia, d. 18 Feb. 999, who became Pope Gregory V, 996-999). (*ES* I.1/12; *CCN* 495).

21. CONRAD II, "the Salic," d. Utrecht, 4 June 1039, King of Germany, 1024-1039; Holy Roman Emperor, 1027-1039; m. as her 3rd husb. 1015/17, **GISELE OF SWABIA** (157-21), b. 11 Nov 995; d. 14 Feb. 1042/3, dau. Herman II, Duke of Swabia. (*CCN* 274, 495).

22. HENRY III, "the Black," b. 28 Oct. 1017, d. Bodfeld, Hartz, 5 Oct. 1056, King of Germany 1039-1056, Emperor 1046-1056; m. (2) 21 Nov. 1043, Agnes of Poitou d. 14 Dec. 1077, dau. of **WILLIAM III** (110-23), Count of Poitou. (Gen. 18-22: *ES* I.1/12).

23. HENRY IV, b. Goslar, 11 Nov. 1050, d. Liège, 7 Aug. 1106, King of Germany 1056-1084, Emperor 1084-1106; m. (1) 13 July 1066, **BERTHA** (274-23) of Turin, b.

1051, d. 27 Dec. 1087, dau. of **EUDES (ODO) I** (274-22), d. 1060, Count of Maurienne (Savoy) and Chablis, Margrave of Susa, by Alix (Adelaide) Duchess of Turin, b. abt. 1015, d. 27 Dec. 1091, dau. of Olderich Manfred II, d. 1035, Marqrave of Turin by Berta, d. aft. 4 Nov. 1037, dau. of Margrave Udalrich Manfred; m. (2) 1089, Eupraksiya, d. 1109, dau. **VSEVOLOD I** (242-6), Grand Prince of Kiev and his wife Maria Monomacha, dau. of Constantine Monomachos, Byzantine Emperor. (*ES* I.1/12, III.3/593, II/190; *Gen. Mag.* 23: 321-326; West Winter, IX.11, XI.37).

    24. AGNES, of Germany, by (1), b. 1072/3, d. 24 Sept 1143; m. (1) 1086/7, (engaged) 24 Mar. 1079, Frederick I, b. abt. 1050, d. 1105, of Hohenstauffen, Duke of Alsace and Swabia, son of Frederick of Buren, and Hildegarde; m. (2) 1106, Leopold III (see 147-26), Margrave of Austria, d. 15 Nov. 1136. (West Winter XII.52. Gens. 18-24: *ES* I.1/12).

    25. FREDERICK II, by (1), of Hohenstauffen, b. 1090, d. 6 Apr. 1147, Duke of Swabia; m. **JUDITH** (166-25), of Bavaria. (*ES* I.1/14).

    26. FREDERICK III, Barbarossa, (Emperor of Germany 1152, as Frederick I), b. 1122, d. 10 June 1190, on the Third Crusade and was bur. somewhere in the Holy Land, Duke of Alsace and Swabia; m. (2) 1156, Beatrix of Burgundy, d. 15 Nov. 1184/5, dau. of Renaud III, d. 1148, Count of Burgundy, by his wife, Agatha, dau. of Simon I, d. 1138, Duke of Upper Lorraine. (*ES* I.1/14, 15).

    27. PHILIP II, by (2), b. 1177/81, murdered 21 June 1208, at Bamberg, by Otto V of Wittelsbach, d. 1209 (son of Otto IV, and grandson of **OTTO II** (252C-26) Count Palatine of Wittelsbach), Duke of Swabia, Margrave of Tuscany, Emperor of Germany, 1198; m. 25 May 1197, Irene (or Maria) b. 1181, d. 1208, dau. of Isaac II Angelus, d. 1204, Eastern Roman Emperor, son of Andronicus Angelus (m. Euphrosyne Castamonitia), son of Theodora Comnena (m. Constantinus Angelus), dau. of Alexius I Comnenus, b. 1048, d. 15 Aug. 1118, Byzantine Emperor, who m. abt. 1078, Irene, dau. of Andronicus Ducas, by wife Maria, dau. of Trojan of Bulgaria, son of Ivan (John) Vladislav, Tsar of West Bulgaria, d. 1018,. (*CCN* 802; *ES* II/168. Gens. 21-27: Thatcher 322; G.P. Fisher, *op. cit.* 259; Moriarty, *The Plantagenet Ancestry*, p. 137-139, 174).

    28. MARIE OF SWABIA (MARY OF HOHENSTAUFFEN), d. abt. 1240; m. (1) 1215, **HENRY II** (155-27), Duke of Brabant, d. 1 Feb. 1247/8. (*CP* VII: 386; Gens. 26-28: *ES* I.1/15).

    29. MATILDA OF BRABANT, b. 1196, d. 29 Sept. 1288; m. (1) 1237, **ROBERT** (113-29), Count of Artois, son of **LOUIS VIII** (101-27), King of France. (*CP* VII: 386).

    30. BLANCHE OF ARTOIS, b. abt. 1245/50, d. Paris, 2 May 1302; m. (1) 1269, as 2nd wife, Henry III (I), Count of Champagne and Brie, King of Navarre, d. 22 July 1274; m. (2) 29 Oct. 1276, **EDMUND** "Crouchback" (17-28), b. 16 Jan. 1244/5, d. Bayonne, 5 June 1296, Earl of Lancaster. (*CP* VII: 378-387; *ES* II/47; *CCN*, 588).

    31. JEANNE OF NAVARRE, by (1), b. Jan. 1272, d. 2 Apr. 1305; m. 16 Aug. 1284, **PHILIP IV** (101-30), d. 1314, King of France. (*ES* II/47. Gens. 17-31: "The Origin of the Conradins," by G.A. Moriarty in *NEHGR* 99: 243; 101: 41; Chaume, *Les Origins de Duché de Burgoyne*, I, 542, 551-552; Thatcher, 322; *Boston Evening Transcript*, 9 Nov. 1926, Note 2257, Part XV Brabant; Turton; *TAG* 9: 113; Moriarty, *The Plantagenet Ancestry*).

Line 46

    34. SIR WILLIAM HARINGTON, (35-34); m. **MARGARET DE NEVILLE** (247-31).

    35. ISABEL HARINGTON, d. 1441; m. 1411, Sir John Boteler, Knt., of Bewsey, b. Bewsey, 26 Feb. 1402/4; d. 12 Sept. 1430, Baron of Warrington, M.P. 1426.

36. SIR JOHN BOTELER, KNT., of Bewsey, b. 24 Aug. 1429, d. 26 Feb. 1463, Baron of Warrington, knighted 1447, Knight of the Shire 1449, M.P. 1449; m. 1460, as 3rd wife, **MARGARET STANLEY** (20-34). (Gens. 34-36: *CP* IV: 205; *VCH Lanc.* VIII: 194, 202).

37. THOMAS BOTELER, KNT., of Bewsey, b. 1461, d. 27 Apr. 1522, knighted 1485, J.P. 1486, Baron of Warrington; m. Margaret Delves, dau. of John Delves of Doddington, Knt.

38. MARGERY BOTELER; m. 1518, **SIR THOMAS SOUTHWORTH** (9-38). (Gens. 36-38: *VCH Lanc.* I: 345-349).

Line 47

30. MAUD LA ZOUCHE (32-30); m. by 1309/10 Sir Robert de Holand, 1st Lord Holand, of Upholland, co. Lancaster, d. 7 Oct. 1328. (*CP* VI: 530).

31. SIR THOMAS DE HOLAND, K.G., Earl of Kent, d. 26 or 28 Dec. 1360; m. bef. May 1340, as her 1st husb., **JOAN** (236-12), "Fair Maid of Kent," d. 7 or 8 Aug. 1385, dau. of **EDMUND**, of Woodstock (155-31), executed 19 Mar. 1329/30, son of **EDWARD I** (1-27) and **MARGUERITE OF FRANCE** (155-30). (*CP* VI: 533, VII: 150-154).

32. SIR THOMAS DE HOLAND, K.G., of Woodstock, 2nd Earl of Kent, d. 25 Apr. 1397; m. 1364, **ALICE FITZ ALAN** (78-33). (*CP* VI: 533, VII: 154-156, XII (1): 44).

33. MARGARET DE HOLAND, d. 30 Dec. 1439; m. (1) **JOHN BEAUFORT** (1-31); m. (2) Thomas, Duke of Clarence. (*CP* XII (1): 44; Clay, 230).

Line 47A   Prepared for an earlier edition by Douglas Richardson

30. MAUD LA ZOUCHE (32-30, 47-30); m. by 1309/10 Sir Robert de Holand, b. abt. 1283 (*Eng. Hist Rev.* 86: 449-472), first Lord Holand, of Upholland, co. Lancaster. (*CP* VI: 528-531).

31. SIR ROBERT DE HOLAND, Lord Holand, s. and h., b. abt. 1312 (ae. 16 in 1328), d. 16 Mar. 1372/3, Halse or Hawes, Brackley, co. Northampton, guardian of Garendon Abbey 1360; m. Elizabeth, who died bef. his death. (*CP* VI: 531).

32. ROBERT DE HOLAND, s. and h. apparent, d.v.p. 1372/3; m. in or by 1355 Joan (or Alice) when his father in that year settled on them by fine the manors of Nether Kellet, Wanborough, and Denford. (*CP* VI: 532).

33. MAUD DE HOLAND, b. abt. 1356 (ae. 17 in 1373), h. to her grandfather Lord Holand, d. 7 May 1423; m. **SIR JOHN LOVEL, K.G.** (215-32), Lord Lovel and Holand of Titmarsh, d. 10 Sept. 1408. (*CP* VI: 532, VIII: 219-221).

Line 47B   Prepared for an earlier edition by Douglas Richardson

30. MAUD LA ZOUCHE (32-30, 47-30, 47A-30), b. 1283 (*Eng. Hist. Rev.* 86: 449-472), d. 31 May 1349; m. by 1309/10 Sir Robert de Holand, first Lord Holand, of Upholland, co. Lancaster. (*CP* VI: 528-530).

31. MARGARET DE HOLAND, d. 20 or 22 Aug. 1349; m. by 1326 John la Warre, d. shortly bef. 24 June 1331, son of Sir John la Warre, 2nd Baron la Warre*, by his wife, **JOAN DE GRELLE** (99-31). (*CP* IV: 144-147, VII: chart 452-453; Cal. Inq.p.m. 9: 239-240).

32. ROGER LA WARRE, Baron la Warre*, b. 30 Nov. 1326, d. Gascony, 27 Aug. 1370; m. (3) bef. 23 July 1358, **ELEANOR** (or **ALIANORE**) **MOWBRAY** (18-31), dau. of John de Mowbray, 3rd Lord Mowbray by his wife, Joan of Lancaster. (*CP* IV: 144-147).

   * This title was created as "la Warre" and became "de la Warre" in 1570.

Line 47C   Prepared for an earlier edition by Douglas Richardson

   31. SIR THOMAS DE HOLAND (47-31), Earl of Kent; m. **JOAN**, "Fair Maid of Kent." (236-12).

   32. SIR JOHN DE HOLAND, K.G., b. aft. 1350, d. 1400, Duke of Exeter, Earl of Huntingdon, Lieutenant of Ireland, Justice of Chester, Admiral of Fleet; m. 24 June 1386, Elizabeth, d. 1425, dau. of **JOHN OF GAUNT** (1-30), d. 1399, Duke of Lancaster, by his 1st wife, Blanche, d. 1369, dau. and h. of **HENRY** (72-33), d. 1361, Duke of Lancaster. She m. (2) bef. 12 Dec. 1400, Sir John Cornwall, d. 1443, Lord Fanhope. (*CP* V: 195-200, 253-254, VII: 401-416).

   33. CONSTANCE DE HOLAND, b. abt. 1387, d. 1437; m. (1) bef. 1 June 1402, Thomas Mowbray, d. 1405, Earl of Norfolk, Earl of Nottingham, Earl Marshal, Lord Mowbray and Segrave; m. (2) bef. 24 Feb. 1412/3, **SIR JOHN GREY, K.G.** (93B-33), d. 27 Aug. 1439, s. and h. ap. of Sir Reynold Grey, Lord Grey of Ruthin, Co. Denbigh. (*CP* VI: 155-159, IX: 604-605).

Line 47D   Prepared for an earlier edition by Douglas Richardson

   32. SIR THOMAS DE HOLAND (47-32), Earl of Kent; m. **ALICE FITZ ALAN** (78-33).

   33. ELEANOR DE HOLAND, d. 6 (or 18) Oct. 1405; m (1) abt. 1388, Roger de Mortimer, d. 1398, Earl of March & Ulster, Lord Mortimer, s. of **EDMUND DE MORTIMER** (29-34), 3rd Earl of March, by his wife **PHILIPPA**, Countess of Ulster (5-32); m. (2) June 1399, as 1st wife, Sir Edward Cherleton, K.G., b. abt. 1371, d. 14 Mar. 1420/1, Lord Cherleton, feudal lord of Powis, son of John Cherleton, Lord Cherleton, by Alice, dau. of **SIR RICHARD FITZ ALAN** (20-31) (60-33), by **ELIZABETH BOHUN** (15-31). (*CP* III: 161-162, VIII: 445-450).

   34. JOAN CHERLETON, dau. by (2), h. to Lordship of Powis, co. Montgomery, b. abt. 1400, d. 17 Sept. 1425; m. Sir John Grey (or Gray), K.G., created Earl of Tankerville in Normandy, b. aft. 1384, d. 22 Mar. 1420/1, son of Sir Thomas Gray, d. 1400, of Heton & Wark-on-Tweed, co. Northumberland, by his wife Joan. (*CP* III: 161-162, VI: 136-138).

   35. SIR HENRY GREY, b. abt. 1419, d. 13 Jan. 1449/50, 2nd Earl of Tankerville in Normandy; m. aft. 3 Jan. 1434/5, **ANTIGONE** (IA-34), illegitimate daughter of Humphrey, Duke of Gloucester, d. 1447. (*CP* V: 736 (n), VI: 138-9, 699; *Visit. Salop.* (1623), 105, 295.

Line 48   Revised for 8th Edition

   8. CHARIBERT, d. bef. 638, noble in Neustria.

   9. CHRODOBERTUS (Robert), noble in Nuestria.

   10. LANTBERTUS (Lambert), d. abt. 650, noble in Nuestria.

   11. CHRODOBERTUS (Robert II), mar. Doda.

12. LANTBERTUS (Lambert) II, adult abt. 690, dead 741, count in Nuestria and Austrasia. (see esp. Milton Rubincam, "Ancestry of Robert the Strong,..." *NEHGR* 117: 268-271 for Gens. 12-20).

13. RUTPERT I, Count in the Upper Rhine and Wormsgau, d. bef. 764; m. Williswint, d. 768, heiress of Count Adelhelm. (Note: Rutpert is often used interchangeably with Robert).

14. TURINCBERTUS (Thuringbert), d. aft. 1 June 770.

15. RUTPERT II, Count in the Upper Rhine and Wormsgau, d. 12 July 807; m. (1) Theoderata, d. by 789; m. (2) Isingard, seen 789.

16. RUTPERT III, by (1), Count in Wormsgau, seen 812-825, d. by. 834; m. abt. 808, as 2nd husb., Wiltrud (Waldrada) of Orléans, dau. of Count Hadrian of Orléans and Waldrat. (Said by de Vajay to be dau. of St. William d. 812, Count of Toulouse (see "Der Eintritt des Ungarischen Stammesbundes in die *Europäische Geschichte* (862-933)" (1968)) Prof. Kelley doubts this identification.

17. RUTPERT IV (called **ROBERT THE STRONG**), Count of Wormsgau, Paris, Anjou, and Blois, seen 836, killed 15 Sep 866; m. (1) per. Agnes; m. (2) abt. 864, **ADELAIDE** (or **AELIS**) (181-6), of Tours and Alsace, b. abt. 819, d. abt. 866, wid. of Conrad I, Count of Aargau and Auxerre, d. 863, dau. of Hugh III, Count of Alsace and Tours, by his wife Bava. He had chn by (2) wife: (1) Odo or Eudes, King of the Franks (France), and (2) **ROBERT I** (48-18) (53-18), Count of Paris 888, King of the Franks 922-3, father of **HUGH MAGNUS** (53-19). (*NEHGR* 110: 290-291).

18. ROBERT I, b. posthumously 866, d. 15 June 923, Count of Poitiers, Count of Paris, Marquis of Neustria, King of the West Franks (France); m. (1) Aelis; m. (2) abt. 890, Beatrix of Vermandois, d. aft. Mar. 931, dau. of **HERBERT I** (50-17), Count of Vermandois. (*TAG* 58 (1982): 164-165).

19. LIEGARDE (or Hildebrante) of France, dau. by (1); m. **HERBERT II** (50-18, 136-18), d. 943, Count of Vermandois and Troyes. (Gens. 8-19: *ES* II/10)

20. ALIX DE VERMANDOIS, b. 910/15, d. Bruges, 960; m. 934, **ARNOLD I** (162-18), the Old, d. 27 Mar. 964, Count of Flanders. (Gens: 17-20: Crispin, *Falaise Roll*, 186-187; Turton; Thatcher 320).

Line 49 Revised for 8th Edition

17. ROGER (RODGER), Count of Maine, d. 900; m. Rothilde, dau. of **CHARLES II** (148-15) "The Bald," and his 2nd wife, Richaut, dau. of Bouvin, Count of Metz, by unkn. dau. of Boso of Arles, Count in Italy. (*Foundations for Med. Gen.* 1 (2003): 3-4; *ES* II/189, II/186).

18. RICHILDE; m. Theobald (Tetbald), d. 904, Viscount of Troyes, Count of Blois, d. by 942. (*ES* II/46; West Winter, VII.6; K.S.B. Keats-Rohan, *Family Trees and the Roots of Politics*, Chapt. 10, pp 189-210; K.S.B. Keats-Rohan and C. Settipani, *Onomastique et Parente dans l'Occident Medieval*, pp. 57-68).

19. THEOBALD I, "The Devious," Count of Chartres and Blois, d. 16 Jan 975; m. 942/5 as 2nd husb. **LUITGARDE DE VERMANDOIS** (136-19), d. 978, wid. of **WILLIAM I** (121E-19) of Normandy, d. 942, and dau. of **HERBERT II DE VERMANDOIS** (50-18). (Gens. 16-19: G.A. Moriarty: "The Robertins" in *NEHGR* 99: 130-131, 101: 112 chart, corrected by Moriarty, *The Plantagenet Ancestry*, p. 36; *ES* II/46, III/48; Seversmith, 2,488-9; West Winter, VII.6).

11. ROTROU, d. 724; m. **CHARLES MARTEL** (190-11, 191-11), Mayor of the Palace in Austrasia, victor over the Saracens at Tours, 732.

12. PEPIN III THE SHORT, b. 714, d. 768, Mayor of the Palace, first king of the Franks of the second race, 751-768; m. **BERTHE** (240A-12), d. 783, dau. of **CHARIBERT** (240A-11) Count of Laon. (*ES* I.1/3 says Bertha dau. of Count Herbert).

13. CHARLEMAGNE, b. 2 Apr. 747, d. Aix la Chapelle, 28 Jan. 813/4, King of France 768-814, crowned Holy Roman Emperor 25 Dec. 800; m. (2) bef. 30 Apr. 771, **HILDEGARDE** (182-5), b. 758, d. 30 Apr. 783, dau. of Gerold of Swabia, Ct. on Linzgau, Prefect in Bavaria. (For their descendants, see Lines 50 to 169 inclusive).

14. PEPIN, bapt. at Rome, 12 Apr. 781, by Pope Adrian I, d. Milan, 8 July 810, King of Italy 781-810, consecrated King of Lombardy 15 Apr. 781. Apparently by a dau. of Duke Bernard, yngr. bro. of Pepin the Short, he had Bernard a natural son. (*NEHGR* 109: 175-178. West Winter, II.4).

15. BERNARD, natural son, b. 797, d. Milan, 17 Apr. 818, King of Italy 813-Dec. 817; m. Cunigunde, d. abt. 835. (West Winter, III.3)

16. PEPIN, b. 817/8, d. aft. 840, Count of Senlis, Peronne and St. Quentin. West Winter, IV.3)

17. HERBERT I DE VERMANDOIS, b. abt. 850, d. 6 Nov. bet. 900/907, Count of Soissons, Count of Méaux, Count of Vermandois 877/900; m. Bertha ?de Morvois, dau. Guerri I, Count of Morvois, by his wife, Eve of Roussillon?. (*ES* III.1/49 does not give wife, West Winter, V.3 questions Bertha's parentage, Saillot; Moriarty, *The Plantagenet Ancestry*, pp. 6, 21, 23, 37).

18. HERBERT II, b. 880-890, d. St. Quentin, 23 Feb. 943, Count of Vermandois, Soissons, and Troyes; m. bef. 907, **LIEGARDE** (Hildebrante) (Adela) (48-19), of France, dau. of **ROBERT I** (48-18), King of the West Franks, by his first wife, Aelis. (*ES* II/1, III.1/49).

19. ALBERT I, the Pious, b. abt. 920, d. 8 Sept. 987, Count of Vermandois; m bef. 954, **GERBERGA OF LORRAINE** (140-19), dau. of Giselbert, Duke of Lorraine and Gerberga, dau. of **HENRY I**, "the Fowler" (141-18), of Saxony.

20. HERBERT III, Count of Vermandois, b. abt. 955, d. 993; m. (1) Ogiva of England, dau. of **EDWARD I** "the Elder (1-15), wid. of **CHARLES III** "the Simple" (148-17); m. (2) Ermengarde, d. aft. 1035, wid. of Milon II, of Tonnerre, dau. of Reinald, Count of Bar-sur-Seine. (*ES* III.1/49, III.4/730; West Winter, VIII.4 doubts that Ermengarde was of Bar, or was wid. of Milon; *ES* III.4/681 shows Ingeltrudis, m. Milon, Count of Tonnerre, as a questionable dau. of Englebert I of Brienne).

21. OTHO (EUDES or **OTTO)**, by (2), Count of Vermandois, b. abt. 1000, d. 25 May 1045; m. Parvie.

22. HERBERT IV, b. abt. 1032, d. abt. 1080, Count of Vermandois and Valois; m. bef. 1068, Adela of Vexin, dau. of Raoul III "the Great," Count of Valois and Vexin.

23. ADELAIDE DE VERMANDOIS, d. abt. 1120, Countess of Vermandois and Valois; m. (1) bef. 1080, **HUGH MAGNUS (II)** (53-23), d. 1101, Duke of France and Burgundy, Marquis of Orleans, Count of Amiens, Chaumont, Paris, Valois, and Vermandois, a leader of the First Crusade; m. (2) abt. 1102, bef. 1103, Reinald, Count of Clermont d. 1162. (*CP* X: 351. Gens. 13-23: *ES* III.1/49).

24. ISABEL DE VERMANDOIS, d. 13 Feb. 1131, Countess of Leicester; m. (1) 1096, Sir Robert de Beaumont, b. abt. 1049, d. 5 June 1118, Lord of Beaumont, Pont-Audemer and Brionne, Count of Meulan, cr. 1st Earl of Leicester, Companion of William the Conqueror at Hastings 1066, son of Roger de Beaumont and Adeline (or Adelise), dau. of

Waleran, Count of Meulan; m. (2) 1118, William de Warenne (see 83-24), d. 11 May 1138, 2nd Earl of Surrey, son of William de Warenne and Gundred, sis. of Gerbod the Fleming, Earl of Chester. (*CP* IV: 670 chart III, VII: 520, 523-526, 737, X: 351).

25. WALERAN DE BEAUMONT, b. 1104, d. 10 Apr. 1166, Count of Meulan, Earl of Worcester; m. abt. 1141, Agnes de Montfort, d. 15 Dec. 1181, dau. of Amauri de Montfort, Count of Evreux, and Agnes, dau. of Anseau (Ansel) de Garlande, d. 1117/8, seigneur de Garlande, seneschal of France. (*CP* VII: 520, 708-717, 737-738; *Dict. de Biographie Francaise*, sub. Garlande).

26. SIR ROBERT DE BEAUMONT, d. 1207, Count of Meulan; m. 1166, Maud, dau. of **REGINALD FITZ ROY** (121-26), Earl of Cornwall (base son of King **HENRY I** (121-25) of England), by Mabel, d. 1162, dau. of William Fitz Richard, Lord of Cardinand, co. Cornwall. (*CP* VII: 520, 739-740).

27. MAUD (MABEL) DE BEAUMONT, of Meulan, liv. 1 May 1204; m. William de Reviers (called "de Vernon"), b. 1155, d. Sept. 1217, Earl of Devon, son of Baldwin de Reviers, cr. Earl of Devon by June 1141, d. 1155, by Adelise. (*CP* IV: 317, 673 chart VI, VII: 520, 740 note *i*).

28. MARY DE VERNON (or **DE REVIERS**), m. (1) 1200, Sir Peter de Preaux of Chagford, co. Devon; m. (2) **SIR ROBERT DE COURTENAY** (138-27), d. 26 July 1242, feudal baron of Oakhampton. (*CP* IV: 317, 335, 673, III: 465 note *c*, X: 125 note *h*, IV: App. H 675; Seversmith, 2,407-2,413). (See also *Devon & Cornwall N & Q* IV: 229).

29. SIR JOHN DE COURTENAY, b. abt. 1220, d. 3 May 1274, Baron of Oakhampton; m. aft. May 1274, Isabel de Vere, dau. of Hugh de Vere, Earl of Oxford, and **HAWISE DE QUINCY** (60-28). Hugh was son of **ROBERT DE VERE** (246-27), b. aft. 1164, d. bef. 25 Oct. 1221, 3rd Earl of Oxford, Lord Chamberlain of England, Magna Charta Surety, 1215, and his wife Isabel de Bolebec, d. 2 or 3 Feb. 1245. (Hedley, *Northumberland Fams.* I, 24-26; *CP* IV: 317, 335, X: 210-213, 125 note *h*; Seversmith, 2,407-2,413).

30. SIR HUGH DE COURTENAY, b. 25 Mar. 1251, d. 28 Feb. 1291, Baron of Oakhampton; m. Eleanor le Despenser, d. 1 Oct. 1328, dau. Hugh le Despenser, Justiciar of England, d. 1306, and Aline Basset (see 72-31). (*CP* IV: 335, 673 chart VI; *CP* VI: 124; Waters, in *Proceedings of the Essex Institute*, XVII: 16; Seversmith, 2,402-2,406; Vivian, *Visit. of Devon*, 243-244).

31. SIR HUGH DE COURTENAY, b. 14 Sept. 1276, d. Tiverton, co. Devon, 23 Dec. 1340; m. abt. 1293, **AGNES DE ST. JOHN** (262-32), d. 1340. (Seversmith, 2,392-2,402).

NOTE: Line breaks here. There is no proof that Eleanor de Courtenay (Gen. 32 in previous editions) is the dau. of Sir Hugh de Courtenay, Gen. 31. However, See: Line 140, Gens. 31-42, for the descendants of Sir Henry de Grey by Eleanor de Courtenay.

Line 51

30. SIR HUGH DE COURTENAY (50-30), b. Mar. 1251, d. 28 Feb. 1291/2, Baron of Oakhampton; m. Eleanor le Despenser, dau. Hugh le Despenser and Aline Basset, dau. & h. Sir Philip Basset (see 72-31) of Wycombe, co. Buckingham, etc. (*CP* IV: 261, 323-4, 335; *TAG* 38: 180).

31. SIR HUGH DE COURTENAY, b. 14 Sept. 1276, d. Tiverton co. Devon, 23 Dec. 1340, Earl of Devon; m. 1293, **AGNES DE ST. JOHN** (262-32), d. 1345. (*CP* IV: 324).

32. HUGH DE COURTENAY, K.G., b. 12 July 1303, d. Tiverton, 2 May 1377, Earl of Devon; m. 11 Aug. 1325, **MARGARET DE BOHUN** (6-30), d. 16 Dec. 1391. (*CP* IV: 324).

33. SIR PHILIP COURTENAY, d. 29 July 1406, of Powderham, Lord Lieutenant of Ireland, 1383; m. Anne Wake, dau. of Sir Thomas Wake of Blysworth. (*CP* IV: 335).

34.   SIR JOHN COURTENAY, m. Joan Champernoun, wid. of **SIR JAMES CHUDLEIGH, KNT** (217-37), dau. of Alexander Champernoun of Bere Ferrers by Joan Ferrers, dau. of Martin Ferrers, and granddau. of Sir Richard Champernoun, of Modbury, by his 2nd wife, Alice, dau. of Thomas, Lord Astley. (Collins VI: 260; *CP* IV: 335; *Devon & Cornwall N. & Q.* XVIII: 225).

35.   SIR PHILIP COURTENAY, of Powderham, d. 16 Dec. 1463; m. Elizabeth Hungerford, d. 14 Dec. 1476, dau. of Sir Walter Hungerford, K.G., 1st Lord Hungerford, Lord Treasurer of England, and wife Catherine Peverell, dau. of Sir Thomas Peverell and **MARGARET DE COURTENAY** (51A-33). (*CP* IV: 335).

36.   SIR PHILIP COURTENAY, of Molland, b. 18 Jan. 1403/4 Sheriff of Devon, 1471; m. Elizabeth Hingston, dau. of Robert Hingston.

37.   MARGARET COURTENAY, m. Sir John Champernoun, of Modbury, d. 30 Apr. 1503, son of William Champernoun, by Elizabeth Chidderley, dau. of John Chidderley. (*CP* IV: 673, VI: 124; Waters: Champernoun Pedigree in *Essex Institute Proceedings* XVII: 16. Generations 30-37: Vivian, *Visit. of Devon*, 162, 244, 246, 251; *Devon & Cornwall N & Q* VIII: 340-342; Paget 2: 460).

38. SIR PHILIP CHAMPERNOUN, of Modbury, b. 18 Jan. 1403/4, d. 2 Aug. 1545, will pro. 3 Feb. 1545/6; m. **KATHERINE CAREW** (6-37). (Vivian, *Visit. of Devon*, 160, 162-163, 379-380; Waters: Pedigree of Champernoun, in *Essex Institute Proceedings* XVII: 16; *Devon & Cornwall N & Q, cit.*).

Line 51A   Prepared for an earlier edition by Douglas Richardson

31. SIR HUGH DE COURTENAY (51-31); m. **AGNES ST. JOHN** (262-32).

32. SIR THOMAS DE COURTENAY, d. 1356, 4th son, of Woodhuish and Dunterton, co. Devon, and Wootton Courtenay and Cricket Malherbe, co. Somerset; m. by 1337, Muriel Moels, b. abt. 1322, dau. & coh. of Sir John de Moels, d. 1337, 4th Lord Moels, of Maperton and North Cadbury, co. Somerset, by his wife, Joan Lovel, dau. of Sir Richard Lovel, d. 1351, Lord Lovel of Castle Cary, co. Somerset. (*CP* IV: 373-374, VI: 613-616, IX: 7-8; Vivian, *Visit. of Devon*, p. 244).

33. MARGARET COURTENAY, dau. & h., d. abt. 8 Dec. 1422; m. Thomas Peverell of Parke, Hamatethy, and Penhale, Cornwall. (*CP* IV: 7-8, VI: 613-616).

34. CATHERINE PEVERELL, dau. & h., liv. 14 June 1426; m. bef. 18 Sept. 1402, Sir Walter Hungerford, b. abt. 1378, d. 9 Aug. 1449, 1st Lord Hungerford, Speaker of the House of Parliament, Sheriff of Somerset and Dorset, Constable of Windsor Castle, Steward to the Household of Henry V and Henry VI, Lord High Treasurer, son of Sir Thomas Hungerford of Farleigh and Wellow, co. Somerset, by his 2nd wife, Joan Hussey, dau. & coh. of Sir Edmund Hussey of Holbrook, co. Somerset. (*CP* VI: 613-616).

35. ROBERT HUNGERFORD, d. 18 May 1493, 2nd Lord Hungerford, of Heytesbury, co. Wilts; m. Margaret Botreaux, d. 7 Feb. 1477/8, dau. & h. of William de Botreaux, d. 1462, 3rd Lord Botreaux, of Boscastle, Cornwall, by his 1st wife, Elizabeth Beaumont, dau. of **JOHN BEAUMONT** (17-32), Lord Beaumont. (*CP* II: 61, 242-243, VI: 617-618).

36. KATHERINE HUNGERFORD, d. 12 May 1493; m. bef. 10 June 1451, **RICHARD WEST** (18-34), b. 28 Oct. 1430, d. 10 Mar. 1475/6, 4th Lord West, 7th Lord La Warre (or de la Warre), son of Reynold West, d. 1450, Lord West and Lord La Warre, by 1st wife, Margaret Thorley. (*CP* IV: 154-155, XII (2): 521-522; *CP* XIV: 243). See footnote end of Line 47B.

36. ELEANOR HUNGERFORD, (dau. of Gen. 35), m. (1) John White; m. (2) 1470, as 2nd wife, Sir William Tyrrell, Knt. (Note: Ancestor of Edward Rainsford, immig. to N.E., d. Boston, 1680. For this descent see: Douglas Richardson, "Plantagenet Ancestry of Edward Rainsford (1609-1680) of Boston Massachusetts," in *NEHGR* 154 (2000): 219-226).

Line 52 Revised for 8th Edition

32. WILLIAM LE PROUZ (217-32), sheriff of Devon 1269, Inq.p.m. writ 21 Oct. 1270, held Gidley, Stodbury, Cumesheved, Hacche and Colton, co. Devon; m. (1) Alice de Widworthy, prob. dead 1250, dau. of William de Widworthy, liv. 1244, by 1st wife, unkn., and in her issue heir to her bro. Hugh de Widworthy, d. 1292; m. (2) abt. 1250, Alice de Ferrers, dau. and h. Sir Fulk de Ferrers (son of Gilbert de Ferrers), of Throwleigh by his wife Alice de Helion, dau. and event. h. Sir Hervey de Helion, of Ashton.

33. SIR WILLIAM LE PROUZ, by (1), b. abt. 1245 (age 25 in 1270), d. sh. bef. 26 Apr. 1316 when Inq.p.m. writ, bur. first at Holbeton, co. Devon, but under Bishop Grandisson's mandate of 19 Oct. 1329, his bones rebur. at Lustleigh, co. Devon, in accordance with his will, held manors of Aveton Gifford, Gidleigh, Holbeton and Lustleigh, co. Devon, Conservator of Peace, co. Devon, 1308, Commissioner re Statute of Winchester, 1310; m. by 1275, Alice de Wydworthy, liv. 1318, dau. of William de Wydworthy by an unkn. dau. of John de Reigney. Alice, (granddau. of John de Reigny, adult by 1222, d. 1246, lord of Aisholt, Aley and Doniford, Somerset, Brixton Reigney in Brixton, co. Devon, and Newton Reigny, co. Cumberland), was coh. with her three sisters, in 1275, to her nephew Sir William de Reigny (Reyny). (*Knights of Edward* I, 4: 103; *Notes and Gleanings*, Vol. 4, chart labelled Appendix B bef. p. 133; *VCH Somerset* 5: 152-153 (manor of Doniford, Somerset); Pole, *Collections towards a History of the County of Devon*, pp. 245-324; Cal. Inq.p.m. 1: 236; 2: 18, 94-95, 141-142, 177, 353; *Gen. Mag.* 16 (1971): 552-553).

34. ALICE PROUZ, age 30+ in 1316, d. sh. bef. 15 Nov. 1335, held the manors of Aveton Gifford, Widworthy, Lustleigh, Holbeton, Gidleigh and Clist Widworthy, writ to partition her estates between her daus. 12 Mar. 1336; m. (1) abt. 1300, Roger de Moels, of Lustleigh, Devon, d. Dec. 1323, son of Sir Roger Moels, Knt., who died 1295, son of Nicholas de Moels, d. sh. aft. 1264, by Hawise de Newmarch, dau. of James de Newmarch. (*CP* XIV: 478, IX: 1-8, esp. note c, p. 5; *Gen. Mag.* 16 (1971): 552-553)

35. JOAN DE MOELS, b. by 1306 (age 30 or more at mother's death), inher. Widworthy, Devon; m. (1) John de Wotton, died bef. 1 Jan. 1335/6; m. (2) by 21 Sept. 1336, John de Northcote, Sheriff of Devon 1353, liv. 1356/7 (see Mark Hughes in *Devon & Cornwall N & Q* XXXV: 310-312, with refs.). She was living 13 Oct. 1343. (*Notes and Gleanings* IV: 133-143; List of Sheriffs of England and Wales, List and Indexes IX: 35).

36. RICHARD WOTTON, by (1); m. Julian, perh. a dau. William le Prouz of Chagford, his cousin. She m. (2) Thomas Jewe.

37. WILLIAM WOTTON; m. by 1374 Gundred Wyger, one of three daus. and coh. Thomas Wyger of co. Devon, and Christian his wife. (*Notes and Gleanings* IV: 133-143; *Somerset and Dorset Notes & Queries* VII: 49-55).

38. JOHN WOTTON, lord of Widworthy, Devon; m. by 8 Mar. 1408/9 Englesia (or Engaret) Dymoke, dau. of Walter Dymoke. (*Notes and Gleanings* IV: 133-143).

39. ALICE WOTTON; m. by 1424, Sir John Chichester, Knt., lord of Raleigh in parish of Pilton, co. Devon, b. 1386, d. 14 Dec. 1437, son John Chichester, d. by 1399, by wife Thomasine Raleigh, dau. and sole h. of John Raleigh, lord of Raleigh, co. Devon. (Sir Alex. P.B. Chichester, *History of the Family of Chichester*, 13-25).

40.   RICHARD CHICHESTER, ESQ., b. 23 Feb. 1424, d. 25 Dec. 1498, bur. Pilton, Devon, Sheriff of Devon, 1463, 1468, 1474, held manors of Raleigh, Arlington, Rokysford, Widworthy and Sutton Sachefield, Devon; m. (1) Margaret Keynes, dau. of Sir Nicholas Keynes of Winkley. (Chichester, *op. cit.* 25-28; List of Sheriffs of England and Wales, List and Indexes IX: 36; Cal. Inq.p.m. Henry VII II: 82-84).

41.   NICHOLAS CHICHESTER, b. abt. 1452 (age 31 in 1483), d.v.p. 1498; m. Christina or Christian Paulet, wid. of Henry Hall, dau. of Sir William Paulet by Elizabeth Denebaud, dau. and h. John Denebaud of Hinton St. George, co. Somerset. (Chichester, *op. cit.* 26-27; *Proc. Som. Arch. & Nat. Hist. Soc.*, 81, Part III (1935): 112-113 for biography of Christian's brother, Sir Amias Paulet).

42.   SIR JOHN CHICHESTER, of Raleigh in Pilton, co. Devon, b. abt. 1475 (age 24 in 1499), d. 22 Feb. 1537/8; m. (2) by 1527, Joan Brett, dau. of Robert Brett, Esq., Escheator of Devon, 1527. (Cal. Inq.p.m. Henry VII II: 82-84; *List of Early Chancery Proceedings* VI: 346 (John Chichester vs. Robert Trett & Joan Chichester); *List of Escheators for England and Wales*, List and Index Society 72: 38; *NEHGR* 51: 214. Gens. 37-40: Burke's *Peerage* (1953, 1967) "Chichester").

43.   AMYAS CHICHESTER, b. abt. 1527, d. 4 July 1577, age 50, of Arlington, co. Devon; m. by 1545, **JANE GIFFARD** (25-37), dau. of Sir Roger Giffard of Brightleigh, in parish of Chittlehampton, Devon; her will was probated 16 Apr. 1596. (Gens. 28-41: Crispin, *Falaise Roll*, Table IX; Vivian, *Visit. of Devon*, 172-173, 179, 397, 400, 626, 823; v. Redlich 105-106; Chichester, *op. cit.*, 32, 67-70, 77-80; Bolton, *Ancestry of Margaret Wyatt*, chart; *NEHGR* 51: 214. See Wm. R. Drake, *Notes of the Family of Chichester* (London 1886), 324 et seq.).

44.   FRANCES CHICHESTER, bur. Braunton, co. Devon, 5 Apr. 1626; m. Braunton, co. Devon, by 19 Oct 1584 John Wyatt, gentleman, bapt. Braunton 11 Nov. 1557, bur. 29 Nov. 1598, Braunton, son of Philip Wyatt, of Braunton, and Joan Paty. (*NEHGR* 51: 214; Vivian, *Devon*, 823; *TAG* 57: 115-119).

45.   MARGARET WYATT, bapt. Braunton, co. Devon, 8 Mar. 1594/5; m. Braunton 2 Feb. 1626/7, Matthew Allyn (or Allen), bapt. Braunton, 17 Apr. 1605, d. Windsor, Conn., 1 Feb. 1670/1, son Richard Allyn of Braunton and Margaret Wyatt. They were the ancestors of President Grover Cleveland. (Vivian, *Chichester and Bolton*, as above; v. Redlich 106; Waters II: 932, 1212-1213; *TAG* 57: 115-119). (Amended by Douglas Richardson).

Line 53

18.   ROBERT I (48-18), b. posth. 866, d. Soissons 15 June 923, Count of Poitiers, Marquis of Neustria and Orleans, Count of Paris, Duke of France, King of the West Franks; m. (2) aft. 893, Beatrix of Vermandois, d. aft. Mar. 931, dau. **HERBERT I** (50-17), Count of Vermandois, by his wife Bertha de Morvois. (*TAG* 58: 164-5; *ES* II/10; Saillot, *Sang de Charlemagne*, p. 5; Sirjean, *Encyclopédie Généalogique...* III: 53-56).

19.   HUGH MAGNUS, b. abt. 895, d. Deurdan 16 June 956, bur. St. Denis, Count of Paris, Orleans, Vexin and Le Mans, Duke of France; m. (2) at Mainz oder Ingelheim 938, **HEDWIG** of Saxony (141-19), d. 10 May aft. 965, dau. of **HENRY I** (141-18), "the Fowler," King of the Saxons. (*ES* II/10-11 says that Hedwig, 3rd wife).

20.   HUGH CAPET, b. winter 941, d. Les Juifs, Chartres 24 Oct. 996, bur. St. Denis, King of France 987-996, Count of Poitou, Count of Orleans, first of the Capetian Kings of France; m. summer 968 **ADELAIDE** (or **ALIX**) **OF POITOU** (144A-20), b. abt. 945, d. 15

June 1006. (*ES* II/11; See Richard Barre, Lord Ashburton, *Genealogical Memorial to the Royal House of France* (London, 1825) -- but use with care).

21. ROBERT II, the Pious, b. Orleans 27 Mar 972 (*ES*; Moriarty says 970/1), d. Melun 20 July 1031, bur. St. Denis, King of France, 1 Jan 996-1031, Count of Paris; m. (3) **CONSTANCE OF PROVENCE** (141A-21), b. abt. 986, d. Melun 25 Jul 1032, bur. St. Denis, dau. of William II, Count of Arles and Provence, by his wife, Adelaide (or Blanche), dau. of Fulk II, Count of Anjou. (*ES* II/11; Moriarty, *The Plantagenet Ancestry*, p. 24; West Winter X.77).

22. HENRY I (101-22), b. 1008, d. Vitry-en-Brie 4 Aug. 1060, bur. St. Denis, King of France 1031-1060, Count of Paris; m. (3) 20 Jan. 1044/5 **ANNE OF KIEV** (241-6), b. 1036, d. aft. 1075, dau. of **IAROSLAV I** (241-5), Grand Prince of Kiev, d. 1054, and Ingigerd, dau. of Olav II Skotkonung, King of Sweden. (*CP* X: 351; N. de Baumgarten, *Orientalia Christiana* (Rome, 1927); *ES, cit.*; Moriarty, *cit.*).

23. HUGH MAGNUS, b. 1057, d. Tarsus 18 Oct 1102, Count of Vermandois and Valois, Duke of France, etc.; m. aft. 1967 as her 1st husb., **ADELAIDE DE VERMANDOIS** (50-23), Countess of Vermandois. (*CP* X: 351).

24. ISABEL (ELIZABETH) DE VERMANDOIS (50-24), d. 13 Feb. 1131; m. (1) 1096, Sir Robert de Beaumont, 1st Earl of Leicester, d. 5 June 1118. (*CP* VII: 520, 523-526, 737, X: 351; *ES* III.1/55).

25. SIR ROBERT DE BEAUMONT, 2nd Earl of Leicester, b. 1104, d. 5 Apr. 1168, knighted 1122, Justiciar of England, 1155-1168; m. aft. Nov. 1120, Amice de Montfort, dau. of Ralph de Gael de Montford, Seigneur of Montford de Gael in Brittany, son of Ralph de Gael, 1st Earl of Norfolk, Suffolk, and Cambridge, Seigneur of Montford de Gael in Brittany, and Emma, dau. of William Fitz Osbern, a Companion of William the Conqueror at the Battle of Hastings, 1066, Earl of Hereford. (*CP* IV: 672-673 chart, V: 736, VII: 520, 527-530, IX: 568-574 and note *n* 574).

26. SIR ROBERT DE BEAUMONT, b. bef. 1135, d. 1190, 3rd Earl of Leicester, Crusader 1179; m. abt. 1155, Petronilla (or Pernell) de Grandmesnil, d. 1 Apr. 1212, dau. of Hugh de Grandmesnil, and great-granddau. of Hugh de Grandmesnil, a Companion of William the Conqueror at the Battle of Hastings, 1066. (*CP* IV: 670 chart III, VII: 520, 530-533, X: Appendix I, p. 106 note *b*, XIV: 429, Old-*CP* VIII: 168; Gen. Mag. 9 (1943): 350).

27. MARGARET DE BEAUMONT, d. prob. on 12 Jan. 1234/5 but sh. bef. 12 Feb. 1234/5; m. bef. 1173, Saher IV de Quincy, b. 1155, d. 3 Nov. 1219, 1st Earl of Winchester, Magna Charta Surety, 1215, Crusader 1219 (son of Robert de Quincy, d. bef. 1197, Lord of Buckley and of Fawside, Justiciar of Scotland, Crusader; m. Orabel, dau. of Ness fitz William, Lord of Leuchars; and grandson of **MAUD DE ST. LIZ (SENLIS** or **SENLIZ)** (130-27) by her 2nd husb., Saher I de Quincy of Lord of Daventry. (See George Bellew, Esq., Somerset Herald, College of Arms, London, "The Family of de Quincy and Quincy" (typescript, vol. 2) at N.E.H.G.S., Boston; also Lundie W. Barlow, "The Ancestry of Saher de Quincy, Earl of Winchester," *NEHGR* 112: 61 et seq.; *CP* VII: 520, 536, XII (2): 746-751; *VCH Lancs.* I: 312; Sydney Painter: *The House of Quincy 1136-1264, Med. et Hum.* XI: 3-9; *ES* III.4/708).

28. ROGER DE QUINCY, d. 25 Apr. 1264, 2nd Earl of Winchester, Constable of Scotland; m. (1) **HELEN OF GALLOWAY** (38-27), dau. of Alan, Lord of Galloway, Constable of Scotland, and a descendant of the English and Scottish Kings. (*SP* IV: 142; Old-*CP* VIII: 169-170; XII(2): 934; Banks I: 469).

29. ELENA (ELLEN) DE QUINCY, of Brackley, d. bef. 20 Aug. 1296; m. by 1242, **SIR ALAN LA ZOUCHE** (see 38-28), d. 10 Aug. 1270, Baron Zouche of Ashby la Zouche, co.

Leicester, Constable of the Tower of London, a descendant in the male line of the Counts of Porhoet in Brittany. (*SP* IV: 142; Old-*CP* VIII: 222, XII (2): 932 934; Banks I: 469).

    30. SIR ROGER LA ZOUCHE, d. sh. bef. 15 Oct 1285, Baron Zouche of Ashby, m. abt. 1267, **ELA LONGESPEE** (31-28), a great-granddau. of **HENRY II** (1-24), King of England. (Old-*CP* VIII: 222, XII(2): 934-5).

Line 54

    28. ROBERT II DE QUINCY, d.v.p. bef. 1232, son of Saher IV de Quincy and **MARGARET DE BEAUMONT** (53-27); m. **HAWISE OF CHESTER** (125-29), b. 1180, d. 1241/3, Countess of Lincoln. (*CP* IV: 670 chart IV, VII: 677, XII(2): 748 note *g* and cited refs.; *VCH Lanc.* I: 306; *The Genealogist* 5 (1984): 221-225).

    29. MARGARET DE QUINCY, b. abt. 1209, d. Hempstead Marshall, Mar. 1266 (sole surv. dau. of Hawise, yngst sis. and eventual coh. of Ranulf III, Earl of Chester and Lincoln); m. (1) bef. 21 June 1221, John de Lacy, b. 1192, d. 22 July 1240, cr. Earl of Lincoln, 1232, Constable of Chester, Magna Charta Surety 1215, son of Roger de Lacy and Maud de Clare. (Margaret m. (2) 1242, Walter Marshal, d. 1245, Earl of Pembroke. It is doubtful that she ever m. (3) Richard of Wiltshire, attributed to her in some sources.) (Louise Wilkinson, "Pawn and Political Player: Observations on the Life of a Thirteenth-Century Countess," *Historical Research* 73 (2000): 105-123, esp. p. 1116; *CP* IV: 670 chart iv, V: 695, 736 chart, VII: 676-680; *VCH Lanc.* I: 306).

    30. MAUD DE LACY, d. bef. 10 Mar. 1288/9; m. 25 Jan. 1237/8, **SIR RICHARD DE CLARE**, (63-29), b. 4 Aug. 1222, d. 15 July 1262, Earl of Clare, Hertford and Gloucester. (*CP* IV: 670 chart iv, V: 696-702, cf. 700, 736 chart, VII: 677-680).

    31. THOMAS DE CLARE, 2nd son, d. Ireland, Feb. 1287/8, Governor of London, Lord of Thomand, Lord of Inchequin and Yougha; m. 1275, **JULIANA FITZ MAURICE**, of Offaly (178-7), dau. of **MAURICE FITZ MAURICE FITZ GERALD** (178-6), Lord of Offaly. (*CP* VII: 200, V: 701; Banks I: 112, 155).

    32. MARGARET DE CLARE, d. 1333; m. (1) 1289, Gilbert d'Umfraville, son of Gilbert d'Umfraville (see 224-30), Earl of Angus, d.s.p. 1303; m. (2) by 1308, Bartholomew de Badlesmere, 1st Lord Badlesmere, b. abt. 1275, hanged at Canterbury, co. Kent, 14 Apr. 1322, of Badlesmere and Chilham Castle, Kent, Steward of the King's household, Ambassador to France, Savoy, and the Pope, son of Sir Guncelin de Badlesmere (see 70-33), d. 1301, of Badlesmere, Kent, Justice of Chester, Custodian of Chester Castle, by his wife Joan. Margaret de Clare was heiress to her nephew Thomas de Clare, son of Richard de Clare, 2nd son of Thomas and Juliane (Cal.Inq.p.m. VI #275, p. 159). She was therefore <u>sister</u> to Richard, 2nd son, and to Thomas, 1st son (Goddard Orpen, *Ireland Under the Normans*; IV 94-6; *CP* I: 371-372 and 373 note c, X: 223; Banks I: 112; M. Altschul, *The Clares*, 187-197, and ped. fac. p. 332).

    33. MARGERY DE BADLESMERE, by (2), b. 1306, d. 18 Oct. 1363; m. bef. 25 Nov. 1326, **WILLIAM DE ROS** (89-31), 2nd Lord Ros of Helmsley, d. 1343. (*CP* I: 373 note c, VIII: 633; Cal.Inq.p.m. VI #275, p. 159).

    34. ALICE DE ROS, d. bef. 4 July 1344; m. **NICHOLAS DE MEINELL** (88-32), d. bef. 20 Nov. 1341, 1st Baron Meinell of Whorlton. (*CP* IV: 60, VIII: 632-634).

Line 55 Supplied by Laurence Eliot Bunker, Wellesley Hills, Mass.; Gens. 25-26 added by Douglas Richardson. (Editorial additions to 8th Edition)

25. FULK PAYNEL (PAGANEL), of Dudley, co. Worcester, founder of Tickford Priory near Newport Pagnell, co. Buckingham, living 1130; m. an heir (possibly a dau., Beatrice) of William Fitz Ansculf (from Picquigny), his Domesday tenancy-in-chief, later known as the barony of Dudley, Worcester,. (*EYC* VI: 47-48; Keats-Rohan, *Domesday People* I, 484; Sanders, *English Baronies*, 113; Cleveland, *Battle Abbey Roll*, II: 392, III: 8).

26. RALPH PAYNEL, of Dudley, co. Worcester, heir of William Fitz Ansculf, one of the rebels against King Stephen in 1138, when he held the castle of Dudley against him, liv. 1141, d. by 1153; m. NN, prob. dau.of Robert de Ferrers, d. 1139, 1st Earl of Derby, by his wife, Hawise de Vitré, reputedly a dau. of Andre, d. 1139, Seigneur of Vitré in Brittany, by Agnes, dau. of Robert, Count of Mortain. Evidence of the identity of the wife of Ralph Paynel is her maritagium which consisted of the manor of Greenham, co. Berks (a Ferrers fee). (*EYC* VI: 48; *CP* IV: 191; Keats-Rohan, *Domesday Desc. II*: 459).

27. HAWISE PAYNEL, dau. & in her issue coh., sister of Gervase Paynel, d. 1194; m. (1) **JOHN DE SOMERY** (81-27); m. (2) abt. 1196 Roger IV de Berkeley, of Dursley, d. 1190. (*CP* X: 320; Banks I: 398; *EYC* VI: 49-50. Gens.: 25-27: Keats-Rohan, *Domesday Desc. II*: 1055-1057).

28. RALPH DE SOMERY (81-28), Baron Dudley, d. 1210; m. Margaret Marshal, sis. of William Marshal, 3rd Earl of Pembroke, and dau. of John Fitz Gilbert (styled John the Marshal) (see 66-27). (CP XII (1): 110-111, XIV: 586).

29. ROGER DE SOMERY (81-29), Lord Dudley, co. Worcester, d. by 26 Aug. 1273; m. (1) **NICHOLE D'AUBIGNY** (126-30, 210-30). (*CP* II: 1-2, VI: 174, XII (1): 112-113; *DNB* 3: 385).

30. MARGARET DE SOMERY (210-30), d. aft. 18 June 1293; m. (1) Ralph Basset, Baron Basset of Drayton, co. Stafford, slain at Evesham, 4 Aug. 1265; custos pacis for Shropshire and Staffordshire, 1264; M.P. 1264, son of Ralph Basset of Drayton, co. Stafford; m. (2) bef. 26 Jan. 1270/1, Ralph de Cromwell, d. sh. bef. 18 Sept. 1289. (See 210-31). (*CP* I: 237, 239,II: 1-2, III: 551, VI: 174; Banks I: 115; *DNB* 3: 385).

30. RALPH BASSET, d. Drayton, 31 Dec. 1299, Lord Basset of Drayton, M.P, 1295-1299; m. Hawise, par. unkn. (*CP* II: 2).

31. MARGARET BASSET, d. 17 Mar. 1336/7; m. (1) in or bef. 1298, Edmund de Stafford, b. 15 July 1273, 1st Baron Stafford, M.P. 1300, d. by 12 Aug. 1308, son of Nicholas de Stafford, d. 1287. (*CP* XII (1): 172-173, XIV: 589; Banks I: 115, 408-414; *DNB* 53: 456).

32. SIR RALPH DE STAFFORD, K.G., b. 24 Sept. 1301, d. 31 Aug. 1372; K.G. 23 Apr. 1349, 1st Earl of Stafford; m. (1) abt. 1326/7 Katharine de Hastang (see *MC* 28-6, 136-6), dau. Sir John de Hastang of Chebsey, co. Stafford, by Eve; m. (2) bef. 6 July 1336, **MARGARET DE AUDLEY** (9-31). (*CP* VI: 338-345, XI: 100-101, XII (1): 173-177; *TAG* 9: 213; Banks I: 115, 408; *DNB* 53: 456-459; Weever, 323).

33. MARGARET STAFFORD, 4th dau. by (1); m. as 2nd wife, Sir John Stafford, Knt., of Bramshall, co. Stafford, son of Sir William Stafford of Bramshall.

34. RALPH DE STAFFORD, of Grafton, in the Parish of Bromsgrove, co. Worcester, d. 1 Mar. 1410 (Inq.p.m., 3 July 1410); m. betw. 20 Aug. 1373 and 24 Feb. 1374/5, Maud de Hastang, bapt. 2 Feb. 1358/9, Chebsey, co. Stafford, age 15 in 1374, dau. & coh. of John de Hastang, of Leamington House, co. Warwick. (See *MC* 28-8.) (*CP* VI: 343 & note f, 344; *TAG* 9: 213).

35. SIR HUMPHREY STAFFORD, KNT., of Grafton co. Warwick b. 1384, age 26 in 1410, d. 20 Feb. 1419 (Inq.p.m., 8 June 1419); m. Elizabeth Burdet, dau. of Sir John

Burdet, Knt., of Huncote and Leire, co. Leicester. (*TAG* 9: 213 (in *TAG* article given as Bindette, pos. error in reading original Inq.p.m.); Nichols, *Leicestershire* III, 820).

36. **SIR HUMPHREY STAFFORD, KNT.**, of Grafton, b. 1400, commissioner 1436, liv. 1467; m. **ELEANOR AYLESBURY** (187·11), dau. of Sir Thomas Aylesbury, Knt., of Blatherwyck. (*TAG* 9: 213).

37. **ELIZABETH STAFFORD**, m. **SIR RICHARD DE BEAUCHAMP** (84·34). (Gens. 32-37: *Gen.* (n.s.) 31: 173; Deighton pedigree certified by A.T. Butler, College of Arms, 11 Dec. 1928, in *TAG* 9: 213). (Burdet ancestry, see Wm. Burton's *Descr. of Leics.*, 2 ed, p. 129; Betham's *Baronetage* (1801), pp. 180·1).

Line 56

27. **MARGARET DE BEAUMONT** (53·27); m. Saher IV de Quincy, 1st Earl of Winchester, Magna Charta Surety 1215, d. 1219. (*CP* VII: 520, 677; *VCH Lanc.* I: 312). (Ancestry of Saher de Quincy, *NEHGR* 112: 61 et seq.; *CP* XII (2): 745·751; *Med. et Hum.* XI: 3·9, reprinted in Painter's *Feudalism and Liberty*, 231·239).

28. **ARABELLA (ORABELLA) DE QUINCY**, m. Sir Richard de Harcourt, d. 1258, son of William de Harcourt, Governor of Tamworth Castle, co. Warwick, 2 Henry III, and Alice Noel, dau. of Thomas Noel of Ellenhall, co. Stafford. (Collins IV: 434; *Wm .Salt Soc.* (n.s.) (1914): 189·193).

29. **WILLIAM DE HARCOURT**, m. (1) Alice la Zouche, dau. of **ROGER LA ZOUCHE** (39·28) and wife Margaret (mother of Arabella de Harcourt who follows, and Margery de Harcourt who m. John de Cauntelou); m. (2) **HILLARY (HILLARIA)** (or **ELEANOR) DE HASTINGS** (93·28), mother of **RICHARD DE HARCOURT** (93·29). (*CP* XII (2): 932, note *i*, cites Cal. Inq.p.m. II no. 305 Inq.p.m. of Henry de Penebrigge (Pembrugge) & Cal. Pat. Rolls 1266·72 p. 120, shows Orabella & Margery were nieces (not gr.daus.) of Alan la Zouche; Eyton, *Antiq. of Shropshire* II: 208·209, 221·222, also shows Alice, dau. of Roger & sis. of Alan; Collins IV: 434 in error; *Wm. Salt Soc.* n.s. (1914) 193·194 also in error; Burke's *Peerage*, 1953 and 1967).

30. **ARABELLA (ORABELLA) DE HARCOURT**, m. Sir Fulke de Pembrugge. (Burke's *Peerage* (1953) p. 984. Gens. 28·30: *ES* X/139).

Line 56A   Supplied for an earlier edition by Neil D. Thompson

31. **FULKE DE PEMBRUGGE**, b. 1271, d. by 20 Feb. 1296; m. Isabel (living 17 Feb. 1297). She m. (2) John de Dene, of co. Huntingdon.

32. **FULKE DE PEMBRUGGE**, b. abt. 1291/2, d. by 21 Jan. 1325/6; m. Maud (living 17 Mar. 1326).

33. **ROBERT DE PEMBRUGGE**, living Michaelmas term, 1350, dead by 1 Aug. 1364; m. Juliana la Zouche (living 1345).

34. **JULIANA DE PEMBRUGGE**, b. 1349 or bef. (age 60, 1409), heiress of her brother Fulke (d.s.p. 26 May 1409); m. (1) **SIR RICHARD DE VERNON, KNT.** (63A·35) of Haddon and Harlaston (d. 1376).

35. **SIR RICHARD VERNON, KNT.**, b. 1370, d. 1409, of Hadley, co. Derby, Harlaston, co. Stafford; m. Joanna (or Joan) dau. of Rhys ap Griffith, b. 1370, liv. 1412, granddau. & h. Richard Stackpole. (*Llyfr Baglan* (London, 1910), p. 149; *Cal. Fine Rolls*; DWB). <u>Note</u>: Proof that Joanna (Joan) was dau. of Rhys ap Griffith is given in Shaw's *Hist. & Antiquities of Staffordshire* I: 122, 126, and app. p. 38, which quotes an indenture made by William Marshal & wife Margaret, wid. of Sir Rhys ap Griffith, Knt., together with Margaret's son, Thomas, eldest son & heir of Sir Rhys, for properties of Sir Rhys, showing remainder for the estates, after Thomas, son of Rhys, to his sister Joan, Aid. of Sir Richard Vernon. Joan is also called "heir of Stackpole," in *Cartae et Alia Munimenta quae ad Dominium de Glamorgancia pertinent*, 4 (Cardiff, 1910), pp. 1466-69, calling her "dau. of Richard de Stackpole & heiress of Isabel dau. of Richard de Stackpole & granddau. of Margaret Turberville, sis. of Richard Turberville, lord of Coity." From the dates known of these people, and ages of death, it is evident that Joan had to be the granddau., not dau., of Sir Richard de Stackpole.

36. SIR RICHARD VERNON, KNT., a minor 1402/3, Treasurer of Calais, Speaker of the House of Commons, d. 24 Aug. 1451; m. by 25 Nov. 1410, Benedicta Ludlow, dau. of Sir John Ludlow, Knt., of Hodnet and Stokesay, living 1427.

37. SIR WILLIAM VERNON, b. 1416, d. 31 July 1467 (will PCC Godyn 9); m. Margaret, daughter of William Swinfen (Swynfen) by Joyce (Jocosa) Durvassal, dau. of William Durvassal *alias* Spernore and heiress also of Sir Robert Pype (d. 1490). (See: *Gen. Mag.* 15: 119-120, for an excellent Swinfen pedigree drawn from primary sources).

38. SIR HENRY VERNON, KNT., b. 1445, d. 13 Apr. 1515 (will PCC 9 Holder), Sheriff, Governor of Arthur, Pr. of Wales, built Haddon Hall; m. 1467, Anne Talbot, d. 17 May 1494, dau. of Sir John Talbot, K.G., 2nd Earl of Shrewsbury, etc., by **ELIZABETH BUTLER** (8-35, 7-34).

39. ELIZABETH VERNON, d. 29 Mar. 1563; m. **SIR ROBERT CORBET, KNT.** (56B-39) of Moreton Corbet, b. abt. 1477, d. 11 Apr. 1513, sheriff of Shropshire.

40. DOROTHY CORBET; m. Sir Richard Mainwaring, Knt., of Ightfield, b. abt. 1494, d. 30 Sept. 1558, Sheriff of Shropshire.

41. SIR ARTHUR MAINWARING, KNT., of Ightfield, b. abt. 1520, d. 4 Sept. 1590 (will PCC 49 Sainberbe); m. abt. 1540 to Margaret Mainwaring, daughter of Sir Randall Mainwaring, Knt., of Over Peover, by Elizabeth Brereton.

42. MARY MAINWARING, b. abt. 1541, d. before 14 June 1578; m. Combermere 6 Jan. 1559/60, as 1st wife, Richard Cotton of Combermere, b. abt. 1539, d. Stoke 14 June 1602.

43. FRANCES COTTON, b. abt. 1573, prob. dead by 16 Apr. 1646; m. George Abell of Hemington, Master of the Middle Temple, b. Stapenhill, co. Derby, abt. 1561, bur. Lockington, co. Leicester, 13 Sept. 1630 (will PCC St. John 10).

44. ROBERT ABELL (2nd son), b. abt. 1605, d. Rehoboth, Mass. 20 June 1663; m. Joanna. Early settler of Weymouth and Rehoboth, Mass. (Gens. 31-38: G. Keith Thomson, "The Descent of the Manor (Aylestone, Leics.)," *Transactions of the Leicester Archaeological Society* 17:206-21 (1932-33); George Morris, *Shropshire Genealogies* (Ms. 2792, Local Studies Library, Shrewsbury, Salop, microfilm copy GSU, SLC) (31-34) 5: 120, (35-38) 5: 89-90. Gens. 34-39: G. Le Blanc Smith, Haddon: *The Manor, The Hall, Its Lords and Traditions* (London, 1906), pp. 15-21, 94-103. Gens. 39-40: Corbet, *The Family of Corbet, Its Life and Times* (2 vols., London, 1918), v. 2, 262-264; Gens. 39-44: Neil D. Thompson, "Abell-Cotton-Mainwaring," *The Genealogist* 5 (1984): 158-171, 9 (1988): 89).

Line 56B Supplied for an earlier edition by Neil Thompson

34. SIR ROBERT DE FERRERS of Chartley (61-34); m. (2) **MARGARET LE DESPENSER** (70-36).

35. SIR EDMUND FERRERS, Lord Ferrers of Chartley, age 26 or 27, at father's death, d. 17 Dec. 1435; m. Ellen Roche, dau. of Thomas Roche of Castle Bromwich, co.

Worcs. by Elizabeth Birmingham, dau. of Thomas Birmingham, d. 4 Nov. 1440 (she m. (2) as 1st wife, Sir Philip Chetwynd). (*CP* V: 317-19).

36. SIR WILLLIAM FERRERS of Chartley, age 23 in 1435, d. 9 June 1450; m. Elizabeth Bealknap, dau. of Hamon Bealknap of Seintlynge in St. Mary Cray, co. Kent, etc., d. 28 May 1471. (*CP* V: 320-21).

37. ANNE FERRERS, b. Nov. 1438, d. 9 Jan. 1468/9; m., bef. 26 Nov. 1446, as 1st wife, Sir Walter Devereux, Lord Ferrers, killed at Bosworth 22 Aug. 1485 and attainted, son of Sir Walter Devereux and Elizabeth Merbery, dau. of John Merbery. (*CP* V: 321-25).

38. ELIZABETH DEVEREUX, d. 1541; m. (1) Sir Richard Corbet, Knt., b. 1451, d. 6 Dec. 1493, son of Sir Roger Corbet of Moreton Corbet, Knt., d. 1467, by Elizabeth Hopton, d. 22 June 1498 (who m. (2) John Tiptoft, Earl of Worcester, and (3) Sir William Stanley) and grandson of **SIR ROBERT CORBET**, Sheriff of Shropshire (29B-33) and **MARGARET MALLORY** (16A-34). (Corbet 2: 243-58; *CP* XII (2): 842-46).

39. SIR ROBERT CORBET m. **ELIZABETH VERNON** (56A-39).

Line 57   Line restored for an earlier edition by research of Claude W. Faulkner

28. ROGER DE QUINCY (53-28); m. **HELEN OF GALLOWAY** (38-27).

29. MARGARET DE QUINCY, d. abt. 12 Mar. 1280/1; m. abt. 1238, **WILLIAM DE FERRERS** (127-30), 5th Earl of Derby, bur. 31 Mar. 1254. (*CP* II: 128, IV: 197, V: 340, chart betw. pp. 320-321; *SP* III: 142).

30. ROBERT DE FERRERS, 6th Earl of Derby, b. 1239, d. 1279; m. (2) 26 June 1269 **ALIANORE DE BOHUN** (68-30), d. 20 Feb. 1313/4. (*CP* IV: 198-202, V: 305, 340, chart, *cit.*).

31. SIR JOHN DE FERRERS, b. Cardiff, 20 June 1271, d. Gascony, Aug. 1312, of Southoe and Keyston, 1st Lord Ferrers of Chartley, co. Stafford; m. bet. 2 Feb 1297/8 and 13 Sept. 1300, **HAWISE DE MUSCEGROS** (189-5) of Charlton, b. 21 Dec. 1276, d. after June 1340, by Dec. 1350. (See 61-31 for male line continuation). (*CP* IV: 205, V: 305-310, chart, *cit.*).

32. ELEANOR DE FERRERS, m. bef. 21 May 1329, Sir Thomas de Lathom of Lathom and Knowsley, co. Lancaster, b. 1300, d. 17 Sept. 1370, son of Sir Robert de Lathom of Lathom, and Katherine, dau. of Thomas de Knowsley. (*CP* IV: 205, V: chart, *cit.*).

33. SIR THOMAS DE LATHOM, KNT., of Lathom, co. Lancaster, d. bef. 20 Mar. 1381/2; m. (1) NN (2) Joan, parentage unkn.(*CP* IV: 205, XII (1): 249-250; *Collectanea Topographica et Genealogica* 7 (1841): 20 chart, says Thomas m. Johanna, dau. of Hugh Venables, Baron of Kinderton, and sis. of Hugh Venables, Sheriff of Cheshire).

34. ISABEL DE LATHOM, prob. by (1), d. 26 Oct. 1414 (Inq.p.m.); m. in or bef. 1385, Sir John Stanley, K.G., b. 1350, d. Ardee, Ireland, bef. 28 Jan. 1413/4, Lord Lieutenant of Ireland 1385, Constable of Rokesbergh, Scotland; Constable of Windsor Castle, Steward of the King's Household, K.G., 1413, son of William Stanley, of Storeton in Wirral., d. 1360, said to have mar. Alice Massey, dau. of Hugh Massey of Timperley (but there is no proof of marr.). (*CP* IV: 205 chart, XII (1): 247-249; Collins III, 59; *DNB* 54: 75-76; Weever, 651).

35. SIR JOHN STANLEY, KNT., of Knowsley and Lathom, co. Lancaster, b. abt. 1386, d. 27 Nov. 1437, Knight of the Shire of Lancaster 1415, Justice of Chester 1426-1427, sheriff of Anglesey, Constable of Caernarvon Castle 1427; m. **ISABEL HARINGTON** (40-33). (*CP* XII (I): 249-250; Collins III: 54-55; *DNB* 54: 76. Gens. 32-35: *Collectanea Topographica et Genealogica* (London, 1841), VII: 1-21, esp. 14, 19-20, article "Lathom").

36. SIR THOMAS STANLEY, K.G., b. 1406, d. 20 Feb. 1459, Lord Stanley of Lathom and Knowsley, M.P. 1432, K.G. 1456, Lord Lieutenant of Ireland; m. **JOAN GOUSHILL** (20-33), liv. 1460, dau. of Sir Robert Goushill of Hoveringham. (*CP* IV 205, XII (I): 250; Collins III: 56; *DNB* 54: 75; *VCH Lanc.* I: 345-349; *Visit. Cheshire* (1580), pp. 9, 201, 203-4; *Visit. Gloucs.* (1623), pp. 144-145; Barry Coward, "The Stanleys, Lords Stanleys and Earls of Derby 1385-1672," Chetham Soc. (3rd ser.) (1983) v. XXX: 2:9, 194 chart).

37. KATHERINE STANLEY (233-37); m. Sir John Savage, K.G., of Clifton & Rocksavage, b. abt. 1422, d. 22 Nov. 1495, son of Sir John Savage and Eleanor Brereton.

38. SIR CHRISTOPHER SAVAGE, lord of manors of Aston Subedge, Camden, Burlington and Westington, co. Gloucester, d. 1513; m. Anne Stanley, dau. of Sir John Stanley of Elford, co. Warwick, his cousin.

39. CHRISTOPHER SAVAGE, s. and h., d. 1546; m. Anne Lygon, dau. of **SIR RICHARD LYGON** (84-36) Knt., of Arle Court, co. Worcester and Margaret Greville.

40. BRIDGET SAVAGE, of Elmley, b. prob. abt. 1540, d. by May 1609; m. abt. 1557/60, Anthony Bonner, gent., of Camden, Burlington and Wetington, d. 1580, son of Thomas Bonner and Joan Skinner.

41. MARY BONNER of Camden, b. abt. 1560, d. 5 Apr. 1617 at Stratford-on-Avon, co. Warwick; m. (1) by 1 Nov. 1579, William Yonge, gent., d. Dec. 1583, son of John Yonge of Caynton and Tiberton, co. Salop, and Mathilda Bull; m. (2) 10 Jan. 158_, Thomas Combe, gent., of Stratford, will dtd 22 Dec. 1608, pro. 10 Feb. 1608/9.

42. BRIDGET YONGE of Caynton and Stratford, b. 1580, bur. at Fenny Compton, co. Worcester, 11 Mar. 1629; m. Holy Trinity, Stratford, 2 Nov. 1609, George Wyllys, of manor of Fenny Compton, went to Hartford, Conn. 1638, Gov. of Conn. 1642, d. 9 Mar. 1645, son of Richard Wyllys and Hester Chambers. All his children returned to or remained in England, except

43. AMY WYLLYS, b. abt. 1625, to America with father, d. Springfield, Mass., 9 Jan. 1698/9; m. Hartford, 6 Nov. 1645, Maj. John Pynchon, b. abt. 1625, d. 17 Jan. 1702/3, son of William Pynchon and Anne Andrew. (Gens. 36-43: see *TAG* 39: 88-89; D.L. Jacobus, *Bulkeley Gen.* Currier-Briggs, *English Wills of Colonial Families* 2-8, and ancestral fan).

Line 58

29. MARGARET DE QUINCY (57-29); m. **WILLLIAM DE FERRERS** (127-30), 5th Earl of Derby. (*CP* V: 333 top; *SP* VI: 142).

30. SIR WILLIAM FERRERS, of Groby, b. abt. 1240, d. sh. bef. 20 Dec. 1287; m. (1) Anne le Despenser (said. to be dau. of Sir Hugh le Despenser of Ryhall, Rutland, Loughborough, co. Leicester & Parlington, co. York, by Aline Basset, d. & h. of Sir Philip Basset of Wycombe Bucks); m. (2) by fine 18 Feb. 1290/1, Eleanor de Lovaine, liv. 3 May 1326, dau. of Sir Matthew de Lovaine of Little Easton, co. Essex. Eleanor m. (2) Sir William de Douglass (Duglas), d. bef. 24 Jan. 1298/9; m. (3) bef. 6 Oct. 1305, Sir William Bagot of Hide & Patshull, co. Stafford, d. by 3 May 1326. (*CP* V: 332 chart, 340-342; *SP* III: 139).

31. SIR WILLIAM FERRERS, s. & h. by (1), 1st Lord Ferrers of Groby, b. Yoxall, co. Stafford, 30 Jan. 1271/2, d. 20 Mar. 1324/5, ae. 53; m. Ellen Segrave, liv. 9 Feb. 1316/17, said to be dau. of Sir John de Segrave of Chacombe, co. Northampton, Lord Segrave, by Christine Plescy, dau. of Sir Hugh de Plescy of Hooknorton & Kidlington, co. Oxford. (*CP* V: chart 332, 343-344, X: 549 note c, XI: 605-608).

32. HENRY FERRERS, b. abt. 1294, d. Groby, co. Leicester, 15 Sept. 1343, 3rd Lord Ferrers of Groby, m. bef. 20 Feb. 1330/1, **ISABEL DE VERDUN** (11-31). (*CP* V: chart 332, 344-347, XII (2): 252, Old *CP* VIII: 25).

Line 59

29. MARGARET DE QUINCY (57-29); m. **WILLIAM DE FERRERS** (127-30), 5th Earl of Derby.

30. JOAN DE FERRERS, d. 19 Mar. 1309/10; m. 1267, **SIR THOMAS DE BERKELEY** (26-29), d. 23 July 1321. (*CP* II: 128, IV: 190-202).

31. SIR MAURICE DE BERKELEY, b. 1281, d. 31 May 1326, Lord Berkeley of Berkeley Castle; m. (1) 1289, neither being over 8 yrs. of age, **EVA LA ZOUCHE** (39-30), d. 5 Dec. 1314. (*CP* II: 128-129, VIII: 584).

32. MILICENT (ELA) DE BERKELEY, d. aft. 1322; m., as his 1st wife, abt. 1313, John Mautravers, b. abt. 1290, d. 1364, Lord Mautravers, knighted 22 May 1306, son of Sir John Mautravers & wife Eleanor, dau. of Sir Ralph de Gorges of Litton and Wraxall. (*CP* VIII: 581-585, cf. 584).

33. SIR JOHN MAUTRAVERS, d.v.p. 22 Jan. 1348/9; m. Gwenthlin (or Welthiana), d. bet. July 1364 and Oct. 1375. (*CP* VIII: 585, XI: 102-103).

34. ELEANOR MAUTRAVERS, b. 1345, d. 10 Jan. 1405/6; m. **SIR JOHN D'ARUNDEL** (21-31), 1st Lord Arundel, d. 1379, Marshal of England. (*CP* VIII: 586, XI: 102-103).

35. JOAN D'ARUNDEL, d. 1 Sept 1404; m. (1) Sir William de Brien; m. (2) abt. 1401, Sir William de Echyngham of Echyngham, Sussex, d. 20 Mar 1412/13. (*Gen.* (n.s.) XXI (1905): 244). Note: Mary Gye, wife of Rev. John Maverick, is a desc. by 2nd husband.

36. SIR THOMAS DE ECHYNGHAM, lord of Echyngham, Sussex, b. abt. 1401, d. 15 Oct. 1444; m. 1415-1424 Margaret Knyvet, liv. 1467, dau. of John Knyvet, Sr.. and wife Joan of Norfolk, wid. of Sir Robert de Tye of Barsham, ds.p. 1415. (*Gen* (n.s.) XXI (1905): 245-246).

37. SIR THOMAS DE ECHYNGHAM of Echyngham, b. abt. 1425, d. 20 Jan. 1482/3, bur. at Echyngham, Sussex; m. Margaret West, dau. of **SIR REYNOLD DE WEST** (18-33). (*CP* IV: 152-154, IX: 336-337; Old-*CP* VII: 185; *Gen., op. cit.*).

38. MARGARET DE ECHYNGHAM, liv. 11 July 1482 when pr. 2nd husband's will, d. Shoreditch, co. Middlesex; m. (1) Sir William Blount, d. 14 Apr. 1471, Knight of the Shire of Derby, 1467, son of Sir Walter Blount, K.G., Lord Mountjoy, Treasurer of England, and Ellen Byron dau. of Sir John Byron of Clayton, co. Lancs.; m. (2) abt. 1478 Sir John Elrington, Knt., Treas. household of Edw. IV. (*CP* IX: 336-337; Old-*CP* VIII: 185; Banks III: 536; *The Gen., op. cit.*)

39. ELIZABETH BLOUNT, b. abt. 1471, liv. 1535, but predeceased her husb.; m. abt. 1490, **SIR ANDREWS WINDSOR, K.B.** (12-36), d. 30 Mar 1543, Baron of Stanwell, Middlesex, M.P., attended the "Cloth of Gold," 1520, son of **SIR THOMAS WINDSOR** (12A-35) of Stanwell and **ELIZABETH ANDREWS** (12-35), dau. of John Andrews, Esq., of Bayleham, Suffolk. (*CP* IX: 337 note *d*, XII (2): 792-794; Seversmith, 2,193-2,209; Banks, 466; Waters I: 275-276).

27. **MARGARET DE BEAUMONT** (53-27); m. Saher IV de Quincy, 1st Earl of Winchester, Magna Charta Surety, 1215. (*CP* IX: 215).

28. **HAWISE DE QUINCY,** m. aft. 11 Feb. 1222/3, Hugh de Vere, b. abt. 1210, d. bef. 23 Dec. 1263, 4th Earl of Oxford, Hereditary Master Chamberlain of England, son of **ROBERT DE VERE** (246-27), Earl of Oxford, bapt. 1164, d. bef. 25 Oct. 1221, Hereditary Master Chamberlain of England, Magna Charta Surety, 1215, by wife **ISABELLA DE BOLEBEC** (267-27), d. 3 Feb. 1245. (*CP* X: 210-216).

29. **ROBERT DE VERE,** b. 1240, d. bef. 7 Sept. 1296, 5th Earl of Oxford, M.P. 1283, 1295-1296; m. by 22 Feb. 1252, Alice de Sanford, d. bef. 9 Sept 1312, dau. of Gilbert de Sanford, by Loretta (or Lora) la Zouche, dau. of **ROGER LA ZOUCHE** (39-28). (*CP* X: 216-218, XII (2): 932 note *i*; *TAG* 49 (1973): 1).

30. **JOAN DE VERE,** d. 1293; m. prob. 1285, **WILLIAM DE WARENNE** (83-29), b. 1256, d. 1286, 7th Earl of Surrey. (*CP* I: 242, IV: 670 chart, X: 218 note *b*.)

31. **ALICE DE WARENNE,** d. bef. 23 May 1338; m. 1305, **SIR EDMUND FITZ ALAN (D'ARUNDEL)** (28-32), b. 1 May 1285, beheaded at Hereford, 17 Nov. 1326, 8th Earl of Arundel. (*CP* I: 241-242, 253, IV: 670 chart; *ES* III.2/355).

32. **SIR RICHARD FITZ ALAN,** b. abt. 1313, d. 24 Jan. 1375/6, 9th Earl of Arundel, Earl of Warenne, Earl of Surrey; m. (1) (both minors) 9 Feb. 1320/1, **ISABEL LE DESPENSER** (8-31); m. (2) Ditton, 5 Feb. 1344/5, **ELEANOR** (17-36) of Lancaster, d. 1372. (*CP* I: 242-244, 253, IV: 670 chart, IX: 604).

33. **SIR RICHARD (FITZ ALAN), K.G.**,(illeg.) son by (2), b. 1346, beheaded 1397, 10th Earl of Arundel & Surrey; m. **ELIZABETH DE BOHUN** (15-31), d. 1385. (*CP* I: 244-245, 253, IV: 670 chart, IX: 604).

31. **SIR JOHN DE FERRERS** (57-31), m. **HAWISE DE MUSCEGROS** (189-5). (*CP* V: 305-310).

32. **SIR ROBERT DE FERRERS,** of Chartley, co. Somerset, b. 25 Mar. 1309, d. 28 Aug. 1350; m. (1) bet. 21 Nov. 1324 and 20 Oct. 1330, Margaret, liv. in Aug. 1331 (*CP* V: 310-312).

33. **SIR JOHN DE FERRERS,** by (1), of Chartley, bapt. Southoe on or abt. 10 Aug. 1333, slain at Najera, Spain, 3 Apr. 1367; m. 19 Oct 1349, as 2nd husb., Elizabeth de Stafford (who m. (3) as 2nd wife Sir Reynold de Cobham, Lord Cobham), d. 7 Aug. 1375, dau. of **RALPH DE STAFFORD** (55-32), 1st Earl of Stafford, and **MARGARET DE AUDLEY** (9-31). (*CP* V: 313).

34. **SIR ROBERT DE FERRERS,** of Chartley, b. 31 Oct. 1357 or 1359, d. 12 or 13 Mar. 1412/13; m. **MARGARET LE DESPENSER** (70-36), d. 3 Nov. 1415.

35. **PHILIPPA DE FERRERS,** buried at Norton; m. by 16 Dec. 1421, **SIR THOMAS GREENE** (14-34), d. Jan. 1461/2. (Gens. 31-35: *CP* V: 320 chart).

32. SIR ROBERT DE FERRERS (61-32), of Chartley, d. 28 Aug. 1350; m. (2) Joan de la Mote, d. London, 29 June 1375, prob. wid. of Edmund de la Mote (*CP* V:312 and note *b*, 320 chart).

33. SIR ROBERT DE FERRERS, of Willisham, b. abt. 1350, d. abt. 31 Dec. 1380; m. by lic. 27 Sept. 1369, **ELIZABETH LE BOTILLER** (or **BUTLER**) (77-34), of Wem and Oversley. (*CP* II: 230-233, V: 320 chart, XIV: 101).

34. SIR ROBERT DE FERRERS, age 8 in 1380, d. bef. 29 Nov. 1396; m. **JOAN BEAUFORT** (2-32), d. Howden, 13 Nov. 1440, dau. of **JOHN OF GAUNT** (1-30), Duke of Lancaster. (*CP* V: 320 chart, XIV: 102).

35. ELIZABETH DE FERRERS, Lady of Wem, age 18 and more in 1411, d. 1434, buried York; m. contract. 28 Oct. 1407, **JOHN DE GREYSTOKE** (265-35), Lord Greystoke, b. bef. 1389, d. 8 Aug. 1436, son of Ralph de Greystoke and **KATHARINE CLIFFORD** (202-33). (*CP* V: 320 chart).

36. JOAN GREYSTOKE, m. **JOHN DARCY** (13A-34), 2nd son of **JOHN DARCY** (88-35) 5th Lord Darcy of Knayth, by **MARGARET DE GREY** (13A-33). (*CP* IV: 71, V: 320 chart).

25. SIR ROBERT DE BEAUMONT (53-25), 2nd Earl of Leicester. b. 1104, d. 5 Apr. 1168; m. Amice de Gael, d. 31 Aug. aft. 1168, dau. of Ralph de Gael de Montfort. (*CP* V: 688, 736, VII: 520; Keats-Rohan, *Domesday Desc. II:* 479; *ES* III.2/354).

26. HAWISE DE BEAUMONT, OF LEICESTER, d. 24 Apr. 1197; m. abt. 1150, **WILLLIAM FITZ ROBERT** (124-27), 2nd Earl of Gloucester, d. 23 Nov. 1183, Lord of the manor of Glamorgan and of Cardiff Castle, son of **ROBERT DE CAEN** (124-26), Earl of Gloucester, d. 1147, and Maud, dau. of Robert Fitz Hamon, by Sybil Montgomery. (*CP* V: 687-688, 736, VII: 520; *ES* III.4/700).

27. AMICE, Countess of Gloucester, d. 1 Jan. 1224/5; m. abt. 1180, Richard de Clare, b. abt. 1153, d.. 28 Nov. 1217, 6th Earl of Clare, Hertford and Gloucester, Magna Charta Surety, 1215, son of **ROGER DE CLARE** (246B-26), Earl of Hertford, and Maud de St. Hilary, dau. of James de St. Hilary. (*CP* V: 736, VI: 500-503).

28. SIR GILBERT DE CLARE, b. abt. 1180, d. Penros, Brittany, 25 Oct. 1230, 7th Earl of Clare, Earl of Hertford and Gloucester, Magna Charta Surety, 1215; m. 9 Oct. 1217, Isabel Marshal, d. Berkhampstead, 17 Jan. 1239/40, dau. of William Marshal, 3rd Earl of Pembroke, and **ISABEL DE CLARE** (66-27). Isabel m. (2) 30 Mar. 1231, Richard, 1st Earl of Cornwall. (*CP* I: 22, IV: 670 chart iii, V: 694-695, 736, X: 364 and note *e*).

29. SIR RICHARD DE CLARE, b. 4 Aug. 1222, d. 15 July 1262 , 8th Earl of Clare, Earl of Hertford and Gloucester; m. (2) abt. 25 Jan. 1237/8, **MAUD DE LACY** (54-30), Countess of Lincoln, d. bef. 10 Mar. 1288/9. (*CP* V: 696-702, 736; Banks I: 155).

30. SIR GILBERT DE CLARE, KNT., "the Red," b. Christ Church, Hampshire, 2 Sept. 1243, d. Monmouth Castle, 7 Dec. 1295, 6th Earl of Gloucester and Hertford, and 9th Earl of Clare, knighted 14 May 1264; m. (1) 1253, (mar. annulled 1285) **ALICE DE LUSIGNAN** (117-29), dau. of **HUGH XI DE LUSIGNAN** (275-28, 117-29) and **YOLANDE DE DREUX** (135-30); m. (2) Westminster Abbey, abt. 30 Apr. 1290, as her 1st husb., **JOAN OF ACRE** (8-29), b. Acre, Holy Land, 1272, d. 23 Apr. 1307, dau. of **EDWARD I** (1-27) King of England and **ELEANOR OF CASTILE** (110-30) Joan m. (2) 1297, Ralph de Monthermer, d. 1325, 1st Lord Monthermer. (*CP* V: 702-710, 736. Gens. 26-30: *CP* IV: 670 chart III;

Michael Altschul, *A Baronial Family of Medieval England: The Clares, 1217-1314* (1965), 332 chart).

Line 63A   Prepared for an earlier edition by Douglas Richardson

27. **AMICE OF GLOUCESTER** (63-27), d. 1225, Countess of Gloucester; m. Richard de Clare, Earl of Hertford and Gloucester, Magna Charta Surety, 1215.

28. **MATILDA (MAUD) (ISABEL) DE CLARE**, whose maritagium was the manor of Buckingham, co. Bucks; m. William de Braose, murdered 1210, at Corfe or Windsor Castle, s. & h. app. of **WILLIAM DE BRAOSE** (177-6), d. France 9 Aug. 1211, of Bramber, Sussex and Totnes, Devon, by wife, Maud de St. Valery "Lady of La Haie." (*TAG* 56: 1-11; *VCH Bucks.* 3: 480; *CP* I: 22; *Moriarty Notebooks*; Lipscomb, *The History and Antiquities of the County of Buckingham,* II: 558, I: 202; *The Gen.* 4 (1880): 235-244).

29. **MAUD DE BRAOSE**, rec'd manor of Tavistock, co. Devon from aunt, Laurette de Braose (wife of Robert, Earl of Leicester); m. Henry de Tracy, d. 1274, of Barnstaple, co. Devon, s. of Oliver de Tracy, d. 1210, of the same, by wife, Eve. (Note: Additional proof of Maud de Braose's identity, see Cal. of Entries in the Papal Registers (Papal Letters), I 282, 405, wherein Maud's son, Master Oliver de Tracy, archdeacon of Surrey, is called "kinsman" by Maud's first cousin, Richard de Clare, d. 1262, Earl of Gloucester). (*CP* III: 3-4, VIII: 535; Sanders, 104-105; *The Gen.* 6: 16 [chart]).

30. **EVE DE TRACY**, m. Guy de Brian, of Laugharne, co. Cornwall. (*CP* III: 3-4; Sanders, 104-105; *Devon & Cornwall Notes & Queries* 19 (1936/7): 8).

31. **MAUD (MATILDA) DE BRIAN**, h. of grandfather, Henry de Tracy, b. abt. 1242, living 1274; m. (1) by 1257, Nicholas Martin, b. abt. 1236, d. abt. 1260, s. & h. ap. of Sir Nicholas Fitz Martin, d. 1282, of Blagdon, co. Somerset, by unknown (1) wife; m. (2) by 1268, Geoffrey de Canville (or Camville), d. 1308, 1st Lord Canville, of Clifton Campville, co. Stafford, and Llanstephan, co. Carmarthen, s. & h. of William de Canville, d. 1260, of same, by wife, Lucy. (*CP* III: 3-4, VIII: 533-535; Sanders, 104-105, 15, 49).

32. **WILLIAM DE CANVILLE**, s. by (2), b. abt. 1268, d. abt. 27 July 1338, 2nd Lord Canville, of Clifton Campville, co. Stafford, and Llanstephan, co. Carmarthen. (*CP* III: 4-5).

33. **MAUD (MATILDA) DE CANVILLE**, liv. 1342, heiress of Clifton Campville, co. Stafford; m. Sir Richard de Vernon, d. 1323, s. & h. app. of Sir Richard de Vernon, liv. 1330, of Haddon, co. Derby, and Harlaston, co. Stafford, by wife, **JULIANA DE VESCY** (269A-28). (*CP* III: 4-5; *VCH Bucks.* IV: 90; Burke, *Peerage & Baronetage* (1953): 2134).

34. **SIR WILLIAM DE VERNON**, b. abt. 1313, d. by 1346, of Haddon, co. Derby, and Harlaston, co. Stafford, sd. to have m. Margaret, dau. of Robert de Stockport. (*VCH Bucks.* IV: 90).

35. **SIR RICHARD DE VERNON**, d. 1376, of Haddon, co. Derby, and Harlaston, co. Stafford; m. **JULIANA DE PEMBRUGGE** (56A-34), b. abt. 1349, liv. 1409, dau. Robert de Pembrugge. (*VCH Bucks.* IV: 90; Farnham, *Leics. Medieval Pedigrees,* p. 7, Burke , *Ibid.*).

Line 64

31. **THOMAS DE CLARE** (54-31), m. **JULIANA FITZ MAURICE** (178-7). (*CP* III: 291).

32. **MAUD DE CLARE**, d. bet. 4 Mar. 1326/7 and 24 May 1327; m. (1) 13 Nov. 1295, **ROBERT DE CLIFFORD** (82-32), 1st Lord Clifford, b. Easter 1274, slain at Bannockburn, 24 June 1314 (age 39); m. (2) 1315 (without royal lic.), Sir Robert de

Welles, Lord Welles, liv. 29 Aug. 1326. (*CP* III: 290-291, V: 437, X: 461-462, XII (2): 440 note *b*, XIV: 188; *TAG* 18: 149-153; Banks I: 155; Inq. p.m., 1315, No. 62; *ES*: III.1/156).

33. MARGARET DE CLIFFORD ('said by some to have been dau. of' Robert and Maud, Gen. 32), d. 8 Aug. 1382; m. **PIERS V DE MAULEY** (156-30), 3ʳᵈ Lord Mauley, d. 18 Jan. 1354/5. (*CP* VIII: 565-567 and note *c*; Banks I: 312).

Line 65

33. MARGARET DE CLARE (54-32); m. (2) by 1308, Bartholomew de Badlesmere, 1ˢᵗ Lord Badlesmere.

34. ELIZABETH DE BADLESMERE, b. 1313, d. 1356; m. (1) **EDMUND DE MORTIMER** (29-32), of Wigmore, d. 1331; m. (2) 1338, **SIR WILLIAM DE BOHUN** (15-30), d. 1360, 1ˢᵗ Earl of Northampton. (*CP* I: 373 note *c*; Banks I: 112, 336).

Line 65A   Prepared for an earlier edition by Douglas Richardson

33. MARGARET DE CLARE (54-32); m. (2) Bartholomew de Badlesmere, 1ˢᵗ Lord Badlesmere.

34. MAUD (MARGARET) DE BADLESMERE, d. 1344/7; m. bef. 24 July 1337, as 1ˢᵗ wife, Sir John Tybotot, b. 20 July 1313, d. 13 Apr. 1367, 2ⁿᵈ Lord Tybotot, Keeper of Berwick-on-Tweed, s. Payn Tybotot, d. 1314, 1ˢᵗ Lord Tybotot, by wife, Agnes de Ros, dau. **WILLIAM DE ROS** (89-30), d. 1316, 1ˢᵗ Lord Ros of Helmsley by wife Maud de Vaux. (*CP* XII (2) 94-97; RJ. Mitchell, *John Tiptoft (1427-1470)*).

35. SIR ROBERT TYBOTOT, bapt Nettlestead, co. Suff. 11 June 1341, d.s.p.m. 13 Apr. 1372, 3ʳᵈ Lord Tybotot, of Nettlestead, co. Suff.; m. 1348 **MARGARET DEINCOURT** (200-33), d. 1380, dau. **SIR WILLIAM DEINCOURT** (247A-30), d. 1364, 2ⁿᵈ Lord Deincourt. She m. (2) by 14 Nov. 1373 John Cheyne. (*CP* XII (2): 97-98; *John Tiptoft (1427-1470), cit*).

Line 66

24. ISABEL DE VERMANDOIS (50-24, 53-24); m. (1) Sir Robert de Beaumont, 1ˢᵗ Earl of Leicester. (*CP* X: 351; West Winter, XIII.519).

25. ISABEL (or **ELIZABETH) DE BEAUMONT**, m. (1) **GILBERT DE CLARE** (184-4), d. 6 Jan. 1147/8, 1ˢᵗ Earl of Pembroke, 1138, son of **GILBERT FITZ RICHARD** (184-3), d. 1117, 2ⁿᵈ Earl of Clare, Suffolk, Tunbridge, Kent, and Cardigan, Wales, by **ADELAIDE** (or **ADELIZA) DE CLERMONT-EN-BEAUVAISIS** (246-24). (*CP* IV: 670 chart, V: 736, VII: 520, X: 348-352, cf. 351; Sanders, 34-35).

26. RICHARD DE CLARE, "Strongbow," b. abt. 1130, d. Dublin, abt. 20 Apr. 1176, 2ⁿᵈ Earl of Pembroke, Lord of Leicester, Justiciar of Ireland; m. at Waterford, Ireland abt. 26 Aug. 1171, **AOIFFE** (or **EVA) OF LEINSTER** (175-7), liv. 1186, dau. of **DAIRMAIT MACMURCHADA** (175-6) (also called Dermot MacMurrough), King of Leinster in Ireland; "Haec jacet Ricarduo Strongbow, filius Gilberti, Comitis de Pembroke." GS in the Chapter House, Gloucester Cathedral. (*CP* I: 22, IV: 670 chart III, V: 736, IX: 590, X: 352-357; West Winter, XIV.72).

27. ISABEL DE CLARE, d. 1220, heiress of Pembroke, Leinster, Bienfaite and Orbec; m. London, Aug. 1189, Sir William Marshal, b. prob. 1146, d. 14 May 1219 at

Caversham, bur. in the Temple Church, London, 3rd Earl of Pembroke, Marshal of England, Protector, Regent of the Kingdom, 1216-1219, son of John Fitz Gilbert (styled John the Marshal) (son of Gilbert Marshal), by his 2nd wife, Sibyl of Salisbury, dau. of Walter of Salisbury, d. 1147, of Chitterne, co. Wilts, sheriff of Wiltshire, founder of Bradenstock Priory. (*CP* I: 22, IV: 670 chart, V: 736, X: 358-364; Gens. 24-27: *ES* III.1/156).

28. EVE (or **EVA) MARSHAL**, d. bef. 1246; m. **WILLIAM DE BRAOSE** (or **BRAIOSE**) (177-8), d. 2 May 1230, 6th Baron de Braose and a descendant of **GRUFFYDD I AP LLYWELYN** (176-2), Prince of North Wales. (*CP* I: 22, IV: 670 chart III, IX: 276, X: 364 note *e*).

29. EVE DE BRAOSE, h. of Abergavenny, d. 1255; m. bef. 15 Feb. 1247/8, William de Cantelou (Cantilou or Cantilupe), d. 25 Sept. 1254, Baron Abergavenny, son of William de Cantelou of Calne, Wilts. (*CP* I: 22; Banks I: 97, 149-150).

30. MILICENT DE CANTELOU, d. abt. 1299; m. **EUDO LA ZOUCHE** (39-29, 39A-29, 253-29), d. 1279. (*CP* II: 129, I: 23 note *a*. Gens. 26-30: Dudley Pedigree).

Line 67

28. EVE (or **EVA) MARSHAL** (66-28), m. **WILLIAM DE BRAOSE** (177-8).

29. MAUD DE BRAOSE, d. bef. 23 Mar. 1300/1; m. 1247, **ROGER DE MORTIMER** (176B-29), b. 1231, d. bef. 30 Oct. 1282, 6th Baron Mortimer of Wigmore and a great-grandson of **JOHN** (1-25), King of England. (*CP* I: 240, IX: 276).

Line 68

28. EVE (or **EVA) MARSHAL** (66-28), m. **WILLIAM DE BRAOSE** (177-8).

29. ELEANOR DE BRAOSE, m. **SIR HUMPHREY VI DE BOHUN** (97-29), d.v.p. 27 Aug. 1267. (*CP* V: 320 chart).

30. ALIANORE DE BOHUN, d. 20 Feb. 1313/4; m. 26 June 1269, **ROBERT DE FERRERS** (57-30), d. 1279, 6th Earl of Derby. (*CP* IV: 198-202, V: 320 chart).

Line 69   Revised for 8th Edition

27. ISABEL DE CLARE (66-27); m. William Marshal, 3rd Earl of Pembroke. (*CP* X: 364, and note a).

28. MAUD MARSHAL, d. 27 Mar. 1248; m. (1) 1207/12, Hugh Bigod, d. Feb. 1224/5, 3rd Earl of Norfolk, Feb. 1221, Magna Charta Surety, 1215, son of Roger Bigod, b. abt. 1150, d. bef. Aug. 1221, Baron le Bigod, Lord High Steward of England, 2nd Earl of Norfolk, 1189, Magna Charta Surety, 1215, and Ida; m. (2) 1225, **WILLIAM DE WARENNE** (83-27), 6th Earl of Surrey. (*CP* IV: 670 chart, IX: 586-590, X: 364; Turton, 138; Weever, 829; *CCN*).

29. SIR HUGH BIGOD, d. sh. bef. 7 May 1266, Chief Justice of England, 22 June 1257-1260; m. bef. 5 Feb. 1243/4 **JOAN DE STUTEVILLE** (270-29) , d. sh. bef. 6 Apr. 1276, dau. of **NICHOLAS II DE STUTEVILLE** (270-28) of Liddel, Cumb., by wife Devorguilla of Galloway, dau. **ROLAND** (38-25) Lord of Galloway, d. bef. 18 Dec. 1241 in the Holy Land. Their son, Roger Bigod was the 5th Earl of Norfolk. (*CP* IX: 593, 590 note c, XII (2): 298-299; *DNB* 5: 24-25; *CCN*).

30. SIR JOHN BIGOD, KNT., of Stockton, co. Norf., and Settrington, co. York, b. by 1266, (age 40 yrs. in 1306), h. to his bro., Roger Bigod, 5th Earl of Norfolk; m. Isabel, par. unkn., d. 1311. (*CP* IX: 590 note *c*, 596; *DNB* 5: 21; Cal.Inq.p.m., IV, 320, V, 302; Rev. C. Moor, *Knights of Edward I* 1: 92-93).

31. SIR ROGER BIGOD, KNT., d. 1362, of Settrington, co. York. (CP IX: 590, 596; Gerrish, *Sir Henry Chauncy, Knight*, pp. 4-5, which is in error in generations 31 and 32).

32. JOAN BIGOD, liv. 9 Sept. 1398; m. 1358, Sir William de Chauncy, Knt., Lord of the Manor of Skirpenbeck, co. York, 1399, and of Stepney, co. Middlesex, son of Sir Thomas de Chauncy, b. abt. 1345, son of William de Chauncy (Chancy), age 30+ on 29 Apr. 1308 (Inq.p.m. Feb. 1343). (GS, Weever, 549; Inq.p.m., 9 Sept. 1398, in Cal.Inq.p.m. II: 246; Gerrish, *op. cit.*, pp. 4-5).

33. JOHN CHAUNCY, of Skirpenbeck, co. York, and Stepney, co. Middlesex, d. 22 Feb. 1444/5; m. bef. 25 June 1418, Margaret Giffard, dau. of William Giffard of Samford, co. Essex and Gedleston co. Herts, sis. & h. of John Giffard, Inq.p.m. 2 Jan 1448/9. (GS, Weever, 549).

34. JOHN CHAUNCY, ESQ., of Gedelston, co. Herts, Lord of the Manor of Skirpenbeck, co. York, d. 27 May 1478/9; m. Anne Leventhorp, d. 2 Dec. 1477, dau. of John Leventhorp, Esq., d. 27 May 1433, of Shingey Hall, Herts., (one of the executors of the will of King Henry V of England), by wife Katherine Rilay. (GS, Weever, 549. For the parentage of Anne Leventhorp, see: F. N. Craig, "Some Additions to the Ancestry of Charles Chauncy, President of Harvard College," *The Genealogist* 16 (2002): 183-188).

35. JOHN CHAUNCY, of Gedelston (now Gilston), co. Herts., b. abt 1452 (age 27+ 5 Aug 1479), d. 8 June 1510; m. (perh.) Alice Boyce, dau. of Thomas Boyce.

36. JOHN CHAUNCY, ESQ., of Sawbridgeworth, Herts., and Crayford, Kent, Lord of the Manor of Netherhall (purch. 1533) in Geldelston, co. Herts., d. 8 June 1546, will dtd 30 Nov. 1543; m. (1) bef. 4 Nov. 1509, Elizabeth Profitt, d. 10 Nov. 1531, dau. and coh. of John Proffitt of Barcombe, Sussex by Alice Horne, wid. of Richard Manfield of co. Middlesex, and dau. of John Horne; m. (2) Katherine, d. Apr. 1535. Monumental brass for John Chauncy and his two wives preserved in parish church of Sawbridgeworth, co. Herts. (Mill Stephenson, *A List of Monumental Brasses in the British Isles* (1926), p. 196; *Misc. Gen. et Her.* (2nd ser.) I: 28)

37. HENRY CHAUNCY by (1), of New Place, Gedelston Lord of the Manors Giffards and Netherhall, d. 14 Apr. 1587, Inq.p.m. 5 Oct. 1587; m. (1) Lucy, d. 25 Apr. 1566; m. (2) lic. 27 Apr. 1574 Jane Salisbury, widow, of Harlow, co. Essex, liv. 1580, dead 1587.

38. GEORGE CHAUNCY, by (1), of New Place, Gedelston, Herts., d. 1625-7, Lord of the Manors of Giffords etc.; m. (1) 26 Sept. 1569, Jane Cornwell, bur. 25 July 1582, dau. & h. John Cornwell, of Stebbing, Essex; m. (2) aft. 1582, Anne Welsh, wid. of Edward Humberston, dau. of Edward Welsh, of Great Wymondley, Herts.

39. THE REVEREND CHARLES CHAUNCY (CHAUNCEY), B.D., by (2), bapt. 5 Nov. 1592, d. Cambridge, Mass., 19 Feb. 1671/2; Vicar of Ware, co. Herts, 1623-1633, emig. to Plymouth, Mass., Dec. 1637, minister at Scituate and Plymouth, Mass. and 2nd President of Harvard College, 1654-1672; m. 17 Mar. 1631, Catherine Eyre, bapt. 2 Nov. 1604, d. 23 June 1667, dau. of Robert Eyre, of Salisbury, Wilts. and Anne Still, dau. of Rev. John Still. (Gens. 31-39: William Blyth Gerrish, *Sir Henry Chauncy, Knt.*, 1907, pp. 4-8; Sir Henry Chauncy, *The Historical Antiquities of Hertfordshire* (London, 1700), pp. 57-60; William Chauncy Fowler, *Chauncy Memorial*, in *NEHGR* 10: 259-262; Waters I: 107-109; Weever, 549-, Weis, *Colonial Clergy of New England* (1934), 53; *Visit. of Hertfordshire* (1634), 39; *Boston Evening Transcript*, 13 Oct. 1933, Note 6914, corrected as above. Also, Gens. 32-39, http://www.Burkes-peerage.net, "Chauncy formerly of Skirpenbeck"). They were parents of the following:

40. REV. ISAAC CHAUNCY, M.D., b. Ware, co. Hertford, Eng., 23 Aug. 1632; A.B., Harvard Coll., 1651, A.M., M.D.; sett. London, Eng. (Berry St. Charterhouse); physician and clergyman; d. London, 28 Feb. 1712, ae. 80. Issue.

40. REV. BARNABAS CHAUNCY, A.M., (son of Gen. 39), b. Marston-St. Laurence, Eng., 1637; A.B., H.C., 1657, A.M.; sett. Saco, Me., 1665-1666; d. 1675.

40. REV. NATHANIEL CHAUNCY, A.M., (son of Gen. 39), b. Plymouth, Mass., 1639; A.B., H.C., 1661, A.M.; Tutor and Fellow, H.C., 1663-1666; sett. Windsor, Conn., 1667-1680; sett. Hatfield, Mass., 1682-1685; physician and minister; d. Hatfield, 4 Nov. 1685; m. 12 Nov. 1673 Abigail Strong dau. of Elder John Strong. Issue.

40. REV. ISRAEL CHAUNCY, A.M., (son of Gen. 39), b. Scituate, Mass., 1644; A.B., H.C., 1661, A.M.; Founder and Trustee, Yale Coll.; ord. Stratford, Conn., Dec. 1666-1703; chaplain, King Philip's War, 1675/6; chosen Pres. of Y.C., but declined; d. Stratford, 14 Mar. 1702/3, will pro. 1 Apr. 1703; m. (1) Mary Nichols, d. Fairfield, Conn., 8 Jan. 1669, (had issue), dau. Isaac Nichols & Margaret Washburn; m. (2) 11 Nov. 1684 Sarah Hudson, d. 1711, no issue, dau. John Hudson (C.L. Torrey, *N.E. Mars.*; Jacobus, *Fams. of Old Fairfield*, I: 140.).

40. SARAH CHAUNCEY, (dau. of Gen. 39), b. 13, bapt. 22 June 1631 at Ware, d. Wethersfield, Conn. 3 June 1699; m. Concord, Mass., 6 Oct. 1659 Rev. Gershom Bulkeley, b. Cambridge, Mass., Jan. 1635/6, d. Glastonbury, Conn., 2 Dec. 1713, son of **REV. PETER BULKELEY** (31-40). (Gens. 32-40: See *Misc. Gen. et Her.* (2nd Ser.) I: 21-22, 35; Gens. 38-40: Weis, *Colonial Clergy of N.E.* (1934), 53).

Line 69A   Line was developed for an earlier edition by the late Sir Anthony Richard Wagner, KCVO, Garter

35. JOHN CHAUNCY (69-35), m. Alice Boyce.
36. WILLIAM CHAUNCEY of Sawbridgeworth, seen in brother's will 1520; m. a Garland, liv. 1557. (*NEHGR* 120: 244).
37. HENRY CHAUNCEY of Sawbridgeworth, seen in will of uncle, 1520, d. 1558; m. Joan, sister of Robert Tenderyng of Sawbridgeworth, whose will 20 July 1562, pro. 20 Mar. 1653. Her will 7 Nov. 1562, no probate date. (*NEHGR* 120: 244-5).
38. ELIZABETH CHAUNCEY, d. bet. 5 Dec. 1577 & 6 Nov. 1579; m. well bef. 1562, Richard Huberd of Birchanger, Essex, churchwarden "lately deceased," 5 Dec. 1577. (*NEHGR* 120: 245).
39. EDWARD HUBERD, ESQ., (also **HUBERT**) of Stansted-Montfichet, Essex, one of the six clerks in Chancery, will 16 Mar. 1601, pr. 14 May 1602; m. (1) well bef. 1590, Jane Southall, dau. of John Southall, citizen & clothworker, London, b. Albrighton, co. Salop., will 4 Oct. 1590, pro. 31 May 1592; m. (2) Eleanor, ment. in husband's will. (*NEHGR* 120: 245-6).
40. MARGARET HUBERD, dau. by (1) (named in admin. of estate of John Southall), under 21 in 1592, bur. Earls Colne, Essex, 4 June 1632 (Inq. p.m., 6 June 1632); m. St. Dunstan-in-the-West, 11 Feb. 1592/3, Richard Harlakenden of Earls Colne, b. 22 July 1568, d. 22 Aug. 1631, bur. Earls Colne, Inq. p.m. 1631, will 29 June 1631, pro. 19 Oct. 1631, heir of Roger Harlakenden and Elizabeth Hardres. (*NEHGR, loc cit.*;.*Topo. et Gen.*, I: 234-235; see *MC* 89-17).

41. COLONEL ROGER HARLAKENDEN, ESQ., of Earls Colne, bapt. 1 Oct. 1611, d. Cambridge, Massachusetts, 17 Nov. 1638, came to N.E. 1635; m. (2) 4 June 1635, Elizabeth Bosvile, b. abt. 1617, dau. of Geoffrey Bosvile by Margaret Greville, dau. of Edward Greville. She m. (2) **HERBERT PELHAM III, ESQ.** (1-39).

41. MABEL HARLAKENDEN (dau. of Gen. 40), bapt. Earl's Colne Priory, Essex, 27 Dec. 1614, d. July 1655; m. (1) abt. 1626, as 2nd wife, Colonel John Haynes, b. England, abt. 1594, d. Hartford, Connecticut, 1 Mar. 1653/4, Governor of Massachusetts, 1635-1636, Colonel, 1636, 1st Governor of Connecticut, 1639, and Governor or Deputy-Governor thereafter until his death; m. (2) 17 Nov. 1654, Samuel Eaton. (*NEHGR* 120: 246; Adams, *Soc. of Col. Wars in the State of Conn.* (1941), pp. 3, 1179, etc.; see *MC* 89-18).

42. RUTH HAYNES, b. Hartford, Conn., 1639, d. there abt. 1688; m. abt. 1654, Samuel Wyllys, A.B. (H.C.), 1643), bapt. Fenny Compton, co. Warwick, 19 Feb. 1631/2, d. Hartford, Conn., 30 May 1709, son of Governor George Wyllys and Mary (Smith) Bisby. (G.S. Steinman, "Pedigree of Harlakenden, of Kent and Essex" in *Topographer and Genealogist*, (1846) I: 233-234; Metcalfe, *Visitations of Essex...1582*, 210-212; see *MC* 89-19).

Line 70

28. MAUD MARSHAL (69-28); m. 1207/12, Hugh Bigod, 3rd Earl of Norfolk. (*CP* XII (2): 248).

29. ISABEL BIGOD, m. (1) **GILBERT DE LACY** (177A-8), of Ewyas Lacy, co. Hereford, and of Trim and Weoberley, d. 1230, son of Walter de Lacy, Lord of Meath, and Margaret de Braose, dau. of **WILLLAM DE BRAOSE** (177-6) 5th Baron Braose, & Maud de St. Valery, of Haie. (*CP* V 437, IX 589-590, XII (2): 169, note *d*; Banks I: 221).

30. MARGARET DE LACY, d. 1256, Lady of Dulek; m. as 1st wife, 14 May 1244, John de Verdun, d. 1274. (*CP* I: 239-240, XII (2): 246-248; Banks I: 221, 445).

31. THEOBALD DE VERDUN, b. abt. 1248, d. Alton, co. Stafford, 24 Aug. 1309, M.P. 1289/90, 1st Lord Verdun, Constable of Ireland, Lord of Dulek; m. by 6 Nov. 1276, Margery (or Eleanor), h. of ¼ hundred of Bisley, co. Gloucester. (*CP* XII (2): 249-250; Banks I: 221, 445).

32. SIR THEOBALD DE VERDUN, KNT., of Alton, co. Stafford, b. 8 Sept. 1278, Lord of Weoberley, 2nd Lord Verdun, Justiciar of Ireland, Knt. 1298, M.P. 1299-1314, d. Alton 27 July 1316; m. (1) Wigmore, co. Hereford, 29 July 1302, Maud de Mortimer, d. Sept. 1312, dau. of **SIR EDMUND DE MORTIMER** (176B-30) and **MARGARET DE FENLIS** (120-32); m. (2) 4 Feb. 1316, **ELIZABETH DE CLARE** (11-30). (*CP* II: 426, XII (2): 250-252; Banks I: 445). Note: By Maud, Theobald, also had daus. Joan de Verdun, b. 1304, d. 1334, who m. Thomas Furnival, and Margaret de Verdun, who m. Sir William Blount; and. by Elizabeth, he had dau. Isabella de Verdun, who m. Henry Ferrers, of Groby.

33. ELIZABETH DE VERDUN, by (1), d. 1360; m. bef. 11 June 1320, Sir Bartholomew de Burghersh, Lord Burghersh, d. 3 Aug. 1355, son of Robert, Lord Burghersh, and Maud de Badlesmere, dau. of Guncelin de Badlesmere. (*CP* II: 426-427, XII (2): 426, 252; Banks I: 445).

34. BARTHOLOMEW DE BURGHERSH, K.G., d. 5 Apr. 1369, Lord Burghersh, fought at Crecy, 1346, original Knight of the Garter, 23 Apr. 1349; m. (1) bef. 10 May 1335, Cicely de Weyland, liv. Aug. 1354, dau. of Sir Richard de Weyland. (*CP* II: 426-427, IV: 269-277, V: 736).

35. ELIZABETH DE BURGHERSH, *suo jure*, Baroness Burghersh, b. 1342, d. Aug. 1409; m. bef. Dec. 1364, **SIR EDWARD DESPENSER, K.G.** (74-34), b. abt. 24 Mar. 1335/6, d. 11 Nov. 1375, Lord le Despenser. (*CP* II: 427, IV: 274-277, V: 320, 736 charts).

36. MARGARET LE DESPENSER, m. **SIR ROBERT DE FERRERS** (61-34) of Chartley.

Line 70A   New to 8th Edition

25. BERTRAN I DE VERDUN, liv. 1086 -1120, Domesday Tenant.

26. NORMAN DE VERDUN, liv. 1120 · 1153; m. Lescelina de Clinton, dau. of Geoffrey I de Clinton, by Lescelina. (Keats-Rohan, *Domesday Desc.* II: 403, 404, 766).

27. BERTRAN II DE VERDUN, liv. 1153 · 1192; m. (1) Maud (or Matilda) de Ferrers, dau. of Robert I de Ferrers; m. (2) Rohesia. (*DNB* 20: 217).

28. NICHOLAS DE VERDUN, d. 1231; m. Clemencia.

29. ROHESIA DE VERDUN, d. 10 Feb. 1247; m. Thomas (Theobald) le Boteler (Butler). (*CP* XII (2): 246-247; Richard Dace, "Bertran de Verdun: ...," in *Medieval Prosopography* 20 (1999): pp 75-93, esp. 84, 90, 91, 92).(Note: their dau. Maud le Boteler, d. 27 Nov. 1283; m. **JOHN FITZ ALAN,** (149-28), Lord of Clun and Oswestry, *de jure* Earl of Arundel. (*CP* I: 239).

30. JOHN DE VERDUN; d. 1 Oct. 1274; m. 14 May 1244, **MARGARET DE LACY** (70-30). (*CP* XII (2): 247-248).

Line 71   Revised for 8th Edition

29. ISABEL BIGOD (70-29), m. (1) **GILBERT DE LACY** (177A-8) of Ewyas Lacy. (*CP* V: 437; IX: 589-590).

30. MAUD DE LACY, d. 11 Apr. 1304; m. (2) **SIR GEOFFREY DE GENEVILLE** (71A-70), d. 1314, son of **SIMON DE JOINVILLE** (71A-29), Senechal of Champagne, Seigneur de Vaucouleurs in France. (*CP* V: 628-631; Banks I: 220-221).

31. SIR PIERS DE GENEVILLE, d. bef. 8 June 1292, Baron de Geneville of Trim and Ludlow Castle; m. **JEANNE DE LUSIGNAN** (135-32), d. bet. Aug. & 14 Sept. 1322. (*CP* I: 339, V: 632-634; Banks I: 221).

32. JOAN DE GENEVILLE, b. 2 Feb. 1285/6, d. 19 Oct. 1356; m. bef. 6 Oct. 1306, **SIR ROGER DE MORTIMER** (176B-31,120-33), 8th Baron Mortimer of Wigmore, 1st Earl of March. (*CP* I: 339, V: 634, XIV: 87; Banks I: 220-221).

33. JOAN DE MORTIMER (176B-32), d. 1337/51; m. bef. 13 June 1330, as 1ST wife, **SIR JAMES AUDLEY, K.G.** (122-33), 2nd Lord Audley, of Redcastle, co. Salop, b. Knesale, co. Nottingham, 8 Jan. 1312/3, d. 1 Apr. 1386, will dated 1385; fought at Poitiers, M.P. 1331-1386, son of Nicholas, 1st Lord Audley of Heleigh, and Joan Martin, dau. of William Martin, Lord Martin and Eleanor, dau. of **SIR REGINALD** (or **REYNOLD) FITZ PIERS** (262-30), wid. of Henry de Lacy, Earl of Lincoln. (*CP* I: 339-340; Banks I: 100-102; *Gen.* (n.s.) 36 (1919): 15). Note: Sir James Audley m. (2) by 1351, Isabel, living 1366, said to be dau. of Robert, Lord Fitz Walter of Knokyn and had issue by both wives. (See *Gen., cit.*)

24. **ÉTIENNE (STEPHEN) DE VAUX**, 1st Sire de Joinville, Count of Joigny, m. bef. 1027 a dau. of Engelbert de Brienne and Adelaide (Alix), Countess of Joigny, dau. of Renaud I de Joigny, son of Fromond I de Joigny, son of Garnie de Joigny. (*ES* VII/6; Stokvis II: 92-93).

25. **GEOFFROI DE JOINVILLE**, Seigneur de Joinville, d. 1080; m. Blanche of Reynel, dau. of Arnoul, Count of Reynel. (*ES* VII/4, 6, 7).

26. **ROGER I DE JOINVILLE**, Seigneur de Joinville ,d. aft.1137; m. Aldéarde (Hodiarde) de Vignory, d. aft. 1140, dau. of Guy III, Seigneur de Vignory (son of Guy II, Seigneur de Vignory and Hildegarde) and **BEATRICE OF BURGUNDY** (71B-25). (West Winter, XIV.33, XIII.24, XIII.165, XII.754, XII.104, XI.61; *ES* II/20).

27. **GEOFFROI III DE JOINVILLE**, Sénéchal of Champagne, 1127-1188 and of Bar-sur-Seine, d. 1188; m. bef. 1141, Félicité de Brienne, d. 21 July 1178, wid. of Simon de Broyes, d. 1132, dau. of Erard I, Count of Brienne, d. 1114/1115, by **ALIX DE RAMERU** (151A-24), dau. of **ANDRE I DE RAMERU** (151A-23). (*ES* VII/4, 6, III.4/681; West-Winter, XIII.1028-1029).

28. **GEOFFROI IV DE JOINVILLE**, Sénéchal of Champagne, d. Acre, in battle, Aug. 1190; m. **HELVIS (HELVIDE) DE DAMPIERRE** (264-28), d. aft. 1195, dau. of Gautier (Guy) I de Moëlan, Seigneur de Dampierre, Viscount of Troyes and Helvis de Baudemont. (West Winter, XIII.1028).

29. **SIMON DE JOINVILLE**, Sénéchal of Champagne, Seigneur de Vaucouleurs in France, d. Palestine, May 1233; m. (1) by 1209, Ermengarde de Walcourt (surn. de Moncler), d. in or aft. 1218, dau. of Jean de Walcourt (surn. de Moncler); m. (2) Béatrix d'Auxonne, d. 11 Apr. 1260, wid. of Aymon de Faucigny, dau. of Étienne III de Bourgogne, Count d'Auxonne, by Béatrix de Thiers, Countess of Châlon-sur-Saône. (*ES* VII/6; West Winter, XIV.1370).

30. **GEOFFREY DE GENEVILLE**, by (2), Seigneur de Vaucouleurs 1252, Lord of Trim, b. abt. 1226, d. Trim, co. Meath, Ireland 21 Oct. 1314; m. 1252, **MAUD DE LACY** (71-30), wid. of Peter (Pierre) of Geneva, the son of Humbert of Geneva, dau. of Gilbert de Lacy of Ewyas Lacy, co. Hereford. (*ES* VII/9; *CP* V: 628-631; T. W. Moody Ed., et al, *A New History of Ireland* (1984) IX: 173).

31. **SIR PIERS DE GENEVILLE** (71-31) Lord of Walterstone-Staunton-Lacy, Ludlow, Malmeshull, Wulveslowe and Ewyas-Lacy, d. 8 June 1292; m. **JEANNE DE LUSIGNAN** (135-32) de la Marche, d. sh. bef. 18 Apr. 1323, wid. of Bernard Ézy I, Sire d'Albret in Gascony, d. 1281, dau. of **HUGH XII DE LUSIGNAN** (135-31, 275-29), called le Brun, Comte de La Marche et Angoulême and **JEANNE DE FOUGÈRES** (214A-30), dau. of **RAOUL III DE FOUGÈRES** (214A-29), Seigneur de Fougères in Brittany; she m. (2) her husb. bro., Pierre de Joinville. (*CP* V: 630, 632-633).

32. **JOAN DE GENEVILLE** (71-32), b. 2 Feb. 1285/1286, d. 19 Oct. 2356; m. **ROGER DE MORTIMER** (176B-31, 120-33), 8th Baron Mortimer of Wigmore, 1st Earl of March, Lord of Leix, Ireland, b. 25 Apr. or May 3, 1287, d. 29 Nov. 1330, granted seisin of lands in Ireland, 1308, by Joan's grandfather, Geoffrey. (*CP* V: 643; T. W. Moody, Ed., et al, *A New History of Ireland* (1982) VIII: 120). (For early gen. see also, G. W. White, "The Families of Lacy, Geneva, Joinville, and La Marche, *Gen.* (n.s.) 21 (1904/5): 1-16, 73-82, 163-172, 234-243; *CP* VI: 63).

30. **JEAN (JOHN) DE GENEVILLE**, (son of Gen. 29), Sénéschal of Champagne, b. 1224/1225, d. 24 Dec. 1317; m. (1) 11 Aug. 1230, Alix de Grandpre, d. 1261; m. (2) 11 Dec. 1261, Alix de Reynel, d. 1288, dau. of Gautier de Reynel, by Hélisende. (ES VII/4).

31. ALIX DE GENEVILLE, by (2), d. 19 Apr. 1336; m. (1) Jean d'Arcis, d. 1307; m. (2) as 2nd wife, **HENRY** (17-29), "of Lancaster," 3rd Earl of Lancaster. (*ES* VII/6).

Line 71 B   New to 8th Edition

24. HENRY I, of Burgundy, "le damoiseau de Bourgogne," (108-23) b. abt. 1035, d. 27 Jan. 1066/7; m. abt. 1056, Sibylle of Barcelona, b. abt. 1035, d. aft. 6 July 1074, dau. of Berenger Ramon I. (*ES* II/20).

25. BEATRICE OF BURGUNDY, d. aft. 1110; m. aft. 1082 **GUY III DE VIGNORY** (71C-25), d. 1125. (*ES* II/20, XV/197)

26. ALDÉARDE (HODIARDE) DE VIGNORY, d. aft. 1140, m. **ROGER I DE JOINVILLE** (71A-26). (*ES* II/20).

Line 71C   New to 8th Edition

22. RODOLFUS barbatus, Normanne.

23. GUY I DE VIGNORY, d. abt.. 1040

24. ROGER I DE VIGNORY, d. abt. 1059; m. (1) Mathilde; m. (2) as her 3rd husb., Alice de Bar-sur-Aube. (*ES* XV/729A).

25. GUY II DE VIGNORY "le Rouge"; m. Hildegarde de Bar-sur-Aube. Both liv. 1081?

26. GUY III DE VIGNORY, d. 1126; m. aft. 1082, **BEATRICE OF BURGUNDY** (71B-25). (*ES* XV/197).

Line 72

29. ISABEL BIGOD (70-29), wid. Gilbert de Lacy of Ewyas Lacy; m. (2) aft. 1230, **SIR JOHN FITZ GEOFFREY** (246C-28), d. 23 Nov. 1258, of Shere, Farnbridge, etc., Justiciar of Ireland, 1245-1256, son of Geoffrey Fitz Piers, 1st Earl of Essex and **AVELINE DE CLARE** (246B-27). (*CP* V: 433-434, 437).

30. MAUD FITZ JOHN, d. 16 or 18 Apr. 1301; m. (2) bef. 1270, **WILLIAM DE BEAUCHAMP** (86-29), b. 1237, bur. 22 June 1298, 9th Earl of Warwick; she had m. (1) Gerard de Furnival, of Sheffield, co. York. (*CP* IV: 265, 670 chart III, V: 437, 439-441).

31. ISABEL DE BEAUCHAMP, d. sh. bef. 30 May 1306; m. (1) Sir Patrick de Chaworth, Knt, d. abt. 7 July 1283, Lord of Kidwelly, co. Carmarthen, Wales, son of Patrick de Chaworth, of Kempsford, co. Gloucester, d. 1258, by his wife, Hawise, d. 1273, dau. & h. of Thomas de London, Lord of Kidwelly, d. by 1221; m. (2) 1286, Sir Hugh le Despenser, b. 1 Mar. 1260/1, hanged Oct. 1326, 1st Earl of Winchester (s. of Sir Hugh le Despenser, sum. 14 Dec. 1264 Lord Despenser, d. Evesham Aug. 1265, & Aline Basset (m. 2nd Roger Bigod), dau. of Sir Philip Basset of Wycombe, Bucks, Justiciar, and Hawise de Lovaine, dau. of **SIR MATTHEW DE LOVAINE** (155A-27) of Little Easton, Essex). (Sanders, 125; *CP* IV: 261, 265).

32. MAUD DE CHAWORTH by (1); m. bef. 2 Mar. 1297 **HENRY** (17-29), "of Lancaster," 3rd Earl of Lancaster, b. 1281, d. 22 Sept. 1345. (*CP* I: 244, *CP* VII: 396, 400-401).

33. HENRY "The Wryneck," b. Grosmont, abt. 1300, d. 24 Mar. 1361, 4th Earl of Lancaster and Leicester, Earl of Lincoln, Duke of Lancaster 1352, Steward of England, Earl of Moray (Scotland); m. abt. 1334 **ISABEL DE BEAUMONT,** liv. 1361, dau. of **HENRY DE BEAUMONT** (114-30), d. 1340, 1st Lord Beaumont, *jure uxoris* Earl of Buchan

(Scotland), Constable of Scotland, and **ALICE COMYN** (114A-29) Countess of Buchan. (*CP* VII: 401-410; *SP* II: 258-261).

Line 73

29. ISABEL BIGOD (70-29); m. (2) **SIR JOHN FITZ GEOFFREY** (246C-28). (*CP* V: 437).

30. JOAN FITZ JOHN, d. 4 May 1303; m. abt. 1268, Theobald Butler (le Boteler), b. abt. 1242, d. 26 Sept. 1285, son of Theobald le Boteler, d. 1248, and Margery de Burgh, dau. of Richard de Burgh. (*CP* II: 449, V: 437).

31. EDMUND BOTILLER (BUTLER), d. London, 13 Sept. 1321, Justiciar and Governor of Ireland; m. 1302, **JOAN FITZ GERALD** (178A-8), dau. of **JOHN FITZ THOMAS FITZ GERALD** (178A-7), 1st Earl of Kildare, and Blanche Roche, dau. of John Roche of Fermoy. (*CP* II: 449-450, III: 60, V: 437).

32. JAMES BOTILLER (BUTLER), b. abt. 1305, d. 6 Jan. 1337/8, cr. 1st Earl of Ormond; m. 1327, **ELEANOR DE BOHUN** (7-30). (*CP* V: 437, X: 116-119).

33. PETRONILLA (or **PERNEL**) **BOTILLER (BUTLER)** (13-31), liv. 28 May 1365, dead 1368, m. 8 Sept. 1352, **GILBERT TALBOT** (95-32), b. abt. 1332, M.P. 1362, d. 24 Apr. 1387, 3rd Lord Talbot. (*CP* XII (1): 614-617).

Line 74

30. MAUD FITZ JOHN (72-30); m. (2) **WILLIAM DE BEAUCHAMP** (86-29), 9th Earl of Warwick. (*CP* IV: 265, 670 chart III).

31. ISABEL DE BEAUCHAMP (72-31), d. 1306; m. (2) 1286, Sir Hugh le Despenser, d. 27 Oct. 1326, 1st Earl of Winchester. (*CP* IV: 262-265, V: 433-434, 437).

32. SIR HUGH LE DESPENSER, hanged and quartered 29 Nov. 1326, Baron Despenser; m. in 1306 bef. 14 June, **ELEANOR DE CLARE** (8-30), b. Oct. 1292, d. 30 June 1337. (*CP* IV: 267-271, cf. 269, 670 chart III, V: 763).

33. SIR EDWARD DESPENSER, d. 30 Sept. 1342; m. Groby, 20 Apr. 1335, Anne de Ferrers, d. 8 Aug. 1367, dau. of **SIR WILLIAM FERRERS** (58-31), of Groby. (*CP* IV: 274-275, 670, chart III, V: 343-344, 736).

34. SIR EDWARD DESPENSER K.G., bapt. 24 Mar. 1335/6, d. 11 Nov. 1375; m. bef. 2 Aug. 1354, **ELIZABETH DE BURGHERSH** (70-35), d. abt. 26 July 1409. (*CP* II: 425-427, IV: 274-278, 670 chart III, V: 736).

35. ELIZABETH DESPENSER, m. **SIR JOHN FITZ ALAN** (21-32), b. 30 Nov. 1364, d. 14 Aug. 1390. (*CP* I: 253, V: 736, Banks I: 378).

Line 74A

31. ISABEL DE BEAUCHAMP (74-31), d. 1306; m. (2) 1286 Sir Hugh le Despenser, 1st Earl of Winchester, d. 27 Oct. 1326. (*NEHGR* 145: 268 and refs).

32. SIR PHILIP LE DESPENSER, yngr. s., d. 24 Sept. 1313; m. Margaret de Goushill, b. 12 May 1294, d. 29 July 1349, dau. of Sir Ralph de Goushill of Goxhill, co. Lincs., & Hawise, dau. Fulk Fitz Warin. (*CP* IV: 288-90, VI: 42-43; *NEHGR*, cit).

33. SIR PHILIP LE DESPENSER, of Camoys Manor in Toppesfield, co. Essex, b. 6 Apr. 1313, co. Lincs., d. there 22 or 23 Aug. 1349; m. Joan de Cobham, prob. dau. of Sir John de Cobham. (*CP* IV: 288-90; *NEHGR, cit*).

34. HAWISE LE DESPENSER, b. abt. 1345, d. 10 Apr. 1414; m. as 2nd wife, 7 Sept. 1363, Sir Andrew Luttrell, Lord Luttrell, b. 1313, d. 6 Sept. 1390, son of Sir Geoffrey Luttrell & Agnes de Sutton, dau. Sir Richard de Sutton of Warsop & Sutton on Trent, co. Notts. (*CP* VIII: 287-288, notes *k, n*; *NEHGR, cit*. 267).

35. SIR ANDREW LUTTRELL, b. abt. 1364, d. 31 Dec. 1397, Lord Luttrell; m. by 1379 Joan Tailboys, d. bef. 1397, dau. of Henry Tailboys (or Talbois), b. abt. 1335, d. 23 Feb. 1368/9, and **ELEANOR DE BOROUGHDON** (224-33), Baroness Kyme. (*NEHGR, cit*. 265-268).

36. HAWISE LUTTRELL, b. abt. 1393, d. 24 Mar. 1421/2; m. (1) Sir Thomas Belesby, d. 20 Sept. 1415; m. (2) Sir Godfrey Hilton, d. 5 Aug. 1459. (*CP* VIII: 289; *NEHGR, cit*. 267).

37. SIR GODFREY HILTON, b. 9 Nov. 1419, d. 18 May 1472; prob. m. 1453 Margery, d. 14 Nov. 1495, par. unknwn., who. m. 2nd William Walron. (*NEHGR, cit.*, 67-268).

38. ELIZABETH HILTON, dau. & event. coh., b. abt. 1455, d. betw. 1496 & 1522, acquired manor of Irnham on death of her bro. Sir Godfrey Hilton; m. Richard Thimbleby (or Thimelby), Esq., d. 24 Apr. 1522. (*NEHGR, cit.*, 268).

39. ANNE THIMBLEBY, liv. 1537; m. **JOHN BOOTH** (224A-39), b. 1487/8, dead by 22 or 23 May 1537. (*NEHGR, cit.*, 266, 268).

Line 75

29. ISABEL BIGOD (70-29); m. (2) **SIR JOHN FITZ GEOFFREY** (246C-28), Justiciar of Ireland. (*CP* V: 437, IX: 589-590).

30. AVELINA FITZ JOHN, d. abt. 20 May 1274; m. **WALTER DE BURGH** (177B-9), d. 28 July 1271, 2nd Earl of Ulster. (*CP* V: 437, XII (2): 171-3).

31. RICHARD DE BURGH, b. abt. 1259, d. Athassel, 29 July 1326, 3rd Earl of Ulster; m. by 27 Feb 1280/1, Margaret, d. 1304, dau. prob. of **ARNOULD III** (272-30), Count of Guines (see 94A-31). (*CP* V: 437, IX: 403-404, XII (2): 173-7, XIV: 619; *Gen. Mag.* 20 (10): 335-340).

32. ELEANOR DE BURGH, m. 3 Jan. 1297, **THOMAS DE MULTON** (40-30), b. 21 Feb. 1276, d. 1321, 1st Lord Multon of Egremont. (*CP* V: 437, IX: 403-404).

Line 75A   Prepared for an earlier edition by Douglas Richardson

30. AVELINA FITZ JOHN (75-30), d. abt. 20 May 1274; m. abt. 1257 **WALTER DE BURGH** (177B-9), b. abt. 1230, d. 28 July 1271, 2nd Earl of Ulster, son of Richard de Burgh, Lord of Connaught (died 1242), by wife, Egidia (or Gille) de Lacy, dau. of Walter de Lacy (died 1241), Lord of Meath. (Orpen, *Ireland under the Normans*, III, chart p. 286-287, IV, chart p. 159; *CP* XII (2): 171).

31. EGIDIA DE BURGH, m. James Stewart, 5th High Steward of Scotland, b. abt. 1243, d. 1309, son of Alexander Stewart of Dundonald, 4th High Steward of Scotland, d. abt. 1282, by wife, Jean, said to be dau. of James, Earl of Bute. (Orpen, *op. cit.*, IV, chart p. 159; *SP* I:1 3-14; *Calendar of Documents Scotland* II, no. 847).

32. WALTER STEWART, 6th High Steward of Scotland, b. 1292, d. 9 Apr. 1326; m. (1) 1315, **MARJORIE BRUCE** (252-31), b. bef. 1297, d. 2 Mar 1316, dau. of Robert Bruce, Earl of Carrick, King of Scotland, by Isabel (also called Matilda), dau. of Donald, 6th Earl of Mar. (*SP* I: 14-15, V: 577-578; *CP* I: 310-311).

Line 76

27. ISABEL DE CLARE (66-27); m. William Marshal, 3rd Earl of Pembroke. (*CP* I: 22, X: 364).

28. MAUD MARSHAL, d. 27 Mar. 1248; m. (2) **WILLIAM DE WARENNE** (83-27), d. 1240, 6th Earl of Surrey. (*CP* IV: 670, X: 364 note *e*).

Line 77

29. MAUD DE BRAOSE (67-29); m. **ROGER DE MORTIMER** (28-29, 176B-29).

30. ISABELLA MORTIMER; m. **JOHN FITZ ALAN** (149-29), Lord of Clun and Oswestry.

31. SIR RICHARD FITZ ALAN (28-31), 1st Earl of Arundel; m. Alasia di Saluzzo. (*CP* I: 240-241, 250).

32. MARGARET FITZ ALAN; m., as 1st wife, William le Botiller (or Butler), of Wem and Oversley, b. 8 Sept. 1298, d. Dec. 1361, son of William le Botiller of Oversley, co. Warwick, by his 1st wife, Beatrice. He m. (2) abt. 1354, **JOAN DE SUDELEY** (222-35). (*Gen. Mag.* 13: 173-174; *CP* II: 230-233; *Wm. Salt Soc.* n.s. (1945-6), pp. 40-43).

33. WILLIAM LE BOTILLER (or Butler), Lord le Botiller of Wem and Oversley, b. bef. 1331, d. 14 Aug. 1369, M.P. 1368-1369; m. bef. July 1343, Elizabeth, perh. Holand of Upholand. (*CP* II: 230-235, V: 320 chart, XII (1): 417-418, XIV: 320; *Wm. Salt Soc.* n.s. (1945-6), pp. 42-43). Note: Elizabeth was not dau. of Robert, Lord Holand, since his daughter, Elizabeth, married by 1340 **SIR HENRY FITZ ROGER** (261-35). See refs. cited under that line & generation.

34. ELIZABETH LE BOTILLER (or Butler), of Wem and Oversley, b. bef. 1345, d. 19 June 1411, will 6 Jan. 1410/11, pro. June 1411; m. abt. 27 Sept. 1369, **SIR ROBERT DE FERRERS** (62-33), of Willisham. (*CP* II: 230-235, V: 320 chart; *Wm. Salt Soc.*, *cit.*).

Line 78

32. SIR RICHARD FITZ ALAN (60-32), 9th Earl of Arundel; m. **ELEANOR OF LANCASTER** (17-30). (*CP* XII (1): 44; Muskett II: 175).

33. ALICE FITZ ALAN, d. 17 Mar. 1415/6; m. 1364, **SIR THOMAS DE HOLAND, K.G.** (47-32), 2nd Earl of Kent. (*CP* VII: 154-156, XII (1): 44; Muskett II: 175).

34. ELEANOR DE HOLAND (2nd dau. of the name, 5th child); m. 1399, **THOMAS DE MONTAGU, K.G.** (8A-33), d. abt. 3 Nov. 1428, Earl of Salisbury. (*CP* V: 429, VII: 156 note *e*, XI: 394-395, XII (2): 305 note *a*; *Warwick Castle and Its Earls*, I: 144, II: 829 chart).

35. ALICE DE MONTAGU, *suo jure* Countess of Salisbury, d. by Feb. 1462/3; m. in or bef. Feb. 1420/1, Sir Richard de Neville, K.G., beheaded at Pontefract, 31 Dec. 1460, *jure uxoris* 4th Earl of Salisbury, son of **RALPH DE NEVILLE, K.G.** (207-34), 1st Earl of Westmorland, and **JOAN BEAUFORT** (2-32). (*CP* V: 429, XI: 395-398; *Warwick Castle*, etc., *Ibid.*).

36. ALICE DE NEVILLE, liv. 22 Nov. 1503 (sis. of Richard de Neville, Earl of Warwick and Earl of Salisbury, the "King Maker"); m. **HENRY FITZ HUGH** (219-35), Lord Fitz Hugh, d. 8 June 1472, son of William Fitz Hugh and Margery Willoughby. (*CP* V: 427-429, X: 309).

37. ELIZABETH FITZ HUGH, m. as 2nd wife, Sir William Parr, K.G., of Kendal, b. 1434, d. abt. 26 Feb. 1483/4. (*CP* V: 428 note *h*, X: 309, XI: 398).

38. WILLIAM PARR d. bef. 13 Dec. 1547, Baron Parr of Horton, co. Northampton (uncle to Queen Katherine Parr), Sheriff of Northamptonshire, Knt. 1513; m. bef. 1511, Mary Salisbury, d. 10 July 1555, dau. of William Salisbury of Horton and Elizabeth Wylde, dau. of Thomas Wylde. (*CP* X: 309-311).

39. ELIZABETH PARR, m. abt. 1523, as 2nd wife, **SIR NICHOLAS WODHULL** (150-39), d. 5 May 1531. (*TAG* 21: 72).

Line 79

29. ROBERT DE VERE (60-29), 5th Earl of Oxford; m. Alice de Sanford, d. Sept.1312. (*CP* X: 216-218).

30. ALFONSO DE VERE, KNT., of Great Hormean, Herts., d. abt. 20 Dec. 1329; m. Joan, prob. dau. of Sir Richard Foliot. (*CP* X: 222, note *a*).

31. JOHN DE VERE, 7th Earl of Oxford, b. abt. 12 Mar. 1311/2, d. Rheims, Jan. 1359/60, Hereditary Chamberlain to the King of England, served in France and Spain; m. bef. 27 Mar. 1336, Margaret (or Maud) de Badlesmere, b. abt. 1308/9, d. prob. 24 May 1366, wid. of Robert Fitz Payn, d. 1322, dau. of Bartholomew de Badlesmere and **MARGARET DE CLARE** (54-32). (*CP* I: 373, X: 222-223).

32. MARGARET DE VERE, d. 15 June 1398; m. (1) **HENRY DE BEAUMONT** (17-31), Lord Beaumont, d. 17 June 1369; m. (2) abt. 1370, Sir Nicholas de Lovaine, b. abt. 1325, d. 1376, of Penhurst, Kent, (his first wife was Margaret de Bereford, dau. of John de Bereford, wid. Sir John de Pulteney, d. abt. 1349); m. (3) Sir John Devereux, Lord Devereux, d. 22 Feb. 1392/3. (*CP* I: 373 note *e*, II: 60-61, IV: 296-299, X: 224 note *a*; *Gen. Mag.* 15: 251-255, 284-292; *ES* III.4/714).

33. MARGARET DE LOVAINE by (2), b. abt. 1372, d. 1408; m. bef. 1398, Sir Philip St. Clair (de Seyntclere), d. 1408. (*CP* IV: 299 footnote *c*; *VCH Oxford* V: 284-285).

34. THOMAS ST. CLAIR (yngr. bro. and h. of John St. Clair), d. 6 May 1434, held Chalgrove, co. Oxford, and extensive property in co. Sussex and co. Suffolk; m. bef. 8 Feb. 1424 (fined for m. w/o a lic.) Margaret Hoo, dau. of Sir William Hoo & Alice St. Omer. (*CP* VI: 567; Cal. Pat. Rolls 1424; Inq.p.m. 2 Hen VII on Thomas Hoo, nephew of Margaret, vol. 1, p. 93 no. 205; *Gen.* (n.s.) 18 (1902): 101).

35. EDITH ST. CLAIR, b. abt. 1425, dau. & coh. h. 1451; m. **SIR RICHARD HARCOURT** (143-35), sheriff of Oxford 1461, d. 1486.

Line 80   Revised for 8th Edition

27. ISABEL DE CLARE (66-27); m. William Marshal, 3rd Earl of Pembroke.

28. JOAN MARSHAL, m. as 1st wife, Warin de Munchensi, d. abt. July 1255, (Fuedal) Lord of Swanscombe. (*CP* X 364 note *a*, 377-382, IX: 421-2; West Winter, XVI.541).

29. JOAN DE MUNCHENSI, d. bef. 30 Sept. 1307; m. 13 Aug. 1247, **SIR WILLIAM DE VALENCE** (154-29), b. abt. 1225/6, d. bef. 18 May 1296, titular Earl of Pembroke, Lord of Valence, Montignac, Bellac, Rancon and Champagnac, knighted 13 Oct. 1247, crusader 6 Mar. 1250, 4th son of **HUGH X DE LUSIGNAN**, (275-27) "le Brun," Sire de Lusignan, Count of la Marche and Angoulême, Lord of Lusignan, and **ISABELLA OF ANGOULÊME** (153-28), wid. of **JOHN** (1-25), King of England. (*CP* X: 364 note *a*, 377. Gens. 27-29: *CP* IV: 670 chart III).

Line 81

27. **JOHN DE SOMERY**, m. **HAWISE PAYNEL** (55-27), sis. of Gervase Paynel and dau. of Ralph Paynel. (*CP* X: 320; Sanders, 113).

28. **RALPH DE SOMERY** (55-28), Baron Dudley, held Dudley and Dinas Powis, d. 1210; m. Margaret, sis. of William Marshal, 3rd Earl of Pembroke & dau. of John Fitz Gilbert (styled John the Marshal), by 2nd wife Sibyl, dau. Walter of Salisbury. (*CP* X: 320, corrected by XII (1): 111).

29. **ROGER DE SOMERY** (55-29), d. on or bef. 26 Aug. 1273, Lord Dudley, held Dinas Powis; m. (1) **NICHOLE D'AUBIGNY** (126-30, 210-30); m. (2) in or bef. 1254, Amabil de Chaucombe, d. abt. 1278, dau. & coh. of Sir Robert de Chaucombe and widow of **SIR GILBERT DE SEGRAVE** (16B-26). (*CP* X: 320, XII (1): 112-113; Segrave, *The Segrave Family 1066 to 1935*, pp. 13-16, which may or may not be correct in stating that this Gilbert d. 8 Oct.--but year prob. not 1254 as shown here.)

30. **ROGER DE SOMERY** by (2), b. 24 June 1255 (age 18 in 1273), Baron Dudley, 1290, held Dinas Powis, d. on or bef. 11 Oct. 1291; m. Agnes, par. unkn., d. by 23 Nov. 1308. (*CP* XII (1): 114).

31. **MARGARET DE SOMERY**, b. 1290, d. 1384, Baroness Dudley; m. John I de Sutton, Knt., Lord of Dudley Castle, co. Stafford, 1326, liv. 1337, son of Sir Richard de Sutton, b. abt. 1266, liv. 1346, Lord of Warsop, Sutton, Eakring and Cotham, co. Nottingham, by his wife, Isabel Patrick, b. abt. 1260, d. by 1318, wid. of Philip Burnel, dau. & h. of William Patrick, d. by 1279, by his wife, Beatrice de Malpas, d. 1290. Margaret de Somery was sis. & h. of John de Somery, b. 1278, d.s.p. 29 Dec. 1321. (*CP* XII (1): 109-115 & 115 note *g*, 351-352; *DNB* 16: 107-109; C. J. Holdsworth, ed., *Rufford Charters*, pub. 1972-1981 as Thoroton Record Series, vol. 29-34; Farrer; *VCH Huntingdon*, vol. 3).

32. **JOHN II DE SUTTON**, d. 21 Nov. 1359, seen 25 Feb. 1341/2, M.P. 25 Feb. 1341/2; m. Isabel de Cherleton, d. 10 Apr. 1397, dau. of John de Cherleton, Lord of Powis. (*CP* IV: 479 note *e*; Old-*CP* VII: 190; *DNB* 16: 108; *MC* 30-7).

33. **JOHN III DE SUTTON**, of Dudley Castle, co. Stafford, b. 1338, d. 1369/70; m. (1) 25 Dec. 1357, Katharine Stafford, b. in or bef. 1347/8, d. by 25 Dec. 1361, dau. of **RALPH DE STAFFORD** (55-32) and **MARGARET DE AUDLEY** (9-31); m. (2) aft. 1361, Joan Clinton, b. 1341/2, d. by 1386, wid. of Sir John Montfort, Knt, liv. 25 May 1361, dau. of Sir John Clinton of Coleshill. (*CP* IV: 479 note *e*; *DNB* 16: 107-109; *Hist. Cols. of Staffs.* XIII (1892): 38). (See also Elmendorf, *Anc of Gov. Thomas Dudley*, p. 11. Marriage certificate shows she would be a minor for four years after marriage).

34. **JOHN IV DE SUTTON**, by (1), of Dudley Castle, co. Stafford, b. 6 Dec. 1361, d. 10 Mar. 1396, Inq.p.m. 1401; m. Jane (or Joan), d. Apr. 1408. (*CP* IV 479 note *e*; *DNB* 16:107-109; *The Genealogist* 5 (1984): 134).

35. **JOHN V SUTTON**, Baron of Dudley, b. Feb. 1380, d. 28 Aug. 1406; m. Constance Blount, d. 23 Sept. 1432, dau. of Sir Walter Blount of Barton, co. Derby. (*CP* IV: 479; *DNB* 16: 107-109).

36. **JOHN VI SUTTON (ALIAS DUDLEY), K.G.**, b. 25 Dec. 1400, bapt. at Barton-under-Needwood, co. Derby, d. 30 Sept. 1487, will 17 Aug. 1487, cr. 1st Lord Dudley

1440, Lord Lieutenant of Ireland, 1428-1430, Constable of Clun Castle 1435, M.P. 1440-1487, Constable of Wigmore Castle 1459, K.G. bef. 1459, wounded at Bloreheath, 1459; m. as 2nd husb., aft. 14 Mar. 1420/1, Elizabeth Berkeley, d. 1478, wid. of Edward Cherleton, Lord Cherleton, d. abt. 8 Dec. 1478, dau. of Sir John Berkeley of Beverstone, co. Gloucester, by his 1st wife, Elizabeth Betteshorne, dau. of Sir John Betteshorne. Sir John Berkeley was yngr. son of **THOMAS DE BERKELEY** (39-31), by his 2nd wife, Katherine de Clyvedon. (*CP* IV: 479-480; *DNB* 16: 107-109; *Her. and Gen.*, vols, V and VI; *Wm. Salt Soc.*, vol. IX. Gens. 31-36: see *The Genealogist* 5 (1984): 131-139).

37. SIR EDMUND SUTTON (alias Dudley), d. aft. 6 July 1483, but bef. 1487; m. (2) **MATILDA CLIFFORD** (5-36). (*CP* IV 480. Gens. 32-38: George Adlard, *The Sutton-Dudleys of England and New England* (N.Y.C., 1862), Pedigree A; The Suttons; *Warwick Castle and Its Earls* I, 224-227. Gens. 28-31: *CP* XII (1): 109-115 note e, XII (1): 351-352).

Line 81A   Prepared for an earlier edition by Patrick W. Montague-Smith

36. SIR JOHN VI SUTTON, K.G. (81-36), 1st Baron of Dudley, K.G. (1459), sum. Lord Dudley (1440), b. Barton 25 Dec. 1400, d. 10 Sept. 1487; m. Elizabeth, d. sh. bef. 8 Dec. 1478, wid. of Edward, Lord Cherleton, dau. of Sir John Berkeley, d. 30 Sept. 1487 in 87th yr., of Beverstone Castle, co. Gloucester (only son of 3rd Lord Berkeley by his 2nd wife Katherine, dead 8 Dec. 1478) and his (1) wife Elizabeth Betteshorne , dau. of Sir John Betteshorne. (*CP* IV: 479-80; Henry S. Grazebrook, "The Barons of Dudley," note 2, pp. 65-70; *Hist. of Staffordshire*, (Dudley) 9 (2): 1-152).

37. ELEANOR SUTTON, prob. d. 1513; m. (1) **SIR HENRY BEAUMONT, KNT.** (17-35), of Wednesbury, co. Stafford, and Thorpe-in-Balne, co. York, high sheriff of Staffordshire, d. 16 Nov. 1471; m. (2) George Stanley, of Hammerwich, Lichfield, co. Stafford, b. abt. 1440, d. 1508/9, bur. Lichfield Cathedral, son of Thomas Stanley, of Elford, co. Stafford, d. 1463 (3rd son of Sir John Stanley and **ISABEL DE LATHOM** (57-34)), by his 2nd wife, Elizabeth Langton.

38. ANNE STANLEY by (2), b. aft. 1472, liv. 1532/3; m. John Wolseley, Lord of Wolseley, co. Stafford, b. abt. 1475, d. 1553, son of Ralph Wolseley, of Wolseley, d. 1504. (*Visit. of Staffs*, 1614).

39. ELLEN WOLSELEY, 6th dau., d. 3 Dec. 1571; m. (1) George Abney, Lord of Willesley, co. Derby, d. 1 Mar. 1578, bur. Willesley, will dtd. 4 Jan. 1571, pro. PCC 27 Jan. 1579.

40. EDMUND ABNEY, 4th s., bur. St. Mary's, Leicester, 1 Apr. 1604, will pro. 25 Jan. 1604, Freeman of Leicester 1594, member of Council 1599; m. 1587 Catherine Ludlam, dau. William Ludlam, Alderman & Mayor of Leicester.

41. PAUL ABNEY, eldest s., entered ped. in *Visit. of Leicester* (1634), will pro. 18 June 1635, d. Leicester 10 June 1635; m. 1611 Mary Brokesby, dau. George Brokesby of Stapleford, co. Leicester.

42. GEORGE ABNEY, eldest s., bapt. St. Mary's, Leicester, 11 July 1613, bur. same 3 May 1661; m. Bathusa (of unknown parentage), will dtd. 2 Jan. 1706, pro. Leicester 22 Sept. 1712. She m. (2) Rev. Joseph Lee, rector of Cotesbach near Lutterworth, co. Leicester.

43. DANNETT ABNEY, 4th s., 3rd surv., bapt. St. Mary's, Leicester, 26 Feb. 1660, will pro. 5 Mar. 1733, Spotsylvania Co., Virginia, patented land in Spotsylvania 28 Sept. 1728; m. (2) abt. 1702 Mary Lee, dau. Rev. Joseph Lee (husband's stepfather) by his 1st wife. (Gens. 36-43: see *The Genealogist*. 5 (1984): 131-157).

38. ANNE STANLEY (81A-38), b. aft. 1472, liv. 1532; m. John Wolseley, Lord of Wolseley, co. Stafford, b. 1475, d. 1553.

39. ANTHONY WOLSELEY, eldest son, Lord of Wolseley, b.c. 1510, d. 1571; m. Margaret Blythe, d. by 1570, dau. William Blythe, Lord of Norton, co. Derby.

40. ERASMUS WOLSELEY, eldest surv. s., Lord of Wolseley, bur. Colwich, co. Stafford, 15 Jan. 1599, recusant; m. 1562 Cassandra Gifford, bur. Colwich as a recusant 5 Jan. 1616, dau. Sir Thomas Gifford of Chillington, co. Stafford.

41. SIR THOMAS WOLSELEY, eldest surv. s., Lord of Wolseley, b. 1564, bur. Colwich 21 Mar. 1630, Knt. 28 Aug. 1617, conveyed Wolseley to cousin Sir Robert Wolseley, will dtd. 13 Mar. 1630, pr. PCC 30 Mar. 1630; m. (1) 1584, a dau. Sir Thomas Gresley, bur. Colwich, 6 Sept. 1591, n.i.; m. (2) 1592 Anne Moseley, d. 1606, dau. Humphrey Moseley, 3 sons d.s.p., 3 daus.; m. (3) as 1st husb., Colwich, 1607/8, Helen Brocton, dau. Edward Brocton of Broughton Hall, Longdon, co. Stafford.

42. WALTER WOLSELEY, elder survs. s. of 3rd mar., of Wolseley Bridge, co. Stafford, later of Ravenstone, co. Leicester, bapt. Colwich 25 Sept. 1612, d. by 1661; m. Mary Beauchamp, liv. 1661 a wid., dau. John Beauchamp of Reigate, co. Surrey and of London.

43. MARY WOLSELEY, liv. in Maryland 20 Apr. 1685 when named exec. of will of her aunt Winifred (Wolseley) Mullett; to Maryland 1673/4 to join her aunt Mary (Wolseley) Calvert, at whose home she m. bef. 1687 as his 2nd wife Roger Brooke of Battle Creek, Calvert Co., Md., b. Brecon, 20 Sept. 1637, d. 8 Apr. 1700.

44. ANNE BROOKE, d. 1733; m. (1) James Dawkins d. 1701; m. (2) James Mackall, b. 1671, will pr. 26 Dec. 1716. By (2) 3 sons, 3 daus. (Gens. 39-44: *The Genealogist* 5 (1984): 131-157).

41. SIR THOMAS WOLSELEY (81B-41), b. 1564, bur. Colwich 21 Mar. 1630; m. (1) 1584 a dau. Sir Thomas Gresley, bur. Colwich, 6 Sept. 1591, n.i.; m. (2) 1592 Anne Moseley, d. 1606, dau. Humphrey Moseley, 3 sons d.s.p., 3 daus.; m. (3) as 1st husb., Colwich, 1607/8, Helen Brocton, dau. Edward Brocton of Broughton Hall, Longdon, co. Stafford.

42. COL. DEVEREUX WOLSELEY, ynst. s. by (3), bapt. Colwich 24 Nov. 1617, d. 1648; m. Elizabeth Zouche, liv. 1663, dau. Sir John Zouche of Codnor Castle, co. Derby, by Isabel Lowe, dau. Patrick Lowe of Denby Park, co. Derby. Their dau.

43. ANNE WOLSELEY, b. 164_, d. 24 Aug. 1685, bur. Westminster Abbey; m. as 1st wife, Rev. Thomas Knipe, Prebendary of Westminster, then Headmaster, Westminster School b. 1639, d. 5 Aug. 1711, bur. Westminster Abbey. Only dau.

44. ANNE KNIPE, b. 1676, bur. Westminster Abbey 30 Sept. 1703; m. 16 Feb. 1697, Michael Arnold of par. of St. Margaret, Westminster, d. 3 Nov. 1735, bur. St. Margaret, Westminster. Their dau.

45. ALICIA ARNOLD, bapt. St. Margaret, Westminster, 30 July 1700; d. Annapolis, Maryland, 9 July 1746, came to Maryland 1723; m. St. James, Westminster 20 Oct. 1720, John Ross, b. 13 Aug. 1696, d. Annapolis, Md. 18 Sept. 1766, to Maryland 1721 when served as Lord Baltimore's agent and Clerk of the Maryland Council 1732-1764, Alderman of Annapolis. Their elder dau.

46. ANNE ARNOLD ROSS, b. 9 Oct. 1727, d. Belvoir, Maryland., 5 Jan. 1811; m. 12 Dec. 1752 Francis Key, b. 1731/2, St. Paul's Covent Garden, London, d. Charlestown, Cecil Co., Md. Nov. 1770. Their elder son

47. JOHN ROSS KEY, a soldier in the Revolution, b. 19 Sept. 1754, d. Redlands, Frederick Co., Md., 13 Oct. 1821; m. 19 Oct. 1778, Ann Phoebe Penn Dagworthy Charlton, b. 6 Feb. 1756, d. 8 July 1830. They had, among other children, son Francis Scott Key (1779-1843), author of the Star Spangled Banner, and Ann Key, wife of Roger Brooke Taney (1777-1864), 2nd Chief Justice of the United States. (*The Genealogist, cit.*).

Note: Mr. Montague-Smith in his referenced article (*The Genealogist* 5 (1984): 131-157) includes 4th line, this from Anne Stanley and John Wolseley (81A-38), ten generations, by way of Ireland, to Robert Warren St. John Wolseley (1848-1910) who came to N.Y., and including three further generations into Texas.

Line 82

29. ISABEL BIGOD (70-29); m. **SIR JOHN FITZ GEOFFREY** (246C-28).

30. ISABEL FITZ JOHN, (sis. of Richard Fitz John); m. Robert de Vipont (or Vieuxpont), b. 1239, d. 7 June 1264, Lord of Appleby, Westmorland, hereditary sheriff of Westmorland, son of John de Vipont, b. 1210, d. 1241, Lord of Appleby, by Sibyl de Ferrers, dau. of **WILLIAM DE FERRERS** (194-7), d. 1247, 4th Earl of Derby, by his wife, **AGNES OF CHESTER** (127-29).

31. ISABEL DE VIPONT, b. 1254, d. 14 May 1292, heiress of Appleby, Westmorland; m. Roger de Clifford, of Tenbury, co. Worcester, Justice of the Forests, drowned, 6 Nov. 1282, son of Sir Roger de Clifford, of Tenbury, Justice of Wales, Justice of the Forest south of Trent, crusader, d. 1285.

32. ROBERT DE CLIFFORD, 1st Lord Clifford, b. 1274, d. 1314; m. **MAUD DE CLARE** (64-32). (*CP* III: 290-291. Gens. 29-32: *CP* V: 437).

Line 83

24. ISABEL DE VERMANDOIS (50-24, 53-24); m. (2) 1118, William de Warenne, 2nd Earl of Surrey, d. 1138, son of William de Warenne, 1st Earl of Surrey, d. 1088, by wife, Gundred. (*CP* IV: 670, VII: 642, XII (1): 492-495).

25. WILLIAM DE WARENNE, b. 1118, d. 1148, 3rd Earl of Surrey; m. **ELA TALVAS** (108-26), d. 1178. (*CP* IV: 670).

26. ISABEL DE WARENNE, Countess of Surrey, sole dau. and h., d. 13 July 1199; m. (1) William of Blois, d.s.p. 1159, yr. son of **STEPHEN OF BLOIS** (169-25), King of England; m. (2) 1163, **HAMELIN (PLANTAGENET)** 5th Earl of Surrey (123-26), d. 7 May 1202, , natural son of **GEOFFREY V (PLANTAGENET)**, Count of Anjou (118-25, 123-25). (*CP* IV: 670; *ES* III.2/355).

27. WILLIAM DE WARENNE by (2), d. 27 May 1240, 6th Earl of Surrey; m. (2) 13 Oct. 1225, **MAUD MARSHAL** (69-28, 76-28), d. Apr.1248, wid. of Hugh Bigod. (*CP* IV: 670).

28. JOHN DE WARENNE, b. 1231, d. 1304, 7th Earl of Surrey, m. Aug. 1247, **ALICE (ALFAIS) DE LUSIGNAN** (153-29), d. 9 Feb. 1256/6, dau. of **HUGH X DE LUSIGNAN** (275-27). (*CP* IV: 670, XII (1): 449-508; *ES* III.2/355, III.4/816).

29. WILLIAM DE WARENNE, Earl of Surrey, b. 1256, killed in a tournament at Croydon, 15 Dec. 1286; m. abt. 1285, **JOAN DE VERE** (60-30), d. 1293. (*CP* I: 242, IV: 670).

30. ALICE DE WARENNE, d. bef. 23 May 1338; m. 1305, **SIR EDMUND FITZ ALAN** (28-32), b. 1 May 1285, beheaded at Hereford, 17 Nov. 1326, 8th Earl of Arundel. (*CP* I: 241-243, 253, IV: 670. Gens. 26-30: *ES* III.2/355).

Line 84   Revised for 8th Edition

24. ISABEL DE VERMANDOIS (50-24, 53-24); m. William de Warenne, 2nd Earl of Surrey.

25. GUNDRED DE WARENNE (88-25), liv. 1166; m. bef. 1130 (1) **ROGER DE BEAUMONT** (151-25), d. 1153, 2nd Earl of Warwick, crusader, son of Henry de Beaumont, d. 20 June 1123, 1st Earl of Warwick, 1090. (*CP* XII (2): 362; Old-*CP* VIII 53-56).

26. WALERAN DE BEAUMONT, 4th Earl of Warwick, b. bef. 1153, d. 24 Dec. 1203 or bef. 13 Oct. 1204; m. (2) abt. 1196, as her 2nd husb., Alice de Harcourt, liv. 1212, wid. of John de Limesy, Lord of Cavendish, co. Suffolk, dau. of Robert de Harcourt of Stanton-Harcourt, co. Oxford, and wife Isabel Camville, liv. 1207/8, dau. of Richard de Camville of Stanton. (*CP* XII (2): 363-364; *Wm. Salt Soc.* (n.s.) vol. 35, chart). <u>Note</u>: Rosie Bevan, "A Realignment of the 12th and 13th Century Pedigree of the Earls of Warwick - A *Complete Peerage* Correction," in *Foundations*, (see at http://www.fmg) v. 1 #3, Jan. 2004, pp 194-197, shows that Waleran de Beaumont m. (1) Margery d'Oilly, dau. of Henry d'Oilly, of Hook Norton, co. Oxen., by Maud de Bohun, dau. of Humphrey de Bohun, thus correcting *CP* XII (II): 363-364. Waleran and Margery were the parents of Henry, 5th Earl of Warwick.

27. ALICE DE BEAUMONT, d. 1246-1263; m. William Mauduit, d. Apr. 1257, Lord of Hanslope, and Hartley Mauduit, co. Bucks., Chamberlain of the Exchequer, son of Robert Mauduit, d. 1222, Lord of Hanslope, Chamberlain of the Eschequer, by his wife Isabel Basset. Robert Mauduit's maternal grandfather was Simon de St. Liz, d. 1153, Earl of Huntingdon. (*CP* XII (2): 364 note *f*, 366-368; Sanders, 50-51).

28. ISABEL MAUDUIT (see 197-28), buried at the Nunnery of Cokehill; m. William de Beauchamp, 5th Baron Beauchamp of Elmley Castle, co. Worcester, will dtd. 7 Jan. 1268/9. (*CP* II: 44; Old-*CP* VIII: 53-56. Gens. 24-28: *Warwick Castle and Its Earls*, II: 827-828; *CP* IV: 670 chart III).

29. WALTER DE BEAUCHAMP, d. 1303, of Beauchamp's Court, in Alcester, co. Warwick, and Powyck, co. Worcester, Steward of the Household of King Edward I, Constable of Gloucester Castle; m. abt. 1275 (papal dispensation dtd. 1289) Alice de Toeni, liv. 1307, dau. of **ROGER V DE TOENI** (98-29) of Flamstead, co. Hertford, perh. by (1) Alice de Bohun, dau. of **HUMPHREY DE BOHUN** (97-28), 2nd Earl of Hereford & Essex. Alice de Toeni had as maritagium the manor of East Coulston, co. Wilts, which manor previously part of maritagium of her mother Alice de Bohun, (*CP* II: 46 note *f*; W.H. Bliss, ed., *Cal. of Entries in the Papal Registrars: Papal Letters*, 1: 503 (calls Alice dau. Ralph de Toeni, apparent scribal error as that relationship chronologically impossible); Rev. C. Moor, *Knights of Edward I*, 1: 74-74; Emma Mason, ed., *The Beauchamp Cartulary Charters*, pub. 1980 as Publ. Pipe Roll Soc., (n.s.) XLIII: pp. iviij-ix, 216).

30. GILES DE BEAUCHAMP, of Beauchamp's Court, d. Oct. 1361; m. abt. 1329, **CATHERINE DE BURES** (189-6), dau. of Sir John de Bures. (*CP* II: 46 note *f*, V: 320 chart).

31. SIR JOHN DE BEAUCHAMP, d. 1378-1401; m. Elizabeth, d. 1411, parentage unproven. (*CP* II: 46 note *f*).

32. SIR WILLIAM DE BEAUCHAMP, of Powyke and Alcester, d. bef. 1431, Constable of the Castle of Gloucester, sheriff of Worcestershire and Gloucestershire; m. bef. Mar. 1414/5, Catharine Ufflete, dau. of Sir Gerard de Ufflete. (*CP* II: 46-47).

33. SIR JOHN DE BEAUCHAMP, K.G., d. bef. 19 Apr. 1475, cr. Baron Beauchamp of Powyke, 2 May 1447, Justice of South Wales, Lord Treasurer of England, 1450-1452; m. abt. 1434, Margaret Ferrers, sister of Richard Ferrers. (*CP* II: 46-47).

34. SIR RICHARD DE BEAUCHAMP, K.B., b. 1435, d. 19 Jan. 1502/3, 2nd Baron Beauchamp of Powyke; m. 27 Jan. 1446/7, **ELIZABETH STAFFORD** (55-37), dau. of Sir Humphrey Stafford, Knt., of Grafton, co. Worcester. (*CP* II: 47; Inq.p.m. 21 Nov. 1504).

35. ANNE DE BEAUCHAMP, b. 1462/1472, d. 1535; m. Thomas Lygon, of Madresfield, co. Worcester, d. 1515, J. P. for Worc. 1509/10, son of Thomas Lygon, d. 1507, by Ann Giffard, dau. of Nicholas Giffard. (http://www.Burkes-peerage.net "Ligon formerly of Madresfield I"; *CP* II: 47 note e; *Visit. of Gloucester* (1623): 204-206).

36. SIR RICHARD LYGON, KNT., of Arle Court, d. 1557, Sheriff of Gloucester, 1534, Sheriff of Worcester 1547; m. Margaret Greville, dau. of William Greville, Esq., of Arle Court, par. Cheltenham, co. Gloucester, Justice of the common pleas, d. 1513. Monumental brass for William Greville in parish church of Cheltenham. (*Visit. of Gloucester* (1623), 204-206; Mill Stephenson, *A List of Monumental Brasses in the British Isles* (1926), 147; Burkes, *Peerage* (1967): 194-195).

37. HENRY LYGON, of Upton St. Leonard, co. Gloucester, d. abt. 1577, will dtd. 30 July 1577, pro. 15 Aug. 1577; m. **ELIZABETH BERKELEY** (187-16), dau. of Sir John Berkeley. (*Visit of Gloucester* (1623), 204-206; *Visit. of Worcester* (1569), 90-91).

38. ELIZABETH LYGON, m. Edward Basset of Uley, co. Gloucester, will dated 3 June 1601, pro. 5 Nov. 1602, son of William Basset, of Uley. (*Visit. of Gloucester* (1623), 204-206).

39. JANE BASSET, d. 23 Apr. 1631; m. 12 Apr. 1605, Dr. John Deighton, Gent., d. 16 May 1640, of St. Nicholas, Gloucester, will dated 30 Jan. 1639, pro. 21 May 1640. (*Basset Genealogy*, 245-246; *The Genealogist* 6 (1985): 197 chart).

40. FRANCES DEIGHTON, bapt. St. Nicholas, Gloucester, 1 Mar. 1611; d. Taunton, Mass., Feb. 1705/6; m. Witcombe Magna, Gloucester, 11 Feb. 1632, Richard Williams, bapt. Wootton-under-Edge, 28 Jan. 1607, d. Taunton, Mass., Aug. 1693. (Waters I: 551-552).

40. JANE DEIGHTON (dau. of Gen. 39), bapt. St. Nicholas, 5 Apr. 1609, living in Boston, Mass., 1671; m. (1) St. Nicholas, 3 Jan. 1627, John Lugg, of co. Glouc. and Boston, Mass., came to N.E., 1638, d. aft. 1644; m. (2) abt. 1647, Jonathan Negus, b. 1602, living 1678; children by both husbands. (*TAG* 9: 221-222; *The Genealogist* 6 (1985): Dorothy Chapman Saunders, :"Jonathan and Benjamin Negus of Boston and Some of Their Descendants," pp. 195-231). (Gens. 34-40: Certified by A.T. Butler, 11 Dec. 1928, of the College of Arms, London, cf. W.L. Holman in *TAG* 9: 213-214. Gens. 38-40: Waters I: 551-552; *NEHGR* 45: 303, 96: 342-343; v. Redlich 158. See also *Boston Evening Transcript*, 9 July 1938).

40. KATHERINE DEIGHTON, (dau. of Gen. 39), bapt. Gloucester, England, 16 Jan. 1614/5, d. 29 Aug. 1671, wid. of Samuel Hackburne; m. (2) Roxbury, Mass., 14 Apr. 1644, as his 2nd wife, **GOVERNOR THOMAS DUDLEY** (143-41), d. 31 July 1653; besides Joseph Dudley (below) she was the mother of Deborah Dudley, who m. Jonathan Wade; and Hon. Paul Dudley, who m. Mary Leverett. Katherine (Deighton) (Hackburne) Dudley m. (3) the Rev. John Allin of Dedham, Mass., and had children by all three husbands.

41. GOVERNOR JOSEPH DUDLEY, A.M., (Harvard College, 1665), b. Roxbury, 23 Sept. 1647, buried Roxbury 8 Apr. 1720; m. 1669, Rebecca Tyng, dau. of Maj.-Gen. Edward Tyng. He was Governor of Massachusetts, 1702-1715. (See Sibley, *Harvard Graduates*, II: 166-188).

Line 84A   Prepared for an earlier edition by Douglas Richardson

   28. ISABEL MAUDUIT (84-28), m. William de Beauchamp, 5th Baron Beauchamp.

   29. SARAH DE BEAUCHAMP, liv. July 1317; m. aft. 7 Jan. 1268/9, Richard Talbot, Lord of Eccleswall, co. Hereford, sheriff of Gloucestershire, b. abt. 1250, d. abt. 3 Sept. 1306, son of Gilbert Talbot, of the same, d. 1274, by wife Gwenthlian, dau. & event. h. Rhys Mechyll, lord of Dynevor. (*CP* XII (1): 608-610).

   30. GILBERT TALBOT, 1st Lord Talbot, of Eccleswall, co. Hereford, b. 18 Oct. 1276, d. 24 Feb. 1345/6, sd. to have m. Anne, dau. of William le Botiler, of Wem, co. Salop. (*CP* XII (1): 610-612).

   31. SIR RICHARD TALBOT, 2nd Lord Talbot, steward of the King's household, b. abt. 1305, d. 23 Oct. 1356; m. 1326/7 **ELIZABETH COMYN** (95-31), b. 1 Nov. 1299, d. 20 Nov. 1372, dau. & coh. **JOHN COMYN** (95-30), lord of Badenoch, by wife **JOAN DE VALENCE** (154-30). (*CP* XII (1): 612-614).

Line 84B   Prepared for an earlier edition by Douglas Richardson

   30. GILBERT TALBOT (84A-30), 1st Lord Talbot; m. Anne le Botiler.

   31. PHILIPPA TALBOT, m. Sir Philip de Clanvowe, d. abt. 1347, of Michaelchurch-on-Arrow, co. Radnor, and Yazor, King's Pyon, Hergast and Ocle Pichard, co. Hereford, hereditary bailiff in fee in the lordship of Gladestry, co. Radnor, deputy to Gilbert Talbot (his father-in-law), then Justice of S. Wales, commissioner for Gilbert Talbot's castles, s. & h. William ap Hywel, liv. 1286. (MacFarlane, *Lancastrian Kings and Lollard Knights*, p. 230; Cal. Pat. Rolls, 1334-1338, p. 20; Cal. Close Rolls, 1339-1341, pp. 316-9; Cal. Inq. Misc., 1307-1349, p. 404; *Visit. Gloucs.* (*Harl. Soc. Publ.* XXI: 128); *Bulletin, Board of Celtic Studies*, 28: 270; *Welsh Hist. Review*, 8: 139, et seq.; *Cal. of Papal Reg. (Petitions)*, 1342-1419, p. 261).

   32. ELIZABETH DE CLANVOWE, h. in her issue to Yazor, co. Hereford; m. by 1343, **SIR JOHN POYNTZ** (234A-33), d. 24 Feb. 1376, Lord of Iron Acton, Winston and Elkstone, co. Gloucester.

84C   New to 8th Edition

   36. SIR RICHARD LYGON, KNT. (209-36), d. 1557; m. Margaret Greville. (*Visit. of Gloucester* (1623): 204-206; Mill Stephenson, *A List of Monumental Brasses in the British Isles* (1926), p. 147; Burke's *Peerage* (1967): 194-195).

   37. WILLIAM LYGON (209-37), of Madresfield, co. Worc. sheriff of Worcester 1549, d. 1567; m. Eleanor Dennis, dau. of Sir William Dennis and Anne Berkeley.

   38. THOMAS LYGON, 2nd son; m. his cousin, Frances Dennis, dau. of Hugh Dennis.

   39. THOMAS LYGON (LIGON), farmer, of Stoke-by-Coventry, and Calouden, co. Warwick, c. 1577-1626, m. 1623 Elizabeth Pratt, 1602-1631.

   40. COL. THOMAS LYGON (LIGON), bp. Sowe, co. Warwick, 11 Jan. 1623/4, d. 1675; emig. to Virginia 1641/2, mem. House of Burgesses from Henrico Co, 1655/6; m. 1648/1650 Mary Harris, b.c. 1625, d. 1703/4. (Gens. 36-40: *The Va. Gen.* 22 (1978): 253-5; 23 (1979): 80; 38 (1994): 48-51).

Line 85

30. GILES DE BEAUCHAMP (84-30); m. **CATHERINE DE BURES** (189-6).

31. ROGER DE BEAUCHAMP, d. 3 Jan. 1379/80, 1st Baron Beauchamp of Bletsoe, Chamberlain to the Household of King Edward III; M.P. 1364-1380; m. (1) bef. 1336/7, **SIBYL DE PATESHULL** (184A-13, 263-32), liv. 26 Oct. 1351, dau. of Sir John de Pateshull and Mabel de Grandison. (*CP* II: 44-45; Banks I: 118-119, II: 136-137).

32. ROGER DE BEAUCHAMP, d.v.p. 1373/4; m. (1) NN; m. (2) Joan Clopton, wid. of Sir Walter Walcot, of co. Norf., d. 1366, dau. of Walter Clopton. (*CP* II: 45; XIV: 75).

33. ROGER DE BEAUCHAMP, KNT., by (1), bapt. 14 Aug. 1363, d. 13 May 1406, 2nd Baron Beauchamp of Bletsoe and Lydiard Tregoz, m. Mary, par. unkn. (*CP* II: 45, XIV: 75 (corrects gen. 32 and 33); Banks as above).

34. SIR JOHN DE BEAUCHAMP, KNT., 3rd Baron Beauchamp of Bletsoe, d. Apr. 1412; m. (1) by Jan. 1405/6, Margaret Holand, dau. of Sir John Holand; m. (2) Esther Stourton, dau, of Sir John Stourton. (*CP* II: 45, XIV: 75).

35. MARGARET DE BEAUCHAMP, prob. but not certainly by (1), d. 1482; m. (1) Sir Oliver St. John, Knt., d. 1437, of Penmark, co. Gloucester. (*CP* II: 45 note c, 206, XI: 545, XII (2): 444; Banks as above; *Gen.* (n.s.) XVI: 13).

36. SIR JOHN ST. JOHN, b. abt. 1437/1442, of Penmark, 1488; m. Alice Bradshagh, dau. of Sir Thomas Bradshagh of Haigh, co. Lancs. (*CP* II: 206; Collins VI: 741).

37. SIR JOHN ST. JOHN, K.B., of Bletsoe, co. Bedford, K.B., 1502; m. Sybil, dau. of Morgan ap Jenkyns ap Philip. (*CP* II: 206; Collins VI: 742).

38. ALEXANDER ST. JOHN, ESQ., of Thurley, co. Bedford; m. Jane (Anne) Dallison, dau. of George Dallison of Cranesley, co. Northampton. She m. (2) Thomas Leventhorpe, Esq., of Shinglehall, co. Hertford. Monumental brass for Jane and her second husband in parish church of Sawbridgeworth, co. Herford. (Collins VI: 742. Gens. 35-38: *Visit. of the County of Huntingdon* (1613), Camden Society 1849, p. 2; Mill Stephenson, *A List of Monumental Brasses in the British Isles* (1926), 195-196).

39. HENRY ST. JOHN, d. 1598, of Keysoe, co. Bedford; m. Jane Neale, d. 1618, sister of John Neale of Wollaston. (Gens. 37-41: *The Gen. Mag.*, 16: 93-96; *Visit. of Bedfordshire* (1566), 44).

40. SIR OLIVER ST. JOHN, GENT., of Keysoe (Heishoe), co. Bedford, b. abt. 1575, d. Keysoe, 23 Mar. 1625/6, will made 13 Mar. 1625/6, pro. 1 May 1626; m. (1) 1597, **SARAH BULKELEY** (31D-40, 245-40) b. 1580, d. 1611, dau. of **REV. EDWARD BULKELEY, D.D.** (31-39) and Olive Irby; m. (2) at Goldington, co. Bedford, 16 Aug. 1611, Alice Haselden, half-sister of Jane Allen, 1st wife of the **REV. PETER BULKELEY** (31-40). (Waters II: 1420-1421).

41. ELIZABETH ST. JOHN, bapt. Bletsoe, co. Bedford, 12 Jan. 1604/5, d. Lynn, Mass., 3 Mar. 1676/7; m. Boston, co. Lincoln, Eng., 6 Aug. 1629, Rev. Samuel Whiting, A.M., b. Boston, co. Lincoln, 20 Nov. 1597, d. Lynn, Mass., 11 Dec. 1679, minister at Lynn, 1636-1679, son of the Hon. John Whiting, Mayor of Boston, co. Lincoln. (Gens. 39-41: *Bulkeley Genealogy*, 17, 30-31; Waters II: 1420-1421; Weis, *Colonial Clergy of N.E.*, 223; *Harleian Soc.*, vol. 19, *Visit. of Bedfordshire*, 51-55).

42. REV. SAMUEL WHITING, Jr., A.M., b. Skirbeck, co. Lincoln, Eng., 25 Mar. 1633; minister, Billerica, Mass., 1658-1713, d. Billerica, 28 Feb. 1712/3, ae. 79.

42. REV. JOSEPH WHITING, A.M., b. Lynn, Mass., 6 Apr. 1641; A.B., H.C., 1661, A.M., Fellow, 1664-1665; ord. Lynn, 6 Oct. 1680-1682; sett. Southampton, L.I., N.Y.,

1682-1723; d. Southampton, 7 Apr. 1723, age 82. (Donald L. Jacobus in *TAG* 45: 256, 34: 15-17, supports this line, Gens. 38-41).

Line 86   Revised for 8th Edition

28.   **ISABEL MAUDUIT** (84-28), d. 1268; m. William de Beauchamp, 5th Baron Beauchamp of Elmley Castle. (Old-*CP* VIII: 54).

29.   **WILLIAM DE BEAUCHAMP**, b. 1237, bur. 22 June 1298, 9th Earl of Warwick; m. bef. 1270, **MAUD FITZ JOHN** (72-30), d. 16 or 18 Apr. 1301, bur. 7 May 1301. (Gens. 28-29: *CP* IV: 670 chart III, V :437; XII (2): 368-370; *Warwick Castle and Its Earls*, II: 828).

30.   **SIR GUY DE BEAUCHAMP, KNT.**, b. 1278, 10th Earl of Warwick, knighted 25 Mar. 1296, will made 25 July 1315, d. Warwick Castle, 10 Aug. 1315; m. bet. 12 Jan and 28 Feb. 1309/10, **ALICE DE TOENI** (98-31), d. abt. 8 Jan. 1324/5, wid. of Thomas Leyburne, d. 1307, dau. of **RALPH VII DE TOENI** (98-30), sis. of Robert de Toeni, 1st Lord Tony. She m. (3) William Zouche, Lord Zouche of Mortimer. (*CP* XI: 477; XII (1): 774, note *i*, XII (2): 370-372).

31.   **MAUD DE BEAUCHAMP**, b. 1310/15, d. 28 July 1369; m. (1) Geoffrey IV de Say, b. abt. 1304/5, knight-banneret, Admiral of the Fleet, d. 26 June 1359. (*CP* XI: 475-477).

32.   **IDONEA DE SAY**, d. by 1384; m. prob. abt. 1350 as 1st wife of Sir John de Clinton, b. 1325/6, 3rd Lord Clinton of Maxstoke, co. Warwick, d. 6 Sept. 1398, son of John de Clinton, 2nd Lord Clinton, b. abt. 1300, d. abt. 1335 and Margaret Corbet, liv. May 1343, dau. of Sir William Corbet of Chaddesley Corbet, co. Worcester. John de Clinton, 2nd Lord Clinton was s. & h. of John de Clinton, 1st Lord Clinton (s. and h. of Thomas de Clinton by Maud, dau. Sir Ralph Bracebridge of Kinsbury, co. Worcester), b. abt. 1258, d. 1310; m. abt. 1290, Ida d'Odingsells, dau. of Sir William d'Odingsells of Maxstoke by **ELA** (30-29), dau. of **WALTER FITZ ROBERT** (148-28). (*CP* XI: 478 note *g*, III: 314-315, XIV: 191; *Gen. Mag.* 16 (1971): 550-551).

33.   **MARGARET DE CLINTON**; m. Sir Baldwin de Montfort, of Coleshill, co. Warwick, d. Spain, 1385, son of Sir John de Montfort of Coleshill, liv. 1361 (illeg. son of Peter de Montfort, of Beaudesert), by Joan Clinton, dau. & h. Sir John Clinton, of Coleshill, d. 1353/4, and Joan Hillary. (*Gen. Mag.* 16 (1971): 550-551; *TAG* 26 (1950): 22-23; *Topo. et Geneal.* I: 359-360; *VCH Warwick* IV: 50-51; *The Genealogist* 5: (1984): 131-139; *Boston Evening Transcript*, Sept. 5, 1928, #7409).

34.   **SIR WILLIAM DE MONTFORT**, of Coleshill, sheriff for Warwick. and Leicestershire 1431, 1441, 1450, d. 1452; m. (1) Margaret Peele; (2) Joanne Alderwich.

35.   **BALDWIN DE MONTFORT**, of Coleshill; m. Joan Vernon, dau. of Richard Vernon. (*Visit. of Warwick* (1619), 54-55; *Boston Evening Transcript, ibid.*).

36.   **ROBERT MONTFORT, ESQ.**, of Bescote, co. Stafford, and Monkspath, co. Warwick; m. Mary Stapleton, dau. and h. of Leonard Stapleton. (*Ancient Deeds* V, 163, #A 11549; *VCH Warwick* IV: 50-51).

37.   **KATHARINE MONTFORT**, m. **SIR GEORGE BOOTH** (33-36), d. 1483, of Dunham-Massie, co. Chester. (*Warwick Castle and Its Earls*, II: 828; *Ancestry of John Barber White*, 200, corrected by v. Redlich, 121-122; Ormerod (Helsby) I: 524).

30. GUY DE BEAUCHAMP (86-30), 10th Earl of Warwick; m. **ALICE DE TOENI** (98-31). (*CP* II: 50).

31. THOMAS BEAUCHAMP, 11th Earl of Warwick, prob. b. Warwick Castle, 14 Feb. 1313/14, K.G., 23 Apr. 1349, will made 6 Sept. 1369, d. Calais, 13 Nov. 1369; m. 1337, **CATHERINE DE MORTIMER** (120-34), will made 4 Aug. 1369. (*CP* II: 50, XII (2): 372-374).

32. THOMAS BEAUCHAMP, 2nd son, 12th Earl of Warwick, b. bef. 16 Mar. 1338/9, K.G., abt. Jan. 1372/3, will made 1 Apr. 1400, d. 8 Apr. 1401; m. bef. Apr. 1381, Margaret de Ferrers, d. 22 Jan. 1406/7, dau. of **WILLIAM DE FERRERS** (11-32), 3rd Lord Ferrers of Groby. (Gens. 30-34: *CP* XII (2) 375-377).

33. RICHARD BEAUCHAMP, K.G., b. 25 or 28 Jan. 1381/2, 13th Earl of Warwick and Albemarle, d. Rouen, 30 Apr. 1439; m. (1) Sept. 1393, **ELIZABETH DE BERKELEY** (39-34), b. abt. 1386 (under 7 in 1392), d.s.p.m. 28 Dec. 1422, only dau. of Thomas Berkeley, 5th Lord Berkeley, and Margaret, dau. of Warin de Lisle, 2nd Lord Lisle, and Lord Teyes. He m. (2) Isabel le Despenser, dau. and event. h. of Thomas le Despenser, 1st Earl of Gloucester, wid. of Richard Beauchamp, 1st Earl of Worcester. (*CP* II: 131 note c, IV: 282, XII (2): 378-382).

34. ELEANOR BEAUCHAMP, dau. by (1), b. 1407, d. 6 Mar 1466/7, wid. of Thomas, Lord Ros; m. (2) by **1436 EDMUND BEAUFORT** (1-32), 1st Duke of Somerset; m. (3) Walter Rokesley, Esq. (*CP* II 131 note c, 145, IV 417. Gens. 30-34: *CP* XII (1): 49, 53, XII (2): 370-382; *Warwick Castle and Its Earls*, II: 828-829).

Line 88   Revised for 8th Edition

23. ELDRED THE THANE, of Workington, "poss. a scion of the great house of Dunbar."

24. GODITHA (See 34-24), sis. of Ketel, 3rd Baron Kendal, husb. of Christian, perh. dau. of Ivo de Tailbois, 2nd Baron of Kendal; m. Gilbert, a Norman knight, 4th Baron Kendal in right of his wife. (Ketel was the father of Orm of Seaton, husb. of **GUNNILDA** (34-23) of Dunbar. (*Trans. Cumberland. and Westmoreland Ant. and Arch. Soc.* 62 (1962): 95-100).

25. WILLIAM I DE LANCASTER, 5th Baron of Kendal of Workington, in Coupland, served as castellan of William Fitz Duncan's castle of Egremont 1138, Gov. of Castle of Lancaster, d. 1170; m. (1) NN; m. (2) **GUNDRED DE WARENNE** (84-25), wid. of **ROGER DE BEAUMONT** (151-25), 2nd Earl of Warwick. (*CP* VII: 371-373; *VCH Lancs.* I: 357-366; *Trans. Cumb. & West., ibid.*).

26. WILLIAM II DE LANCASTER, by (1), b. abt. 1110, 6th Baron Kendal, d. 1184; m. **HELEWISE DE STUTEVILLE** (270C-27), dau. of **ROBERT III (IV) DE STUTEVILLE** (270-26) of Lazenby, co. Cumberland, and Hawise (Helwise), poss. niece of Geoffrey Murdac. Helewise m. (2) Hugh de Morville (see 40-26); m. (3) **WILLIAM FITZ RANULF** (265A-27), Lord of Greystoke. (*VCH Lanc.* I: 357-366; *NEHGR* 79: 373-378, 96: 103-104; *Trans. Cumb. & West., ibid.*).

27. HAWISE (or **HELWISE) DE LANCASTER** only child, Baroness Kendal, liv. Sept. 1226; m. bef. 20 July 1189, Gilbert [Fitz Roger] Fitz Reinfrid, Lord of Kendal, in right of his wife. Gilbert was Steward to Henry II, in France 1180-1189, and later to Richard I; was justice of the King's Court 1185, sheriff of Lancashire 1205-1216, and of Yorkshire 1209-1212, and d. sh. bef. 5 May 1220. His father, Roger Fitz Reinfrid, was witness to the

King's will, Judge 1176, 1198, sheriff of Sussex 1176, and of Berkshire 1186-1187. (*CP* V: 269, VII: 371, 672-673; *VCH Lanc.* I: 357-366).

28. HAWISE (or **HELWISE**) **DE LANCASTER**, m. **PIERS (PETER) DE BRUS** (136-26), d. bef. 1247, Crusader, Lord of Skelton, son of Piers de Brus and Joan le Grammaire. (*CP* V: 269; *VCH Lanc.* I: 357-366).

29. LUCY DE BRUS; m. Sir Marmaduke de Thwenge, Lord of Kilton Castle in Cleveland, and Daneby, co. York, M.P. 1294. (*CP* V: 269 note *b*, VII: 373; Banks I: 432; *NEHGR* 96: 120).

30. SIR ROBERT DE THWENGE, of Kilton Castle in Cleveland, d.s.p.m. legit. (*CP* VII: 373, 467-8, note c, 467; XII (1): 738-739 notes *h*. & *i* 739; Banks I: 432).

31. LUCY DE THWENGE, (dau. & h. of Robert de Thwenge, by uncertain mother), b. Kilton Castle, 24 Mar. 1278/9, d. 8 Jan. 1346/7; m. bef. 20 Apr. 1295, William Latimer, Lord Latimer, from whom sought divorce on grounds of consanguinity, also claimed cruelty & fear for her life. She had a son (below) by **NICHOLAS DE MEINELL** (268-31). (*CP* VII: 467-468, note *d* 467, VIII: 568, 619-635, cf. 632-634).

32. SIR NICHOLAS DE MEINILL (268-32), (natural son of Nicholas de Meinill by Lucy de Thwenge, above), d. bef. 20 Nov. 1341, 1st Baron Meinill of Whorlton (of the second creation of that barony); m. **ALICE DE ROS** (54-34), d. bef. 4 July 1344. (*CP* IV: 60, VIII: 632-634).

33. ELIZABETH DE MEINILL (268-33), b. Whorlton, 15 Oct. 1331, d. 9 July 1368, Baroness Meinill of Whorlton; m. (1) as 2nd wife, abt. 7 Jan. 1344/5, Sir John Darcy, 2nd Lord Darcy of Knayth, b. 1317, slain at Crécy, 5 Mar. 1355/6, son of Sir John Darcy, 1st Lord Darcy, co. Lincoln, and Emmeline Heron, dau. of Walter Heron, of Silkstone, co. York., and Alice de Hastings, dau. of Sir Nicholas de Hastings of Allerton, co. York, and Gissing, Norfolk; m. (2) bef. 18 Nov. 1356, **SIR PIERS VI DE MAULEY** (156-31), b. 1330, d. 20 Mar. 1382/3, 4th Lord Mauley of Mulgrave Castle. (John Darcy, had m. (1) Alianore de Holand, dau. of Robert de Holand, by **MAUD LA ZOUCHE** (32-30), dau. of **SIR ALAN LA ZOUCHE** (31-29). (*CP* IV: 58-61, 71, VIII: 567-568, 632-634, XIV: 234).

34. SIR PHILIP DARCY, b. 21 May 1352, d. 24 Apr. 1399, 4th Lord Darcy of Knayth; m. Elizabeth Gray, d. 11 Aug. 1412, dau. of Sir Thomas Gray of Heton, co. Northampshire, and Margaret Presfen, dau. of William Presfen, of Northumberland. (*CP* IV: 61-63, 71).

35. JOHN DARCY, b. abt. 1377, d. 9 Dec. 1411, 5th Lord Darcy of Knyath, m. **MARGARET DE GREY** (13A-33), d. 1 June 1454. (*CP* IV: 63-65, 71).

Line 89

24. ISABEL DE VERMANDOIS (50-24); m.(2) William de Warenne, Earl of Surrey.

25. ADA DE WARENNE, d. 1178; m. 1139, **HENRY OF HUNTINGDON** (170-23), b. 1114, d. 12 June 1152, son of **DAVID I** (170-22), King of Scots, and **MAUD OF HUNTINGDON** (130-26). (*CP* IV: 670 chart iv, VI: 642; *SP* I: 4).

26. WILLIAM THE LION (170-24), King of Scots, 9 Dec. 1165-1214, b. 1143, d. Stirling, 4 Dec. 1214. (*CP* IV: 670 chart iv, VI: 644-645; Old-*CP* VI: 400; *SP* I: 4; Gardiner, 216).

27. ISABEL (natural dau. of **WILLIAM THE LION** (170-24) by a dau. of Richard Avenal); m. (2) Haddington, 1191, Robert de Ros (see 170-25), d. bef. 23 Dec. 1226, of Helmsley in Holderness, co. York, Magna Charta Surety, 1215, Knight Templar, son of Everard de Ros, d. 1196, and Roese Trussebut (1st sis. and in her iss. sole heir of Robert Trussebut, and dau. of William Trussebut by Aubreye de Harcourt), and grandson of

Robert de Ros and Sibyl de Valognes (Valoines). (*CP* XI: 90-93; *SP* I: 4; Banks I 377; *DNB* 49: 216-219).

28. SIR WILLIAM DE ROS (see also 170-26), of Helmsley, M.P. 1235/6, d. abt. 1264; m. **LUCY FITZ PIERS** (237-7), dau. of **PIERS FITZ HERBERT** (262-29), of Brecknock, Wales. (*CP* XI: 93-94).

29. SIR ROBERT DE ROS, of Helmsley and Belvoir, co. Leicester, M.P. 1261, 1265, d. 17 May 1285; m. bet. 5 June 1243 and 17 May 1244, Isabel d'Aubigny, d. 15 June 1301, of Belvoir Castle, dau. of William d'Aubigny Lord of Belvoir, and granddau. of William d'Aubigny (see *MC* 1-1), d. 1236, Lord of Belvoir Castle, Magna Charta Surety, 1215. (*CP* XI: 95-96; Banks I: 377).

30. WILLIAM DE ROS, b. abt. 1255, d. bet. 12 May/16 Aug. 1316, 1st Lord Ros of Helmsley, M.P. 1295-1316, a competitor for the crown of Scotland 1291; m. 1287, Maud de Vaux, dau. of John de Vaux of Freiston, co. Lincoln, and Walton in Norfolk, son of Sir Oliver de Vaux, (*CP* XI: 96-97; *SP* I: 4; Sanders, 47-48).

31. WILLIAM DE ROS, 2nd Lord Ros of Helmsley, M.P. 1317-1340, served in Scotland 1316-1335, sheriff of Yorkshire 1326, d. 3 Feb. 1342/3; m. bef. 25 Nov. 1316, **MARGERY DE BADLESMERE** (54-33), b. 1306, d. 18 Oct. 1363. (*CP* VIII: 632-634, XI: 98-99; *DNB* 49: 216-219).

32. THOMAS DE ROS, KNT., 2nd son, b. Stoke Albany, co. Northampton, 13 Jan. 1336/7, d. Uffington, co. Lincoln, 8 June 1384, 4th Lord Ros of Helmsley, M.P. 1362-1384, served in France 1369 and 1371, Warden of Scotland 1367, Knt. Banneret 1372; m. (royal lic.) abt. 1 Jan. 1358/9, **BEATRICE STAFFORD** (9-32), wid. of Maurice (Fitz Maurice) Earl of Desmond, d. 1358. (*CP* V: 736, XI: 100-101. Gens. 25-32: *CP* XI: 90-101; Old-*CP* VI: 400-401; Banks I: 377-378; *DNB* 49: 216-219; Robert Thoroton, *The Antiquities of Nottinghamshire* (London, 1677), p. 115; John Nichols, *History of Leicestershire*, II Part 1: 27 ff.; W.T. Lancaster, *Early History of the Ripley and the Ingilby Family* (1918)).

33. ELIZABETH DE ROS, d. Mar. 1424; m. **THOMAS DE CLIFFORD** (26-33), 6th Lord Clifford.

33. MARGARET DE ROS; m. abt. 25 Nov. 1378, **SIR REYNOLD DE GREY** (93A-32), Lord of Ruthin. (*CP* VI: 157).

Line 90 Line cancelled

Line 91 Line cancelled

Line 92 Line cancelled

Line 93

24. ISABEL DE VERMANDOIS (83-24); m. (2) 1118, William de Warenne, 2nd Earl of Surrey.

25. ADA DE WARENNE, d. 1178; m. 1139, **HENRY OF HUNTINGDON** (170-23), b. 1114, d. 12 June 1152, Earl of Northumberland and Huntingdon. (*CP* IV: 670 chart IV, V: 736, VI: 642 note *m*; *SP* I: 4).

26. DAVID OF SCOTLAND (styled **DAVID OF HUNTINGDON**) (252-26), 9th Earl of Huntingdon, b. 1144, d. Yardley, 17 June 1219; m. 26 Aug. 1190, **MAUD OF CHESTER** (131-29), b. 1171, d. 1233, dau. of **HUGH OF KEVELIOC** (125-28), 3rd Earl of Chester. (*CP* IV: 670 chart iv, V: 736, VII: 646-647; *SP* I: 4,7; Dunbar, 65, 280-281).

27. ADA OF HUNTINGDON, m. Sir Henry de Hastings, d. sh. bef. Aug. 1250, of Ashill, Norfolk, Blunham, co. Bedford & Lidgate, Suffolk, hereditary steward of the Liberty of the Abbey of Bury St. Edmunds, son of William de Hastings and Margaret Bigod, and grandson of **ROGER BIGOD**, (see at Line 69-28) Magna Charta Surety, 1215. (*CP* IV: 670 ch. IV, V: 736, VI: 345, 646-647 note *I*; *SP* I: 4; Dunbar, 281; Dudley Pedigree; Gardiner 216; K.J. Stringer, *Earl David of Huntingdon* (1985), chart pp. 180-181, 185).

28. HILLARY (or ELEANOR) DE HASTINGS, m. as (2) wife **SIR WILLIAM DE HARCOURT** (56-29), of Stanton Harcourt, co. Oxford, and Naylston, co. Leicester, son of Sir Richard de Harcourt of Stanton-Harcourt, d. 1278. (Burk's *Peerage* (1967), 1164; Collins-Brydges IV: 434).

29. RICHARD DE HARCOURT, of Stanton Harcourt, co. Oxford, and Bosworth, co. Leicester, b. abt. 1256, d. 1293; m. (1) Margaret Beke (Inq.p.m. on her brother Walter's estate, 1333), dau. of John Beke, d. abt. 1303/4, Lord of Eresby, co. Lincoln, son of Walter Beke, Lord of Eresby, and Eve Grey, niece of Walter de Grey, Archbishop of York. (Collins-Brydges IV: 434-5; Rev. C. Moor, *Knights of Edward I*, 2: 183-184).

30. SIR JOHN DE HARCOURT, KNT., by (1), of Stanton Harcourt, co. Oxford, and Bosworth, co. Leicester, d. 1330, knighted 1306; m. (1) **ELEANOR (or ELLEN) LA ZOUCHE** (39A-30). (Gens. 27-30: Dudley Pedigree; Banks I: 122; Nichols, L*eicestershire*, IV, Part II: 519a-520a for the Harcourt pedigree; Collins-Brydges IV: 434-6; *Wm. Salt Soc.* (n.s.) (1914), 187-204).

Line 93A   Revised for 8th Edition. Corrections incorporated into Line originally prepared by Douglas Richardson.

27. ADA OF HUNTINGDON (93-27); m. Sir Henry de Hastings.

28. SIR HENRY DE HASTINGS, constable of Winchester Castle, b. abt. 1235, d. abt. 5 Mar. 1268/9; m. Joan de Cantelou, d. by June 1271, dau. & coh. Sir William de Cantelou, of Calne, co. Wilts, d. 1254, by wife **EVA DE BRAOSE** (66-29). (*CP* VI: 345-346).

29. SIR JOHN DE HASTINGS, 1st Lord Hastings, lieutenant & seneschal of Gascony, b. 1262, d. 1313; in 1292 claimed third part of Kingdom of Scotland as a gr.s. of Ada, 4th dau. & coh. of David, Earl of Huntingdon, claim rejected; m. (1) Isabel de Valence, d. 1305, dau. of **SIR WILLIAM DE VALENCE** (154-29), Lord of Valence, titular Earl of Pembroke (half bro. of **HENRY III** (1-26)), by wife **JOAN DE MUNCHENSI** (80-29); m. (2) Isabel, dau. of Hugh le Despenser, Earl of Winchester, by wife **ISABEL DE BEAUCHAMP** (74-31). (*CP* VI: 346).

30. ELIZABETH DE HASTINGS, dau. by (1); m. Sir Roger de Grey, 1st Lord Grey of Ruthin, of Ruthin, co. Denbigh, d. 6 Mar. 1352/3, younger s. Sir John de Grey, Lord Grey of Wilton, d. 1323. (*CP* VI: 151-153, 173-174, X: Append. L, 127-129).

31. REYNOLD DE GREY, Lord Grey of Ruthin, b. abt. 1319, d. 28 July or 4 Aug. 1388; m. bef. 29 Nov. 1360, Alianore (Eleanor) le Strange, d. 20 Apr. 1396, sister of Hamond le Strange, dau. of John le Strange, of Blackmere, 2nd Lord Strange. (*CP* XIV: 354, VI: 154-155, XII (1): 354).

32. SIR REYNOLD GREY, Lord Grey of Ruthin, b. abt. 1362, d. 30 Sept. 1440; m. (1) abt. 25 Nov. 1378, **MARGARET DE ROS** (89-33), dau. **SIR THOMAS DE ROS** (89-32), Lord Ros of Helmsley, d. 1384, by wife **BEATRICE DE STAFFORD** (9-32); m. (2) by 7 Feb.

1414/5, Joan Asteley, d. 1448, widow of Thomas Raleigh, & dau. & h. Sir William Asteley, 4th Lord Astley, of Astley, Co. Warwick. (*CP* VI: 155-158, XI: 100-101, XIV: 355).

    33. MARGARET GREY; m. abt. 12 Dec. 1414, as 1st wife, **SIR WILLIAM BONVILLE, K.G.** (261A-38), Lord Bonville, sheriff of Devonshire, seneschal of Aquitaine, b. 1393, beheaded 18 Feb. 1460/1. (*CP* II: 218-219). (Identification of William Bonville's wife Margaret Grey made by Robert Behra based on Cal. Close Rolls, 1413-1419, p. 199).

Line 93B   Prepared for an earlier edition by Douglas Richardson

    32. SIR REYNOLD GREY (93A-32), Lord Grey of Ruthin; m. Margaret de Ros.

    33. SIR JOHN GREY, K.G., s. & h. app., d. 27 Aug. 1439, captain of the town and castle of Gournay; m. bef. 24 Feb. 1412/3, **CONSTANCE DE HOLAND** (47C-33), b. abt. 1387, d. 1437, wid. Thomas Mowbray, d. 1405, Earl of Norfolk, dau. John de Holand, d. 1400, Earl of Huntingdon, 1st Duke of Exeter, by Elizabeth, dau. **JOHN OF GAUNT** (1-30), 2nd Duke of Lancaster. (*CP* VI: 155-159, IX: 604-605).

    34. ALICE GREY, d. 1474; m. as (1) wife, **SIR WILLIAM KNYVET** (188-12), b. abt. 1440, d. 1515, of Buckenham, Norfolk, M.P., sheriff of Norfolk and Suffolk, 1470, 1479, s. **JOHN KNYVET** (188-12), d. 1490, of the same, by wife, Alice Lynne (or Linne). (Banks I: 158).

Line 94

    26. DAVID OF SCOTLAND (styled **DAVID OF HUNTINGDON**) (93-26); m. **MAUD OF CHESTER** (131-29).

    27. MARGARET OF HUNTINGDON, d. abt. 6 Jan. 1233; m. 1209, **ALAN** (38-26), Lord of Galloway, d. 1234, hereditary Constable of Scotland. (*CP* IV: 670 chart IV, V: 675, VII: 646-647; *SP* I: 4, 7, IV: 142-143; *ES* II/90).

    28. DEVORGUILLA OF GALLOWAY (95-28), d. 28 Jan. 1289/90; m. 1233, John de Baliol, d. 1269, of Barnard Castle; they were the founders of Balliol College, Oxford. (*CP* IV: 670 chart iv, V: 675, VII: 646-647; *SP* I: 4, 7, IV: 142-143; *ES* II/91).

    29. CECILY DE BALIOL, d. 1289; m. Sir John de Burgh, d. sh. bef. 3 Mar. 1279/80, feudal Baron Lanvallei of Walkern, son of John de Burgh, Knt., b. 1210, d. 1275 (son of Hubert de Burgh, 1st Earl of Kent, by Beatrice de Warenne, dau. William de Warenne of Wormgay) and Hawise de Lanvallei, d. 1249, and grandson of William de Lanvallei, d. 1217, Magna Charta Surety, 1215, of Great Bromley, Essex. Sir John and Cecily had 3 daus. cohs.: (1) Devorguilla, wife of **SIR ROBERT FITZ WALTER** (130-31); (2) Hawise, wife of **SIR ROBERT DE GRELLE** (99-30); (3) Margery, a nun. (*CP* V: 437; *ES* II/91).

Line 94A

    31. RICHARD DE BURGH (75-31), 2nd Earl of Ulster, b. abt. 1259, d. 29 July 1326; m. by 27 Feb. 1280/1, Margaret, d. 1304, prob. dau. of **ARNOULD III** (272-30), Count of Guines (d. 1282). (*CP* XII (2): 173-177 & note *k* 176, XIV: 619; *Gen. Mag.* 20: 335-340).

    32. JOHN DE BURGH, 2nd but 1st surv. son, b. abt. 1290, d.v.p. 18 June 1313; m. 30 Sept. 1308, **ELIZABETH DE CLARE** (11-30, 70-32), b. 1295, d. 4 Nov. 1360, age 65, leaving a will., dau. and coh. of **SIR GILBERT DE CLARE, KNT.** (63-30), 6th Earl of Gloucester and Hertford, 9th Earl of Clare, and **JOAN OF ACRE** (8-29). Elizabeth m. (2) 4

Feb. 1315/16 as 2nd wife, **THEOBALD DE VERDUN, KNT.** (70-32), Lord Verdun, b. 8 Sept. 1278, d. 27 July 1316; m. (3) by 3 May 1317, Roger Damory, 1st Lord Damory, d. 13-14 Mar. 1321/2. (*CP*, XII (2): 177-8).

   33. WILLIAM DE BURGH, 3rd Earl of Ulster, b. 17 Sept. 1312, murdered at LeFord, Belfast 6 June 1333, age 20; m. (Papal disp. 1 May 1327), Maud of Lancaster, d. 5 May 1377, dau. of **HENRY** (17-29), 3rd Earl of Lancaster by **MAUD DE CHAWORTH** (72-32), dau. Sir Patrick de Chaworth, and **ISABEL DE BEAUCHAMP** (72-31). She m. (2) by 8 Aug. 1343, Sir Ralph d'Ufford, Justiciar of Ireland, d. 9 Apr. 1346. (*CP*, XII (2): 178-179).

   34. ELIZABETH DE BURGH, b. 1332, d. 1363; m. **LIONEL OF ANTWERP** (5-31), *j.u.* Earl of Ulster, b. 1338, Duke of Clarence.

Line 95

   28. DEVORGUILLA OF GALLOWAY (94-28), d. 28 Jan. 1289/90; m. 1233, John de Baliol. (*CP* I: 385, II: 374 note c, IV: 671 chart iv; *SP* I: 4; *Scottish Gen.* 21 (1974): 27).

   29. ELEANOR DE BALIOL, m. 1279/83, **SIR JOHN COMYN** (121A-29), "Black Comyn," Lord of Badenoch, d. 1302. (*SP* I: 507-508, IV: 143; *CP* I: 386 note d; *ES* II/91).

   30. JOHN COMYN, Red Comyn, murdered by **ROBERT THE BRUCE** (252-30), (later Robert I of Scotland), 10 Feb. 1306, Church of the Grey Friars, Dumfries, Lord of Badenoch; m. **JOAN DE VALENCE** (154-30), dau. of **SIR WILLIAM DE VALENCE** (154-29) (or de Lusignan), Lord of Valence, titular Earl of Pembroke, son of **HUGH X DE LUSIGNAN** (275-27). (*CP* II: 374 note c; Gardiner 216; *SP* I: 508-509; Rev. C. Moor, *Knights of Edward I* 1: 232; *Scottish Gen.* 21 (1974): 25; *ES* III.4/816).

   31. ELIZABETH COMYN, b. 1 Nov. 1299, d. 20 Nov. 1372; m. betw. 24 July 1326 & 23 Mar. 1326/7, **SIR RICHARD TALBOT** (84A-31), b. abt. 1305, d. 23 Oct. 1356, Lord Talbot. (*CP* XII (1): 613-617; *SP* I: 509).

   32. GILBERT TALBOT, b. abt. 1332, d. 24 Apr. 1387, Lord Talbot, M.P. 1362; m. (1) bef. 8 Sept. 1352 **PETRONILLA (PERNEL) BOTILLER (BUTLER)** (13-31, 73-33), dau. of **JAMES BOTILLER (BUTLER)** (73-32), 1st Earl of Ormond. (*CP*, XII (1): 613-617, X: 116-119, esp. 119 note d).

Line 96   Revised for 8th Edition

   25. ADA DE WARENNE (93-25), m. **HENRY OF HUNTINGDON** (170-23).

   26. MARGARET OF HUNTINGDON, d. 1201; m. (1) 1159/60, **CONAN IV** (119-27), Duke of Brittany, Earl of Richmond, d. 1171. (*CP* IV: 669; *SP* I: 4).

   27. CONSTANCE, Countess of Brittany, b. abt. 1162, d. 4 Sept. 1201; m. (3) 1199, **GUI DE THOUARS** (271-27), d. 1218, Count of Brittany. (Note: *ES* III.4/810 corrects earlier editions; *CP* X: 794-795).

   28. ALIX DE THOUARS (271-28), b. 1201, d. Oct. 1221, Countess of Brittany; m. **PIERRE DE DREUX** (135-29), d. 1250, gr. grandson of **LOUIS VI** (101-24) King of France. (*ES* III.4/810; *CP* X: 796).

26. MARGARET OF HUNTINGDON (96-26); m. (2) 1175, **HUMPHREY IV DE BOHUN** (193-6), d. 1182. (*CP* IV: 669, VI: 457; *SP* I: 4).

27.   HENRY DE BOHUN, 5th Earl of Hereford, b. 1176, sheriff of Kent, 1200 Hereditary Constable of England, Magna Charta Surety, 1215, d. on a Pilgrimage to the Holy Land, 1 June 1220; m. Maud Fitz Geoffrey (de Mandeville), d. 27 Aug 1236, and after Henry's death, Countess of Essex, dau. of Geoffrey Fitz Piers (see also 246B-27), d. 1213, 3rd Earl of Essex, by 1st wife Beatrice de Say, dau. of William de Say. She m. (2) Roger de Daunteseye, d. aft. 1238, div. 1232. (*CP* IV: 669 chart, v: 116-117, 135, 437, VI: 457-459).

28.   HUMPHREY V DE BOHUN, 2nd Earl of Hereford and after div. of his mother 1236, 7th Earl of Essex, Constable of England, sheriff of Kent, b. by 1208, d. 24 Sept. 1275; m. (1) **MAUD D'EU** (or de Lusignan) (123-29), d. 14 Aug. 1241. (*CP* IV: 669, V: 135, VI: 459-462, XII (1): 768-777. See also Maclean, *Deanery of Trigg Minor*).

29.   HUMPHREY VI DE BOHUN, d.v.p. 27 Oct. 1265; m. by 15 Feb. 1247/8 (1) **ELEANOR DE BRAOSE**. (*CP* IV: 669, V: 135, VI: 462-463).

30.   HUMPHREY VII DE BOHUN, b. abt. 1249, d. Pleshey, 31 Dec. 1298, 3rd Earl of Hereford and Essex, Constable of England; m. 1275, **MAHAUD (MAUD) DE FIENNES** (158C-29), dau. of **ENGUERRAND (INGELRAM) II DE FIENNES** (152-28, 158C-28). (*CP* IV: 669, VI: 463-466, XIV: 381).

31.   HUMPHREY VIII DE BOHUN, b. abt. 1276, slain at Boroughbridge, 16 Mar. 1321/2, 4th Earl of Hereford and Essex Lord High Constable of England; m. 14 Nov. 1302, **ELIZABETH OF ENGLAND** (6-29), b. 7 Aug. 1282, d. 5 May 1316, dau. of King **EDWARD I** (1-27). (*CP* V: 135, VI: 467-470).

32.   SIR WILLIAM DE BOHUN, K.G. (15-30), d. 1360, created 1st Earl of Northampton; m. **ELIZABETH DE BADLESMERE** (65-34). (*CP* IV: 669).

33.   HUMPHREY DE BOHUN, K.G., d. 1372, 7th Earl of Hereford, Earl of Essex and Northampton; m. Joan Fitz Alan, dau. of **RICHARD FITZ ALAN** (60-32), 3rd Earl of Arundel, by 2nd wife Eleanor de Lancaster. (*CP* IV: 669, VI: 473-4).

34.   ELEANOR DE BOHUN by (2), d. 1399; m. **THOMAS OF WOODSTOCK** (4-31), Duke of Gloucester, son of **EDWARD III** (1-29) and **PHILIPPA OF HAINAUT** (103-34). (*CP* II: 155, IV: 669. Gens. 31-34: Lucy Freeman Sandler, *Gothic Manuscripts, 1285-1385*, v. 1 (1986): 60).

25.   CONSTANCE, bastard dau. of King **HENRY I** (121-25); m. Roscelin (Raoul), d. aft. 1145, Viscount of Maine. (*CP* XI, App. D: 116).

26.   RICHARD I DE BEAUMONT, d. aft. 1194, hereditary viscount of Maine, Seigneur of Beaumont-le-Vicomte, Fresnay and Ste.-Suzanne; m. bef. 1177, Lucie de l'Aigle (Laigle), d. aft. 1217, dau. of Richard II de l'Aigle, Sire de Egenoul. (*CP* XII (1): 768; *ES* III.4/705, 687).

27.   CONSTANCE DE BEAUMONT, liv. 1226; m. by 1190 **ROGER IV DE TOENI, KNT.** (98A-27), also styled de Conches, b. abt. 1160, adult by 1189, d. prob. Jan, 1209, Lord of Flamstead, co. Hertford, seigneur de Toeny, founded the nunnery of St. Giles in the Wood, near Flamstead, co. Hertford. She brought her husband in free marriage the manor of South Tawton (otherwise Ailrichescot), co. Devon. (*CP* XII (1): 765-769; Sanders, 117-118; The Beauchamp Cartulary Charters 1100-1268, pub. as Vol. 81 (n.s. vol. 43),

Publications of the Pipe Roll Society, pp. xiiii-xivii; Mis. Gen. Her. (5th ser) VII (1929/31): 329; *ES* III.4/705).

28. RALPH VI DE TOENI, b. prob. 1189 or 1190, lord of Flamstead, co. Hertford, Crusader 1239, d. at sea about Michaelmas 1239; m. (1) Nov. 1232/4, Pernel de Lacy, liv. 1288, dau. of Walter de Lacy, d. 1241, Lord of Meath, Ireland, and of Weobley, co. Hereford, by **MARGARET** (or **MARGERY**) **DE BRAOSE** (177A-7), dau. of **WILLIAM DE BRAOSE** (177-6). Pernel had the manors of Britford, co. Wilts, and Yarkhill, co. Hereford, in free marriage. (*CP* XII (1): 769-771; Orpen, *Ireland under the Normans*, III, chart 286-287; Sanders, 117-118; The Beauchamp Cartulary Charters, *op. cit.*; *ES* III.4/706).

29. ROGER V DE TOENI, b. Sept. 1235, lord of Flamstead, co. Hertford, d. bet. 10 June 1263 and 14 May 1264; m. (1) (contract 1239) Alice de Bohun, dau. of **HUMPHREY V DE BOHUN** (97-28), 2nd Earl of Hereford and Essey, by his wife, **MAUD D'EU** (123-29) (Alice had as her maritagium the manors of Newton Toney and East Coulston, co. Wilts); m. (2) after 1255, Isabel, living 1264/5. (Sanders, *op. cit.*; The Beauchamp Cartulary Charters, *op. cit*; See: MC 101A for documentation of correction of *CP* XII (1): 771-772 esp. note *h*; *ES* III.4/706).

30. RALPH VII DE TOENI, by (2), b. 1255, lord of Flamstead, co. Hertford, d. Gascony, bef. 29 July 1295; m. by 1276 Mary, living 1283, prob. a Scotswoman. (*CP* XII (1): 773; Sanders, *op. cit*; The Beauchamp Cartulary Charters, *op. cit.*; *ES* III.4/706).

31. ALICE DE TOENI, b. abt. 1283, sh. bef. 8 Jan., d. Jan. 1324/5; m. (1) Thomas de Leyburn (d.s.p.m. & d.v.p. bef. 30 May 1307); m. (2) bef. 28 Feb. 1309/10, **GUY DE BEAUCHAMP** (86-30), 10th Earl of Warwick; m. (3) as 1st wife, bef. 25 Feb. 1316/7, Sir William la Zouche (formerly de Mortimer), yr. son of Robert de Mortimer (d. 7 Apr. 1287) of Richard's Castle, co. Hereford, by Joyce La Zouche, bur. 13 Mar. 1289/90, dau. & h. William La Zouche, d. by 3 Feb. 1271/2, of King's Nympton, co. Devon, yr. son of **ROGER LA ZOUCHE** (39-28) of Ashby. (*CP* XII (1): 774 note *i*; *ES* III.4/706).

32. JOYCE LA ZOUCHE (DE MORTIMER), by (3), liv. 4 May 1372; m. (1) 31 May 1347, as 2nd wife, **JOHN DE BOTETOURTE** (216-31), Lord Botetourte of Weobley Castle, b. 1318, d. 1386, M.P. 1342-1385. (*CP* II: 234-235, XII (2): 962-963).

33. JOYCE DE BOTETOURTE (216-32), b. 1367/8, d. 13 Aug. 1420; m. (1) as 2nd wife, **SIR BALDWIN III FREVILLE** (230A-33), of Tamworth Castle, co. Warwick, b. 1350/1, d. 30 Dec 1387; m. (2) 1388, Sir Adam de Peshall, d.s.p.m. 1419, son of Adam de Peshale and Joan de Eyton. (Inq.p.m. Sir Adam Peshale, 20 Dec. 1419, mentions wife Joyce, and dau. Margaret, wife of Richard Mytton (Mitton); *Wm. Salt Soc.* XV: 312; *Mis. Gen. Her.* n.s. III: 273; *History and Genealogy of the Pearsall Family in England and America* II 572; *Gen. Mag.* 21: 187-188).

34. MARGARET DE PESHALE, d. 5 Aug. 1420; m. Sir Richard Mytton (Mitton), Knt., d. bef. 26 Oct. 1419. (*Wm. Salt Soc.* I: 367; *CP* XIV: 102; *Visit. of Shropshire*, 360).

35. WILLIAM MYTTON, ESQ., liv. 1485; m. Margaret Corbet, dau. of Thomas Corbet of Lee. (*Wm. Salt Soc.* I: 367; *Visit of Shropshire*, 360).

36. JOHN MYTTON, ESQ., of Weston under Lizard, d. Feb. 1500; m. (1) Anne Swinnerton, dau. of Thomas Swinnerton, co. Stafford; m. (2) Joan Middlemoore. (*Visit. of Warwickshire*, Harleian Soc. XII: 237-238).

37. JOHN MITTON (MYTTON), sheriff of Staffordshire; m. **CONSTANCE BEAUMONT** (17-36), b. abt. 1467.

Note: Descent through this line to Alice Tomes (Gens. 37-41 in previous editions) is still unproven and has been omitted.

Line 98A

23. JUDITH OF LENS (130-25), niece of William the Conqueror, liv. 1086; m. 1070 Waltheof II, beheaded Winchester, 31 May 1076, Earl of Huntingdon, Northampton and Northumberland, son of Sigurd, Earl of Northumberland, by his wife, Aelfled, daughter of Aldred of Bernicia. (*CP* VI: 638-640).

24. ALICE OF NORTHUMBERLAND, dau. and coh., d. aft. 1126; m. 1103, Ralph IV de Toeni, also styled de Conches, adult by 1102, d. abt. 1126, buried Conches, France, lord of Flamstead, co. Hertford, son of Ralph III de Toeni (de Conches) by his wife, Isabel (or Elizabeth) de Montfort, dau. of Simon de Montfort, Seigneur of Montfort l'Amaury (France). (*CP* XII (1): 760-762, VII: 710 notes *e*, *h*; *The Beauchamp Cartulary Charters 1100-1268*, pub. as Vol. 81 (n.s. vol. 43), *Publications of the Pipe Roll Society*, pp. xliii-xlvii).

25. ROGER III DE TOENI, also styled **DE CONCHES**, b. abt. 1104, d. aft. 29 Sept. 1158, lord of Flamstead, co. Hertford; m. abt. 9 Aug. 1138, Ida of Hainaut, dau. of **BALDWIN III** (163-25), Count of Hainaut, by his wife, Yolande of Geldern. With Ida, Roger had in marriage from King Henry I, 20 librates of land out of the royal demesne at East Bergholt, Suffolk. (*CP* XII (1): 762-764; Sanders, 117-118; *The Beauchamp Cartulary Charters, op. cit.; ES* III.4/705).

26. RALPH V DE TOENI, also styled **DE CONCHES**, d. 1162, lord of Flamstead, co. Hertford; m. Margaret de Beaumont, liv. 1185, dau. of **SIR ROBERT DE BEAUMONT** (53-25), 2nd Earl of Leicester, by his wife, Amice de Montfort. (*CP* XII (1): 764-765; Sanders, *op. cit.; The Beauchamp Cartulary Charters, op. cit.*).

27. ROGER IV DE TOENI, also styled **DE CONCHES**, b. abt. 1160, d. prob. Jan. 1209, lord of Flamstead; m. by 1190 **CONSTANCE DE BEAUMONT** (98-27).

Line 99

29. CECILY DE BALIOL (94-29); m. Sir John de Burgh, of Walkern, co. Hertford, & Wakerley, co. Northampton. (*CP* V: 474, VI: 107 (d); Sanders, 92).

30. HAWISE DE BURGH, b. 1256, d. aft. 1282; m. Sir Robert de Grelle, of Manchester, b. 1252, d. 15 Feb. 1282, s. & h. of Robert de Grelle, d. 1261, s. & h. of Thomas de Grelle, s. & h. of Sir Robert de Grelle, b. 1174, d. 1230, with the Barons at Runnemede. (*CP* IV 142-143, VI 107 (d), VII: 450-458, chart 452-453; Baines, *History of Lancashire*, I: 274-275; *VCH Lanc.* I: 326+).

31. JOAN DE GRELLE, d. 20 or 21 Mar. 1352/3, eventual h. of Thomas Grelle, 1st Lord Grelle, lord of Manchester; m. soon aft. 19 Nov. 1294, **JOHN LA WARRE** (255A-32), 2nd Baron la Warre, d. 9 May 1347, famous soldier in Flanders 1297, Scotland 1298-1327, at Sluys 1340 and Crecy 25 Aug. 1346, son of Sir Roger la Warre and **CLARICE DE TREGOZ** (255A-31), dau. of **SIR JOHN DE TREGOZ** (255A-30) of Eywas Harold, co. Hereford, and Mabel Fitz Warin. (*CP* IV: 141-143, VII: 453-454, chart 452-453, XIV: 425; Baines, *op. cit.* I: 277).

32. CATHARINE LA WARRE, d. 9 Aug. 1361, wid. of Robert de Brewes, son of Giles de Brewes; m. (2) 1328, Sir Warin Latimer, Lord Latimer, b. abt. 1300, d. 13 Aug. 1349, son of Thomas le Latimer, Lord Latimer, and Lora de Hastings, d. abt. 2 July 1339, dau. of **HENRY DE HASTINGS** (93A-28), d. 1269, by 1st wife Joan de Cantelou. (*CP* VII: 451-454 esp 453 note *p*, chart 452-453).

33. ELIZABETH LATIMER m. Thomas Griffin, through whom the title of Lord Latimer descended. (*CP* VII: 453 chart, 456-457).

34. RICHARD GRIFFIN, d. by 1411; m. Anne Chamberlain, dau. of Richard Chamberlain. (*CP* VII: 453 chart, 456-457).

35. NICHOLAS GRIFFIN, d. 1436; m. Margaret Pilkington, dau. of Sir John Pilkington; she m. (2) Sir Thomas Saville. (*CP* VII: 457).

36. NICHOLAS GRIFFIN, Lord Latimer, b. Brixworth, 5 June 1426, d. 6 June 1482, sheriff of Northamptonshire 1473; m. (1) Catherine Curzon, dau. of Richard Curzon. (*CP* VII: 457-458, chart 452-453).

37. CATHERINE GRIFFIN, m. as 3rd wife Sir John Digby, of Eye Kettleby, co. Leicester, knighted at Bosworth Field, d. abt. 1533 (will made 1 Aug. 1529, codicil 19 May 1533), son of Everard Digby, Esq., sheriff of Rutlandshire, 1485, 1486, 1499, M.P., (will made 17 Jan. 1508-9, pro. 12 Feb. 1508/9) and Jacquette Ellis, dau. of Sir John Ellis. (*Visit. of Warwick* (1619), 167; *Harleian Soc. XII*: 167; *Visit. of Leicestershire, Harl. Soc.* II: 40; Nichol, *Hist. of Antiq. of Leicestershire* II: 51, 201).

38. WILLIAM DIGBY of Kettleby and Luffenham, co. Leicester, Esq., liv. 1558; m. (1) Rose Prestwich, dau. of William Prestwich of Lubenham and his wife, dau. of Sir Thomas Poultney. (Nichol, *op. cit.*).

39. SIMON DIGBY, executed Mar. 1570, of Bedale, co. York; m. Anne Grey, dau. and h. of Reginald Grey of York, attainted 1569, executed 28 Mar. 1570. (Nichol, *cit.*; Stow, *Annals*).

40. EVERARD DIGBY, m. Katherine, dau. of Stockbridge de Vanderschaff Theuber de Newkirk. (Nichol, *cit.*; *The Diaries of Benjamin Lynde and of Benjamin Lynde, Jr.* (Boston, 1880), cf. Intro., iii-viii, and Pedigree of Lynde in the Appendix).

41. ELIZABETH DIGBY, b. abt. 1584, d. London, 1669; m. Hackney, 25 Oct. 1614, Enoch Lynde, shipping merchant, Netherlands, d. London, 23 Apr. 1636, will pro. 7 Oct. 1636, wid. Elizabeth executrix. (Nichol, *cit.*; Digby pedigree, Sherborne Castle).

42. HON. SIMON LYNDE, bapt. London, June 1624, d. Boston, 22 Nov. 1687; m. Boston, 22 Feb. 1652/3, Hannah Newgate. (Bible, Geneva version, 1597, of Simon Lynde of Boston, "given to Enoch Lynde (of London), the son of Nathan, by his grandmother Elizabeth." Salisbury's *Family Histories*, referred to in previous editions for Gens. 37-41, is not reliable.)

Line 100

25. ADA DE WARENNE (93-25); m. **HENRY (OF SCOTLAND)** (170-23), 4th Earl of Huntingdon.

26. ADA OF HUNTINGDON, m. 1162, **FLORENT III** (100A-26), Count of Holland, d. 1190. (*SP* VII: 231).

27. WILLIAM I, Count of Holland and Zealand, d. 4 Feb. 1223/4; m. Adelaide, d. 1218, dau. of Otto I, Count of Geldern and Zutphen, d. 1207. (*CP* VII: 642).

28. FLORENT IV, Count of Holland, d. 1245; m. bef. Dec. 1224, Mechtild of Brabant, dau. of **HENRY I** (155-26), Duke of Brabant, by Mathilde of Boulogne, dau. of Matthew of Alsace, Count of Boulogne.

29. ADELAIDE OF HOLLAND, d. abt. 1284; m. **JOHN I D'AVESNES** (168-30), d. 1256, Count of Hainaut and Holland.

Line 100A New to 8th Edition

18. DIETRICH I, Count in Kinnemerland, liv. 916-928; m. Geva.

19. DIETRICH II, Count of Westfriesland and Holland, d. 988; m. Hildegard of Flanders, d. 990, dau. of Arnulf I, Count of Flanders by (1) NN. (West-Winter. VII.95).

20. ARNULF, Count of Westfriesland and Holland, d. in battle 993; m. 980, Liutgard, of Luxembourg, d. aft. 1005, dau. of **SIEGFRIED OF LUXEMBOURG** (143-19), d. 998.

21. DIETRICH III, of Holland, d. 27 May 1039; m. Othelendis of Nordmark, d. 1044, pos. dau. of Bernard I Margrave of Nordmark.

22. FLORENT I, Count of Holland, murdered 28 June 1061; m. abt. 1050, as 1st husb., Gertrude of Saxony, d. 4 Aug. 1113, dau. of Bernard II (see 101-23), Duke of Saxony, d. 1059 and Elica (Eilika), dau. of Henrich of Schweinfurt, Margrave in the Nordgau. Gertrude m. 2nd Robert I, Count of Flanders.

23. DIETRICH V, Count of Holland, d. 17 June 1091; m. 1083, Othehilde. (West-Winter, XI.312).

24. FLORENT II, Count of Holland, d. 2 Mar. 1121; m. 1113, Gertrude of Upper Lorraine, d. 23 May 1144, dau. of Dietrich (Thierry) II (see 164-24), Duke of Lorraine, d. 1115. (West-Winter, XII.510).

25. DIETRICH VI, of Holland, d. 5 Aug. 1157; m. bef. 1137, **SOPHIE VON SALM** (100B-26), heiress of Bentheim, d. 1176. (*ES* IV/92, XVIII/56; West-Winter, XIII.799).

26. FLORENT III, Count of Holland, d. Tyre, 1 Aug. 1190; m. **ADA OF HUNTINGTON** (100-26). (*SP* 7: 231. Gens. 18-26: *ES* II/2).

Line 100B New to 8th Edition

20. WIGERIC, Count in the Ardennes (Bidgau), liv. 899-916, d. bef. 919; m. 907/9, Cunigonde, d. aft. 923, granddau. of King **LOUIS II** "the Stammerer" of France (143-16, 148-16). *ES* I.2/203; West Winter, VI.51).

21. SIEGFRIED OF LUXEMBOURG (143-19), Count of Luxembourg, d. abt. 28 Oct. 998; m. Hedwig, d. 13 Dec. abt. 1053, perh. had (ES I.2/202-203, VI/127-128; West Winter VII.111).

22. FREDERICK I OF LUXEMBOURG (143-20), Count of Luxembourg, count in the Mosel area, Admin. of Stable, b. abt. 965, d. 6 Oct. 1019; m. abt. 985, Ermentrude of Gleiberg, d. aft. 985, dau. of Heribert, Count in Gleiberg, count in the Kinziggau, Count Palatine, d. 992 by Ermentrud (Imizi), dau. of Megingoz, count in Avalgau, by Gerberga of Alsace. (West Winter VIII.141, VIII.150; *ES* I.1/8, VI/127-128)

23. GISELBERT, (see 168A-27) Count of Salm-en-Ardennes and Count of Luxembourg, d. 14 Aug. 1056/1059; m. NN.

24. HERMAN I, of Luxembourg, Count of Salm, German King, d. Metz, 28 Sept. 1088; m. Sophie, d. 1056/1059. (*ES* IV/92, VI/128, I.2/203).

25. OTTO VON SALM, Count Palatine of the Rhein, Count of Bentheim, and Rheineck, d. 1150-1165; m. abt. 1115, as 2nd husb., Gertrude von Northeim, h. of Friesland, d. bef. 1165, dau. of Heinrich (the Fat) Count of Northeim. (*ES* IV/92; West-Winter XIII.193).

26. SOPHIE VON SALM, heiress of the county of Bentheim, d. 26 Feb. 1176; m. bef. 1137, **DIETRICH VI** (100A-25) of Holland, d. 5 Aug. 1157. (*ES* IV/92, XVIII/56; West-Winter, XIII.799).

18. ROBERT I (48-18), Duke of France, chosen king 922, d. 15 June 923; m. (2) Beatrix of Vermandois, dau. of **HERBERT I** (50-17), Count of Vermandois.

19. HUGH MAGNUS, d. June 956, Count of Paris; m. (3) **HEDWIG** (141-19), dau. of **HENRY I, THE FOWLER** (141-18), King of the Saxons.

20. HUGH CAPET, b. aft. 939, d. 24 Oct. 996, Count of Paris 956-996, King of France 987-996, first of the Capetian kings of France; m. **ADELAIDE OF POITOU** (144A-20).

21. ROBERT II, "the Pious," King of France, 996-1031, b. Orléans, 985, d. Meulan, 20 July 1031; m. (1) bef. April 988, **ROSELA** (or **SUSANNA**) (146-19) of Ivrea, as (2) husb., repudiated 992; m. (2) 995, **BERTHA OF BURGUNDY** (159-20), repudiated 998, d. 1001, wid. of **EUDES I** (136-20), Count of Blois, dau. of Conrad I, King of Burgundy and King of the West Franks and **MATHILDA OF FRANCE** (157-19, 133-19); m. (3) 1001/2, **CONSTANCE OF PROVENCE** (141A-21), d. 25 July 1032, dau. of **WILLIAM II** (141A-20), Count of Arles and Provence by Adelaide of Anjou, dau. of Fulk II, Count of Anjou. (*ES* II/11).

22. HENRY I, by (3), King of France 1031-1060, b. 1006, d. 4 Aug. 1060; m. (3) 20 Jan. 1051, **ANNE OF KIEV** (241-6), d. aft. 1075.

23. PHILIP I, King of France 1060-1108, Count of Paris, b. 1053, d. Meulan 29 July 1108, bur. Abbaye St-Benoit-sur-Loire; m. (1) 1072, Bertha of Holland, b. abt. 1055, d. Montreuil-sur-Mer early 1094, dau. of **FLORENT I** (100A-22), Count of Holland, d. 1061, by his wife, Gertrude, d. 1113, dau. of Bernard II, Duke in Saxony, d. 1059,. (*ES* II/11).

24. LOUIS VI, "the Fat," King of France 1108-1137, Crusader, b. 1081, d. Chiteau Bethizy, Paris, 1 Aug. 1137; m. (2) Paris, abt. 1115, **ADELAIDE** (274A-25) of Savoy, b. abt. 1092, d. 18 Nov. 1154, dau. of **HUMBERT II** (274A-24), d. 1103, Count of Maurienne, Savoy and Turin, by Gisele, of Burgundy d. 1133, dau. of **WILLLAM I** (132-24), d. 1087, Count Palatine of Burgundy, by his wife, Stephanie. (*Ibid*).

25. LOUIS VII, "the Young," King of France 25 Dec. 1137-1180, b. 1120, d. Paris 18 Sept. 1180, bur. Notre-Dame-de-Barbeau, Fontainebleau; m. (1) Bordeaux 22/25 July 1137, **ELEANOR OF AQUITAINE** (110-26), divorced 1152, d. 1204 (she m. (2) **HENRY II** (1-24) of England); m. (2) Orleans 1153/4, Constance of Castile, b. abt. 1140, d. 4 Oct. 1160, bur. St. Denis, dau. of **ALFONSO VII** (113-25), King of Castile and Leon; m. (3) 18 Oct. 1160, **ALIX OF CHAMPAGNE** (137-25), b. abt. 1140, d. Paris 24 June 1206, bur. Abbaye de Potigny. (*Ibid*)

26. PHILIP II Augustus, by (3), King of France 1180-1223, Count of Artois, Crusader, b. Gonesse 22 Aug. 1165, d. Mantes 14 July 1223, bur. St. Denis; m. (1) Bapaume, 28 Apr. 1180, **ISABELLA OF HAINAUT** (163-28), b. Valenciennes Apr. 1170, d. Paris 15 Mar. 1190, bur. Notre-Dame, Countess of Artois. (*Ibid*).

27. LOUIS VIII, "the Lion," King of France 1223-1226, b. 3 Sept. 1187, d. Montpensier, Auvergne, 8 Nov. 1226; m. 23 May 1200, **BLANCHE OF CASTILE** (113-28), d. 1253. (*ES* II/12, 62).

28. LOUIS IX, "Saint Louis," King of France 1226-1270, Crusader, b. Poissy, 25 Apr. 1215, d. in battle, near Tunis, 25 Aug. 1270; m. Marguerite of Provence, b. 1221, d. Paris Dec. 1285, dau. of **RAYMOND V BERENGER** (111-29), Count of Provence. (See Joinville, *Chronicle of the Crusade of St. Louis*, for an account of his life).

29. PHILIP III, "the Bold," King of France 1270-1285, b. 1245, d. Perpignan, 5 Oct. 1285; m. (1) (with Papal Disp.) 28 May1262, **ISABELLA OF ARAGON** (105-30), b. 1247, d. 1271; m. (2) 21 Aug. 1274, **MARIE OF BRABANT** (155-29), d. 1321.

30. **PHILIP IV,** "the Fair," by (1), King of France 1285-1314, b. Fontainebleau, 1268, d. 29 Nov. 1314; m. Paris 1284, **JEANNE OF NAVARRE** (45-31), b. 1272, d. 1305, dau. of Henry III (I), King of Navarre.

31. **ISABELLA OF FRANCE,** b. 1292, d. 27 Aug. 1357; m. Boulogne, 28 Jan. 1308, **EDWARD II** (1-28), d. 21 Sept. 1327, King of England. (Generations 13-31: Moriarty, *The Plantagenet Ancestry*; Turton; G.P. Fisher, *Outline of Universal History* (1885), p. 287; Thatcher 320, 323; Gardiner xxxi. Gens. 27-31: *ES* II/12).

Line 102

25. **LOUIS VII** (101-25), King of France; m. (1) **ELEANOR OF AQUITAINE** (110-26). (*CCN* 112).

26. **MARIE OF FRANCE,** b. 1145, d. 11 Mar. 1198; m. 1164 Henry, Count of Blois, and Champagne, d. Troyes, 17 Mar. 1181, son of **THEOBALD IV** (137-24), d. 1152. (*ES* II/11, II/46-47).

27. **MARIE OF CHAMPAGNE,** d. 9 Aug. 1204; m. 6 Jan. 1186, **BALDWIN VI** (168-28), d. 11 June 1215, Count of Hainaut and Flanders, a leader of the Fourth Crusade.

Line 103

23. **PHILIP I** (101-23), King of France; m. Bertha, dau. of Count **FLORENT I** (100A-22) Count of Holland.

24. **CONSTANCE OF FRANCE,** b. abt. 1078, d. 1124/26; m. (2) 1106, Bohémond I, b. abt. 1052, d. Canossa, Italy, 8 Mar. 1111, Prince of Antioch, son of Robert Guiscard, a leader of the First Crusade, captured Antioch, d. 17 July 1098. (*ES* II/11, 205; *CCN* 166).

25. **BOHÉMOND II,** Prince of Antioch, b. 1107/8, killed in battle Feb. 1130; m. 1126, **ALIX** (103A-26), of Rethel, dau. of **BALDWIN II** (103A-25), Count of Rethel, King of Jerusalem, d. 21 Aug. 1131. (*ES* II/205; *CCN* 112).

26. **CONSTANCE OF ANTIOCH,** m. (2) abt. 1152/3, Renaud de Châtillon-sur-Loing, *j.u.* Prince of Antioch, d. 1137, son of Geoffroy de Châtillon. (*ES* III/154, II/205).

27. **AGNES** (or **ANNA**) **DE CHÂTILLON,** b. 1154, d. 1184; m. 1172, as 2nd wife, **BÉLA III** (242-10), King of Hungary, b. 1148/1151, d. 23 Apr. 1196, son of Geza II, and a descendant of **HAROLD II** (1B-23), King of England. (*ES* II/154).

28. **ANDREW II,** King of Hungary 1205-1235, b. 1176, d. 21 Sept. 1235, father of St. Elizabeth of Hungary; m. (1) abt. 1203, Gertrude of Meran, d. 1213, dau. of Berthold VI, Duke of Meran. (*ES* II/155).

29. **BÉLA IV,** King of Hungary 1235-1270, b. 1206, d. 3 May. 1270; m. 1218, Maria Lascaris, dau. of Theodore I (Comnenus) Lascaris, d. 1222, by Anna Angelus, the dau. of Alexius III Angelus, and the gr.-gr.-grandau. of **ALEXIUS I COMNENUS** (105A-26) (Gen. Mag. 20 (1980): 85-91 esp. chart p. 89; *ES* II/155; *CCN* 139).

30. **STEPHEN V,** King of Hungary 1270-1272, b. 1239, d. 1 Aug. 1272; m. 1253, Elizabeth of the Cumans, d. abt. 1290, dau. of Kuthen (Zahan), Prince of the Cumans. (*ES* II/155; Otto Forst de Battaglia, *Wissenschaftliche Genealogie*, Tafel II).

31. **MARIE OF HUNGARY,** b. abt. 1257/8, d. Sicily, Mar. 1323; m. 1270 as 2nd wife, **CHARLES II** (104-29), King of Naples, d. abt. 6 May 1309.(*ES* II/155, 15).

32. **MARGARET OF NAPLES,** d. 31 Dec. 1299, Countess of Anjou; m. Corbeil, 16 Aug. 1290, Charles of France, Count of Valois, d. 16 Dec 1325, youngest son of **PHILIP III** (101-29), King of France, and **ISABELLA OF ARAGON** (105-30). (*ES* II/15).

33. JEANNE OF VALOIS, d. 7 Mar. 1342; m. abt. 1305, **WILLLAM III** (168-32), Count of Hainaut and Holland, d. 1337. (*ES* II/4).

34. PHILIPPA OF HAINAUT, b. 24 June 1311, d. Windsor, 15 Aug. 1369; m. 24 Jan. 1327/8, **EDWARD III** (1-29). (*The Genealogist* 1 (1980): 138; *ES* II/4. Gens. 23-34: v. Redlich, 267-268; *TAG* 9: 15; Vambery, *The Story of Hungary* (1894), 120-147).

Line 103A

23. MANASSES III, Count of Rethel 1048, d. 1056; m. Yvette de Roucy, dau. of **GISELBERT** (151-20), Count of Roucy.

24. HUGH I, Count of Rethel 1086, d. 1118; m. Mélisende de Montlhéry, dau. of Guy I de Montlhéry, d. 1095, seigneur of Montlhéry and Bray, by his wife, Hodierne de Gometz. (*ES* III.4/624-625).

25. BALDWIN II, Count of Rethel, b. abt. 1058, d. 21 Aug. 1131, on First Crusade 1098, Count of Edessa 1110, King of Jerusalem 1118; m. Morfia (Malfia), dau. of Gabriel, d. 1103, Armenian gov. of Melitene on the upper Euphrates. Baldwin's dau. Melisende, m. as 2nd wife, **FULK V** (118-24), Count of Anjou, King of Jerusalem, through which marriage the royal line continued. Baldwin's second dau., Alix, through her Antioch marriage, became ancestress to many of the noble families of Outremer. (See Stephen Runciman's *History of the Crusades*, which is in error regarding the parentage of Hugh, Count of Rethel).

26. ALIX, of Rethel, d. aft. 1136; m.1126, **BOHÉMOND II** (103-25), b. 1107, Prince of Antioch. (Moriarty, *The Plantagenet Ancestry*; *Speculum* 17 (1942): table bet. 100-101).

Line 104

27. LOUIS VIII (101-27), King of France; m. **BLANCHE OF CASTILE** (113-28).

28. CHARLES I, Count of Anjou, King of Naples and Sicily, b. 1220, d. 1285; m. Beatrix of Provence, dau. of **RAYMOND V BERENGER** (111-29) and **BEATRIX OF SAVOY** (274C-28, 133-27). (*CCN* 237).

29. CHARLES II, King of Naples, d. abt. 6 May 1309; m. **MARIE OF HUNGARY** (103-31). (*ES* II/5, 155. Gens. 27-29: Thatcher, 323).

Line 105

28. ANDREW II (103-28), King of Hungary; m. (2) **YOLANDE DE COURTENAY** (163A-29), d. 1233, dau. of **PETER DE COURTENAY** (107-27). (Moriarty, *The Plantagenet Ancestry*; *ES* II/155).

29. YOLANDE OF HUNGARY, d. 12 Oct. 1251; m. Barcelona 1235, **JAMES I** (105A-29), King of Aragon, b. 1208, d.25 July 1276, son of Pedro II, King of Aragon. (*ES* II/70)

30. ISABELLA OF ARAGON, b. 1243, d. 1271; m.1262, as 1st wife, **PHILIP III** (101-29), King of France. (*ES* II/12, Isenburg II/45)

Line 105A   Revised for 8th Edition

    21. MANUEL COMNENUS, b. abt. 955, d. 1025; m. (1) NN. (*ES* II/174).

    22. JOHN I COMNENUS, d. 12 July 1056; m. 1042, Anne Dalassene, dau. of Alexius Charon Präfect in Italy and NN Dalassene. (*ES* II/174).

    23. ALEXIUS I COMNENUS, Byzantine Emperor, b. abt. 1048, d. 15 Aug. 1118; m. (2) 1077/8, Irene Ducas, b. abt. 1066, d. 19 Feb. 1133, dau. of Protovestiary Andronicus Ducas by Mary, dau. of Khan or Tzar Trajan, of the West Bulgars. (*ES* II/168, 175; Sturdza, 293).

    24. JOHN II COMNENUS, Byzantine Emperor, b. 13 Sept. 1087, d. Cilicia 8 Apr. 1143; m. 1104/5, **PRISCA (IRENE)** (244A-8) of Hungary, b. abt. 1088, d. Bethinia 13 Aug. 1134. (*ES* II/175, 177).

    25. ANDRONICUS COMNENUS, b. 1108, d. 24 Sept. 1142; m. 1124 Irene, d. 1151. (*ES* II/177).

    26. ALEXIUS COMNENUS, b. abt. 1136, murdered 1183; m. Maria Dukas. (*ES* II/177).

    27. EUDOXIA COMNENUS, b. abt. 1167, div. 1187, d. a nun 1202; m. abt. 1178/9 as 1st wife, William VIII, Seigneur de Montpellier, b. abt. 1158, d. at Rome 1218 (will dtd. Nov. 1202), bur. St. Peters, son of William VII, b. abt. 1130, d. 1172 (will dtd. 20 Sept. 1172), Seigneur of Montpellier, by Matilda (m. 25 Feb. 1159), b. abt. 1130, d. 29 Sept. 1172, dau. of Hugh II, Duke of Burgundy, b. abt. 1085, d. 1143, and Mathilda of Mayenne, d. aft. 1162. Hugh II was son of **EUDES I** (108-24), Duke of Burgundy, by his wife, Matilda of Burgundy. (*ES* II/177). (Gens. 21-27: Mihail D. Sturdza, *Grandes Familles de Grèce* (1983): charts pp 274-276).

    28. MARIA, Dame of Montpellier, b. 1182, d. Rome 1218, bur. St. Peters; m. (3) 15 June 1204, Pedro II, King of Aragon, Count of Barcelona and Gevandur, b. 1176, killed in Battle of Muret fighting for the Albigensians 14 Sept. 1213, son of **ALFONSO II** (111-27), King of Aragon, by his wife, **SANCHA OF CASTILE** (116-26). (*ES* III.3/446, II/70).

    29. JAMES I, King of Aragon 1213, b. Montpellier. 1 Feb. 1207, d. Valencia 27 July 1276; m. (2) 8 Sept. 1235, **YOLANDE** (105-29), d. 12 Oct. 1251, dau. of **ANDREW II** (103-28), King of Hungary, b. abt. 1216, d. 1251. (*ES* II/70).

Line 106

    20. HUGH CAPET (101-20), King of France, d. 24 Oct. 996; m. **ADELAIDE OF POITOU** (144A-20). (*ES* II/11; *NEHGR* 109: 179-182; Moriarty, *The Plantagenet Ancestry*).

    21. HEDWIG, of France, b. abt. 969, d. 1013; m. 996, Regnier IV, b. abt. 950, d. 1013, Count of Hainaut, son of **REGNIER III** (155-19), Count of Hainaut, b. abt. 928, d. 973. (*ES* I.2/236; Moriarty, *cit.*).

    22. REGNIER V, d. aft. 1039, Count of Hainaut 1013; m. abt. 1015, Mathilde of Verdun, d. abt. 1039, dau. of Herman von Enham, Count in Eifelgau, d. 1029, Count in Westphalia, son of Gottfried, Count of Verdun and Mathilde of Saxony, wid. of **BALDWIN III** (162-19), Count of Flanders, dau. of Herman Billung, Duke of Saxony. (*ES* VI/127, I.2/202, VIII/98A, I.1/11; West Winter IX.146, X.254).

    22. BEATRIX OF HAINAUT, (sis. of Régnier V); m. **EBLES I** (151-21), Count of Rheims and Roucy, Archbishop of Rheims. (*ES* I.2/236; Seversmith, 2,555, 2,544; *Boston Evening Transcript*, Feb. 1928, Note 2257, Part XV Brabant; Moriarty, *cit.*; *ES* I.2/236).

19. **HUGH CAPET** (101-20) King of France, d. 24 Oct. 996; m. **ADELAIDE OF POITOU** (144A-20).

20. **ROBERT II,** (101-21), "the Pious," King of France; m. (3) 1001/2 **CONSTANCE OF PROVENCE** (141A-21).

21. **ADÈLE OF FRANCE,** Countess of Auxerre, b. abt. 1003, d. abt. 1063; m. about 1015, Renaud I, Count of Nevers 1000-1040, d. 29 May 1040. (*ES* II/11, III.4/716).

22. **WILLIAM I,** Count of Nevers, b. abt. 1030, d. 20 Jun 1100; m. 1045, Ermengarde, dau. & h. of Renaud, Count of Tonnerre.

23. **RENAUD II,** Count of Nevers and Auxerre, d. 5 Aug. 1089; m. (1) Ida, dau. of Artald (II) III, Count of Lyon and Forez. (*ES* III.4/716, 737)

24. **ERMENGARDE DE NEVERS,** m. abt. 1095 Milo (or Miles), Sire de Courtenay, b. abt. 1075 or bef., d. 1127, son of Jocelin de Courtenay, 1065, and Isabel de Montlhéry, dau. of Guy de Montlhéry.

25. **RENAUD DE COURTENAY,** Sire de Courtenay, d. 1189/90; m. Helvis, a sister of Frederick (or Guy) du Donjon and Corbeil. (*ES* III.4/629; Seversmith 2,421).

26. **ELIZABETH DE COURTENAY,** heiress of Courtenay, liv. 1205; m. abt. 1150, **PETER OF FRANCE** (117-25), b. abt. 1121, d. 1179-10 Apr. 1183, Count of Montargis & Courtenay, *j.u.*

27. **PETER DE COURTENAY,** Count of Courtenay, Marquis of Namur, Emperor of Constantinople, b. abt. 1155, d. Epirus, bef. Jan. 1218; m. betw. 24 June & 1 July 1193 **YOLANDE OF FLANDERS** (163A-28), Countess and h. of Namur, b. abt. 1175, d. Constantinople Aug. 1219. (Gens. 21-26: Moriarty, *The Plantagenet Ancestry*, 63-64 (which, however, identifies Renaud de Courtenay (Gen. 25) as the Reginald de Courtenay (see 138-24) of the English manor of Sutton, Berks; *ES* III.4/629, II/17).

21. **ROBERT II** (101-21), King of France; m. (3) 998, **CONSTANCE OF PROVENCE** (141A-21).

22. **ROBERT THE OLD,** Duke of Burgundy, b. abt. 1011, d. 21 Mar. 1076; m. (1) abt. 1033, Hélie (Eleanor), b. 1016, repudiated 1046, d. a nun, 22 Apr. aft. 1055, dau. of Dalmas I Sire of Semur-en-Brionnais, by his wife Aremburge, dau. of Henry I Count of Nevers, Duke of Lower Burgundy by 3rd wife Mathilda de Châlon, dau. of Count Lambert of Châlon; m. (2) abt. 1048, **ERMENGARDE OF ANJOU** (118-22); m. (3) Hildegarde of Metz. (*ES* II/11, II/20, III.3/433-4, III.1/116; Saillot, *Sang de Charlemagne* 43, 71; Annales de Bourgogne, vol. 32, pp. 34, 158-161, 167).

23. **HENRY,** by (1), of Burgundy, d.v.p. 27 Jan 1066/1074; m. Sibylle of Barcelona, d. 6 July aft. 1074, dau. of Berenger Ramon I [not Raymond Berenger], d. 26 May 1035 (son of Ramon Borrell I, Count of Barcelona, d. 1018), by (2) Gisla (Gisela) de Lluca, dau. of Sunifredo II, Signeur de Lluca and Vilanova and Ermegende de Balsareny. (*ES* II/20, 69; see also, de Vajay, *Annales de Bourgogne*, vol. 32 (1960), pp. 158-161).

24. **EUDES I,** Duke of Burgundy, d. Cilicia, 23 Mar. 1102/3; m. 1080, Sibylle (aka Matilda) of Burgundy-Ivrea, d. aft. 1103, dau. of **WILLLAM I** (132-24), d. 1087, Count of Burgundy, by his wife, Stephanie de Longwy. (*CP* XI 697, XII (1) 497; *ES* II/20. 59; West Winter XII.282).

25. **HÉLIE (ELA, ALIX) OF BURGUNDY,** b. 1080, d. 28 Feb. 1142, m. (1) 1095, Bertrand, Count of Toulouse, d. 1112; m. (2) abt. 1115, William I (III) Talvas, Count of

Alençon & Ponthieu, d. 30 June 1171, son of Robert II de Bellême, 3rd Earl of Shrewsbury, Seigneur of Bellême, Domfront and Alençon, bapt. Sées 1056, d. 8 May, aft. 1130, by his wife, Agnes, liv. 1100, dau. of Guy I, d. 1100, Count of Ponthieu and Montreuil. (*CP* XI: 689, 696-697, XII(1): 497; *ES* II/20, III.4/635, 638; Anselme III: 289-292, 299).

    26. ELA (TALVAS), of Alençon and Ponthieu, d. 10 Oct. 1174; m. (1) **WILLIAM DE WARENNE** (83-25), 3rd Earl of Surrey, b. 1118, d. 1148; m. (2) in or bef. 1152 Patrick of Salisbury, 1st Earl of Salisbury, slain Poitou, abt. 7 Apr. 1168, son of Walter of Salisbury (also styled Walter Fitz Edward, and Walter the Sheriff), d. 1147, of Chitterne, co. Wilts, sheriff of Wiltshire, founder of Bradenstock Priory, by his wife, Sibyl de Chaworth, d. bef 1147, dau. of Patrick de Chaworth, liv. 1133, of Kempsford, co. Gloucester, by Maud, dau. of Ernulf de Hesden. (*CP* IV: 670 chart II, XI: 377, 697, XII(1): 496-7; Sanders, pp. 112, 125; *ES* III.2/355, III.4/638; Anselme III: 292).

    27. WILLIAM FITZ PATRICK (by 2), 2nd Earl of Salisbury, b. abt. 1150, d. 17 Apr. 1196; m. abt. 1190, as her 3rd husb., Eleanor de Vitré, d. 1232/3, dau. of Robert III de Vitré (son of Robert II de Vitré by Emma NN; the son of Andre de Vitré, 1055/67-1139 by Agnes de Mortain, dau. of Robert, Ct. of Mortain; the son of Robert I de Vitre) and Emma de Dinan, d. 18 Dec 1205/1208, dau. of Alan de Dinan, d. 1157, Lord of Dinan and Becherel, in Brittany, son of Geoffrey de Dinan, d. 1127. (*CP* XI: 374-379, XII(1): 497-8; *ES* XIV: 136; Keats-Rohan, *Domesday Desc.* II, p. 433; *VCH Lanc.* I: 312).

    28. ELA, Countess of Salisbury, b. Amesbury, co. Wilts., abt. 1191, d. 24 Aug. 1261; m. 1198, **WILLIAM DE LONGESPEE** (30-26), Earl of Salisbury, b. abt. 1176, d. 7 Mar. 1226, natural son of **HENRY II** (1-24) King of England. (*VCH Lanc,* I: 312; *CP* V: 472, XI: 379-382, XII(1): 497-8; *ES* III(2): 356a. Gens. 21-28: D.L.J. in *Boston Evening Transcript* (1927), Note 2257, Part XIII; Turton; Dudley Pedigree; *Gen. Mag.* 14: 361-368).

Line 109

    25. HÉLIE (ELA, ALIX) OF BURGUNDY (108-25); m. (2) William I (III) Talvas.

    26. GUY II, Count of Ponthieu, d. 1147; m. bef. 18 Dec. 1139, Ida. (*CP* X: 697; *ES* III.4/638).

    27. JOHN I, Count of Ponthieu, d. Acre, 1191; m. (1) Matilda; m. (2) Laurie of St. Valery (Valerie), dau. of Bernard III of St. Valerie; m. (3) bef. 4 Dec. 1170, Beatrice Candavaine of St. Pol, dau. of Anselme Candavaine, Count of St. Pol, d. 1164, and **EUSTACHIE OF CHAMPAGNE** (169A-27) (*ES* III.4/638; West Winter XIV.640; *Gen. Mag.* 15: 186-187)).

    28. WILLIAM II (TALVAS), prob. by (3), Count of Ponthieu, b. 1179, d. 6 Oct. 1221; m. Meudon, 20 Aug. 1195, Alice (or Alix) of France, Countess of Vexin, b. abt. 1170, d. 18 July 1218, dau. of **LOUIS VII** (101-25), King of France, by **ALIX OF CHAMPAGNE** (137-25). (*ES* III.4/638).

    29. MARIE, Countess of Ponthieu, b. bef. 17 Apr. 1199, d. Sept. 1250; m. (1) 1208/11, **SIMON DE DAMMARTIN** (144-27), d. 1239, Count of Aumale, 2nd son of of Albri de Luzarches and **MATHILDA, OF CLERMONT, PONTHIEU & DAMMARTIN** (144-26); m. (2) Mathieu de Montmorency, killed Feb. 1250. (Gens. 25-29: Moriarty, *The Plantagenet Ancestry*, 113; *ES* III.4/649).

    30. JEANNE DE DAMMARTIN, Countess of Ponthieu, 1251, d. 15/16 Mar. 1279; m. (1) 1237, as his 2nd wife, **FERNANDO III**, "the Saint" (110-29), King of Castile 1217-1252, King of Leon 1230-1252, b. 1191 (1201), d. 15 Mar. 1252, canonized by Pope Clement X in 1671. (*CP* II: 59 note *b*; *ES* II/63, III.4/649; *N&Q* (4th Ser.) VII: 437-438. Gens. 25-30: *Gen Mag.* 15: 53-63).

Line 110

22. ROBERT THE OLD (108-22), Duke of Burgundy. b. abt. 1011, d. 1075/6; m. (2) **ERMENGARDE OF ANJOU** (118-22), b. abt. 1018, d. Mar. 1076, wid. of Aubri Geoffrey (Geoffroy Ferréol), Count of Gâtinais, dau. of **FULK III** (118-21), "the Black," Count of Anjou by (2) Hildegarde.. (ES II/20, 82, III.1/116, West Winter, X.31).

23. HILDEGARDE, b. abt. 1050, d. aft. 1104; m. 1068/9 as 3ʳᵈ wife, Geoffrey (called William VI) Count of Poitou, b. abt. 1024, d. 25 Sept. 1086, s. of William III, Count of Poitou, Duke of Aquitaine, s. of William II, Count of Poitou, s. of **WILLIAM I OF POITOU** (144A-19). (ES II/20; West Winter, XI.8, X.22; Garnier, table XXXIX; Moriarty 27, 35, 36,).

24. WILLIAM VII OF POITOU (IX OF AQUITAINE), b. abt. 22 Oct. 1071, d. 10 Feb. 1126/7, Count of Poitou 1086-1126, Duke of Aquitaine, crusader 1101, first known singer-poet in the vernacular; m. 1094, **PHILIPPA (MATHILDA) OF TOULOUSE** (185-3), b. abt. 1073, d. 28 Nov. 1117. div. 1115/16, dau. of William IV Count of Toulouse and **EMMA OF MORTAIN** (185-2). (West Winter, XI.40; Moriarty 36, 42; Larousse, *Ency. of Music*, pp. 74-75; Done Stone, *Some Ancient and Medieval Descents*, Chart 72, "Descent from Theuderic," and note 11).

25. WILLIAM VIII OF POITOU (X OF AQUITAINE), b. 1099, d. 9 Apr. 1137, Count of Poitou 1126-1137, Duke of Aquitaine; m. (1) 1121, **ELEANOR** (or **AENOR**) **DE CHATELLERAULT** (183-4), d. aft. Mar. 1130, dau. of Almeric (or Aimery) I, Viscount of Chatellerault. (West Winter, XII.54; Sugar, *Vie de Louis VI*, 127; *Chronique des eglises d'Anjou*, p. 432).

26. ELEANOR OF AQUITAINE (and **POITOU**), b. abt. 1124, d. 31 Mar. or 1 Apr. 1204; m. (1) 1137, **LOUIS VII** (101-25), King of France, divorced 8 Mar. 1152; m. (2) 18 May 1152, **HENRY II** (1-24), King of England, b. 5 Mar. 1132/3, d. 6 July 1189. (Brandenburg; Winkhaus. Gens. 23-26: *ES* II/76; Done Stone, *Some Ancient and Medieval Descents*, Chart 11, "Descent from William the Conqueror," and note 4).

27. ELEANOR OF ENGLAND, b. 1161, d. 1214; m. Sept. 1177, **ALFONSO VIII** (113-27), King of Castile, b. 1155, d. 1214. (*ES* II/62).

28. BERENGARIA OF CASTILE, b. abt. 1180, d. 8 Nov. 1246; m. (2) 1197, **ALFONSO IX** (114-27), King of Leon, b. 1166, d. 1230. (*CP* II: 59 note *b*; *ES* II/62; *CCN* 385).

29. FERNANDO III, "the Saint," King of Castile 1217, and of Leon 1230, b. 1201, d. Seville 30 May 1252; m. (2) 1237, **JEANNE DE DAMMARTIN** (109-30), d. 1279. (*CP* II: 59 note *b*; *ES* II/63; *CCN* 385).

30. ELEANOR OF CASTILE, Countess of Ponthieu, b. 1241, d. 28 Nov. 1290; m. 18 Oct. 1254, **EDWARD I** (1-27), King of England. (*CP* II: 59 note *b*, X: 118; *ES* II/63; *Medieval Studies* 46 (1984): 248; Don Stone, *Some Ancient and Medieval Descents...*: Chart 11, "Descent from William the Conqueror," and note 4).

31. JOAN (OF ACRE), b. Acre, 1272, d. 23 Apr. 1307; m. (1) Westminster Abbey 30 April 1290, as 2ⁿᵈ wife, **SIR GILBERT DE CLARE** (63-30). (*CP* V: 708-710. Gens. 22-30: Turton; Watts, *Christian Recovery of Spain*, 307; *Medieval Studies* 46 (1984): 261; *Burke's Guide to the Royal Family* (1973), 197).

24. WILLIAM VII OF POITOU (IX OF AQUITAINE) (110-24), Count of Poitou, Duke of Aquitaine, b. abt. 22 Oct. 1071, d. 10 Feb. 1126/7; m. **PHILIPPA (MATHILDA** or **MAUD) OF TOULOUSE** (185-3).

25. AGNES OF POITOU AND AQUITAINE, m. (1) **AIMERY VI DE THOUARS** (271-25), d. 1127; m. (2) 1135, Ramiro II "the Monk," King of Aragon, d. 1157, s. of Sancho I (IV) Ramirez, King of Aragon & Navarre, d. 1094, by his wife, Felicie de Roucy, d. 1086, dau. of **HILDUIN III (IV) DE RAMERU** (151A-22), Count of Montdidier and Roucy, by his wife, **ADELE DE ROUCY** (151-22). (Moriarty, *The Plantagenet Ancestry*, 36, 68, 78; *CCN* 38; *Gen. Mag.* 19 (1977): 55-59; *ES* II/58, 76).

26. PETRONILLA OF ARAGON, by (2), b. 1135, d. 17 Oct 1174 (or 13 Oct. 1173); m. 1151, Raymond IV Berenger, b. abt. 1113, d. 6 Aug. 1162, Marquis of Barcelona, son of Raymond III Berenger, Count of Barcelona, by his 3rd wife, Dulce de Gevaudan, heiress of Provence, d. of Gilbert, Count of Gevauden, Vicomte de Carlat, Count of Provence and Gerberga of Provence, Countess of Arles, dau. of Fulk (Bertrand) Count of Provence. (*ES* II/58, 69, 187; *CCN* 38).

27. ALFONSO II, b. 1157, d. 25 Apr. 1195, King of Aragon; m. 18 Jan. 1174, **SANCHA OF CASTILE** (116-26), d. 1208. (*ES* II/70, 62; *CCN* 38).

28. ALFONSO, d. 1209, Count of Provence; m. 1193, Gersenda of Sabran, dau. of Rainou, Count of Forcalquier. (*ES* II/70, XIV/182).

29. RAYMOND V BERENGER, Count of Provence and Forcalquier, b. 1198, d. 19 Aug. 1245; m. Dec. 1220, **BEATRIX OF SAVOY** (133-27), d. Dec. 1266. (See also Line 104-28. *CP* IV 321; *ES* II/70, 190; Moriarty, *cit.*).

30. ELEANOR OF PROVENCE, d. Amesbury, 25 June 1291; m. Canterbury, 14 Jan. 1236/7, **HENRY III** (1-26) King of England. (*CP* IV 321; V 736; *ES* II/70. Gens. 24-30: Garnier; Moriarty, *cit.*).

23. HENRY (108-23), of Burgundy; m. Sibylle of Barcelona, d, 6 July aft. 1074, dau. of Berenger Ramon I. (*ES* II/69, 38).

24. HENRY I, Count of Portugal, b. 1069, d. 1 Nov. 1112; m. 1093, Theresa of Leon and Castile, d. 1130, natural dau. of Alfonso VI, d. 1109, King of Castile & Leon (see 113-23), by his mistress, Ximena Nunia de Guzman. (Moriarty, *The Plantagenet Ancestry*, 83, 109; *ES* II/38; *CCN* 38).

25. ALFONSO I (or **HENRIQUEZ**), 1st King of Portugal, reigned 1128-1185, b. 15 July 1110, d. 6 Dec. 1185; m. 1146, **MAUD** (or **MATHILDA**) (274B-26). of Savoy, d. 1157, dau. of **AMADEUS III** (274B-25) Count of Savoy. (Moriarty 104, 109;*ES* II/38; *CCN* 38).

26. URRACA OF PORTUGAL, b. abt. 1150, d. 16 Oct. 1188; m. 1165 (annulled June 1175), **FERNANDO II** (114-26), King of Leon, d. 1188. (Moriarty 109; *ES* II/38).

Line 113

22. ROBERT THE OLD (108-22), Duke of Burgundy, m. (1) abt. 1033, Hélie (Eleanor), b. 1016, repudiated 1046, d. a nun, 22 Apr. aft. 1055, dau. of Dalmas I Sire of Semur-en-Brionnais. (*ES* II/20, III.4/344, 343; Moriarty, *The Plantagenet Ancestry*, 40-41).

23. CONSTANCE OF BURGUNDY, d. 1092; m. (1) Hugh II, Count de Chalon-sur-Saône, d. 1078; m. (2) as 2nd wife, Alfonso VI, b. 1039, d. 1109, King of Castile and Leon, son of Fernando I the Great, d. 1065, King of Castile and Leon, by his wife, Sancha, dau. of Alfonso V, d. 1027, King of Leon. (*CCN*, 37; Moriarty, 40, 82).

24. URRACA I, by (2) d. & h., Queen of Leon & Castile, b. 1082, d. 8 Mar. 1126; m. **RAYMOND OF BURGUNDY** (132-25), b. abt. 1060, d. 26 Mar. 1107. (Moriarty, 62, 81, 83; *ES* II/57).

25. ALFONSO VII, King of Castile and Leon, b. 1 Mar. 1105, d. 21 Aug. 1157; m. (1) 1128, as 2nd husb., Berenguela of Barcelona, d. 3 Feb. 1148/9, dau. of Raymond III Berenger, Count of Barcelona, by his 3rd wife, Dulce de Gevaudan (see 111-26); m. (2) July 1152 as 1st husb., **RICHENZA**, of Poland (147-27). (W. Dworzaczek, *Genealogia*, v. 2: chart 5; *CCN*, 38; Moriarty, 81, 108).

26. SANCHO III, by (1), King of Castile, b. 1134, d. 1158; m. 30 Jan. 1151, **BLANCHE OF NAVARRE** (113A-26), d. 12 Aug. 1156. (*CCN*, 37; *EB* 25: 544).

27. ALFONSO VIII, "the Good," King of Castile 1158-1214, b. 1155, d. 1214; m. 1177, **ELEANOR OF ENGLAND** (110-27), b. 1162, d. 1214. (*ES* II/62; *CCN*, 37; *EB* 25: 544-545).

28. BLANCHE OF CASTILE, b. 1188, d. Paris, 27 Nov. 1252; m. 23 May 1200, **LOUIS VIII** (101-27), b. 1187, d. 1226, King of France. (*CP* VII: 386. Gens. 24-28: *ES* II/62, 12).

29. ROBERT, Count of Artois, b. 1216, d. 1250; m. 14 June 1237, **MATILDA OF BRABANT** (45-29), d. 1288. (*CP* VII: 386. *ES* III.1/70. Gens. 22-29: Turton).

Line 113A   Revised for 8th Edition. Original Gens. 23-26, provided by Claude W. Faulkner. Gens. 17-22 have been added to 8th Edition.

17. LAIN CALVO, Judge in Castile.

18. FERNÁN LAINEZ.

19. LAIN FERNANDEZ.

20. NUÑO LAINEZ; m. Eilone, dau. of Ferán Ruiz.

21. LAIN NUÑEZ, liv. 1045-1063, a noble of Castile, at the Court of Fernando I of Leon and Castile.

22. DIEGO LAINEZ, Señor de Bibar in Castile, d. abt. 1058; m. ?Teresa?, dau. of Rodrigo Alvarez, Count in the Asturias, liv. 1038-1066, son of Alvaro, a noble of Castile. (Gens. 17-22: *NEHGR* 117 (1963): 95).

23. EL CID (Rodrigo Diaz, Señor de Bibar), Count of Valencia, "El Campeador," b. abt. 1042, d. Valencia, 10 July 1099, (great national hero of Spain, subj. of epic poems & ballads); m. 14 July 1074, Ximina (Jimena), d. abt. 1115, dau. of Diego, Count of Orviedo, and Christina dau. of Fernando Gundemariz and his wife Ximina, nat. dau. of Alfonso V, King of Leon and Castile. (Moriarty, *The Plantagenet Ancestry*, pp. 82, 109-110; Joseph R. Strayer, ed., *Dict. of the Middle Ages*, vol. 3, p. 386). (*Gen. Mag.* 5 (1931): 361; *NEHGR* 117 (1963): 94-96; *Journal of Medieval Hisory* 6 (1980): 37-60).

24. CHRISTINA (or **ELVIRA**) b. abt. 1077; m. abt. 1095, Ramiro, Count of Monçon, the disinherited Infante of Navarre, d. aft. 1 Feb. 1116, went on First Crusade. (Moriarty, *op. cit.*).

25. GARCIA VII, King of Navarre, "el Restaurador," d. 21 Nov. 1150; m. (1) abt. 1130 Margaret (or Marguerite) de l'Aigle, d. 25 May 1141, dau. of Gilbert, Seigneur de l'Aigle in Normandy, (see also 18A-23) listed as tenant in England in Domesday Book (1086), and Juliana of Mortagne and Perche, dau. of Geoffrey IV, Count of Perche and Mortagne, seen 1079, fought at Hastings 14 Oct. 1066, d. Oct. 1100, by his wife, **BEATRIX DE MONTDIDIER** (151-23, 153-23). (Moriarty 49, 109, 111, *Gen. Mag.* 19: (1977): 55-59; *ES* II/56, III.4/689)

26. BLANCHE (or **SANCHA**) **OF NAVARRE**, d. 12 Aug 1155/6; m. 4 Feb. 1151 (betrothed 15 Oct. 1140), **SANCHO III** (113-26), b. 1134, d. 31 Aug. 1158, King of Castile 1157-1158. (Moriarty, 108-109; *ES* II/55, 62).

Line 114

25. ALFONSO VII (113-25), m. (1) 1128. Berenguela of Barcelona.

26. FERNANDO II, King of Leon, 1157-1188, b. 1137, d. 22 Jan. 1188; m. (1) 1165 (annulled June 1175), **URRACA OF PORTUGAL** (112-26), d. 1188. (*ES* II/62, 38; *CCN*, 37, 38).

27. ALFONSO IX, King of Leon 1188-1229, b. Zamora, 15 Aug. 1171, d. 24 Sept. 1230; m. (2) 1197 (mar. annulled 1204) **BERENGARIA OF CASTILE** (110-28), d. 1246, wid. of Konrad II of Swabia. (*CP* II: 59 note *b*; *ES* II/63).

28. BERENGARIA OF LEON (120-29), b. 1204, d. 12 Apr. 1237; m. Toledo. 1224, as 3rd wife, Jean de Brienne, b. abt. 1168, d. 21 Mar. 1237, King of Jerusalem, 1210-1215, Emperor of Constantinople, Crusader. Jean de Brienne was yr. son of Erard II, Count of Brienne (who fought in the 3rd Crusade, being killed at Acre, 8 Feb. 1191), by Agnes de Montfaucon (m. 1166), dau. of Richard II de Montbéliard, Seigneur de Montfaucon by Sophie de Montbéliard. Jean de Brienne m. (1) 15 Sept. 1210, Mary, dau. Conrad de Montferrat, by 3rd wife Isabella d'Anjou, dau. Amaury I, King of Jerusalem, He became King of Jerusalem by election of the Barons, in right of his wife, who died shortly leaving a daughter and heiress, in whose right he reigned; m. (2) 1214, Stephanie, dau. and h. Leo II, King of Armenia. On mar. of his dau. Yolande, he returned to Europe. He was elected Latin Emperor of Constantinople 1228. (*CP* II: 59 note *b*; *ES* II/62, 200, III.4/683, 681; John L. La Monte, *Feudal Monarchy in the Latin Kingdom of Jerusalem 1100-1291* (1932) (the best & most accurate work on this subject); West Winter XIV.27). (See Moncrieff, in Burke's *Peerage* (1963) 202).

29. LOUIS DE BRIENNE, d'Acre, d. 1297, Vicount of Beaumont-au-Maine; m.12 Feb. 1253 Agnes de Beaumont, liv. 28 Nov. 1304. dau. & h. of Raoul VIII de Beaumont-au-Maine, d. 1235, hereditary vicomte of Maine, Seigneur de Beaumont-le-Vicomte, by his (2) wife, Agnes. Raoul VIII de Beaumont was son of **RICHARD I DE BEAUMONT** (98-26). (*CP* II: 59 note *b*; *ES* III.4/683).

30. HENRY DE BEAUMONT, KNT., d. 10 Mar. 1339/40, knighted 1308, M.P. 1308/9-1332, Lord Beaumont, 8th Earl of Buchan, Justiciar of Scotland 1338; m. abt. 1310, **ALICE COMYN** (114A-29), d. 1349, bef. 10 Aug., dau. of Alexander Comyn, Sheriff of Aberdeen. (*CP* II: 59-60, 375-376; *ES* III.4/685).

31. JOHN DE BEAUMONT, KNT., 2nd Lord Beaumont, M.P. 1342/3, b. 1317/8; m. by June 1337, **ELEANOR** (17-30) of Lancaster. (*ES* III.4/685. Gens. 28-31: Michael

Maclagan, "Ancestry of the English Beaumonts," pp. 190-194, and chart VI, in: Lindsay Brook, Editor, *Studies in Genealogy and Family History in Tribute to Charles Evans...* (1989)).

Line 114A

26. WILLIAM COMYN (121A-26), d. 1233; m. (2) in or bef. 1210, as her 2nd husb., Margaret, Countess of Buchan, d. 1242/3, dau. & h. of Fergus, 4th Earl of Buchan, d. bef. 1199,. (*CP* II: 374).

27. ALEXANDER COMYN, 6th Earl of Buchan d. 1290, bef. Apr. 6; m. **ELIZABETH** (or **ISABEL**) **DE QUINCY** (224-29), 2nd dau. and coh. of **ROGER DE QUINCY** (53-28), Earl of Winchester, by 1st wife **HELEN OF GALLOWAY** (38-27), eldest dau. and coh. of **ALAN** (38-26) Lord of Galloway, liv. 1282. (*CP* II: 374-375).

28. ALEXANDER COMYN, yr. son, Sheriff of Aberdeen 1305; m. prob. Joan, sister of William le Latimer. (*CP* II: 375-376, 60, XIV: 119).

29. ALICE COMYN, of Buchan, d. 1349, eldest dau. and coh.; m. by 14 July 1310, **HENRY DE BEAUMONT** (114-30), Lord Beaumont, sum. as 8th Earl of Buchan, d. sh. bef. 10 Mar. 1340. (*CP* II: 59-60, 375-376. Gens. 26-29: *Scottish Gen.* 21 (1974): 25, 27).

Line 115   Line cancelled

Line 116

25. ALFONSO VII (113-25), King of Castile and Leon, b. 1103, d. 1157; m. (3) 1152, **RICHENZA OF POLAND** (147-27), d. bef. 1176.

26. SANCHA OF CASTILE, b. 1155/1157, d. 1208; m. 18 Jan. 1174, **ALFONSO II** (111-27), King of Aragon, b. 1157, d. 1196. (*ES* II/62; ... *Tribute to Charles Evans...* (1989), 375, 403 note 43).

Line 117

24. LOUIS VI (101-24) King of France, b. 1081, d. 1 Aug. 1137; m. (2) 1115, **ADELAIDE** (274A-25) of Savoy, d. 1 Aug. 1154, granddau. of **WILLIAM I** (132-24), Count Palatine of Burgundy, Count of Macon.

25. PETER OF FRANCE, Seigneur de Courteney, b. abt. 1125, d. Palastine 1179/1183, Crusader 1147; m. aft. 1150, **ELIZABETH (ISABEL) DE COURTENAY** (107-26), Dame de Courteney, liv. 1205. (West Winte,r XIII.150).

26. ALICE (ALIX) DE COURTENAY, d. 1218; m. (2) 1186, **AYMER "TAILLIFER" DE VALENCE** (153A-27), d. abt. 1202, Count of Angoulême. (*ES* II/17, III.4/818; West Winter, XIV.258).

27. ISABELLA OF ANGOULÊME, (153A-28), b. abt. 1189, d. 3 or 4 June 1246; m. (1) 24 Aug. 1200, **JOHN** (1-25) King of England; m. (2) 10 May 1220, **HUGH X DE LUSIGNAN** (275-27), Count of la Marche and of Angoulême, d. 1249. (*CP* V: 697; *ES* III.4/816, 818, 725; *CCN*, 547-548; Painter, *Speculum* 30: 374-384, 32: 27-47; *Gen. Mag.* 12: 484).

28. HUGH XI DE LUSIGNAN (275-28), b. 1221, d. Damette 1250, Count of la Marche and Angoulême, Count of Ponthieu; m. 1238 **YOLANDE DE DREUX** (135-30).

29. ALICE DE LUSIGNAN, (aka Alice de La Marche) d. May 1290; m. abt. 1253, (annulled May 1285) **GILBERT DE CLARE** (63-30), b. 1243, d. 7 Dec. 1299, Earl of Gloucester and Hereford, d. 1295. (*CP* V: 702-710, 736; ES III.4/816. Gens. 24-27: Turton; see Watson on the Lusignans, *The Gen.* (n.s.) 21: 78+).

Line 118

17. HERBERT I (50-17), Count de Vermandois; m. Bertha (or Beatrice) of Morvois, dau. of Guerri I, Count of Morvois, by his wife, Eve of Roussillon. (*ES* III.1/49; Saillot; Moriarty, *The Plantagenet Ancestry*, pp. 6, 21, 23, 37).

18. HERBERT II, d. 943, Count de Vermandois and Troyes; m. by 907, **LIEGARDE OF FRANCE** (48-19). (Seversmith, 2,483; *ES* II/10).

19. ROBERT, Count of Troyes and Meaux, b. abt. 920, d. Aug.. 967; m. (1) by 950 Adelaide of Burgundy, dau. of Giselbert, Count of Burgundy, and Ermengarde of Burgundy.

20. ADELAIDE DE VERMANDOIS (121-20) b. 950, d. 975/8; m. (2) 979 Geoffroy I, "Grisonelle," d. 21 Jul 987, Count of Anjou, son of Fulk II, "the Good," Count of Anjou, and Gerberga. (*ES* III.1/49; *NEHGR* 99: 130-131, 101: 112).

21. FULK III, "the Black," of Maine, Count of Anjou, d. 21 June 1040; m. (2) aft. 1000, Hildegarde, d. Jerusalem, 1 Apr. 1040.

22. ERMENGARDE OF ANJOU, b. abt. 1018, d. 21 Mar. 1076; m. (1) abt. 1035, Aubri Geoffrey (Geoffroy Ferréol), d. 11 Apr. 1046, Count of the Gâtinais, 1034-1043, son of Geoffrey III, Count of the Gâtinais, and Beatrix of Mâcon. (*ES* III.1/116; *NEHGR* 99: 34-37; *ES* II/82, XV/92).

23. FULK IV, "Rechin," Count of Anjou, b. 1043, d. 14 Apr. 1109; m. (5) 1089, Bertrade (or Beatrice) de Montfort (div. abt. 1092), d. 1117, dau. of Simon I, d. abt. 1087, Seigneur of Montfort l'Amauri, and Agnes of Evreux, dau. of Richard, Count of Evreux, and gr.-grandau. of **RICHARD I** (121E-20) Duke of Normandy. (*CP* XI: App. D, 114).

24. FULK V, "the Young," Count of Anjou, King of Jerusalem, b. 1092, d. at Jerusalem, 10 Nov. 1144; m. (1) 1110, Erembourg, Countess of Maine d. 1126, dau. of Helie de la Flêche, Count of Maine; m. (2) 2 June 1129, Melisende de Rethel, d. 11 Sept. 1161, eldest dau. of **BALDWIN II** (103A-25), King of Jerusalem (by whom he was father of Baldwin III, King of Jerusalem, b. 1130, d.s.p. 10 Feb. 1162, and of Amaury I, King of Jerusalem, b. 1136, d. 11 July 1174). (*NEHGR* 99: 34-37; *ES* II/82, III.4/692).

25. GEOFFREY V (PLANTAGENET), (see 123-25), Count of Anjou, Duke of Normandy b. 24 Aug. 1113, d. 7 Sept. 1151,; m. Le Mans 22 May. 1127, as her 2nd husb., **MATILDA** (1-23), b. 1104, d. 10 Sept. 1167, dau. of **HENRY I** (121-25), King of England. (*CP* V: 736; *SP* I: 1-2; Burke, (1967): lxi).

Line 119

23. FULK IV (118-23), Count of Anjou, b. 1043, d. 14 Apr. 1109; m. (1) Hildegarde of Baugency, d. bef. 1070, dau. of Lancelin II, Seigneur of Baugency, d. 1098, by his wife, Alberge. (*CP* XI: App. D, 114; *ES* II/82, XII/45).

24. ERMENGARDE OF ANJOU, d. 1 June 1147; m. (2) abt. 1093, **ALAN IV** (119A-25) "Fergent," d. 1119, Duke of Brittany, son of Hoel, Duke of Brittany and Hawise, d. 1072, dau. of Alan III, Duke of Brittany, d. 1040, and Bertha, d. 1084, dau. of **EUDES I**

(136-20), Count of Blois & Chartres. Alan III was a grandson of **RICHARD I**, (121E-20) Duke of Normandy. (*CP* X: 788-789, and chart of the Dukes of Brittany opp. 781; *ES* II/75 NEU).

25. CONAN III, Duke of Brittany, d. 17 Sept. 1148; m. Maud, natural dau. of **HENRY I** (121-25), King of England. (*CP* X: 790, XI: App. D, 114; *ES* II/75 NEU).

26. BERTHA OF BRITTANY, d. 1158/1164; m. (1) abt. 1137 **ALAN II** (227-25), Earl of Richmond, son of **STEPHEN I** (214-24), Count of Brittany, Lord of Richmond. (*CP* X: 790, XI: App. D, 114).

27. CONAN IV, Duke of Brittany, Earl of Richmond, d. 20 Feb. 1171; m. 1160, **MARGARET OF HUNTINGDON** (96-26), dau. of **HENRY OF HUNTINGDON** (170-23), Earl of Huntingdon. (*CP* X: 791-793).

Line 119A   Revised for 8th Edition. This was Line 39, Gens. 21-25 in previous editions.

21. ERMENGARDE OF ANJOU (121-21); m. (2) 980, Conan I, Count of Rennes, Duke of Brittany, abt. 970-990, killed 27 June 992, son of Jubel Berenger, d abt. 930, by Gerberge. Jubel Berenger was son of Pascwitann Count of Rennes, son of Alan I, King of Brittany, d. 907, by Oreguen. (*ES* II/75 NEU).

22. GEOFFREY, Duke of Brittany, d. 20 Nov. 1008; m. 996, Hawise, of Normandy; d. 21 Feb. 1034; illeg. dau. of **RICHARD I** (121E-20), Duke of Normandy. (*ES* II/75 NEU).

23. ALAN III, Duke of Brittany, d. 1 Oct. 1040; m. 1018, Bertha of Blois, d. Apr. 1085, dau. of **EUDES II** (136-21), Count of Blois, by his wife Ermengarde of Auvergne. (Saillot, 36).

24. HAWISE, d. 1072; m. Hoel, Count of Cornouille, Leon, and Nantes, *jure uxoris* Duke of Brittany 1066, d. 13 Apr. 1084.

25. ALAN IV "Fergent," Duke of Brittany, d. 13 Oct. 1119; m. (2) abt. 1093, **ERMENGARDE OF ANJOU** (119-24), d. 1147, dau. **FULK IV** (118-23), Count of Anjou.

Line 120

28. BERENGARIA OF CASTILE (110-28), d. 1244; m. (2) **ALFONSO IX** (114-27), King of Leon, b. 1166, d. 1229. (*ES* II/62).

29. BERENGARIA OF LEON (114-28), m. as 3rd wife, Jean de Brienne (see 114-28), d. 1237, King of Jerusalem. (*ES* III.4/683).

30. JEAN DE BRIENNE, of Acre, d. 1296, Grand Butler of France, 1258; m. (1) Mary, d.s.p., wid. of Alexander II, King of Scotland, dau. of **ENGUERRAND III DE COUCY** (273-29); m. (2) 1251, Jeanne, dau. of Geoffrey VI, d. 1249, Vicomte of Châteaudun, by his wife, Clemence, dau. of William des Roches, d. 1222, Seneschal of Anjou, Maine & Touraine, by his wife, Marguerite de Sablé. (Anselme, III: 314-316, VI: 134; *ES* III.4/690, 718 B).

31. BLANCHE DE BRIENNE, Lady of Loupeland, liv. 1265/9; m. Sir William de Fenlis. She was 2nd cousin of **ELEANOR OF CASTILE** (110-30). (*CP* VIII: 433, IX: 384). (See Moncrieff, Burke's *Peerage* (1963) 202).

32. MARGARET DE FENLIS, m. abt. 1285, **SIR EDMUND DE MORTIMER** (176B-30), 7th Baron Mortimer of Wigmore, b. 1261, d. 1304. (*CP* VIII: 433, IX: 283).

33. SIR ROGER DE MORTIMER (176B-31), 8th Baron Mortimer of Wigmore, 1st Earl of March; m. **JOAN DE GENEVILLE** (71-32, 71A-32). (*CP* VIII: 441).

34. CATHERINE DE MORTIMER, d. bet. 4 Aug. and 6 Sept. 1369; m. **THOMAS DE BEAUCHAMP, K.G.** (87-31), 11th Earl of Warwick, d. 1369. (*CP* XII (2): 374).

35. WILLIAM BEAUCHAMP, d. 1411, Baron Abergavenny; m. Joan Fitz Alan, dau. of **RICHARD FITZ ALAN** (60-33) and **ELIZABETH DE BOHUN** (15-31). (*CP* X: 125).

36. JOAN BEAUCHAMP, d. 1430; m. abt. 1413, **JAMES BOTILLER (BUTLER)** (7-33), 4th Earl of Ormond, b. abt. 1390, d. 1452. (*CP* X: 125).

37. THOMAS BUTLER, K.B., 7th Earl of Ormond, Baron Ormond de Rocheford, d.s.p.m. 3 Aug. 1515, K.B., 6 July 1483; m. (1) bef. 11 July 1445, Anne Hankeford, d. 1485, dau. of Sir Richard Hankeford and Anne Montagu; m. (2) bef. Nov. 1496, Lora Berkeley, d. bef. 30 Dec. 1501, dau. of Sir Edward Berkeley of Beverton, co. Gloucester, by Christian Holt, dau. Richard Holt of Coldrey, Hants. (*CP* X: 131-133).

38. MARGARET BUTLER, by (1), b. 1465 (age 20 in 1485), d. 1539; m. 1485, Sir William Boleyn, Knt. (*CP* X: 133 note *b*; *Gen. Mag.* 13 (1960): 206).

39. SIR THOMAS BOLEYN, b. 1477, d. 12 Mar. 1539, cr. Earl of Wiltshire; m. **ELIZABETH HOWARD** (22-36), dau. of Thomas Howard, 2nd Duke of Norfolk. (*CP* X: 137-140; *Gen. Mag.* 13 (1960): 205-6). They were par. of Anne Boleyn, mother of Queen Elizabeth I.

Line 121

20. ADELAIDE DE VERMANDOIS (118-20), m. Geoffroy I, "Grisgonelle," Count of Anjou.

21. ERMENGARDE OF ANJOU, m. (2) 980, Conan I of Rennes, d. 992, Duke of Brittany. (*ES* II/75).

22. JUDITH OF BRITTANY, b. 982, d. 16 June 1017; m. abt. 1000, **RICHARD II**, "the Good" (121E-21), d. 28 Aug. 1026, Duke of Normandy. (Moriarty, *ES* II/75).

23. ROBERT I, d. 22 July 1035, Duke of Normandy; by his mistress Herleve (or Harlette), dau. of Fulbert of Falais, tanner. (*CP* I: 351-352; *Eng. Hist. Rev.* 101, pp. 399-404; Moriarty; *ES* II/79), had

24. WILLIAM I, the Conqueror (natural son by Herleve), b. Falaise, 1027, d. Rouen, 9 Sept. 1087, Duke of Normandy, King of England 1066-1087; m. 1053, **MAUD** (or **MATILDA) OF FLANDERS** (162-23), b. 1032, d. 3 Nov. 1083. (*CCN*, 494; Moriarty; *ES* II/81).

25. HENRY I, "Beauclerc," King of England 1100-1135, b. 1068, d. 1 Dec. 1135; m. 11 Nov. 1100, **MATILDA OF SCOTLAND** (1-22), b. 1079, d. 1 May 1118. (*CP* V: 736, VII: 737; *SP* I: 1-2; *ES* II/81, 89; *CCN*, 494). He had issue by a number of mistresses.

26. REGINALD (REINALD) FITZ ROY (or **FITZ HENRY) DE MORTAIN**, Earl of Cornwall, d. 1 July 1175 (natural son by Sybil Corbet, dau. of Robert Corbet of Alcester), sheriff of Devon, 1173; m. Mabel, d. by 1162, dau. of William Fitz Richard, Lord of Cardinan, Cornwall, and granddau. of **ROBERT DE MORTAIN** (185-1), Earl of Cornwall. (*CP* III: 429, VII: 737-740, XI: Append. D, 107-108; Ordericus Vitalis; *TAG* 29: 13-17, 31: 118; Powley, *House of de la Pomerai; Devon & Cornwall Rec. Soc.*, n.s. XXX (Cart. of Launceston Priory); Sanders; *The Genealogist* 9 (1988) 206-7; *ES* III.2/354).

Line 121A

23. DONALD BANE, King of Scots, son of **DUNCAN I MAC CRINAN** (170-20), King of Scots, 1093-1094, by an unnamed wife had (*SP* I: 3, 504)

24. BETHOC, m. Huctred of Tyndale, son of Waldef. (*SP* I: 3).

25. HEXTILDA, m. Richard Comyn of Northallerton and Badenoch (son of William, son of John, son of Robert); m. abt. 1145. He d. 1176-82, when wid. m. (2) Malcolm, Earl of Athol. (*SP* I 504-555).

26. WILLIAM COMYN, d. 1233, *j.u.* Earl of Buchan; m. (1) Sarah, liv. 1204, dau. & h. of Robert Fitz Hugh, d. abt. 1201; m. (2) by 1214, Margaret, Countess of Buchan, d. abt. 1242, dau. & h. of Fergus, d.abt.1199, 4th Earl of Buchan. (*CP* II: 374-375, *SP* I: 3, 505, II: 252).

27. RICHARD COMYN, by (1), Lord of Badenoch, d. 1244-9, by unknown wife, had (*SP* I: 505-506).

28. SIR JOHN COMYN, "The Red Comyn #1," seen 1242, d. aft. 1273; m. Amabilia (or Alicia), liv. 1280. (*SP* I: 506-507; Rev. C. Moor, *Knights of Edward I* 1: 231).

29. SIR JOHN COMYN, ""The Black Comyn," seen 1281, d. abt. 1303, claimant of the Crown of Scotland on the above cited descent from Donald Bane; m. **ELEANOR** (or **ALIANORA) DE BALIOL** (95-29), dau. of John de Baliol and **DEVORGUILLA OF GALLOWAY** (95-28). (*SP* I: 507-508).

Line 121B

26. ELIZABETH (ISABEL), yngst illeg. dau. of **HENRY I** (121-25), King of England, by Elizabeth de Beaumont, dau. of Robert I de Beaumont; m. Fergus, Lord of Galloway, seen 1136-47, d. Holyrood Abbey, 1161 or 1166. (*SP* IV: 135-137, esp. 136; *CP* XIV: 582. Note: *ES* III.2/354 and *CP* XI, Appendix D: 105 note *d*, 120, do not credit Elizabeth (Isabel) as having had issue.). But, perhaps by Elizabeth, Fergus had

27. UCHTRED, seen 1136, killed 22 Sept. 1174 at Loch Fergus by nephew Malcolm, s. of Gilbert, his bro.; m. **GUNNILD**, dau. of **WALDEVE** (or **WALTHEOF**) (38-23), Lord of Allerdale, bro. of Gospatric, 2nd Earl of Dunbar. (*SP* IV: 136-138).

Line 121C

26. FERGUS, Lord of Galloway, d. 1161; m. (1) **ELIZABETH (ISABEL)** (121B-26); m. (2) NN. (*SP* IV: 136, II: 421).

27. GILBERT, by (2), seen 1174, d. 1 Jan. 1185. (*SP* II: 421-422, IV: 136).

28. DUNCAN, Lord of Carrick, prob. a minor 1185, cr. Earl of Carrick 1225-30, d. 13 June 1250; m. prob. Avelina, dau. of Alan Fitz Walter, High Sheriff of Scotland, who may or may not be mother of his son. (*SP* II: 422-423; *CP* III: 55; Duncan Stewart, *Hist. of Scotland* 48).

29. NEIL, Earl of Carrick, d. 1256, Regent of Scotland, and Guardian of Alexander III, 1255; m. Isabella or Margaret, parents not surely identified. (*SP* IV: 423-426, IX: 55; *CP* III: 55).

30. MARJORIE (or MARGARET) (one of four daus.), *s.j.* Countess of Carrick, d. by 27 Oct. 1292- m. (1) Adam de Kilconquhar, d. Acre 1270; m. (2) 1271, **ROBERT BRUCE** (252-29), son of Robert de Bruce of Annandale and Cleveland, *j.u.* Earl of Carrick, which title he resigned to his son Robert (later **ROBERT I** (252-30) King of Scots), 27 Oct. 1292. (*SP* II: 426-427; *CP* III: 55; Farrer, *Early Yorkshire Charters* II 14-15).

Line 121D

30. ELIZABETH COMYN (224-30), d. bef. 17 Feb. 1328/9, 3rd dau. of **ALEXANDER COMYN** (114A-27), Earl of Buchan, by **ELIZABETH DE QUINCY** (224-29), 3rd dau. and coh. of **ROGER DE QUINCY** (53-28), Earl of Winchester; m. Gilbert d'Umfreville, d. 1307, Earl of Angus, son of Gilbert d'Umfreville, Baron of Prudhoe, etc., by 1st wife, Mathilda, Countess of Angus. (*CP* I: 147-148; Clay, 224-225).

31. ROBERT D'UMFREVILLE (224-31), Earl of Angus, aged 30+ in 1307, d. 30 Mar. 1325; m. (1) by 20 Sept. 1303, Lucy Kyme, dau. & event. h. of Philip de Kyme, 1st Lord Kyme, by Joan Bigod, dau. of **HUGH BIGOD** (69-29); m. (2) Eleanore (or Alienor), d. 31 Mar. 1368, who m. (2) aft. 1327 without lic., Sir Roger Mauduit, d. bef. 24 Feb. 1350/1. (Clay, 224; *CP* I: 149-150, VII: 352-354).

32. THOMAS D'UMFREVILLE, by (2), of Harbottle, and of Hessel, co. York., d. 21 May 1387; m. Joan de Roddam, dau. of Adam de Roddam (or Retdam). (Clay, *op. cit.*; *CP* I: 151, VII: 363).

33. THOMAS D'UMFREVILLE, b. abt. 1361, M.P., Northumb. 1387-1388, d. 12 Feb. or 8 Mar. 1390/1; m. Agnes, d. 25 Oct. 1420, pos. dau. of Thomas Grey of Heton. (Clay, *op. cit*; *CP*, *op. cit*).

34. MARGARET D'UMFREVILLE, age 47 in 1437, d. 23 June 1444; m. (1) William Lodington, d. 9 Jan. 1419/20; m. (2) by 26 Apr. 1423, John Constable, of Halsham and Burton Constable, will 23 Nov. 1449, pro. 17 Jan. 1451. (Clay, 28, 225; *CP* I: 152-153).

35. SIR JOHN CONSTABLE of Halsham, nunc. will 20 Dec. 1477, pro. 18 Mar. 1477/8; m. Lora, dau. of **WILLIAM** (219-34), Lord Fitz Hugh. (Clay, 28-29; *CP* I: 153; *NEHGR* 111: 196-198. Gens. 30-35: *Gen.* (n.s.) 26 (1910): 193-205).

36. ISABEL CONSTABLE, will dated 20 July, pro. 12 Dec. 1505; m. abt. 1482 as (2) wife, Stephen de Thorpe of Thorpe and Welwyk, b. abt. 1446; Stephen m. (1) 1466-71, Dyonis, dau. William Eland of Hull, d. test. 1503. (*NEHGR* 114: 224-225).

37. MARGARET THORPE; m. aft. 20 July 1505, John Newton of Ryhill, co. York, and Burstwick juxta Skeklyng, d. 9 June 1515. (*NEHGR* 111: 198).

38. JOHN NEWTON, b. abt. 7 Nov. 1515, dead 1562/3; m. Margaret Grimston, bur. 14 Dec. 1587, dau. of John Grimston, d. 1534, and Elizabeth Eure of Aldbrough. (*NEHGR* 94: 13-14, 111: 199). (For the Grimston-Eure anc., see *NEHGR* 111: 261-265).

39. JOHN NEWTON of Flinton, bur. 2 Apr. 1587; m. Marie, who m. (2) 18 July 1587, William Skipsey. (*NEHGR* 94: 14-15).

40. LANCELOT NEWTON of Hedon, b. abt. 1580, bur. Hedon, 30 Aug. 1622; m. at Barmeston, 3 Jan. 1610, Mary Lee, bur. 12 Mar. 1632 at Hedon. (*NEHGR* 94: 15, 17-18).

41. ELLEN NEWTON, bapt. 24 Feb. 1614; m. St. Martin Michelgate, York, 3 Nov. 1636, **EDWARD CARLETON** (2-42), b. Hornsea, co. York, bapt. Beeford, co. York, 20 Oct. 1610. (*NEHGR, cit*; Sheppard, "Ancestry of Edward Carleton and Ellen Newton his wife").

Line 121E

14. HALFDAN, the Old.
15. IVAR OPLAENDINGE, Jarl, fl. abt. 800.

16. EYSTEIN GLUMRA, Jarl of the Upplands, abt. 830, sd. to have fathered two known children: Swanhild, who m. **HARALD** (243A-17) King of Norway, and

17. RAGNVALD I, "the Wise," Jarl of North and South More, and of Ramsdal in Norway, seen 867, d. 890; m. Hiltrude (or Raginhilde), dau. of Hrolf Nefia.

18. GANGER ROLF, "the Viking" (or **ROLLO**), 1st Count of Normandy, banished from Norway to the Hebrides abt. 876, 890 participated in Viking attack on Bayeux, where Count Berenger of Bayeux was killed, and his dau. Poppa captured and taken 886, by Rollo (now called Count of Rouen) as his "Danish" wife. Under Treaty of St. Claire, 911, rec'd the County of Normandy from **CHARLES III**, (148-17) "the Simple"; d. 929, bur. Notre Dame, Rouen. (*Eng. Hist. Rev.* 57: 417-436). Besides a dau. Adele Gerloc (or Gerloc) who m. 935, **WILLLAM I** (144A-19), Count of Poitou, Rollo had

19. WILLIAM I, "Longsword," b. abt. 891, prob. Rouen, abt. 927 succ. to County of Normandy, abt. 930 the Bretons rebelled, he subdued them, taking Brittany, the Channel Islands, the Contentin, and the Averanchin; killed in treacherous ambush 17 Dec. 942 by servants of Theobald of Blois and Arnulf of Flanders. (Isenburg; Onslow, pp. 46-62). He m. (1) Sprota; m. (2) **LUITGARDE DE VERMANDOIS** (136-19), n.i., dau. of **HERBERT II** (50-18), Count of Vermandois and Troyes.

20. RICHARD I, by (1), "the Fearless," Duke of Normandy, b. Fecamp abt. 933, named father's h. 29 May 942, d. 20 Nov. 996; m. (1) (Danish wife) Gunnora, d. 1027 or 1031, dau. of the forester of Arques; but betrothed abt. 945 & event. m. (2) 960, Emma, d. abt. 968, dau. of Hugh Capet (see 53-20), Count of Paris. After Emma's death, m. (Christian marriage) Gunnora to legit. their children. (Onslow). By Gunnora, Richard had

21. RICHARD II, "the Good," Duke of Normandy, d. 28 Aug. 1026; m. (1) abt. 1000, **JUDITH** (121-22) of Brittany, b. abt. 982, d. 1017, dau. of Conan I, Count of Rennes; m. (2) 1017 Astrid (Margaret), dau. of Swen I, King of Denmark; m. (3) abt. 1024, Poppa. He had many children by (1) and (3).

22. ROBERT I (121-23), by (1), Duke of Normandy, d. 22 July 1035; m. (Danish wife) Herleve (or Harlette), dau. of Fulbert of Falais. By Arletta he was the father of **WILLIAM I** (121-24). (Gens. 14-22: Moriarty, *The Plantagenet Ancestry*, pp. 10-11, 13; *ES* II/79).

Line 122

28. ELA (108-28), Countess of Salisbury, m. **WILLIAM LONGESPEE** (30-26), natural son of **HENRY II** (1-24), King of England. (*CP* XI 379-382; *Gen. Mag.* 14: 361-367).

29. SIR WILLIAM II LONGESPEE (30-27), slain in battle with the Saracens, 8 Feb. 1250; m. 1226, Idonea de Camville, dau. and h. of Richard de Camville, by Eustache Basset, dau. of Gilbert Basset. (Inq.p.m. 1299; *CP* I: 338, XI: 382-383, App. F, 126-127; *VCH Lanc*. I: 312).

30. ELA LONGESPEE, d. bef. 22 Nov. 1299; m. 1244, James de Audley (or Aldithley), b. abt. 1220, d. abt. 11 June 1272, of Heleigh, co. Stafford, Keeper of the Castle of Newcastle-under-Lynn, 30 Oct. 1250, Lord Marcher, Sheriff of Salop 1261-1262, and Staffordshire 1270-1271, Justiciar of Ireland. (*CP* I: 337-338; *ES* III.2/356a).

31. NICHOLAS AUDLEY, Lord Audley, b. bef. 1258, d. 28 Aug. 1299 (Inq.p.m. 1299); m. Catherine Gifford, b. 1272, liv. 1322, dau. of John Gifford, 1st Lord Gifford of Brimsfield, by Maud de Clifford, dau. of Walter de Clifford and wid. of William III Longespee, earl of Salisbury (son of No. 29). (*CP* I: 338-339; Banks I: 100). (See 29A-29).

32. NICHOLAS AUDLEY, of Heleigh, co. Stafford, 3rd Lord Audley, b. 11 Nov. 1289, d. Dec. 1316, age 27, M.P. 1312-1316; m. 1312, Joan de Martin, d. 1319/22, wid. of

Henry, Earl of Lincoln, younger daughter of William Martin, 1st Lord Martin, and Eleanor, dau. of **SIR REYNOLD FITZ PIERS** (262-30) and **JOAN DE VIVONIA** (261-32). (*CP* I: 339, VIII: 535-538; Banks I: 101).

33. SIR JAMES AUDLEY, K.G., b. Knesale, co. Nottingham, 8 Jan. 1312/3, d. Apr. 1386; m. (1) bef. 13 June 1330, **JOAN DE MORTIMER** (71-33, 176B-32), d. aft. 1337. (*CP* I: 340, XI: App. F, 127; Banks I: 100-103).

Line 122A   Prepared for an earlier edition by Douglas Richardson

28. ELA (108-28), Countess of Salisbury; m. **WILLIAM LONGESPEE** (30-26), natural son of **HENRY II** (1-24), King of England. (*CP* XI: 379-382).

29. IDA (or **IDONEA**) **DE LONGESPEE**, liv. 1266/7; m. (1) as a child, Ralph de Somery, d. 1212, son and h. of **RALPH DE SOMERY** (55-28, 81-28) Baron Dudley, by his wife, Margaret Marshal; m. (2) by 1220, as his 2nd wife, William de Beauchamp, b. say 1185, d. 1260, held barony of Bedford, co. Bedford, Baron of the Exchequer, Sheriff of Bedford and Bucks, son of Simon de Beauchamp (dead by 1206/7) by his wife Isabella. (*CP* XII (1): 110-111, 382; *Pubs. of the Bedfordshire Hist. Rec. Soc.* I: 10-16, esp. chart p. 25). (See also *ES* III.2/356a).

30. BEATRICE DE BEAUCHAMP, 3rd dau. and coh., d. abt. 1280/1; m. (1) by 1264, Sir Thomas Fitz Otto (or Fitz Otes) of Mendelsham, Suffolk, b. abt. 1231 (age 30 in 1261), d. by 28 Mar. 1274, holding lands in Hunts., Essex, Beds., Bucks., Glouc. and Worc.; m. (2) by 26 June 1278, Sir William de Montchensy of Edwardeston, Suffolk, d. sh. bef. 15 May 1302. (*CP* II: 233-235; *Pubs. of the Bedfordshire Hist. Rec. Soc.* II 233-235; *Knights of Edward I*, II: 49-50; III: 279-180).

31. MAUD (or **MATILDA**) **FITZ THOMAS** (**FITZ OTTO** or **FITZ OTES**) (also seen as **FITZ OTHO**), living 28 May 1329; m. by June 1292 **JOHN DE BOTETOURTE** (216-29), d. 25 Nov. 1324, 1st Lord Botetourte. (*CP* II: 233-235; *Pubs. of the Bedfordshire Hist. Rec. Soc.* I, chart p. 25).

Line 123

25. GEOFFREY V (PLANTAGENET) (118-25), Count of Anjou, Duke of Normandy, b. 23 Aug. 1113, d. 7 Sept. 1151; by unknown mistress had

26. HAMELIN (PLANTAGENET), Earl of Surrey, d. 7 May 1202; m. 1164, as her 2nd husb., **ISABEL DE WARENNE** (83-26). (*CP* IV: 670 chart II).

27. MAUD DE WARENNE, d. bef. 13 Dec. 1228; m. (1) **HENRY** (139-27), Count d'Eu, Lord of Hastings, d. 11 Mar. 1183; m. (2) Henry de Stouteville, d. 1232/1236, Lord of Eckingtonn Seigneur de Valmont, son of Robert de Stouteville and Leonia, of Salisbury, Dame of Rames. (*CP* V: 158-160, XII (1): 500; *ES* XIII/103. Gens. 25-27: *ES* III.2/355).

28. ALICE D'EU, Countess of Eu, Lady of Hastings, d. 15 May 1246; m. 1194, Raoul I de Lusignan, Count of Eu, d. 1 May 1219, bro. of **HUGH DE LUSIGNAN** (275-25), d. bef. 11 Mar. 1169, and son of **HUGH VIII DE LUSIGNAN** (275-24). (Painter, *Speculum* 30: 374-384, 32: 27-44; *CP* V: 160-166).

29. MAUD D'EU (or **DE LUSIGNAN**), d. 14 Aug. 1241; m., as 1st wife **HUMPHREY DE BOHUN V** (97-28), 2nd Earl of Hereford and Earl of Essex, b. by 1208, d. 24 Sept. 1275. (Painter, *Speculum* 30: 374-384, 32: 27-44; *CP* V: 163 note *d*, IV: 669).

Line 124

25. **HENRY I** (121-25), King of England, b. 1070, d. 1 Dec. 1135. (*CP* IV: 670 chart III, V: 736, VII: 677).

26. **ROBERT DE CAEN**, Earl of Gloucester, 1122-1147 (natural son of Henry I, prob. by a NN dau. of the Gay or Gayt family of N. Oxfordshire (<u>See</u>: David Crouch, "Robert of Gloucester's Mother and Sexual Politics in Norman Oxfordshire," *Bull. of the Inst. of Hist. Research* 72 (Oct. 1999): 323-333)), b. abt. 1090, d. Bristol, 31 Oct. 1147, called "the Consul"; m. Maud Fitz Hamon, dau. & h. of Robert Fitz Hamon, d. 1107, seigneur of Crelly in Calvados, Normandy, Lord of Thoringni, etc., and Sybil de Montgomery, dau. of Roger de Montgomery, Earl of Shrewsbury. (*CP* IV: 670 chart iii, V 736, VII: 677, XI: 683-687 App. D, 106; *DNB*).

27. **WILLIAM FITZ ROBERT**, 2nd Earl of Gloucester, Lord of Tewkesbury and Glamorgan, b. abt. 1128, d. 23 Nov. 1183; m. abt. 1150, **HAWISE DE BEAUMONT** (63-26), d. 24 Apr. 1197. (*CP* IV: 670 chart III, V: 687, 736, VII: 520).

Line 124A   Prepared for an earlier edition by Douglas Richardson

26. **ROBERT DE CAEN** (124-26), Earl of Gloucester; m. Maud, dau. of Robert Fitz Hamon.

27. **MABIRA DE CAEN**, of Gloucester, seen abt. 1190; m. Jordan de Cambernon (also Campernon or Campo Ernulfi), seen 1172, seigneur de Cambernon and Maisoncelles, France; held 7 knts fees of the honor of Gloucester in England 1166, and three knts fees under the Duke of Normandy 1172. English fees: Umberleigh and High Bickington, Devon & other properties in Oxford, Northants, and Somerset. (*Devon and Cornwall N & Q*, vol. 18 (1934-35), pp. 3-7; C. Elizabeth Champernowne, *History of the Champernowne Family* (1943), pp. 4-6; J. Horace Round, *Cal. of Doc. Preserved in France*, pp. 192, 195; *VCH Oxford*, VII: 185).

28. **HENRY DE CHAMBERNON**, d. abt. 1203, younger son, of Ilfracombe, Devon; m. Isabel, liv. 1218.

29. **HENRY DE CHAMBERNON**, d. abt. 1210, of Ilfracombe, Devon; m. Rose (or Rohese), liv. 1237, app. dau. & h. Sir William de Tracy, b. say 1135, seen 1170, of Bradninch, Devon, one of the 4 murderers of Thomas A Beckett, Archbishop of Canterbury, s. of **WILLIAM DE TRACY** (222-26), d. abt. 1135, lord of Bradninch, Devon. Rose m. (2) Robert de Sechevill (or Sacchville), d. abt. 1218, of Braunton, Cowley, Dunsford & Rewe, Devon. Rose was h. to Clistwick, Devon (Clyst St. George or Clist Champernowne). Manor previously the maritagium of Sir William de Tracy's wife, given name unknown. The lords of Bradninch held Clyst St. George of the Pomeroy family; so Sir William de Tracy's wife likely dau. of Henry de Pomeroy, seen 1156, lord of Berry Pomeroy, Devon, by **ROHESE** (195-26). Rohese was a sister of **REGINALD FITZ ROY** (121-26), Earl of Cornwall, a bastard son of King Henry I. Earl Reginald had several half-siblings by his mother, Sibyl Corbet's marriage to **HERBERT FITZ HERBERT** (262-27); [so poss. Rohese de Pomeroy was a child of her mother's marriage to Herbert Fitz Herbert, because as her dau.'s. husb. Sir William de Tracy, himself a gr.s. of **HENRY I** (121-25), would be his wife's first cousin if she were also Henry's grandchild. This previously undetected Tracy-Pomeroy match gives strong circumstantial evidence that King Henry I was not Rohese de Pomeroy's father]. (Book of Fees, Part I, pp. 97, 612-613; Pipe Rolls 12th King John [A.D. 1210], ed. S. F. Slade (1951), *Pub. of the Pipe Roll Soc.*, Vol. 64 [or

n.s., Vol. 26], pp. 167-168; George Oliver, *Monasticon Dioecesis Exoniensis* (1846), pp. 346-347; *History of the Champernowne Family, cit.*, p. 10; Sanders, 20-21, 106-107). [Ed. note, See: Powley, *The House of Pomerai...* (1944), p. 16, note 12: "Tregothnan charter (1141-5/6) in which Reginald, styling himself son of Henry, earl of Cornwall, names Rohesia de Pomeria as his sister.]

30. **OLIVER DE CHAMBERNON**, dead by 1232, of Ilfracombe, Birch and Southcott, Devon; m. Wymarca, &. 1238. She had a suit in 1232, regarding land in Gillescot, Devon. (*Devon & Cornwall N & Q*, Vol. 18 (1934-1935), pp. 3-7; *Champernowne Family, cit.*, pp. 10-11; Book of Fees, Part II, pp. 778, 784; Curia Regis Rolls, XIV, p. 428).

31. **SIR HENRY DE CHAMBERNON**, b. say 1225 (still minor in 1242/3), liv. 1281, of Ilfracombe, Jacobstowe, Coryton and Alphington, Devon, and Tywardreath and Ludgvan, Cornwall; m. Dionisia English, dau. of Sir Robert English of Stockleigh English, Devon. (*Devon & Cornwall N & Q*, Vol. 18 (1934-1935), pp. 3-7; *Champernowne Family, cit.*, pp. 11-12; Book of Fees, Part II, pp. 778, 784; Vivian, *Visit. of Devon*, p. 160).

32. **WILLLIAM DE CHAMBERNON**, d. 1304, of Ilfracombe & Warcomb, Devon, and Otterham and Tywardreath, Cornwall; m. Joan de Ferrers, dau. of William de Ferrers. (*Champernowne Family*, pp. 12-21; Vivian, *Visit. of Devon*, p. 169).

33. **HENRY DE CHAMBERNON** (or **CHAMPERNON**), b. abt. 1274, d. 1330, of Ilfracombe, Devon, and Tywardreath, Cornwall; m. Joan Bodrugan, dau. Sir Henry Bodrugan. (*Champernowne Family, cit.*, pp. 12-21; Vivian, *Visit. of Devon*, p. 160).

34. **JOAN DE CHAMPERNON**, m. Sir Nicholas de Bonville, b. abt. 1293, d. abt. 1354, of Shute, Devon, and Sock Dennis, Somerset, M.P., Somerset, 1324, son of Sir Nicholas de Bonville, d. 1295, of Sock Dennis, Somerset, and Wiscombe, Devon, by his wife, Hawise de Shute, alive 1304, widow of Thomas de Pyne. (Vivian, *Visit of Devon*, pp. 101, 160; *Somerset Arch. & Nat. Hist. Soc.*, LXXIX App. II, p. 27; *Champernowne Family, cit.*, pp. 12-21).

35. **SIR WILLLAM BONVILLE**, b. abt. 1340, d. 1408, large landowner in west of England, property including Shute, co. Devon, and Sock Dennis, Somerset; M.P. 8 times for Somerset and 12 times for Devon; sheriff of Somerset and Dorset, 1380-1; sheriff of Devon 1389, 1400; m. (1) Margaret Daumarle, b. abt. 1347, d. 1399, dau. & coh. of Sir William Daumarle (or de Albemarle) of Woodbury and Lympstone, co. Devon, and Middle Chynnock, Somerset, d. 1361, by Agnes de Meriet; m. (2) abt. 1402 Alice, d. 1426, widow succ. **JOHN FITZ ROGER** (261-36), Sir Edmund de Clyvedon, Sir Ralph Carminow, and Sir John Rodeney (issue only by (1) marriage). (Vivian, *Visit of Devon*, p. 101; *Proc. Somerset Arch. & Nat Hist. Soc.*, LXXX, App. II, pp. 54-55).

36. **SIR JOHN BONVILLE**, by (1), b. abt. 1371 (aged 11 in 1382), d. 21 Oct. 1396; m. by 18 Oct. 1377, **ELIZABETH FITZ ROGER** (261-37), b. 15 Aug. 1370, d. 15 Apr. 1414, heiress of Chewton, Somerset, Glen Magna, co. Leicester, Merston, Sussex, and other properties. She m. (2) by 2 Dec. 1398 Richard Stucle (or Stukeley), gent., d. sh. bef. 28 Nov. 1441, King's Esquire of Ridgewell, Essex, escheator of Somerset and Dorset, 1412-3, (prob. s. of Geoffrey de Styuecle, King's Esquire, of co. Bucks, London & Ireland, seen 1348-1380). (*CP* II: 218; *VCH Sussex* IV: 158-159; *VCH Leics.* V: 77,104; *NGSQ* 59: 254-262, 60: 25-35; Feudal Aids III: 123; Cal. Close Rolls (Henry VI), I: 194, (Richard II), VI: 364,368; Vivian, *Visit. of Devon*, pp. 101, 721; Cal. Inq. p.m. 15: 203, 16: 92-93, 209-210; Inq. p.m. for John Bonville, Year: 20 Richard II).

Line 125

26. ROBERT DE CAEN (124-26); m. Maud, dau. of Robert Fitz Hamon.

27. MAUD DE CAEN, of Gloucester, d. 29 July 1189; m. abt. 1141, **RANULPH DE GERNON** (132A-27), b. abt. 1100, d. 16 Dec. 1153, Earl of Chester, Vicomte d'Avranches, son of Ranulph le Meschin, Earl of Chester, and Lucy. (*CP* III: 166-167, IV: 670 chart iv, V: 736, VII: 677; *ES* III.2/354).

28. HUGH OF KEVELIOC, b. 1147, Kevelioc, co. Monmouth, d. 30 June 1181, Leek, co. Stafford, 3rd Earl of Chester, Vicomte d'Avranches in Normandy; m. 1169, Bertrade de Montfort, dau. of Simon de Montfort, d. 1180/1, Count of Evreux, and Maud. (*CP* III: 167, V: 670 chart iv, VII: App. D, 708-717; Wagner, *Pedigree and Progress*, chart p. 204).

29. HAWISE OF CHESTER, Countess of Lincoln, b. 1180, d. 1241/3; m. **ROBERT II DE QUINCY** (54-28). (*CP* III: 167, 169 note *a*, IV: 670 chart iv, VII: 677; *VCH Lanc.* I: 312; *Eng. Hist. Rev.* 35: 27-28; *ES* III.4/708).

Line 126

28. HUGH OF KEVELIOC (125-28), Earl of Chester; m. 1169, Bertrade de Montfort. (*CP* II: 167).

29. MABEL OF CHESTER, m. **WILLIAM D'AUBIGNY** (149-27), 3rd Earl of Arundel, d. Mar. 1220/1. (*CP* I: 233-238).

30. NICHOLE D'AUBIGNY (210-30), m. as 1st wife **ROGER DE SOMERY** (55-29, 81-29), of Dudley, co. Warwick. He m. (2) Amabil de Chaucombe, wid. of Gilbert de Segrave, dau. of Robert de Chaucombe. (Gens. 28-29: *CP* I: 236-237, II: 1-2, *CP* III: 169 note *a*, IV: 670 chart iv, VI: 174; *DNB* 3: 285).

Line 127

28. HUGH OF KEVELIOC (125-28), Earl of Chester; m. Bertrade de Montfort. (*CP* II: 167).

29. AGNES (ALICE) OF CHESTER, d. 2 Nov. 1247; m. 1192, **WILLIAM DE FERRERS** (194-7), 4th Earl of Derby, d. 22 Sept. 1247. (*CP* III: 169 note *a*, IV: 194-196).

30. WILLIAM DE FERRERS, 5th Earl of Derby, b. abt. 1193, bur. 31 Mar. 1254; m. (1) by 14 May 1219, Sibyl Marshal, 3rd dau. of William Marshal, 3rd Earl of Pembroke, by **ISABEL DE CLARE** (66-27), d.s.p.m.; m. (2) abt. 1238, **MARGARET DE QUINCY** (57-29), d. sh. bef. 12 Mar. 1280/1. (Gens. 28-30: IV: 192-198, chart 199, V: 320 chart, vii: 677; *SP* III: 142).

Line 128

21. ROBERT II (53-21, 101-21), King of France; m. (3) Constance of Provence, b abt. 986, d. 1032. (*Falaise Roll*, 187-197; *ES* II/11).

22. ADELE (or **AELIS**) **OF FRANCE**, Countess of Contentin, b. abt. 1009, d. Messines, 8 Jan. 1079; m. (1) 10 Jan 1027, **RICHARD III** (132A-23), Duke of Normandy, d. 6 Aug. 1027, m. (2) Paris, 1028, **BALDWIN V** (162-22), Count of Flanders, d. Lille, 1 Sept. 1067. (M. Jackson Crispin, *Falaise Roll* (London, 1938), 186-187; *ES* II/11, II/79; West Winter, IX.125, X.30, XI.12).

Line 129

24. FULK V (118-24), Count of Anjou, King of Jerusalem; m. Erembourg, Countess of Maine, dau. of Helie de la Flêche, Count of Maine. (*NEHGR* 99: 34).

25. SYBIL OF ANJOU, b. 1112, d. 1165; m. (2) 1131, **THIERRY I OF LORRAINE** (164-25), Count of Flanders, d. 17 Jan. 1168. (*ES* II/82) (Note: Thierry was also known as Dietrich I, Count of Alsace.)

Line 130

23. ROBERT I (121-23), Duke of Normandy d. 22 July 1035; left issue by his mistress, Herleve (or Herleva), dau. of Fulbert of Falais. (*CP* I: 351-352; *Eng. Hist. Rev.* 101: 399-404).

24. ADELAIDE (or **ADELA**) of Normandy, Countess of Aumale, b. abt. 1030, d. 1081/4-1090, sister of **WILLIAM I** (121-24) the Conqueror; m. (1) Enguerrand II, Count of Ponthieu, slain at the siege of Arques, 1053, son of Hugh II, d. 20 Nov. 1052, Count of Ponthieu and Bertha of Aumale; m. (2) **LAMBERT OF BOULOGNE** (148-22), Count of Lens in Artois, slain at the battle of Lille, 1054; m. (3) 1054/6, **EUDES** (136-23), Count of Champagne and Aumale (of which he was deprived by his uncle Theobald bef. 1071), Earl of Holderness, imprisoned 1096. (*CP* I: 350-353, V: 736).

25. JUDITH OF LENS (see also 98A-23), prob. by (1), b. 1054; m. 1070, Waltheof II, Earl of Northumberland, beheaded Winchester 31 May 1076, son of Sigurd, Earl of Northumberland, and Aelfled, dau. of Aldred of Bernicia. (*CP* I: 350-353, IV: 670 chart iv, V: 472, 736, VII: 640-641).

26. MAUD OF HUNTINGDON, b. 1072 (age 18 yrs. in 1090), d. 1130/1, Countess of Huntingdon and Northumberland; m. (1) abt. 1090, Simon de St. Liz (Senlis/Senliz) , d. 1111, Earl of Huntingdon and Northampton, Crusader, son of Ranulph the Rich, a Norman; m. (2) 1113, **DAVID I** (170-22), "The Saint," King of Scots. (*CP* IV: 670 chart iv, V: 472 note *f*, VII: 640-642; *SP* I: 1; Dunbar 59).

27. MAUD DE ST. LIZ, d. 1140 (or 1158/63?); m. (1) Robert Fitz Richard, d. 1134/6, steward of **HENRY II** (see 1-24), lord of Little Dunmow, Essex, son of Richard I Fitz Gilbert, d. abt. 1090, seigneur of Bienfaite & Orbec, Normandy & of Clare, Suffolk, by (1) wife **ROHESE GIFFARD** (184-2), and grandson of Gilbert, Count of Brionne in Normandy; m. (2) aft. 1136, Saher I de Quincy (see 53-27), Lord of Daventry. (*CP* IV: 670 chart iv, V: 472 note *f*, VI: 641 note *b*).

28. WALTER FITZ ROBERT, d. 1198, of Little Dunmow, Essex; m. (1) Maud de Bohun; m. (2) Maud Lucy (who had as maritagium Diss, Norfolk), dau. of Sir Richard de Lucy, Knt., Justiciar of England, d. 1179, of Chipping Ongar, Essex, & Diss, Norfolk, by Rohese (Roesia). (*CP* V: 472 note *f*, VIII: 257 note *n*; Weever 336-337; Sanders, 129-130).

29. ROBERT FITZ WALTER, by (2), of Woodham, d. 9 Dec. 1235; leader of the barons who revolted against King John in 1215 and obtained the Magna Charta; m. Rohese. (*CP* V: 472 note *f*; Weever 632).

30. SIR WALTER FITZ ROBERT, d. sh. bef. 10 Apr. 1258, of Woodham-Walter, Burnham, Roydon, Dunmow, Henham, Wimbish and Tey; m. **IDA LONGESPEE** (30-28). (*CP* V: 472, XI: 382; *Dudley Pedigree*; Turton; D.L. Jacobus in *Boston Evening Transcript* (1 Feb. 1928) note 2257, Part XIII).

31. SIR ROBERT FITZ WALTER, b. 1247, d. 18 Jan. 1325/6, 1ˢᵗ Lord Fitz Walter; m. (1) Devorguilla de Burgh, d. 1284, dau. of Sir John de Burgh and **CECILY DE BALIOL** (99-29); m. (2) 1289, Alianore de Ferrers, dau. of **SIR ROBERT DE FERRERS** (57-30) of Chartley, Earl of Derby, by (2) wife **ALIANORE DE BOHUN** (68-30); m. (3) 1308, Alice de Montfort, wid. of Sir Warin de Lisle, dau. of Piers de Montfort. (CP IV: 474, VIII: 71).

Line 131

28. HUGH OF KEVELIOC (125-28), 3ʳᵈ Earl of Chester; m. Bertrade de Montfort. (CP IV: 640 chart iv, VII: 677; VCH Lanc. I: 312).

29. MAUD OF CHESTER, b. 1171, d. 1233; m. 26 Aug. 1190, **DAVID OF SCOTLAND** (styled **DAVID OF HUNTINGDON**) (93-26, 252-26), b. 1144, d. 17 June 1219, Earl of Huntingdon. (CP IV: 670 chart iv, V: 736, VII: 677; SP I: 4; ES II/90).

Line 132

22. JUDITH OF BRITTANY (121-22), b. 982, d. 1017; m. abt. 1000, **RICHARD II** (121E-21), Duke of Normandy.

23. ADELAIDE (or **JUDITH**) **OF NORMANDY**, m. 1016, Renaude I, Count of Burgundy, d. 1057. (ES II/79).

24. WILLIAM I, "the Great," Count of Burgundy, Count of Mâcon, d. 12 Nov. 1087; m. 1049/57 Stephanie, parentage unknown (see note at 144-22). de Longwy, b. abt. 1035, liv. 1088, , by wife, Clemence de Foix,. (Garnier xxviii; Moriarty, The Plantagenet Ancestry; Annales de Bourgogne, XXXII: 247-267, article by Szabolcs de Vajay; ES II/59).

25. RAYMOND OF BURGUNDY, d. 1107; m. Toledo 1087, **URRACA I** (113-24), Queen of Leon and Castile, d. 1126. (Turton; Moriarty, cit.; ES II/59, 62).

Line 132A   Prepared for an earlier edition by Douglas Richardson

22. JUDITH OF BRITTANY (121-22, 132-22), founded abbey of Bernay, Normandy, abt. 1026; m. abt. 1000-1008 **RICHARD II** (121E-21) "the Good," d. 28 Aug 1026, Duke of Normandy, 20 Nov. 996-1026. (Onslow, The Dukes of Normandy, pp. 63-112, chart 176; Ed. Garnier, Table xlviii; Douglas, William the Conqueror, pp. 15, 29, 109, chart Table I; Salliot, 36; Moriarty Notebooks).

23. RICHARD III, eldest s., Duke of Normandy 1026-1028, d. 6 Aug 1028; by unk. mistress had (Onslow, cit. pp. 113-114; Douglas, cit. pp. 92-93, chart Table I; Douglas, "The Rise of Normandy," Proc. of the British Academy (1947), Vol. 33; Garnier, cit.).(See also ES II/79).

24. ALICE OF NORMANDY, illeg. dau.; m. Ranulph I, vicomte of the Bessin, fought at the Battle of Val-es-Dunes, 1047, son of Anschitil, living 1031, vicomte of the Bessin. (Douglas, cit., pp. 92-93; Douglas, "The Rise of Normandy," pp. 127-128; Gallia Christiana, Vol. XI, Instrumenta, col. 70; Chronique de Robert de Torigni (ed. L. Delisle), Vol. 1, p. 34; Recueil des Actes des Ducs de Normandie (911-1066), ed. M. Faroux, no. III).

25. RANULPH II, adult by 1066, living April 1089, vicomte of Bayeux in Normandy; m. Margaret (or Maud), dau. of Richard (le Goz), living 1084, vicomte d'Avranches, by wife Emma (alleged to be a half-sister of William the Conqueror; Prof. Douglas says "fictitious.") (Douglas, *cit*, pp. 92-93; Douglas, "The Rise of Normandy," pp. 127-128; *CP* III: 166, XII (1) App. K, 32-33).

26. RANULPH III le Meschin, de Briquessart, d. abt. 1129, bur. St. Werburg's, Chester, lord of Cumberland, vicomte of Bayeux in Normandy, Earl of Chester in 1120, foll. the death of his first cousin, Hugh d'Avranches, Earl of Chester; in 1124 commander of the Royal Forces in Normandy; m. prob. abt. 1098 Lucy, liv. 1130, wid., successively, of Ivo de Tailbois and Roger Fitz Gerold. (*CP* III: 166, VII, App. J, 743-746; Douglas, *cit.*, pp. 92-93; Sanders, 32-33; Douglas, "The Rise of Normandy," pp. 127-128).

27. RANULPH DE GERNON, Earl of Chester, Vicomte d'Avranches in Normandy, b. abt. 1100, Castle of Gernon in Normandy, d. 16 Dec. 1153, bur. St. Werburg's, Chester; m. abt. 1141, **MAUD DE CAEN** (125-27) of Gloucester, d. 29 July 1189, dau. of Robert, d. 1147, Earl of Gloucester. (*CP* III: 166-167; Sanders, 32-33).

Line 132B   Prepared for an earlier edition by Douglas Richardson

25. RANULPH II (132A-25), vicomte of Bayeux in Normandy, living Apr. 1089; m. Margaret (or Maud), dau. of Richard (le Goz), vicomte d'Avranches. (Douglas, *William the Conqueror*, pp. 92-93; *CP* III: 166; Douglas, "The Rise of Normandy," *Proc. of British Academy* (1947), 33: 127-128).

26. WILLIAM LE MESCHIN, lord of Skipton-in-Craven, co. York; m. Cecily de Rumilly, dau. and h. of Robert de Rumilly. (*CP* IX: 270-272, XII (2): 930-931; Eyton, *Antiquities of Shropshire*, 2: 201-205).

27. MAUD LA MESCHIN, dau. and coh., inherited manor of Molland, Devon, held by her maternal gr.f., Robert de Rumilly; m. (1) by 1139. Philip de Belmeis, adult by 1127, lord of Tong, Salop, and Ashby, co. Leicester, son of Walter de Belmeis; m. (2) Hugh de Mortimer, d. 1180/1, lord of Wigmore, co. Hereford. (*CP* IX: 270-272, XII (2): 930-931; Eyton, *op. cit.*; Farrer, *Early Yorkshire Charters*, 3: 470; Farrer, *Honours and Knight's Fees*, 3: 35).

28. ALICE DE BELMEIS, dau. by (1); m. **ALAN CEOCHE** or **LA COCHE**, or **LA ZOUCHE** (39-27), adult by 1153, d. 1190, lord of North Molton, Devon, son of Geoffrey, vicomte of Porhoët, by Hawise, dau. Alan Fergent, Duke of Brittany. (*CP* XII (2): 930-931).

Line 132C   Prepared for an earlier edition by Douglas Richardson

27. MAUD (or **MATILDA**) **LA MESCHIN** (132B-27); m. (1) by 1138/9 Philip de Belmeis, lord of Tong, Salop, and Ashby, co. Leicester; m. (2) Hugh de Mortimer, d. 1180/1, Lord Mortimer of Wigmore, co. Hereford, son of Hugh de Mortimer, d. 1148/50, Lord Mortimer of Wigmore. (*CP* IX: 268-272).

28. ROGER DE MORTIMER, d. bef. 19 Aug. 1214, Lord Mortimer of Wigmore, co. Hereford; m. Isabel, d. bef. 29 Apr. 1252, granted a life interest in Lechlade, co. Gloucester, & Oakham, Rutland, which her brother Henry lost at time of conquest of Normandy, dau. of Walkelin de Ferrieres, seigneur of Ferrieres-Saint-Hilaire, and lord of Oakham, Rutland. (*CP* IV: 191, IX: 272-273).

29. RALPH DE MORTIMER, d. 6 Aug. 1246, bur. Wigmore, co. Hereford, Lord Mortimer of Wigmore; m. 1230, **GLADYS DHU** (176B-28), d. 1251, widow of Reynold de Braose and dau. of **LLYWELYN AP IORWERTH** (176-7), Prince of North Wales. (*CP* IX: 275-276).

Line 132D   Prepared for an earlier edition by Douglas Richardson

26. RANULPH III (styled le Meschin) (132A-26), Earl of Chester; m. Lucy.

27. ADELIZ (or **ALICE**), m. (1) **RICHARD FITZ GILBERT** (also styled de Clare) (246B-25), lord of Clare, Suffolk, d. 1136; m. (2) Robert de Condet (or Cundy), d. abt. 1141, lord of Thorngate Castle in the city of Lincoln, and of Wickhambreaux, Kent, Grimston, co. Nottingham, and South Carlton, Thurlby, Eagle and Skellingthorpe, co. Lincoln, s. Osbert de Condet (or Cundy), d. by 1130, lord of Wickhambreux, Kent, Grimston, co. Nottingham, and South Carlton, Eagle and Skellingthorpe, co. Lincoln, by Adelaide de Chesney, dau. & h. William de Chesney, lord of Caenby and Glentham, co. Lincoln. (*CP* III: 243; "Thorngate and the Condet Family," pub. in *The Registrum Antiquissimum of the Cathedral Church of Lincoln*, Vol. I (published 1931, as Publications of the Lincoln Record Society, vol. 27), ed. by C. W. Foster, Appendix II, pp. 277-295).

28. ISABEL DE CONDET (or **CUNDY**), living 1166, had land in South Carlton, co. Lincoln and app. also in Grimston, co. Nottingham as maritagium; m. Hugh Bardolf the elder, d. abt. 1176, lord of Waddington, Riseholm and Scothern, co. Lincoln, bro. & h. Hamelin Bardolf, living 1162, lord of Bungay, Suffolk. The parentage of Hugh and Hamelin Bardolf is unknown, but they were closely related to Thomas Bardolf, ancestor of the Lords Bardolf of Wormegay. (*Lincolnshire History and Archaeology*, I:4-28 (1966), "Thorngate and the Condet Family," *cit.* Note: Isabel's identity is proved by her maritagium in South Carlton, co. Lincoln, which land was part of her mother's known holding in that locality, temp. King Stephen, 1135-1154).

29. JULIANA BARDOLF, d. by 1219, dau. & in her issue coh.; m., as (1) wife, Nicholas Poyntz, b. by 1173, d. by 2 Nov. 1223, lord of Tockington and Swell, co. Gloucester, steward of Gilbert, Earl of Gloucester, 1217-30, keeper of Gloucester Castle, keeper of the Honour of Dunster, son of Pons Fitz Simon, living 1166, lord of Tockington and Swell, co. Gloucester. (*CP* X: 670-672; *Lincolnshire History and Archaeology*, I: 4-28 (1966); Reading Abbey Cartularies, ed. by B. R. Kemp, vol. I (pub. 1986 as Camden, 4th ser., vol. 31), pp. 321-347, re. Hoo, Kent, a Bardolf property inherited jointly by the Poyntz and Grey families).

30. SIR HUGH POYNTZ, d. abt. 4 Apr. 1220; m. bef. 23 Mar. 1216/7 **HAWISE MALET** (234A-29), living 1287, elder dau. & coh. William Malet, lord of Curry Malet, Somerset. (*CP* X: 672).

Line 133   Revised for 8th Edition

19. MATHILDA of the West Franks (157-19), b. abt. 943, d. 26 Nov. 981, dau. of **LOUIS IV** (148-18), King of France and of **GERBERGA OF SAXONY** (142-18); m. abt. 964, Conrad I of Burgundy, "the Peaceful," d. 19 Oct. 993, King of Burgundy, King of the West Franks, son of Rudolph II, King of Burgundy, and Bertha of Swabia. (*ES* I.1/6).

20. MATILDA OF BURGUNDY, m. pos. Robert, Count of Geneva. (Armin Wolf, "Ein Kamp um Genf: ...," in Rechtsgeschichte Interdisziplinaritat (2001):, 63-74).

21. BERTHA OF BURGUNDY, m. a Gerard III, Count of Dagsburg-Egisheim, d. 1038.

22. GÉROLD OF GENEVA, d. by 1080, Count of Geneva, bef. 1034; m. (1) Gisele; m. (2) Tetberge.

23. AIMON I OF GENEVA, by (2), Count of Geneva, 1091, b. abt. 1050, d. bef. 1128; m. Ita. (Moriarity, 261; Gens. 19-23: Foundations I(2) 2003: 111-115).

24. AMADEUS I OF GENEVA, Count of Geneva, b. 1100, d. 26 June 1178; m. (1) by 1130, Matilda of Cuiseau, d. by 2 July 1137, dau. of Hugh, Seigneur de Cuiseau and Clairvaux. (*ES* XV/87).

25. WILLIAM I OF GENEVA, Count of Geneva, b. 1130, d. 25 July 1195; m. (1) **AGNES** (274B-26) of Savoy, d. by 1172, dau. of **AMADEUS III** (274B-25), Count of Savoy; m. (2) Beatrix de Faucigny, dau. of Aimon I of Faucigny and of Clementia, d. 1178. (*ES* XI: 158; Moriarity, 104, 107).

26. MARGARET (BEATRIX) OF GENEVA, by (2), b. abt. 1180, d. Pierre Chatel, 8 Sept. 1257 (13 Apr 1236); m. May 1195, **THOMAS I** (274C-27) Count of Savoy and Maurienne, b. 20 May 1178, d. 1 Mar. 1233, son of **HUMBERT III** (247C-26) Count of Savoy by his 4th wife, Beatrix of Mâcon. (*CP* IX: 805; *ES* XI/158, II/190, III.1/122; Moriarty, 107, 261; Brandenburg, p. 10 #52, #59; p. 11 #65, #67; p. 50, #138, #216; p. 51 #396, #393; Winkhaus, pp. 85, 95).

27. BEATRIX OF SAVOY (247C-28), d. 1266; m. 5 Dec 1220, **RAYMOND V BERENGER** (111-29), b. 1198, d. 19 Aug. 1245, Count of Provence and Forcalquier. (*CP* IV: 321; *ES* II/190).

Line 134   Line cancelled

Line 135   Revised for 8th Edition

26. LOUIS VI (101-24), King of France; m. 1115, **ADELAIDE** (274A-25) of Savoy, d. 1154, dau. of **HUMBERT II** (274A-24), d. 1103, Count of Maurienne & Savoy, by his wife, Gisele of Burgundy, d. 1133, dau. of **WILLIAM I** (132-24), Count of Burgundy and his wife, Stephanie. (*ES* II/11)

27. ROBERT I, Count of Dreux, b. abt. 1123, d. 1188; m. (3) 1152, Agnes de Baudemont, dau. of Gui de Baudemont. [Not Vaudemont as in earlier editions]. (*ES* III.1/63, XIV/51).

28. ROBERT II, Count of Dreux & Braine, b. abt. 1154, d. 28 Dec. 1218; m. (2) 1184, Yolande de Coucy, d. 18 Mar. 1222, dau. of Raoul de Coucy, killed at Acre 1191 in Third Crusade, Seigneur of Coucy and Marie, by his wife, Agnes de Hainaut, d. 1174, dau. of **BALDWIN IV** (163-26), Count of Hainaut, by his wife, Alice of Namur. (Moriarty, *The Plantagenet Ancestry*, p. 150, 195; LaChesnaye VI: 283).

29. PIERRE (DE BRAINE) DE DREUX (also styled Mauclerc), d. 22 June 1250; m. (1) March 1213, **ALIX DE THOUARS** (96-28, 271-28), d. 1221, Countess of Brittany, m. (2) 1235 Margaret de Montagu.

30. YOLANDE DE DREUX by (1), b. 1218, d. 10 or 16 Oct. 1272; m. 1238, **HUGH XI DE LUSIGNAN** (275-28, 117-28), "le Brun," b. 1221, d. 1250, Count of Ponthieu, la Marche and Angoulême. (Gens: 29-30: Garnier xxxi; Painter, *Feudalism & Liberty*, 115, 116; *ES* III.4/816).

31. HUGH XII DE LUSIGNAN (275-29), d. 1270, Count of la Marche and Angoulême; m. 29 Jan. 1253/4 **JEANNE DE FOUGÈRES** (214A-30) Dame of Fougères, dau. & h. **RAOUL III DE FOUGÈRES** (214A-29) and Isabel de Craon. (*CP* V: 632, 634).

32. JEANNE DE LUSIGNAN, (de la March), d. betw. Aug. & 14 Sept. 1322; m. (2) bef. 11 Oct. 1283, **SIR PIERS DE GENEVILLE** (71-31), d. bef. 8 June 1292, Baron Geneville of Trim. She m. (1) Bernard I Ézy, Sire d'Albret, who d. soon after. (*CP* V: 632-634 [789-790]; Turton; *ES* III.4/816).

Line 136   Revised for 8th Edition, Gens. 18-27. Gens. 27-34 originally prepared by Douglas Richardson

18. HERBERT II (50-18), d. 943, Count of Vermandois and Troyes; m. **LIEGARDE** (or Hildebrante) (48-19), dau. of Robert I, King of France, by 1st wife, wife Aelis. (Isenburg).

19. LUITGARDE DE VERMANDOIS, d. aft. 978; m. (2) 943 **THEOBALD I** (49-19),"le Tricheur," d. 978, Count of Blois. (Saillot, 45).

20. EUDES I, Count of Blois, d. 12 Mar. 995/6; m. abt. 983, **BERTHA OF BURGUNDY** (159-20), b. abt. 964, d. aft. 1010. (Saillot, 45).

21. EUDES II, b. 990, d. 15 Nov. 1037, Count of Blois, 1004, and of Champagne, 1019; m. (2) abt. 1010, Ermengarde of Auvergne, d. 10 Mar. 1040, dau. of Robert I, d. 1032, Count of Auvergne, by his wife, Ermengarde, dau. of **WILLIAM II** (141A-20), d. 994, Marquis of Provence, by his wife, Adelaide of Anjou. (Saillot, 45).

22. STEPHEN II, Count of Champagne, b. abt. 1015, d. 1047; m. Adela. (*CP* I: 350-352).

23. EUDES, Count of Champagne & Aumale, Earl of Holderness; m. 1054/60, **ADELAIDE** (130-24) of Normandy, b. bef. 1030, d. bef. 1090, Countess of Aumale, sister of **WILLIAM THE CONQUEROR** (121-24). (*CP* I: 350-353).

24. STEPHEN, Count of Aumale, b. abt. 1070, d. 1127, Earl of Holderness, Crusader, 1096; m. Hawise de Mortimer, d. 1189, dau. of Ralph de Mortimer, liv. 1104, lord of Wigmore, co. Hereford, Seigneur of St. Victor-en-Caux in Normandy, by his 1st wife, Millicent. (*CP* I: 352-353).

25. AGNES; m. (1) William de Roumare, d. 1151; m. (2) Piers (Peter) I de Brus, Lord of Skelton, d. Feb. 1218/9, son of Adam de Brus, by Joan le Grammaire, dau. Richard le Grammaire of Knottington, co. York. (West Winter XIII.84; *ES* II/46; *CP* V: 269, VII 373).

26. PIERS (PETER) II DE BRUS, d. bef. 1222, bur. Guisborough, Lord of Skelton, co. York, Crusader; m. abt. 1210/15, **HAWISE (or HELWISE) DE LANCASTER** (88-28). (*CP* V: 267; West Winter, XIV.145; *VCH Lanc.* I: 357-366; Banks I: 431-432; Farrer, *EYC* II: 15, III: 87).

27. AGNES DE BRUS, (coh. of bro. Piers (Peter) III de Brus, d. 18 Sept. 1272), d. abt. 1280; m. by Nov. 1243, **SIR WALTER DE FAUCONBERGE** (184B-8), d. 1-2 Nov. 1304, 1st Lord Fauconberge, of Rise & Withernwick in Holderness, s. Sir Peter de Fauconberge, liv. 1230, of same, by Margaret de Montfichet, dau. & coh. of Richard de Montfichet of Stanstead Mountfitchet, Essex. (*CP* V: 267-269, West Winter, XV.209; Clay, 69).

28. AGNES DE FAUCONBERGE, seen 1323; m. Sir Nicholas Engaine, d. 1322, of Colne Engaine, Essex & Coton, co. Cambridge, son of Sir John Engaine, d. 1297, of Laxton, co. Northampton, by his wife, Joan de Greinville. (*CP* V: 75).

29. SIR JOHN ENGAINE, b. 30 May 1302, d. 16 Feb. 1357/8, 2nd Lord Engaine, of Laxton, co. Northampton, & Colne Engaine, Essex; m. abt. 12 Nov. 1318, Joan Peverel, liv. 1358, dau. Sir Robert Peverel of Castle Ashby, co. Northampton, & Alice. (*CP* V: 75-77).

30. ELIZABETH ENGAINE, b. abt. 1341, d. in or bef. 1387, h. of Laxton & Engaine, co. Northampton, & Engaine, co. Huntingdon; m. Sir Lawrence Pabenham, b. 1334, d. 10 June 1399, of Pabenham, co. Bedford, knt. of the shire, 1378, 1383, son of Thomas de Pabenham, d. 1345, of same, by wife Alice. (*CP* V: chart p. 80; Katherine S. Naughton, *The Gentry of Bedfordshire in the 13th & 14th Centuries*, p. 34 (chart); *VCH Cambridge* IX: 294; *VCH Hunt.* II: 326, III: 49).

31. KATHERINE PABENHAM, b. 1372, d. 17 June 1436, h. of Ilchester & Laxton, co. Northampton & Pabenham & Eaton, co. Bedford; m. (1) Sir William Cheyney (or Cheyne), d. abt. 1394, of Fen Ditton, co. Cambridge, sheriff of Cambridge & Huntingdon, son of John Cheyney (or Cheyne) of Long Stanton, co. Cambridge, by wife Joan Muschet; m. (2) **SIR THOMAS AYLESBURY** (187-10), b. abt. 1369, d. 9 Sept. 1418, of Milton Keynes, co. Buckingham, & Blatherwick, co. Northampton. (Naughton, *cit*, p. 34 (chart); *CP* V: chart p. 80; *VCH Cambridge* IX: 294; *VCH Hunt.* II: 326, III: 49; *VCH Beds*. III: 191).

32. LAURENCE CHENEY (or Cheyne), b. 1393, d. 30 Dec. 1461, of Fen Ditton, co. Cambridge; M.P.; Escheator of Bedford & Buckingham, 1423; sheriff of Cambridge & Huntingdon, 1430, 1435; m. (1) Elizabeth Cokayne, alive 1422, widow of Sir Philip Butler, dau. Sir John Cokayne, d. 1427, of Bury Hatley, co. Bedford, chief baron of the exechequer. (*CP* V chart 80, IX: 612-615; *VCH Cambridge* IX: 223, 294).

33. ELIZABETH CHENEY, dau. by (1); m. Sir Frederick Tylney, d. by 1447, of Ashwellthorpe, Norfolk, & Boston, co. Lincoln, son of Sir Philip Tylney, d. 1453, of Boston, co. Lincoln, Canon Residentiary of Lincoln Cathedral, by wife, Isabel Thorpe, d. 1436, dau. & h. Edmund, 5th Lord Thorpe, d. 1418, of Ashwellthorpe, Norfolk. (*CP* XII (1): 723-725, IX: 612-615).

34. ELIZABETH TYLNEY, h. of Ashwellthorpe, Norfolk, d. 4 Apr. 1497; m. (1) **SIR HUMPHREY BOURCHIER** (4-34), d. 14 Apr. 1471, s. & h. app. of Sir John Bourchier, Lord Berners; m. (2) as his 1st wife, 30 Apr. 1472, **SIR THOMAS HOWARD** (22-35), b. 1443, d. 21 May 1524, Duke of Norfolk, Earl of Surrey, Earl Marshal, s. John Howard, d. 1485, Duke of Norfolk, by (1) wife, Catherine Moleyns, dau. of Sir William Moleyns. (*CP* II: 153-154, IX: 610-615, XII (1): 723-725).

Line 137

21. EUDES II (136-21), Count of Blois, d. 15 Nov. 1037; m. (2) abt. 1010, Ermengarde, dau. of Robert I, d. 1032, Count de Auvergne, and Ermengarde, dau. **WILLIAM II** (141A-20), d. 994, Marquis of Provence, and Adelaide of Anjou. (Saillot, 45).

22. THEOBALD III, Count of Blois and Champagne, d. 1089; m. (3) .Alix (Adela) de Crepy. (West Winter X.11, XI.18).

23. STEPHEN OF BLOIS, b. 1046, a leader of the First Crusade, 1096, d. 1101; m. abt. 1080, bef. 1085, **ADELA OF NORMANDY** (169-24), b. abt. 1062, d. 1137, dau. of **WILLIAM THE CONQUEROR** (121-24). (Robinson, *Readings in European History*, I: 321-325; Moriarty, *The Plantagenet Ancestry*).

24. THEOBALD IV, Count of Blois and Champagne, d. 1152, (bro. of **STEPHEN** (169-25, 169A-25, King of England); m. 1126, Matilda (or Maud), d. 1161, dau. of Engelbert, d. 1141, Duke of Carinthia, Marquis of Istria, by his wife, Uta, dau. of Ulrich the Rich, Count of Passau. (*ES* II/46-47).

25. ADELAIDE (or **ALIX**) **DE CHAMPAGNE**, b. abt. 1140, d. 4 June 1209; m. as (3) wife, 18 Oct. 1160, **LOUIS VII** (101-25), b. 1120, d. 18 Sept. 1180, King of France. (Isenburg). (Gens. 21-25: Moriarty, *The Plantagenet Ancestry*, p. 117).

24. ERMENGARDE DE NEVERS (107-24), m. abt. 1095 Milo (or Miles), Sire of Courtenay, b. abt. 1075 or bef., d. 1127, son of Jocelin de Courtenay, 1065, and Isabel de Montlhéry, dau. of Guy de Montlhéry.

25. RENAUD DE COURTENAY, Sire de Courtenay, d. 1189/90; m. (1) Helvis, a sister of Frederick (or Guy) du Donjon and Corbeil; m. (2) Maud, dau. Robert Fitz Edith (illegitimate son of **HENRY I** (121-25) King of England). (*ES* III.4/629; Seversmith 2,421).

26. RENAUD (or REGINALD) DE COURTENAY, by (1), b. abt. 1150, d. 27 Sept. 1194, bur. Ford Abbey, co. Devon; held barony of Oakhampton *j.u.*; m. abt. 1175, Hawise de Courcy, d. 31 July 1219, dau. & h. William de Courcy, by Maud d'Avranches, lady of Oakhampton, and of du Sap in Normandy, dau. & h. Robert d'Avranches, lord of Oakhampton, co. Devon. (Seversmith, 2,419).

27. SIR ROBERT DE COURTENAY, feudal baron of Oakhampton, sheriff of Devon 1216, b. abt. 1183, perh. bef., d. 26 July 1242, bur. Ford Abbey, co. Devon; m. **MARY DE VERNON** (or **DE REVIERS**) (50-28). (*CP* IV: 317, 673; Seversmith, 2,413-2,419; *ES* III.4/629).

Line 139

23. STEPHEN OF BLOIS (137-23), Count of Champagne, Brie, Blois, and Chartres, a leader of the First Crusade, 1096, d. 1101, killed by Turks in Crusade of 1101; m. abt. 1080, bef. 1085, **ADELA** (169-24), b. abt. 1062, d. 1137, dau. of **WILLIAM THE CONQUEROR** (121-24). (*CP* V: 156).

24. WILLIAM OF CHAMPAGNE, Sire of Sully, elder brother of **STEPHEN** (169-25), King of England; m. Agnes de Sully dau. of Gilles de Sully, liv. 1098, Seigneur of Sully-sur-Loire and la Chapelle, and Eldeburge of Bourges. (*CP* V: 156; *ES* II/46).

25. MARGARET OF CHAMPAGNE, d. 15 Dec. 1145; m. (3) Henry, Count d'Eu, Lord of Hastings, d. 12 July 1140, s. of William, Count d'Eu, Lord of Hastings, and Beatrice de Builly, sis. & event. h. in her issue of Roger de Builly, lord of Tickhill, co. York. (*CP* V: 155-156; *ES* III.1/110; for the Norman pedigrees, see Moriarty, *The Plantagenet Ancestry*).

26. JOHN, Count d'Eu, Lord of Hastings, d. 26 June 1170, held 56 knight's fees; m. Alice (or Adelise) d'Aubigny, d. 11 Sept. 1188, dau. of William d'Aubigny, 1st Earl of Arundel, and **ADELIZA OF LOUVAIN** (149-25). (*CP* V: 156-158).

27. HENRY, d. 16 or 17 Mar. 1183, Count of Eu, Lord of Hastings; m. **MAUD DE WARENNE** (123-27), d. abt. 1212. (*CP* V: 158-160, esp. 159 note *d*; Gens. 25-27: *ES* III.4/693).

Line 140

13. CHARLEMAGNE (50-13); m. **HILDEGARDE (182-5).**

14. LOUIS I, the Fair, b. Aug. 778, d. near Mainz, 20 June 840, Emperor 814-840; m. (1) 794/5, Ermengarde, d. abt. 3 Oct. 818, dau. of Ingerman, Count of Hesbaye; m. (2) Feb. 819, Judith of Bavaria, d. 19 Apr. 843, dau. of Welf I, Duke of Bavaria. (*CCN*, 623).

15. LOTHAIR I, by (1), b. 795, d. Pruem, Germany, 29 Sept. 855, King of Italy 817-855, Holy Roman Emperor 840-855; m. 15 Oct. 821, Ermengarde, d. 20 Mar. 851, dau.

of Hugh II, Count of Tours. (*ES* I.1/4; Saillot, *Sang de Charlemagne*, p. 9; Brandenburg III 8a. See Line 240).

16. HELLETRUDE (perhaps **ERMENGARDE)** of Lorraine; m. 846, Count **GISELBERT** (240-16), count of Darnau.

17. REGINAR I, (155-17, 240-17), Count of Hainaut, d. aft. 25 Oct. 915, bef. 19 Jan 916; m. (2) Alberade, of Mons?, d. 916, Dame of Hainaut. (*ES* I.1/4, 1.2/236; West Winter, V.11).

18. GISELBERT, (240-18), Duke of Lorraine, b. abt. 880, d. 939; m. 929, **GERBERGA OF SAXONY** (142-18), d. 5 May 984. (She m. 2nd, 939, **LOUIS IV,** d'Outre-Mer (148-18) King of France).

19. GERBERGA of Lorraine, b. abt. 935, d. 978; m. bef. 954, **ALBERT I** (50-19), the Pious, Count de Vermandois, b. abt. 920, d. 987/88.

20. HERBERT III, Count de Vermandois, b. abt. 955, d. 993; m. by 987, Ermengarde, liv. 1021-1043, dau. of Reinald, Count of Bar.

21. OTHO, Count de Vermandois, b. abt. 1000, d. 25 May 1045; m. Parvie, par. unknown.

22. HERBERT IV, Count de Vermandois, b. abt. 1032, d. abt. 1080; m. Adela de Valois and Vexin, dau. of Raoul III, the Great, Count of Valois, Vexin, etc.

23. ADELAIDE DE VERMANDOIS, d.. 1120/24, Countess de Vermandois and Valois; m. (1) **HUGH MAGNUS (II)** (53-23), d. 1101, Duke of France, etc. (*CP* X: 351. Gens. 20-23: *ES* I.1/7).

24. ISABEL DE VERMANDOIS (50-24, 53-24), d. 13 Feb. 1131, Countess of Leicester; m. (1) 1096, Sir Robert de Beaumont, 1st Earl of Leicester, b. abt. 1049, d. 5 June 1118; m. (2) abt. 1118, William de Warenne, d. 1138, 2nd Earl of Surrey. (*CP* IV: 670 chart iii, VII: 520, 523-526, 737, X: 351. Gens. 13-15: Larousse, *Histoire de France*, I: 79 chart; Voltaire, *Oeuvres* (1827), vol, 33, Annales de l'Empire II, Catalogue des Empereurs, 381-383, and for many other lines covered in this section, see Voltaire, *Oeuvres*, vol. 20, Essai sur les Moeurs, *passim*, but verify details. Gens. 13-16: *Boston Evening Transcript*, 9 Nov. 1927, Note 2257, by D.L.J. Part X Carolingians. Gens. 16-19: *Ibid* Part XV Brabant. Gens. 19-24: *Ibid* Part IX Vermandois. See also refs. end of Line 50, and Moriarty, *The Plantagenet Ancestry*).

Line 141   Revised for 8th Edition

16. LUDOLPH, b. abt. 816, d. 6 Sept. 864, Duke of Saxony 859; m. Oda, d. 913, age 107. (*ES* I.1/10).

17. OTTO, "the Illustrious," Duke of Saxony, b. abt. 836, d. 30 Nov. 912; m. abt. 869/70, Haduich (Hedwig), d. 24 Dec. 903, dau. of Henrich, Marquis of France, Duke of Austrasia, d. in battle, Paris, 28 Aug. 886. (*ES* III.1/54).

18. HENRY I, "the Fowler" (147-18), b. 876, d. Memleben, 2 July 936, Duke of Saxony, King of the Saxons 912-936; m. (2) 909, Mechtilde of Ringelheim, b. abt. 896, d. 14 March 968, dau. of Dietrich, Count of Ringelheim. (*ES* I.1/10; *CCN*, 495).

19. HEDWIG OF SAXONY, d. aft. 958; m. 937, **HUGH MAGNUS** (53-19, 101-19), d. June 956, Count of Paris. (*ES* I.1/10; *CCN*, 517).

20. HUGH CAPET, b. aft. 939, d. 24 Oct. 996, King of France 987-996, first of the Capetian kings of France; m. **ADELAIDE OF POITOU** (144A-20). (*CCN*, 517).

21. ROBERT II, King of France, b. 27 Mar. 872, d. 20 July 1031; m. (3) 1001/2, **CONSTANCE OF PROVENCE** (141A-21), d. 25 July 1032. (*ES* II/11; *CCN*, 859).

22. HENRY I, King of France, b. 1005/6, d. Aug. 1060; m. 20 Jan. 1044, **ANNE OF KIEV** (241-6). (*CP* X: 351).

23. HUGH MAGNUS (II), b. 1057, d. 1101, Duke of France and Burgundy, Marquis of Orleans, Count of Amiens, Chaumont, Paris, Valois and Vermandois; m. **ADELAIDE DE VERMANDOIS** (50-23, 140-23), Countess of Vermandois and Valois. (*CP* X: 351).

24. ISABEL DE VERMANDOIS (50-24, 53-24), d. 13 Feb. 1131; m. (1) 1096, Sir Robert de Beaumont, b. abt. 1049, d. 5 June 1118, 1st Earl of Leicester; m. (2) abt. 1118, William de Warenne, d. 1138, 2nd Earl of Surrey. (*CP* X: 351; *ES* III.1/55. Gens. 16-24: *Cambridge Medieval History*; *EB*; Dudley Pedigree; *NEHGR* 99: 243 chart; *Boston Evening Transcript*, 9 Nov. 1927, Note 2257, Part X Carolingians; Moriarty, *The Plantagenet Ancestry*).

Line 141A   Provided by David H. Kelley

15. EUDOCIA INGERINA, b. abt. 840, d. 882/3, mistress of Michael III, Emp. of Byzantium 842-867; m. Basil I, Emp. of Byzantium 867-886 (founder of the "Macedonian" family), his sucessor. Uncertain whether Leo was son of Michael or of Basil.

16. LEO VI, b. 1 Sept. 866, d. 12 May 912, Emperor of Byzantium 886-912; m. (2) 898, Zoe Tzautzina, previously his mistress.

17. ANNA, of Byzantium, b. 886/8, d. abt. 914; m. abt. 900 **LOUIS III** (141B-18) "the Blind," b. abt. 883, d. 5 June 928, King of Provence and Italy. (Brandenburg).

18. CHARLES CONSTANTINE, Count of Vienne, b. abt. 900/1, d. abt. Jan. 962; m. Teutberg, d. abt. 960, dau. of Garnier de Troyes, Viscount of Sens. (Brandenburg; C. W. Previte-Orton, "Charles Constantine of Vienne," *English Historical Review* 29 (1914): 703-706; West Winter, VII.17).

19. CONSTANCE OF PROVENCE, d. 961-965; m. abt. 930, Boso II, d. 965/67, Count of Provence, Avignon & Arles, son of Rotbald I. (*ES* II/187).

20. WILLIAM (or **GUILLAUME**) **II**, b. 950, d. 993/4, Count of Arles, Count of Provence 979-993, m. (1) Arsenda de Comminges; m. (2). as her 4th husb., Adelaide of Anjou, d. 1026, dau. Fulk II, Count of Anjou. (*ES* II/187; Don Stone, *Some Ancient and Medieval Descents...*: Chart 30, "Descent from Charlemagne," and note 9).

21. CONSTANCE OF PROVENCE, dau. by (2), b. abt. 986, d. 25 July 1032; m. as (3) wife, 1001/2 **ROBERT II** (101-21, 107-20, 141-21) the Pious, King of France, b. 27 Mar. 972, d. 20 July 1031. (See Lindsay Brooks, "The Byzantine Ancestry of H.R.H. Prince Charles, Prince of Wales," *The Genealogist* (1981) vol. 2, pp. 3-51 and notes 11-13, 131; Christian Settipani, "Des Capetiens a Ramses II ... pourquois pas?" *Heraldique et Genealogie* (Aug. 1985), vol. 17, no. 3, pp. 263-268, Moriarty, *The Plantagenet Ancestry*, p. 24; Don Stone, *Some Ancient and Medieval Descents...*: Chart 31, "Descent from HGugh Capet").

Line 141B

15. LOTHAIR I (140-15), b. 795, d. 29 Sept. 855, King of Italy 817-855, Holy Roman Emperor; m. 15 Oct. 821 Ermengarde d. 20 Mar. 851, dau. of Hugh II, Count of Tours. (Brandenburg, Table 1; West Winter, III.9).

16. LOUIS II, b. abt. 825, d. 12 Aug. 875, Holy Roman Emperor; m. bef. 5 Oct. 851, Engelberge, d. abt. 900, dau. of Gui I, Duke of Spoleto. (*ES* I.1/4; Brandenburg, *cit.*; West Winter, IV.8).

17. ERMENGARDE, b. 852/855, d. 897, bef. 2 Apr., said to be mistress before 866 of "an Emperor of Byzantium"; m. 3 June 876 Count Boso, King of Provence, King of Burgundy, Count of Vienne, b. 835, d. 887. (Brandenburg, *cit.*; West Winter, V.10).

18. LOUIS III, "the Blind," b. abt. 883, d. 5 June 928, King of Provence and Italy 900; m. (1) **ANNA** (141A-17), of Byzantium, dau. of **LEO VI** (141A-16), Emperor of Byzantium. (ES II/189 NEU; Brandenburg, *cit.*; West Winter, VI.12. Gens. 15-18: Don Stone, *Some Ancient and Medieval Descents...:* Chart 30, "Descent from Charlemagne").

Line 142

17. HENRY I (141-18), "the Fowler," b. 876, d. 2 July 936, King of the Saxons; m. (2) 909 Mechtilde of Ringelheim, b. abt. 890, d. 14 Mar 968, dau. of Dietrich, Count of Saxon-Hamelant. (*ES* I.1/10).

18. GERBERGA OF SAXONY, b. 913/14, d. 5 May 984; m. (1) 929, **GISELBERT** (140-18), Duke of Lorraine, b. abt. 890, d. 939; m. (2) 939/940, **LOUIS IV**, d'Outre-Mer (148-18), King of the West Franks, d. Reims 10 Sept. 954.

19. GERBERGA OF LORRAINE (140-19), b. abt. 935; m. **ALBERT I** (50-19), Count of Vermandois, b. 915/920, d. 987/88. (Moriarty, *The Plantagenet Ancestry*; Seversmith, 2,481-2,483).

Line 143   Revised for 8th Edition. Gens. 31-42 transposed from Line 50, Gens. 32-43 in previous editions. See note at Gen. 30.

16. LOUIS II (148-16), "the Stammerer," King of the Franks; m. (3) 868/70, Adelaide (or Aelis) of Paris, d. abt. 10 Nov. 901, poss. (not proven) dau. of Bego, Count of Paris (d. 861) (Brandenburg), or dau. of Count Girard of Paris. (Saillot, *Sang de Charlemagne* 201; West Winter V.53).

17. ERMENTRUDE OF FRANCE, b. 870; m. N.N. (Winkhaus 103).

18. CUNEGONDE, b. abt. 890; m. (1) 907/8 Wigeric, d. by 919, Count in the Ardennes (Bidgau), Count Palatine; m. (2) 916/19, Richwin, d. aft. 923, Count of Verdun. (Saillot, 21; Parisse, chart p. 112; *ES* I.2/202).

19. SIEGFRIED OF LUXEMBOURG (perh. by (1) but more prob. by (2)) Count of Luxembourg 943, d. 28 Oct. 998; m. abt. 950, Hedwig, d. 13 Dec. 992, perh. dau. of Count Eberhard, Count in the Nordgau. (ES I.2/202-203; Parisse, charts pp. 112, 119).

20. FREDERICK I OF LUXEMBOURG, b. abt. 965, d. 1019, Count of Salm and Luxembourg; m. bef. 995, NN heiress (Ermentrude?) of Gleiberg, dau. of Heribert I, d. 992, Count of Gleiberg, Count in the Kinziggau, by his wife, by Ermentrud (Imizi), dau. of Megingoz, count in Avalgau, by Gerberga of Alsace (Herbert I was son of Udo, Count in the Wetterau, by his wife, a dau. of **HERBERT I** (50-17), Count of Vermandois). (Saillot 5, 6 ,51; Brandenburg. Gens. 18-20: *ES* I.2/203, 205; *TAG* 58 (1982): 14-17).

21. GISELE (or **GISLA) OF LUXEMBOURG**, liv. 1058, bur. Chapel of St. Lawrence, Ghent; m. Rudolph I of Aalst (or Alost) (also called Ralph of Gand or Ghent), liv. 1058, Lord of Aalst (or Alost) in Flanders, hereditary Advocate or Protector of St. Peter of Ghent 1036-1056. (Brandenburg 7; Winkhaus 19, 21, 117; Clay, 83; *Gen. Mag.* 9: 1-7; *ES* VIII/22a).

22. GILBERT DE GANT (GAUNT or **GHENT**), d. abt. 1095, bur. Bardney, probably arrived in England in 1066; was a commander in York, 1068, and was taken prisoner there by the Danes in 1069. He was a tenant-in-chief and one of the largest landholders in co. Lincoln in 1086, Folkingham being the head of his barony; m. Alice de Montfort, dau. of Lord Hugh de Montfort-sur-Risle. (*Gen. Mag.* 9: 1-7; *CP* VII: 672 note *b*; Sanders, 114; *NEHGR* 115 (1961): 209-210. For Gens. 17-22: see *Boston Evening Transcript*, 9 Nov. 1927, Note 2257, Part XV Brabant).

23. WALTER DE GAUNT (156-24), d. 1139, held barony of Folkingham, co. Lincoln, a commander in the battle of the Standard 1138, founder Bridlington Priory, co. York, bef. 1113-14; m. by 1120, Maud (or Matilda) of Brittany, dau. of **STEPHEN I** (214-24), Count of Brittany, Lord of Richmond. (*CP* VII: 672, X: 786-787, chart 780, XII (1): 674; Sanders, 114; Brandenburg 10, 11, 66; Milton Rubincam, in *Gen. Mag.* 9 (1940): 1-7; Winkhaus 21; *Monasticon* VI: 284-291).

24. AGNES DE GAUNT, m. William de Mohun, adult by 1131, d. in or bef. 1155, Earl of Somerset, held barony of Dunster, Somerset, son of Sir William de Mohun, d. aft. 1190, lord of Dunster, Somerset, Sheriff of Somerset, 1084, 1086, by his wife Adeliz. The proof of Agnes de Gaunt's identity is the manor of Whichford, co. Warwick, a Gaunt family property, which she received as her maritagium. Agnes and her husband William de Mohun later gave the church at Whichford to Bridlington Priory, which priory was founded by Agnes' father, Walter de Gaunt. (*CP* IX: 17-18 and note *h*, XII (1): 37-39; *VCH Warwick* V: 205; Maxwell Lyte, *A History of Dunster*, Part I, pp. 5-9; Sanders, 114; Keats-Rohan, *Domesday Desc.* 2, 470, 587).

25. WILLIAM DE MOHUN, seen 1142, died 1176, held barony of Dunster, Somerset; m. by 1160, **GODEHEUT** (or **GODEHOLD) DE TOENI**, dead by 1186, dau. of **ROGER III DE TOENI** (98A-25), lord of Flamstead, co. Hertford, by his wife, Ida of Hainaut, dau. of **BALDWIN III**, Count of Hainaut (163-25). Godeheut's maritagium, the manor of Brinkley, co. Cambridge, shows her identity to be Toeni. This manor came into possession of the Toeni family upon the marriage of Godeheut's grandmother, **ALICE OF NORTHUMBERLAND** (98A-24), to Ralph IV de Toeni. (*CP* IX: 18; Maxwell Lyte, *A History of Dunster*, Part I, pp. 9-11, Sanders, 114; *VCH Cambridge* VI (Brinkley Fee), 136; *Beauchamp Cartulary*, pub. of the Pipe Roll Society, New Series, XLIII: 206, 207, 217, 218; *Calendar of Documents preserved in France*, I: 174, 282-3; *The Gen.* 5: 10 & note; *ES* III.4/705).

26. WILLIAM DE MOHUN, s. and h., minor 1176, adult by 1177, pilgrimage to Jerusalem, d. Oct. 1193, held barony of Dunster, Somerset, benefactor of Bruton Priory; m. Lucy, who is seen 1201 with seven knts. fees in Cambridge. (*CP* IX: 19; Maxwell Lyte, *A History of Dunster*, Part I: 11-15; Sanders, 114).

27. SIR REYNOLD DE MOHUN, adult by 1204, d. 1213, held barony of Dunster, Somerset; m. Alice Briwere, liv. 1233, 4th dau. and event. coh. of Sir William de Briwere, d. 1226, lord of Torre, co. Devon, and Horsley, co. Derby, sheriff of Devon temp. Hen. II, and of Dorset, Oxfordshire, Bucks, Berks, Northants & Derbyshire, by his wife Beatrice de Valle (or de Vaux). Alice m. (2) by 1224, William Paynel of Bampton, co. Devon, d. 1228. (*CP* IX: 19; Maxwell Lyte, *A History of Dunster*, Part I, pp. 15-17; *DNB* (Brewer); Sanders, 114, 122-123; *Notebook of Tristram Risdon*, p. 71).

28. SIR REYNOLD DE MOHUN, born say 1206, minor in 1213 and 1222, adult by 1227, d. Torre Mohun 20 Jan. 1257/8, bur. Newenham Abbey, held barony of Dunster, Somerset, Justice of Common Pleas, Chief Justice of the Forests South of Trent, Gov. of Saubey Castle; m. (1) by 1227, **HAWISE FITZ GEOFFREY** (246B-28), dead 1243, dau. of Geoffrey Fitz Piers, Earl of Essex by his (2) wife, Aveline de Clare (Hawise received as her maritagium the manor of Streatley, Berkshire from her half-brother, William de Mandeville, Earl of Essex); m. (2) in or bef. 1243 Isabel de Ferrers, d. 26 Nov. 1260, wid. of Gilbert Basset, dau. of **WILLIAM DE FERRERS**, Earl of Derby (127-30), by Sibyl, dau. of **WILLIAM MARSHAL**, 3rd Earl of Pembroke (177-8). Sir Reynold's arms were, Gules, a maunch ermine. (*CP* IX: 19-20, V: 116-117, 433, footnote *e*, 437; *Roll of Arms Henry III*, ed. Tremlett & London, pp. 126-127; Sanders, 114; *VCH Berks*. III: 512 (manor of Streatley); Maxwell Lyte, *A History of Dunster* Part I: 15-34).

29. LUCY DE MOHUN, dau. prob. by (1); m. Sir John de Grey of Codnor, co. Derby, d. bef. 5 Jan. 1271/2, son of Sir Richard de Grey and Lucy de Humez. (*CP* VI: 123-135, IX: 19; Maxwell-Lyte, *A History of Dunster*, Part I 32, considers Lucy as child of her father's first marriage).

30. SIR HENRY DE GREY, 1st Lord Grey, of Codnor, co. Derby, Grays Thurrocks, Essex, Ayilsford and Hoo, Kent, d. 1308; m. (1) Eleanor de Courtenay. (Note: said perhaps to have been the dau. of **HUGH DE COURTENAY** (50-31); however, there is no proof of her parentage). (*CP* VI: 123-124, chart bet. 128-129, 133, 135).

31. SIR RICHARD DE GREY of Codnor, b. 1281, d. 10 Mar. 1334/5; m. Joan Fitz Payn, dau. of Sir Robert, Lord Fitz Payn, and Isabella de Clifford, dau. & coh. Sir John Clifford, of Frampton-on-Severn, co. Gloucester. (*CP* V: 448-451, VI: 124-125).

32. JANE DE GREY, (she was sis., not dau., of Sir John de Grey, Knt, d. 1392, Lord Grey of Codnor); m. (1) by 1344, **SIR WILLIAM DE HARCOURT, KNT**. (39A-31), d. 6 June 1349, of Stanton-Harcourt, co. Oxford. (CP VI: 126 note *g*; Dudley Pedigree). (See Josiah C. Wedgewood, "Harcourt of Ellenhall," *Wm. Salt Soc.* n.s. v. 35, pp. 195-196; Burke, *Peerage and Baronetage* (1953), 984).

33. SIR THOMAS DE HARCOURT, KNT., of Stanton-Harcourt, co. Oxford, Market Bosworth, co. Leicester, and Ellenhall, co. Stafford; d. 12 Apr. 1417, knt. 1366, M.P. for Oxfordshire 1376; m. 1370, **MAUD DE GREY** (30-32), wid. of Sir John Botetourte, dau. of **JOHN DE GREY** (30-31) of Rotherfield. (Wedgewood, *cit.*, pp. 196-197).

34. SIR THOMAS II DE HARCOURT, KNT., of Stanton-Harcourt, b. 1377, d. 1420; m. Jane Franceys (Francis), dau. of Sir Robert Franceys (Francis) of Formark, co. Derby. (Wedgewood, *cit.*, pp. 197-198).

35. SIR RICHARD HARCOURT, KNT., d. 1 Oct. 1486, of Wytham, co. Berks, will made 27 Apr. 1486, pro. 25 Oct. 1486; m. (1) bef. 16 Dec. 1445, **EDITH ST. CLAIR** (79-35), liv. 16 Sept. 1462, d. bef. 8 Nov. 1472, dau. of **THOMAS ST. CLAIR** (79-34) of Wethersfield, Legham and Chalgrove, Suffolk. (*CP* V: 397, VII: 64-65; Wedgewood, *cit*, pp. 204-205; Gens. 33-36: *ES* X/139).

36. ALICE HARCOURT; m. William Bessiles, of Bessiles-Leigh, co. Berks, d. 1515. Her will pro. 19 June 1526. (*Misc. Gen. Her.* (5th ser.) V: 64-82; Wedgewood, *cit.*, chart).

37. ELIZABETH BESSILES, dau. & h.; m. Richard Fettiplace, of East Shefford, co. Berks, d. at Bessiles-Leigh, 1511, s. of John Fettiplace, of East Shefford, d. 1464, by wife, Joan Fabian, wid. of Robert Horne of London. John Fettiplace was s. of Thomas Fettiplace, d. 1442/46, M.P., sheriff of Oxfordshire & Berkshire, by wife Beatrice, d. 1447. Her parentage unkn., but Royal arms of Portugal impaled on her seal. (*Misc. Gen. Her.*, (5th ser.) II: 186, V: 64; *CP* XII(1): 617-620, esp. 619 notes *d* and *g*, I: 246, XIV: 38, V: 209-210; *NEHGR* 123: 254-255).

38. ANNE FETTIPLACE, b. Little Shefford, co. Berks, 16 July 1496, d. 16 Aug. 1568; m. Edward Purefoy, of Shalston, co. Buckingham, b. 13 Jan. 1494, d. 1558, son of Nicholas Purefoy and Alice Denton. (*Misc. Gen. Her.*, (5th ser.) II: 186; Lipscombe, *Hist. of Bucks* III, 71). (For Purefoy, see F. N. Craig, "Corrections and Additions to the Purefoy Line in the Maternal Ancestry of Governor Thomas Dudley of the Massachusetts Bay," *TAG* 77 (2002): 57-65).

39. MARY PUREFOY, of Yardley-Hastings, co. Northampton, sister of John Purefoy and mentioned in his will, 1579; m. Thomas Thorne, Gent., of Yardley-Hastings, will made 29 Oct. 1588, pro. 9 May 1589 (*Northampton Reg. of Wills*, V: 328-330). Thomas Thorne bequeaths "To the Children of Susan Dudley, my Daughter, widow, £ 10, to be equally divided." These children were (Gov.) Thomas Dudley, bapt. 12 Oct. 1576 (see below), and Mary Dudley, bapt. 16 Oct 1580.

40. SUSAN (or **SUSANNA) THORNE**, bapt. Yardley-Hastings, 5 Mar. 1559/60, liv. 29 Oct. 1588 (Parish Reg. at Yardley-Hastings, see *NEHGR* 68: 341-342); m. 8 June 1575 at Lidlington, co. Bedford, Captain Roger Dudley, d. 1585. The will of John Purefoy, 1579, mentions Thomas Dudley. The arms of Thorne are: Sable, three fusills in fess, argent. (*NEHGR* 139: 60).

41. GOVERNOR THOMAS DUDLEY, bapt. Yardley-Hastings, co. Northampton, 12 Oct. 1576, bur. at Roxbury, Mass., 31 July 1653, ae. 76 yrs.; m. (1) Hardingstone, near Northampton, 25 Apr. 1603, Dorothy Yorke, buried at Roxbury, 27 Dec. 1643, dau. of Edmund Yorke, of Cotton End, co. Northampton; m. (2) Roxbury, 14 Apr. 1644, **KATHERINE DEIGHTON** (84-40), wid. of Samuel Hackburne, dau. of John Deighton by **JANE BASSET** (84-39). The Reverend Cotton Mather, D.D., of Boston, stated that Thomas Dudley was baptized at Yardley-Hastings. The will of Edmund Yorke was dated 18 Nov. 1614, and mentions his grandchildren Samuel and Anne Dudley, and appoints Thomas Dudley one of his overseers. (*NEHGR* 47: 120). Governor Dudley lived in Northampton as a young man, served under King Henry IV of France at the siege of Amiens, settled in Mass. 1630, Governor and Deputy-Governor of Mass. 1630-1653, a man of large and noble character. (Gens. 34-43: Dudley Pedigree, Herald's College, 28 Jan. 1937, approved by A.T. Butler, Windsor Herald. Gens. 9-13: G.A. Moriarty: Chart of the Robertins in *NEHGR* 99: 130-131, corrected by chart in 101:112; see also references under line 48-13. Gens. 13-24: D.L. Jacobus in *Boston Evening Transcript*, 12 Oct. 1927, Note 2257, Part IX, Note 5980, 28 Nov. 1927; Pere Anselme; v. Redlich I: 120-121; *CP* I: 22, IV: 670, 672-674, V: 736, VII: 520, 737, X: 351. Gens. 24-27: *CP* IV: 317, 670 chart III, VII: 520, 708-737, 771; *NEHGR* 97: 342; Jackson, *Falaise Roll*, table IX; Waters: "Pedigrees of Courtenay and Champernoun," in *Proceedings of the Essex Institute*, XVII: 16. Gens. 30-34: *CP* IV: 676, VI: 123-126; Dudley Pedigree; Collins IV: 240-241; *Stokes Records* I: 99-102. Gens. 38-43: *Visit of Berks*, I: Publications of the Harleian Soc, vol. 56 (Visit. of Bucks) 58:199; Purefoy pedigree in Brit. Museum Harleian ms. 1189, folios 18 and 19; Nichols, *Hist. of Leicestershire*, IV Part II pp. 519a-520a; *Stokes Records* I: 93; Mary K. Talcott in *NEHGR* 47: 120, 49: 507, 56: 189, 206, 66: 340-343, 97: 342; Waters II: 1087; Publications of the Dudley Family Association; *Northamptonshire Past & Present*, vol. V, no. 4, pp. 325-332 (1976)).

42. REV. SAMUEL DUDLEY, by (1), bapt. All Saints, Northampton, Eng., 30 Nov. 1608, matric. Emmanuel College, Camb., 1626, came to N.E. 1630, minister at Exeter, N.H., 30 May 1650-1683, d. Exeter, 10 Feb. 1682/3. For his descendants, see *Gen. Dict. of Me. & N.H.*, pp. 209-210.

42. ANNE DUDLEY, (dau. of Gen. 41, by (1)), b. Northants., abt. 1612, poetess, ancestress of many N.E. Clergymen, d. Andover, Mass., 16 Sept. 1672; m. 1628, Gov. Simon Bradstreet.

42. MERCY DUDLEY, (dau. of Gen. 41, by (1)), b. Eng., 1621, ancestress of sixteen colonial clergymen by name of Woodbridge and many bearing other names, d. Newbury, Mass., 1 July 1691; m. 1639, Rev. John Woodbridge of Andover, Mass.

Line 144   Revised for 8th Edition

22. WILLLAM I (132-24), "the Great," d. 1087, Count of Burgundy; m. Stephanie, parentage NN. *(Note:* Prof. David H. Kelley believes her parentage unproven (2003)). (De Vajay, in *Annales de Bourgogne* vol. 32 (1960) 258-261, identifies Stephanie (Etiennette) as dau. of Clemence de Foix & Albert de Longwy, Duke of Lorraine, d. 1048. Clemence is identified as dau. of Bernard I Roger, Comte de Foix, d. 1035, & Garsinde de Bigorre; & Bernard as son of Roger I de Carcassonne & wife Adelaide. Moriarty, *cit.*, supplies pedigree charts for these families, but does not agree with de Vajay as to her identity. Garnier (table XXVIII) shows her as dau. of Raymond II, Count of Barcelona).

23. ERMENTRUDE OF BURGUNDY, d. aft. 1105; m. 1076, **THIERRY I** (167-23), Count of Montbéliard and Bar-le-Duc, d. 1105, son of Louis, Count of Montbéliard, d. 1073, , and Sophia, Countess of Bar-le-Duc, d. 1092. *(ES* I.2/223, 204; Parisse, charts pp. 115, 354).

24. REINALD (RENAUD) I, Count of Mousson, Count of Bar-le-Duc *j.u.*, d. 1150; m. Gisele of Vaudemont, dau. of Gerard, of Lorraine, Count of Vaudemont, d. abt. 1120, and Edith (Helvide) of Egisheim, d. 1118, dau. of Gerard II, Count of Egisheim, d. 1098, and Richarde NN. (LaChasnaye, *Dict. de la Noblesse,* VIII/40; Wagner, *Ped. & Prog.,* 161; Parisse, charts pp. 89, 354, 444).

25. CLÉMENCE DE BAR-LE-DUC, liv. 1183, Countess of Dammartin; m. (1) Lancelin I, Count of Dammartin, d.s.p.; m. (2) by 1153, Renaud II (at least 7 ch.), d. abt. 1162, Count of Clermont in Beauvaisis, son of Hugh de Creil, d. 1101, Count of Clermont in Beauvaisis, by his wife, **MARGARET DE ROUCY** (246-23); m. (3) Thibaut III, Seigneur of Nanteuil-le-Handouin & de Crepi (Crepy). (Michel Parisse, *Noblesse et Chevalerie en Lorraine Medievale,* chart p. 354 (1982); LaChasnaye, *Dict. de la Noblesse,* VIII/40; Wagner, *Ped. & Prog.,* 161; *ES* III.4/649, 653).

26. MATILDA, (MAUD, MABILIE) OF CLERMONT, PONTHIEU & DAMMARTIN,. by (2), d. Oct. 1200; m. **ALBRI DE LUZARCHES** (152-26), Chamberlain of France 1155-1160, *j.u.* Count of Dammartin, d. 19 Sept. 1200. *(Gen. Mag.* 15 (2): 53-63, esp. 55; *ES* III.4/649, 653)

27. SIMON DE DAMMARTIN, Count of Aumale, d. 1239; m. as (1) husb. 1208-1211, **MARIE** (109-29), Countess of Ponthieu, d. 1250. Marie m. (2) Mathieu de Montmorency, Seigneur d'Attichy, killed 1250. (Gens. 22-23: Garnier xxviii; Gens. 23-27: *N&Q* (4th ser.), VII: 437-438; Moriarty, *The Plantagenet Ancestry; Gen. Mag.* 15: 53-63, 16: 94, 23: 281-288; William M. Newman, *Les Seigneurs de Nestle en Picardie,* pp. 73, 81-88 (1971); *ES* XIV/117, III.4/638).

14.   LOUIS I, "the Fair" (140-14), Emperor 814-840; m. (1) Ermengarde. (*NEHGR* 109: 179-182).

15.   ROTRUDE (prob.); m. abt. 814, Count Gerard of Auvergne, d. 25 June 841. (Prof. Leonce Auzias, in *Revue Historique* 173: 91-102; G. Andrews Moriarty, *NEHGR* 109: 179-182; West Winter, III.11; *ES* II/76, I.1/4).

16.   RANULF I, Duke of Aquitaine, d. 866; m. abt. 845, Blichilde of Maine, dau. of Rorick, Count of Maine. (West Winter, IV.18; *ES* II/76; *NEHGR*, *cit*.; Brandenburg, 63, 66).

17.   RANULF II, Count of Poitou, b. abt. 855, d. 5 Aug. 890; m. Ada, d. 935 (not mother of gen. 18). (*ES* II/76; West Winter, V.17)

18.   EBLES MANCER, (bastard of Ranulf II by Ermengarde, prob. a concubine), b. 868, d. 932, Count of Poitou 890-892, 903,; m. (1) 892, Aremburge; m. (2) 911, Emiliane. (Moriarty, *The Plantagenet Ancestry*, p. 26; West Winter, VI.22).

19.   WILLIAM I OF POITOU (III OF AQUITAINE), by (1), b. 900, d. 3 Apr. 963; m. 935, Adele (Gerloc) of Normandy, d. aft. 969, dau. of **ROLLO** (121E-18), Duke of Normandy. (Brandenburg, p. 66).

20.   ADELAIDE (ALIX) OF POITOU, b. 945, d. 15 June 1006; m. bef. 969, **HUGH CAPET** (53-20, 101-20, 106-20, 141-20), d. 24 Oct. 996, King of France 987-996. (Brandenburg, p. 67; Moriarty, *The Plantagenet Ancestry*, pp. 24, 27; *ES* II/11).

21.   HEDWIG OF FRANCE, d. aft. 1013; m. **REGNIER IV** (106-21), Count of Hainaut, b. abt. 950, d. 1013. (Gens. 15-20, *ES* II/76).

22.   BEATRIX OF HAINAUT, m. (1) **EBLES I** (151-21), d. 11 May 1033, Count of Rheims and Roucy, Archbishop of Rheims; m. (2) Manasses Calva Asina de Rameru, son of **HILDUIN II** (151A-21), Seigneur de Rameru. (*ES* III/675, 678).

Line 145

15.   LOTHAIR I (140-15); m. 821, Ermengarde of Tours. (*CCN*, 623).

16.   LOTHAIR II, the Saxon, b. 827, d. 8 Aug. 869, King of Lorraine; m. (2) 862, Waldrada, d. 868.

17.   BERTHA, of Lorraine, b. 863, d. 8 Mar. 925; m. (1) abt. 879, Theobald, Count of Arles, d. 887/895.

18.   BOSO, b. 885, d. 936, Count of Arles, Margrave of Tuscany, 913-936; m. Willa of Tuscany, dau. of Rudolf I, King of Upper-Burgundy.

19.   WILLA, d. aft. 963; m. 936, **BERENGARIUS II** (146-18), King of Italy, Margrave of Burgundy-Ivrea, d. 966. (*CCN*, 147.   Gens. 15-19: See *Boston Evening Transcript*, 9 Nov. 1927, Note 2257, Part X, Carolingians. Gens. 17-19: *ES* II/186 NEU).

Line 146

13.   CHARLEMAGNE (50-13); m. **HILDEGARDE** (182-5).

14.   LOUIS I (140-14), the Fair; m. (2) Judith of Bavaria.

15.   GISÈLE (250-15), b. 820, d. 1 July 874; m. bef. 840, **EBERHARD** (191A-16), d. abt. 864, Margrave of Friuli. (*NEHGR* 99: 243, chart; *ES* II/188A).

16.   BERENGARIUS I, b. 850, d. 7 Apr. 924, King of Italy, Jan. 888-924, Emperor Dec. 915-924; m. 899, Bertila of Spoleto, d. Dec. 915, dau. of Suppo, Margrave of

Spoleto in Perugia, Italy. (West Winter IV.35; *ES* II/59; Seversmith, 2,472-2,473; *CCN* 147).

17. GISÈLE, of Fruili, d. 910; m. Adalbert, d. 923, Margrave of Ivrea in Turin, Italy.

18. BERENGARIUS II, d. 6 Aug. 966, Margrave of Ivrea, King of Italy 950-966; m. 936, **WILLA** (145-19).

19. ROSELA (or **SUSANNA**), of Ivrea, b. abt. 952, d. 1003; m. (1) bef. 968, **ARNOLD II** (162-20), d. 30 Mar. 987, Count of Flanders; m. (2) 988, **ROBERT II** of France (101-21), repudiated. (Gens. 15-19: Crispin, *Falaise Roll* (London, 1938), 186-187; de Vajay, *Annales de Bourgogne*; *ES* II/59 NEU).

Line 147   Revised for 8th Edition

18. HENRY I, the Fowler (141-18), Duke of Saxony, King of the Saxons; m. Mechtilde of Ringelheim. (*ES* I.1/10; *CCN*, 767).

19. OTTO I, the Great, b. 23 Nov. 912, d. Memleben, 7 May 973, King of Germany 939-973, Emperor 962-973; m. (1) **EDITH** (45-17), d. 947, granddau. of **ALFRED THE GREAT** (1-14); m. (2) Oct/Nov. 951, Adelaide of Burgundy, b. 931/2, d. Selz, Alsace, 16 Dec. 999, dau. of Rudolph II, King of Burgundy, and wid. of Lothair of Italy (to whom m. 947 as infant). (*CCN*, 767; Moriarty, 33, 34, 87; *ES* II/186NEU).

20. OTTO II, by (2), b. abt. 955, d. Rome, 7 Dec., 983, King of Germany 973-983; m. (2) 14 Apr. 972, Theophana, b. abt. 956/958, d. 15 June 991, niece of John I Tsimices, and poss. dau. of Romanus II, Emperor of the East, 959-963, by 2nd wife, Theophana. (Anthony Wagner, *Ped. and Prog.*, 202, 258; *The Genealogist* 2 (1981): 7, 38-39 esp. note 15; *ES* I.2/201, I.1/84. I.1/10).

21. MATILDA OF SAXONY, b. 978, d. 1025; m. 991, **EZZO** (147A-21), d. 1034, Count of Lorraine. (Gens. 18-21: *ES* I.1/10).

22. RICHENZA, (**RIXA**), d. 21 Mar. 1063; m. abt. 1013, Mieszislav II Lambert, d. 10 May 1034, King of Poland.

23. KAZIMIERZ (CASIMIR I), b. 25 July 1016, d. 28 Nov. 1058, King of Poland; m. 1038, **DOBRONEGA** (241-5), b. aft. 1011, d. 1087, dau. of **ST. VLADIMIR I** (241-4), Grand Prince of Kiev. (*ES* II/120).

24. WLADISLAS I, b. abt. 1043, d. 4 June 1102, King of Poland; m. (1) abt. 1080, **JUDITH** (244-8) Princess of Bohemia, d. 1085, dau. of Vratislav II, King of Bohemia and **ADELAIDE** (244-7) of Hungary.

25. BOLESLAS III, b. 20 Aug. 1085, d. 28 Oct. 1138, King of Poland; m. (1) abt. 1103, **ZBYSLAVA,** of Kiev (241-8), d. 1113, dau. of **SVIATOPOLK II** (241-7) Grand Prince of Kiev.

26. WLADISLAS II, "the exile," b. 1105, d. 1159, King of Poland; m. abt. 1125/27, Agnes of Babenberg, b. 1108/1113, d. 1160/63, dau. of St. Leopold III, "the Saint," b. 1073, d. 1136, Margrave of Austria and **AGNES** (45-24) of Germany, son of Leopold II "the Fair," Margrave of Austria, by Ita, of Retelberg. (*ES* III/9).

27. RICHENZA, of Poland, b. abt. 1135, d. 16 Oct. 1185; m. (1) 1152, **ALFONSO VII** (113-25), b. 1103, d. 1157, King of Castile and Leon; m. (2) Raymond V Berenger, Count of Provence, d, 1166. (*ES* III/9, II/69. Gens. 19-27: G.A. Moriarty in *NEHGR* 101: 39-40; Brandenburg; N. de Baumgarten, *Orientalia Christiana* (Rome, 1927). Gens. 22-27: Wlodzimierz Dworzaczek, *Genealogia*, Warsaw, 1959, v. 2: charts 1 and 5. Gens. 25-27: West Winter XII.532, XII.831, XIII.963, XII.612, XII.52, XII.280, XI.185).

17. ERENFRIED I, liv. 877-904, of the Ezzonen family in Ripuaria, son of Adalhard, liv. in Ripuaria 920s, and Adelheid; m. Adelgunde of Burgundy, dau. of Konrad II, Margrave of Burgundy. (Donald C. Jackman, *Criticism and Critique*; ... (1997) 67-68).

18. EBERHARD I, liv. 904-937, Count in the area of Keldach and Bonn; m. NN.

19. ERENFRIED II, d. by 970, Count in the area of Bonn and Ruhr-Keldach; m. Richwara, d. by 983.

20. HERMAN PUSILLUS, d. 996; m. Helwig, of the family of Ulrich, Bishop of Augsburg.

21. EZZO (ERENFRIED), d. 21 May 1034, Count Palatine of Lorraine; m. bef. 15 June 991, **MATILDA OF SAXONY** (147-21). (Gens. 17-21: *ES* I.2/201).

Line 148   Revised for 8th Edition

13. CHARLEMAGNE (50-13); m. **HILDEGARDE** (182-5), of Swabia.

14. LOUIS I (140-14), "the Fair," b. 778, d. 20 June 840; Emperor 814-840; m. (2) 819, Judith of Bavaria, b. abt. 805, d. Tours 19 Apr. 843, dau. of Welf. (*ES* I.1/4; West Winter, IV.48).

15. CHARLES II, "the Bald," b. Frankfort-am-Main, 13 June 823, d. near Mt. Cenis in the Alps, 6 Oct. 877, King of the Franks 840-877, Emperor 25 Dec. 875-877; m. (1) 14 Dec. 842, Ermentrude of Orléans, b. abt. 830, d. 6 Oct. 869, dau. of Odo (Eudes), Count of Orléans, and Engeltrude. (*ES* I.1/4, 6, 116; *CCN*, 236, 642).

16. LOUIS II, "the Stammerer," b. 846, d. Compiegne, 10 Apr. 879, King of the Franks 877-879; m. (2) abt. 868, Adelaide, of Paris, d. aft. 9 Nov. 901, dau. of Adelhard, of Paris. (*ES* I.1/6; *CCN*, 624).

17. CHARLES III, "the Simple," b. 17 Sept. 879, d. Peronne, 7 Oct. 929, King of the Franks; m. (3) 918, Ogiva of England, d. 951, dau. of **EDWARD I** "the Elder" (1-15). (*ES* II/78).

18. LOUIS IV, d'Outre-Mer, b. 10 Sept. 920, d. 10 Sept. 954, King of the Franks 936-954; m. 939/40, **GERBERGA OF SAXONY** (142-18), d. 5 May 984, dau. of **HENRY I, THE FOWLER** (141-18), and wid. of Giselbert, Duke of Lorraine. (*ES* I.1/6; *CCN*, 624. Gens. 13-18: Thatcher 319-320).

19. CHARLES OF LORRAINE, b. 953, d. 991, Duke of Lower Lorraine; m. bef. 979 Adelheid, parentage unknown. (Gens. 13-20: Brandenburg; Thatcher, 319-320; Fisher, 238; Moriarty; Winkhaus; Saillot, 192).

20. GERBERGA, b. abt. 975, d. aft. 1017; m. abt. 990, **LAMBERT I** (155-20), the Bearded, Count of Louvain. (*CP* I: 352; *ES* I.1/6).

21. MAUD, m. Eustace I, d. 1049, Count of Boulogne. (*CP* I: 352).

22. LAMBERT OF BOULOGNE, Count of Lens in Artois, slain at the battle of Lille, 1054; m. as 2nd husb. **ADELAIDE** (130-24) of Normandy, b. 1030, d. 1081/84, Countess of Aumale, sister of **WILLIAM I** (121-24), the Conqueror. Adelaide m. (1): Enguerrand II, Count of Ponthieu. (*CP* I: 350-353, V: 736).

Note: Judith of Lens (Gen. 23 in previous editions) appears to have been Adelaide's child by her first marriage to Enguerrand II. See **JUDITH OF LENS** (130-25, 98A-23), for her descendants (See: Catharine Morton & Hope Muntz, *The Carmen de Hastingae Poelio of Guy, Bishop of Amiens* (Oxford, 1972), p. 27. See also *Gen. Mag.* 19 (1978): 257; The Genealogist 10 (1989): 4; *TAG* 54: 231-2; Seversmith, 2,583, 2,595).

26. WALTER FITZ ROBERT (130-28); m. (1) Maud de Bohun; m. (2) Maud de Lucy.

27. MAUD FITZ WALTER, b. abt. 1161, liv. 1196; m. (1) William de Luvetot of Sheffield, co. York, d. 1181, s. Richard de Luvetot of Sheffield, d. 1171, by 1st wife Cecily de Brito; m. (2) Ernulf de Magnaville. (*CP* V: 580; *EYC* III: 3-6, VI: 209-211).

28. MAUD DE LUVETOT, b. abt. 1178, d. 1250, h. of Sheffield, co. York, and Worksop, co. Nottingham; m. Gerard de Furnival, d. 1218, s. Gerard de Furnival. (*CP* V: 580; *EYC* III: 3-6, VI: 209-211).

29. THOMAS DE FURNIVAL, of Sheffield, co. York, d. abt. 1238; m. Bertha, liv. 1267. She m. (2) Ralph le Bigod, d. abt. 1260. (*CP* V: 580).

30. THOMAS DE FURNIVAL, younger s., of Worksop, co. Nottingham, & Sheffield, co. York, d. 1291. (*CP* V: 580-581).

31. SIR THOMAS DE FURNIVAL, b. abt. 1270, d. 1332, 1st Lord Furnival, of Worksop, co. Nottingham, and Sheffield, co. York; m. (1) by Jan. 1272/3 Joan le Despenser, d. abt. 1322, dau. Sir Hugh le Despenser, b. 1223, d. 1265, Justiciar of England, of Loughborough and Arnesby, co. Leicester, by wife Aline Basset, b. 1246, d. 1281, dau. & h. Sir Philip Basset, d. 1272, Justiciar of England, of Wycombe, co. Buckingham, and Wootton Basset, co. Wilts, by 1st wife, Hawise de Louvaine, dau. **SIR MATTHEW DE LOVAINE** (155A-27). (*CP* V: 581-582).

32. MAUD DE FURNIVAL, liv. 1348; m. **SIR JOHN MARMION** (218-30), b. abt. 1292, d. 30 Apr. 1335, Lord Marmion. (*CP* V: 581-582, VIII: 520-521).

19. CHARLES OF LORRAINE (148-19), Duke of Lower Lorraine; m. bef. 979, Adelheid, parentage unknown. (*ES* I.1/6).

20. ERMENGARDE OF LORRAINE, d. aft. 1012; m. 990, Albert I, Count of Namur, d. 998/1011, son of Robert I, Count of Lomme. (*ES* VII/68)

21. ALBERT II, Count of Namur, b. abt. 1000, d. 1064; m. Regilinde of Lorraine, d. 1064, dau. of Gozelon I, d. 1044, Duke of Lower Lorraine, gt.-gr.son of **CUNEGONDE** (143-18), wife of Wigeric. (*CP* I: 235; *ES* VII/68, VI/127; Moriarty, *The Plantagenet Ancestry*, for the connecting line).

22. ALBERT III, Count of Namur, d. 22 June 1102; m. 1065/6, Ida of Saxony, dau. prob. of Bernard II, Duke in Saxony, b. abt. 995, d. 1057, and Elica (m. abt. 1020), dau. of Henrich, Markgrave of Schweinfurt. (*CP* I: 235; Moriarty, *The Plantagenet Ancestry*).

23. ADELAIDE OF NAMUR, b. 1068, d. 1124; m., as 2nd wife, Otto II, Count of Chiny, d. 28 Mar. 1125, son of Arnold II, Count of Chiny, d. 1106, by his wife, Adela, dau. of **HILDUIN III** (or **IV**) **DE RAMERU** (151A-22), d. abt. 1063, Count of Montdidier, Count of Roucy, Seigneur of Rameru, and **ADELE DE ROUCY** (151-22). (*ES* VII/42, 68; Brandenburg, 52-56).

24. IDA OF CHINY AND NAMUR, b. abt. 1083, d. abt. 1117/22; m. abt. 1105, **GODFREY I** (155-23), Duke of Lower Lorraine, Margrave of Antwerp, Count of Louvain, son of Henry II, Count of Louvain. (*CP* I: 235; Seversmith, 2,666).

25. ADELIZA (ADELA) OF LOUVAIN, b. abt. 1103, bur. 23 Apr. 1151 (age abt. 48 yrs.); m. (1) 1120, as 2nd wife, **HENRY I** (121-25), King of England, s.p.; m. (2) 1138, William d'Aubigny, d. 12 Oct. 1176, 1st Earl of Arundel, 1141-1176. (*CP* I: 233-235, IV: 670 chart *i*; *ES* I.2/236).

26. **WILLIAM D'AUBIGNY,** 2nd Earl of Arundel and Sussex, d. 24 Dec. 1193, Crusader; m. Maud de St. Hilary, d. 1173, wid. of **ROGER DE CLARE** (246B-26), Earl of Hertford, dau. and h. of James de St. Hilary (Hilaire) du Harcourt, d. abt. 1154, of Field Dalling, Norfolk, by his wife, Aveline. (*CP* I: 236, IV: 670 chart *i*; Sanders, 44).

27. **WILLIAM D'AUBIGNY,** 3rd Earl of Arundel, d. near Rome, Mar. 1220/1, Crusader, named in the Magna Charta, 1215; m. **MABEL OF CHESTER** (126-29). (*CP* I: 236-237, IV: 670 chart *i*).

28. **ISABEL D'AUBIGNY;** m. John Fitz Alan, feudal Lord of Clun and Oswestry, Salop. (*CP* I: 239, 253, IV: 670 chart *i*).

29. **JOHN FITZ ALAN,** Lord of Clun and Oswestry, 1243, made his will Oct. 1267, d. bef. 10 Nov. 1267; m. Maud le Boteler, d. 27 Nov. 1283, dau. of Theobald le Boteler and Rohese de Verdun, dau. of Nicholas de Verdun of Alton, co. Stafford. (See 70A-29). (*CP* I: 239-240, 253, IV: 670 chart *i*).

30. **JOHN FITZ ALAN,** Lord of Clun and Oswestry, b. 14 Sept. 1246, d. 18 Mar. 1271/2; m. **ISABELLA DE MORTIMER** (28-30), d. sh. bef. 1 Apr. 1292. (*CP* I: 240,253, IV: 670 chart *i*, XIV: 38. Gens. 19-24: Brandenburg; *Boston Evening Transcript*, 9 Nov. 1927, Note 2257, Part X Carolingians, Feb. 1928, Part XV Brabant).

Line 150

27. **ROGER DE MOHAUT,** of Elford, co. Stafford, dead 1230/1 (when his h. was Agnes de Orreby), yr. son of Robert de Mohaut, of Howarden, succ. abt. 1141, d. abt. 1162, hereditary seneschal of the co. of Chester, and Leucha, living 1162, perh. dau. of William Fitz Neel of Halton, Constable of Cheshire. (*CP* IX: 10-11, X: 168-170; *Wm. Salt Soc.* III: 89, IV: 24, 46). This Roger de Mohaut was misidentified in the early editions and in von Redlich. He did not marry Cecily d'Aubigny. That Roger de Mohaut was his nephew.

28. **LEUCA DE MOHAUT,** m. 1227, Philip de Orreby, b. abt. 1190, d. by 1230, of Elford, co. Stafford, and Alvarley, co. Chester, son of Sir Philip de Orreby, Knt., b. abt. 1160, d. abt. 1230, Justiciar of Chester 1208-1229, Constable to Gilbert de Gant, Earl of Lincoln, by 1st wife, Emma de Coventre, dau. of Walter de Coventre, d. by 1235, of Coventry, co. Warwick, and Ashby & Thurlby, co. Lincoln. (*CP* X: 169-170; Farrer, *Honours & Knights Fees* II, 100-101).

29. **AGNES DE ORREBY,** only dau.; m. Sir Walkelin de Arderne, Knt., seen 1235/6, d. abt. 1265, Justiciar of Chester. (*CP* X: 170).

30. **SIR PETER DE ARDERNE, KNT.,** of Alford, seen 1262/3, d. 1292; m. Margery. (Gens. 27-30: Farrer, *Honours & Knights Fees* II, 110-111, 271-273).

31. **AGNES ARDERNE,** m. Sir Warin Mainwaring, Knt., of Wormingham, d. 1289. (*The Genealogist* 7 (1986): 62-63).

32. **MAUD** (or **MATILDA**) **MAINWARING,** b. abt. 1289, m. Sir William Trussell, Knt., Lord of Cubbleston and Wormingham. (*The Genealogist* 7 (1986): 117 note 632).

33. **SIR WARIN TRUSSELL,** liv. 1325/6-1352, of Cubbleston; said to have m. a dau. of Sir John Stafford. (See: *The Genealogist.* v. 7 (1986) 117 note 639 regarding his wife. Her correct identity has not been satisfactorily resolved.).

34. **SIR LAWRENCE TRUSSELL,** d. by 18 Sept. 1399, of Cubbleston; m. Maud Charnells, dau. of Thomas Charnells, Lord of Elmesthorpe, co. Leic.

35. **SIR WILLIAM TRUSSELL,** b. abt. 1385/6, d. 1463/4, of Elmesthorpe; m. bef. 1383, Margery Ludlow, dau. of Sir John Ludlow and Isabel Lingen. (*The Genealogist* 7 (1986): 63-65).

36. ISABEL TRUSSELL, m. bef. 1435, Thomas Wodhull, of Warkworth, b. 1411, d. 8 Aug. 1441, son of Thomas Wodhull and Elizabeth Chetwode, dau. of Sir John Chetwode of Warkworth.

37. JOHN WODHULL, of Warkworth, b. 1435, d. 12 Sept. 1490; m. bef. Feb. 1456, Joan Etwell, dau. of Henry Etwell, L.L.D., of London.

38. FULK WODHULL, of Warkworth and Thenford, b. 1459, d. 1508, Sheriff of Northamptonshire, 1500/1; m. (1) Anne Newenham, dau. of William Newenham, of Thenford, co. Northampton, and Margaret Lamporte, dau. of Thomas Lamporte.

39. SIR NICHOLAS WODHULL, of Warkworth, b. 1482, d. .5 May 1531, Sheriff of Northampton 1516, 1518; m. (1) 1508, Mary Raleigh, d. bef. 1522/3, dau. of **SIR EDWARD RALEIGH, KNT.**, (14-36), of Farnborough, co. Warwick; m. (2) **ELIZABETH PARR** (78-39), one of the heirs of William Parr, and cousin to Queen Katherine Parr. (*TAG* 21: 72).

40. ANTHONY WODHULL, of Warkworth (by the first wife), b. 1518, d. 4 Feb. 1541/2; m. Anne Smith, dau. of Sir John Smith, Baron of the Exchequer. (*NEHGR* 145 (1991): 20).

41. AGNES WODHULL only dau., b. 1542, d. 1575/6; m. by Jan. 1555/6, Sir Richard Chetwode, d. 1559/1560, son of Roger Chetwode by Ellen Masterson, dau. of Thomas Masterson. (*Visit. of Shropshire* (1580), 62; *Visit. of Bedfordshire* (1556), 69, 61; *Mis. Gen. et Her.* (5ᵗʰ ser.) I: 242-243).

42. SIR RICHARD CHETWODE, b. posthumously 1560, d. aft. 1631; m. as 2ⁿᵈ wife, Dorothy Needham. (Gens. 27-40: Dr. Arthur Adams, *The Elkington Family* (Hartford, 1945), pp. 16, 18; Ormerod, *History of Chester*; Wodhull Pedigree in *Mis. Gen. Her.* (2ⁿᵈ ser.) I: 69-75, 80; F.B. Smith, *The Chetwode Family in England* (Worcester, 1945), p. 71 chart, corrected by D.L. Jacobus, *The Bulkeley Genealogy*, pp. 61-62. Richard Woodhull of Setauket, L.I., N.Y., may be of this family though his parentage is currently unknown. However, such relationship if it exists can not be close. See *TAG* 21: 72).

Line 151

18. GISELBERT (140-18), Duke of Lorraine, d. 939; m. **GERBERGA OF SAXONY** (142-18), d. 5 May 984.

19. ALBERADE OF LORRAINE, m. Reinald (Ragenold), d. 10 May 967, comes de Roucy. (Seversmith, 2,549).

20. GISELBERT, Count of Roucy, b. bef. 956, d. 19 Apr. 991/1000; m. NN. (Seversmith, 2, 548 says he was liv. 994, but d. by 997).

21. EBLES I, b. abt. 980, d. 11 May 1033, Count of Rheims and Roucy, Archbishop of Rheims; m. **BEATRIX OF HAINAUT** (106-22). (*ES* I.2/236; Seversmith, 2,542).

22. ADELE DE ROUCY, b. abt. 1014, d. 1062; m. 1031, **HILDUIN III** (or **IV**) **DE RAMERU** (151A-22), b. abt. 1010, d. 1063, Count of Montdidier & Roucy, Seigneur of Rameru. (Seversmith, 2,542, 2,547; Brandenburg, p. 78. Gens. 19-22: *ES* III.4/675A, 676). (See: *Gen.* (n.s.) X (1893): 85, for Montdidier).

23. BEATRIX DE MONTDIDIER, d. 2 Sept. aft. 1129; m. Geoffroy, Count of Mortagne, 1ˢᵗ Count de Perche, d. 1100, son of Routrou II, Count of Mortagne, Viscount of Chateaudun, and Adeline de Bellesme, Dame de Domfront, dau. of Warin de Bellesme, Seigneur de Domfront. (*CP* XI Append. D, 112-113; West Winter XII.70, XI.198, XI.461c; Brandenburg 78; *ES* III.4/689; Anselme III: 307-8).

24. MARGARET DE PERCHE, elder dau., living 1156; m. bef. 1100, Henry de Beaumont, b. abt. 1046, d. 1119, cr. 1ˢᵗ Earl of Warwick abt. 1090, son of Roger de

Beaumont, Seigneur of Beaumont Pont-Audemar, and Adeline of Meulan, dau. of Waleran, Count of Meulan, and brother of Sir Robert de Beaumont, 1st Earl of Leicester, who m. **ISABEL DE VERMANDOIS** (50-24). (*Gen. Mag.* 19: 567 chart; *Med. Proso*pography 19 (1998): 2).

    25. ROGER DE BEAUMONT, d. 12 June 1153, 2nd Earl of Warwick; m. bef. 1130, **GUNDRED DE WARENNE** (84-25). (Gens. 18-26: *Boston Evening Transcript*, Note 2257, Part XV Brabant, Feb. 1928, also 14 Nov. 1936; Turton; *Genealogist* (n.s.) X (1893): 85; *Warwick Castle and Its Earls* II: 827-829; *CP* IV: 672-673, VIII: 53-56, XII (2): 361-362, Append. A, 3-6).

Line 151A   New to 8th Edition

    19. HELPUIN I, b. abt. 925, Comte d'Arcis-sur-Aube; m. Hersende, Countess of Rameru.

    20. HILDUIN I (or **II**), b. abt. 950, d. bef. 1000.

    21. HILDUIN II (or **III**) **DE RAMERU**, b. abt. 985, d. abt. 1037.

    22. HILDUIN III (or **IV**) **DE RAMERU**, b. abt. 1010, d. 1063, Count of Montdidier, Lord of Rameru 1061, Count of Roucy 1032; m. abt. 1031 **ADELE DE ROUCY** (151-22, 246-22), d. 1062. (Seversmith, 2,542-2,543, 2,546; *ES* III.4/676-677).

    23. ANDRE I DE RAMERU and d'Arcis-sur-Aube, d. 1118; m. (1) Adele; m. (2) Guisemode, founded Abbey de Bassefontaine, 1143, widow of Hugue of Pleurs (Theodore Evergates, *Feudal Society in The Bailliage of Troyes under the Counts of Champagne* (1975), 196-198).

    24. ALIX DE RAMERU (71A-27), Dame of Rameru; m. Erard I, Count of Brienne, son of Gautier I (son of Englebert), d. 1090, by Eustace of Bar-sur-Seine, dau. of Milo I, Count of Tonnerre, d, 1046. (Theodore Evergates, *Feudal Society in The Bailliage of Troyes under the Counts of Champagne* (1975), 164-165, 196-197).

Line 152   Revised for 8th Edition

    26. ALBRI DE LUZARCHES, Chamberlain of France 1155-1160, *j.u.* Count of Dammartin, d. 19 Sept. 1200; m. **MATHILDA, (MAUD, MABILIE) OF CLERMONT, PONTHIEU & DAMMARTIN** (144-26), d. Oct. 1200. (*Gen. Mag.* 15 (2): 53-63, esp. 55; *ES* III.4/653) (144-26), Count of Dammartin, d. 1200; m. Maud. (Anselme VIII: 401-402).

    27. JULIANE DE DAMMARTIN, m. Hugh V de Gournay, d. 1238. They parents of Juliane de Gournay who m. William Bardolf (or Bardolph), of Wormegay, Norfolk, who were the parents of Hugh Bardolf (or Bardolph) (see 257-31). (*Gen. Mag.* 23 (7): 261).

    27. AGNES DE DAMMARTIN, (dau. of Gen. 26), d. 1237; m. 1190, **GUILLAUME (WILLIAM) DE FIENNES** (158B-27, 158C-27), liv. 1220-1233. (Anthony Wagner, *Pedigree & Progress* (1975): 161; LaChesnaye, *Dict. de la Noblesse*, VIII/40).

    28. ENGUERRAND II DE FIENNES (158C-28) m. Isabel, dau. of Nicholas I, Seigneur de Conde (*CP* XIV: 381; *ES* XIII/139).

23. BEATRIX DE MONTDIDIER (151-23); m. Geoffrey IV, Count de Perche. (*ES* III.4/689).

24. ROUTROU III, d. Apr. 1144, Count de Perche, Comte de Belleme; m. (1) **MATILDA**, b. 1086, d. 25 Nov. 1120, natural dau. of **HENRY I** (121-25), King of England, by Edith. (*CP* XI Append. D, 112; West Winter, XII.313, says he mar. first NN, Maud being 2nd wife; Brandenburg 79, #343).

Line 153A   New to 8th Edition

23. BEATRIX DE MONTDIDIER (151-23); m. Geoffrey IV, Count de Perche.(*ES* III.4/689).

24. MAUD (MATHILDE) DE PERCHE, b. 1105, d. 28 May 1143; m. (1) Raymond I, d. abt. 1122, Vicount of Turenne, son of Boson I, Vicount de Turenne, d. 1092, and Gerberge. (West Winter, XII.316 corrects Brandenburg which incorrectly identified her; *ES* III.4/766).

25. MARGUERITE DE TURENNE; m. (3) abt. 1147, William VI (Taillifer), d. 7 Aug. 1179, Count of Angoulême, son of Wulgrin II, Count of Angoulême, and Ponce de la Marche. (*ES* III.4/766).

26. Note: Generation 25 are the parents of Generation 27.

27. AYMER (ADHÉMAR) "TAILLIFER" DE VALENCE, d. 16 July 1202, Count of Angoulême (see also 275-26); m. 1186, as her 2nd husb., **ALICE (ALIX) DE COURTENAY** (117-26). (*ES* III.4/818).

28. ISABELLA OF ANGOULÊME, (117-27), b. 1187, d. 31 May 1246; m. (1) 10 May 1200, **JOHN** (1-25), King of England, d. 1216; m. (2) Mar./Apr.1220, **HUGH X DE LUSIGNAN** (275-27) (see 117-27). (*ES* III.4/819; *CP* X: 377-382).

29. ALICE (ALFAIS) DE LUSIGNAN, by (2), d. 9 Feb. 1256; m. Aug. 1247, **JOHN DE WARENNE** (83-28), 7th Earl of Surrey. (*CP* IV: 670 chart ii, XII (1): 449-508; *ES* III.2/355; West Winter, XV.368, XVI.544).

30. ELEANOR DE WARENNE, b. 1251; m. York, 8 Sept. 1268, **SIR HENRY DE PERCY, KNT.** (161-27), b. abt. 1235, d. 29 Aug. 1272.

Line 154

28. ISABELLA OF ANGOULÊME (117-27, 153A-28); m. (2) 1217, **HUGH X DE LUSIGNAN** (275-27). (*CP* X: 377-382; *ES* III.4/818, 816).

29. SIR WILLIAM DE VALENCE (or **DE LUSIGNAN**), **KNT.**, Lord of Valence, titular Earl of Pembroke, b bef. 1225, d. bef. 18 May 1296-, m. 13 Aug. 1247, **JOAN DE MUNCHENSI** (80-29) d. 1307,. (*CP* X: 346 note *a*, 377-382, Append. L. 127-129).

30. JOAN DE VALENCE; m. by 1291, **JOHN COMYN** (95-30), Lord of Badenoch. (*CP* X: 381; *SP* I: 508-509; *ES* III.4/818).

17. REGINAR I (140-17, 240-17), Count of Hainaut, d. aft. 25 Oct. 915, bef. 19 Jan. 916; m. Alberade, of Mons?. (*ES* I.2/236).

18. REGINAR II, Count of Hainaut, b. abt. 890, d. 932; m. NN, poss. a dau. of a Count Boso. (*ES* I.2/236; West Winter,VI.14).

19. REGINAR III, Count of Hainaut, b. 920, d. 973; m. Adela (or Alix), d. 961, whose parentage is in question. (*ES* I.2/236; West Winter, VII.22; *Das Haus Brabant*, p. 14).

20. LAMBERT I, "the Bearded," Count of Louvain, b. abt. 950, d. 12 Sept. 1015; m. 985-990 **GERBERGA OF LORRAINE** (148-20), b. abt. 975, d. 27 Jan. aft. 1018. (*CP* I: 335; West Winter, VIII.43).

21. LAMBERT II, Count of Louvain, b. abt. 991, d. aft. 21 Sept. 1062; m. Oda, dau. of Gozelon I, d. 19 Apr. 1044, Count of Verdun, Duke of Lower Lorraine, gt.-gr.son of **CUNEGONDE** (143-18). (*ES* I.2/202).

22. HENRY II, b. abt. 1021, d. 1078/9, Count of Louvain and Lorraine; m. Adelheid (Adela), d. aft. 1086, dau. of Eberhard, Count in the Betuwe. (Brandenburg; Moriarty, *cit.*, 125; *Das Haus Brabant*, p. 18; *ES* I.2/201, 236).

23. GODFREY I of Brabant, "the Bearded," b. abt. 1060, d. 25 Jan. 1139/40, Count of Louvain, Duke of Lower Lorraine; m. (1) abt. 1100, **IDA OF CHINY AND NAMUR** (149-24), d. 1117/22; m. (2) Clemence of Burgundy. (*CP* I: 235; *Das Haus Brabant*, pp 18-19; *ES* I.2/236).

24. GODFREY II, d. 1142, Count of Louvain; m. 1139, Luitgarde of Sulzbach, dau. of Berenger I, Count of Sulzbach. (*Das Haus Brabant*, p. 19).

25. GODFREY III, Count of Louvain, Duke of Lorraine, b. 1142, d. 10 Aug. 1190; m. (1) 1158, Margaret of Limbourg, d. 1172/3, dau. of Henry II, Count of Limbourg, and Matilda, dau. of Adolph, Count of Saffenberg; m. (2) Imaine of Looz (sis. of Agnes of Looz who m. **OTTO I (III)** (252C-27)), dau. of Louis I, Count of Looz. (*Das Haus Brabant*, p. 20; *ES* XVIII/56).

26. HENRY I, b. 1165, d. 5 Sept. 1235, Duke of and Lorraine, Louvain and Brabant; m. (1) 1179, **MATHILDE OF FLANDERS** (165-27), dau. of **MATTHEW OF ALSACE** (165-26), Count of Boulogne. (See also 100-28) (*Das Haus Brabant*, p. 21. Gens. 17-26 see also: Milton Rubincam, "The House of Brabant," in *TAG* 25 (1949): 224-232).

27. HENRY II, d. 1 Feb. 1248, Duke of Lorraine and Brabant, 1235-1248; m. (1) **MARIE OF SWABIA** (45-28), d. 1235. (*Das Haus Brabant*, pp 24-25).

28. HENRY III, d. 28 Feb. 1261, Duke of Lourraine and Brabant; m. 1251 Alix of Burgundy, d. 23 Oct. 1273, dau. of Hugh IV, b. 9 Mar. 1212, d. 27 Oct. 1272, Duke of Burgundy by (1) Yolande de Dreux, d. 30 Oct. 1248, dau. of Robert III, Count of Dreux and Braine, d. 1234, and Aenor de St. Valery. (*Das Haus Brabant*, p. 27; *ES* I.2/237, II/20, III.1/63; Garnier xxvii).

29. MARIE OF BRABANT, b. abt. 1256, d. 12 Jan. 1321; m., as 2nd wife, 21 Aug. 1274, **PHILIP III** (101-29), King of France, b. May 1245, d. 5 Oct. 1285. ((*Das Haus Brabant*, p. 34; *ES* II/12; Weever 775).

30. MARGUERITE OF FRANCE, b. abt. 1275, d. Marlborough Castle 14 Feb. 1317/18; m. Canterbury Cathedral 8 Sept. 1299, as 2nd wife, **EDWARD I** (1-27), King of England. (*CP* V: 736; *ES* II/12, 83. Gens. 17-30: *Das Haus Brabant*, Tables, I, II, III. Gens. 19-30: *Boston Evening Transcript*, 1927, Note 2257, Part XV Brabant, Part XII Early Plantagenets).

31. THOMAS "of Brotherton," (16-29), Earl of Norfolk, b. 1 June 1300, d. Aug. 1338; m. (1) abt. 1316, Alice Hales, dau. of Sir Roger Hales (Hayles), Knt., of Harwich, by whom he left, an heiress **MARGARET** (16-30); m. (2) abt. 1328, Mary de Ros, wid. of Sir Ralph

Cobham, dau. of William, 2nd Lord Ros, no surv. issue. (Burke's *Peerage*, 1973. pp 197-8; *ES* II/84; *DNB* 56: 152).

31. EDMUND OF WOODSTOCK, Earl of Kent, (son of Gen. 30), b. 5 Aug. 1301, beheaded 19 Mar. 1330, m. 1327, **MARGARET WAKE** (236-11), wid. of John Comyn of Badenoch and dau. of John, 1st Lord Wake, by whom he left a dau. **JOAN** (236-12), "Fair Maid of Kent," his event. heiress. (Burke's *Peerage*, 1967, p. lxiii; *ES* II/84; *DNB* 16 :410).

Line 155A   Prepared for an earlier edition by Douglas Richardson

25. GODFREY III (155-25), Count of Louvain, Duke of Brabant; m. (2) Imaine (Imagina), dau. Louis I, Count of Looz.

26. SIR GODFREY DE LOVAINE, custodian of the honour and castle of Eye, Suffolk, d. abt. 26 Apr. 1226; m. abt. 1199, Alice de Hastings, wid. of Ralph de Cornhill, dau. & h. Robert de Hastings, of Little Easton, Essex, by wife, Maud de Flamville. (*CP* VIII: 178; *Early Yorkshire Families* (*Yorkshire Arch. Soc.*, Record Ser, vol. CXXXV) 29-32 (re Flamville); Sanders, 130).

27. MATTHEW DE LOVAINE, of Little Easton, Essex, custodian of the honour of Eye, Suffolk, d. by June 1258; m. Muriel, liv. 1275. (*CP* VIII: 178-179; Sanders, 130).

28. MATTHEW DE LOVAINE, b. abt. 1237, of Little Easton, Essex, and Bildeston, Suffolk, steward of Eye, d. 1302; m. (1) on or bef. 31 May 1268, Helisant, kinswoman of King Henry III, by whom besides Thomas, his h., he had a dau. Eleanor, m. Sir William de Ferrers of Groby; m. (2) Maud Poyntz, liv. 1306. By (2) he had a dau. Alice, h. to her mother 1319. (*CP* VIII: 179-180; Sanders, 130).

29. SIR THOMAS DE LOVAINE, by (1), b. 11 July 1291, d. 9 Apr. 1345, of Little Easton, Essex, and Bildeston, Suffolk; m. Joan, d. 1318. (*CP* VIII: 180-181; Sanders, 130).

30. JOHN DE LOVAINE, b. abt. 1318, of Little Easton, Essex, and Bildeston, Suffolk, d. 30 Jan. 1346/7; m. (1) Joan; m. (2) Margaret de Weston, d. 25 July 1349, dau. & coh. Sir Thomas de Weston. She m. (2) William de Wauton. (*CP* VIII: 181).

31. ELEANOR DE LOVAINE, by (2), b. 27 Mar. 1345, h. of Little Easton and Broxsted, Essex, and Bildeston, Suffolk, d. 5 Oct. 1397; m. by June 1359, Sir William de Bourchier (or Bourghchier, Bourgchier), d. 1375, younger s. Robert Bourchier, d. 1349, 1st Lord Bourchier, by wife, Margaret, d. & h. of Sir Thomas Prayers of Sible Hedingham, Essex. (*CP* II: 246-248, V: 176-178, VIII: 181-182).

32. SIR WILLIAM BOURCHIER (or **BOURGHCHIER**) (or **BOURGCHIER**), created Count of Eu in Normandy, constable of the Tower of London, d. Troyes, 28 May 1420; m. **ANNE** (4-32), Countess of Buckingham, Hereford and Northampton, b. abt. 1383, d. 1438, widow successively of Thomas and Edmund de Stafford, both Earls of Stafford, dau. & h. of **THOMAS OF WOODSTOCK** (4-31), Duke of Gloucester. (*CP* II: 388, V: 176-178, XII (1): 179-181).

Line 156 Revised for 8th Edition

24. WALTER DE GAUNT (143-23), d. 1139; m. Maud, dau. of **STEPHEN** (214-24), Count of Brittany. (*CP* VII: 672, IX: 18).

25. ROBERT DE GAUNT, d. 1191; m. (1) by 1167, Alice Paynel, wid. of Richard de Courcy (Cursy), dau. & h. of William Paynel of Drax; m. (2) Gunnor, dau. & coh. of Ralph D'Aubigny. Gunnor m. (2) **NICHOLAS I DE STUTEVILLE** (270-27). (*CP* VII: 674-675).

26. SIR GILBERT DE GAUNT, son by (2), minor in 1191, adult by 1201, d. sh. bef. 22 Jan. 1241/2, Earl of Lincoln; m. NN. (*CP* V: 625, VII: 674-675).

27. SIR GILBERT DE GAUNT, of Folkingham, co. Lincoln, M.P. 1264, d. Folkingham, 5 Jan. 1273/4; m. NN. (*CP* V: 625-627, VIII: 554-556).

28. NICHOLE DE GAUNT, d. 1284; m. abt. 1273, Sir Piers III de Mauley, 1st Lord Mulgrave and Doncaster, co. York, b. 22 Jul 1249, d. 8 Sept. 1308, son of Sir Piers II de Mauley, d. 1279 (by 2nd wife) and grandson of Sir Piers I de Mauley, d. abt. 1241, and Isabel de Turnham, dau. of Robert de Turnham. (*CP* V: 625-627, VII: 672-677, VIII: 554-562; Banks I: 220).

29. PIERS IV DE MAULEY, 2nd Lord Mauley of Mulgrave Castle, b. 10 Mar. 1280/1, bapt. 19 Mar. 1290/1, d. aft. 23 May 1348; m. bef. 1299, Eleanor de Furnival, dau. of Thomas, Lord Furnival. (*CP* VIII: 562-565).

30. PIERS V DE MAULEY, 3rd Lord Mauley of Mulgrave Castle, b. abt. 1300, d. 18 Jan. 1354/5; m. in or bef. 1322, **MARGARET DE CLIFFORD** (64-33), d. 8 Aug. 1382, said to be dau. of **ROBERT DE CLIFFORD** (82-32). (*CP* VIII: 565-567; Banks I: 312).

31. SIR PIERS VI DE MAULEY, 4th Lord Mauley of Mulgrave Castle, b. abt. 1330, d. 20 Mar. 1382/3; m. (1) as 2nd husb., bef. 18 Nov. 1356, **ELIZABETH DE MEINILL** (88-33) (268-33), Baroness Meinill of Whorlton, b. 15 Oct. 1331, d. 9 July 1368; m. (2) abt. 1371, Constance Sutton, elder dau. of Sir Thomas Sutton. (*CP* IV: 60-61, VIII: 567-568, 632-634).

32. PIERS VII DE MAULEY, 5th Lord Mauley of Mulgrave Castle, d. bef. Jan. 1377/8 and Mar. 1382/3; m. abt. 1371, Margery Sutton, d. 10 Oct. 1391, yngr. dau. of Sir Thomas Sutton and sist. of his father's 2nd wife. (*CP* VIII: 568-569).

33. CONSTANCE DE MAULEY, will dated 1 Jan. 1449/50; m. (2) Sir John Bigod of Settrington, d. abt. 1425, son of Sir John Bigod, Knt., of Settrington, d. 1389, and grandson of **SIR ROGER BIGOD, KNT.** (69-31), of Settrington, d. 1362. (*CP* VIII: 571, IX: 593-596; John Burke, *History of the Commoners* I: 673).

Line 157

18. LOUIS IV (148-18), d'Outre-Mer, b. 919, King of the Franks, d. 10 Sept. 954; m. 939, **GERBERGA OF SAXONY** (142-18), dau. of **HENRY I** (141-18), "the Fowler," King of the Saxons.

19. MATHILDA, of the West Franks, b. 933, d. abt. 981; m., as 2nd wife, aft. 964, Conrad I, King of Burgundy, King of the West Franks, d. 19 Oct. 993, son of Rudolph II, King of Burgundy. (See 133-19). (*ES* I.1/6).

20. GERBERGA OF BURGUNDY, b. 965, d. aft. 1016; m. (2) abt. 988, Herman II, Duke of Swabia, d. 4 May 1003. (*ES* III.4/736).

21. GISELE OF SWABIA, b. 11 Nov. 995, d. 14 Feb. 1042/3; m. (3) 1016, **CONRAD II** (45-21), the Salic, Emperor of Germany, d. 4 June 1039. (*ES* I.1/9; *CCN* 274, 495).

Line 158

21. MAUD OF LOUVAIN (148-21); m. Eustace I, Count of Boulogne, d. 1049. (*CP* I: 352; *ES* III.4/621).

22. EUSTACE II, Count of Boulogne, a companion of William I, The Conqueror, at the battle of Hastings, 1066, d. abt. 1080; m. (2) 1057, Ida, d. 13 Aug. 1113, dau. of Godfrey the Bearded, d. 1069, Duke of Upper and Lower Lorraine, by his wife Dada (or Ida). (*CCN* 444; Brandenburg p. 11; Anthony Wagner, *Pedigree and Progress*, chart p. 159).

23. EUSTACE III, d. aft. 1125, Count of Boulogne and Lens, Crusader; m. 1102, Mary (Marie), of Scotland, d. 18 Apr. 1118, dau. of **MALCOLM III CANMORE** (170-21) and **MARGARET** (1-21), dau. of **EDWARD**, the Atheling (1-20), by Agatha of Kiev.

24. MATILDA OF BOULOGNE, b. abt. 1105, d. Hedingham Castle, Kent, 3 July 1151; m. abt. 1119, **STEPHEN OF BLOIS** (169-25), King of England. (*ES* III.4/621; *CCN* 956-957).

Line 158A   Text supplied by Prof. David H. Kelley

22. EUSTACE II, Count of Boulogne (158-22), d. abt. 1080; m. (2) 1057 Ida, d. 13 Aug. 1113, dau. of Godfrey the Bearded, d. 1069, Duke of Upper and Lower Lorraine, by his wife Dada (or Ida). (Brandenburg p. 11; Anthony Wagner, *Pedigree and Progress* chart p. 159).

23. GODFREY (or **GEOFFREY**), Count of Boulogne, Duke of Lower Lorraine, prob. born earlier than the 1061 usually given, at Baisy (?), Brabant, d. Jerusalem 18 July 1100; Domesday tenant 1086 at Carshalton, Surrey, a leader of the First Crusade, elected King of Jerusalem, but took the title Advocate of the Holy Sepulcher (as Godfrey I); succeeded by his next younger brother Baldwin, Count of Edessa, who became Baldwin I, King of Jerusalem, d. 2 Apr. 1118, surviving issue, if any, unknown; m. Beatrice de Mandeville, daughter of Geoffrey de Mandeville and aunt of the first Earl of Essex. (Wagner considers Godfrey, father of William (No. 24), "prob. illeg." and not identical with the Advocate of the Holy Sepulcher, *op. cit.*, and explanatory note p. 253).

Note: Although the Lotharingian name, Godofred, borne by the famous leader of the First Crusade, has been transcribed into modern English as "Godfrey" this is etymologically incorrect.   The name is, instead, the equivalent of the name which normally appears in contemporary French or Anglo-Norman documents in such forms as "Goisfrid" and "Gauzfrid," the prototypes of modern "Geoffrey."   There is every reason to believe that bearers of the name might be as well aware of that as many a modern William knows that his name is the etymological equivalent of French Guillaume or Spanish Guillermo.   J. Horace Round (1895, p. 256), citing Domesday references to property held by Goisfrid, son of Count Eustace in right of his wife, daughter of Geoffrey de Mandeville, says that "Dr. Liebermann asks whether Geoffrey's daughter was not thus 'the first wife, else unknown, of the future King of Jerusalem.'"   The reference is presumably to the linguistically sophisticated Anglo-Saxonist, Felix Liebermann, who would have known the equation.   However, in an article published a year later, on Faramus, grandson of "Goisfrid," Round makes no mention of this identification.   He had come to recognize that "Goisfrid" was the equivalent of later Geoffrey and had been informed by his friend, M.V.J. Vaillant, of Boulogne that "the sons of Eustace are known and that Geoffrey is not among them."   What M. Vaillant should have written was that there was no Godfrey among them.   However, Round accepted the testimony of his linguistically naive friend against that of Liebermann and therefore invented a non-existent bastard son, Geoffrey, of Eustace of Boulogne. The truth was later recognized by Joseph Armitage Robinson in his study of the Crispins, and by H.W.C. Davis (1913), who drew attention to the fact that "Godfrey" of Jerusalem married Beatrice, daughter of Geoffrey de Mandeville and aunt of the first Earl of Essex.

While the holdings of Geoffrey de Mandeville were not nearly as great as those of Eustace of Boulogne, he was a very substantial landholder in 11 counties and his daughter a suitable match for "Godfrey," who had already inherited a great deal from his maternal uncle. That De Mandeville would have alienated property in order to give his daughter in marriage to a bastard son of Count Eustace, lacking any substantial prospects, is highly unlikely.

More recently, Johnson and Cronne, good historians but poor linguists, have used Round's article to "correct" Davis. The true identity of Geoffrey/Godfrey was recognized again by Miss Catherine Morton, who has been in touch with DHK and with Sir Anthony Wagner on this matter. Wagner (1975, p. 253, with an unfortunate misprint) mentions the "confusion" between "Godfrey" and "Geoffrey." It was there assumed that the confusion was ancient and that Eustace's son, Godofred, was genuinely a Godfrey. It should be emphasized, however, that actually the confusion is entirely modern due to the use of "Godfrey" to transcribe a name which is etymologically "Geoffrey" (the Germans use "Gottfried" both for the leader of the first crusade and for Geoffrey Plantagenet, Count of Anjou--one may regard this either as desirable consistency or doubled error).

Wagner cites the views of Stephen Runciman, a historian of the crusades, pointing out that crusader sources make no suggestion of a wife for "Godfrey" and emphasizing his chastity. However, a wife and child left in England would not necessarily have been known to such sources, nor was there anything notable in a Crusader leaving a wife behind, though certainly noteworthy if he brought a wife with him. Runciman's further suggestion that "Godfrey" might have made some sort of "morganatic" alliance must be rejected. The concept is completely foreign to the period, save, perhaps, among the Welsh, and would, in any case, hardly apply to a marriage of "Godfrey"/Geoffrey with Beatrice de Mandeville, of a family whose status was fully comparable to his own. It is extremely unlikely that "maritagium," the term used for Goisfrid's marriage, would be applied to a union which was in any way irregular. Runciman is looking back from the days of Godfrey's greatness, rather than realistically appraising the situation at the time of his marriage.

The child left by "Godfrey" in England was William de Boulogne, bearer of one of the oldest English surnames, for William was neither Count of Boulogne nor from Boulogne. He should appear with some frequency in the English records, for his son, Faramus, held extensive estates in widely separated parts of England (Somerset, Surrey, Essex, Oxford, Buckinghamshire, Suffolk, probably Kent and Northumberland). William appears as a witness to a document of 1106 and in a couple of later documents. Perhaps he is a still-unrecognized William Fitz-Geoffrey of other documents.

The heir of Faramus was his daughter, Sybil, who married Enguerrand de Fiennes, whose heirs are the extant Fiennes family. However, Faramus had two younger brothers, Eustace and Simon, who witnessed his charter confirming land grants at Balham by Clapham made to the Abbey of Bec by their father and grandfather. The Eustace de Boulogne of that document may well be the Eustace de Boulogne who appears in a document of 1145-7 with his brother, Baldwin de Boulogne, the king's chaplain, who could, therefore, be another brother of Faramus. Widicumbe and Ash, in Martock, which had been held by Count Eustace before the Norman conquest, passed to his heir, William, Count of Boulogne (son of King Stephen), who granted these properties to his cousin,

Faramus de Boulogne, from which the overlordship passed to the Fiennes family. The sub-holders, however, were Boulognes, and in 1227 the sub-holder was a second Faramus de Boulogne, son of Thomas. Presumably Thomas was a grandson or great-grandson of a brother of the first Faramus.

In the later mediaeval period, "de Boulogne" (de Bolonia, de Bononia) became "Boleyn" and still later "Bullen." Admiral Sir Charles Bullen, a hero of Trafalgar, and his relatives probably have a male line descent from "Godfrey"/Geoffrey, as may also the Somerset families of Ashe, Martock, Crewkerne, Widicumbe/Whitcomb; the Boulognes, alias Bamptons, of Oxford; the Bernes, of Kent; and perhaps the Rochesters and Lavers of Essex. An apparent female relationship connected the Boulognes of Somerset with the Beaumonts of Northumberland, and the Boulognes and Widicumbs of Yorkshire may be of the family.

However, the name Boulogne also came into England much later with merchants from the Boullonnais, and it is apparently from one such family that Queen Anne Boleyn derived. Much remains to be done before fully documented unbroken pedigrees can be established, but Godfrey's English wife and child can now be recognized. Marjorie Chibnall, ed., *Select Documents of the English Lands of the Abbey of Bec*, Camden, (3rd Ser.) 73 (1951): 25-26).

24. WILLLIAM DE BOULOGNE, adult by 1106, d. about 1159. (Wagner, *op. cit.*; Chibnall, *cit.*).

25. FARRAMUS DE BOULOGNE, Seigneur de Tingry, adult by 1130, in charge of Dover Castle and of the Honour of Peverel of Dover in 1157-8, held lands at Eaton, Bedford, and Wendover, Bucks, d. abt. 1183/4; m. Maud (Matilda). (West Winter, XVI.85; *ES* III.4/621; LaChesnaye, *Dict. de la Noblesse*, VIII/39-40; Wagner, *op. cit.*; *Bedfordshire Hist. Rec. Soc.* V: 211-212; *Gen. Mag.* 20: 335-340).

26. SIBYLLE DE TINGRY, dau. and h. (she had two brothers, William and Thomas, apparently both died before her, s.p.); m. **ENGUERRAND I DE FIENNES** (158B-26), Seigneur de Fiennes, liv. 1197. (For Gen. 27 in previous editions, see at 158B-27, 158C-27).

Line 158B   New to 8th Edition

23. EUSTACHE, Seigneur and Baron de Fiennes, liv. abt. 1020; m. Adèle de Selvesse, Dame d'Ardres, dau. of Erard (Everard) de Furnes and Adèle de Selvesse, Dame d'Ardres, niece of François, Bishop of Thérouanne. (*Dict. de la Noblesse*, VIII: 39).

24. CONAN, Seigneur and Baron de Fiennes, liv. 1099-1112; m. Alix de Bournonville, dau. of Louis, Seigneur de Bournonville and Silvie, par. unkwn. (West-Winter calls her illeg. dau. of William the Conqueror, but this is not correct, see: Sheppard, *NEHGR*, Apr. 1965, pp 94-95 and Oct. 1970, p. 306). (*Dict. de la Noblesse*, VIII: 39).

25. EUSTACHE II (The Old), Seigneur de Fiennes; m. NN. (Keats-Rohan, *Domesday Desc.* II: 460; *Dict. de la Noblesse*, VIII: 39).

26. ENGUERRAND I DE FIENNES (158B-26), liv. 1197, Seigneur de Fiennes, Crusader, 1207; m. **SIBYLLE DE TINGRY** (158A-26). (*Dict. de la Noblesse*, VIII: 39-40; West Winter, XVI.85; *ES* III.4/621; Wagner, *Ped. & Prog.*, chart p. 159).

27. GUILLAUME (or WILLIAM) DE FIENNES, Seigneur de Fienes, Baron de Tingry, liv. 1220-1233; m.1190, **AGNES DE DAMMARTIN** (152-27). (Wagner, *Ped. & Prog.*, chart p. 161; *Dict. de la Noblesse*, VIII: 40).

28. MAHAUD (MATHILDA) DE FIENNES, m. **BALDWIN (BAUDOIN) III** (272-29), Count of Guines.

27. GUILLAUME (or **WILLIAM**) **DE FIENNES** (158B-27), Seigneur de Fiennes, Baron de Tingry, liv. 1220-1233; m.1190, **AGNES DE DAMMARTIN** (152-27). (Wagner, *Ped. & Prog.*, chart p. 161; *Dict. de la Noblesse*, VIII: 40)

28. ENGUERRAND II DE FIENNES, Seigneur de Fiennes, Baron de Tingry and de Ruminghen, d. 1265; m. Isabel de Conde, dau. of Nicholas de Conde, Seigneur de Bailleul and Elizabeth de Morialmé, Dame de Fraire. Isabel was the sister of Jacques, Seigneur de Conde, not the dau. (West Winter, XIX.1,519d; *ES* XVIII/116; *Dict. de la Noblesse*, VIII: 40).

29. MAHAUD (MAUD) DE FIENNES, d. bef. 31 Dec. 1298; m. 1275. **HUMPHREY VII DE BOHUN** (97-30), b. abt. 1249, d. 31 Dec. 1298. (*Dict. de la Noblesse*, VIII/40.; *CP* VI: 463-466).

Line 159

19. MATILDA (157-19) of the West Franks; m. aft. 964, Conrad I, King of Burgundy and King of the West Franks. (See 133-19).

20. BERTHA OF BURGUNDY, b. abt. 964, d. aft. 1010; m. (1) abt. 983, **EUDES I** (136-20), Count of Blois.

22. HENRY II (155-22), of Brabant, Count of Louvain and Lorraine, d. 1078/9; m. Adelheid (Adela), dau. of Eberhard, Count in the Betuwe.

23. IDA OF LOUVAIN, d. 1139; m. 1084, **BALDWIN II** (163-24), Count of Hainaut, d. 1099. (*ES* I.2/236; *Boston Evening Transcript*, 9 Nov. 1927, Note 2257, Part VI Flanders, Part XV Brabant).

Line 161

23. GODFREY I (155-23), of Brabant, "the Bearded," b. abt. 1060, d. 25 Jan. 1139/40, Count of Louvain, Duke of Lower Lorraine; m. (2) abt. 1125, Clemence of Burgundy, wid. of Robert II, Count of Flanders, dau. of **WILLIAM I** (132-24), Count of Burgundy. (*CP* I: 235, X: 445-448; Collins, *Peerage*, (1756), IV: 23-26; Garnier, Table xxviii).

24. JOCELIN OF LOUVAIN (natural son of Godfrey I by an unknown mistress), d. 1180, lord of Petworth, Sussex, castellan of Arundel; m. aft. 1154, Agnes de Percy, b. 1134, d. bet. 1201-13 Oct. 1204, dau. & coh. of William de Percy, d. 1174/5, lord of Topcliffe, co. York, by his 1st wife, Adeliza de Clare (alias de Tonbridge), dau. **RICHARD FITZ GILBERT** (246B-25), d. 1136, lord of Clare, Suffolk. (*CP* X: 440-443, 445-448; Collins IV: 25-26; Sanders, 148; *ES* III.4/710. See Knetsch, *Das Haus Brabant.* p. 20).

25. HENRY DE PERCY, d. 1198; m. Isabel de Brus, liv. 1230, dau. of Adam II de Brus, of Skelton in Cleveland, and sister of Piers (Peter) I de Brus, Lord of Skelton; she m. (2) Sir Roger Mauduit. (*CP* X: 448-449; Collins IV: 29-30).

26. WILLIAM DE PERCY, b. abt. 1193, lord of Topcliffe, co. York, d. sh. bef. 28 July 1245; m. (2) abt. 1233, Ellen de Baliol, d. bef. 22 Nov. 1281, dau. of Ingram (or Enguerrand) de Baliol, d. abt. 1244, of Tours-en-Vimeu, Picardy, by his wife, N.N., heiress of Redcastle (Inverkeilor) in Angus & Urr in Galloway, dau. of Walter de Berkeley. (*CP* X: 452-455; Sanders, 148; Geoffrey Steil, "The Balliol Family and the Great Cause of 1291-2," in *Essays on the Nobility of Medieval Scotland*, esp. pp. 153-154; G.W.S. Barrow, *The Anglo-Norman Era in Scottish History*, (1980), 174-175).

27. SIR HENRY DE PERCY, KNT., b. abt. 1235, knighted 1257, d. 29 Aug. 1272; m. York, 8 Sept. 1268, **ELEANOR DE WARENNE** (153A-30), b. 1251, liv. 1282. (*CP* X: 455-456).

28. SIR HENRY PERCY, KNT., 1st Lord Percy, b. abt. 25 Mar. 1273, knighted 1296, M.P. 1299-1314, Baron of Alnwick, co. Northumberland, 1309, d. Oct. 1314; m. NN. (*CP* X: 456-459; Clay, 161; Burke (1953) p. 1583).

29. HENRY DE PERCY, K.G., 2nd Lord Percy of Alnwick, b. 1299, M.P. 1322-1352, knighted 1323, Constable of Scarborough Castle, Warden of the Marches of Scotland, d. 26 Feb. 1351/2; m. **IDOINE (IDONEA) DE CLIFFORD** (205-33), d. 24 Aug. 1365, dau. of **ROBERT DE CLIFFORD** (82-32), 1st Lord Clifford. (*CP* X: 459-464).

30. HENRY DE PERCY, 3rd Lord Percy, b. 1320, fought at Crecy, 26 Aug. 1346, d. abt. 18 May 1368; m. (1) Sept. 1334, **MARY**, of Lancaster (19-30), dau. of **HENRY** (17-29), 3rd Earl of Lancaster. (*CP* I: 244, X: 462-463. Gens. 24-30: *ES* III.4/711).

Line 162

16. JUDITH, b. abt. 844/6, d. 870, dau. **CHARLES II**, the Bald (148-15), King of the Franks, and Emperor, and Ermentrude of Orléans; m. (3) 862, Baldwin I "Bras de Fer," d. 879, Count of Flanders. (*CCN* 112).

17. BALDWIN II, the Bald, b. 863/5, Count of Flanders and Artois, d. 918; m. 884, **ALFTHRYTH (ETHELSWITH)** (44-16) of Wessex, d. 7 June 929, dau. of **ALFRED THE GREAT** (1-14). (*CCN* 112).

18. ARNOLD I, the Old, b. abt. 890, Count of Flanders and Artois, d. 27 Mar. 964; m. 934, **ALIX DE VERMANDOIS** (48-20), d. Bruges, 960.

19. BALDWIN III, Count of Flanders, b. abt. 940, d. 1 Jan. 961/2; m. abt. 961, Mathilde of Saxony, d. 25 May 1008, dau. of Herman Billung, Duke of Saxony. (*ES* I.2/11).

20. ARNOLD II, the Young, b. abt. 961/2, Count of Flanders, d. 30 Mar. 987; m. 968, **ROSELA** (or **SUSANNA**) (146-19) of Ivrea, d. 26 Jan. 1003. She m. (2) **ROBERT II** (101-21), King of France as (1) wife, repudiated.

21. BALDWIN IV, the Bearded, b. 980, Count of Valenciennes, 1007, and Count of Flanders, d. 30 May 1035; m. abt. 1012, Ogive (or Otgiva) of Luxembourg, b. abt. 995, d. 21 Feb. 1030 or 1036, dau. of **FREDERICK I** (143-20), Count of Luxembourg, by his wife Ermentrude of Gleiberg. (*ES* I.2/203, II/5; West Winter, VIII.114).

22. BALDWIN V, de Lille, Count of Flanders, b. 1012, d. Lille, 1 Sept. 1067; m. 1028, as 2nd husb., **ADELE** (or **AELIS**) **DE FRANCE** (128-22), d. 8 Jan. 1079, wid. of **RICHARD III** (132A-23), Duke of Normandy. (*ES* II/79; West Winter, IX.125, X.30, XI.12).

23. MAUD (or **MATILDA**) **OF FLANDERS**, b. 1032, d. 3 Nov. 1083; m. 1053, **WILLIAM I**, the Conqueror (121-24), Duke of Normandy, King of England. (Gens. 16-23: *ES* II/5. See also: Crispin, *Falaise Roll*, (1938). 186-187; *Boston Evening Transcript*, 26 Sept. 1927, Note 2257, D.L.J., Part VI Flanders).

22. BALDWIN V (162-22), de Lille, Count of Flanders; m. **ADELE** (or **AELIS**) **DE FRANCE** (128-22).

23. BALDWIN VI (I), de Mons, b. abt. 1030, Count of Flanders, and (as Baldwin I) Count of Hainaut, d. 10 July 1070; m. abt. 1055, Richilde of Mons, d. 15 Mar. 1086, wid. of Herman, Count of Hainaut, dau. & h. of Renier V, Count of Mons, niece or gr.-niece of Pope Leo IX (Bruno of Egisheim). Richilde m. (3) sh. bef. 1071, William Fitz Osbern, Earl of Hereford. (See 53-25). (*CP* VI: 447-449, IX: 18, XIV: 380;   *ES* I.2/236, II/5; Brandenburg, p. 84; Moriarty, *The Plantagenet Ancestry*, 124; *Encyc. Brit.* (1952) 15: 738).

24. BALDWIN II, Count of Hainaut, d. 1099; m. 1084, **IDA OF LOUVAIN** (160-23), d. 1139. (*ES* II/5-6, I.2/236).

25. BALDWIN III, Count of Hainaut, d. 1120; m. Yolande of Geldern, dau. of Gerald (Gerhard) I Flaminius de Wassenberg, Count of Geldern. (*ES* II/6, XVIII/26).

26. BALDWIN IV, Count of Hainaut, d. 8 Nov. 1171; m. abt. 1130, Alix (or Adelaide) de Namur, d. July 1169, dau. of Godfrey, d. 1139, Count of Namur, and Ermesinde, d. 1143, dau. of Conrad I, d. 1086, Count of Luxembourg. Godfrey, s. **ALBERT III** (149-22), Count of Namur, d. 1102, and Ida of Saxony.

27. BALDWIN V, Count of Hainaut, Margrave of Namur, b. 1150, d. 17 Dec. 1195; m. Apr. 1169, as 2nd husb., **MARGARITE OF LORRAINE** (164-26), heiress of Flanders, d. 17 Dec. 1195. (*ES* II/6).

28. ISABELLA OF HAINAUT, b. abt. 1170, d. 15 Mar. 1190; m. 28 Apr. 1180, **PHILIP II** (101-26), b. 22 Aug. 1165, d. 14 Jul 1223, King of France. (*ES* II/6; Gens. 22-28: *Boston Evening Transcript*, 1927, Note 2257, Part VI Flanders).

Line 163A

27. BALDWIN V (163-27), Count of Hainaut, Margrave of Namur, VIII of Flanders, b. 1150, d. 17 Dec. 1195; m. Apr. 1169 as 2nd husb., **MARGARITE OF LORRAINE** (164-26), dau. & h. of **THIERRY I OF LORRAINE** (164-25), Count of Flanders, b. abt. 1150, d. 12 Nov. 1194. (*ES* II/6).

28. YOLANDE OF FLANDERS, b. abt. 1175, d. Constantinople Aug. 1219, heiress and Countess of Namur; m. as 2nd wife, I July 1193, **PETER DE COURTENAY** (107-27), b. 1155, d. Epirus bef. Jan. 1218, Count de Courtenay and de Nevers, Marquis of Namur, Emperor of Constantinople,. (ES II/6, 17).

29. YOLANDE DE COURTENAY, b. abt. 1200, d. 1233; m. 1215, as 2nd wife, **ANDREW II** (105-28), King of Hungary, b. 1176, d. 21 Sept. 1235. (*ES* II/17; Moriarty, *The Plantagenet Ancestry*).

Line 164

22. BALDWIN V (162-22) de Lille, Count of Flanders; m. **ADELE** (or **AELIS**) **DE FRANCE** (128-22).

23. ROBERT I, Count of Flanders, b. abt. 1035, d. 3 Oct. 1093; m. 1063, Gertrude of Saxony, d. 4 Aug. 1113, widow of Florent I, Count of Holland, daughter of Bernard II (Billung), Duke of Saxony. (*ES* I.2/11).

24. GERTRUDE OF FLANDERS, b. abt. 1070, d. 1117; m. (2) 1095/6 Thierry (Dietrich) II, Duke of Lorraine, d. 1115, s. of Gerard IV, d. 1070, Count of Alsace, Duke of Upper Lorraine, by Hadwide, d. abt. 1080, dau. of Albert I, d. 1012, Count of Namur & **ERMENGARDE OF LORRAINE** (149-20). (*ES* II/6).

25. THIERRY (DIETRICH) I OF LORRAINE, Count of Flanders, d. 17 Jan 1168; m. (2) 1131, **SYBIL OF ANJOU** (129-25).

26. MARGARITE OF LORRAINE, and heiress of Flanders, b. abt. 1140/5, d. 17 Dec. 1195; m. (1) abt. 1160, Rudolph (Raoul) II, Count of Vermandois, d. 17 Jun 1167; m. (2) 1169, **BALDWIN V** (163-27), Count of Hainaut. (*ES* II/6; Brandenburg).

Line 165

25. THIERRY I OF LORRAINE (164-25), Count of Flanders; m. (2) 1131, **SYBIL OF ANJOU** (129-25).

26. MATTHEW OF ALSACE, Count of Boulogne; m. **MARY (MARIE) OF BLOIS** (169-26), b. 1136, d. 1182, Countess of Boulogne in her own right, dau. of **STEPHEN OF BLOIS** (169-25), King of England, by **MATILDA OF BOULOGNE** (158-24).

27. MATHILDE OF FLANDERS, d. 1210/11; m. 1179, **HENRY I** (155-26), Duke of Brabant, d. 5 Sep, 1235; he m. (2) 1213, Marie, dau. of **PHILIP II** (101-26), King of France.

Line 166   Revised for 8th Edition

22. RICHARD III, (132A-23) Duke of Normandy, b. abt. 1001, d. 6 Aug. 1027, son of **RICHARD II** (121E-21), Duke of Normandy by **JUDITH OF BRITTANY** (121-22); m. as her 1st husb., **ADELE (AELIS)** (128-22) of France.

23. JUDITH, of Normandy, b. posthum. 1028, d. 4 Mar. 1094; m. (1) Tostig, d. 25 Sept. 1066, Earl of Northumbria, son of Godwin, Earl of Wessex; m. (2) 1071, Welf IV, Duke of Bavaria, d. 6 Nov. 1101. (Gens. 22-23: *ES* II/79, West Winter, XI.12, XI.59. This corrects the paternity of Judith.).

24. HENRY I, b. 1074, d. 13 Dec. 1126, Duke of Bavaria; m. abt. 1100, **WULFHILDA** (243-8), d. 29 Dec. 1126, dau. of **MAGNUS** (243A-23), Duke of Saxony, and **SOPHIA** (243-7), dau. of **BÉLA I**, King of Hungary (243-6).

25. JUDITH OF BAVARIA, b. 1100, d. 1130; m. **FREDERICK II** (45-25) of Hohenstauffen, b. 1090, d. 6 Apr. 1147, Duke of Swabia. (Gens. 22-25: ES II/79, I.1/18; Brandenburg).

Line 167

20. GERBERGA OF BURGUNDY (157-20); m. (2) Herman(n) II, d. 1003, Duke of Swabia and Alsace, son of Konrad, d. 997, Count in the Rheingau, Duke of Swabia.

21. MATHILDE OF SWABIA, d. bef. 1033; m. (2) Frederick II, Duke of Upper Lorraine, b. abt. 995, d. 1026, son of Thierry (Dietrich) I, Duke of Upper Lorraine, by Richilde von Blieskastel, dau. of Folmar, dead 993, Count in the Bliesgau. (Michel Parisse, *Noblesse el Chevalerie en Lorraine Medievale* (1982), 115, 354; *ES* VI/156).

22. SOPHIE (or **SOPHIA**), Countess of Bar-le-Duc, d. 21 Jan. 1093; m. abt. 1040, Louis, Count of Montbéliard, d. 1073/6, son of Richwin, Count of Scarpone, by Hildegarde of Egisheim, dau. of Hugo VI, Count in Nordgau and of Egisheim, sis. of Pope Leo IX. (Brandenburg X/26; *ES* I.2/200B, I.2/226; Parisse, *cit*. Gens. 21-22: *ES* VI/127).

23. THIERRY (DIETRICH) I, Count of Montbéliard and Bar-le-Duc, d. 1105; m. abt. 1065, **ERMENTRUDE OF BURGUNDY** (144-23). (*ES* I.2/226; West Winter, XI.98; Parisse, *cit*).

Line 168

27. BALDWIN V (163-27), Count of Hainaut, d. 17 Dec. 1195; m. abt. 1169, **MARGARITE OF LORRAINE** (164-26), heiress of Flanders, d. 15 Nov. 1194.

28. BALDWIN VI, Count of Hainaut and Flanders, b. Valenciennes, July 1171, a leader of the Fourth Crusade, Emperor of Constantinople, d. 11 June 1205 or 1206; m. **MARIE OF CHAMPAGNE** (102-27). (*ES* II/6).

29. MARGARET DE HAINAUT, Countess of Hainaut and Flanders, b. 1202, d. 10 Feb. 1279; m. (1) abt. 1212 (annulled 1221), **BOUCHARD D'AVESNES** (168A-29), Archdeacon of Laon and Canon of St. Pierre de Lille, d. 1244.

30. JOHN I D'AVESNES, Count of Hainaut and Holland, b. 1 May 1218, d. 24 Dec. 1257, m. 9 Oct. 1246, **ADELAIDE OF HOLLAND** (100-29), Countess of Holland, d. abt. 1284. (*Speculum* 23 (1948): 81-101).

31. JOHN, Count of Hainaut and Holland, b. 11 Sept. 1247, d. 22 Aug. 1304; m. abt. 1265, Philippine of Luxembourg, d. 6 Apr. 1311, dau. of **HEINRICH II** (234B-26), Count of Luxembourg, by his wife, Margareta of Bar, d. 1275, dau. of Henry II, Count of Bar, d. 1239, whose wife, Philippa, d. 1242, was dau. of **ROBERT II DE DREUX** (135-28).

32. WILLIAM III, Count of Hainaut and Holland, b. abt. 1286, d. 7 June 1337; m. 19 May 1305, **JEANNE OF VALOIS** (103-33), d. 1342, granddau. of **PHILIP III** (101-29), King of France and **ISABELLA OF ARAGON** (105-30). (Gens. 27-32: Moriarty, *The Plantagenet Ancestry*, 124, 175, 177, 192, 193, 194; Gens. 29-32: *ES* II/4. See also Stokvis III, Chapt. 10, tables 21-22).

Line 168A New to 8th Edition

24. FASTRÉ I, Admin. of Tournay (Doornick), d. bef. 1092; m. Ade, pos. dau. of Wédric II d'Avesnes.

25. FASTRÉ II D'OISY, noble in Tournay (Doornick), d. aft. 1111; m. Richilde.

26. WAUTER (WALTER) I D'OISY, Seigneur d'Avesnes, Conde, Leuse, advocate of Tournai, d. 1147; m. Ida de Mortagne, dau. of Everard, Seigneur de Mortagne, by Richilde, dau. of Baldwin III, Count of Hainaut. (West-Winter XI.459).

27. NICHOLAS D'OISY, Seigneur d'Avesnes, Leuse and Conde, d. 1169/1171; m. by 1150, Matilda (Maud) de La Roche, wid. of Thierry (Dietrich) I de Walcourt, dau. of Henry I Count de Namur and de La Roche, by Mathilde von Limburg (Limbourg), d. aft. 1148. Henry I was son of **ALBERT III** (149-22, 246A-22), Count of Namur. Mathilde von Limburg was dau. of Heinrich I, Count von Limburg-Arlon, d. 1119, by NN, dau. of Walrun II Count of Arlon. Heinrich I was son of Udo, Count of Limburg and Judith of Luxembourg, dau. of **GISELBERT** (100B-22), Count of Luxembourg. (*ES* VII/68, I.2/229, VI/26, I.2/203, IV/92; West-Winter, XII.749, XI.440, XII.156).

28. JAMES (JACQUES) D'AVESNES, Seigneur d'Avesnes, Conde, Leuse, d. in battle, Arsuf, Palestine, 7 Sept. 1191; m. 1163/8, Alix (Adeline) de Guise, dau. of Bouchard, Seigneur de Guise, by Alix. (West-Winter, XII.719, XIV.787, XIII.565).

29. BOUCHARD D'AVESNES, Knight of Hainaut, d. 1244; m. bef. 23 July 1212 (mar. annulled 1221) as her 1st husb., **MARGARET DE HAINAUT** (168-29), Countess of Hainaut and Flanders, d. & h. of **BALDWIN VI (IX)** (168-28), Count of Hainaut and Flanders, Emperor of Constantinople and **MARIE OF CHAMPAGNE** (102-27), d. 1204. (West-Winter, XIII.1119, XIV.1498, XIII.1085, XIV.109. Gens. 24-29: *ES* III.1/50).

30. JOHN I D'AVESNES (168-30), Count of Hainaut, b. 1218, d. 1257; m. 1246 **ADELAIDE OF HOLLAND** (100-29), d. 1284. (Gens. 25-30: *ES* III.1/50; *Herald. Genealog. Zeitschrift*, 1888; A. duChesne, *Histoire de la Maison de Chastillon sur Marne* (1621), p. 89. Gens. 29-30: *ES* II/4).

Line 169

23. MAUD OF FLANDERS (162-23); m. 1053, **WILLIAM I**, the Conqueror (121-24), Duke of Normandy, King of England. (*CCN* 494).

24. ADELA OF NORMANDY, b. 1062, d. 1137; m. abt. 1080, bef. 1085, **STEPHEN OF BLOIS** (137-23), Count of Blois, a leader of the First Crusade.

25. STEPHEN OF BLOIS, King of England, b. 1095/6, d. 25 Oct. 1154; m. abt. 1119, **MATILDA OF BOULOGNE** (158-24), b. abt. 1105, d. 3 July 1151, dau. of **EUSTACE III** (158-23), Count of Boulogne, and Mary (Marie), dau. of **MALCOLM III CANMORE** (170-21), King of Scots, and **MARGARET** (1-21), dau. of Edward, the Atheling. (*CP* VII: 641-642; *SP* I: 2; Weever 278; Dunbar 32; Thatcher 324; *ES* III.4/621, III.2/355, II/46).

26. MARY (MARIE) OF BLOIS, b. 1136, d. 1182; m. **MATTHEW OF ALSACE** (165-26), son of Thierry, Count of Flanders, and Sybil, dau. of **FULK V** (118-24), Count of Anjou.

Line 169A

25. STEPHEN OF BLOIS, King of England (169-25), b. 1095/6, d. 25 Oct. 1154; m. abt. 1119, **MATILDA OF BOULOGNE** (158-24).

26. EUSTACE IV, Count of Boulogne, 1150, son and h. app., b. abt. 1120, d.v.p. 10 Aug. 1153; m. abt. Feb. 1140, Constance, d. abt. 1180 s.p., dau. of **LOUIS VI** (101-24), King of France. Eustace had by unknown mistress,

27. EUSTACHIE, of Champagne, d. bef. 1164; m. (1) Geoffrey de Mandeville, d.s.p., Earl of Essex, (div.); m. (2) Anselme Candavaine, Count of Saint-Pol, son of Hugh III Candavaine. (*ES* III.4/622).

28. BEATRICE CANDAVAINE, de Saint Pol, m., as 3rd wife, **JOHN I** (109-27), Count of Ponthieu, d. 1191. (*Gen. Mag.* 15: 186-187).

Line 170   Revised by Prof. David H. Kelley, Calgary, Alberta, Canada

1. ERCC, King of Dalriada, in northern Ireland, son of Eochaid Muinremur, King of Dalriada, d. 474. (*Annals of the Four Masters*). Several sons including Loarn and Fergus.

2. FERGUS, established an Irish kingdom of Dalriada in Argyle, now Scotland. Ruled (for three years ?) in succession to his brother, Loarn, at an uncertain date 498-501?). He has sometimes been confused with Ercc, a son of Loarn's daughter.

3. DOMONGART, apparently briefly King of Dalriada in Scotland, at an uncertain date for a short time following his father's death. According to *Book of Leinster* (12th cent.) and *Book of Ballymote* (14th cent.), he m. Feldelm Foltchain, dau. of Brion, son of Eochaid Mugmedon. Brion was a half-brother of the famous Niall of the Nine Hostages. This marriage is in good agreement with the revised chronology of Carney (*Studies in Irish Literature and History*) for the fifth century, which puts the death of Niall at about 542 A.D., and the death of Patrick about 490 A.D.

4. GABRAN. He and his son are both called, in Welsh sources, "the Treacherous." Welsh pedigrees make him a son of Dyfnwal Hen, allegedly of the line of Ceretic Guletic, regarded by later Welsh writers as an important ruler in northern Britain. According to Welsh sources, his wife was Lleian, dau. of Brychan, the ruler who gave his name to Brecknock.

5. AEDAN. Details of his life and those of his children and grandchildren are well attested in the near-contemporary life of St. Columba, by Adamnan. Died about 608 A.D., after ruling Dalriada in Scotland for about 37 years.

6. EOCHU BUIDE (sometimes **EOCHAID BUIDE**), a younger son of Aedan, succeeded his father, as his brothers had been killed, d. abt. 630. Also called King of the Picts.

7. DOMNALL BRECC, killed at the battle of Strathcarron, prob. about 642 A.D. He is apparently the last king of Dalriada known to early Welsh tradition.

8. DOMONGART, did not reign.

9. EOCHAID II, King of Dalriada, killed about 697 A.D. (aft. ruling three years?).

9A. EOCHAID III, King of Dalriada, about 721-733.

10. AED FIND, "the White," King of Dalriada, d. 778, aft. ruling 30 years.

11. EOCHAID, "the Poisonous," King of Dalriada, 781 ff.

12. ALPIN, slain in Galloway, abt. 837.

13. CINAED. This is the famous Kenneth MacAlpin, King of the Picts and Scots, 843-d. 858. (For more details on generations 1-13, see also H. Pirie-Gordon, "Succession of the Kingdom of Strathclyde," *The Armorial* vol. I: 35-40, 79-87, 143-148, 192-196; vol. II: 9-14, 92-102 with cited authorities. This reference also provides the descent to Kenneth MacAlpin of the lines of the Kings of Strathclyde and of the Picts).

14. CAUSANTIN (CONSTANTINE), King of Scots, 862, d. 877, slain in battle by the Norse.

15. DOMNALL, King of Scots, 889, killed 900.

16. MAEL-COLUIM (MALCOLM), King of Scots, 943, killed by the men of Moray, 954.

17. CINAED (KENNETH), King of Scots, 971, killed 995 by his own men. (Berchan's *Prophecy* indicates that his wife was a Leinster woman).

18. MAEL-COLUIM (MALCOLM II), King of Scots, 25 Mar. 1005-1034; fought a battle in 1008 at Carham with Uchtred (d. 1016), son of Waltheof, Earl of the Northumbrians, and overcame the Danes, 1017; published a code of laws; was murdered, 25 Nov. 1034. "1004. Malcolm the son of Kenneth, a most victorious king, reigned 30 years. 1034. Malcolm king of Scots died." (Ritson II: 104-109; Dunbar I: 280; *ASC*; at this point the *New Revised Complete Peerage* (G.E. Cokayne, vols. I-XII pts. I & 2) and the *Scots Peerage* (Sir James Balfour Paul, 9 vols., 1904-1914) begin the list of Scots kings. *CP* IX: 704; *SP* I: 1; *CP* X: Append. A, p. 9 shows Malcolm MacKenneth had 3 daus: Bethoc; Donada m. Sigurd II, Earl of Orkney; and (?) Anleta. See also Marjorie Anderson, *Kings & Kingship in Early Scotland*).

19. BETHOC (BEATRIX), m. 1000, Crinan the Thane (also called Albanach or Grimus), b. 978, d. 1045, Lay Abbot of Dunkeld, Governor of the Scots Islands. "1045. A battle between the Scots themselves, where fell Crinan abbot of Duncaillen." (Dunbar, 4, 28; Ritson II: 116; *CP* IV: 504, IX: 704; *SP* I: 1).

20. DUNCAN I MAC CRINAN, King of Scots, 1034-1040; murdered by Macbeth near Elgin, 14 Aug. 1040; m. a dau. of Siward, Danish Earl of Northumbria. He besieged

Durham, 1035. "1034. Duncan, the son of Crinan, abbot of Dunkeld, and Bethoc, daughter of Malcolm, the son of Kenneth, reigned six years." Now being on solid ground, with the backing of *CP* and *SP*, we leave Ritson's *Annals of the Scots*. The above unbroken succession of the kings of the Scots from Fergus to Malcolm II is thus soundly and convincingly authenticated. (Dunbar, 12-13, 280; Ritson II: 111-116; *CP* IV: 504 note *b*, IX: 704; *SP* I: 1, III: 240).

21. MALCOLM III CANMORE, King of Scots 1058-1093, b. 1031, crowned at Scone, 17 Mar. 1057/8, slain while besieging Alnwick Castle, 13 Nov. 1093; m. (1) 1059, Ingibiorg, dau. of Earl Finn Arnason, and wid. of Thorfill Sigurdson, Earl of Orkney; m. (2) Dunfermline, 1068/9, **MARGARET** (1-21), St. Margaret of Scotland, d. 16 Nov. 1093, dau. of Prince **EDWARD** (1-20) the Exile, and a descendant of **ALFRED THE GREAT** (1-14), **CLOVIS I** (240A-3), **CERDIC** (1-1), and perhaps Hengist, and ancestress of the royal line of England. (*CP* V: 736, VI: 641-642; *SP* I: 1; Dunbar, 25-34, 280-281. Gens. 12-21: Lang (1901) I: 56-57. For the whole line above the following sources are given by Ritson. Gens. 2-20; *Cronica regum Scottorum; Nomina regum Scot. et Pict.; Annals of Tigernach* (d. 1080, cf. Roderic O'Flaherty, *Ogygia*, published in Latin, 1685, in English, 1793, pp. 477-478); Duan, a Gaelic or Irish poem, abt. 1050. Gens. 4-20: *Annalles Ultonianses* (Annals of Ulster), a faithful chronology of great antiquity but uncertain date. Gens. 11-20: *Cronica de Mailros* (Chronicle of Melrose). Gens. 12-22: William of Malmesbury (d. aft. 1142), 56; *ASC*; Florence of Worcester (d. 1118). Gens. 13-17: *Cronica de origine antiquorum Pictonan et Scotorum*, ends 994, written at the time of Kenneth II. The *Chronicon elegiacum* extends to Gen. 20. Gens. 16-20: *Historia de Dunelmensis ecclesia*, pp. 156-178 (by Turgotus, d. 1115, or Simon of Durham, d. 1130); *Chronicle of Innisfallen; Synchronisms* of Flan of Bute (d. 1056); *Scala Chronica*, 1365).

22. DAVID I, "The Saint," b. abt. 1080, King of Scots, 23 Apr. 1124-1153, d. Carlisle, 24 May 1153; m. 1113/4, **MAUD OF HUNTINGDON** (130-26), Countess of Huntingdon, d. 1130/1. (*CP* IV: 670 chart iv, V: 736, VI: 640-642; *SP* I: 3-4; Dunbar, 58-70, 280-281; *Handbook of British Chronology*, p. 55).

23. HENRY OF HUNTINGDON, b. 1114, Earl of Northumberland and Huntingdon, d. 12 June 1152; m. 1139, **ADA DE WARENNE** (89-25), d. 1178. (*CP* IV: 670 chart iv, V: 736, VI: 642; *SP* I: 4; Dudley Pedigree; Dunbar, 64-65, 280-281).

24. WILLIAM THE LION, King of Scots, 9 Dec. 1165-1214, b. 1143, d. Stirling, 4 Dec. 1214. (*CP* IV: 670 chart iv, VI: 644-645; *SP* I: 4; Gardiner 216).

25. ISABEL (89-27) (natural dau. of William the Lion by a dau. of Richard Avenal); m. (2) Haddington, 1191, Robert de Ros, d. bef. 23 Dec. 1226, of Helmsley in Holderness, co. York, Magna Charta Surety, 1215, Knight Templar, grandson of Robert de Ros and Sibyl de Valognes. (*CP* XI: 90-92; *SP* I: 4; Banks I: 377; *DNB* 45: 216-219).

26. SIR WILLIAM DE ROS, d. abt. 1264, of Helmsley, M.P. 1235/6; m. **LUCY FITZ PIERS** (237-7), of Brecknock. (*CP* XI: 93-94).

27. SIR WILLIAM DE ROS, of Ingmanthorpe, 3rd son, served in Scotland, 1257-1258, and in Gascony, 1294, d. abt. 28 May 1310; m. 1268, Eustache, wid. of Sir Nicholas de Cauntelo, dau. & h. of Ralph Fitz Hugh, son of Hugh Fitz Ralph by Agnes, dau. & h. of Ralph de Gresley. (*CP* XI: 117-118).

28. LUCY (or **LUCIA**) **DE ROS**, m. Sir Robert Plumpton of Plumpton, Knt., fl. 1307, d. 1325, of an ancient family settled in Yorkshire since the time of the Conquest, 1066. (*CP* XI: 117-118; York Deeds, *York Record Society*, V: 273, 306; W.T. Lancaster, *Early History of the Ripley and the Ingilby Family*, 1918; Foster, *Visit. of Yorkshire* (1584/5 and 1612), "Plumpton of Plumpton").

29. SIR WILLIAM DE PLUMPTON, of Plumpton, d. 1362; m. (1) abt. 1330, Alice, dau. of Sir Henry Byaufiz (Beaufitz) (mar. sett. 1322). Her property did not go to the

Plumptons, but to a distant cousin, so Alice No. 30 was not her dau.; m. (2) by 1338, Christianna Mowbray, wid. of Richard de Emildon, d. 1333. (See *MC* 116-5). (Foster, *op. cit*, 386; *VCH Lanc*. I: 345; IV: 143; ms. dated 1487).

30. ALICE DE PLUMPTON, by (2), living 21 Mar. 1400; m. (1) 1352, Sir Richard Shireburne (Sherburne), Knt., of Aighton, d. 1361, son of Sir John Shireburne; m. (2) 1364, Sir John (Robert?) Boteler of Bewsey in Warrington, co. Lancaster, d. 1400, son of William le Boteler of Bewsey and Elizabeth de Havering, dau. of Nicholas de Havering. Sir John Boteler was M.P. 1366, 1372, 1376-1378, 1380, Knight of the Shire of Lancaster 1388, 1397-1398, Baron of Warrington 1380-1400; fought in Gascony 1369-1370, in Aquitaine 1372-1373. (*VCH Lanc*. I: 345, IV: 143, Foster 386; *Dugdale's Visitations of Yorkshire* II: 390).

31. ALICE BOTELER, d. 27 Feb. 1441/2; m. **JOHN GERARD** (233B-35) of Kingsley and Bryn, b. 1386, d. 6 Nov. 1431, lord of the manors of Kingsley and Bryn, 1416-1431. (Inq.p.m. 10 Henry VI; *VCH Lanc*. IV: 143; Gerard of Kingsley, see Ormerod (Helsby) II: 96, 131-132).

32. CONSTANCE GERARD, b. 1402, living 1468; m. abt. 1421-3, Sir Alexander Standish of Standish, d. 1445, eldest son of Lawrence Standish and Lora Pilkington. (Marriage settlement between Lawrence de Standish and John Gerard of Bryn that Alexander his son shall marry Constance, dau. of the said John Gerard, in Earwaker, *The Standish family of Standish...Charters and Deeds* (Manchester, 1898), No. 111, P. 40; VCH Lanc. VI: 194).

33. RALPH STANDISH, ESQ., of Standish, eldest son, h. abt. 1424, living in 1468; m. Margaret Radcliffe, d. 1476, dau. of Richard Radcliffe of Chadderton. (Ralph de Standish and his wife participate in the division of the manor of Chadderton, formerly belonging to Sir John Radcliffe, Knt., dated 1454/5. Earwaker, op. cit., No. 139, p. 48; *VCH Lanc*. VI: 194).

34. SIR ALEXANDER STANDISH, KNT., of Standish, eldest son, b. 1452 (ae. 24 in 1476), d. 1507; m. Sibyl de Bold, living as wid., 1507, dau. of Sir Henry Bold of Bold. Sir Alexander was knighted for service at the battle of Hutton Field, Scotland, 1482. (Ralph de Standish contracts for the marriage of his son and h. Alexander de Standish with Sibyl, dau. of Henry Bold, Esq., of Bold. Apparently a child marriage. Earwaker, No. 135, p. 47; *VCH Lanc*. VI: 194-195).

35. RALPH STANDISH, of Standish, eldest son, b. 1479 (ae. 28 in 1507), d. 1538; m. abt. 16 Aug. 1498, **ALICE HARINGTON** (34-38). (Marriage contract between Alice, dau. of Sir James Harington, Knt., and Ralph, son of Sir Alexander Standish, Knt., dated 16 Aug. 1498. Inq.p.m., Sir James Harington, 14 Nov. 1498; Earwaker, No. 182, p. 61; *VCH Lanc*. VI: 194-195).

Line 170A   New to 8th Edition. Suggestion for descent was supplied by Ralph N. Thompson, Yardley, PA.

30. SIR RICHARD SHERBURNE, d. 1379, son of John Sherburne; m. 1351, **ALICE DE PLUMPTON** (170-30), dau. of **SIR WILLIAM DE PLUMPTON** (170-29) and Alice Byaufiz (Beaufits). (J. W. Clay, ed., *Dugdale's Visitations of Yorkshire* II: 390).

31. MARGARET SHERBURNE; m. abt. 1377/8, Richard de Bayley, of Stoneyhurst, son of John de Bayley.

32. SIR RICHARD SHERBURNE (formerly **DE BAYLEY**), b. 12 Oct. 1381, d. 1441; m. Agnes Stanley, bur. Mitton, 3 Nov. 1444, dau. of William Stanley, of Hooton, co. Chester.

33. ALICE SHERBURNE; m. Sir John Tempest, Knt., of Bracewell, co. Yorks., Sheriff of Yorkshire 1440, 1459. son of Sir Peter Tempest. (Gens. 30-33: Charles Davis Sherburne, *History of the Family of Sherburn*, 1901, pp 10-16).

34. AGNES TEMPEST; m. 1441, **SIR WILLIAM CALVERLEY** (9A-35), of Calverley of Oulton Hall, d. 1488.

35. JOAN CALVERLEY (9A-36), m. 20 June 1467, Christopher Lister, of Medhope, co. Yorkshire, d. aft. 17 Apr. 1509, son and h. of Lawrence Lister, and Ellen Banestre, dau. of Richard Banester (Banestre) of Brokden. (*Dugdale's Visitations of Yorkshire II*: 134).

36. WILLIAM LISTER, ESQ., (9A-37) of Midhope, d. abt. 1537, will proved, York, 3 June 1540; m. Elizabeth Banestre (Banester), dau. and h. of Thurstone Banestre of Swindon, co. Wilts. (Whitaker 35, 95).

37. CHRISTOPHER LISTER, of Midhope, and *j.u.* of Clayton Hall, co. Lancs., b. 1498, named s. and h. of father in deed of 1521/2; m. (mar. set. 2 Apr. 1522), Ellen Clayton, dau. of John Clayton, Esq., of Clayton, co. Lancashire. (Whitaker 35, 95; Foster, *Visit. of Yorks.* (1584/5, and 1612), p. 290). (Burkes, *Landed Gentry* (1952), 1,532; Whitaker, 35, 95; Foster, *Visit. of Yorks.* (1584/5 and 1612), "Lister of Medhope").

38. WILLIAM LISTER, only son, of Midhope, purch. Thornton-in-Craven, d. 1582, will pro. 1582, mentions son-in-law Thomas Southworth; m. (1) Anne Midhope, d. bef. June 1553, dau. of Roger (Richard) Midhope; m. (2) 1557, Bridget Pigot, (will 1 Mar. 1600/1 mentions son-in-law-Thomas Southworth and dau. Rosamond Southworth, and gr.-dau. Bridget Southworth) wid. of Thomas Banister of Brockden dau. of Bartholomew Pigot of Aston Rowen, co. Oxford. (Whitaker, 35, 95; Foster, *Visit. of Yorks.* (1563/4), 191-192; 290. James Stow, *Survey of London* (1633)).

39. ROSAMOND LISTER, d. abt. 1617, (betrothed 1st to Gresham Clapham, who broke the engagement); m. **THOMAS SOUTHWORTH** (9-40), son and heir of **SIR JOHN SOUTHWORTH** (9-39) of Samlesbury, co. Lanc., by Mary Assheton, dau. of Sir Richard Assheton (Whitaker 35, 95; J. W. Clay, *Dugdale's Visit. of Yorkshire*, II, 134-135; Stow, *Survey of London* (1633). See also Henry Lyster Denny, *Memorials of Ancient House: A Story of the Family of Lister or Lyster*, Edinburgh, 1913). <u>Note</u>: More research is needed to adequately verify descent of the last two generations.

Line 171

21. MALCOLM III CANMORE (170-21); m. (1) Ingibiorg.

22. DUNCAN II, b. abt. 1060, King of Scots, 1093-1094, d. 12 Nov. 1094; m. **ATHELREDA OF DUNBAR** (40-23), his cousin. (*SP* I: 2-3).

Line 172

19. BETHOC (BEATRIX) (170-19); m. 1000, Crinan the Thane, b. 978, d. 1045, Lay Abbot of Dunkeld. (*CP* IV: 504, IX: 704).

20. MALDRED (brother of **DUNCAN I MAC CRINAN** (170-20) King of Scots), slain in battle 1045, Lord of Carlisle and Allerdale; m. **EALDGYTFH (ALDGITHA)** (34-21), granddau. of **ÆTHELRED II** (1-18), the Redeless, King of England. (*CP* IV: 504, IX: 704; *SP* III: 240-241; Dunbar 4, 280).

Line 173   Line cancelled

Line 174   Line cancelled

Line 175   Revised by Prof. David H. Kelley, Calgary, Alberta, Canada

    1. BRIAN of the Tributes (**BORAMA, BOROIMHE, BORU**), King of the Dalcassians, then King of Munster (976-1002), and finally usurped the high kingship of Ireland (1002-1014). Killed at the battle of Clontarf, 1014 A.D., fighting a mixed force of Norse and Leinstermen. He had at least three wives, the mother of his son, Donnchad, being Gormflaith of Naas, dau. of Murchad, King of Leinster (d. 972). Gormflaith was the wid. of Anlaf (Olaf), King of Dublin (d. 981), and had been the wife of Mael-Sechnaill, King of Ireland. She d. 1030. (Brian's ancestry table depends solely on tradition and is not accepted as proven).
    2. DONNCHAD, King of Munster, 1023. On pilgrimage to Rome 1064, and d. the same year.
    3. DARBFORGAILL, d. 1080; m. Diarmait MacMael nam Bo, King of Hy Kinsale, who subsequently usurped the high kingship of Leinster. Held the overlordship of Ossory, Dublin, and other local kingdoms. Died 23 Feb. 1072.
    4. MURCHAD, d. in Dublin, v.p., 8 Dec. 1070; m. Sadb, dau. of MacBricc.
    5. DONNCHAD MACMURCHADA, King of Dublin, killed in battle against Domnall Ua Briain, 1115. Of his wives, Orlaith was the mother of Diarmait.
    6. DIARMAIT MACMURCHADA, b. 1100, King of Leinster 1135, d. 1 Jan. 1171. He had several wives, of whom Mor, dau. of Muirchertach Ua Tuathail (O'Toole) and sis. of St. Laurence O'Toole, was the mother of his dau. Aoife. Mor d. 1164. (Brian de Breffny, *Heritage of Ireland*, p. 52).
    7. AOIFE (or **EVE**) **OF LEINSTER**, liv. 1186; m. abt. 1171, **RICHARD DE CLARE** (66-26), Earl of Pembroke, d. abt. 20 Apr. 1176. (*CP* X: 352-357).

Line 176   Revised for 8th Edition

    1. LLYWELYN AP SEISYLL, Prince of North Wales 980-1023, king of Deheubarth & Gwynedd; m. 994, Angharad, dau. of Maredudd ap Owain ap Hywel Dda. (*Dict. of Welsh Biography* (1959), . 600-601).
    2. GRUFFYDD I AP LLYWELYN, Prince of North Wales, king of Gwynedd & Powys, 1039, and of Deheubarth, 1055, slain 5 Aug. 1063; m., as 1st husb., abt. 1057, **EDITH** (or **ALDGYTH**) (176A-4), dau. of **AELFGAR** (176A-3). (*ASC* 1035, 1051, 1053, 1055, 1057, 1058; *CCN* 444,604). She m. (2) abt. 1064, (**HAROLD II** (IB-23), King of England. (*CP* VI, 451-453; *DNB* 23: 307; *NGSQ* 50 (1962): 76-77; *Dict of Welsh Biog.*, cit., p. 312).
    3. NESTA, (177-2), b. abt. 1055/7, m. Osborn Fitz Richard.

Line 176A

    1. LEOFWINE, d. by 1032, Earl of Mercia. (See refs. 176-2).
    2. LEOFRIC, d. Bromley, co. Stafford, 31 Aug. 1057, founder of the church of Coventry, seen as thegn from 1005, "dux" from 1026, Earl of Mercia by 1032; m. prob. by

1030 (pos. as her 2nd husb.) Godgifu (or Godiva), b. prob. abt. 1010, sister of Thorold of Buckingham, sheriff of Lincolnshire. Godgifu's ancestry is uncertain, but she was evidently of an old, noble family. She is the "Lady Godiva" of legend. They had one known child. (*NGSQ* 50 (1962): 74-78; See also other refs. at 176-2).

3. AELFGAR, of age 1051, d. shortly after 1062, Earl of East Anglia 1053, Earl of Mercia 1057, banished 1058; m. Aelfgifu, by whom 3 known sons: Eadwine, Morkere and Burchard whose issue is unknown, and a dau. Aldgyth.

4. EDITH (or **ALDGYTH**), seen at "Doomsday" 1086, death date unknown; m. (1) abt. 1057, **GRUFFYDD I AP LLYWELYN** (176-2), slain 5 Aug. 1063; m. (2) prob. 1064 **HAROLD II** (IB-23). By Gruffydd she had a dau. **NESTA** (176-3, 177-2). By Harold she had a son Harold, seen at Domesday 1086, later life unknown, and possibly King Harold's son Ulf. (*NGSQ*, vol. 50, pp. 74-78 and cited references; *ES* II/78).

Line 176B   New to 8th Edition

24. LLYWARCH AP TRAHAEARN, s. of Trahaern, d. abt. 1129; m. Dyddgu, of Builth.

25. GLADYS, m. as (1) wife, **OWAIN I GWYNEDD** (239-6), d. 1170, Prince of North Wales. He m. (2) (outside church) his cousin Christina ferch Gronw ap Owen ap Edwin. (*Dict. of Welsh Biog.*, *cit.*, pp. 692-3).

26. IORWERTH DRWYNDWN, by (1), Prince of North Wales, prob. d. abt. 1174; m. Marared, dau. of Madog ap Maredudd, d. 1160, ruler of Powys, by his wife, Susanna, dau. of Gryffydd ap Cynan, d. 1137, ruler of Gwynedd [North Wales]. (*CP* IX: 276; *Dict. of Welsh Biog.*, *cit.*, pp. 417, 608. Note error in *Dict. of Welsh Biog.* which shows Susanna as dau. of Owen Gryffydd. Correct father shown in *DNB*, etc.).

27. LLYWELYN AP IORWERTH, the Great, Prince of North Wales, b. 1173, d. 11 Apr. 1240; m. 1205 **JOAN** (29A-27), Princess of Wales, natural dau. of **JOHN** (1-25), King of England. (*CP* IX: 276; *ASC*; Jacobus, *Bulkeley Genealogy*, 87-88). (*Dict. of Welsh Biog.*, *cit.*, pp. 599, 600). He had a number of mistresses, one of whom, Tangwystl, was the mother of

28. GLADYS DHU, d. 1251, widow of Reynold de Braose; m. 1230, **RALPH DE MORTIMER** (132C-29), d. 6 Aug. 1246. (*CP* IX: 276; *Burke's Guide to the Royal Family* (1973) p. 323; *TAG* 41: 122).

29. ROGER DE MORTIMER, b. abt. 1231, d. Kingsland, bef. 30 Oct. 1282, 6th Baron Mortimer of Wigmore; m. 1247, **MAUD DE BRAOSE** (67-29), d. bef. 23 Mar. 1300/1. (*CP* IX: 276-281).

30. SIR EDMUND DE MORTIMER, b. 1261, d. 17 July 1304, 7th Baron Mortimer of Wigmore; m. (2) abt. 1280, **MARGARET DE FENLIS** (120-32), d. 7 Feb. 1333/4. (*CP* VIII: 433, IX: 281-283).

31. SIR ROGER DE MORTIMER (120-33), b. 25 Apr. 1287, d. 29 Nov. 1330, 8th Baron Mortimer of Wigmore, cr. Earl of March, Oct. 1328; m. bef. 6 Oct. 1306, **JOAN DE GENEVILLE** (71-32, 71A-32), b. 2 Feb. 1285/6, d. 19 Oct. 1356. (*CP* VIII: 433-442, IX: 284; Banks I: 220-221; Turton, 72).

32. JOAN DE MORTIMER (71-33), d. bet. 1337-1351; m. by 13 June 1330 as 1st wife, **SIR JAMES DE AUDLEY, K.G.** (122-33), b. 1312/3, d. 1386, 2nd Lord Audley; he m. (2) by Dec. 1351 Isabel Fitz Walter, liv. 1366, dau. of Robert, 2nd Lord Fitz Walter, son of **SIR ROBERT FITZ WALTER** (130-31). (*CP* I: 339-340, XII (2): 59, V: 501; XIV: 50; *Gen.* (n.s.) 36 (1920): 9-16).

33. JOAN DE AUDLEY, b. abt. 1332; m. (1) **JOHN TUCHET** (176C-33), b. 25 July 1327, dead 10 Jan 1361. (*CP, Cit.*).hh

34. JOHN TUCHET, minor in 1361, d. 23 June 1372; m. an unidentified wife, said in some refs. to be Margaret (or Maud), dau. **SIR ROGER MORTIMER** (29-33), 2nd Earl of March. (*CP* I: 340, XII (2): 59-60; Banks I: 100-101).

35. SIR JOHN TUCHET, b. 23 Apr. 1371, d. 19 Dec. 1408 (aged 38), Lord Audley, M.P. 1406-1408; m. Isabel (Elizabeth), living June 1405. (*CP* I: 340-341, XII (2): 60; Banks I: 100-102).

36. JAMES TUCHET, styled Lord Audley, b. abt. 1398, d. 23 Sept. 1459; M.P. 1421-1455; m. (1) abt. 1415, **MARGARET DE ROS** (9-34), living 1423. (*CP* I: 341, XI: 102-103; Banks I: 100-102).

37. ANNE DE AUDLEY (TUCHET), d. 1503; m. **SIR THOMAS DUTTON** (32-35), of Dutton, d. 23 Sept. 1459. (*VCH Lanc.* VI: 305; *Gen.* (n.s.) 36 (1920): 9-16).

38. ANNE DUTTON, d. 22 Oct. 1520; m. abt. 11 July 1463, **SIR THOMAS MOLYNEUX**, (23-35), d. 12 July 1483. (Ormerod, *History ... of Chester* (Helsby ed.), I: 662; *VCH Lanc.* III: 69).

Line 176C   New to 8th Edition

24. JOSCELIN TUCHET, held in 1086, manors os Ashwell, Rutland and Mackworth, co. Derby.

25. HENRY TUCHET, lord of Low Clawson, co. Leics. 1124-1129, d. bef. 1143/9.

26. HENRY TUCHET, liv. 1143/1149, d. prob. 1178; m. Maud.

27. SIMON TUCHET, of age 1178, d. aft. 1203/5; m. Pernel (Petronilla) de Cumbrai, liv. 1218, prob. dau. of Roger de Cumbrai.

28. THOMAS TUCHET, of age 1205, d. bef. 2 Jan. 1234/5; m. Elizabeth, prob. liv. Sept. 1248.

29. ROBERT TUCHET, d. 13 Oct. 1248,(bro. and h. of Henry Touchet); m. Alice.

30. THOMAS TUCHET, b. 1244, d. sh. bef. 1 May 1315; m. Margery.

31. ROBERT TUCHET, b. 1264, d. prob. bef. Dec. 1341; m. Agnes. (*Visit. of Cheshire* (1580), 224).

32. THOMAS TUCHET, d. 18 Aug. 1349; m. Joan. (Gens. 24-32: *CP* XII(2): 53-58).

33. JOHN TUCHET, b. 1327, d. sh. bef. 10 Jan. 1361; m. **JOAN DE AUDLEY** (176B-33). (*CP* XII(2): 59).

Line 177

1. GRUFFYDD I AP LLYWELYN (176-2), Prince of North Wales, slain 5 Aug. 1063; m. (1) abt. 1057 **EDITH (or ALDGYTH)** (176A-4). (*CP* VI: 451-453; *DNB* 23: 307; *NGSQ* 50 (1962): 74-78; *Dict. of Welsh Biog.*, 312).

2. NESTA, of North Wales, b. abt. 1055/7; m. Osborn (or Osbert) Fitz Richard, liv. 1100, of Richard's Castle, co. Hereford, sheriff of Hereford, 1060, son of Richard Fitz Scrob, d. 1067, of Richard's Castle. (*CP* VI: 452-453; J.E. Lloyd, *Hist. of Wales* II: 369, 395, 397 and note 135; *DNB* 23: 307; *NGSQ* 50: 76-77; Sanders, 75; R.R. Darlington, ed., *The Cartulary of Worcester Cathedral Priory* (Register I), (1968) (being vol. 38, New Series, Publications of the Pipe Roll Society)).

3. NESTA, m. Bernard de Neufmarche, d. 1093, Lord of Brecon, son of Geoffrey (son of Thurcytel) by Ada, dau. of Richard Fitz Gilbert, seigneur of Hugleville and Auffay in Normandy, seen 1025-1053 (s. Gilbert de St. Valerie (Valery), seen 1011, advocate of St. Valerie, protector of the monastery of Fecamp), by N., said to be Papia, illeg. dau. of

RICHARD I (121E-20), d. 996, Duke of Normandy. (*CP* I: 20, VI: 452-453; Eleanor Searle, *Predatory Kinship and the Creation of Norman Power* (1988), 840-1066; David C. Douglas, *William the Conqueror* (1964)).

4. SIBYL DE NEUFMARCHE; m. 1121 Miles of Gloucester, Earl of Hereford 1141, Constable, d. 24 Dec. 1143, son of Walter of Gloucester, son of Roger de Pitres. (*CP* I: 20, VI: 452-453; VIII: 677; XIV: 380-381).

5. BERTHA OF HEREFORD, m. abt. 1150, William de Braose, d. abt. 1192/3, of Brecknock, Abergavenney and Gower, 1st Baron of Gwentland, son of Philip de Braose of Bramber, Sussex, and Aenor, dau. & h. of Juhel (Judhael) de Toteneis, liv.. 1123, of Totnes & Barnstable, co. Devon, son of Alved, Lord of Barnstable and Totnes. (*CP* I: 21- 22; Sanders, 89, 104).

6. WILLIAM DE BRAOSE, 5th Lord de Braose, b. 1175, d. Corbeil, 9 Aug. 1211; m. Maud de St. Valery of Haie, d. 1210, murdered by King John who had her walled up alive in her castle walls with her young son William. (*CP* I: 22, VI 456 note *j*, 457 note *c*).

7. REYNOLD (REGINALD) DE BRAOSE, d. 1227/8; m. (1) Grace (or Gracia) de Briwere, d. bef. 1215, dau. of William de Briwere (see 143-27) and Beatrice de Vaux; m. (2) **GLADYS DHU** (176B-28), dau. of **LLYWELYN AP IORWERTH** (176B-27), by Tangwystl. (*CP* I: 22).

8. WILLIAM DE BRAOSE, by (1), 6th Lord de Braose, d. 2 May 1230; m. **EVE** (or **EVA**) **MARSHAL** (66-28), d. bef. 1246. (*CP* I: 22; *Dudley* Pedigree. Gens. 5-8: *Gen.* (orig. ser.) 4: 133-141, 235-244).

Line 177A   Prepared for an earlier edition by Douglas Richardson

6. WILLIAM DE BRAOSE (177-6), Lord of Braose (Briouze), Bramber, Brecon, Over Gwent, etc., Sheriff of Hereford 1192-9, d. Corbeil, near Paris, France, 9 Aug. 1211; m. Maud de St. Valerie, starved to death by King John, 1210. (*CP* I: 22).

7. MARGERET (or MARGARY) DE BRAOSE, d. 19 Nov. 1200; m. Walter de Lacy, b. abt. 1172, d. 1241, lord of Meath, Ireland, and of Weobley, co. Hereford, son of Hugh de Lacy, d. 1186, by his wife Rohese de Monmouth, dau. of Badeion de Monmouth, 1170/76, of Monmouth, co. Monmouth, by his wife, Rohese, dau. of **GILBERT FITZ RICHARD** (184-3), d. 1114/7, Lord of Clare, of Suffolk & Cardigan, Wales, by his wife, **ADELAIDE (or ADELIZA) DE CLERMONT-EN-BEAUVAISIS** (246-24). (Orpen, *Ireland under the Normans*, III, chart pp. 286-287; *CP* XII (2): 169, footnote *d*, Sanders, 64-65).

8. GILBERT DE LACY, of Ewyas Lacy, co. Hereford, and of Trim and Weobley, d. 1230; m. **ISABEL BIGOD** (70-29, 71-29), dau. of Hugh Bigod, Earl of Norfolk, by his wife, Maud Marshal. (*CP* V: 437, IX: 589-590; Orpen, *op. cit.*, III, chart pp. 286-287).

Line 177B   Prepared for an earlier edition by Douglas Richardson

7. MARGERET (or MARGARY) DE BRAOSE (177A-7), d. 19 Nov. 1200; m. Walter de Lacy, b. abt. 1172, d. 1241, lord of Meath, Ireland, and of Weobley, co. Hereford, son of Hugh de Lacy, d. 1186, by his wife, Rohese de Monmouth. (Orpen, *Ireland under the Normans*, III, chart pp. 286-287; *CP* XII (2): 169, footnote *d*).

8. EGIDIA (or GILLE) DE LACY, m. Richard de Burgh, lord of Connaught, d. 1242, son of William de Burgh (died 1205), lord of Connaught, by his wife, a daughter of Donnell O'Brien, K.T. (Orpen, *op. cit.* III, chart pp. 286-287, IV, chart p. 159; *DNB* 3: 328).

9. WALTER DE BURGH, b. abt. 1230, Earl of Ulster, d. 28 July 1271; m. abt. 1257, **AVELINA FITZ JOHN** (75-30, 75A-30), d. abt. 20 May 1274, dau. of Sir John Fitz Geoffrey, Justiciar of Ireland, by his wife, Isabel Bigod. (Orpen, *op. cit.* IV, chart p. 159).

Line 178

1. **RHYS AP TUDOR MAWR**, Prince of South Wales, d. 1093; m. Gwladus, dau. of Rhiwallon ap Cynfyn of Powys. (*CP* X: 11; *Handbook of British Chronology*, p. 50; *Dict. of Welsh Biog.*, pp. 837, 840. See J.E. Lloyd, *Hist. of Wales* II: 767 for his ancestry).

2. **NEST**, of Wales; m. (2) Gerald of Windsor, d. bef. 1136, Constable of Pembroke Castle, 1092, son of **WALTER FITZ OTHER** (12A-21). (*CP* VII: 200, X: 10-11).

3. **MAURICE FITZ GERALD**, b. abt. 1100, of Windsor, Lord of Lanstephen, Wales, Steward of St. Davids (brother of David Fitz Gerald, Bishop of St. Davids), landed in Wexford, 1 Sept. 1176; m. Alice de Montgomery, dau. of Arnulph de Montgomery, son of Roger de Montgomery. (*CP* VII: 200, X: 11-12; *Mis. Gen. et Her.* (n.s.) I (1974): 266).

4. **GERALD FITZ MAURICE**, b. abt. 1150, 1st Baron of Offaly, was at the siege of Dublin, 1171, d. bef. 15 Jan. 1203/4; m. abt. 1193, as her 1st husb., Eve de Bermingham, d. bef. Dec. 1226, dau. & h. of Robert de Bermingham. She brought Offaly to Gerald Fitz Maurice and his heirs. She m. (2) Geoffrey Fitz Robert, baron of Kells, and (3) Geoffrey de Marisco. (*CP* VII: 200, X: 12-14; Orpen, *Ireland under the Normans*, IV: chart p. 128).

5. **MAURICE FITZ GERALD, KNT.**, b. abt. 1194, 2nd Baron Offaly, knighted July 1217, Lord of Lea, Justiciar of Ireland, Sept. 1232-1245, Commissioner of the Treasury and Councillor, 1250, d. Youghal, 1257; m. Juliane. (*CP* VII: 200, X: 14-16).

6. **MAURICE FITZ MAURICE FITZ GERALD**, Lord of Offaly in Ireland, Justiciar, d. 1286; m., prob. 1266, Emmeline Longespee, b. abt. 1250, d. 1291, dau. & coh. of **STEPHEN LONGESPEE** (31-27), and **EMELINE DE RIDELISFORD** (33A-27). (*CP* VII: 200, X: 16 note c; *ES* III(2): 356a).

7. **JULIANA FITZ MAURICE**, m. **THOMAS DE CLARE** (54-31). (*CP* VII: 200, X: 16, note c.)

Line 178A   Prepared for an earlier edition by Douglas Richardson

5. **MAURICE FITZ GERALD, KNT.** (178-5), b. 1190, 2nd Baron of Offaly, Justiciar of Ireland, d. 1257; m. Juliane. (*CP* VII: 200, X: 14-16).

6. **THOMAS FITZ MAURICE FITZ GERALD**, d. enfeoffed in Banada, co. Sligo, by Maurice Fitz Maurice, d. 1271. (Orpen, *Ireland under the Normans*, IV: 128-129).

7. **JOHN FITZ THOMAS FITZ GERALD**, 5th Baron of Offaly, 1st Earl of Kildare, d. 12 Sept. 1316 at Laraghbryan near Maynooth, bur. Church of the Friars Minor at Kildare; m. Blanche Roche, dau. of John Roche of Fermoy. (Orpen, *op. cit.*; *CP* VII: 218-221).

8. **JOAN FITZ GERALD**, m. 1302 **EDMUND BUTLER (BOTILLER)** (73-31), Justiciar and Governor of Ireland, d. London 13 Sept. 1321. (*CP* II: 449-450).

Line 179

Note: This line, as originally included in the 1st Edition (1950), offered a 17 generation pedigree from Twdur (Tudor) Mawr, Prince (not king) of South Wales, down to

Griffith Bowen, of Boston, 1638/9, copied from a pedigree certified by the York Herald in 1891 as a true copy of one filed at the Herald's Office, College of Arms, London. The only references added to the Herald's pedigree and used "to correct minor errors" in it were Clark's *Genealogies of Morgan and Glamorgan* (1886),193-211, and the pedigree of "Berry of Berrynarbor" in Vivian, *Visit. of Devon*, 74. Due to the absence of dates and the lack of cited contemporary evidence, the pedigree was dropped from later editions. However, in Sept. 1979 Lt. Gen. Herman Nickerson, Jr., USMC Ret, published in *NGSQ*: 67: pp. 163-165,a short discussion of the pedigree with cited references for each generation referring to better researched material, the bulk of which were to Welsh compilations and translations of early Welsh manuscripts. A footnote to the article advises the readers that full documentation has been filed in the Society's library where it may be consulted. The pedigree has therefore been reinstated, except that to conform to Gen. Nickerson's work the first seven generations have been changed to carry the pedigree back to the Norman earls of Gloucester instead of to Twdur, Prince of South Wales. However, in the absence of dates, pedigrees kept by bards consisting of strings of names without biographical data on the majority of the generations are not the most convincing to the experienced genealogist.

    1. NN (?MABEL?), illegitimate dau. of "The Earl of Gloucester," living (infant) 1128, d. 23 Nov. 1183 (identified by Nickerson (*NGSQ* 67: 163-166) as ch. of **WILLIAM,** 2nd Earl of Gloucester (124-27)); m., abt. 1158, **GRUFFUDD AP IFOR BACH,** d. 1211. (Patterson, ed., *Earldom of Gloucester Charters*, p. 115, states that Mabel (No. 1) was illegit. dau. of **ROBERT**, Earl of Gloucester (124-26), rather than his son William, citing Clark, *Cartae et alia*, I: 149 n. Bartrum in his article, "The Ancestors of My Lord Herbert," *National Library of Wales Journal*, xvii, no. 3, (Summer 1972), 237-248, shows Mabel as dau. of William as indicated by Peniarth MS 134, 137 & 225. Mabel's husband, Gruffudd ap Ifor Bach, held the lordship of Senghenydd of the honour of Glamorgan. Bartrum, *Welsh Genealogies* A.D. 300-1400, p. 209, chart Cydrich 2). Note: William, 2nd Earl of Gloucester, had a legitimate dau., Mabel, who mar. Amaury V de Montfort, Count of Evreux, see *CP* VII: Append. D, p. 716 and note *b*.

    2. RHYS AP GRUFFUDD, had by an unknown wife (David Edward's "Rice Merrick ms."; Bartrum, *ibid*).

    3. JOAN FERCH RHYS, m. Sir Ralph Maelog. (Edwards, *cit.*; Bartrum, *cit.* and chart Maelog).

    4. ANN MAELOG, m. SIR GWRGI GHANT (Bartrum, *op. cit*, p. 439, chart Grant 1).

    5. JENKIN AP GWRGI, by unknown consort had (Bartrum, *op. cit.*, chart Grant 2).

    6. GWILYM AP JENKIN, by unknown consort had (Bartrum, *ibid*).

    7. ANN, m. **HYWEL AP GRUFFUDD** FAB. (Bartrum, Glam. 241, p. 115, chart Bleddyn ap Maenyrch 31).

    8. HYWEL FYCHAN AP HYWEL, m. Catrin, dau. of Ieuan Llwyd of Castell Odyn. (Bartrum, *ibid*).

    9. GWILYM GAM AP HYWEL FYCHAN, m. Gwenllian, dau. of Gwilym ap Ieuan. (Bartrum, 117, 563).

    10. HYWEL MELYN AP GWILYM GAM of Ynys Derw, by an unknown consort (but said in the Herald pedigree to be Catharine, dau. Griffith Llywelyn Voythys.) (Bartrum, *op. cit.*, p. 117, chart Bleddyn ap Maenrych 33; Bartrum says no. 10 m. Mabel ferch Gruffudd, by whom he had No. 11).

    11. IEUAN GWYN AP HYWEL MELYN, m. Mabel, dau. of Wilcock Cradock. (Bartrum, *ibid*).

12. JENKIN AP IEUAN, m. Jonet (or in the Herald's pedigree, Joan, dau. of 'Thomas ap Gwilim Vachan).

13. OWAIN (OWEN AP JENKIN), living 1566; m. Alice ferch John of Swansea.

14. GRUFFUDD BOWEN of Slade, seen 1557 and 1566; m. Anne Berry, dau. of Nicholas Berry, d. 1565, lord of Berrynarbor and Martinhoe, Devon, by his first wife, Elizabeth, dau. & sole h. of John Bowden of Bradwill, co. Devon. (Vivian, *Visit. of Devon*, p. 74).

15. PHILIP BOWEN of Slade; m. Elsbeth Vaughan, dau. of Hopkin John Vaughan.

16. FRANCIS BOWEN, renewed the lease on Slade, 10 Aug. 1591; m. Ellen Franklyn, dau. of Thomas Franklyn.

17. GRIFFITH BOWEN, b. abt. 1600 prob. at Langwith, d. abt. 1675; m. 1627 Margaret Fleming, dau. of Henry Fleming. They emigrated to Boston, Mass. 1638/9, returned to Wales abt. 1650 to Swanzey, then to London 1669. (See also Suffolk, Mass., Deeds, I: 48).

Line 180   Revised for 8th Edition by David H. Kelley, with additional information from Don C. Stone

1. FLAVIUS AFRANIUS SYAGRIUS, liv. 379-382, of Lyons, Gallo-Roman Senator. (Note: Christian Settipani, *Continuite Gentilice Familiale dans les Familles Senatoriales Romaines a l'Epoque Imperiale*, p. 380, has a possible ancestry for Flavius Afranius Syagrius).

2. A DAUGHTER of Syagrius; m. Ferreolus.

3. TONANTIUS FERREOLUS, Praetorian Prefect of Gaul, 451-453, at Rome 469, 475; m. Papianilla, a relative of Sidonius Apollinaris' wife, Papianilla, dau. of the emperor Avitus.

4. TONANTIUS FERREOLUS, a senator of Narbonne (brother of Ruricius, Bishop of Uzes, d. 506); m. Industria.

5. FERREOLUS, a senator in the Narbonne region; m. Dode, abbess of St. Pierre de Rheims.

6. ANSBERTUS, the Gallo-Roman Senator (see 190-9); m. perh. Bilichilde, whose ancestry is unproven. (See also: *NEHGR* 101: 109-112, 110: 38-40).

7. ARNOALDUS, Bishop of Metz, 601-611.

8. DODE (CLOTHILDE); m. **ST. ARNULF** (190-8). (Gens. 1-8: Don C. Stone, *Some Ancient and Medieval Descents of Edward I of England*, (Philadelphia, PA, 2003) Chart 50: "Descent from Flavius Afranius Syagrius").

Line 181

1. ADALRIC (or ETHIC), obtained the Duchy of Alsace 662, d. 20 Feb. 690, head of the Alsatian House of the Ethiconides, Duke of Alsace 662-690; m. Berswinde.

2. ADELBERT, Duke of Alsace, d. 722.

3. LUITFRIDE I, Duke of Alsace, d. 731.

4. LUITFRIDE II, Count of Alsace, d. 800; m. Hiltrude.

5. HUGH III, Count of Alsace and Tours, d. 20 Oct. 837; m. Bava (Ava), d. 4 Nov. 839. (Gens. 1-5: Stokvis III: 15-16).

6. ADELAIDE (or AELIS), d.aft. 866, wid. of Conrad I, Count of Auxerre, m. as his second wife, **ROBERT THE STRONG** (48-17), Count of Wormgau, Paris, Anjou, and Blois,

d. 866; ancestor of the Kings of France. (Gens. 1-6: J.D. Schoepflin, *L'Alsace Ilustree* (1851), III: 566, corrected; Isenburg, *ES* III.4/736; Gens. 5-6: *ES* I.2/200A).

Line 182

1. **GODEFRIED**, Duke of Alemania (or, of the Alamans) 687-709, d. 709.
2. **HOUCHING**, b. abt. 675, Count in Alemania.
3. **NEBI**, b. 700, d. abt. 775, Count in Alemania.
4. **EMMA**, b. 735, d. abt. 788; m. Gerold of Swabia, d. abt. 795, Count in Linzgau and Prefect in Bavaria.
5. **HILDEGARDE**, of Swabia, b. 758, d. 30 Apr. 783; m. 771, as 2nd wife, the Emperor **CHARLEMAGNE** (50-13); parents of **PEPIN** (50-14), King of Italy, and of **LOUIS I**, "the Fair," (140-16) Emperor. Their descendants are given in Lines 50 to 169 inclusive. (Christian Settipani, *Les Ancêstres de Charlemagne* (1989), Update (1990) pp 8-10; *ES* XII/24; Gaston Sirjean, *Encyclopédie Généalogique des Maisons Souveraines du Monde*, II: *Les Carolingiens*, p. 40; Chaume, *Les Origines du Duché de Bourgogne* I: 550-551).

Line 183   Revised for 8th Edition

1. **AIMERY IV DE THOUARS** (271-23), Viscount de Thouars, b. Hastings, 1030, d. 1093, companion of William the Conqueror at the battle of Hastings, 1066, son of Geoffroy de Thoars, Viscount de Thouars; m. (1) Aurengarde de Mauléon. (*ES* III.4/810; Brown, *Anglo-Norman Studies* (1985)).
2. **ALIÉNOR (ELEANOR) DE THOUARS**; m. 1075, Boso II, Viscount de Chatellerault, d. 1092, son of Hugh de Chatellerault and Gerberga de la Rochefoucauld. (*ES* III.4/813). Aliénor's sister, Hildegarde (Aldéarde) de Thoars, m. **HUGH VI DE LUSIGNAN** (275-22)
3. **AIMERY I**, Viscount de Chatellerault, d. bef. 1144, as monk at Notre Dame de Noyers; m. Dangerose (Dangereuse), dau. of Bartholomew, Seigneur de l'Isle-Bouchard and wife Gerberga. Dangerose was also mistress of **WILLIAM VII OF POITOU (IX OF AQUITAINE)** (110-24).
4. **ELEANOR** (or **AENOR**) **DE CHATELLERAULT**, m. 1121, **WILLIAM VIII OF POITOU (X OF AQUITAINE)** (110-25), Count of Poitou, Duke of Aquitaine, d. 9 Apr. 1137. (*ES* III.4/813, II/76; West Winter XII.54. Gens. 1-4: Moriarty, *The Plantagenet Ancestry*, pp. 45-46; Marion Meade, *Eleanor of Aquitaine*, pp. 15-17).

Line 184   Revised for 8th Edition

1. **WALTER II GIFFARD**, 1st Earl of Buckingham, b. abt. 1015, called aged Earl of Buckingham 1085/6, d. 15 July 1102, bur. Longueville, Normandy; m. (1) NN; m. (2) Agnes Ribemont, sis. of Anselm Ribemont of Longueville-sur-Scie, Lord of Longueville. Walter II Giffard, was the son of Walter I Giffard, b. abt. 985, d. sh. aft. 1066; m. (Agnes) Flaitel, dau. of Gerald Flaitel. Walter I Giffard was son of Osbern de Bolebec, b. abt. 945/950 seigneur of Longueville-sur-Scie in Normandy 1028-1035, and Avelina (Duvelina), of Denmark, sister of the Duchess Gunnora, wife of **RICHARD I** (121E-20), Duke of Normandy. (Seversmith, 2,533-2,537; *CP* II: 386-7; *The Ancestor*, #12 (1905) 192-194).

2. **ROHESE GIFFARD**, liv. 1113; m. Richard Fitz Gilbert of Clare and Tonbridge, d. bef. Apr. 1088. (Seversmith, 2,530-2,533).

3. **GILBERT FITZ RICHARD**, b. abt. 1060, Lord of Clare, Tonbridge, and Cardigan, Wales, d. 1114 or 1117; m. **ADELAIDE** (or **ADELIZA**) **DE CLERMONT-EN-BEAUVAISIS** (246-24). (Seversmith, 2,529-2,530; *CP* II: 386-7, III 242-3, IX: Append. I, 66; Sanders, 34-35).

4. **GILBERT DE CLARE**, b. abt. 1100, Earl of Pembroke, 1138, d. 6 Jan. 1147/8; m. **ISABEL DE BEAUMONT** (66-25). (Generations 2-4: *CP* IV: 670 chart III; Altschul, *A Baronial Family in Medieval England: The Clares, 1217-1314*, Table III).

Line 184A   Prepared for an earlier edition by Douglas Richardson

3. **GILBERT FITZ RICHARD** (184-3); m. **ADELAIDE** (or **ADELIZA**) **DE CLERMONT-EN-BEAUVAISIS** (246-24).

4. **BALDWIN FITZ GILBERT DE CLARE**, lord of Bourne, Deeping and Skellingthorpe, co. Lincoln, founder of Bourne Abbey, d. 1154; m. Adeline, h. of barony of Bourne, co. Lincoln, dau. Richard de Rollos (Rullos) by wife Godiva, dau. Hugh d'Envermeu, lord of Deeping and Skellingthorpe, co. Lincoln. (R. Allen Brown, ed., *Anglo-Norman Studies* XI (1989), chart p. 262; Sanders, 107-108; *Northamptonshire Past & Present* V: 167-176; *Gen. Mag.* 15 (1967): 359-369).

5. **EMMA FITZ BALDWIN**, h. of barony of Bourne, co. Lincoln, d. by 1168; m. Hugh Wake, d. 1175/6, seigneur of Negreville in Normandy, founder of Longues Abbey, son of Geoffrey Wac. (*CP* XII (2) 295-296; *Northamptonshire Past & Present* V: 167-176).

6. **BALDWIN WAKE**, held barony of Bourne, co. Lincoln, seigneur of Negreville in Normandy, d. abt. 1198; m. Agnes du Hommet, dau. William du Hommet, d. abt. 1213, seigneur of Le Hommet in Normandy, by wife Lucy. (*CP* XII (2): 297; Sanders, 107-108; *Northamptonshire Past & Present* V: 167-176).

7. **BALDWIN WAKE**, b. abt. 1180, held barony of Bourne, co. Lincoln, lost his lands in France after 1204, d. bef. 20 July 1213; m. Isabel, d. 1233, widow of Fulbert de Dover, dau. & event. coh. Sir William Briwerre (Briwere), d. 1226, by wife Beatrice de Valle (or Vaux). (*CP* XII (2) 297-298; Sanders, 107-108).

8. **HUGH WAKE**, held barony of Bourne, co. Lincoln, sheriff of Yorkshire, constable of Scarborough Castle, d. bef. 18 Dec. 1241; m. bef. 29 May 1229, as 1st husb., **JOAN DE STUTEVILLE** (270-29), d. 1276, dau. & h. of **NICHOLAS DE STUTEVILLE** (270-28), d. 1233, lord of baronies of Cottingham, co. York, and Liddel Strength, Cumberland, by wife Devorguilla of Galloway, dau. **ROLAND** (38-25), Lord of Galloway. (*CP* XII (2): 298-299; *Eng. Hist. Rev.*, 65: 89-91; *EYC* IX: 20-22; *ES* XIII/104).

9. BALDWIN WAKE, b. abt. 1238, held barony of Bourne, co. Lincoln, d. 1282; m. (1) Ela, d. by 1265, dau. & h. William de Beauchamp, d. 1260, lord of barony of Bedford, co. Bedford, by wife **IDA LONGESPEE** (122A-29); m. (2) **HAWISE DE QUINCY** (236-9), b. abt. 1250, d. 1285, dau. & h. Robert de Quincy, d. 1257, by wife Helen (or Ellen), dau. Llywelyn ap lorwerth, Prince of North Wales. (*CP* XII (2): 299-301; Sanders, 10-12, 107-108; *ES* III.4/708).

10. IDA WAKE, by (1), h. of 1/9th interest in barony of Bedford, co. Bedford; m. by 1273 Sir John de Stonegrave (or Steyngreve), d. 1295, lord of Stonegrave and Nunnington, co. York, son of Simon de Stonegrave of same, & Beatrice Foliot, dau. Jordan Foliot, liv. 1225, of Norton, co. York, and Frisby, co. Lincoln, s. & h. of Richard Foliot of Norton, & Beatrice or Cecily Bardolf, dau. & h. in her issue of Hugh Bardolf, d. abt. 1176, of Waddington, co. Lincoln, & **ISABEL DE CONDET** (or **CUNDY**) (132D-28). (*CP* Old CP V: 538, VII: 757 note c, XII (1): 276, XII (2): 300 note f; Sanders, 10-12; *EYC* 6:119-122).

11. ISABELLA DE STONEGRAVE, b. abt. 1271, h. of Stonegrave and Nunnington, co. York, d. abt. 1324; m. (1) abt. 1286/7 Simon de Pateshull, d. 1295, lord of Pateshull, co. Northampton, and Bletsoe, co. Bedford, son of Sir John de Pateshull, d. 1290, of same, by wife Hawise. (*CP* X 314-315; Sanders, 10-12).

12. SIR JOHN DE PATESHULL, b. abt. 1291, lord of Pateshull, co. Northampton, and Bletsoe, co. Bedford, d. 1349; m. in or bef. 1312 Mabel de Grandison, dau. & event. coh. Sir William de Grandison, d. 1335, 1st Lord Grandison, by wife Sibyl de Tregoz, d. 1334, yr. dau. & coh. **SIR JOHN DE TREGOZ** (255A-30), Lord Tregoz. (*CP* X: 315316, VI: 60-68, XII (2): 20-22; Sanders, 10-12).

13. SIBYL DE PATESHULL, liv. 26 Oct. 1331; m. bef. 133/7, as (1) wife, **ROGER DE BEAUCHAMP** (85-31), d. 3 Jan. 1379/80, 1st Lord Beauchamp of Bletsoe, Chamberlain to the Household of King Edward III, M.P. 1364-1380. (*CP* II: 44-45, VI: 67-68 and note f; Banks I: 118-119, II: 136-137).

Line 184B   Prepared for an earlier edition by Douglas Richardson

3. GILBERT FITZ RICHARD (184-3); m. **ADELAIDE** (or **ADELIZA**) **DE CLERMONT-EN-BEAUVAISIS** (246-24).

4. MARGARET DE CLARE, liv. 1185; m. William de Montfitchet, d. 1135/36, whose lands formed the barony of Stanstead Mountfitchet, Essex; founder of Stratford Langthorne Abbey, Essex. (Sanders, 83; J .H. Round, *Feudal England*, 357-359, 432).

5. GILBERT DE MONTFITCHET, held barony of Stanstead Mountfitchet, Essex, d. 1186-7; m. Aveline de Lucy, dau. Sir Richard de Lucy, d. 1179, Justiciar of King Henry II, of Chipping Ongar, Essex, and Diss, Norfolk, by wife Rohese. (Sanders, 83; *DNB*).

6. RICHARD DE MONTFITCHET, held barony of Stanstead Mountfitchet, Essex, sheriff of Essex, 1200-1202, d. 1204; m. Millicent. (*CP* V: 267-269, X: 537-538; Sanders, 83).

7. MARGARET DE MONTFITCHET, dau. & coh.; m. (1) **HUGH III DE BOLEBEC** (267A-27), d. abt. 1194, of Styford, Northumberland; m. (2) Sir Peter de Fauconberge, liv. 1230, of Rise & Withernwick in Holderness, s. & h. Walter de Fauconberge of the same, d. abt. 1216, by wife Agnes Fitz Simon, dau. & h. Simon Fitz Simon of Brentworth, co. Northampton, and Bilborough, co. Nottingham. (*CP* V: 267-269; Sanders, 83-85).

8. SIR WALTER DE FAUCONBERGE, 1st Lord Fauconberge, lord of Rise & Withernwick in Holderness, d. 1/2 Nov. 1304; m. by Nov, 1243, **AGNES DE BRUS** (136-27), d. abt. 1280, dau. & coh. **PIERS (PETER) II DE BRUS** (136-26), d. 1222, Lord of

Skelton, co. York, and **HAWISE** (or **HELEWISE**) **DE LANCASTER** (88-28). (*CP* V: 267-269; Clay, 69).

Line 185   Revised for 8th Edition

    1. ROBERT OF MORTAIN, b. 1031, d. 8 Dec. 1090, Earl of Cornwall, half bro. of **WILLIAM I** (121-24), the Conqueror and a companion at the battle of Hastings, 1066; m. (1) Mathilda de Montgomery, dau. of Roger de Montgomery, d. 1094, Earl of Shrewsbury, Viscount of the Hiesmois, Seigneur of Montgommeri in Normandy, by his 1st wife, Mabel Talvas, d. 1079, dau. & h. of William Talvas, d. 1070, lord of Belleme, Seigneur of Alençon (a kinsman of Robert, Duke of Normandy). (*CP* III: 427-7, XI: 687; Moriarty, *The Plantagenet Ancestry*, p. 44; *ES* III.4/637, 694B).

    2. EMMA OF MORTAIN, d. 1080; m. abt. 1071, William IV, b. abt. 1040, d. 1093, Count of Toulouse and Péregord, son of Pons, Count de Toulouse, Albi. and Dijon, b. abt. 990, d. 1060, by **ALMODE** (185A-5), d. 1071, dau. of Bernard I, Count of La Marche and Périgord, d. 1047, by Amelia. Pons was son of William III, d. 1037, Count of Toulouse, by his 2nd wife, Emma of Provence, gt.-gr.dau. of Boso II, d. 965/7, Count of Avignon & Arles, and his wife, **CONSTANCE OF PROVENCE** (141A-19). (Moriarty, *cit.*, 42, 44; Anselme II: 684-5; Don Stone, *Some Ancient and Medieval Descents...*: Chart 72, "Descent from Theuderic," and note 8; *ES* III.4/763).

    3. PHILIPPA (MATHILDA or **MAUD) OF TOULOUSE**, b. abt. 1073, div. 1115/16, d. 28 Nov. 1117; m. (1) Sancho Ramiros, King of Aragon; m. (2) 1094, **WILLIAM VII OF POITOU (IX OF AQUITAINE)** (110-24), Count of Poitou, Duke of Aquitaine, b. abt. 22 Oct. 1071, d. 10 Feb. 1126/7, crusader 1101. (Moriarty, *cit.*, 36, 42; *ES* III.4/763; Don Stone, *Some Ancient and Medieval Descents...*: Chart 72, "Descent from Theuderic," and note 11).

Line 185A   New to 8th Edition

    2. BOSO I, "The Old," d. abt. 975; m. 940/950, Emma of Périgord.

    3. ADALBERT I, d. 997, Count of La Marche and Périgord; m. Aisceline? de Limoges, d. 1007/1010, dau. of Geraud, Vicomte de Limoges. (Done Stone, *Some Ancient and Medieval Descents...*: Chart 72, "Descent from Theuderic," and note 7; West Winter, VIII.69).

    4. BERNARD I, d. 1047, Count of La Marche and Périgord; m. Amelia ?d'Angoulême, d. 1072. (Done Stone, *Some Ancient and Medieval Descents...*: Chart 72, "Descent from Theuderic" and note 8).

    5. ALMODE (ALMODIS), d. 1071; m. (div. about 1051) Pons (see 185-2), d. 1063, Count of Toulouse, etc. (Stone, *Some Ancient and Medieval Descents...*: Chart 72, "Descent from Theuderic"; Moriarity, p. 42).

Line 186

    1. JOHN FITZ ROBERT, of Warkworth, co. Northumberland, Magna Charta Surety, 1215, d. 1240; m. (2) Ada de Baliol, d. 1251, sister of John de Baliol who m. **DEVORGUILLA OF GALLOWAY** (94-28). (*NEHGR* 106 (1952): 281; *ES* III.4/707).

    2. ROGER FITZ JOHN, d. 1249; m. Isabel.

3. **ROBERT FITZ ROGER**, b. 1247, Baron of Clavering, d. 1310; m. 1265, Margery la Zouche, dau. of Sir Alan la Zouche (see 38-28, 39-29) (see Dodsworth ms. Bodleian Lib,; Hedley, *Northumberland Fams.*, I: 62; *CP* III: 274-275).

4. **EUPHEME DE CLAVERING**, m. Randolf (Ranulph) de Neville, b. 1262, d. 1331, 1st Lord Neville of Raby, son of Robert de Neville. (*CP* IX: 502 ii-iii chart).

5. **RALPH DE NEVILLE**, b. abt. 1291, 4th Lord Neville of Raby, d. 5 Aug. 1367; m. 1326/7 **ALICE DE AUDLEY** (207-32), d. 12 Jan. 1373/4, wid. of **RALPH DE GREYSTOKE** (265-32), dau. of Hugh de Audley, Lord Audley, d. 1325, and **ISOLDE DE MORTIMER** (207-31). (*CP* IX: 499-501; *Bulkeley Genealogy*, 77).

6. **MARGARET DE NEVILLE**, d. 12 May 1372; m. (1) William de Ros, of Helmsley, d. by 3 Dec. 1352; m. (2) 1358, **HENRY DE PERCY, K.G.** (19-31). (*CP* IX: 99-100).

Line 187

1. **ROGER DE HUNTINGFIELD**, Lord of East Bradenham, Norfolk; m. Alice de Senlis, d. 1204. (*CP* VI: 671).

2. **SIR WILLIAM DE HUNTINGFIELD**, Magna Charta Surety, 1215, of Frampton, b. abt. 1165, Keeper of Dover Castle 1203, Warden of the Cinque Ports, sheriff of Norfolk and Suffolk 1210-1212, 1215 excommunicated by the Pope, d. on a crusade, bef. 25 Jan. 1220/1; m. by 1194, Isabel, d. 1207, wid. of **OSMOND DE STUTEVILLE** (270B-27), dau. of William Fitz Roger of Gressinghall, Norfolk. (*CP* VI: 671).

3. **SIR ROGER DE HUNTINGFIELD**, of Huntingfield, Suffolk, and Frampton, d. abt. 10 July 1257; m. (2) 1236, Joan de Hobrugg, d. abt. 7 Sept. 1297, dau. of William de Hobrugg, of Hobridge, Essex & Agnes Picot, dau. & coh. Sir William Picot, d. abt. 1218, of Quy, Waterbeach, & Huntingfield, co. Cambridge. (*CP* IV: 674-665, 671; *VCH Cambridge* IX: 243, 272-3).

4. **SIR WILLIAM DE HUNTINGFIELD**, of Huntingfield, b. 24 Aug. 1237, d. bef. 2 Nov. 1290; m. (1) Emma de Grey, d. 1264, dau. of Sir John de Grey of Shirland, co. Derby, and Emma de Glanville, dau. of Geoffrey de Glanville. (*CP* VI: 664-666, 671).

5. **SIR ROGER DE HUNTINGFIELD**, of Huntingfield and Frampton, summoned for military service 14 June 1294, d. bef. 5 Dec. 1302; m. abt. 1277, Joice d'Engaine, d. 1312, dau. of Sir John d'Engaine of Colne Engaine and Laxton, co. Northampton, and Joan de Greinville, dau. of Sir Gilbert de Greinville of Hallaton, co. Leic. (*CP* VI: 666).

6. **JOAN DE HUNTINGFIELD**, m. Sir Richard Basset, 1st Lord Basset of Weldon, Great Weldon, co. Northampton, b. abt. 1273, minor in 1291, taken prisoner at Bannockburn, d. bef. 18 Aug. 1314.

7. **RALPH BASSET** of Great Weldon, b. 27 Aug. 1300, custody of father's lands 1314 to Richard Grey of Codnor until of age on 29 Mar 1322; m. Joan, sd. to be a Sturdon of Winterbourne, co. Gloucester. He d. shortly bef. 4 May 1341. She m. (2) bef. 1346, Robert de Fourneux. (*CP* II: 10-11; *Northamptonshire Past and Present*, vol. V, no. 3, pp. 167-176 (1975)).

8. **JOAN BASSET**, m. Thomas de Aylesbury of Aylesbury, d. bef. 1350. (*CP* II: 13).

9. **SIR JOHN AYLESBURY**, of Milton Keynes, co. Buckingham, d. 1410; m. Isabel, dau. of Eubolo le Strange of Knokyn. (*Le Strange Records*, Hamon le Strange (1916), pp. 321, 337-8. This citation offers no proof of wife or heirs of this Ebulo, rector of Gresford.).

10. **SIR THOMAS AYLESBURY**, of Milton Keynes, b. abt. 1369, d. 9 Sept. 1418; m. **KATHERINE PABENHAM** (136-31), b. 1372, d. 17 June 1436, dau. of Sir Lawrence Pabenham of Pabenham, co. Bedford, d. 10 June 1399, and Elizabeth, dau. of Sir John d'Engaine, 2nd Lord Engaine. (*CP* V: 80 chart).

11. ELEANOR AYLESBURY, m. **SIR HUMPHREY STAFFORD, KNT.** (55-37), of Grafton, co. Warwick, b. 1400, living 1467.

12. SIR HUMPHREY STAFFORD, KNT., of Grafton, co. Worcester, executed at Tyburn, 8 July 1486; m. Catherine, dau. of Sir John Fray, Chief Baron of the Exchequer. (*CP* II: 136; *Gen.*(n.s.) 31: 173).

13. ANNE STAFFORD, m. Sir William Berkeley, K.B., of Stoke-Gifford, sheriff of Gloucester, 1485. (*CP* II: 136).

14. RICHARD BERKELEY, of Stoke-Gifford; m. Elizabeth, dau. of Sir Humphrey Conningsby, Knt., of cos. Worc. And Herts. (*Visit. of Glouc.* (1623), 8).

15. SIR JOHN BERKELEY, d. 1546, of Stoke-Gifford, co. Glouc.; m. Isabel, dau. of Sir William Dennis, Knt., of Dunham, co. Gloucester, & Anne, dau. Maurice, Lord Berkeley, d. 1506 (MC 66-10). (*The Genealogist* 6 (1985): 195-197; *Visit. of Glouc.* (1623), 51).

16. ELIZABETH BERKELEY, m. **HENRY LYGON** (84-37). (*Visit. of Glouc.*(1623), 204-206. Gens. 1-14: *Boston Evening Transcript*, 9 July 1938; with continuation to Deighton (Line 84)).

Line 188

6. JOAN DE HUNTINGFIELD (187-6), m. Sir Richard Basset. (*CP* II: 10-13).

7. RALPH BASSET, b. 27 Aug. 1300, summoned for service against the Scots, 5 Apr. 1327, d. bef. 4 May 1341; m. Joan. (*CP* II: 10-13).

8. ELEANOR (or **ALIANORE**) **BASSET**, b. abt. 1325, heiress of Weldon, co. Northampton, d. 1388; m. Sir John Knyvet, d. 1381, of Southwick, co. Northampton, Chief Justice of the King's Bench, Lord Chancellor of England. (Banks I: 158; *DNB*; *CP* II: 10-13; *Northamptonshire Past and Present*, vol. V, no. 3, pp. 167-176 (1975)).

9. SIR JOHN KNYVET, b. abt. 1358, d. 1418; m. **JOAN BOTETOURTE** (216A-32), liv. 1428. (Banks I 158. Gens. 6-9: *CP* II: 10-13).

10. SIR JOHN KNYVET, b. abt. 1380, d. 1445; m. **ELIZABETH CLIFTON** (218-35), liv. 1447, heiress of Buckenham, Norfolk, dau. of Constantine Clifton, 2nd Lord Clifton, and Margaret Howard, dau. of Sir John Howard. (*CP* III: 308).

11. SIR JOHN KNYVET; m. Alice Lynne, dau. of William Lynne Esq., of co. Norfolk. (*Surtees Soc. Pub.* 144: 10, 155).

12. SIR WILLIAM KNYVET, b. abt. 1440, of Buckenham, Norfolk, M.P., sheriff of Norfolk and Suffolk, 1470, 1479, d. 1515; m. (1) **ALICE GREY** (93B-34), d. 1474. (Banks I: 158).

13. SIR EDMUND KNYVET, Knt. of Buckenham, co. Norf., d. in a sea fight, temp. Henry VIII; m. Eleanor Tyrrel, dau. of Sir William Tyrrel, Knt., co. Essex, by Margaret Darcy. (Banks I: 158).

14. SIR EDMUND KNYVET, d. 1539, of Ashwellthorpe, co. Norf.; m. **JANE** (or **JOAN**) **BOURCHIER** (4-36), d. 1561/2. Monumental brass, dated 1561, for Jane Bourchier, widow of Edmund Knyvett, in Ashwellthorpe parish church. (Gens. 6-14: Banks I: 158; *Surtees Soc.* 144; Banks, *Dormant and Peerage* (1837) IV, and App. I: 20; Meredith B. Colket, Jr., in *TAG* 14: 10-12; Berry, *Berkshire Pedigrees* 55; Mill Stephenson, *A List of Monumental Brasses in the British Isles* (1926)).

Line 189

1. **SIR WILLIAM MALET** (234A-28), held barony of Curry Malet, Somerset, sheriff of Somerset and Devon, Magna Charta Surety, 1215, d. abt. 1216; m. Alice Basset, dau. of Thomas Basset.

2. **HAWISE MALET** (234A-29); m. (1) **SIR HUGH POYNTZ** (132D-30), d. sh. bef. 4 Apr. 1220; m. (2) bef. 11 Feb. 1220/1, Sir Robert de Muscegros, of Charlton, Somerset, d. sh. bef. 29 Jan. 1253/4.

3. **SIR JOHN DE MUSCEGROS**, of Charlton, b. 10 Aug. 1232, d. 8 May 1275; m. Cecily Avenal, d. sh. Bef. 10 Aug. 1301, dau. of Sir William Avenal. (*CP* V: 308 and notes *a*, *b*, *c*, *e*, chart betw. pp. 320-321).

4. **SIR ROBERT DE MUSCEGROS**, b. abt. 1252, d. 27 Dec. 1280; m. Agnes de Ferrers, liv. 9 May 1281, dau. of **SIR WILLIAM DE FERRERS** (127-30) and **MARGARET DE QUINCY** (57-29), dau. of **ROGER DE QUINCY** (53-28). (Sir Christopher Hatton's Book of Seals in *Northants Rec-Soc.* (1950), No. 98, p. 64; *CP*, *cit*, esp. notes *a* and *b*; Hatton, *cit.*, appears to answer note *c* completely; *ES* III.4/708).

5. **HAWISE DE MUSCEGROS**, b. 21 Dec. 1276, (betrothed but not married to William de Mortimer, who d. aft. June 1340); m. (1) bet. 2 Feb. 1297/8 and 13 Sept. 1300 **SIR JOHN DE FERRERS** (57-31), of Southoe and Keystone, b. Cardiff, 20 June 1271, Lord Ferrers of Chartley, d. Gascony, Aug. 1312; m. (2) Sir John de Bures, d. Bodington, 21 or 22 Dec. 1350. (*CP* V: 305-310).

6. **CATHERINE DE BURES**, b. bef. 1315, liv. Oct. 1355; m. bef. 21 May 1329, **SIR GILES DE BEAUCHAMP** (84-30), d. 1361. (Gens. 1-6: *CP* V: 320-321 chart).

Line 190

1. **CLOVIS THE RIPARIAN**, Frankish King of Cologne, living 420, kinsman of **CLOVIS I** (240A-3).

2. **CHILDEBERT**, King of Cologne, living 450.

3. **SIGEBERT THE LAME**, King of Cologne, murdered 509 by his own son at the instigation of Clovis I, King of the Salic Franks, 481-511.

4. **CLODERIC** the Parricide, King of Cologne, murdered 509, by agents of his kinsman, Clovis I, King of the Salic Franks. The identity of his wife is uncertain.

5. **MUNDERIC**, of Vitry-en-Perthois, very young in 509, when his father was murdered; revolted against Thierry I, who killed him.

6. **ST. GONDOLFUS**, Bishop of Tongres, consecrated 599 (brother of Bodegeisel I). He was almost certainly father of Bodegeisel II (Gen. 7), not Bodegeisel I as shown in earlier editions. (Correction by Prof. Kelley, see in *NEHGR* 101: 110-111).

7. **BODEGEISEL II**, m. Oda, a Suevian.

8. **ST. ARNULF**, b. abt. 13 Aug. 582, Mayor of the Palace and tutor of Dagobert, Bishop of Metz 612, d. 16 Aug. 640; m. abt. 596, **DODE** (180-8), who became a nun at Treves 612. (They were also the parents of St. Clodulf, Bishop of Metz abt. 650, d. 690).

9. **DUKE ANSEGISEL**, b. 602, (Mayor of the Palace to Siegbert, 632, son of Dagobert), d. bet. 648 and 669; m. bef. 639, St. Begga, d. 693, dau. of Pippin I of Landen, Mayor of the Palace in Austrasia, d. 694, and his wife Itta, presumedly dau. of Arnoaldus, Bishop of Metz, son, it is said, of **ANSBERTUS**, the Senator (180-6).

10. **PEPIN II OF HERISTAL**, b. abt. 645, Mayor of the Palace in Austrasia, d. 714; by concubine, Aupais, he was father of

11. **CHARLES MARTEL**, b. 689, Mayor of the Palace in Austrasia, victor over the Saracens at Poitiers, 732, d. 741; m. (1) **ROTROU** (50-11), d. 724, sister of a Wido, identified without proof by the Abbe Chaume as son of St. Lievin, Bishop of Treves.

12. **PEPIN III THE SHORT** (50-12), b. 714, Mayor of the Palace, deposed the last of the Faineant (Merovingian) kings and became himself the first king of the Franks of the second race, 751-768, d. 768; m. **BERTHE** (240A-12), d. 783, dau. of **CHARIBERT** (240A-11), Count of Laon. (Gens. 8-12: Don C. Stone, *Ancient and Medieval Descents*, Chart 50).

13. **CHARLEMAGNE** (50-13), b. 2 Apr. 747, King of France 768-814, crowned Holy Roman Emperor, 25 Dec. 800, one of the great men in history, d. Aix la Chapelle, 28 Jan. 813/4; m. abt. 771, **HILDEGARDE** (182-5), b. abt. 758, d. 30 Apr. 783, dau. of Count Geroud of Swabia. (Gens. 1-13: *NEHGR* 98: 304-306, and corrected in 101: 109-112 charts, etc.; *Boston Evening Transcript*, 23 Jan. 1936 and 20 May 1937, citing J. Depoin: "Grandes Figures Monocales au Temps Merovingiens', in *Revue Mabillon*, XI (1921), 245-258; XII (1922), 13-15, 105-118; *Cambridge Medieval History*; Turton; L'Abbe Chaume, *Les Origins de Duche de Bourgogne*, I: 530-551. Gens. 8-13: D.L. Jacobus in *Boston Evening Transcript*, Note 2257, Part IX; Anselme; Thatcher, table p. 318).

Line 191   Revised for 8th Edition

11. **CHARLES MARTEL** (190-11), b. 689, Mayor of the Palace, d. 741; m. (1) **ROTROU** (50-11), m. (2) Swanhilde, a Bavarian.

12. **CARLOMAN**, by (1), Mayor of the Palace, d. 754; m. prob. a dau. of Alard, brother of Garnier, ancestor of the Margraves of Spoleto.

13. **ROTRUDE**, m. Girard, Count of Paris 743-755.

14. **BEGUE** (**BOGO**), Count of Paris, Chamberlain of Louis of Aquitaine 776, d. 816; m. (2) Alpais.

Line 191A   Revised for 8th Edition

15. **HUNROCH** (**UNROC**), Margrave of Friuli, d. by 853, parentage unproven; m. Engeltron, whose parentage has not been satisfactorily proven. (See: Chaume, *Les Origins de Duche de Bourgogne*, I: p. 543; Seversmith, 2,472-2,473; *ES* II/188A; Moriarity, *Plantagenet Ancestry*, p. 229).

16. **EBERHARD**, (son of Hunroch by NN), Margrave of Friuli, d. 864/6; m. 836/40 **GISÈLE** (146-15, 250-15), d. 1 July 874, dau. of the Emperor **LOUIS I** (140-14) and Judith of Bavaria. (*ES* I.1/4; Moriarty, "The Conradins," in *NEHGR* 99: 243 and chart).

Line 192   Revised for 8th Edition

19. **WERNER**, Count in Wormsgau.

20. **CONRAD**, the Wise, Count in Wormsgau, Count in Franconia, Duke of Lorraine, killed in battle, Lechfeld, 10 Aug. 955; m. abt. 947 **LUITGARDE** (45-18), dau. of **OTTO I** (147-19) the Great, by **EDITH** (or **EADGYTH**) (45-17). (*ES* I.1/12; *NEHGR* 99: 243).

Line 193

4. SIBYL DE NEUFMARCHE (177-4); m. 1121, Miles of Gloucester, cr. Earl of Hereford 1141, d. 24 Dec 1143. (*CP* I: 20, IV: Append. H, 669 chart, VI: 452-453, XIV: 380-381).

5. MARGARET OF HEREFORD, d. 1146; m. Humphrey III de Bohun, Baron de Bohun, Lord of Hereford. (*CP* I: 22, VI: 545).

6. HUMPHREY DE BOHUN IV, Baron de Bohun, Lord of Hereford, constable of England, d. 1182; m. 1175, **MARGARET OF HUNTINGDON** (97-26). (*CP* I: 22, VII: 457).

Line 194

5. BERTHA OF HEREFORD (177-5); m. abt. 1150, William de Braose.

6. SIBYL DE BRAOSE, prob. living abt. 5 Feb. 1227/8; m. William de Ferrers, 3rd Earl of Derby, d. at Acre 1190, bef. 21 Oct., on a crusade. (*CP* IV: 192-194, 771).

7. WILLIAM DE FERRERS, 4th Earl of Derby, d. 22 Sept. 1247; m. 1192, **AGNES OF CHESTER** (127-29), Lady of Chartley, d. 2 Nov. 1247. (*CP* IV: 192-196, 771, V: 320 chart).

Line 195

25. HENRY I (121-25), King of England, b. 1070, d. 1 Dec. 1135. (*CP* V: 736, VII: 737).

26. ROHESE, (natural dau., by Sibyl Corbet), liv. 1175/6; m. abt. 1146, Henry I de la Pomerai, d. bet. 1156 and 1164, a great Devonshire baron, son and h. of Jocelyn de la Pomerai, commander in Normandy, 1136, d. 1137/1141. (They left sons Henry II (below) and Joscelin. *CP* XI: Append. D, 119; *ES* III.2/354; Keats-Rohan, *Domesday Desc.* II: 641-642).

27. HENRY II DE LA POMERAI, "the younger," liv. 1145/6, d. 1207, lord of Beri Pomeroy; m. (1) Maud (or Matilda) de Vitré, m. (2) Rohesia Bardolf. (*CP* XI: App. D, 119; Edward B. Powley, *House of de la Pomerai*; P. L. Hull, ed., *Cartulary of St. Michael's Mount*, pub. 1962 as Devon & Cornwall Rec. Soc., n.s., 5: 18-19; Sanders, 106).

28. HENRY III DE LA POMEROY, by (1), d. 1222; m. Alice de Vernon, d. 1206. (Powley, *cit.*; *Cartulary of St. Michael's Mount, cit.*, p. 20).

29. HENRY (IV) DE LA POMEROY, d. 1221, Governor of Rougemont Castle, Exeter, 1211-1215, sheriff of Devon 1215; m. Joan de Vautort (Valletort). (Powley, *cit.*).

Line 196   Line cancelled

Line 197

28. ISABEL MAUDUIT (84-28), great-great-granddau. of William de Warenne and **ISABEL DE VERMANDOIS** (50-24); m. William de Beauchamp of Elmley Castle.

29. JOHN DE BEAUCHAMP, of Holt, co. Worcester, living 1297. (*CP* II: 45 note *d*; *VCH Worc.* III: 403).

30. RICHARD DE BEAUCHAMP, d. 1327, of Holt; m. Eustache. (*Ibid*).

31. SIR JOHN BEAUCHAMP, KNT., b. 1319/21, d. 12 May 1388, knighted 1387, Justice of North Wales; m. abt. 1370, Joan Fitzwith, b. 25 Mar. 1352, living 1384, dau. of Robert Fitzwith. (*CP* II: 45-46; *VCH Worc.* III: 403-404; *VCH Warwick* VI: 46).

32. SIR JOHN BEAUCHAMP, b. 1377, Lord Beauchamp of Kidderminster, d.s.p. Sept. 1420; m. by 1398, Isabel Ferrers, a niece of the Countess of Warwick. (*CP* II: 46 note *d*; *VCH Worc.* III: 298; *VCH Warwick* VI: 46).

33. MARGARET BEAUCHAMP, b. 1400; m. (2) aft. 1422, Sir John de Wysham, living 1428. (*CP* II: 46 note *d*; *VCH Worc.* III: 298; *VCH Warwick* VI: 47).

34. ALICE WYSHAM, d. 1487; m. John Guise (or Gyse), Esq., d. by 1485, of Apsley Guise and Holt, sheriff of Gloucestershire 1454, 1470-1471, son of Reynold Gyse and Katharine Clifford, dau. of James Clifford. (*VCH Worc.* III: 298, 404; *VCH Warwick* VI: 47; *Burke's Peerage* (1938), pp. 1174-1175).

35. JOHN GYSE (or **GUISE**), **KNT.**, of Apsley Guise, co. Bedford, and Elmore, co. Gloucester, d. 30 Sept. 1501, (Inq.p.m. 17 Hen. VII no. 18); m. Anne Berkeley, d. aft. 1501, of Stoke Gifford (Papal disp. for m. 15 May 17 Apr. (o.s.) 1484). A monumental brass, dated 1501, for Sir John Guise is preserved in the parish church of Apsley Guise, co. Bedford. (*VCH Worc.* III: 404; *Burke's Peerage* (1938). 1174-1175; *Trans. Bristol and Gloucs. Arch. Soc.* III: 57-58; Mill Stephenson, *A List of Monumental Brasses in the British Isles* (1926), p. 1).

36. JOHN GYSE, ESQ., of Elmore, co. Gloucester, b. abt. 1485 (age 16+ at father's death), d. at Brockworth, co. Gloucester, 20 Dec. 1556, (Inq.p.m. 3 and 4 Philip and Mary pt. 2, no. 73); m. abt. 1510, **TACY** (or **TASY**) **GREY** (207-39), b. abt. 1490, bur. Elmore 15 Nov. 1558. (John Gyse and Tasy, and their son Anselme and his wife Alice (prob. just m.) exchanged manors and lordships of "Asple Gyse, co. Beds., and Wyggyngton, co. Oxon" with the King for manor and lordship of Brockworth, etc. Deed recites that John Gyse had indentured 24 Feb. 10 Hen. VIII (1518-9) covenanting to convey to his young son Anselme on m. to Alice, dau. James Clifford of Frampton-upon-Severne, estates in Wygyngton,and in further agreements same date both parents undertook to share equally the costs of "school learning, meat, drink, apparel of Anselme until aged 17, and if Alice die, Anselme to have another Clifford dau. within 10 years of his age." Anselme d.s.p. 9 May 1563 (Inq.p.m. 5 Eliz No. 22) next heir his brother William aged 49+). (*Bristol and Gloucs., cit.* 59-61; *CP* VI: 181).

37. WILLIAM GYSE, 2nd son but event. h., b. abt. 1514, d. 7 Sept. 1574 (Inq.p.m. 17 Eliz. No. 50), bur. Elmore 9 Sept. 1574, will dated 10 Mar. 1568/9, Gloucs.; m. Mary Rotsy, dau. of John Rotsy of Colmore, King's Norton, co. Worcester, by Margaret Walsh, dau. John Walsh of Sheldeslcy Walsh, co. Worcester, bur. 24 Nov. 1558 at Elmore. (*Cit.* 61-2, 70).

38. JOHN GYSE, of Elmore and Brockworth, s. and h., b. abt. 1540 (age 34+ at father's death), d. 24, bur. 26 Jan. 1587/8, will dated 1 Dec. 1577, pro. 12 Nov. 1588 (Inq.p.m. 30 Eliz. pt. 1, No. 131); m. 27 June 1564, Jane Pauncefort, bur. 27 June 1587, dau. of Richard Pauncefort of Hasefield. (*Cit.* 62-63, 70; *VCH Warwick* V: 148; VI: 47; *Oxford* VI: 9, VIII: 255; see also for all Gyse generations, *Harleian Soc. Pub.* XXI (Gloucs. 1623): 72-73).

39. ELIZABETH GYSE, bapt. Elmore, 1 Aug. 1576; m. at Kenn, Somerset, 7 July 1604, Robert Haviland, Esq. b. 11 Feb. 1576, of Hawkesbury Manor, Tewkesbury, co. Gloucester, signer of the Visitation Pedigree of 1623, d. 1648, son of Matthew Haviland, Mayor of Bristol, and Mary Kytchin, dau. of Robert Kytchin, of Bristol. (*Cit.* 71; *Harleian Soc. Pub.* XXI: 72-73, 78; *NEHGR* 110 (1956): 232; Seversmith, 1,312, 1,317).

40. JANE HAVILAND, bapt. St. Werbergh's Church, Bristol, 2 Aug. 1612, bur. 27 Apr. 1639; m. 17 Mar. 1630, Capt. William Torrey, bapt. 21 Dec. 1608, d. Weymouth,

Mass., 10 June 1690, will made 15 May 1686, pro. at Boston, July 1691, freeman, Weymouth, 1642, deputy, 1642-47, 1648, 1649, 1679-1683, member of the Anc. & Hon. Art. Co., son of Philip Torrey and Alice Richards. (Bishops Register at Welles; *Torrey Gen.*, I: 13, 15-16; Waters, 498-499, 555-556; Seversmith, 1,317; Visit. of Glouc. (1623): 72-73, 78).

41. WILLIAM TORREY, b. England, 1638, d. Weymouth, 11 Jan. 1717/8; m. abt. 1669, Deborah Greene, b. Warwick, Rhode Island, 10 Aug. 1649, d. Weymouth, 8 Feb. 1728/9, dau. of Deputy-Governor John Greene of Rhode Island. They had children, including a son, Deacon Haviland Torrey, b. Weymouth, 1684, who left issue. (*Blake-Torrey Gen.*, 68-76).

Line 198

36. MATILDA CLIFFORD (5-36); m. **SIR EDMUND SUTTON, KNT.** (81-37). (See *MC* Lines 36 & 80A).

37. DOROTHY SUTTON; m. Richard Wrottesley, of Wrottesley, High Sheriff of Staffordshire, 1492, 1502, 1516. (George Adlard, *Sutton Dudleys* (N.Y., 1862), ped. A; Burke's *Peerage* (1938), p. 2631).

38. ELEANOR WROTTESLEY; m. Richard Lee, Esq., of Langley, co. Salop.

39. DOROTHY LEE; m. (mar. settlement 27 July 1566), Thomas Mackworth of Betton Grange, living 10 Jan. 1585, son of John Mackworth and Elizabeth Hosier.

40. RICHARD MACKWORTH, of Betton Grange; m. Dorothy Cranage, dau. of Laurence Cranage, gent. (Gens. 38-40: Burke's *Peerage* (1938), p. 1640).

41. AGNES MACKWORTH (sis. of Col. Humphrey Mackworth of Betton Grange, Governor of Shrewsbury); m. (1) Richard Watts, d. 1635; m. (2) bef. 1640, Col. William Crowne, gent., b. abt. 1617, d. Boston, Mass., will dated 24 Dec. 1682, pro. 28 Feb. 1682/3; appointed Rouge-Dragon, 14 Sept. 1638; Lt.-Col., 1650; at the coronation of Charles II, 23 Apr. 1661. Their son Henry Crowne left issue. (*NEHGR* 5: 46, 249; 58: 406-410; Blore, *Hist. of Rutland*; Lipscombe, Hist. of Buckinghamshire).

Line 199

34. MARGARET STANLEY (20-34); m. 1459 (1) Sir William Troutbeck, Knt., b. abt. 1432, d. 1459, of Dunham-on-the-Hill, co. Chester, son of John Troutbeck and Margaret Hulse; m. (2) 1460, **SIR JOHN BOTELER**, Knt. (46-36), Baron of Warrington, d. 26 Feb. 1463; m. (3) a Lord Grey of Codnor, N.B. (*CP* IV: 205).

35. JOAN TROUTBECK, b. 1459, m. (2) Sir William Griffith d. by 1509/10, of Penrhyn, co. Carnarvon, Chamberlain of North Wales, son of Fychan ap Gwilym and Alice Dalton, dau. of Sir Richard Dalton of co. Northampton. (Dwnn II: 167-168).

36. SIR WILLIAM GRIFFITH, of Penrhyn, living 1520; m. (1) **JANE STRADLING** (199A-36), dau. of Thomas Stradling of St. Donat's, co. Glamorgan; m (2) 1520, Jane Puleston. (Dwnn II: 154-159).

37. DOROTHY GRIFFITH, by (1); m. as 1st wife, William Williams, Esq., of Cochwillan, co. Carnarvon (son, according to Burke, of William Williams and Lowry, dau. of Henry Salusbury, Esq., of Llanrhaidadr). (cf. Burke, *Peerage* (1847), p. 1046). (*Ibid* 166).

38. JANE WILLIAMS, m. William Coytemore, of Coytmore, in Llechwedd Uchav, co. Carnarvon. (Gens. 34-38: Sir Anthony R. Wagner, in *Gen. Mag.* 8 (1938): 204; Lewis Dwnn, *Heraldic Visitations of Wales* (1846), II: 167-168).

39. ROWLAND COYTEMORE, b. abt. 1565/1570, grantee of the second charter of Virginia, 23 May 1607 (undoubtedly identical with the Rowland Coytemore mentioned in Dwnn, *op. cit.*), widower at Wapping, d. 1626, will pro. Canterbury, 24 Nov. 1626; m. (1) Stepney, Middlesex, 13 Jan. 1590/1, Christiana Haynes; m. (2) St. Mary's, Whitechapel, Middlesex, 28 Mar. 1594/5, Dorothy Harris; m. (3) Harwich, Essex, 27 Dec. 1610, Katherine Miles, came as wid. to N.E. abt. 1636, d. Charlestown, Mass., 29 Nov. 1659, wid. of Thomas Gray, bur. Harwich, 7 May 1607, and dau. of Robert Miles of Sutton, co. Suffolk. (Waters I: 160-171, 404; *NEHGR* 106: 15, 108: 172-174).

40. ELIZABETH COYTEMORE, by (3), b. abt. 1617, d. Boston bet. 1642/3-1648/9; m. abt. 1636/7, as 2nd wife, Capt. William Tyng (brother of Col. Edward Tyng of Boston), b. abt. 1605, Treasurer of the Mass. Bay Colony 1640-1644, d. Braintree, Mass., 18 Jan. 1652/3. They were ancestors of President John Quincy Adams and many other distinguished New Englanders. (Waters I: 160-171, 404; *NEHGR* 34: 253, 259; 106: 15; see *TAG* 32: 9-23; see also *MC*, Line 103).

Line 199A

33. JOAN (JANE) BEAUFORT (234-32) natural dau. of **HENRY BEAUFORT** (234-31) by Alice Fitz Alan; m. Sir Edward Stradling,. b. abt. 1389, Knt. of St. Donat's Castle, d. 1453, son of William Stradling, Knt., by Isabel St. Barbe. (*TAG* 32 (1956): 180)

34. SIR HENRY STRADLING, KNT., s. and h., of St. Donat's Castle, b. abt. 1423, age 30 in 1453, knighted at the Holy Sepulchre, Jerusalem, 1477, d. soon after at Famagusta, Cyprus; m. Elizabeth Herbert, dau. of Sir William ap Thomas of Raglan Castle, who d. 1446, and half sis. of Sir William Herbert, cr. Earl of Pembroke, 8 Sept. 1468. (*TAG* 32: 11; *CP* X: 400-401).

35. THOMAS STRADLING, of St. Donat's Castle, b. abt. 1454/5, d. 8 Sept. 1480 "being under the age of 26"; m. Janet Mathew, d. 1485, dau. of Thomas Mathew of Radyr, co. Glamorgan. She m. (2) Sir Rhys ap Thomas, K.G. (*TAG* 32: 11-12; Nichols, II: 559-562).

36. JANE STRADLING, b. abt. 1477/80, d. 1520; m., as 1st wife, **SIR WILLIAM GRIFFITH, KNT.** (199-36), of Penrhyn Castle, co. Carnarvon, Chamberlain of North Wales, High Sheriff of Carnarvon 1493/4, Banneret 1513.

Line 200   Revised for 8th Edition

30. MILICENT DE CANTELOU (66-30), d. 1298/9; m. **EUDO LA ZOUCHE** (39-29), d. 1279.

31. SIR WILLIAM LA ZOUCHE, b. 1276, d. 1351/2, 1st Lord Zouche of Haryngworth; m. bef. 15 Feb. 1295/6, Maud Lovel, d. by 1346, dau. of **JOHN LOVEL** (215-29), of Titmarsh, Co. Northants, 1st Lord Lovel.

32. MILICENT LA ZOUCHE, d. 1379; m. bef. 26 Mar. 1326, Sir William Deincourt of Blankney, co. Lincoln, Lord Deincourt, d. 2 June 1364, son of John Deincourt. (*CP* IV: 121-122, 290).

33. MARGARET DEINCOURT, d. 2 Apr. 1380; m. (1) **SIR ROBERT DE TYBOTOT** (65A-35), d.s.p.m. 13 Apr. 1372, Lord Tybotot, of Nettlestead, Suffolk; m. (2) John Cheyne. (*CP* IV: 290, XII (2): 97-98). (See *MC* 30-9).

34. ELIZABETH DE TYBOTOT, b. abt. 1371, d. bef. June 1424; m. (2) Sir Philip le Despenser, (see *MC* 9-9), Knt., of Goxhill, Camoys Manor, b. abt. 1365/6, d. 20 June 1424. (*CP* IV 290; XII (2): 97 note *i*).

35. MARGERY DESPENSER, b. abt. 1398/1400, d. abt. Apr. 1478; m. (2) bef. 25 June 1423, Sir Roger Wentworth, Knt, of North Elmsall, co. York, d. aft. 5 June 1452, son of John Wentworth. (*CP* IV: 291).

36. HENRY WENTWORTH, of Cobham Hall, Wethersfield, Essex, d. 22 Mar. 1482/3; m. (1) Elizabeth Howard, dau. of Henry Howard, son of Sir John Howard. (*Wentworth Genealogy* (1878) I: 27).

37. MARGERY WENTWORTH, bur. Bures, Suffolk, 7 May 1540; m. bef. 1483, Sir William Waldegrave, K.B., bur. Bures, 30 Jan. 1527/8, son of Sir Thomas Waldgrave and Elizabeth Fray. (*Visit. of Essex* (1558): 124-125; *Collins' Peerage* 4: 234-235).

38. GEORGE WALDEGRAVE, ESQ., b. 1483, d. 1528, of Smallbridge, par. Bures St. Mary, Suffolk; m. **ANNE DRURY** (257-39), d. 1572, dau. of Sir Robert Drury, of Hawstead, Suffolk. She m. (2) Sir Thomas Jermyn of Rushbrook. A monumental brass for Anne Drury and her two husbands is preserved in the parish church of Depden, Suffolk. (J. J. Muskett, *Suffolk Manorial Families* (London, 1900), II: 345; Mill Stephenson, *A List of Monumental Brasses in the British Isles* (1926), p. 454; *Collins' Peerage* 4: 235).

39. PHILLIS WALDEGRAVE (sis. of Sir William Waldegrave); m. Thomas Higham, d. 1554, son of Sir John Higham of Higham, Suffolk. (*Collins' Peerage* 4: 235-236).

40. BRIDGET HIGHAM, living 1595; m. (1) Thomas Burrough, Esq., d. 19 June 1597, will made 12 May 1595, pro. 26 June 1597, arms granted 1596; son of William Burrough, gent.

41. REV. GEORGE BURROUGH, LL.B., bapt. Wickhambrook, 26 Oct. 1579, bur. Pettaugh, 24 Feb. 1653; L.L.B., Trinity Hall, 1600; Rector of Pettaugh, 1604, and of Gosbeck, 1621; m. Frances Sparrow, dau. of Nicholas Sparrow of Wickhambrook, and sister of Nicholas Sparrow of Gosbeck.

42. NATHANIEL BURROUGH, was by 1651/2 on the Patuxent River, Calvert Co., Maryland, travelled frequently between Mass. and Maryland as merchant mariner, last of record in Maryland in 1676, will, of Limehouse, Stepney Parish, Middlesex, England, dtd. 13 Dec. 1681, prob. 23 Mar. 1682; m. Rebecca Stiles (Style) dau. of John Stiles (Style) of Stepney, Middlesex, will made 26 Oct. 1658. On 19 July 1657, Mrs. Rebecca Burrows adm. 1st Church of Roxbury, Mass. 29. 9 mo. 1674, Mrs. Burrows recommended and dismissed, going to England. (*NEHGR* 33: 239, and note; *TAG* 60: 140-142).

43. REV. GEORGE BURROUGH, A.B., b. abt. 1650, executed for witchcraft, Salem, 19 Aug. 1692, age 42; Harvard College, A.B., 1670; minister at Portland, Maine, 1674-1676, 1683-1690; ord. Danvers, Mass., 25 Nov. 1680. (Gens. 34-44: Muskett, *op. cit.*, I: 311-314; Weis, *Colonial Clergy of N.E.* (Lancaster, 1936), 47; Waters I: 737).

37. ELIZABETH FITZ HUGH (78-37); m. (2) Nicholas Vaux, Lord Harrowden, d. 14 May 1523. (*CP* V: 428, VI: 398, X: 309; *Throckmorton Genealogy*, 106; Burke, *Peerage* (1923), pp. 2176, 2223-2224).

38. KATHARINE VAUX, m. Sir George Throckmorton, Knt., of Coughton, co. Warwick, d. 6 Aug. 1552, son of Robert Throckmorton by 1st wife Catherine Marrow, dau. of Sir William Marrow. (*Throckmorton Gen.*, 105, 164-166; *Burke's Peerage* (1953): 2078).

39. CLEMENT THROCKMORTON, of Haseley, co. Warwick, d. 14 Dec. 1573, M.P. 1541, 1562, 1572; m. Katherine Neville, dau. of Sir Edward Neville, Knt., of Aldington Park, co. Kent, d. 1492 (son of George Neville), by Eleanor Windsor (as her 2nd husb.), dau. of **ANDREWS WINDSOR** (12-36), b. 1467, d. 1543, and **ELIZABETH BLOUNT** (59-39). (*Throckmorton Gen.*, 165; *Burke's Peerage* (1953): 2078; Seversmith, 2,193, 2,204).

40. KATHERINE THROCKMORTON, m. as 3rd wife, Thomas Harby of Adston, co. Northampton, son of William Harby of Ashby. (*Throckmorton Gen.*, 166).

41. KATHERINE HARBY, d. 1651; m. Daniel Oxenbridge, d. London, 1642, "Dr. of Phisick," of Daventry, co. Northampton, son of the Rev. John Oxenbridge, scholar and divine. (*NEHGR* 108: 178; *Throckmorton Gen.*, 166).

42. REVEREND JOHN OXENBRIDGE, A.M., b. Daventry, 30 Jan. 1608/9; matric. Emmanuel Coll., Cambridge, 1626; Magdalen Hall, Oxford, A.B., 1628, A.M., 1631; installed First Chh. in Boston, Mass., 10 Apr. 1670; d. Boston, 28 Dec. 1674; m. (2) Frances Woodward, d. 1659, dau. of Rev. Hezekiah Woodward of Uxbridge, England. (Waters I: 418-423, 442; Weis, *Colonial Clergy of N.E.*, 155; *NEHGR* 112: 169).

43. THEODORA OXENBRIDGE, b. 1659, d. Milton, Mass., 18 Nov. 1697; m. 21 Nov. 1677, Rev. Peter Thacher, A.M. (H.C., 1671), of Milton, Massachusetts. The various Oxenbridge Thachers (H.C., 1698, 1738, 1796 and 1901) were among their descendants. (Weis, *op. cit*, 155, 210, etc.; *NEHGR* 108: 178).

Line 202

32. ROGER DE CLIFFORD (26-32), 5th Lord Clifford, d. 13 July 1389; m. Maud de Beauchamp, dau. of **THOMAS DE BEAUCHAMP** (87-31), and **CATHERINE DE MORTIMER** (120-34). (*CP* III: 292).

33. KATHARINE CLIFFORD, d. 23 Apr. 1413; m. **RALPH DE GREYSTOKE** (265-34), b. 18 Oct. 1353, d. Apr. 1418, 3rd Lord Greystoke. (*CP* VI: 195-196).

34. MAUD DE GREYSTOKE, m. Eudo de Welles, eldest son Sir John de Welles, Lord Welles, of Gainsby, and Eleanor Mowbray, dau. of John de Mowbray and **ELIZABETH DE SEGRAVE** (16-31). (*CP* VI 196; v.Redlich 216; *TAG* 37:114-115; 38:180).

35. SIR LIONEL DE WELLES, K.G., d. Towton, 29 Mar. 1461, 6th Lord Welles, Governor of Ireland 1438-1442; m. (1) 15 Aug. 1417, Joan (or Cecily) de Waterton, dau. of Robert de Waterton, of Methley, co. York, by Alice de Everingham, wid. of Sir William Ellis, dau. of William de Everingham: Sir Lionel de Welles m. (2) as her 3rd husb., **MARGARET DE BEAUCHAMP** (85-35). (*CP* XII (2): 443-4; v.Redlich 216).

36. MARGARET DE WELLES, d. 13 July 1480; m. Sir Thomas Dymoke, Knt., of Scrivelsby, co. Lincoln, son of Sir Philip Dymoke, b. abt. 1428, beheaded 12 Mar. 1470; ancestors of President George Washington. (*CP, cit*; v.Redlich 216; *Harleian Soc. Pub.* (Linc. Pedigrees) 53: 1204; Samuel Lodge, *Scrivelsby, Home of the Champions*, 56; Burke, *Landed Gentry* (1937): 372).

37. SIR LIONEL DYMOKE, KNT., d. 17 Aug. 1519; twice m. and by Joan, prob. dau. of Richard Griffith, he had (*Harl. Soc.*, 53:1204; Lodge 56; Burke 372).

38. ANNE DYMOKE; m. John Goodrick, of Kirby, co. Lincoln. (*Gen.* 4 (1880): 31; *Harl. Soc.Pub.* (Linc. Pedigrees) 51: 416; Early Chancery Proceedings, Bundle 444/43, which identifies her as Anne and her mother as Johanne).

39. LIONEL GOODRICK; m. prob. Winifred Sapcott, dau. of Henry Sapcott, of co. Lincoln. (Authorities as for generation 38).

40. ANN GOODRICK; m. Benjamin Bolles of Osberton, co. Nottingham. (*Gen.* 4 (1880): 31; *Harl.Soc.Pub.* 4: 94; 51: 416; 53: 1204; *Nottinghamshire Visitations*).

41. THOMAS BOLLES, of Osberton, 1614; m. (1) Elizabeth Perkins, dau. of Thomas Perkins, of Fishlake, co. York. (*NEHGR* 82 (1928): 152; Authorities as for generation 40; Charles Thornton Libby, Noyes & Davis, *Genealogical Dictionary of Maine and New Hampshire*, 101).

42. JOSEPH BOLLES (or **BOWLES**), bapt. at Worksop, 19 Feb. 1608/9; to NE by 1640, res. at Winter Harbor and Wells, Maine, d. 1678; m. Mary Howell, prob. sister of Morgan Howell. (Waters I: 606-607; *Genealogy of Edward Small* III: 1289-1294; *TAG* 37: 114-115, 38: 120).

Line 203

39. REV. EDWARD BULKELEY, D.D. (31-39); m. Olive Irby, b. abt. 1547, d. 1614/15.

40. DORCAS BULKELEY (31E-40), m. Anthony Ingoldsby.

41. OLIVE INGOLDSBY, bapt. 1602; m. 20 Apr. 1620, Rev. Thomas James, A.M., bapt. Boston, co. Lincoln, England, 5 Oct. 1595, A.B., Emanuel Coll., Cambridge, 1614/5, A.M. 1618; ord. Charlestown, Mass., 2 Nov. 1632-1636; sett. New Haven, Conn., 1636-1642; d. Needham-Market, England, Feb. 1682/3, age 90 years.

42. REV. THOMAS JAMES, b. England, 1620/22; d. East Hampton, L.I., N.Y., 1696; first minister at Southampton, 1650-1696; m. Ruth Jones, b. abt. 1628, d. abt. 1668. (*Bulkeley Gen*, 11-16.; *TAG* 11: 26-30, 143-145; Weis, *Col. Clergy of N.E.*, 116).

Line 204 Corrections to 8th Edition

35. SIR RALPH DE EURE, b. abt. 1350/3, sheriff of Northumberland 1389-1397, Governor of the Castle of Newcastle, Constable of York Castle, d. 10 Mar. 1422; m. (1) Isabel de Athol; m. (2) by 1387 **CATHERINE DE ATON** (206-35). (*Gen. Mag.* 17 (1972): 86-87, 219; *VCH Yorks*. N. Riding II, 303; Clay, *Dormant & Extinct Peerages of the Northern Cos.*, pp. 3-4, 54-55, with errors).

36. CATHERINE EURE, by (2), d. bef. 31 Aug. 1459; m. Sir Alexander Neville, of Thornton Bridge, d. 1457, will pro., York, 25 June 1457.

37. WILLIAM NEVILLE, b. abt. 1425/6, Squire of Thornton Bridge; m. NN.

38. WILLIAM NEVILLE, b. abt. 1450, d. ah. bef. 1484; m. (1) (under age), 1457, Joan Boynton; m. (2) Alice.

39. RALPH NEVILLE, s. and h. by (1), d. 1522, of Thornton Bridge; m. **ANNE WARD** (2-37). (see also: *New County History of Northumberland* XII: 494-495; Gens. 36-40: "Neville of Thornton Bridge" in *Gen.* (n.s.) 33: 15, which has one too many Williams; *TAG* 17: 108; see ms. notes of G. Andrews Moriarty, at NEHGS, Boston; *Gen. Mag.* 13 (1959): 104-105).

Line 205

32. ROBERT DE CLIFFORD (82-32), 1ˢᵗ Lord Clifford, b. 1274, d. 1314; m. **MAUD DE CLARE** (64-32).

    33. IDOINE (IDONEA) DE CLIFFORD, d. 24 Aug 1365; **HENRY DE PERCY** (161-29), 2ⁿᵈ Lord Percy, b. abt. 1299, d. abt. 26 Feb. 1351/2. (*CP* X: 459-462 & note *a* 462).

    34. MAUD PERCY (see 2-32), d. bef. 18 Feb. 1378/9; m. **JOHN DE NEVILLE, K.G.** (207-33). (*CP* IX: 502-503).

Line 206

    33. IDOINE (IDONEA) DE CLIFFORD (205-33), m. **HENRY DE PERCY** (161-29) 2ⁿᵈ Lord Percy (will mentions. Isabel, wife of William, Lord Aton). (*CP* X: 462, note *a*).

    34. ISABEL DE PERCY, d. bef. 25 May 1368; m. bef. Jan. 1326/7 Sir William de Aton, Knt., 2ⁿᵈ Lord Aton, d.s.p.m. sh. bef. Mar. 1388/9. age 81, son of Sir Gilbert de Aton, of Aton Malton. (*CP* X: 459-462).

    35. CATHERINE DE ATON, m. **SIR RALPH DE EURE, KNT.** (204-35). (*CP* I: 324-326). (Gens. 33-35: Clay, pp 3-4).

Line 207   Revised for 8ᵗʰ Edition

    30. SIR EDMUND DE MORTIMER (9-30), 7ᵗʰ Baron Mortimer of Wigmore; had, prob. by unkn, 1ˢᵗ wife, (*NEHGR* 116: 16-17).

    31. ISOLDE DE MORTIMER, d. 1338; m. (1) Walter de Balun; m. (2) Hugh de Audley, Lord Audley, d. 1325, Ambassador to France, son of James de Audley and **ELA LONGESPEE** (122-30). (*CP* I: 347-348, IX: 499-501).

    32. ALICE DE AUDLEY, d. 12 Jan. 1373/4; m. (2) abt. 14 Jan. 1326/7, **RALPH DE NEVILLE** (186-5), b. abt. 1291, d. 5 Aug. 1367, Baron Neville of Raby. She had m. (1) **RALPH GREYSTOKE** (265-32), 1ˢᵗ Lord of Greystoke. (*CP* IX: 499-501, IV: 190).

    33. JOHN DE NEVILLE, K.G., Lord Neville of Raby (See 2-32), b. abt. 1331, d. Newcastle, 17 Oct. 1388, Knt. 1360, K.G. 1369; m. (1) **MAUD PERCY** (205-34), d. 1378/9. (*CP* IX: 502-503; *ES* III.4/711).

    34. RALPH DE NEVILLE, K.G., b. bef. 1364, d. Raby, 21 Oct. 1425, cr. 1ˢᵗ Earl of Westmorland 1397; m. (1) **MARGARET STAFFORD** (10-33); m. (2) **JOAN BEAUFORT** (2-32, 3-32, 78-35), granddau. of **KING EDWARD III** (1-29) and **PHILIPPA OF HAINAUT** (103-34). (*CP* IX: 503; Edward Blore, *The Monumental Remains of Noble and Eminent Persons, etc.* (London, 1826), section 21, p. 9).

    35. ELEANOR NEVILLE (3-33) by (2), wid. of Richard le Despenser; m. (2) **SIR HENRY PERCY, K.G.** (19-33). (*CP* X: 464; Collins IV: 84).

    36. KATHERINE PERCY, b. 28 May 1423; m. well bef. 1458/9, Edmund Grey of Ruthin, cr. Earl of Kent 1465, b. 26 Oct. 1416, d. 22 May 1490, son of Sir John Grey, K.C., d. 27 Aug. 1439 and (m. by 24 Feb. 1412/13) Constance Holand, d. Nov. 1437, dau. of John de Holand (son of **SIR THOMAS DE HOLAND, K.G.** (47-31) and **JOAN** (236-12), "Fair Maid of Kent"), by his wife Elizabeth, dau. of **JOHN OF GAUNT** (1-30). (*CP* VI: 159, 180, VII: 164-165; Weever 425; *ES* III.4/712).

37. ANNE GREY; m. abt. 1468, as 1st wife, John Grey, 8th Lord Grey of Wilton, d. 3 Apr. 1499, who m. (2) Elizabeth Vaughn, d. 15 Jan. 1514/5, wid. of Sir Thomas Cokesey (otherwise Grevile), Knight of Cooksey, age 28+ in 1480, d.s.p, 6 Mar, 1497/8, and dau. of Thomas Vaughn. (*CP* VI: 180-181, VII: 165 note *e*, 166 note *f*, XII (1): 48 note *a*). "Gyse of Elmore" (*Trans. Bristol & Gloucs.*, *cit*. III: 59, 70) and *Visit. of Gloucs.* (1623), p. 72 *Harleian Soc. Pub.* XXI) show that **JOHN GYSE** (197-36) of Elmore, b. 1485, d. 20 Dec. 1556, mar. bef. 1518 (actually abt. 1510), **TACY** (or **TASY**) **DE GREY** (Gen.-39 below), dau. of "Lord Grey of Wilton." In some pedigrees he appears as "Lord Grey of Ruthin" though the former is that which is recorded by "the Heralds' College" (*Bristol & Gloucs.*, cit III 77). Anne's father, Edmund Grey (Gen. 36 above) was a member of the family of Ruthin, which may be the source of the confusion. John Grey of Wilton was the proper age to be Tase's grandfather, and his mother bore the same name. Though there is no positive evidence seen identifying John and Anne as grandparents of Tacy, wife of John Gyse, everything fits chronologically and the identification appears most probable.

38. EDMUND GREY, Lord Grey of Wilton, b. abt. 1469, d. 5 May 1511; m. bef. May 1505, Florence Hastings, living 5 May 1511, dau. of Sir Ralph and Anne Hastings. (*CP* VI: 181-182; v.Redlich, 199).

39. TACY (or **TASY**) **GREY**, dau. perh. by an earlier marriage, b. abt. 1490, bur. at Elmore, co. Gloucester, 15 Nov. 1558; m. abt. 1510, **JOHN GYSE, ESQ.** (197-36), b. abt. 1485, d. 20 Dec. 1556. (Sir Robert Atkyns,...*State of Gloucestershire...* (1712), 325).

Line 208

29. SIR ROBERT DE ROS (89-29), d. 1285; m. Isabel d'Aubigny.

30. ISABEL DE ROS; m., as 1st wife. Walter de Fauconberge, 2nd Lord Fauconberge, d. 31 Dec. 1318, son of **SIR WALTER DE FAUCONBERGE** (184B-8), d. 1304, and **AGNES DE BRUS** (136-27). (*CP* V: 270).

31. JOHN DE FAUCONBERGE, b. 1290, 3rd Lord Fauconberge, d. 17/18 Sept. 1349; m. Eve Bulmere, prob. dau. of Sir Ralph de Bulmere, of Wilton and Bulmer. (*CP* V: 271-272, XI: 95-96).

32. JOAN DE FAUCONBERGE; m. (2) 1376/7, Sir William Colville of Arncliffe, d. abt. 1380/1. (Brown: "Ingleby and Arncliffe" in *Yorks. Arch. Journ.* XVI: 159-170, 211).

33. SIR JOHN DE COLVILLE, of Arncliffe and Dale, beheaded at Durham, 20 Aug. 1405 with his wife; m. Alice Darcy, dau. of John Darcy, Lord Darcy. (*Yorks. Arch.Jnl.*, *cit.*).

34. ISABEL DE COLVILLE, liv. 1442/3; m. (1) John Wandesford, of Kirklington, d. abt. 1400, son of John Wandesford, by Elizabeth Musters. (*Y.A.J.*, *cit.* 217-219; H.B. McCall, *The Wandesfords of Kirklington and Castle Camer* (1904); *The Ancestor* X: 98-99; Clay, 231).

35. THOMAS WANDESFORD, merchant of London, Sheriff of London, Alderman of London, d. 13 Oct. 1448; m. Idonea. (*The Ancestor*, *cit.*; *The Wandesfords*, *cit*; Bevan, *Aldermen of London* I: 206, 336, II: 7; *Dugdale's Visit. of Yorkshire* I: 341).

36. ALICE WANDESFORD, coh.; m. William Mulso of Creatingham, Suffolk, d. 1495. (Rot. Parl. VI 493; Wedgewood, *Hist. of Parliament. Biogs.* 1439-1509, pp. 557, 618; Coppinger's *Manors of Suffolk* IV: 243).

37. ANNE MULSO, m. Thomas Louthe (Lowthe), of Sawtry, co. Huntingdon, M.P., d. 1533. (Authorities at 208-36; *Camden Soc* 77: 4 and App. 2).

38. EDMUND LOUTHE, d.v.p. (killed 1522); m. Edith Stukeley, dau. of John Stukeley of Stukeley, co. Huntingdon. (Authorities as above).

39. ANNE LOUTHE, d. 1577; m. Simon Throckmorton of Barsham, Suffolk, d. 10 July 1527. (Authorities as above; Metcalf, *Visit. Suffolk*; *NEHGR* 98: 67-72, 111-123).

40. LIONEL THROCKMORTON b. 1525, of South Elmham and Bungay, Suffolk, d. 1599; m. (2) 1561, Elizabeth Blennerhasset, dau. of John Blennerhasset of Barsham by his 1st wife, Elizabeth Cornwallis. (Metcalf, *op. cit.*; *NEHGR* 98: 67-72,111-123).

41. BASSINGBOURNE THROCKMORTON, ESQ., grocer, citizen, and Alderman of Norwich, b. 1564, d. 21 Sept. 1638; m. (1), lic. 7 Dec. 1591, Mary Hill, d. 1615, dau. of William Hill, gent., of Bury St. Edmunds, and his wife, Joan Annabel. (*NEHGR* 98: 67-72, 111-123; Rye, *Calendar of the Freemen of Norwich 1317-1608*, p. 137).

42. JOHN THROCKMORTON, of Providence, Rhode Island, bapt. St. Paul's, Norwich, 9 May 1601, d. bet. 17 Mar. 1683 and 4-25 Apr. 1684; m. Rebecca Farrand (*TAG* 77: 110). (Gens. 29-42: Moriarty Notebook XIV: 17-18. *NEHGR* 98 (1944): 67-72, 111-123). For Eng. ancestry of Rebecca Ferrand, *see* Paul C. Reed and Leslie Maher, "The English Ancestry of Rebecca Farrand...," *TAG* 77 (2002), pp 110-124, 229-234, 290-297.

Line 209

36. SIR RICHARD LYGON, KNT. (84-36), of Arle Court, d. 20 Mar. 1557; m. Margaret Greville. (Wm. D. Ligon, *The Ligon Family* (1947), pp. 33-34, 37-38, 45-46; *TAG* 52: 176-7, 247; *Visit. of Worcestershire* (1569): 90-91).

37. WILLLAM LYGON (84C-37), of Redgrove and Madresfield, b. 1518, d. 29 Sept. 1567, sheriff of Worcestershire 1550, 1560; m. 1529, Eleanor Dennis, dau. of Sir William Dennis (or Denys), of Durham, co. Gloucester, and his wife Anne Berkeley, dau. of Maurice Berkeley. (*Ibid*, 45-46).

38. CICELY LYGON, of Madresfield, co. Worcester; m. 1559, Edward Gorges, Esq., of Wraxall, co. Somerset, b. 1537, d. 29 Aug. 1568, son of Edmund Gorges, Esq., and Anne Walsh. (*Ibid*, 45-60, 101, 177-178).

39. SIR FERDINANDO GORGES, KNT., of Kinterbury, co. Devon colonizer of Me., b. abt. 1565, d. Ashton Court near Bristol, England, 4/14 May 1647; m. (1) Westminster, 24 Feb. 1589/90, Anne Bell, d. 26 Aug. 1620, bur. London, 6 Aug. 1620, dau. of Edward Bell, will 20 Nov. 1576, of Writtle, co. Essex, and Margaret Barley, of Writtle, Essex; m. (2), lic. 21 Dec. 1621, Mary Fulford, d. 1622, wid. of Thomas Achym, d. 1618, dau. of Sir Thomas Fulford, Esq., by Ursula Bamfield, and sister of Bridget Fulford, wife of **ARTHUR CHAMPERNOUN, ESQ.** (6-40). (*Ibid*, 178; Noyes, Libbey and Davis, *Gen. Dict. of Maine and N.H.*, II: 274; Devon & Cornwall N. & Q. 18 (1933/5): 134-138; *Mis. Gen. et Her.* (n.s.) 4 (1888): 55; see also *Genealogist* 14 (2002): 3-45, esp. 12-13, 9 note 47).

Line 210   Revised for 8th Edition

30. NICHOLE D'AUBIGNY (126-30); m. (1) **ROGER DE SOMERY** (55-29, 81-29).

31. MARGARET DE SOMERY (55-30), wid. of Ralph Basset of Drayton co. Staff., slain 1265; m. (2) bef. 26 Jan. 1270/1, as 2nd wife, Ralph de Cromwell, d. bef. 18 Sept. 1289. (*CP* III: 551).

32. RALPH DE CROMWELL, d. abt. 2 Mar. 1298/9. (*CP* III: 551).

33. RALPH DE CROMWELL, d. 1291/2; m. Joan de la Mare, d. 9 Aug. 1348. (*CP* III: 551).

34. RALPH DE CROMWELL, of Cromwell and West Hallam, d. bef. 28 Oct. 1364; m. 1351, Anice (or Amice) Bellers, dau. of Roger de Bellers, d. 1326, of Bunny, co.

Nottingham, Edward II's notorious chief baron of the Exchequer. (*CP, ibid*; Simon Payling, *Political Society in Lancastrian England: The Greater Gentry of Nottingham* (Oxford, 1991), pp. 95-96 (re Cromwell); *DNB* (re Roger de Bellers)).

35. SIR RALPH CROMWELL, Lord Cromwell of Tattershall, co. Lincoln, M.P. 1375-1397, d. 27 Aug. 1398; m. bef. 20 June 1366, **MAUD BERNAKE** (218-32), d. 10 Apr. 1419, dau. of John Bernake by **JOAN MARMION** (218-31), and great-great-granddau. of Robert de Tateshal of Tattershall. (*CP* III: 551-552, V: 519, XII (1): 653 notes c and d; Banks I: 168-170).

36. MAUD CROMWELL, m. Sir William Fitz William, of Sprotborough, co. Yorks., Lord of Emley, d. 8 Apr. 1398. (*CP* V: 519; Banks I: 170).

37. SIR JOHN FITZ WILLIAM, KNT., d. 5 July 1417/8, Lord of Emley and Sprotborough; m. Eleanor Green, dau. of Sir Henry Green of Drayton. (*CP* V: 519; Clay, 77; *Visit. of Essex* (1612): 198).

Line 211   The ancestry of Philippa Bradbury needs further research.

38. MARGARET ROKELL, prob. granddau. of Thomas, the "sick and aged" coroner of co. Hertford 1427; m. William Bradbury of Littleton & Wicken Bonhunt, Essex, son of Robert Bradbury, of Olerset, co. Derby. (*TAG* 18 (1942): 220-221; Feet of Fines, Essex, IV: 80; Close Rolls, *Bradbury Memorial*.) (Provided by John B. Threlfall).

39. PHILIPPA BRADBURY, d. aft. 14 Oct. 1530; m. (1) John Barley; m. (2) aft. 7 July 1502, John Josselyn, d. July 14, 1525, son of George Josselyn, of Newell Josselyn and Hide Hall in Sawbridgeworth, co. Hertford, and High Roding, Essex, by Maud Bardolf, dau. of Edmund Bardolf. (*TAG* 52: 177; *NEHGR* 71 (1917): 20-21, 241-242. The *Visit. of Herts.* (1546) Appendix II, p. 129, does not list Phillipa as a dau. for William).

40. SIR THOMAS JOSSELYN, K.B., of Hide Hall, Sawbridgeworth, and Newell Josselyn, High Roding, b. abt. 1507, d. 24 Oct. 1562, bur. at Sawbridgeworth; Knight of the Bath, 1547/8; m. 1524, Dorothy Gates, d. 11 Feb. 1582/3, dau. of Sir Jeffrey Gates, Knt., and Elizabeth Clopton, dau. of Sir William Clopton, Knt., of Kentwell, Suffolk. (*NEHGR* 71: 22-23, 242-245; *Visitations. of Essex* (1558): 65, (1612): 229-230).

41. HENRY JOSSELYN, b. Willingale-Doe, Essex, abt. 1540, bur. there 25 Aug. 1587; m. abt. 1562, Anne Torrell, b. abt. 12 Dec. 1542, d. 30 May 1589, dau. of Humphrey Torrell, of Torrell's Hall in Willingale-Doe, and Alice Leventhorpe. (*NEHGR* 71: 23, 245-246).

42. SIR THOMAS JOSSELYN, KNT.,b. abt. 1560/67 of Torrell's Hall, Knt., 1603; appointed by **SIR FERDINANDO GORGES** (209-39) deputy-governor of his possessions in N.E.; arriv. Black Point, Me., 14 July 1638, returned to Eng., 3 Sept. 1639; m. (2) abt. 1603, Theodora Cooke, bur. Boxley, Kent, 13 Aug. 1635, wid. of Clement Bere of Dartford, co. Kent, dau. of Edmund Cooke by Elizabeth Nichols, dau. of John Nichols. (*NEHGR* 71: 246, 248-250; *Visit. of Kent* (1619): 118).

43. HENRY JOSSELYN, b. abt. 1606, d. Maine, bef. 10 May 1683, Corpus Christi Coll., Camb., 1623; sett. Black Point, Me. 1634, later at Pemequid; dep. gov. of Maine 1645; m. Margaret (__) Cammock, living 12 May 1680, wid. of Thomas Cammock. (*NEHGR* 71: 249).

43. JOHN JOSSELYN, son of Gen. 42, b. abt. 1608, d.s.p, Eng. aft. 1675; sett. Black Point, Me., 1638; traveller, writer and naturalist; published *New Rarities Discovered* and *An Account of Two Voyages to New England.* (*NEHGR* 71: 249-250; *DNB* X: 1096;

Publications, Colonial Soc. Mass., 28:24-36. Weis states that Thomas Josselyn (Joslin), 1591-1661, of Lancaster, Mass., was fifth cousin to Henry and John above).

Line 212

    30. MILICENT DE CANTELOU (66-30, 200-30), d. abt. 1299; m. **EUDO LA ZOUCHE** (38-29), of Haryngworth, d. 1279.

    31. WILLIAM LA ZOUCHE, of Haryngworth, 1st Lord Zouche, b. Haryngworth, 18 or 21 Dec. 1276, Knt. 1306, M.P. 1308-1348, d. Mar. 1351/2; m. before 15 Feb. 1295/6 Maud Lovel, d. bef. 1346, dau. of **JOHN LOVEL**, 1st Lord Lovel (215-29) by his 1st wife, Isabel du Bois. (*CP* XII (2): 97, 938-940; *TAG* 49: 2-3).

    32. EUDO LA ZOUCHE, of Haryngworth, b. 1297/8, d.v.p. Paris, 24 Apr. 1326; m. bef. June 1322, Joan Inge, age 22 or 23 in 1322, d. by Jan. 1359/60, dau. of William Inge, Chief Justice, 1325/6, by Margery Grapinel. (*CP* XII (2): 940-941).

    33. WILLIAM LA ZOUCHE of Haryngworth, 2nd Lord Zouche, b. 1321, d. 23 Apr. 1382, M.P. 1348-1351; m. bef. 16 July 1334, Elizabeth de Ros, will dtd. 16 May 1380, dau. of **WILLIAM DE ROS** (89-31), 2nd Lord Ros of Helmsley, and **MARGERY DE BADLESMERE** (54-34). (*CP* XII (2): 941-942).

    34. WILLIAM LA ZOUCHE, of Haryngworth, 3rd Lord Zouche, b. abt. 1342, M.P. 1382/3, d. 13 May 1396; m. (1) Agnes Green, prob. dau. of Sir Henry Green, d. bet. 2 Dec. 1391 and 28 Apr. 1393; m. (2) aft. 28 Apr. 1393, **ELIZABETH DESPENSER** (74-35), d. 10 or 11 Apr. 1408, wid. of **SIR JOHN FITZ ALAN** (21-32), dau. of **SIR EDWARD DESPENSER** (74-34). (*CP* XII (2): 942-943).

    35. SIR WILLIAM LA ZOUCHE, K.G., of Haryngworth, 4th Lord Zouche, b. abt. 1373 or 1374, M.P. 1396, K.G. 1415, d. 3 Nov. 1415; m. by 1402, Elizabeth Crosse, d. sh. bef. 20 Nov. 1425, said to be dau. of Sir William Crosse. (*CP* XII (2): 943-944 and note *j*).

    36. WILLIAM LA ZOUCHE, of Haryngworth, 5th Lord Zouche, b. abt. 1402, M.P. 1425/6, d. 25 Dec. 1462; m. (1) bef. 8 Mar. 1423/4, **ALICE ST. MAUR** (or SEYMOUR) (213-34); m. (2) by 2 Apr. 1450, Elizabeth de St. John, dau. of Sir Oliver St. John of Bletsoe, by **MARGARET DE BEAUCHAMP** (85-35), d. 1482. (*CP* II: 45 note c, XI 362, XII (2): 944-945).

    37. WILLIAM LA ZOUCHE, by (1), 6th Lord Zouche, and *jure matris* Lord St. Maur, b. abt. 1432, age 30+ at father's death, MP 1455/6, d. 15 Jan. 1467/8; m. (1) Katharine Lenthall (dau. of Sir Rowland Lenthall, by Lucy Grey, dau. Richard Grey, 4th Lord Grey, aunt and in her issue coh. of Henry Grey, 7th Lord Grey of Codnor); m. (2) Katharine Plumpton, dau. of Sir William Plumpton, by 1st wife, Elizabeth Stapleton, dau. of Sir Brian Stapleton. (*CP* XII (2): 946; *Gen.* (n.s.) 22: 41).

    38. JOHN LA ZOUCHE, by (1), 7th Lord Zouche of Haryngworth, Lord St. Maur and Lovel, d. abt. 1525/6; m. bef. 26 Feb. 1486/7 **JOAN DYNHAM** (214-36), d. aft. 1507. (*CP* IV: 381, XII (2): 946-947).

Line 213

30. ELENA (ELLEN) LA ZOUCHE (31-30); m. (1) Apr. 1314, as his 2nd wife, Nicholas de St. Maur (Seymour), M.P. 1314/5, Knt. of the Shire for Gloucester, 1312/3, 1st Lord St. Maur, d. 8 Nov. 1316, son of Sir Lawrence de St. Maur, and grandson of Nicholas de St. Maur, d. abt. May 1267. (*CP* XI: 359).

31. NICHOLAS DE ST. MAUR (SEYMOUR), KNT., 2nd Lord St. Maur, Knt. 1346, J.P. for Somersetshire 1351, M.P. 1351-1360, d. 8 Aug. 1361; m. Muriel Lovel, d. bef. 1361, dau. of James Lovel and granddau. of Richard Lovel, d. 1350/1, 1st Lord Lovel of Castle Cary, co. Somerset. (*CP* XI: 359-360).

32. RICHARD SEYMOUR, KNT., 2nd son, 4th Lord St. Maur and Lovel, M.P. 1380-1400, Knt. 1382, d. 15 May 1401; m. aft. 1374, Ela de St. Lo, d. 1409/10, wid. of Thomas de Bradeston, dau. of Sir John de St. Lo, by Alice de Pavely, dau. of John de Pavely. (*CP* XI: 360-361).

33. RICHARD SEYMOUR, 5th Lord St. Maur and Lovel, J.P. 1405, M.P. 1402-1407, d. Jan. 1408/9; m. Mary Peyvre, d. July 1409, wid. of John Broughton, dau. of Thomas Peyvre of Toddington, co. Beds., by Margaret Loring, dau. of Sir Nele Loring, K.G. (See 40-33). (*CP* XI: 361).

34. ALICE SEYMOUR (ST. MAUR), Baroness St. Maur and Lovel, b. 24 July 1409, seen 1430/1; m. bef. 8 Mar. 1423/4, **WILLIAM LA ZOUCHE** (212-36), Lord Zouche of Haryngworth, d. 25 Dec. 1462. (Gens. 30-34: *CP* XI: 356-362).

Line 214   Revised for 8th Edition

21. ERMENGARDE OF ANJOU (121-21); m. 973, Conan I, Duke of Brittany, Count of Rennes, d. 27 June 992, son of Judicael Berenger, (*ES* II/75 NEU; Anselme III: 45).

22. GEOFFREY (119A-22), b. abt. 980, Duke of Brittany, d. 20 Nov. 1008; m. 996, Hawise of Normandy, d. 21 Feb. 1034, illeg. dau. of **RICHARD I** (121E-20), Duke of Normandy. (*CP* X: 779; Anselme III: 46).

23. EUDES I, b. 999, Co-Reageant of Brittany, and Count of Penthièvre, 1034, d. 7 Jan. 1062; m. Orguen, liv. 1056, whose origin is unkn. (*CP* X: 781 and note *b*; *ES* II/75 NEU).

24. STEPHEN (ETIENNE) I, (perh. by Orguen), a count of Brittany, Count of Tréguier and Lamballe, held honour of Richmond in England, founder of Augustinian abbey of Ste. Croix at Guincamp abt. 1110, founder of Cistercian abbey of Begard, d. 21 Apr. 1135 or 1136; m. Hawise (par. unkn.), liv. 1135. (*CP* X: 786-787 and note *e*; *ES* II/75 NEU).

25. AGNORIA of Brittany, m. 1135, Oliver II, Sire de Dinan, d. abt. 1155/1156, son of Geoffrey, Sire de Dinan in Brittany, d. 1123, by Orieldis NN. (*ES* II/75 NEU).

26. OLIVER III DE DINAN, liv. 1173, bro. and h. of Geoffrey de Dinan, founder of Hartland Abbey.

27. GEOFFREY DE DINAN, son and heir. (*CP* X: 781 and note *b*; Keats-Rohan, *Domesday Desc.* II: 434; Also, Gens. 22-26: Brandenburg).

28. OLIVER DE DINANT, d. sh. bef. 28 June 1221. (Gens. 25-28: *CP* IV: 369 note c).

29. SIR GEOFFREY DE DINHAM, of Hartland, d. sh. bef. 26 Dec. 1258. (*CP* IV: 369).

30. SIR OLIVER DE DINHAM (or **DINAUNT**), age 24 at his father's death, of Hartland and Nutwell, co. Devon, and Buckland Dinham, Somerset, b. 1234, Constable of Exeter and Taunton Castles, d. 26 Feb. 1298/9; m. (1) NN; m. (2) bef. 24 Jan. 1276/7, Isabel de Vere, wid. of **SIR JOHN DE COURTENAY** (50-29), d. 1274, dau. of Hugh de Vere, Earl of

Oxford, (son of **ROBERT DE VERE** (246-27)), and **HAWISE DE QUINCY** (60-28). (*CP* IV: 369-371).

   31. SIR JOSCE DE DINHAM, by (1), age 24+ or 26+ at father's death, of Hartland, Buckland, Denham and Cardinham, d. 30 Mar. 1300/1; m. bef. 23 Apr. 1292, Margaret de Hydon, d. 15 May 1357, dau. of Sir Richard de Hydon of Clayhidon and Hemock, co. Devon. (*CP* IV: 371-372).

   32. SIR JOHN DE DINHAM, b. Nutwell, 14 Sept. 1295, of Hartland, d. 14 Apr. 1332, age 36; m. abt. 1310, Margaret NN, d. 28 Mar. 1361. (*CP* IV: 372-373).

   33. SIR JOHN DE DINHAM, KNT., b. abt. 1315/8, murd. 7 Jan. 1382/3, age 64; m. Muriel de Courtenay, d. bef. 12 Aug. 1369, dau. of Sir Thomas de Courtenay and Muriel de Moels, dau. of John de Moels, and granddau. of **SIR HUGH DE COURTENAY** (51-31) and **AGNES ST. JOHN** (262-32). (*CP* IV: 373-374).

   34. SIR JOHN DE DINHAM, b. co. Devon, 1359/60, d. 25 Dec. 1428, age 69; m. (3) aft. 1 Nov. 1402, **PHILIPPE LOVEL** (215-34), d. 15 May 1465, dau. of Sir John Lovel of Titchmarsh, co. Northants and Alianore la Zouche, dau. of Sir William la Zouche. (*CP* IV: 374-377; *Gen. Mag.* 7 (1935): 120).

   35. SIR JOHN DYNHAM, KNT., b. abt. 1405, Lord Dynham of Hartland, co. Devon, d. Nuthwell, co. Devon 25 Jan. 1457/8; m. bef. 12 July 1434, Joan (Jane) Arches, d. 1497, dau. of Richard Arches of co. Bucks. (*CP* IV: 377-378).

   36. JOAN DE DYNHAM, age 40/45 in 1501, & aft. 1507, (sis. & coh. of her bro., John Dynham, 7th Lord Dynham; m. **JOHN LA ZOUCHE** (212-38), d. 23 June 1526, 7th Lord Zouche of Haryngworth. (*CP* IV: 377, 381; Old-*CP* VIII: 223-224).

   37. JOHN LA ZOUCHE, 8th Lord Zouche of Haryngworth, b. abt. 1486, Lord of St. Maur and Lovel, d. 10 Aug. 1550; m. (1) bef. 1510, Dorothy Capell, dau. of Sir William Capell, Lord Mayor of London, and Margaret Arundel, dau. of Sir John Arundel of Lanherne, Cornwall, by Katherine Chideoke. (*CP* XII (2): 948; Burkes *Peerage and Baronetage*: Arundell of Wardour; *Visit. of Cornwall* (1620): 3, 5).

   38. RICHARD LA ZOUCHE, 9th Lord Zouche of Haryngworth, b. abt. 1510, M.P., d. 1552. (*CP* VI: 186-187, XII (2): 948-949).

   39. DOROTHY LA ZOUCHE (nat. dau.); m. abt. 1553, Sir Arthur Grey, K.G., Lord Grey of Wilton, Gov. of Ireland. (*CP* VI: 186-187).

Line 214A   Prepared for an earlier edition by Douglas Richardson

   24. STEPHEN I (214-24), d. 1135 or 1136; m. Hawise.

   25. OLIVE OF BRITTANY, to whom her father gave Long Bennington, co. Lincoln; m. (1) Henry de Fougères, seigneur of Fougères, d. 1154; m. (2) William de St. John. (Moriarty Notebooks; *Sir Christopher Hatton's Book of Seals*, 172-173).

   26. RAOUL III DE FOUGÈRES, son by (1), seigneur of Fougères, d. 1194; m. Jeanne, dau. of Geldouin I, seigneur of Dol. (Hatton, *cit*; Moriarty).

   27. WILLIAM DE FOUGÈRES, d. 7 June 1187; m. Agatha, dau. of William of Hummet, d. 1180, seigneur of Le Hommet in Normandy, constable of Normandy, by wife Lucy. (Hatton, *cit.*; Moriarty).

   28. GEOFFREY DE FOUGÈRES, seigneur of Fougères, d. 15 Dec. 1212; M. Maud, dau. of Eudo, d. 1239, Count of Porhoët in Brittany, by wife Margaret. (Hatton, *cit.*; Moriarty).

   29. RAOUL DE FOUGÈRES, Sire of Fourgères in Brittany, d. 1256; m. Isabel de Craon, dau. of Amaury de Craon, d. 1226, seigneur of Craon, by wife Jeanne des Roches. (Moriarty).

30.   JEANNE DE FOUGÈRES, dau. & h.; m. 29 Jan. 1253/4, **HUGH XII DE LUSIGNAN** (275-29, 135-31), d. 1270, Count de la Marche and Angoulême. (*ES* III.4/816; Moriarty).

Line 215

24.   ISABEL DE VERMANDOIS (50-24), d. 1131; m. (1) Robert de Beaumont, Lord of Beaumont, Earl of Leicester, b. abt. 1049, d. 1118.

25.   MAUD DE BEAUMONT, liv. 1189; m. William de Lovel, d. 1166/70, Seigneur d'Ivry and Breval, son of Ascelin Goel and Isabel, illeg. dau. of William de Bréteuil, son of William fitz Osbern. (*CP* VIII: 211-212).

26.   WILLIAM LOVEL, (aka William d'Ivry) of Minster (Lovel), co. Oxford, crusader, d. abt. 1212/13; m. bef. 1190, Isabel. (*CP* VIII: 213-214).

27.   SIR JOHN LOVEL, KNT., d. bef. 23 Dec. 1252; m. bef. Aug. 1216, Katherine Basset, dau. of Alan Basset, lord of Wycombe, co. Buckingham, d. 1231, and Aline Grey, dau. & coh. Philip de Grey, lord of Wooton Basset & Broadtown, co. Wilts, by wife Sedzilia. (*CP* VIII: 214).

28.   JOHN LOVEL, b. 1222, d. 1287; m. Maud de Sydenham, dau. of Sir William de Sydenham. (*CP* VIII: 215).

29.   SIR JOHN LOVEL, KNT., 1st Lord Lovel, b. 1252, M.P. 1298-1307, d. bef. 1 Oct. 1310; m. (1) Isabel du Bois, d.s.p.m. bef. 1280, dau. of Arnold du Bois; m. (2) Joan de Ros, d. 13 Oct. 1348, dau. of **ROBERT DE ROS** (89-29) and Isabel d'Aubigny, granddau. of William d'Aubigny, M.C. 1215. (*CP* VIII: 215-217, XI: 95-96, XII (2): 940).

30.   JOHN LOVEL, by (2), 2nd Lord Lovel, b. 1288, M.P. 1311-1314, killed at Bannockburn 24 June 1314; m. Maud Burnell b. 1290, d. 17 May 1341, dau. of Sir Philip Burnell, of Acton Burnell, and Maud Fitz Alan, dau. of **JOHN FITZ ALAN** (149-29), and sister of **RICHARD FITZ ALAN** (28-31), Earl of Arundel. (*CP* VIII: 217-218).

31.   SIR JOHN LOVEL, 3rd Lord Lovel, b. posthum. abt. Sept. 1314, d. 3 Nov. 1347; m. in or bef. 1340, Isabel, d. 2 July 1349. (*CP* VIII 218-219).

32.   SIR JOHN LOVEL, K.G., 5th Lord Lovel, K.G. 1405, M.P. 1375-1407, d. 10 Sept. 1408 (bro. of John, 4th Lord Lovel); m. abt. 1372, **MAUD DE HOLAND** (47A-33), d. 7 May 1423, dau. of Robert de Holand, and granddau. of Robert, Lord Holand, d. 16 Mar. 1372/3. (*CP* VIII: 219-221).

33.   JOHN LOVEL, 6th Lord Lovel of Titchmarsh, M.P. 1409-1414, d. 19 Oct. 1414; m. perh. Alianore la Zouche, dau. of William la Zouche of Harringworth, Northants, Lord Zouche.(*CP* VIII: 221).

34.   PHILIPPE LOVEL, d. 15 May 1465; m. **SIR JOHN DE DINHAM** (214-34).

Line 216

29. JOHN DE BOTETOURTE, (illeg. son of **EDWARD I** (1-28)), 1ˢᵗ Lord Botetourte, admiral, governor of Famlingham Castle 1304, M.P. 1305-1324, d. 25 Nov. 1324; m. 1285/92, **MAUD** (or **MATILDA) FITZ THOMAS** **(FITZ OTTO, FITZ OTES, FITZ OTHO)**, (122A-31), liv. 28 May 1329, dau. of Thomas Fitz Otto (Otes) of Mendlesham, Suffolk, and **BEATRICE DE BEAUCHAMP** (122A-30), dau. of William de Beauchamp feudal lord of Bedford. (*CP* II: 233-234, XIV: 102; *TAG* 63: 145-153. For a possible identification of his mother, see *NEHGR* 120: 259).

30. THOMAS DE BOTETOURTE, perh. named after Thomas de Clare, d.v.p. 1322; m. Joan de Somery, liv. 18 Jan. 132617, sis. and coh. of John de Somery, Lord Somery, dau. of **ROGER DE SOMERY** (81-30). (*CP* II: 234-235).

31. JOHN DE BOTETOURTE, Lord Botetourte of Weobley Castle, b. 1318, M.P. 1342-1385, d. 4 Apr. 1386; m. bef. 31 May 1347, **JOYCE ZOUCHE DE MORTIMER** (98-32), living 4 May 1372, dau. of William Zouche, Lord Zouche of Mortimer. (*CP* II 234-235, XII (2): 962-963; *Gen. Mag.* 21 (1984): 188; *ES* III.4/706. Gens. 29-31: *DNB* 5: 447).

32. JOYCE DE BOTETOURTE (98-33), b. 1367/8, d. 13 Aug. 1420; m. (1) as his 2ⁿᵈ wife, **SIR BALDWIN III FREVILLE** (230A-33), b. 1350/1, of Tamworth Castle, co. Warwick, d. 30 Dec. 1387; m. (2) 1389, Sir Adam de Peshale of Weston under Lizard, co. Staffs, d.s.p.m. 1420. (*CP* V: chart 332, 357 note *a*; *Gen Mag.* 21 (1984): 187-188, 252).

33. SIR BALDWIN IV FREVILLE (230A-34) of Tamworth Castle, b. Woebley Castle, co. Worcester 1368, d. 1401; m. (1) Joan Greene, d.s.p., dau. Sir Thomas Greene; m. (2) Maud, d. 1397. (*Gen Mag.* 21 (1984): 187-188).

34. ELIZABETH FREVILLE, b. abt. 1393/4, ae. 24 in 1418; m. **THOMAS FERRERS, ESQ.,** (11-35), of Groby, d. 6 Jan. 1458/9. (*CP* V: chart 332, 357 note *a*; *Gen Mag.* 21 (1984): 189).

Line 216A

29. JOHN DE BOTETOURTE (216-29), 1ˢᵗ Lord Botetourte; m. **MAUD FITZ THOMAS** (122A-31). (*CP* II: 233-235).

30. SIR OTTO (or **OTES) DE BOTETOURTE**, yngr. s., of Mendlesham, Suffolk, and Hamerton, co. Huntingdon, d. 1345; m. Sibyl. (*VCH Hunts.* III: 67; Cal. Pat. Rolls, 1324-1327, p. 207).

31. SIR JOHN DE BOTETOURTE, b. abt. 1333, of Mendlesham, Suffolk, and Hamerton, co. Huntingdon, d. 1377; m. Katherine Weyland, liv. 1377, dau. of Sir Robert Weyland, liv. 1330, of Charsfield, Suffolk, by wife Cecily, dau. Thomas de Baldock. (*VCH Hunts.* III: 67).

32. JOAN DE BOTETOURTE, liv. 1428, h. of Mendlesham, Suffolk, and Hamerton, co. Huntingdon; m. **SIR JOHN KNYVET** (188-9), b. abt. 1358, d. 1418. (*VCH Hunts.* III: 67).

Line 217   Revised for 8ᵗʰ Edition. Correction submitted by Todd A. Farmerie

32. SIR WILLIAM LE PROUZ, KNT. (52-32), of Gidley Castle, co. Devon, d. 1270; m. (2) Alice de Ferrers, dau. of Sir Fulk Fitz Gilbert de Ferrers. (Crispin, *Falaise Roll*, Table IX; Vivian, *Visit. of Devon*, p. 626; W.H. Hamilton Rogers, *Antient Sepulchral Effigies and*

Monumental and Memorial Sculptures of Devon, Exeter (1876), pp. 34, 41, 198-189, 279; and references at (52-32)).

33. SIR RICHARD PROUZ, of Ashton (Ashreston), 2nd son, b. abt. 1250, d. by 1303; m. Margaret Helion, dau. of William de Helion, of Credy Helion.. (Rogers, 29, 34, 199; Vivian, 199, 597, 626).

34. RICHARD PROUZ, 2nd son (succ. his bro. William Prouz, at Ashton) fl. 1340; m. Margaret.

35. THOMASINE PROUZ; m. (1) abt. 1320, Sir John Chudleigh, Knt., son of John Chudleigh. (*Trans. Devonshire Assoc.* 72: 179-183, corrects Vivian).

36. JOHN CHUDLEIGH, of Broadclyst; m. **JANE BEAUCHAMP** (246B-32), dau. of Sir John Beauchamp of Ryme, by Alice, dau. of Sir Roger Nonant, Lord of Broadclyst. (Vivian, 199, 597, 626).

37. SIR JAMES CHUDLEIGH, KNT., b. bet. 1337-1340 (of age in 1361), 1358 held Ashton as a minor; d. 1401 or later; m. as her 1st husb. Joan Champernoun, d. aft. 1433, dau. of Sir Alexander Champernoun and Joan Ferrers dau. of Martin Ferrers. She m. (2) by 1403/4, **SIR JOHN COURTENAY** (51-34) said to have d. by 29 July 1406. (Collins VI: (1812): 260; *Devon and Cornwall N & Q* XII: 340-342, XVIII: 225).

Line 217A   New to 8th Edition

38. THOMAS GERARD, (233B-39); m. **MARGARET** (or **MARGERY**) **TRAFFORD** (233A-39)

39. THOMAS GERARD, Knt., b. abt. 1512, of Kingsley, co. Chester and Bryn, co. Lanc.; m. Jane Legh, dau. of Sir Peter Legh, of Haydock, co. Lincs., and Lyme, co. Chester, by 1st wife, Margaret Tyldesley, dau. of Nicholas Tyldesley. (Joseph Foster, *Ped. co. Fam. of England. Vol. 1: Lancashire* (1873), "Legh, of Lyme Hall").

40. CATHERINE GERARD; m. William Torbock (Tarbock) Esq., b. abt. 1526, d.s.p.m. sh. bef. 1558. (Gens. 38-40: Joseph Foster, *Ped. co. Fam. of England. Vol. 1: Lancashire* (1873), "Gerard, of Bryn").

41. MARGARET TORBOCK, d. aft. 1587; m. Oliver Mainwaring, liv. 1587, d. bef. 1634.

42. OLIVER MAINWARING, Gent., d. 14 Mar. 1672; m. 1618, Prudence Esshe (Eshe, Ashe), bapt. Sowton, 23 Dec. 1599, dau. of Henry Esshe, by wife Loveday Moyle, dau. of Richard Moyle, of St. Austle, co. Cornwall. (Sowton Parish Registers; Vivian 25; *NEHGR* 79: 110-111; *Visit. Cornwall* (1530, 1573, 1620); *Visit. Devon* (1620): 14).

43. OLIVER MAINWARING, of Salem, Mass. and New London, Conn., mariner, bapt. Dawlish, co. Devon, 16 Mar. 1633/4, d. New London, Conn., 3 Nov. 1723, age 89; m. Hannah Raymond, b. Salem, Mass. 12 Feb. 1643, d. New London, Conn. 18 Dec. 1717. (*Hempstead's Diary*; *NEHGR* 79: 110-111).

Line 218

27.　**RICHARD FITZ ROY** (26-27), Lord of Chilham, nat. son of King **JOHN** "Lackland" (1-25) by a dau. of **HAMELIN PLANTAGENET** (123-26); m. Rohese (Rose) de Douvres, d. 1264/5, dau. of Foubert de Douvres, d. abt. 1204, and Isabel Briwere, dau. of William de Briwere. (*CP* I: 305, II: 127, VIII: 518, XIV: 468, 46, 87; *Gen.* (n.s.) 22: 105-110, cf. 109; *NEHGR* 105 (1951): 36-42, esp. p. 40).

28.　**LORETTE (LORI) DE DOUVRES**, m. 1248, Sir William Marmion, received Budington and Northampton in right of his wife, d. by 1276, son of Robert Marmion, the younger, d. 1241/2, and Avice de Tanfield, liv. 1284, dau. of Gernegan de Tanfield. (*CP* VIII: 509, 510 note *a*, 514-518, XIV: 46, 87, 468).

29.　**SIR JOHN MARMION**, Lord Marmion, M.P. 1313-1322, d. bef. 7 May 1322; m. Isabel. (*CP* VIII: 518-520).

30.　**JOHN MARMION**, b. abt. 1292, Lord Marmion, M.P. 1326, d. 30 Apr. 1335; m. **MAUD DE FURNIVAL** (148A-32), liv. 1348. (*CP* V: 581-582, VIII: 520-521).

31.　**JOAN MARMION**, d. 1362; m. Sir John Bernake, b. 1309, d. 1349, of Tattershall, co. Lincoln, son of Sir William Bernake and Alice Driby, dau. of Robert Driby by Joan Tateshal, sis. of Robert de Tateshal (Tateshale) of Tattershall. (*CP* VIII: 521 note *j*, 522).

32.　**MAUD BERNAKE**, d. 10 Apr. 1419; m. bef. 20 June 1366, **SIR RALPH CROMWELL** (210-35), 1st Lord Cromwell.

33.　**ELIZABETH CROMWELL**, d. 1393/4; m. (1) John Clifton, b. abt. 1353, 1st Lord Clifton, of Buckenham Castle, co. Norfolk, d. Rhodes, 10 Aug. 1388, son of Constantine Clifton, d. by 1372, of Buckenham, co. Norfolk, by wife Catherine de la Pole, dau. of Sir William de la Pole, Mayor of Hull, baron of the Exchequer, d. 1366; m. (2) Sir Edward Bensted. (*CP* III: 307-308).

34.　**CONSTANTINE CLIFTON**, by (1), b. 1372, 2nd Lord Clifton, of Buckenham Castle, co. Norfolk, d. 1395; m. aft. Feb. 1389/90, Margaret Howard, d. 1433, dau. of Sir John Howard, d. 1438, of Wigenhall, Norfolk, by (1) wife Margaret Plaiz, d. 1391, dau. Sir John Plaiz, 5th Lord Plaiz, d. 1389. (*CP* III: 308, X: 541-542).

35.　**ELIZABETH CLIFTON**, liv. 1447, h. of Buckenham, co. Norfolk; m. **SIR JOHN KNYVET** (188-10), d. 1445. (*CP* IV: 308). (Gens. 33-35 added by Douglas Richardson).

Line 219

30.　**JOHN MARMION** (218-30); m. **MAUD DE FURNIVAL** (148A-32).

31.　**AVICE MARMION**; m. as (2) wife, **SIR JOHN DE GREY** (30-31), 1st Lord Grey of Rotherfield. (*CP* VI: 145-147, VIII: 521, note *j*, 522). Their dau. **MAUD DE GREY** (30-32), m. (1) John de Botetourte; m. (2) **SIR THOMAS DE HARCOURT, KNT.** (50-35).

32.　**SIR ROBERT DE GREY**, Lord of Wilcote, Co. Oxford, d.s.p.m. bef. 30 Nov. 1367; m. Lora de St. Quintin, yr. dau. & coh. of Sir Herbert de St. Quintin, d. 1347, Lord of Stanton St. Quintin, co. Wilts, and Frome St. Quintin, Dorset. (*CP* V: 421-425, VI: 147, VIII: 522 XI: 368, esp. notes *a* and *e*).

33.　**ELIZABETH DE GREY**, d. Dec. 1427; m. Henry (Fitz Hugh), Lord Fitz Hugh, K.G., b. abt. 1358, d. Ravensworth, 11 Jan. 1424/5, age 60, son of Henry Fitz Hugh by Joan Lescrope, dau. of Sir Henry Lescrope of Masham. (*CP* V: 420-425, VI: 147 note *a*, VIII: 522).

34.　**WILLIAM FITZ HUGH, KNT.** (3rd but 1st surv. son), Lord Fitz Hugh, b. abt. 1399, d. 22 Oct. 1452, M.P. 1429-1450; m. bef. 18 Nov. 1406, Margery de Willoughby, d. bef.

1452, dau. of William de Willoughby, Lord Willoughby of Eresby, co. Linc., by Lucy le Strange, dau. of Sir Roger le Strange of Knokyn, co. Salop. (*CP* V: 426-427).

35. HENRY FITZ HUGH, age 23+ in 1452, d. 8 June 1472, Lord Fitz Hugh; m. **ALICE DE NEVILLE** (78-36), liv. 1503.

Line 220

41. CAPTAIN JEREMY CLARKE (11-41); m. Frances (Latham) Dungan, b. 1609/10, d. 1677, wid. of Thomas Dungan, dau. of Lewis Latham.

42. MARY CLARKE, b. abt. 1641, d. 7 Apr. 1711; m. (1) 3 June 1658, Governor John Cranston (son of Rev. James Cranstoun, A.M., of St. Saviour's, Southwark, London; chaplain to King Charles I), b. 1626, came to N.E. with Captain Jeremy Clarke, his future father-in-law in 1638, age 12 yrs., Deputy-Gov. of Rhode Island 1672-1678, Gov. of Rhode Island 1678-1680, d. Newport, Rhode Island, 12 Mar. 1680. Mary Clarke m. (2) Philip Jones, of New York; m. (3): John Stanton of Newport, Rhode Island. (See *MC* Line 41 for the ancestry of Governor John Cranston).

43. GOVERNOR SAMUEL CRANSTON, b. Newport, Rhode Island, Aug. 1658, Gov. of Rhode Island 1698-1717; m. 1680, Mary Hart, a granddau. of Rev. Roger Williams of Rhode Island. (Gens. 41-43: *NEHGR* 79: 57-66).

Line 221

36. JOHN VI SUTTON, K.G. (81-36), b. 1400, d. 1487, Lord Dudley, m. aft. 1422, Elizabeth Berkeley.

37. ELEANOR SUTTON, m. **SIR HENRY BEAUMONT, KNT.**, (17-35), of Wednesbury, d. 16 Nov. 1471, sheriff of Staffordshire.

Line 222   Revised for 8th Edition

25. HENRY I (121-25), had the following child by an unknown mistress. (*CP* XI: Append. D, 109-110 note; Sanders, 20; Keats-Rohan, Domesday Desc. II: 743, citing Pipe Roll 31 Henry I, 79-gl; http://burkes-peerage.net, "Sudeley" Lineage of Tracy).

26. WILLIAM DE TRACY, (natural son)., d. abt. 1136; m. NN.

27. GRACE DE TRACY, (prob. dau.); m. by 1130, **JOHN DE SUDELEY** (235-23), d. bef. 1166. (*ES* III.2/354; Atkins, *Gloucestershire*, p. 369; *VCH Warwick* V: 70; *Hist. Mon. St. Peter, Glouc.*, ii: 180; Sanders, 85-86).

28. RALPH DE SUDELEY, of age 1135, d. 1192, held 3 knight's fees 1166 (bro. of William de Tracy of Toddington, ancestor of the Viscounts Tracy); m. Emma de Beauchamp, dau. of William I de Beauchamp, d. 1170, of Elmley, co. Worcester, by his wife, Bertha de Braose, dau. of William de Braose, d. abt. 1192/3, Baron of Gwentland, of Bramber, Sussex, by his wife, **BERTHA OF HEREFORD** (177-5). (*CP* XII (1): 413; Burke's *Peerage and Baronetage* (1967): 2413. Authorities as before; Emma Mason, ed., *The Beauchamp Cartulary Charters 1100-1268*, pub. 1980 as *Publ. Pipe Roll Soc.*, (n.s.), vol. 43, chart *p.* lviii).

29. RALPH DE SUDELEY, accounted for £100 in 1201 for having his father's lands, d. 1221/2; m. Isabel, living 1241/2, presumably dau. of Maud de Stafford of Theddlethorpe, co. Lincoln. (*Ibid*; Farrer, 2:116; Gens. 25-29: *CP* XII (1): 413-414).

30. RALPH DE SUDELEY, of Great Dassent, later Burton Dassent, d. on or bef. 19 Mar. 1241/2; m. Imenia, living 1247. (*CP* VII (1): 414-415; *VCH Warwick* V 70; Atkins 369).

31. BARTHOLOMEW DE SUDELEY, KNT., of Great Dassett and Chilvers Coton, co. Warwick, and Sudeley, co. Gloucester, 1269, Sheriff of Hereford 1272, M.P. 1278, Gov. of the Castle of Hereford, temp. Henry III, d. abt. 29 June 1280; m. Joan, liv. 1298. (*CP* XII (1): 415).

32. JOHN DE SUDELEY, 1st Lord Sudeley, M.P. 1299-1321, b. abt. 1257, d. on or bef. 1336, of Great Dassett, co. Warwick, and Sudeley, co. Gloucester, was a soldier, temp. Edward I, Lord Chamberlain, served in the French and Scottish wars; m. NN. (*CP* XII (1): 416).

33. BARTHOLOMEW DE SUDELEY, d.v.p. 1327; m. Maud de Montfort, sis. of Piers de Montfort, 3rd Lord Montfort. (*CP* XII (1): 416-417, XIV: 600).

34. JOHN DE SUDELEY, 2nd Lord Sudeley, b. abt. 1304/5, d. 1340; m. Eleanor (or Isabelle), d. 1361, perh. dau. of Robert de Scales, 2nd Lord Scales, b. abt. 1279, d. 20 Mar. 1324/5, M.P. 1306-1321/22, (son of Robert de Scales, M.P., and Isabel de Burnell), who m. Edeline de Courtenay, d. abt. 1 Oct. 1335, dau. of **SIR HUGH DE COURTENAY** (50-30) and Eleanor Le Despenser. (*CP* XI: 499-501; *VCH Warwick* V: 70; Atkins, 369).

35. JOAN DE SUDELEY, (coh. of bro. John de Sudeley, b. abt. 1337/8, d.s.p. 11 Aug. 1367); m. as (2) wife, abt. 1354, William le Botiller (Butler) (see 77-32), 2nd Lord Botiller of Wem, by whom mother of Thomas le Botiller, 4th Lord Sudeley. (*CP* XII (1): 417-419; Gens. 30-35: *The Gen. Mag.* 13: 173-174; *Wm. Salt Soc.*(n.s.) v. (1945-6): 41-42).

Line 223   Revised for 8th Edition

33. ELIZABETH DE SEGRAVE (16-31), b. 25 Oct. 1338, d. by 1368; m. abt. 1349, John de Mowbray, 4th Lord Mowbray, b. 1340, d. 1368. (*CP* IX: 383-384).

34. JOAN DE MOWBRAY; m. Sir Thomas Grey of Wark. (*NEHGR* 104: chart bet. pp. 270 and 271, as corrected by vol. 105, p. 155, which also corrects *CP*, Clay, and other established references).

35. MAUD GREY, liv. 22 Aug. 1451; m. abt. 21 May 1399, Sir Robert Ogle, Knt., b. 1379/83, d. 12 Aug. 1436, warden of Roxborough Castle. (*CP* VI: 488, X: 28-29; Clay, *op. cit.*)

36. ANNE OGLE; m. (1) Sir William Heron, Knt., b. abt. 8 Nov. 1400, d.s.p.m. 1 Sept. 1425, son of William Heron, by Isabel Scott, dau. of Richard Scott; m. perh. (2) Sir John Middleton (Mydelton). (*CP* VI: 487-488; Clay, 152-153 as corrected by Surtees; see *Surtees Soc. Pub.* 45: 321).

37. ELIZABETH HERON, b. 1422; m. her cousin, under dispensation, 11 July 1438, Sir John Heron, Knt., b. 1415/18, Sheriff of Northumberland 1440/1, 1451/2, 1456/7, slain at the battle of Towton, 29 Mar. 1461, son of William Heron, b. 1395/6, d. 1427/8, by Isabel Scott, dau. of Richard Scott. [William Heron being the son of John Heron, d. 1408, being the son or grandson of Sir William Heron I, d. 1379]. (*CP* VI: 488-489; v.Redlich 212; *Harl. Soc. Pub.* 52: 946; Foster, *op. cit.* III: 860-861, gives her line back to King Edward I).

(Gens. 36-37 corrected by: http://www.medievalgenealogy.org.uk; *Foundations* (2003) 1 (2): 132-135, Tony Ingham, Chris Phillips and Rosie Bevan, "Additions and Corrections to the *Complete Peerage*, The Herons of Ford and Thornton.")

38. ELIZABETH HERON; m. bef. 1467, **SIR ROBERT TAILBOYS, KNT.** (224-37), Lord Kyme, M.P. 1472-1478, d. 30 Jan. 1494/5; ancestors of President George Washington. (*CP* VII: 356, 361; *Harl. Soc. Pub.* 52: 946; v.Redlich, 212).

39. MAUD TAILBOYS, m. by 1546, Sir Robert Tyrwhit, Knt., of Kettleby, co. Linc. b. 1482, knighted at Touraine 1513, High Sheriff of Lincolnshire, d. 4 July 1548; son of William Tyrwhit by Ann Constable, grandau. of **ROGER WENTWORTH** (200-36). Robert Tyrwhit was a descendant of **MARGARET DE CLARE** (54-32). (*CP* VII: 361 note *h*; *Harl. Soc. Pub.* 52: 1019).

40. KATHARINE TYRWHIT; m., as 2nd wife, Sir Richard Thimbleby of Irnham, Lord of the manor of East Bridgeford, co. Nottingham, d. 28 Sept. 1558/9, son of John Thimbleby, Knt., and Margaret Boys, dau. of John Boys.

41. ELIZABETH THIMBLEBY, m. (1) John St. Paul, of Nettleby; m. (2) 20 July 1560, Thomas Welby of Moulton, d. Bath 1570. (*Harl. Soc. Pub.* reverses the correct order of these marriages).

42. RICHARD WELBY, of Moulton, co. Linc., 2nd son, bapt. 1564; m. abt. 1595, **FRANCES BULKELEY** (31B-40).

43. OLIVE WELBY (31B-41), b. abt. 1604, d. 1 Mar. 1691/2; m. Boston, co. Linc., 16 Apr. 1629, Dea. Henry Farwell, d. Concord, Mass., 1 Aug. 1670.

Line 224

28. ROGER DE QUINCY (53-28), Earl of Winchester, Constable of Scotland; m. **HELEN OF GALLOWAY** (38-27). (Gen. 28-37: v.Redlich 211-212).

29. ELIZABETH DE QUINCY; m. **ALEXANDER COMYN** (114A-27), 6th Earl of Buchan, Constable of Scotland, Justiciar, d. 1290, son of **WILLIAM COMYN** (121A-26), d. 1233, and Margaret, Countess of Buchan, (*CP* I: 148, II: 374-275).

30. ELIZABETH COMYN, d. bef. 17 Feb. 1328/9; m. Gilbert d'Umfreville, Earl of Angus, b. 1244, d. sh. bef. 13 Oct. 1307, son of Gilbert d'Umfreville and Maud (Matilda), dau. of Malcolm, d. by 1242, Earl of Angus. (*CP* I: 147-148).

31. ROBERT D'UMFREVILLE, 3rd Earl of Angus, Lord Umfreville, d. 30 Mar. 1325; m. (1) 1303, Lucy de Kyme, dau. of Philip, 1st Lord Kyme, of Kyme, co. Linc., M.P. 1295, d. bef 2 Apr. 1323, and his wife, Joan Bigod, dau. of **SIR HUGH BIGOD** (69-29), Chief Justice of England. (*CP* I: 148-150, VII: 357; *SP* I: 168).

32. ELIZABETH D'UMFREVILLE; m. Gilbert de Boroughdon (or Burrodon, Burdon), lord of Boroughdon, sheriff of Northumberland 1323-1324,1339-1341. (*CP* VII: 358).

33. ELEANOR DE BOROUGHDON, b. abt. 1340, Baroness Kyme, liv. 1381; m. bef. 1352 Henry Tailboys (or Talboys), b. abt. 1335, d. 23 Feb. 1368/9, son of William Tailboys (or Talboys). (*CP* I: 151 note *a*, VII: 358).

34. SIR WALTER TAILBOYS (or **TALBOYS**), *de jure* Lord Kyme, sheriff of Lincolnshire 1389, b. abt. 1351, d. 20 or 21 Sept. 1417; m. Margaret. (*CP* VII: 358).

35. WALTER TAILBOYS (or **TALBOYS**), sheriff of Lincolnshire 1423, J.P. 1442-1443, *de jure* Lord Kyme, b. 1391, d. 13 Apr. 1444; m. (1) NN; m. (2) Alice Stafford, heiress of the Stafford Earls of Devon, d. by 24 Apr. 1448, wid. of Sir Edmund (not Henry) Cheyney, Knt., and dau. of Sir Humphrey Stafford. (*CP* VII: 358-359, XIV: 420).

36. SIR WILLIAM TAILBOYS (or **TALBOYS**), **KNT.**, by (1) (received none of the inheritance of Alice Stafford), *de jure* Lord Kyme, knighted 19 Feb. 1460/1, b. abt. 1415, d. abt. 26 May 1464; m. **ELIZABETH BONVILLE** (261A-39), d. 14 Feb. 1490/1, dau. of **SIR WILLIAM BONVILLE** (261A-38), by 1st wife, **MARGARET GREY** (93A-33). (*CP* VII: 359-361).

37. SIR ROBERT TAILBOYS (or **TALBOYS**), **KNT.**, b. 1451, *de jure* Lord Kyme, M.P. 1472, 1477-1478, sheriff of Lincolnshire 1480, d. 30 Jan. 1494/5; m. Elizabeth Heron (223-38), dau. of John Heron. (*CP* VII: 361).

Line 224A

34. SIR WALTER TAILBOYS (or **TALBOYS**) (224-34), b. abt. 1357, d. 20 or 21 Sept. 1417, M.P. 1382 & 1386, sheriff of Lincolnshire 1389; m. Margaret. (*NEHGR* 145 (1991): 266 and refs there cited.).

35. SIR JOHN TALBOYS, of Stallingborough, sheriff of Lincolnshire 1426, d. 16 Apr. 1467; m. Agnes Cokefield, dau. & h. of Sir Roger Cokefield of Nuthall, co. Nottingham, and Cecily Charnells, dau. & h. Robert Charnells. (*CP* VII: 358 note *j*; *NEHGR*, *cit* and cited refs.).

36. JOHN TALBOYS, ESQ., "the Younger," of Stallingborough ("sometimes called Walter"), d.v.p. bef. Apr. 1467; m. Katharine Gibthorpe, dau. of Sir William Gibthorpe. (*NEHGR*, *cit.*).

37. MARGARET TALBOYS, dau. & h., b. abt. 1446 (age abt. 21 in 1467), d. bef. July 1491; m. John Ayscough, d. 20 July 1491, s. & h. of Sir William Ayscough, Knt., Chief Justice of Common Pleas, d. 1456, by Elizabeth Claythorpe. (*NEHGR*, *cit.*).

38. ELIZABETH (called **MARGARET** in Lincs. Peds.) **AYSCOUGH**, b. prob. abt. 1465; m. William Booth, d. 20 Oct. 1509, son of Henry Booth of Middle Soyle, Killingholme, co. Lincoln, and Elizabeth Gascaryk, dau. & h. William Gascaryk. (*NEHGR*, *cit.*).

39. JOHN BOOTH, b. 1487/8 (age 22+ on 30 Sept. 1510), d. by 22 or 23 May 1537; m. **ANNE THIMBLEBY** (74A-39), liv. 1537, dau. of Richard Thimbleby, Esq., and Elizabeth Hilton. (*NEHGR*, *cit.*, 266-267).

40. ELIZABETH (or **ELEANOR**) **BOOTH**, b. prob. Killingholme, co. Lincoln, abt. 1510, d. 13 July 1547, bur. Brocklesby, co. Lincoln; m. prob. Brocklesby abt. 1531 Edward Hamby, b. 1512/3, d. Brocklesby 29 June 1559, son of George Hamby (whether by (1) wife Margaret Green, or (2) wife Margaret Cutleer uncertain). (*NEHGR*, *cit.*, 104-107, 267).

41. REV. WILLIAM HAMBY of Dallinghoo & Little Glenham, co. Suffolk, b. Brocklesby, co. Lincoln, 31 Oct 1543, B.A. 1564/5, M.A. 1568, St. Johns College, Cambridge, rector of Brocklesby, co. Lincoln, chaplain to Thomas Sackville, Lord Buckhurst, 1st Earl of Dorset, d. Dallinghoo, Suffolk 22/27 Jan. 1613; m. abt. 1572, as 2nd husb., Margaret Blewett, liv. Jan. 1613 (a widow of NN by whom a she had dau. Grace), dau. of Edmond Blewett. (*NEHGR*, *cit.* 113-116).

42. ROBERT HAMBY, bapt. Dallinghoo, co. Suffolk, 5 July 1573, claimed land in 5 parishes in Suffolk, steward of Charles Veysey, gent., for manor of Toppesfield Hall, Hadleigh, co. Suffolk, d. Ipswich, co. Suffolk, bet. 7 June and 6 Aug. 1635; m. (perh. (2)) by 1613 when named in will of William Hamby) Elizabeth Arnold, d. aft. 1635, dau. of John Arnold & h. to her bro. John Arnold. (*NEHGR*, *cit.* 117-121).

43. KATHERINE HAMBY, b. bef. 19 Oct. 1615, bapt. psh. of St. Matthew's Ipswich, 10 Dec. 1615, d. bet. 10 June 1649 (b. of last child) and 1651, prob. Boston or Mt. Wollaston, Mass.; m. (lic. 19 Oct. 1636) Lawford parish., Edward Hutchinson, bapt. Alford, co. Linc., 28 May 1613, d. New England. 19 Aug. 1675, killed by Indians in King Philip's War, bur. Springhill cemetery, Marlborough, Mass., son of William Hutchinson and **ANNE MARBURY** (14-41). Edward adm. First Ch. Boston 5 Oct. 1634. Katherine adm. 3 Feb. 1638/39. To Mass. 4 Sept. 1633 w. John Cotton, on the Griffin. After Katherine's death, Edward m. (2) Abigail Firmage (Vermais?), d. 10 Aug. 1689, (wid. of

Robert Button, by whom 4 chn), dau. of Alice (Blessing) Firmage. His will 17 July 1675, pr. 17 Sept. 1675. (*NEHGR, cit.* 120, 258-265; Savage II: 509-510).

Line 225   Revised for 8th Edition

32. PHILIPPA, Countess of Ulster (5-32), granddau. of King **EDWARD III** (1-29); m. 1368, **EDMUND DE MORTIMER** (29-34), 3rd Earl of March. (*DNB*).

33. ROGER DE MORTIMER, 4th Earl of March, Earl of Ulster, Lord Mortimer, b. 11 Apr. 1374, d. 20 July 1398; m. abt. 1388, Eleanor de Holand, d. Oct. 1405, dau. of **THOMAS DE HOLAND** (47-32), Earl of Kent. (*CP* II: 494, VII 156 note e).

34. ANNE DE MORTIMER, d. Sept. 1411, m., as 1st wife, Richard, of Conisburgh, b. 1375, Earl of Cambridge, executed 5 Aug. 1415, (son of Edmund of Langley, b. 1341, 1st Duke of York, Earl of Cambridge, K.G., d. 1402 [5th son of **EDWARD III** (1-29) and **PHILIPPA** (103-34)] by Isabella of Castile, b. 1355, d. 1392, dau. & coh. of Pedro I, "The Cruel," King of Castile & Leon (see at 1-30), d.s.p.m. 1369). Anne m. (2) 1399, Sir Edward Charleton, Lord of Powys. (v. Redlich 208; *DNB; The Augustan,* No. 80, 1977, p 123; *CP* II: 494; Burke's *P. & B.* 1967 "Kings of England"; Burke's *Guide to the Royal Family,* 1972; *ES* II/64).

35. RICHARD (Plantagenet), 3rd Duke of York, b. 21 Sept. 1411, d. 30 Dec. 1460; m. 1424, Cecily de Neville, dau. of **RALPH DE NEVILLE, K.G,** (207-34), 1st Earl of Westmorland. They were parents of Kings Edward IV and Richard III. (*CP* II: 495; Burke's *P. & B.* 1967; Blore, *Monumental Remains,* section 21, pp. 1-5; *DNB*). [Note: See full cit. at *CP* I: 183, note c: "It is much to be wished that the surname "Plantagenet," which, since the time of Charles II, has been freely given to all descendants of Geoffrey of Anjou, had some historical basis which would justify its use, for it forms a most convenient method of referring to the Edwardian kings and their numerous descendants.The fact is, however, ..., that the name, although a personal emblem of the aforesaid Geoffrey, was never borne by any of his descendants before Richard Plantagenet, Duke of York (father of Edward IV), who assumed it apparently about 1448."]).

36. SIR GEORGE, K.G., Duke of Clarence, b. 21 Oct. 1449, d. 18 Feb. 1477; m. 11 July 1469, Isabel Neville, d. 1476, dau. of Sir Richard Neville (see 78-36), Earl of Salisbury and Warwick, "the King Maker," b. 22 Nov. 1428, d. 14 Apr. 1471, by wife Anne Beauchamp, dau. of Richard Beauchamp, Duke of Warwick. (*CP* VI: 656 note e, XI: 398-399; Blore, *op. cit* 21, pp. 1-5; *DNB*).

37. MARGARET (PLANTAGENET), Countess of Salisbury, b. 14 Aug. 1473, executed 28 May 1541; m. prob. Nov. 1487, Sir Richard de la Pole, K.G., d. Nov. 1504, son of Geoffrey de la Pole, of Medmenham and Ellesborough, co. Buckingham, by 1st wife, Edith St. John, dau. of Sir Oliver St. John, by **MARGARET DE BEAUCHAMP** (85-35), sister and h. of Sir John de Beauchamp of Bletsoe. (*CP* II: 399-401, XIV: 567; Burke's *P. & B.* (1967)).

38. SIR HENRY POLE, Lord Montagu (bro. of Reginald, Cardinal Pole); m. bef. May 1520, Jane Neville, b. 1492, d. 1538/9, dau. of George Neville, Lord Abergavenny, by Margaret Fenne, dau. of Hugh Fenne. (*CP* V: 656 note e, IX: 94-97; Blore *op. cit* 21, 1-5).

39. KATHERINE POLE, d. 23 Sept. 1576; m. 15 June 1532, Sir Francis Hastings, K.G., 2nd Earl of Huntingdon, b. abt. 1514, d. 23 June 1560, son of George Hastings, 1st Earl of Huntingdon, by Anne Stafford, wid. of Sir Walter Herbert, and dau. of Henry Stafford, 2nd Duke of Buckingham and Catherine Woodville (Wydvill), b. abt. 1457, dau. of Richard Wydvill (Woodville), 1st Earl Rivers and **JACQUETTA OF LUXEMBOURG** (234B-33). (*CP* VI: 655-656, VII: 694, IX: 96 note f).

40. CATHERINE HASTINGS, b. 11 Aug. 1542; m. Sir Henry Clinton (otherwise Fiennes), b. 1540, K.B.1553, 2nd Earl of Lincoln, 10th Lord Clinton, d. 29 Sept. 1616, son of Sir Edward de Clinton (or Fiennes), Lord of Clinton and Saye, Earl of Lincoln, Lord High Admiral 1550, by his 2nd wife; m. abt. 1541, Ursula Stourton, dau. of William, Baron Stourton, by Elizabeth Dudley, dau. of Edmund Dudley (Sutton), and sister of John, Duke of Northumberland. (*CP* III: 317, VII: 690-694; *I Proc. Mass. Hist. Soc.* II: 212; *CCN* 260).

41. THOMAS CLINTON (otherwise **FIENNES**), b. 1571, 3rd Earl of Lincoln, 11th Lord Clinton, d. 15 Jan. 1618/19; m. abt. 21 Sept. 1584, Elizabeth Knyvet, d. aft. 1619, dau. of Sir Henry Knyvet of Chariton, co. Wilts, & Elizabeth Stumpe, dau. & h. of Sir James Stumpe of Malmesbury, co. Wilts. (*CP* VII: 695-696; *Proc. Mass. Hist. Soc.* as before).

42. SUSAN FIENNES (or **CLINTON**), m., as 2nd wife, Maj.-Gen. John Humphrey, of Chaldon, Dorset, b. 1595, d. 1661, of Dorchester, England, Dep.-Gov. of Mass., came with his wife to New England, July 1634, founder of Lynn, memb. Artillery Co. 1640, held ranks to Gen., 1641, returned to Sandwich, England, 26 Oct. 1641 (see 228-40). (*CP* VII: 696 note c; *I Proc. Mass. Hist. Soc.* II: 212; *Am. Antiquarian Soc.*, Coll. 3: 1, lxxxvi; Farmer, 154; *TAG* 15: 123; Jones, *Thos. Dudley*, 46; Winthrop, *Journal* I: 15, 127; II: 83).

42. ARBELLA FIENNES (or **CLINTON**), (dau. of Gen. 41), d.s.p. Salem, Aug. 1630; m. Isaac Johnson, Esq., d. Boston, 30 Sept. 1630, son of Abraham Johnson of Chilsam, Rutlandshire, by his wife, a dau. of Dr. Chadderton, Master of Emmanuel College, Cambridge, and one of the translators of the King James version of the Bible. Governor Winthrop's flagship, the "Arbella," was named for Lady Arbella. (*CP* VII: 696 note c; Winthrop, *Journal* I: 15, 26, 52; Capt. Edward Johnson, *Wonder Working Providence*, 56, 65; *Am. Antiquarian Society, Collections* III: lxvii-lxviii, 87).

Line 226

23. EUDES I, Co-Regeant of Brittany (214-23), b. 999, d. 7 Jan. 1079; also Count of Penthièvre 1034. (*CP* X 779-780).

24. BARDOLF (nat. son), ancestor of the Lords Fitz Hugh of Ravensworth; brother of Bodin, who held Ravensworth, Mickleton, Romandkirk, etc., in Domesday Book 1086. (*CP* V: 416-417 note d, 781 note b; *Yorkshire Archaeological Society Publications* iv, v, "Early York Charters," vol. V: 196-200, 316-321; *ES* II/75 NEU).

25. AKARIS FITZ BARDOLF of Ravensworth. (*CP* V 416-417, note d).

26. HERVEY FITZ AKARIS, d. 1182/4, of Ravensworth, forester of the New Forest and Arkengarthdale, co. York, by grant of Conan, Duke of Brittany. (*CP* V: 416).

27. HENRY FITZ HERVEY of Ravensworth, Cotherstone, Hinton, etc., Lord of Ravensworth, d. 1202; m. Alice, dau. of Ranulf Fitz Walter of Greystoke. (*CP* V: 416 note d; Keats-Rohan, *Domesday Desc.* II: 910).

28. RANULF FITZ HENRY, of Ravensworth, Hinton, etc., d. bef. 13 Jan. 1243; m. Alice de Staveley, dau. of Adam de Staveley. Clay, 73).

29. AGATHA OF RAVENSWORTH, m. **SIR MICHAEL III LE FLEMING** (34-27), b. 1197.

Line 227

24. STEPHEN I (214-24), Count of Brittany, d. 21 Apr. 1135 or 1136; m. Hawise (or Hedwig). (*CP* X: 786-787).

25. ALAN II, Earl of Richmond, d. 15 Sept. 1146; m. abt. 1137, **BERTHA OF BRITTANY** (119-26). (*CP* X: 780, 788-791).

Line 228

38. ANNE KNOLLYS (1-37); m. **THOMAS WEST** (18-38), Lord de la Warre.

39. ELIZABETH WEST, b. 11 Sept. 1573; m., as 2nd wife, Wherwell, co. Hants, 12 Feb. 1593/4, Herbert Pelham, Esq., b. abt. 1546, of Fordingham, Dorset, and Hellingly, Sussex (father, by 1st wife, of Herbert Pelham (1580-1624) who m. **PENELOPE WEST** (1-38).

40. ELIZABETH PELHAM, b. Hellingly, 27 Apr. 1604, d. 1 Nov. 1628; m. Salisbury, 4 Sept. 1621, Col. John Humphrey, gent., b. 1595, who m. (3) 1630/4, **SUSAN FIENNES** (225-42). (*NEHGR* 33: 288).

41. ANNE HUMPHREY, only surviving child, bapt. Fordingham, Dorset, 17 Dec. 1625; m. (1) William Palmes; m. (2) Rev. John Myles of Swansea, Mass. (Gens. 38-41: Meredith B. Colket, Jr. in *TAG* 15: 123-124).

42. REV. SAMUEL MYLES, A.M. (H.C. 1684), was Rector of King's Chapel, Boston 1689-1728. (Weis, *Colonial Clergy of New England*, 148).

Line 229   See Line 1, Gens. 39 and 40.

Line 230   Revised for 8th Edition. This line requires further research.

32. SIR JOHN DE ARDERNE, KNT., of Alford and Elford, etc., Knight of the Shire of Stafford 1324, held manors of Stockport, Poynton and Woodford, d. abt. 1349; m. (1) 1307/8, Alice de Venables, dau. of Hugh de Venables, Baron of Kinderton. (*Ibid* 474; Inq. p.m. 1349). Note: Adequate proof that he was the son of Sir John de Arderne, Knt. by Margery ferch Gryffud ap Madog (gen. 31 in earlier editions) is lacking. More research is needed.

33. PETER DE ARDERNE of Alvanley and of Harden, b. 1327, d. bef. 1378/9; m. Cicely Bredbury, dau. of Adam de Bredbury, and Cicely his wife. (Ibid, 474).

34. HUGH DE ARDERNE of Harden and Alvanley, fl. 1385, 1419, d. bef. 1423; m. (2) Cicely de Hyde, dau. of Ralph de Hyde, liv. 1378/9. (*Ibid*, 474. Note: The dates to this point are questionable. There may be a missing generation).   **35. ALICE ARDERNE**; m. abt. 1414/5, Christopher Davenport, Esq. of Woodford, b. abt. 1394, d. abt. 1488, son of Nicholas Davenport of Woodford, and his wife, Ellen, living 1371, wid. of Edward Massey. (*Ibid* I 474, II 411).

36. JOHN DAVENPORT of Woodford, living 1476, d. bef. his father, abt. 1480; m. Alice Prestwick, dau. of Ralph Prestwick. (*Ibid*).

37. NICHOLAS DAVENPORT, ESQ., of Woodford, succeeded his grandfather 1488, d. bef. 9 Feb. 1522; m. (1) abt. 1459/60, **MARGARET DAVENPORT** (231-36), dau. of John Davenport, Esq., of Bramhall. She prob. d.s.p. He m. (2) Margaret Savage, by whom issue. (*Ibid* I 436, II 411).

38. CHRISTOPHER DAVENPORT, of Lowcross in Malpas Parish, Cheshire, said to be founder of the branch of the Davenport family in Coventry; m. Emma Blunt, dau. of John Blunt of Stafford. (Earwaker, *East Chester*, I: 436, II: 411; Harleian Mss. 1535, 2094, 2119; *Visit. of the County of Warwick in the Year 1619* in *Harl. Soc, Pub.* XII (London, 1877), 373; Isabel MacB. Calder, *Letters of John Davenport Puritan Divine* (New Haven, 1937), pp. 1, 13-14, notes 4 and 5).

Line 230A   Revised for 8th Edition

33. SIR BALDWIN III FREVILLE, of Tamworth Castle, b. 1350/1, d. 30 Dec. 1387, (son of Sir Baldwin II Freville, b. 1317, d. 1375 and 1st wife, Ida Clinton, wid. of John le Strange, dau. of Sir John Clinton of Stafford Clinton); m. (2) **JOYCE DE BOTETOURTE** (98-33, 216-32), b. 1367/8, d. 13 Aug. 1420. (*Gen. Mag.* 21 (1984): 186-188).

34. SIR BALDWIN IV FREVILLE, of Tamworth Castle, b. Woebley Castle, co. Worcester 1368, d. 1401; m. (1) 1389, Joan Greene, d.s.p., dau. Sir Thomas Greene; m. (2) Maud, surname unkn, d. 1397. (*Gen Mag.* 21 (1984): 187-188).

35. MARGARET FREVILLE, b. 1400/1 (aged 17 in 1418 at death of bro., Sir Baldwin V Freville); m. (1) Sir Hugh Willoughby, Knt., of Middleton, Co. Warwick; m. (2) Sir Richard Bingham, Knt. (Dugdale, *Antiquities of Warwickshire.*, Willoughby ped. in *Visit. of Nottinghamshire* (1569 and 1614), pub. by *Harl. Soc.*; *Gen. Mag.* 21 (1984): 188-189).

36. ELEANOR WILLOUGHBY; m. John Shirley, b. abt. 1426, d. 18 May 1485, of Lower Ettingdon, co. Warwick, and Shirley, co. Derby, son of Ralph Shirley, d. 1466. (*Stemmata Shirleiana* (London, 1873) 53f.; *TAG* 23: 109; *VCH Warwick* 5: 78-79).

37. HUGH SHIRLEY, 4th son, b. say 1467; m. Anne Hevyn, (d. seized of Clyberry 17 Sep 1510), dau. & coh. John Hevyn of Hevyn, psh. of Dilwyn, co. Hereford, and of Clyberry, co. Salop. (*Stemmata Shirleiana* 54 and Table II; *Visit. of Shropshire* (1623) (*Harl. Soc. Pub.*, v. 28: 83, 153).

38. THOMAS SHIRLEY, d.v.p.; m. Margaret Wroth, dau. John Wroth of Durance, psh. of Enfield, Middlesex. (*Stemmata Shirleiana* 54, Table II misidentifies him as "John" Shirley).

39. JOYCE SHIRLEY, only surv. dau. & h.; m. (1) Richard Abington (or Habington), of Brockhamton, co. Hereford; m. (2) Thomas Blount of Sodington, Co. Worcester, as 2nd wife. She had 3 daus., cohs. of father, by (1), and 2 sons by (2). (*Stemmata Shirleiana* 54, Table II, misidentifies 2nd husb. as "Richard," though "Thomas" in text; *Visit. of Worcs.* (1569) (*Harl. Soc. Pub.*, v. 27) 18, 22, 63; Nash, *Hist. of Worcs.* (2nd ed.), I: ped. facing p. 588).

40. MARY ABINGTON (or **HABINGTON**), d. 9 July 1574; m. by 1555, Richard Barnaby, Esq., bur. as widower 4 Dec. 1597, of Acton and the Hull, co. Worcester, son & h. of Thomas Barnaby of the Hull and Joyce Acton, dau. and h. of Walter Acton of Acton, co. Worcester. (Nash, *cit.* I: 115-118; *Visit. of Worcs.* (1569), *cit.* 14; Weaver, *Visit. of Hereford* (London 1884) 2; *TAG* 52: 216-217).

41. WINIFRED BARNABY, 3rd of 4 daus., b. 1569, bur. Holy Trinity, Coventry, co. Warwick, 12 Apr. 1597; m., as 1st wife, abt. 1585, Henry Davenport, b. say 1555, draper, alderman, Mayor of Coventry, bur. Holy Trinity, Coventry, co. Warwick., 29 May 1627, son of Edward Davenport, anc. unkn., Mayor of Coventry, 1551, by Margery Harford, dau. of John Harford, alderman of Coventry. (*Visit. of Warwick* (1619), *cit* 373; parish registers of Holy Trinity, Coventry, in Warwick Co. Record Office, Warwick; Calder I: 13-14). (This information supplied by Gary Boyd Roberts.)

Line 230B

35. ELEANOR WILLOUGHBY (230A-36); m. John Shirley, son of Ralph Shirley, by 1st wife, Margaret Staunton. (see *MC* 122A-10).

36. ROBERT SHIRLEY, 3rd son, b. abt. 1465, liv. 1513. (*Stemmata Shirleiana*, 53).

37. RALPH SHIRLEY, of Repton, co. Derby, b. abt. 1495, d. 15 Jan. 1535; m Amee Lolle, dau. & coh. of William Lolle of Ashby-de-la-Zouch, co. Leicester. (*Stemmata Shirleiana*, 53-54).

38. ELEANOR SHIRLEY, b. abt. 1525, bur. Snelston, co. Derby 28 Apr. 1595; m. (1) (settlement 5 May 1545) Thomas Vernon; m. (2) Nicholas Browne of Snelston, co. Derby, bur. 18 Jan. 1587, son of Thomas Browne and Margaret Chetham. (*Stemmata Shirleiana*, 54; *TAG* 22: 158).

39. SIR WILLIAM BROWNE, b. 1558, d. in the Low Countries Aug. 1610; m. Mary Savage. (*TAG* 22: 158).

40. PERCY BROWNE, b. abt. 1602; m. Anne Rich, dau. of Nicholas Rich, sheriff of London (illeg. son of Richard Rich, 1st Baron Rich, 1496-1568) and Ann Machell. (*TAG* 22: 27-29,158; 60: 91, a note by D.L. Greene identifying Ann Rich's forename).

41. NATHANIEL BROWNE, b. abt. 1625, of Hartford, Springfield and by 1651 Middletown, Conn., d. Middletown bef. 26 Aug. 1658; m. Hartford 23 Dec. 1647, Eleanor Watts, b. abt. 1627, d. Middletown 28 Sept. 1703, dau. of Richard & Elizabeth Watts of Hartford. (*TAG* 22: 159-163; D.L. Jacobus outlined this descent in *TAG* 23: 109).

Line 231

29. WILLIAM DE WARENNE (83-29); m. prob. June 1285, **JOAN DE VERE** (60-30). (*CP* XII (1): 507).

30. JOHN II DE WARENNE, 8th and last Earl of Surrey of this family, said to have been b. 30 June 1286, d.s.p.m. legit., 29 June 1347. (CP XII (1): 508-511 and note *k*, p. 511).

31. SIR EDWARD DE WARENNE, KNT., (said to be nat. son of John de Warenne, by Maud of Nerford), liv. 1347, d. bef. 1369; m. Cicely de Eton, dau. of Sir Nicholas de Eton, Knt., of Poynton and Stockport. (*CP, cit.*; Ormerod, *History of... Chester* III, 682; J.P. Earwaker, *East Chester*, II: 286-7, Warenne of Poynton). Note: The *Visit. of Cheshire*, 1580, p. 242, does not verify connection between Gens. 30 and 31.

32. SIR JOHN DE WARENNE, KNT., of Poynton and Stockport, b. abt. 1343, d. 1387 (Inq.p.m. 1392); m. 1371, Margaret Stafford, d. 6 Apr. 1418 (Inq.p.m. 1418), dau. of Sir John de Stafford, Knt., of Wickham.

33. NICHOLAS DE WARENNE, of Poynton and Stockport, b. 1378, d. 1413; m. Agnes Wynnington, liv. 1417, dau. of Sir Richard de Wynnington, Knt., of Wynnington, co. Chester.

34. SIR LAWRENCE DE WARENNE, KNT., of Poynton and Stockport, b. abt. 1394, d. 1444; m. Margaret Bulkeley, dau. of Richard Bulkeley. (*Visit. of Cheshire* (1580): 242)

35. CICELY DE WARENNE, m. abt. 4 Jan. 1435, John Davenport, Esq., bapt. Stockport, 3 May 1419, d. Oct. 1478 (Inq.p.m.), of Bramhall. (Earwaker, *cit.* I: 436, Davenport of Bramhall, II 411, Davenport of Woodford. Note: Cicely is not shown as dau. of Sir Lawrence in, *Visit. of Cheshire, cit.*).

36. MARGARET DAVENPORT, of Bramhall; m. abt. 1459/60, **NICHOLAS DAVENPORT, ESQ.** (230-37), of Woodford. (Earwaker, *cit.*, I: 436).

28. MAUD MARSHAL (69-28), d. 1248; m. (1) 1207/12, Hugh Bigod, Earl of Norfolk, Magna Charta Surety 1215, d. 1224/5. (*CP* IX: 589-590; Parkin IV: 306).

29. SIR SIMON BIGOD, 3rd son, living 1236, d. bef. 1242; m. Maud de Felbrigge, a wid. seen 1242 and 1275, only dau. and event. sole h. of Richard de Felbrigge, and granddau. of Roger de Felbrigge of Felbrigge, co. Norfolk, and his wife the dau. of Gilbert de Norfolk, Lord of Beeston. (Parkin IV: 305-307).

30. SIR ROGER BIGOD DE FELBRIGGE, liv. in 1275, 1286/7 and 1295; m. Cecilia, living 1295. (*Op. cit.*, IV: 306; *NEHGR* 108 (1954): 252).

31. SIR SIMON FELBRIGGE, KNT., of Felbrigge, liv. 1310, Lord of the Manor of Felbrigge 1316-1349; m. Alice de Thorpe, dau. of Sir George de Thorpe, Knt., Lord of the Manor of Breisworth, Suffolk. (*Op. cit*, IV: 305-307).

32. SIR ROGER FELBRIGGE, of Felbrigge, Lord of the Manor of Felbrigge 1352-1368; m. Elizabeth de Scales, dau. of Robert de Scales, 3rd Lord Scales by Catherine d'Ufford, dau. of Robert d'Ufford, 1st Earl of Suffolk. (*CP* XI: 501 and note *i*, 502, 507; Parkin IV: 305-307).

33. SIR SIMON FELBRIGGE, K.G., of Felbrigge, Lord of the Manors of Felbrigge, Norfolk, and of Breisworth, Suffolk and Lord of Beeston Regis, Norfolk, K.G. 1422, standard bearer to Richard II, fl. 1395, 1399, will made Sept. 1431, pro. 1443; m. (1) Margaret, whose ancestry is undetermined (but perh. related to Anne of Bohemia for whom she was Lady of Honor), d. 1413; m. (2) Katherine Clifton, wid. of Ralph Grene of Drayton, co. Northampton, dau. of Sir John Clifton. (Beltz, p. 369-374, esp. 370-371. See also discussion in Chas. Evans, "Margaret, Lady Felbrygge" in *Blackmansbury* II (Apr. 1965): pp. 207).

34. HELENA (ALANA) FELBRIGGE, by (1); m. Sir William Tyndale of Dene, co. Northampton, d. 1426, son of John Tyndale. (Parkin IV: 205-207; Muskett I: 153).

35. SIR THOMAS TYNDALE, of Dene and Redenhall, Norfolk, Lord of the Manor of Breisworth in Suffolk, d. 1448; m. Margaret Yelverton, dau. of Sir William Yelverton, Justice of the King's Bench 1471. (Muskett I: 153).

36. SIR WILLIAM TYNDAL, K.B., of Dene and Hockwold, co. Norfolk, K.B. 1473, heir of Elizabeth (de Scales) Felbrigge (see at Gen.. 32 above), d. abt. 1488 (Inq.p.m. 13 H VII); m. Mary Mondeford, dau. and h. of Sir Osbert Mondeford (Montford) Esq., of Feltwell, co. Norfolk, by Elizabeth Berney. (*CP* XI: 507; Muskett I: 153).

37. SIR JOHN TYNDAL, K.B., of Hockwold, sold his Suffolk manor 1524; m. Amphillis Coningsby, dau. of Sir Humphrey Coningsby. (Muskett I: 153; Ormerod (Helsby), *History of... Chester* II: 712-713).

38. SIR THOMAS TYNDAL, of Hockwold and Great Maplestead, co. Essex, High Sheriff of the counties of Norfolk and Suffolk 1561; will made 18 Apr. 1583; m. (2) abt. 1533, Anne Fermor, dau. of Sir Henry Fermor of East Bersham, Norfolk. (Muskett I: 153).

39. SIR JOHN TYNDAL, KNT., of Great Maplestead, knt. 1603, will made 17 Jan. 1615/6; d. 12 Nov. 1616; m. Anna Egerton, wid. of William Dean, d. July 1620, dau. of Thomas Egerton, Esq., of Wallegrange, co. Suffolk, and London. (*NEHGR* 18 (1864): 182-183, 185; Muskett I: 153).

40. MARGARET TYNDAL, b. abt. 1591, d. Boston, Mass., 14 June 1647, age 56; m. 28 Apr. 1618, as 3rd wife, John Winthrop, Esq., of Groton, Suffolk, Governor of Mass., b. Groton, co. Suffolk, 12 Jan. 1587, d. Boston, Mass., 26 Mar. 1649, son of Adam Winthrop and Anne Browne. (See abundant material about the last several generations in Winthrop

Papers (M.H.S.) 1929, 1931, 1943, 1944, 1947, 1952, etc.; Lawrence Shaw Mayor, *The Winthrop Family in America* (1948); Muskett I: 153, etc.).

41. COL. STEPHEN WINTHROP, b. 1619, d. 1658; m. Judith Rainsborough.

41. ADAM WINTHROP (son of Gen. 40), b. 1620, d. 1652; m. Elizabeth Glover.

41. DEANE WINTHROP (son of Gen. 40), b. 1623, d. 1704; m. Sarah Glover.

41. CAPT. SAMUEL WINTHROP (son of Gen. 40), b. 1627, d. 1674, (H.C. 1646), Dep.-Gov. of Antigua, W.I., 1667-1669, etc.; m. June 1648, Elizabeth.

Line 233

36. SIR THOMAS STANLEY, K.G., of Lathom (57-36); m. **JOAN GOUSHILL** (20-33).

37. KATHERINE STANLEY, (57-37); m. **SIR JOHN SAVAGE, KNT** (233A-37) of Clifton, d. 22 Nov. 1495, son of Sir John Savage of Clifton, d. 29 June 1463, (son of Sir John Savage of Rocksavage, co. Cheshire and Clifton, Knt., d. 1 Aug. 1450, by **MAUD DE SWYNNERTON** (32-33, see also 57-37)). (*Visit. of Gloucester* (1623): 144. See also *Visit. of Cheshire* (1580): 203, 204; Peter Leycester, *Hist. & Antiq.*, pp. 231, 232).

38. KATHERINE SAVAGE; m. (lic. 4 Nov. 1479) Thomas Legh, Esq., of Adlington, co. Chester, b. 1452, d. Adlington, 8 Aug. 1519 (Inq.p.m.; will dated 4 May, pro. 15 Sept. 1519), son of Robert de Legh of Adlington and Ellen Booth, dau. of Sir Robert Booth, of Dunham Massey, Knt.

39. GEORGE LEGH, ESQ., of Adlington, b. 1497, d. Fleet Prison, 12 June 1529 (Inq. p.m.; will made 11 June 1529); m. abt. 1523, Joan Larke, dau. of Peter Larke of London, and co. Huntingdon. Joan m. (2) George Paulet.

40. THOMAS LEGH, ESQ. of Adlington, b. abt. 1527, d. Eaton, co. Chester, 17 May 1548 (Inq.p.m.); m. Mary Grosvenor, d. 26 Mar., 1599 dau. of Richard Grosvenor of Eaton, Esq.; by Catherine Cotton, dau. of Richard Cotton.

41. THOMAS LEGH, ESQ., of Adlington, b. 1547, d. 25 Jan. 1601/2 (Inq.p.m.; will 20 Nov. 1600), rebuilt Adlington Hall 1581, High Sheriff of Cheshire 1588; m. Cheadle, 29 June 1563, Sybil Brereton, bur. 19 Feb. 1609/10, dau. of Sir Urian Brereton of Honford.

42. SIR URIAN LEGH, KNT., of Adlington, bapt. Cheadle 1566, knighted 26 June 1596, High Sheriff of Chester 1613, bur. 4 June 1627 (Inq. p.m.); m. (settlement 9 Sept. 1586) Margaret Trafford, dau. of Sir Edmund Trafford, of Trafford, co. Lancaster, Knt. (J.P. Earwaker, *East Chester* II: 251-252. Gens. 38-42: *Landed Gentry* (1952): 1497).

43. LUCY LEGH, bapt. Manchester, 12 July 1596, bur. 5 Mar. 1643/4; m. Col. Alexander Rigby, Esq., b. 1594, d. 1650, of Wigan and Peele, co. Lanc., son of Alexander Rigby and Anne Ashaw, dau. of Leonard Ashaw. (*Visit. of Lancashire* (1613): 65). They had four ch., including

44. EDWARD RIGBY, succeeded to his father's rights in Maine; [his bro. Alexander Rigby, was bapt. at Prestbury, 26 Aug. 1620]. (J.P. Earwaker, *East Chester* II: 250-252; *Gen. Dict of Me. and N.H.* II: 587; *Collections of the Massachusetts Historical Society*, 4th ser., VII: 90-91 note, and ff.).

37. SIR JOHN SAVAGE, K.G., of Clifton and Rocksavage; m. **KATHERINE STANLEY** (57-37, 233-37). (*Visit. Cheshire* (1580), *Harl. Soc., Pub.* 18: 203; Ormerod (Helsby), *History of ... Chester* I: 713).

38. MARGARET SAVAGE, m. Sir Edmund Trafford, K.B., of Trafford, co. Lancaster. (*Visit. Cheshire* (1580), p. 204; Ormerod, *cit.*).

39. MARGARET (or **MARGERY**) **TRAFFORD**, of Trafford, co. Lancaster, d. 10 May 1540; m. (1) **SIR THOMAS GERARD** (233B-39), b. 1488, of Kingsley & Bryn, co. Lancaster, will dtd. 13 Sept. 1522, slain fighting Scots at Berwick-upon-Tweed 7 Nov. 1523; m. (2) Sir John Port. (*VCH Lanc.* IV: 143-144, notes 32-33; Ormerod II: 132; Letter to Mr. France, File L. 78, Lancashire Record Office).

40. WILLIAM GERARD, GENT., b. 1515, of the New Hall, Ashton-in-Makerfield, co. Lancaster, yr. s., d. by 1567 (perh. 1540), named in wills of both parents, received in 1542, with s. Thomas Gerard, messuage called the "New Hall" from older bro. Sir Thomas Gerard of Bryn; m. Constance Rowson, liv. 1567 ae. 30. (Duchy of Lancaster records: DL 1/54/B.17, 62/B.13; DL 4/7/3, 8/10, Public Record Office, London).

41. THOMAS GERARD, GENT., of the New Hall, (natural s. & h.), b. abt. 1540/1, d. 1628/9 (will dtd. 21 Dec. 1628, pro. 12 Jan. 1628/9); m. (2) by 1586 Jane (Jaine), liv. 1632. (*VCH Lanc.* IV 144, note 34; Letter of 26 Apr. 1960, File L. 78, Lanc. Rec. off.).

42. JOHN GERARD, GENT., b. 1584, of the New Hall, named in father's will, liv. 1641 Warrington, co. Lancaster; m. 16 Feb. 1607/8, Isabel, d. Dec. 1655. (File L. 78, *cit.*).

43. THOMAS GERARD, GENT., of the New Hall, s. & h., bapt. Winwick 10 Dec. 1608, surgeon and planter, came to St. Mary's Co., Md., first in 1638, brought family over 1650, lord of St. Clement's, Basford & Westwood Manors, moved to Virginia 1664, d. Westmoreland Co., Va., 1673 (will dtd. 1 Feb. 1672, pro. 19 Oct. 1673), bur. St. Clement's Md.; m. (1) Susanna Snow (Snowe) 1629 (marriage covenant, 21 Sept. 1629), dau. of John Snow (Snowe), yeoman, of the Brookhouse, Cheddleton, co. Stafford, and wife Eydreth (or Judith); m. (2) wid. Rose Tucker, n.i. (*Winwick Register*, Lanc. Par. Reg. Soc., p. 77; Walton, "Gerard's Daughters," *Maryland Hist. Mag.* 68: 444-445, and refs. therein. Gens. 39-43: *Stemmata Varia* I, Gerard of Bryn, etc., Pedigrees XI(a) and XI(b), Lanc. Rec. Off.; Gens. 41-43: Edward C. Papenfuse et al., *A Biographical Dictionary of the Maryland Legislature,* 1635-1789, I: 348-349; Gerard Munimenti: DDGe (M) 127, 148, 149, Lanc. Rec. Off.).

34. SIR THOMAS GERARD, of Kingsley & Bryn, co. Lancaster, knight of the shire 1384, 1388, 1394, d. 1416, s. Sir Peter Gerard, Knt., d. 1380; m. Isabel. (*Towneley's Abstracts of Lancashire Inquisitions*, Chetham Soc., xcv, i, 124).

35. JOHN GERARD, of Kingsley & Bryn, b. abt. 1386 (age 30 at d. of father), d. 6 Nov. 1431; m. (contr. 1402) **ALICE BOTELER** (170-31), d. 27 Feb. 1441/2.

36. SIR PETER GERARD, KNT., of Kingsley & Bryn, b. 1407, d. 26 Mar. 1447; m. Isabel (Isabella) Strangeways, liv. 1447, (perhaps) dau. Thomas Strangeways.

37. SIR THOMAS GERARD, KNT., of Kingsley & Bryn, b. 15 July 1431, ward of Thomas Danyell 1449, proof of age 2 Aug. 1452, pension from Edw. IV, d. 27 Mar. 1490; m. abt. 1440 as child (1) Douce (Dulcia) Assheton, dau. Sir Thomas Assheton of Ashton-under-Lyme, co. Lanc. by Elizabeth Byron, dau. of Sir John Byron; m. (2) Cecily Foulshurst, dau. Sir Robert Foulshurst, d. 24 May 1502. (Foster, *Ped. Co. Fam. of Eng. v. I: Lancashire*, "Ped. of Assheton of Ashton-Under-Lyme...").

38. PETER GERARD, (by 2), of Kingsley & Bryn, b. abt. 1460 (ae. 30 at d. of father), d.v.p. 1492, monumental brass in Gerard chantry, Winwick Church; m. (disp. 1476) Margaret (Margery) Stanley, dau. Sir William Stanley, of Hooton, co. Chester, and Margaret Bromley, dau. Sir John Bromley, Knt., of Badington, co. Chester. (Haines, *Manual of Monumenial Brasses*, 113).

39. SIR THOMAS GERARD, KNT., of Kingsley & Bryn, co. Lancaster, b. 1488, slain fighting Scots at Berwick-upon-Tweed 7 Nov. 1523; m. **MARGARET** (or **MARGERY**) **TRAFFORD** (233A-39), of Trafford, co. Lancaster. (Gens. 34-39: Foster, *Ped. Co. Fam. of Eng. v. I: Lancashire* "Ped. of Girard of Bryn..."; Ormerod II: 96, 131, 132, 371, 372, 416; *VCH Lanc.* IV: 143-144, notes 23-33).

Line 234   Revised for 8th Edition

30. JOHN OF GAUNT (1-30), Duke of Lancaster; m. (3) Catherine (Roet) Swynford, b. abt. 1350, d. 1403, (all chn. b. bef. m.). (*DNB*; Armitage-Smith, *John of Gaunt*; *TAG* 32: 9-10).

31. HENRY BEAUFORT, Bishop of Lincoln, Bishop of Winchester, Cardinal of St. Eusebius, b. abt. 1375 (nat. son, legit. 1396), d. Winchester 11 Apr. 1447, bur. Winchester Cathedral; in his youth had an affair with Lady Alice Fitz Alan, b. abt. 1373/5, d.s.p. legit. bef the death of her bro., Thomas Fitz Alan in 1415, dau. of **SIR RICHARD FITZ ALAN** (60-32, 20-31). Alice m. by Mar. 1392, John Cherleton, 4th Lord Cherleton, feudal Lord of Powis, d.s.p. 1401. (*CP* I: 246 note *d*, and XIV: 39; *DNB*; *John of Gaunt*, esp. pp. 389, 462; *TAG* 32: 10-11).

32. JOAN (or **JANE**) **BEAUFORT**, (see 199A-33), (nat. dau.) b. 1391/2; m. Sir Edward Stradling, Knt. of St. Donat's Castle, co. Glamorgan, b. abt. 1389, age 22+ on 23 Nov. 1411, on pilgrimage to Jerusalem 9 Hen. IV (1407-8) and returned, d. 1453, son of Sir William Stradling, by Isabel St. Barbe, dau. of John St. Barbe and **MARY DE LANGLAND** (248A-33). (*TAG* 32: 11).

Line 234A   Prepared for an earlier edition by Douglas Richardson

25. ROBERT MALET, (thought to be grandson of William Malet, d. 1071, of Granville St. Honorine, Normandy, at Battle of Hastings 1066, sheriff of Yorkshire 1068), held barony of Curry Malet, Somerset, 1135, previously held by de Courcelles family, d. by 1156. (Arthur Malet, *Notices of an English Branch of the Malet Family*, 1-73; Sanders, 38-39; *Somerset Arch. and Nat. Hist. Soc.* xxx, 74-75 (Arthur Malet, "Notes on the Malet Family"; Wagner, *English Genealogy* (2nd ed.), 66; Dugdale, *Baronage*, I: 110-111; *Falaise Roll*, Tables III & V).

26. WILLIAM I MALET, d. 1169, steward, favorite of Henry II, held barony of Curry Malet, Somerset, other lands in Kent, Cambridge, and Sussex; signer of the Constitutions of Clarendon in 1164. (Sanders, *op. cit.*; Dugdale, *op. cit.*; *VCH Cambridge* VI: 159-160 (manor of Dullingham, a Malet property); *Som. Arch. & Nat. Hist. Soc.*, *cit*).

27. GILBERT MALET, barony of Curry Malet, Somerset, steward during reign of King Henry II, witnessed the treaty in 1174 betw. Henry II and William, King of Scotland, d. abt.

1194; m. Alice Picot, dau. of Ralph Picot. (*Som. Arch. & Nat. Hist.*, *cit.*; Sanders, *op. cit*, 75-76; Dugdale, *op. cit.*; *VCH Cambridge, op. cit.*).

28. WILLIAM II MALET, adult by 1196, barony of Curry Malet, Somerset, sheriff of Somerset and Dorset 1209, M.C. surety 1215, d. abt. 1216. He was survived by his apparently (2) wife Alice Basset, d. abt. 1263, dau. & coh. Thomas Basset, d. 1220, lord of Headington, Oxford and Colynton and Whitford, co. Devon, by wife, Philippa Malbank. Alice's maritagium, the manor of Deddington, co. Oxford. She m. (2) by 1223 John Bisset (or Biset), d. 1241, by whom 3 daus: Margaret, Ela & Isabel. (Sanders, *op. cit.*, 38-39, 51-52; Malet, *op. cit.*, 77-83; *VCH Cambridge, op. cit.*, VI: 159-160; *DNB* 12: 865-866; Dugdale, *op. cit.*; *VCH Somerset* V 97-98 (manor of Kilve, a Malet property); *CP* X: 672, esp. footnote g. According to *VCH Oxford* V: 160 Alice Basset's three Bisset (Biset) chn. were coh. of Alice's sis. Phillippa Basset, but not the Malet chn; so they must have been chn. of an earlier wife).

29. HAWISE MALET (189-2) aptly. child of first unkn. wife, coh. to barony of Curry Malet, Somerset, liv. 4 May 1287; m. (1) bef. 23 Mar. 1216/7, **SIR HUGH POYNTZ** (132D-30), d. sh. bef. 4 Apr. 1220 (s. & h. app. Nicholas Poyntz, dead by 2 Nov. 1223, lord of Tockington, co. Gloucester, by (1) wife, Juliane Bardolf, dau. of Hugh Bardolf). With father, Hugh joined the Barons agst. King John, captured 17 July 1216, at Worcester and imprisoned. Hawise m. (2) bef. 11 Feb. 1220/1, Robert de Muscegros of Charlton, Somerset, d. sh. bef. 29 Jan. 1253/4. (*CP* X: 672; Sanders, 38-39; Sir John Maclean, *Historical and Genealogical Memoir of the Family of Poyntz*, esp. charts pp. 28-29; *VCH Cambridge, op. cit.*; Cal. Inq.p.m. I: 82).

30. SIR NICHOLAS POYNTZ, b. abt. 1220, d. shortly bef. 7 Oct. 1273, lord of Tockington and Swell, co. Gloucester; 1225, was, through his gr. mother, coh. of Robert Bardolf, and on his step-father's death 1253/4, recd. his mother's portion of half the barony of Curry Malet, Somerset, with 1/3 share of the Basset inheritance. The 1552 *Visitation of Essex* shows his wife as Elizabeth, dau. of Timothy Dyall. The Inq.p.m. of Nicholas Poyntz, dtd. 1273, shows he held the manors of Curry Malet, Somerset, Hoo, Kent, and Sutton, Dorset; and prior to his death, he had given the manor of Tockington, co. Gloucester, and a moiety of the manor of Dullingham, Cambridge, to his son, Hugh. (*CP* X: 673; Sanders, *op. cit.*; *VCH Gloucester* VI: 167 (manor of Swell, a Poyntz property); *VCH Cambridge, op. cit.*; Maclean, *op. cit.*).

31. SIR HUGH POYNTZ, b. 25 Aug. 1252, d. sh. bef. 4 Jan. 1307/8, 1st Lord Poyntz, held manors of Curry Malet, Somerset (with a moiety of the barony), Tockington, co. Gloucester, Hoo St. Werbergh and Lullingstone, Kent, Dullingham, co. Cambridge, and Sutton, Dorset. (Maclean, *Bristol and Glouc. Arch. Soc. Trans.* XII 129, suggests wife of Sir Hugh Poyntz was Margaret, daughter of Sir William Paveley.) (*CP* X: 673-674; Sanders, *op. cit*; *Knights of Edward I*, IV: 89-90; *VCH Cambridge* VI: 159-160 (manor of Dullingham); Maclean, *op. cit.*).

32. SIR NICHOLAS POYNTZ, 2nd Lord Poyntz, b. abt. 1278 (ae. 30+ in 1308), conservator of peace, Dorset, 1307, supervisor of array, Somerset and Dorset, 1311; held manors of Curry Malet, Somerset (including a moiety interest in the barony), Tockington, co. Gloucester, Hoo and Lullingstone, Kent, Dullingham, co. Cambridge, and Sutton and Stoke St. Edwald, Dorset, d. sh. bef. 12 July 1311; m. (1) by 20 Jan. 1287/8, **ELIZABETH LA ZOUCHE** (253-30), liv. 1297, dau. of Eudo La Zouche of Harringworth, co. Northampton, by Milicent, dau. & event. h. Sir William de Cauntelo; m. (2) by 9 Feb. 1308/9, Maud (or Matilda) de Acton, d. 15 Aug. 1361, dau. & event. h. of Sir John II de Acton (d. 1312) of Iron Acton, co. Gloucester, sheriff of Hereford, 1294-9, 1303; sheriff of Shropshire and Staffordshire, 1304-5, knight of the shire, Hereford, 1300, 1301, and Gloucester, 1301, by (1) wife, Helen. Maud m. (2) by 12 Apr. 1315, Sir Roger de

Chaundos (or Chandos), 1st Lord Chaundos, adult by 1303, d. 24 Sept. 1353, lord of Snodhill, Wellington and Fownhope, co. Hereford, sheriff of Hereford, co. Glamorgan and Morganwg, Keeper of Caerphilly Castle, s. of Robert de Chaundos & Alice. (Sanders, *op. cit.*; *CP* X: 674-675, III: 147-148; *VCH Cambridge, op. cit.*; *Visit. of Gloucs.* (1623) *(Harl. Soc. Pub.*, XXI: 128-133) (for Poyntz and Acton pedigrees); Maclean, *op. cit.*; *List of Sheriffs for England and Wales, Lists & Indexes*, no. IX, p. 49; Nigel Saul, *Knights and Esquires: The Gloucestershire Gentry in the 14th Century* (1981), p. 161).

33. SIR JOHN POYNTZ, by (2), b. say 1310, lord of Iron Acton, Winston and Elkstone, co. Gloucester, which he received in 1343, by an agreement with his first cousin, Sir John de Acton; sheriff of Gloucester 1368; d. 24 Feb. 1376; m. (1) by 1343, **ELIZABETH DE CLANVOWE** (84B-32), dau. & coh. of Sir Philip de Clanvowe by his wife, **PHILIPPA TALBOT** (84B-31). (*VCH Gloucester* VII: 212 (manor of Elkstone, an Acton property); Maclean, *op. cit.*, 51-53, and charts pp. 29, 94; *Harl. Soc. Publ.*, XXI: 128-133 (*Visit. of Gloucs.* (1623), for Poyntz and Clanvowe pedigrees; Cal. Inq.p.m. XIV: 303-304, XV: 19-20; *List of Sheriffs for England and Wales, Lists & Indexes*, no. IX, p. 49).

34. ROBERT POYNTZ, ESQ., b. 15 Jun 1359 at Deuchurch in Irchinfeld, co. Hereford; lord of Iron Acton, Winston, Elkstone and Acton Ulgar, co. Gloucester, and *j.u.* lord of Hull alias Hill and Nympsfield, co. Gloucester, escheator of Gloucester, 1395, 1399, 1402, and 1415, sheriff of Gloucester, 1396, d. 15 June 1439, bur. Iron Acton, co. Gloucester; m. (1) Anne, parentage unknown, d.s.p.; m. (2) Katherine, b. abt. 1378 (ae. 40+ in 1418), liv. 8 Feb. 1441, dau. & coh. of Sir Thomas Fitz Nichol, b. abt. 1354, d. 1418, of Hull alias Hill and Nympsfield, co. Gloucester, sheriff of Gloucester 1382-3, knight of the shire 14 times, 1382-1414, J.P. 1382, coroner 1392-5, steward of the Earl of Stafford 1388-9, by (1) wife, Margery. (Maclean, *op. cit.*, 54-57, and chart p. 94; *Harl. Soc. Pub.* XXI, *Visit of Gloucs.* (1623), 128-133, for Poyntz & Fitz Nichol); John Smyth, *The Lives of the Berkeleys* I: 43-50 (for Sir Thomas' lineage back to Robert Fitz Harding); *VCH Gloucs.* VII: 212 (manor of Elkstone); Cal. Close Rolls, Henry V, I: A.D. 1413-1419, 493-494, Henry V, II, A.D. 1413-1422,158-159; Cal. Fine Rolls, XIV, A.D. 1413-1422, 269-270; *List of Escheators for England and Wales, List and Index Society*, 72: 53-54; *CP* II: 124-125 (re Robert Fitz Harding, 1st Lord Berkeley); Cal. Inq.p.m. XV:124-126,184); *List of Sheriffs for England and Wales, Lists & Indexes*, no. IX, p. 50; Nigel Saul, *cit.*, pp. 65, 162; *Trans. Bristol & Gloucs. Arch. Soc.*, p. 145 et seq. (1931)).

35. SIR NICHOLAS POYNTZ, son by (2), adult 1411, lord of Iron Acton, Tockington, Swell, Nympsfield, Winston and Elkstone, co. Gloucester, escheator for Gloucester, 1424, 1434, d. sh. bef. 20 Sept. 1460; m. (1) Elizabeth Mill, dau. of Thomas Mill (Mulle), Esq., d. 1422, lord of Mill, Tiverton psh. co. Devon, and of Harescombe and Duntesborne Rous, co. Gloucester, by Juliana le Rous, dau. & h. Sir Thomas le Rous; m. (2) well bef. 17 Sept. 1450, Elizabeth Hussey, liv. 7 Dec. 1470 when her dower rights were assigned to her, dau. Sir Henry Hussey of Harting, Sussex. (Maclean, *op. cit.*, 57-59, charts pp. 94-95; *Visit. Gloucs.* (1623), 72:36; *VCH Gloucs., op. cit.*; *List of Escheators for England and Wales*, 72: 54; Cal. Close Rolls, Edward IV II, A.D. 1468-1476, 57, 149; *Bristol & Gloucs. Arch. Soc. Trans.* X: 109-129, for Mill & Rous fams.).

36. HUMPHREY POYNTZ, by (1), b. say 1430, lord of Elkstone, co. Gloucester, and, right of wife, lord of Over Woolacome and East Ansty (alias Ansty Cruse), co. Devon, escheator of Devon, 1460, liv. 1461, Tawstock, co. Devon, liv. 1484, Womberlegh and Langlegh, co. Devon, d. 10 Oct. 1487; m. by 1466 Elizabeth Pollard, liv. 1486, dau. & sole h. of Richard Pollard by wife, Thomasin Cruse, dau. & coh. of Robert Cruse (or Cruwys), d. abt. 1406, of Cruwys Morchard, co. Devon. (Maclean, *op. cit*; *Visit. Gloucs.* (1623), 72:36; Vivian, *Visit. Devon*, 59, 256. 597 (for Pollard and Cruse pedigrees); *VCH Gloucs., op. cit.*; *List of Escheators for England and Wales*, 72:36; Inq.p.m. of Fulk Prideaux

22 Henry VIII (A.D. 1530), Chanc. Ser. II; Cal. Fine Rolls, XIX, A.D. 1452-1461, 39-40, *op. cit.*, XXII, A.D. 1485-1509, 84; Sir William Pole, *Collections towards a Description of the County of Devon*, 420 (East Ansty, a Pollard property; *The Genealogist* 9 (1988): 19-20).

37. KATHERINE POYNTZ, m., as 2nd wife, by 1486, Fulk Prideaux, Esq., d. 14 Jan. 1529/30, held manors of Blacheburgh, Yew, Middelmerwode, North Ludbroke, moieties of Overwollacomb and Theuborough, and 1/2 of 1/3 of Curreworthy and Esse Rafe, Devon, son of William Prideaux of Adeston in psh. of Holbeton, Devon, by 3rd wife, Alice Gifford (d. 1511/2), dau. & coh. of Stephen Gifford of Theuborough, co. Devon. (Vivian, *op. cit.*, 619 (for Prideaux pedigree); *Trans. of the Devonshire Association* XXXII, chart p. 214A (descent of manor of Esse Rafe through the families of Esse, Gifford and Prideaux); Pole, *op. cit*, 308-309 (Adeston, a Prideaux property); Abstract of Inq.p.m. for Fulk Prideaux, 22 Henry VIII (A.D. 1530), Chancery Ser. II, Vol. 51, no. 12 on file at Devon Record Office, Exeter, Devon).

38. HUMPHREY PRIDEAUX, b. abt. 1486 (age 44 in 1530), of Theuborough, co. Devon, escheator of Devon 1534, d. 8 May 1550, will dtd. 4 July 1549, pro. 10 Jan. 1550/1 (PCC 15 Code); m. (2) Edith Hatch, dau. of William Hatch of Aller, co. Devon, and Margaret Horton, dau. & sole h. of Thomas Horton of South Molton, co. Devon. Edith's will dtd. 23 Dec. 1562, pro. 13 July 1571, P.R. Exeter. (Vivian, *op. cit.*, 619 and 455 (for Hatch pedigree); *List of Escheators for England and Wales*, 72: 38).

39. ELIZABETH PRIDEAUX, of Theuborough, co. Devon, m. Robert Drake (2nd son of John Drake of Ashe, by his wife Amy Grenville) of Wiscombe Park, co. Devon. (GS of Robert, bur. Southleigh Church, 30 Mar. 1600; Rogers, *Ant. Sepul. Effigies of Devon*, 207; Vivian, 293).

40. WILLIAM DRAKE, of Wiscombe Park, psh. Southleigh, will 4 Dec. 1619, pro. 19 May 1625; m. Philippa Dennys (will 16 July 1647, pro. 5 Oct. 1655), dau. of Sir Robert Dennys, of Holcombe-Burnell, Knt., d. 1592. (Rogers, *op cit.* 207; Vivian, *Visit. of Devon*, 280, 293).

Line 234B   New to 8th Edition

25. WALRAM IV, Duke of Limbourg, d. 1226, son of Heinrich III, Duke of Limbourg, d. 1221 (whose sister, Margaret of Limbourg, m. **GODFREY III**, (155-25) Count of Louvain); m. (2) Ermesinde of Luxembourg, b. 1186, d. 1247, wid. of Theobald I, Count of Bar, dau. of Heinrich "the blind." Count of Luxembourg and Namur, by Agnes, dau. of Henry I, Count of Geldern. (*ES* I.2/229; Moriarty, 185, 192-193).

26. HEINRICH II, Count of Luxembourg, b. 1216/7, d. 24 Dec. 1281; m. Margareta of Bar, d. 1273, dau. of Henry II, Count of Bar, b. 1190, d. 1239, by Philippa de Dreux, dau. of **ROBERT II** (135-28), Count of Dreux. (*ES* I.2/231, 229, 227; Moriarity, 194).

27. WALRAM I OF LUXEMBOURG, d. 5 June 1288, Baron of Ligny-en-Barrois, Roussy, La Roche; m. Jeanne de Beauvoir, liv. 1269/90, d. bef. Dec. 1300, dau. of Mathieu II, Sire de Beauvoir-en-Arrouaise. (*ES* XIII/165. Gens. 27-33: *ES* I.2/231).

28. VALÉRAN II OF LUXEMBOURG, Sire de Beauvoir, de Roussy, and de Ligny, d. aft. 23 Aug. 1366; m. bef. 5 Nov. 1305, Guyotte, Chatelaine de Lille, d. 1338, dau. and h. of Jean IV, Chatelaine de Lille, by Beatrix de Clermont. (*ES* VII/64).

29. JEAN I OF LUXEMBOURG, d. 17 May 1364, Sire de Ligny, de Beauvoir, and de Roussy; m. (1) Alix (Alice) of Flanders (Dampierre), d. 4 May 1346, dau. and h. of Guy V, Seigneur de Richebourg, d. 1345, by Beatrix von Putten. (*ES* II/8).

30. GUY OF LUXEMBOURG, d. 22 Aug. 1371, Count of Ligny, of Saint-Pol, and Roussy; m. 1354, Mahaud de Châtillon, d. 27 Aug. 1371, dau of Jean de Châtillon, Count of Saint-Pol, by Jeanne de Fiennes, d. 1353, dau. of Jean de Fiennes and Isabella of Flanders, dau. of Guy of Dampierre, Count of Flanders and Isabella of Luxembourg, dau. of **HEINRICH II** (234B-26) Count of Luxembourg. (*ES* II/8; De La Chesnaye, *Dict. de la Noblesse* VIII: 41).

    31. JOHN (JEAN) II OF LUXEMBOURG, b. 1370, d. 1397, Seigneur de Beauvoir, Count of Brienne; m., as 3rd husb., Marguerite d'Enghiem, Countess of Conversano, heiress of Engheim, dau. of Louis, Count of Conversano, Count of Brienne, d. 1394. (*ES* VII/79; *The Genealogist* 17 (2003): 250).

    32. PIERRE OF LUXEMBOURG, b. 1390, d. 1433, Count of St. Pol; m. 1405, Marguerite de Baux (del Balzo), b. 1394, d. 1469, dau. of Francesco de Baux (Del Balzo), Duke of Andria by (3) Sueva Orsini, dau. of Niccoló Orsini, Count of Nola. (*The Genealogist* 17 (2003): 250-251 *ES* I.2/231, III.4/750; Lindsay L. Brook, "Bérengère, wife of Bertrand II des Baux, Lord of Bere," *Foundations for Medieval Genealogy* 1(2): 135-136 (2003), (and correction 1(3) p. 197 (2004)) http://genealogy.euweb.cz/baux/baux3.html).

    33. JACQUETTA OF LUXEMBOURG, wid. of John of Lancaster, Duke of Bedford, m. bef. 23 Mar. 1436/7 Richard Woodville (Wydvill), 1st Earl Rivers, d. 1469, son of Richard Wydvill, Esq., d. 1441, and Joan Bittlesgate, dau. of Thomas Bittlesgate by Joan Beauchamp, dau. of John Beauchamp, of Lillesdon, co. Somerset (see *MCS* 153A-11). (*CP* II: 72, XI: 19-22, XIV: 549; *DNB* XXI: 885-887; *The Coat of Arms*, N.S., IX (1992): 178-187; *NEHGR* 147: 3-10).

    34. ANTHONY WOODVILLE (WYDVILL), Baron Scales, 2nd Earl Rivers, d. 1483; m. (1) 1461, Elizabeth Scales, d.s.p. 1473, wid. of Sir Henry Bourchier, dau. of Robert Scales, 3rd Lord Scales; m. (2) Mary Fitz Lewis, dau. of Sir Henry Fitz Lewis and Elizabeth Beaufort, dau. of Edmund Beaufort, Duke of Somerset. He had no legitimate issue by either wife. (*DNB* XXI: 881-884; *CP* XI: 22-24, 507). His sister, Elizabeth Woodville, m. (1), Sir John Grey, d. 1461, son of Edward Grey, Lord Ferrers of Groby, and grandson of **WILLIAM DE FERRERS** (248-34, 11-34), 5th Lord Ferrers of Groby; she m. (2) 1464, Edward IV, King of England. Through her dau. Elizabeth, wife of Henry VII, Elizabeth Woodville is the ancestress of all the following kings and queens of England.

    35. MARGARET WOODVILLE, (natural dau.), m. Sir Robert Poyntz, Knt, of Iron Acton, co. Glouc., b. abt. 1449, d. 1520, son of John Poyntz, Esq., d. 1465, by Alice Cock, dau. of John Cock, and grandson of **SIR NICHOLAS POYNTZ** (234A-35). (*Visit. of Glouc.* (1623): 132-133; *Landed Gentry* (1952): 2,066-2,067).

Line 235

    19. ÆLTHELRED II (1-18), King of England 979-1016; m. (2) 1002, as her 1st husb., Emma of Normandy, d. 6 Mar. 1052, dau. of **RICHARD I** (121E-20), the Fearless, Duke of Normandy, and Gunnora of Denmark. (*CP* VI: 466, XI: Append. D, 109-110 note *1*, XII (1): 411-412).

    20. GODGIFU; m.(1) **DREUX (DROGO)** (250-20), Count of Vexin and Amiens, d. 1035, on pilgrimage to Holy Land with Robert I, Duke of Normandy; m. (2) **EUSTACE II** (158-22), Count of Boulogne. (*CP* XII (1): 411).

    21. RALPH, "Comes" of Hereford, d. 21 Dec. 1057; m. Getha. (*CP* XII (1): 411-412 esp. note *g*).

    22. HAROLD (DE EWYAS) (255-25), of Ewyas Harold, co. Hereford, liv. 1115; m. NN. (*CP* XII (1): 412-413).

    23. JOHN DE SUDELEY, liv. 1140, d. bef. 1166; m. **GRACE DE TRACY** (222-27). (*CP* XII (1): 413-414, VI: 466).

Line 236 Revised for 8th Edition

7. LLYWELYN AP IORWERTH (176B-27), Prince of North Wales; m. **JOAN** (29A-27), dau. of King **JOHN** (1-25).

8. ELLEN (or **HELEN**), (prob. by Joan), d. 1253, bef. 24 Oct., received manors of Bidford, co. Warwick, and Suckley, co. Worcester, as maritagium; m. (1) John of Scotland (le Scot), Earl of Huntingdon; m. (2) bef. 5 Dec. 1237, as 2nd wife, **ROBERT II DE QUINCY** (54-28), d. Aug. 1257, of Colne Quincy, Essex, 3rd son of Saher IV de Quincy, and bro. of **ROGER DE QUINCY** (53-28) (*SP* III: 142; Clay 228). He was the 2nd son named Robert, the first d.s.p. 1217. (*CP* XII (2): 748 note *g*; *ES* III.4/708; *The Genealogist* 1 (1980): 84-86; *VCH Warwick* 3: 52; Close Rolls, Henry III, 1256-1259, p. 164).

9. HAWISE DE QUINCY, b. abt. 1250, d. by 27 Mar. 1284/5, heiress of Bidford, co. Warwick; m. abt. 1267/8, as 2nd wife, **BALDWIN WAKE**, (184A-9), b. abt. 1236/7, d. by 10 Feb. 1281/2, son of Hugh Wake by his wife **JOAN DE STUTEVILLE** (270-29), eldest dau. & coh. **NICHOLAS DE STUTEVILLE** (270-28) of Liddell, Cumberland, by Devorguilla, dau. of **ROLAND OF GALLOWAY** (38-25). (*CP* XII (2) 300-301; Clay, *Early Yorkshire Charters* XI 18-23, chart fac. p. 1; *VCH Warwick* 3:52).

10. JOHN WAKE, 1st Lord Wake, b. abt. 1268, d. sh. bef. 10 Apr. 1300; m. prob. abt. 1286, Jeanne (Joan) de Fennes, d. sh. bef. 26 Oct. 1309 (*CP* 12 (2): 301-302, XIV: 623; *Gen. Mag.* 20 (1982): 336; Clay 228-229; Parsons, *Court and Household of Eleanor de Castile in 1290*, pp. 44-46).

11. MARGARET WAKE, b. abt. 1299, d. 29 Sept. 1349; m. (1) John Comyn of Badenoch, d.s.p. 24 June 1314; m. (2) abt. 25 Dec. 1325, **EDMUND OF WOODSTOCK** (155-31), Earl of Kent. (Gen. Mag. 20 (1982): 336).

12. JOAN, "Fair Maid of Kent," dau. by (2), d. 7 Aug. 1385; m. (1) **SIR THOMAS DE HOLAND, K.G.** (47-31), who assumed Earldom of Kent *j.u.*; m. (2) 10 Oct. 1361, Edward, the Black Prince, by whom mother of Richard II, King of England. (*CP, op. cit.; DNB*, etc.) Her 'defacto' marriage to William Montaqu, Earl of Salisbury, is not a recognized marriage. (See: Karl Wentersdorf, "The Clandestine Marriages of the Fair Maid of Kent," *Journal of Medieval History* 5 (1979) 203-231).

Line 237

4. SIBYL DE NEUFMARCHE (177-4, 193-4), (great-granddau. of **GRUFFYDD I AP LLYWELYN** (176-2) Prince of North Wales); m. 1121, Miles of Gloucester, Earl of Hereford, d. 1143, son of Walter of Gloucester, grandson of Roger de Pitres. (Keats-Rohan, *Domesday People* I: 451).

5. LUCY OF HEREFORD, dau. & coh., liv. 1219/20, Lady of Blaen Llyfni and Bwlch y Dinas, co. Brecknock, bur. Chapter House of Lanthony, near Gloucester, heir to a 1/3 interest in the barony of her father; m. by 1196, **HERBERT FITZ HERBERT** (262-28), adult by 1165, d. sh. bef. June 1204, son and eventual h. of Herbert Fitz Herbert, dead by 1155, by his wife, **SIBYL CORBET** (121-26,195-26).

6. PIERS FITZ HERBERT (262-29), son & event. h., adult by 1204, d. sh. bef. 6 June 1235, bur. at Reading, heir through his mother to a 1/3 interest in the barony of Miles of Gloucester, Earl of Hereford; m. (1) (marriage settlement 28 Nov. 1203), **ALICE FITZ ROBERT** (246D-28) de Warkworth, dau. of Robert Fitz Roger, 2nd Baron of Warkworth and sister of John Fitz Robert, Magna Charta Surety 1215. (Gens. 4-6: *CP* V: 702, note *d*).

7. LUCY FITZ PIERS, liv. 1266; m. **SIR WILLIAM DE ROS** (170-26), b. aft. 1192, d. abt. 1264. (*CP* XI: 93-94).

Line 238

6. JOAN DE HUNTINGFIELD (187-6); m. Sir Richard Basset, Lord Basset.

7. RALPH BASSET, 2nd Lord Basset of Weldon, b. 27 Aug. 1300, d. abt. 4 May 1341; m. Joan, sd. to be a Sturdon of Winterbourne, Co. Glouc. (see 187-6A, 188-7). (*CP* II: 10-13).

8. ALIANORE BASSET, m. Sir John Knyvet of Winwick, co. Northampton, Chief Justice of the King's Bench, Lord Chancellor of England, d. 1381.

9. JOHN KNYVET, ESQ., M.P. for Huntingfield 1397/8, d. 1418; m. Joan Botetourte, dau. of John Botetourte of Mendlesham, Suffolk. (*CP* II: 13).

10. SIR JOHN KNYVET (188-10), sheriff of Northamptonshire 1427, d. 1446; m. Elizabeth Clifton, b. abt. 1392, dau. of Constantine Clifton, Lord Clifton of Buckenham. (*CP* III: 308).

11. MARGARET KNYVET, b. abt. 1412, d. 1458; m., as 2nd wife, Richard Chamberlayne, of Tilsworth, co. Bedford, b. abt. 1392, d. 1439 (for his ancestry see *NEHGR* 79: 358 (1925). (*VCH Beds* III: 433; *VCH Bucks* IV: 340).

12. RICHARD CHAMBERLAYNE, of Coates, par. Titchmarsh, co. Northampton, d. 28 Aug. 1497; m. Sybil Fowler, d. 1525, dau. of Richard Fowler of Shirburn, co. Oxford, Chancellor of the Duchy of Lancaster, by Jane Danvers, d. 1505. Monumental brass for Richard Chamberlain, Esq. "of Cootys, Northampton," and wife Sibyl in Shirburn parish church. (*VCH Beds* III: 433; *VCH Oxford* VIII: 184; Mill Stephenson, *A List of Monumental Brasses in the British Isles* (1926), p. 420).

13. ANNE CHAMBERLAYNE (CHAMBERLAIN); m. **SIR EDWARD RALEIGH, KNT.**, (14-37). (Gens. 6 to 14: Meredith B. Colket, Jr., *Marbury Ancestry* (1936), 41-42; *VCH Oxford* V: 285; correction for Gen. 13, see *NEHGR* 138: 317-320). (For more on the Chamberlain ancestry, see also F. N. Craig, "Chamberlains in the Ancestry of the Marbury Sisters," *The Genealogist* 13 (1999): 189-198).

Line 239   Prepared by David H. Kelley

1. BRIAN BORU (175-1); m. Gormflaith, by whom he had a son **DONNCHAD** (175-2), who may have m. Druella, dau. of Godwin, Earl of Kent, and sister of King Harold. Donnchad was father of **DARBFORGAILL** (175-3), but not by Druella. Brian's dau. (not by Gormflaith) was

2. SLANI, m. Sihtric of the Silken Beard, King of Dublin (son of Olaf Kvaaran, King of York and Dublin, d. in Iona abt. 981, by his wife Gormflaith, dau. of Murchad, King of Leinster, and wife of Brian). Sihtric went on pilgrimage to Rome 1028, and d. 1042.

3. OLAF, of Dublin, prob. the Olaf slain by the "Saxons" while en route to Rome on pilgrimage 1034; m. Maelcorcre, dau. of Dunlang, King of Leinster, who d. 1014.

4. RAGNAILLT; m. Cynan ap Iago, Prince of North Wales, exiled in Dublin.

5. GRIFFITH, b. Dublin 1055, d. 1137, Prince of North Wales; m. abt. 1095, Angharat of Tegaingl, dau. Owain ap Edwin.

6. OWAIN I GWYNEDD, b. abt. 1100, d. 1170, Prince of North Wales; m. (1) **GLADYS** (176B-25); m. (2) Christina (his cousin), dau. Gronw ap Owen ap Edwin. (Arthur Jones, *The History of Gruffydd ap Cynan* (Manchester, 1910), a translation and analysis of a twelfth century biography of Griffith, is the source for this pedigree, with details verified and amplified from the Irish Annals, especially the Annals of Innisfallen, of Ulster, and of the Four Masters).

Line 240   Revised for 8th Edition by David H. Kelley, 2003

   11. ADELA, parentage unknown, mother, by NN, of
   12. AUBRI I, Count of Blois.
   13. AUBRI II, Count of Blois, son of Aubri I and father of Theidlindis.
   14. THEIDLINDIS, dau. of Aubri II, Count of Blois; m. Count Gainfroi, fl. 795, son of Mainier, Count of Sens, Duke of Austrasia 791-796, d. 800, and his wife, a dau. of Duke Haudre.
   15. GISELBERT, Count in the Maasgau (the valley of the Meuse river) 839-342; prob. m. a sister of Echard, Count of Hesbaye.
   16. GISELBERT, Count of Darnau 846-863; m. **HELLETRUDE** of Lorraine (also called **ERMENGARDE**) (140-16), dau. of the Emperor **LOTHAIR I** (140-15).
   17. REGINAR I (140-17, 155-17), b. abt. 850, fl. 877-886, d. aft. 25 Oct. 915, bef. 19 Jan. 915/6, Count of Hainaut, lay Abbot of Echternach (Luxembourg) 897-915; m. Alberade, of Mons?, d. 916. (Gens. 11-18: G.A. Moriarty, in *TAG* 26: 188-189, 28: 23-25; Chaume I: 548-549).
   18. REGINAR (REGNIER) II, b. abt. 890, d. 932, Count of Hainaut; m. NN, poss. a sister of a Count Boso. (*ES* I.2/236. Note: Gens. 17-18 have been altered to reflect current research. See also: (155-17) and (155-18)).

   18. GISELBERT (140-18), (son of Gen. 17), b abt. 880, d. 2 Oct. 939, Duke of Lorraine, lay Abbot of Echternach 915-939; m. 929, as 1st husb., **GERBERGA OF SAXONY** (142-18), d. 5 May 984, dau. of **HENRY I** (141-18), the Fowler, Emperor of Germany. (*Ibid.*)

   From these two brothers are descended the later kings of England, Scotland, France, Spain, Portugal, many of the German emperors, the Dukes of Brabant, Burgundy, Warwick, Northumberland, and Lorraine, the Earls of Chester, Clare, and Pembroke, the Counts of Roucy, Vermandois, Barcelona, Provence, Nevers, Poitou, Burgundy, and Savoy, and the families of Cantelou, Courtenay, Zouche, and many others.

Line 240A   New to 8th Edition. (Suggested by David H. Kelley, 2003)

   3. CLOVIS I, b 466, d. 511; m. St. Clothilde, b. 474, d. 545, dau. of Chilperic, King of Burgundy.
   4. CLOITAIRE I, b. 497, d. 561; m. (2) Arnégonde, b. 515, d. 573, sis. of his 1st wife, Queen Ingonde.
   5. CHILPÉRIC I, b. 539, d. 584; m. Frédégonde, b. 543, d. 597.
   6. CLOTAIRE II, b. 584, d. 629' m. Bertrade, b. 582, d. 618.
   7. DAGOBERT I, b. 604, d. 639; m. (1) Nanthilde, b. 610, d. 642, sis. of Landry (Landegisel).
   8. CLOVIS II, b. 634, d. 657; m. Bathilde, b. 626, d. 680/685.
   9. THIERRY III, b. 654, d. 691; m. Clotilde, b. 650, d. 699.
   10. BERTHE (BERTRÉE), liv. 720, a Merovingian princess; m. NN.

11. **CHARIBERT (HERBERT)**, liv. 720-747, Count of Laon; m. Gisele (Bretrade).

12. **BERTHE (BERTRÉE)**, of Laon, d. 783; m. **PEPIN III THE SHORT**, (50-12, 190-12), d. 778, King of the Franks. (Don Stone, *Some Ancient and Medieval Descents*...: Chart 50, "Descent fron Flavius Afranius Syagrius," Gen. 12. Gens. 3-12: Castries, René de la Croix, duc de, *The Lives of the Kings and Queens of France*; Sirjean, Gaston, *Encyclopédie Généalogique des Maisons Souveraines du Monde*, v. 1: *Les Méovingiens*; Chaume, Maurice (L'Abbé), *Les Origines du Duché de Bourgogne*, v. 1: 546-547; Anselme, v. 1: 4; Cope, Christopher, *The Lost Kingdom of Burgundy*; *Généalogie des Rois de France, Les Mérovingiens*; *ES* 1.1/1-2).

Line 241   Revised for 8th Edition by Norman W. Ingham, Slavic Dept., Univ. of Chicago

1. **RIURIK (HRŒREK)**, legendary Varangian (Viking), Prince of Novgorod, d. 879.

2. **IGOR' (INGVAR)**, (Descendant or kinsman of Riurik, <u>not</u> his son), Prince of Kiev, d. 945; m. St. Ol'ga (Helga), Regent, d. 969.

3. **SVIATOSLAV I**, Prince of Kiev, d. 972; m. Malusha.

4. **ST. VLADIMIR I** (chr. Vasilii, [Basil]), Grand Prince of Kiev, d. 15 July 1015; m. aft. 1011, a dau. (d. 14 Aug. 1014) of Kuno, Count of Ohningen, by Richilde, dau. of **OTTO I**, (147-19) the Great; m. also Rogneda (Ragnheið), dau. of Rogvolod (Rognvald), Prince of Polotsk.

5. **DOBRONEGA** (dau. of St. Vladimir by Rogneda), b. aft. 1011, d. 1087; m. 1038, **CASIMIR (KAZIMIERZ) I** (147-23), b. 28 July 1016, d. 28 Nov. 1058, King of Poland.

5. **IAROSLAV I** (son of St. Vladimir by Rogneda), the Wise (chr. Georgii [George]), Grand Prince of Kiev, d. 20 Feb. 1054; m. (2) 1019, Irina (Ingigerd), d. 10 Feb. 1050, dau. of Olov II Skotkonung, King of Sweden, b. prob. 960s, d. abt. 1020, son of Erik Segersäll, King of Sweden, d. abt. 994, and Sigrid Storråda, dau. of Skoglar-Tosti. Olov's wife is unknown. (Ingigerd's ancestry supplied by Nils William Olsson, sources: *Svenska män och kvinnor* (Stockholm 1942-1955); Brenner, *Nachkommen Gorms des Alten*; Beckman "Tre konungaätter och deras jordegendommer i Sverige," *Personhistorisk tidskrift*, XIV, no. 1, pp. 1-19 (Stockholm 1913)).

6. **ANNE (ANNA) OF KIEV**, d. aft. 1075; m. 20 Jan. 1044[/5?], **HENRY I** (53-22, 101-22), King of France, d. 1060. (Moriarty, *The Plantagenet Ancestry*, pp. 51, 53; *ES* II/11).

6. (prob.) **AGATHA (AGAFIIA)**, (dau. of Iaroslav I), b. 1020s, d. abt. 1068; m. 1040s, **EDWARD THE ATHELING** (1-20), called the Exile, Saxon Prince of England, b. 1016, d. 1057.

Line 241A   Revised for 8th Edition by Norman W. Ingham, Slavic Dept., Univ. of Chicago

5. **IAROSLAV I** (241-5), the Wise, Grand Prince of Kiev, d. 20 Feb. 1054; m. (2) 1019, Irina (Ingigerd), d. 10 Feb. 1050.

6. **ISIASLAV I**, Grand Prince of Kiev, b. 1025, d. 3 Oct. 1078; m. abt. 1043 Gertrude, d. 4 Jan. 1107, dau. of Mieszko II, King of Poland.

7. **SVIATOPOLK** (chr. **MICHAEL**), Grand Prince of Kiev, b. 1050, d. 16 Apr. 1113, had a mistress d. bef. 1094; m. a Kuman (Polovetsian) princess, dau. of Tugor Khan, d. by 1103.

8. ZBYSLAVA (mother uncertain), d. 1113; m. 1103, **BOLESLAW III** (147-25). (Gens. 1-8: cf. Baumgarten, Tables I & II).

Line 242   Revised for 8th Edition

5. IAROSLAV I (241-5); m. (2) 1019, Irina (Ingigerd) of Sweden.
6. VSEVOLOD I, Grand Prince of Kiev, b. 1030, d. 13 Apr. 1093; m. (1) 1046, Maria Monomacha, (d. 1067), dau. of Constantine Monomachos, Byzantine Emperor.
7. VLADIMIR II MONOMAKH, Grand Prince of Kiev, b. 1053, d. 19 May 1125; m. (1) abt. 1070, **GYTHA** (IB-24) of Wessex, dau. of **HAROLD II** (IB-23), Saxon King of England.
8. MSTISLAV II, Grand Prince of Kiev, b. 1076, d. 15 Apr. 1132; m. (2) 1122, a dau. (d. 1168) of Dmitrii?? I, Prince of Novgorod.??
9. EUPHROSYNE, of Kiev, b. abt. 1130, d. by 1186, m. 1146, Géza II, King of Hungary, d. 3 May 1162, son of Béla II, King of Hungary, d. 1141, (the son of Almos, King of Croatia, d. 1129, the son of Géza I, King of Hungary, d. 1077, bro. of **SOPHIA** (243-7) of Hungary). (*ES* II/154).
10. BÉLA III, b. 1148, d. 18 Apr. 1196, King of Hungary, m. abt. 1171, **AGNES DE CHÂTILLON** (103-27). (*TAG* 28: 93; Baumgarten, Table V; *ES* II/155, III.1/154).

Line 243   Revised for 8th Edition

1. ARPÁD, Magyar Prince in Hungary, d. 907; son of Almos, Magyar Prince in Hungary, d. 895.
2. ZOLTÁN, prince in Hungary, d. 947; m. unkwn dau. of Marót, Khagan of Jewis Khazars betw. rivers Theiss (Tisza) and Szamos (Somes).
3. TAKSÓNY, Prince of Hungary, d. 972; m. NN.
4. MICHAEL (MIHALY) Duke betw. Morava and Esztergom (Hron), d. 976/8; m. Adelajda of Poland, d. aft. 997, poss. dau. of Mieszislav I, of Poland. She m. (2) Géza, Grand Prince of Hungary, bro. of Michael.
5. VASUL, pagan Magyar Prince, Duke betw. Morava and Esztergom (Hron), d. Spring 1037. Two sons successively Kings of Hungary, **BÉLA I** (below) and **ANDREW I** (244-6)
6. BÉLA I, King of Hungary, d. abt. 1063; m. 1039/42 Rixa (or Richenza) of Poland, liv. 1051, dau. of Mieszislav II, King of Poland. (see 147-22).
7. SOPHIA, d. 18 June 1095; m. (2) 1070/1, **MAGNUS** (243A-23), Duke of Saxony (see 166-24), b. bef. 1045, d. 23 Aug. 1106. (Dworzaczek, Table 64: Ksiazeta).
8. WULFHILDA of Saxony, b. abt. 1075, d. 29 Dec. 1126; m. 1095/1100, **HENRY I** (166-24), Duke of Bavaria. (Brandenburg). See note under Line 244. (Gens. 1-8: *ES* II/153-154; *NEHGR* 96 (1942): 138-143; Moncrieffe, 83).

Line 243A   Contributed to an earlier edition by Claude W. Faulkner

15. GUDRÖD, "the Magnificent," also called "the Hunting-King," s. Halfdan "White-Leg" and Asa (Moriarty) (Sturleson says gt.-gr.s. Halfdan "White-leg"), King of Vermaland, Vestfold, and Vingulmark, murdered 810-827 at instigation of 2nd wife Asa in revenge for forcibly abducting her and killing, abt. 800, her father and brother; m. (1) Alfhilde, dau. Alfrim, ruler of Vingulmark; m. (2) Asa, dau. Harald, "Red-Beard," King of Agdir. Asa believed bur. in Oseberg ship, richest Scandinavian archeological find. (Moriarty, *The Plantagenet Ancestry*, 170; Snorri Sturleson, *Heimskringla*, tr. Hollander, pp. 45-49 (*Saga of the Ynglings*, chaps. 44-49); Sir Iain Moncreiffe, *Royal Highness: Ancestry of the Royal Child*, p. 109).

16. HALFDAN, "the Black," s. by (2), King of Vestfold, Agdir, Raumarike, and Sogn (827-860), d. abt. 860; m. (1) Thora, dau. Harald, "Goldbeard," ruler of Sogn; m. (2) Ragnhild, dau. Sigurd Hiort, King of Ringerike, and Thyri, dau. Klak-Harald, King of Jutland, b. abt. 830. (Moriarty, *cit.*; Sturleson, pp. 54-58 (*Saga of Halfdan the Black*, chaps. 5-9); Moncreiffe, *cit.*).

17. HARALD, "Fairhair" or "Finehair," s. by (2), b. abt. 848/52, King of Vestfold, King of Norway, had many wives and concubines, undertook conquest of Norway to win Gytha, and until successful refused for ten years to cut or comb hair (called Lufa, "the Slovenly"), became 1st King of all Norway abt. 883/890, cut hair after conquest (then called "Fairhair"), won Gytha, d. abt. 936; m. Swanhild, dau. Eystein Glumra, Jarl of Upplands, father of Ragnvald, "the Wise," Jarl of More, father of **GANGER ROLF** (121E-18), "the Viking," (aka **ROLLO**) 1st Duke of Normandy. (Moriarty, pp. 10-11, 170; Sturleson, pp. 59-88, 94-95 (*Saga of Harald Fairhair*, chaps. 1-33, 42); Moncreiffe, *cit.*).

18. BJÖRN, "the Merchant," under-king in Vestfold, owned merchant ships, murdered abt. 927 by bro. Eric, "Bloodaxe," at Sacheim. (Moriarty, p. 170; Sturleson, pp. 89-90 (*Saga of Harald Fairhair*, chap. 35)).

19. GUDRÖD, under-king of Vestfold, murdered abt. 955 by Harald, "Graycloak," s. Eric, "Bloodaxe"; m. Cacilie. (Moriarty, *cit.*; Sturleson, pp. 89, 97, 137-138 (*Saga of Harald Fairhair*, chap. 35, *Saga of Hakon the Good*, chap. 2, *Saga of Harald Graycloak*, chap. 9)).

20. HARALD, "Grenski" ("the Grenlander"), raised in Grenland, Norway (not Greenland), made under-king of Vingulmark, Vestfold, and Agdir abt. 960 by Harald, "Bluetooth," King of Denmark, murdered abt. 995 by foster sister Sigrid Storråda, "the Haughty," b. abt. 952, dau. Skoglar-Tosti (see 241-5); m. Asta, dau. Gudbrand Kula of the Upplands and wife Ulfhilde. (Moriarty, 54, 170; Sturleson, pp. 138-139, 154, 185-186 (*Saga of Harald Graycloak*, chap. 11, *Saga of Olaf Tryggvason*, chaps. 15, 43)).

21. ST. OLAF II, called Olaf "the Stout" during lifetime, 1st Christian King of Norway, b. abt. 995 (posthumously), patron saint of Norway, with **ÆTHELRED II** (1-18) fought Danes in England, tore down London Bridge (commemorated in nursery rhyme "London Bridge is falling down"), fought in western Europe, became sole ruler of Norway and forcibly Christianized inhabitants, slain during eclipse of 31 Aug. 1030 at Stiklestad fighting Knut (Canute), King of England and Denmark, bur. Trondheim; m. Feb. 1018 (1) Astrid, dau. Olov II Skotkonung (see 241-5), 1st Christian King of Sweden, d. 1021/22. (Moriarty, pp. 54, 171; Sturleson, pp. 245-246, 251-259, 341-342, 350, 393, 510-516, 523-524 (*Saint Olaf's Saga*, chaps. 1-3, 12-30, 92, 95, 124, 224-228, 238); Moncreiffe, p. 113; Magnusson, pp. 248-291).

22. ULFHILDE (or **WULFHILDE**), of Norway, b. abt. 1023, d. 24 May 1070; m. Nov. 1042 Ordulf, Duke of Saxony, b. abt. 1020, d. 28 Mar. 1072, s. Bernard II, Duke of Saxony, and Elica von Schweinfurt (see 246A-22). (Moriarty, pp. 56, 169, 171; Sturleson, p. 474 (*Saint Olaf's Saga*, chap. 180); *EB*, 11th ed., "Saxony," v. 24, p. 268).

23. MAGNUS, Duke of Saxony (see 166-24), b. bef. 1045, d. 23 Aug. 1106, bur. Artlenburg; m. (2) **SOPHIA** (243-7), d. 18 June 1095, dau. **BÉLA I** (243-6), King of Hungary, d. abt. 1063, and Rixa, liv. 1051. (Moriarty, p. 169; *EB*, *cit.*). (See also: *ES* II/105, 108).

Line 244   Revised for 8th Edition

5. **VASUL** (243·5), pagan Magyar Prince, Duke betw. Morava and Esztergom (Hron), d. Spring 1037.

6. **ANDREW (ENDRE) I**, d. 1060, King of Hungary; m. 1040s, Anastasia (Agmunda), liv. 1064, dau. of **IAROSLAV I** (241·5) and Ingigerd.

7. **ADELAIDE**, d. 27 Jan. 1062; m. as 2nd wife, 1057, Vratislav II, b. abt. 1035, d. 24 Jan. 1092, King of Bohemia. Vratislav II was gt.·gt.·grandson of Boleslaw I, "the Cruel," who murdered bro. Duke Venceslav (Václav) (later St. Venceslav and "Good King Wenceslas" of carol) at instigation of their mother Drahomira. (Moriarty, *The Plantagenet Ancestry*, p. 85; Sir Iain Moncreiffe, *Royal Highness.Ancestry of the Royal Child*, pp. 64-65).

8. **JUDITH**, Princess of Bohemia, d. 25 Dec. 1086; m. abt. 1080, **WLADYSLAW I** (147·24), b. abt. 1043, d. 4 June 1102, King of Poland. (*ES* I/155, I.2/177; *TAG* 28: 93. Gens. 6-8: West Winter X.194, XI.330, XII.532).

Line 244A   Revised for 8th Edition

6. **BÉLA I** (243·6), d. abt. 1063, King of Hungary; m. Rixa of Poland.

7. **ST. LADISLAS**, King of Hungary 1077, d. 27 July 1095; m. abt. 1077/79 Adelaide, d. 1090, parentage uncertain.

8. **PRISCA (IRENE) OF HUNGARY**, b. abt. 1088, d. Bethinia 13 Aug. 1134; m. abt. 1105, **JOHN II COMNENUS** (105A·25), Byzantine Emperor, b. 1088, d. 8 Apr. 1134. (Moriarty, *The Plantagenet Ancestry*, 138; Sturdza, 275 chart I).

Line 245   Revised for 8th Edition

39. **REV. EDWARD BULKELEY, D.D.** (31·39); m. Olive Irby.

40. **SARAH BULKELEY** (31D·40), b. 1580, d. 1611; m. 1597, **SIR OLIVER ST. JOHN** (85·40) of Keysoe, co. Bedford, b. abt. 1575, d. Keysoe, 23 Mar. 1625/6, will made 13 Mar. 1625/6, son of Henry St. John and Jane Neale.

41. **ELIZABETH ST. JOHN** (85·41); m. 6 Aug. 1629, Rev. Samuel Whiting, minister at Lynn, Massachusetts, 1635-1679.

42. **REV. SAMUEL WHITING, Jr., A.M.** (85·42).

42. **REV. JOSEPH WHITING, A.M.** (85·42). (For authorities and further data, see Line 85, Gens. 39-42).

Line 246

22. **ADELE (ALIX) DE ROUCY** (151·22); m. 1031, **HILDUIN III (IV) DE RAMERU** (151A·22), d. 1063, Count of Montdidier and Roucy.

23. **MARGARET** (or **MARGUERITE**) **DE RAMERU**, b. abt. 1050; m. abt. 1080, Hugh de Clermont-en-Beauvaisis, d. 1101, Count of Clermont in Beauvaisis. (*CP* X: 348; *ES* III.4/677; Seversmith, 2,542-2,543).

24. **ADELAIDE** (or **ADELIZA**) **DE CLERMONT-EN-BEAUVAISIS**, b. by 1072; m. **GILBERT FITZ RICHARD** (184·3), d. 1114 or 1117, Earl of Clare and Lord of Tonbridge. (*CP* III: 242-243, X: 348; Seversmith, 2,529, 2,530; Sanders, 34-35).

25. ADELIZA (or **ALICE) DE CLARE**, d. 1163; m. Aubrey II de Vere, slain at London, 15 May 1141, of Great Addington and Drayton, co. Northampton, Sheriff of London and Middlesex 1121, 1125, Justice, and Master Chamberlain of England 1133, son of Aubrey de Vere. (*CP* X: 195-213; Seversmith, 2,529).

26. AUBREY DE VERE, 1st Earl of Oxford, d. 26 Dec. 1194; m. (3) 1162/3, Agnes of Essex. dau. of Henry of Essex, Lord of Rayleigh and Haughley (son of Robert Fitz Suein of Essex and Gunnor Bigod) by his wife, Cicely. (*CP* X: 210).

27. ROBERT DE VERE (see 60-28), Earl of Oxford, bapt. 1164, d. bef. 25 Oct. 1221, Hereditary Master Chamberlain of England, Magna Charta Surety, 1215; m. **ISABELLA DE BOLEBEC** (267-27). (*CP* X: 210-216, cf. 213 note *b*; Philip Morant, *Hist. of Essex* (l768), II: 159, 179-182).

28. ELEANOR DE VERE: m., as 1st wife, Sir Ralph de Gernon, d. 1274 (Inq.p.m. 2 Edw. I), Lord of the Manors of East Thorpe and Great Birch, co. Camb., son of William Gernon (d. Dec. 1258, Inq.p.m. 43 Henry III), Marshal of the King's Household. Ralph m. (2) Hawise de Tregoz, sis. & coh. Nicholas de Tregoz of Tolleshunt, founder of Dunkeswell Abbey. (*CP* X: 213 note *b*; Waters, *Chester of Chicheley*, I: 189-194, 199).

29. WILLIAM GERNON, s. and h., age 24 in 1274, of Bakewell, East Thorpe, etc., d. 1327. (Inq.p.m. 7 Edw. III). (*Chester of Chicheley*, I: 194).

30. SIR JOHN GERNON, s. and h. ae. 30+ in 1327; m. Alice de Colville, wid. of Guy Gobaud, dau. of Roger de Colville, b. 1251, d. 1288 and Margery de Braose, d. 1335, dau. of Richard de Braose, d. 1296 (son of John de Braose, and Margaret, d. 1265, ferch **LLYWELYN AP IOWERTH** (176B-27) by Alice de Ros (le Rus), d. 1301. (*The Genealogist* 1 (1980): 83-84, 6 (1985): 91-93; *CP* III: 375 note *d*).

31. SIR JOHN GERNON, b. 1314, age 40+ in 1369/70, d. 13 Jan. 1383/4; m. (1) 1332 at 18, Alice NN, wid. of John Bigot; m. (2) Joan NN, who survived him. (*Chester of Chicheley* I: 196, 198; *CP* III: 375 note *d*).

32. MARGARET GERNON, by (1), b. abt. 1350, d, a wid. 6 June 1413, bur. Wicken, co. Cambridge (Inq.p.m. 2 Henry V); m. Sir John Peyton, Knt., of Peyton Hall in Boxford, Essex. He held *j.u.* East Thorpe and Wicken (Inq.p.m. 7 Richard II), parentage under dispute at this time. (Morant II: 159, 179-182; Augustine Page, *Topographical and Gen. Hist. of Suffolk* (Ipswich, 1847), pp. 155, 919-920; *Harl. Soc.* 71: 3; Burke, *Ext. and Dor. Baronetage*, 408 "*Chester of Chicheley*").

33. JOHN PEYTON of Peyton Hall and Wicken, d.v.p. 1403/4; m. Joan Sutton, dau. of Sir Hamon Sutton of co. Essex. (Morant II: 179-192; Page, 155, 904, 919-920; *Harl. Soc.* 71: 3; Burke, *op. cit*, 408).

34. JOHN PEYTON, ESQ., b. 1392, age 12 in 1404, age 15 in 1407, d. 6 Oct. 1416, age 24 (Inq.p.m. 4 Henry V), Lord of the Manor of East Thorpe 1414-1417; m. Grace Langley, d. 6 Henry VI, dau. ? Langley, of co. Kent; she m. (2) Richard Baynard of Messing. (Morant II: 179-192·, *Harl. Soc.* 71: 3; Burke, 409).

35. SIR THOMAS PEYTON, of Peyton and Ilesham, 1484., bapt. at Dry-Drayton, 14 Feb. 1416/7, d. 30 July 1484, Sheriff of the counties of Camb. and Hunts (21 and 31 Henry VI) 1443 1453; m. Margaret Francis, wid. of Thomas Garneys (Garnish). dau. of Sir Hugh Francis of Giffords Hall in Wickenham, co. Suffolk. His great-grandson, Robert Peyton, sold the Manor of East Thorpe and the Hundred of Lexton on 1 Oct. 1536. (Morant II: 179-180; Burke, 409; *Visit. of Warwick* (1619): 379-380; *Visit. of Suffolk* (1561): 62. Gens. 32-35: Visit. of Cambridge (1575) and (1619) var. pp.).

36. FRANCIS PEYTON, d. 1529, of St. Edmundsbury and Coggeshall, co. Essex,; m. Elizabeth, d. 1536, stated to have been dau. of Reginald Brooke, Esq., of Aspall Stoneham, Suffolk. (*Visit. of Suffolk* (1561): 63-64; Camden in *Harl. Soc.* 12: 379; see Waters, *Chester of Chicheley*, I: 202-203).

37. CHRISTOPHER PEYTON, ESQ., of St. Edmunds Bury; m. Jane (Joanne) Mildmay, dau. of Thomas Mildmay, the son of Thomas Mildmay. (*Her. and Gen.* 6 (1871): 344-345; Morant, *Hist. of Essex* II: 587; *Bradbury Memorial* 32-33; *DNB* 56: 359-362; *CCN*, 351).

38. MARGARET PEYTON; m. (1) 3 Jan. 1574, Richard Eden, of Sudbury, co. Suff., son of Thomas Eden, d. 1568 and Grisella Waldegrave, dau. of Edward Waldgrave, of Sudbury. (Gens. 34-38: *Visit. of Warwickshire* (1619): 378-380. Gens. 35-38: *Visit. of Suffolk* (1561): 3, 62).

Line 246A Provided for the 6th Edition by John Threlfall. (Editorial note added 7th Edition)

22. ALBERT III (149-22), Count of Namur, first mentioned in 1035 next to his father, prob. as a child, next in 1062, d. 22 June 1102; m. abt. 1067 Ida of Saxony, d. 31 July 1102, prob. widow of Frederick of Luxembourg, Duke of Lower Lorraine, d. 28 Aug. 1065, and dau. of Bernard II, Duke of Saxony, b. abt. 995, d. 1059, by his wife Elica (or Eilika), dau. of Henrich, Margrave of Schweinfurt. (Moriarty, *The Plantagenet Ancestry*; Felix Rousseau, *Actes des Comptes de* Namur *de la Premiere Race 946-1195* (Bruxelles 1936); *L'Art de Verifier les Dates des Faits Historiques* (Paris, 1787)).

23. GODFREY OF NAMUR, b. 1067 or 1069, d. 19 Aug. 1139, as a lay brother in the abbey of Floreffe; m. abt. 1087, Sibylle, dau. Roger, Count of Chateau-Porcien, which marriage ended in divorce or annullment because of her affair with a neighbor while Godfrey was away waging war. (*Ibid*).

24. ELIZABETH (or **ISABELL) OF NAMUR**; m. (1) Gervais, Count of Rethel, d. 1124, (3rd son of Hugh I, Count of Rethel and Mélisende de Montlhéry), archdeacon of Rheims, resigned on the death of his father and succeeded him as count of Rethel; m. (2) Clarembald de Rosoy. (*Ibid*; *Chronicon Alberici*; *TAG* 20: 255-6).

25. MILICENT OF RETHEL, m. (1) Robert Marmion, b. prob. 1090-1095 in Normandy, killed 1143 or 1144 at Coventry, son of Roger; first appears in the Lindsey Survey of Lincolnshire 1115-1118; m. (2) Richard de Camville. (C.F.R. Palmer, *Hist of the Baronial Family of Marmion* (1875); *TAG ibid*; Dugdale, *Monasticon Anglicorum*; G. Saige, *Cartulaire de Fontenay de Marmion* (1895); J.H. Round, *Calendar of Documents Preserved in France*; J.H. Round, *Feudal England*, pp. 155-159).

26. ROBERT MARMION, b. bef. 1133, d. abt. 1185. (*Ibid*; *CP* VIII 505-522; *Societe des Antiquaires de Normandie*, Tome 7; *Gallia Christiana*, Vol. XI; Salter, *Boarstall Cartulary*, pub. by Oxfordshire Hist Soc. (1930); John B. Threlfall, *The Ancestry of Thomas Bradbury and his wife Mary Perkins* (1988). See note at end of line).

27. WILLIAM MARMION, b. prob. 1155-1160, d. in or bef. 1220, acquired lordship of Checkenden in Oxfordshire through a series of deeds from his father and brother Geoffrey. (*Ibid*; *Thame Cartulary*, edited by Salter (1948); *Abbreviatio Placitorum*).

28. GEOFFREY MARMION, b. abt. 1198, d. betw. Oct. 1246 and 1255; m. Rosamund, d. betw. 25 Apr 1273 and 2 Feb. 1273/4. (*Ibid*; M.T. Pearman, *Notices of Checkenden* (1898)).

29. WILLIAM MARMION, b. abt. 1229 at Checkenden, d. abt. 1266; m. Maud (or Matilda). (*Ibid*; *The Goring Charters*, vols. 13 & 14, *Oxfordshire Record Society* (1931)).

30. JOHN MARMION, b. abt. 1260 at Checkenden, d. 1330-31; m. abt. 1273 (an arranged child marriage) Margery de Nottingham, dau. of Henry de Nottingham, his guardian. (*Ibid*).

31. THOMAS MARMION, b. abt. 1295-90; m. Agnes. (*Ibid*).

32. ALICE MARMION, b. abt. 1320, d. bef. 1367; m. bef. 1353, William Harlyngrugge of Checkenden. (*Ibid*).

33. CECILY (or **CECILIA**) **HARLYNGRUGGE**, b. prob. 1340-46 at Checkenden, d. 20 May 1428; m. John Rede, d. 20 May 1404, elaborate brass to him in the Checkenden church, brass inscription to her, Rede and Marmion arms, appointed Serjeant-at-law 1396, possibly son of John and Margery Rede of Ascote in the parish of Winkfield, co. Berks. (*Ibid*.; Mill Stephenson, *A List of Monumental Brasses in the British Isles* (1926), p. 401).

34. JOAN REDE, m. (2) as his 2nd wife, Walter Cotton, b. abt. 1376 at Cambridge, d. 13 May 1445 per Inq.p.m. (14 May per former brass), a mercer of London, bought Landwade estate in Cambridgeshire, rebuilt the Landwade church (his tomb is there, Cotton-Rede/Marmion arms in original stained glass window) son of John and Margaret Cotton, his father Mayor of Cambridge in 1378. (*TAG* 57: 35-36).

35. WILLIAM COTTON, b. 1410-11, killed 22 May 1455 in Battle of St. Albans, the beginning of the War of the Roses, his tomb and brass epitaph at Landwade, a London mercer, Vice Chamberlain to Henry VI; m. Alice Abbott, d. 21 Nov. 1473, dau. of John and Agnes Abbott. (*TAG* 56: 13-29, 57: 35-56).

36. CATHERINE COTTON, eldest dau.; m. Thomas V Heigham, b. 1431 (per Inq.p.m.), liv. 1494, of Heigham Hall in Gazeley, Suffolk. (*TAG* 57: 35-44; 58: 168-180).

37. CLEMENT HEIGHAM of Lavenham, Suffolk, d. 26 Sept. 1500; m. Maud (or Matilda) Cooke, dau. of Lawrence Cooke of Lavenham. (*TAG* 58: 168-180).

38. SIR CLEMENT HEIGHAM, KNT., of Barrow Hall, Suffolk, d. 9 Mar. 1570/71, knighted by Queen Mary; m. (1) Anne Munnings of Bury St. Edmunds, d. betw. 26 May and 22 Aug. 1540, dau. of Thomas Munnings and Margaret. (*TAG* 55: 151-155; 58: 168-180).

39. ELIZABETH HEIGHAM, m. (1) Henry Edon of Barningham, Suffolk, d. 30 Jan. 1545/6, son of Thomas and Joan Edon of Bury St. Edmunds; m. (2) Robert Kempe of Spain Hall in Finchingfield, Essex. (*TAG* 55: 5-16).

40. ANN EDON, b. abt. 1542, bur. at Wicken Bonhunt, Essex, 8 Feb. 1611/12; m. William Bradbury, Esq., b. abt. 1544, d. 30 Nov. 1622, son of Matthew and Margaret (Rowse) Bradbury. (*TAG ibid.*)

41. WYMOND BRADBURY, bapt. Newport Pond, Essex 16 May 1574, d. Whitechapel, London, abt. 1649; m., as 3rd husb., Elizabeth Whitgift, b. Clavering, Essex, in March 1574, d. 26 June 1612 ae. 38 yr. 3 mo., buried Croydon, Surrey, dau. of William Whitgift and Margaret Bell; she m. (1) Richard Coles of Leigh, co. Worcester; m. (2) Francis Gill of London. Her uncle, John Whitgift, became Archbishop of Canterbury. (*Bradbury Memorial*, 32-35, 47-48; *TAG* 18: 220-226· Morant, *Hist. of Essex* II: 587; *DNB* 16: 361, 37: 374-6, 56: 359-62; *CCN*, 351; Visit. Pedigrees pub. by Harleian Soc.; Ducarel, *History of Croydon* (1786); *NEHGR* 23: 262). Note: At Croydon is a portrait of her sister Jane, who m. his brother Matthew, recently correctly so identified.

42. THOMAS BRADBURY, CAPT., Gent., 2nd son, bapt. Wicken Bonhunt, 28 Feb. 1610/11, d. Salisbury, Mass., 16 Mar. 1694/5, came to New England 1634 as agent for Sir Ferdinando Gorges (209-39); m. 1636 Mary Perkins, bapt. 3 Sept. 1615 at Hillmorton, co. Warwick, d. 20 Dec, 1700, convicted of witchcraft, but eventually freed, dau. of John Perkins and Judith Gater. A son William Bradbury m. Rebecca Wheelwright, dau. of the Rev. John Wheelwright.

Note: A reviewer of the contributor's book (cited, gen. 26; *The Genealogist*. 9: 80-87) questions the identification of John, gen. 30, as lineal descendant of Robert, gen. 26, based on a quotation from Salter (*cit*.), p. 2. Mr. Threlfall, in response, invites attention to the fact that Mr. H. E. Salter co-authored the edition of the *Goring Charters* (Oxfordshire Record Soc., vol. 13), pub. 1932, after the publication of the cited *Boarstall Cartulary*, and in the introduction of the *Goring Charters*, p. lviii, provided the same lineage of the Marmions, same descent for John Marmion of Checkenden, as did Mr. Threlfall in his book. Also Mr. Threlfall, in his cited book, gives an abbreviated translation of the deed granted by "bro. Henry, prior of the Cathedral Church of Coventry" of the advowson of the church of Checkenden to John Marmion, lord of Checkenden, citing the gift of said advowson to the Cathedral Church by Robert Marmion "for the atonement and good of the soul of the father of the said Robert" and now returned to John Marmion "by a pure and unanimous desire ... (to) absolve ... the souls of the ancestors of the aforesaid John as well as his own" (page M 32 f). It would appear that this answers the question raised by the reviewer and endorses the lineage as presented.

Line 246B   Prepared for an earlier edition by Douglas Richardson. (Editorial addition to 8th Edition)

   24.   ADELAIDE (or **ADELIZA**) **DE CLERMONT-EN-BEAUVAISIS** (246-24); m. **GILBERT FITZ RICHARD** (184-3), Lord of Clare and Tonbridge and Cardigan; (*CP* III: 242-243; Sanders, 34-35, 62-63; Round, *Feudal England*, 468-474; *Registrum Ant. Cath. Church of Lincoln* I (*Pub. Linc. Rec. Soc.* v. 27), App. II: 277-295).
   25.   RICHARD FITZ GILBERT (**DE CLARE**), by (1), Lord of Clare, Suffolk, slain by Welsh near Abergavenny, 15 Apr. 1136, bur. Gloucester; m. **ADELIZ** (or **ALICE**) (132D-27) dau. of **RANULPH LE MESCHIN** (132A-26), Earl of Chester, by Lucy, wid., (1) of Ivo Taillebois and (2) of Roger Fitz Gerold. Adeliz m. (2) Robert de Condet (or Cundy), d. abt. 1141, lord of Thorngate Castle, Lincoln, etc., s. of Osbert de Condet. (*CP* III: 243; Sanders, *op. cit*; *Registrum Ant. Cath. Church of Lincoln* I (*Pub. Linc. Rec. Soc.* v. 27) App. II, 277-295).
   26. ROGER DE CLARE, adult by 1155/6, d. 1173, Earl of Hertford; m., as 1st husb., Maud de St. Hilary, dau. & h. of James de St. Hilary, by wife, Aveline (see at 149-26). (*CP* V: 124-125, VI: 499-501; Sanders, *op. cit*).
   27. AVELINE DE CLARE, liv. 1220, dead by 1225; m. (1) William de Munchanesy of Swanscombe, Kent; Winfarthing, Gooderstone, Norfolk, d. sh. bef. 7 May 1204; m. (2) by 29 May 1205, as 2nd wife, Geoffrey Fitz Piers, adult 1184, died 14 Oct. 1213, bur. Shouldam Priory, Earl of Essex (right of first wife), Justiciar of England, 1198-1213, s. Piers de Lutegareshale, d. by 1198, & Maud de Mandeville, lady of Costow, co. Wilts. (*CP* V: 122-125; Vera C. M. London, ed., *Cartulary of Bradenstock Priory* (London 1979), as Wilts. Rec. Soc. 35: 85).
   28. HAWISE FITZ GEOFFREY, dead 1243, recd. manor of Streatley, co. Berks, from half-brother, William de Mandeville, Earl of Essex; m. by 1227, as 1st wife, **SIR REYNOLD DE MOHUN** (143-28), b. say 1206, minor in 1213 and 1222, adult 1227, d. 20 Jan. 1257/8, at Torre Mohun, co. Devon, bur. Newenham Abbey; Lord of Dunster, Somerset, Justice of Common Pleas, Chief Justice of Forests South of the Trent, s. Reynold de Mohun, Lord of Dunster, by wife, Alice de Briwere, 4th dau. &. event. coh. of Sir William de Briwere, lord of Horsley, co. Derby (d. 1226), by wife, Beatrice de Vaux (Valle). (Sanders, 122-3, 144; *CP* IX: 19-20, V 433, footnote *e*; George Oliver, *Monasticon Dioecesis Exoniensis* 173-174, 190-191; *VCH Berks*. III: 512; Sir H.C. Maxwell Lyte, *History of Dunster and of the Families of Mohun and Luttrell*, Part I: 15-34; *TAG* 57: 32).
   29. ALICE DE MOHUN, liv. 1282, dead 1284; m. (1) as young child, William de Clinton, the younger, d. by 1237; m. (2) by 1246, Robert V de Beauchamp, adult 1244,

liv. 1262-3, dead 1265-6, Lord of Hatch, Somerset, Justice in Eyre for the Western Counties, s. Robert IV de Beauchamp (styled Fitz Simon), Lord of Hatch, Somerset, by prob. wife, Juliana [dau. of the wid., Alice Coleville, see: The Genealogist 9 (1988) 7-8. Ed.]. (*Somersetshire Arch. and Natural History Society* 36:23-34 (Beauchamp of Hatch); Sanders, 51; *CP* II: 48; Maxwell Lyte, *op. cit.*, Part I: 32; *NEHGR* 139: 286-287; Cal. Inq.p.m. I: 19; Cal. Close Rolls, Henry III 3: 505).

30. SIR HUMPHREY DE BEAUCHAMP, KNT., yngr son, b. by Mar. 1253 (adult by 1274), app. liv. 1316, dead 1317, lord of Ryme Intrinseca, Dorset, & Oburnford, Oulescombe, Teignhervy, & Buckerell, co. Devon; m. (1) by 1254 Sibyl Oliver, liv. 1306, dau. & h. of Walter Oliver, lord of Wambrook, Somerset, from whom divorced betw. 1287 and 1290; m. (2) aft. 10 Aug. 1300 Alice, d. sh. bef. 20 Oct. 1317, wid. Peter Corbet. With Alice, Sir Humphrey held the manor of Silferton, co. Devon, in dower for the term of their lives. (*Somerset Arch. and Natural History Society* 36: 33; *VCH Somerset* 4: 224; *Knights of Edward I* I: 71; Coker, *Survey of Dorsetshire*, 125-126; Hutchins, *History and Antiquities of the County of Dorset*, 491; Cal. Inq.p.m. 6: 75; Cal. Patent Rolls, Edward I, A.D. 1272-1281, 46; *NEHGR* 139: 286-287; *CP* III: 417; E.A. Fry and G.S. Fry, ed., *Dorset Records*, V: 234 (being Dorset Feet of Fines from Richard I).

31. SIR JOHN BEAUCHAMP, KNT., yngr. son, event. h., almost certainly by Sibyl, b. say 1285, liv. 1337 when witness to a charter of John, Bishop of Exeter, lord of Ryme, Dorset, & of Oburnford, Oulescombe, Teignhervy & Buckerell, co. Devon, prob. d. by 1346 when a John Beauchamp d. holding manors of Ryme, Dorset, and Oburnford, co. Devon; m. by 1311/2 Joan, surname unknown, when his father settled lands on him in Oburnford, co. Devon. Coker, Risdon, & Pole all state Sir John m., perh. (2), Alice, dau. & coh. of Sir Roger de Nonant, Lord of Cliston (or Brode Clist), co. Devon. Alice reportedly liv. 17 Edward III (A.D. 1343-4). (*Index of Placita de Banco, A.D. 1327-1328*, Part I, 116; Inq. Ad Quod Damnum, Part I, 125; Cal. Inq.p.m. Vol. 7: 314-315; Dugdale, *Monasticon*, Vol. 3: 60; Coker, *Survey of Dorsetshire*, 125-126; Hutchins, *Hist. of the Co. of Dorset*, 491; *Notebook of Tristram Risdon*, 124-125; Sir William Pole, *Collections towards a Description of the County of Devon*, 169-170, 255; *Feudal Aids*, Vol. 1: 432, Vol. 2: 59). Note: Charles Fitz Northern, *The Genealogist* 9 (1988): p. 9, and p. 30 note 86, says that John mar., by 1311, Joan (not Alice) de Nonant, dau. of Roger de Nonant of Broad Clyst, co. Devon, and Isabella Bonville.

32. JANE (or **JOAN**) **BEAUCHAMP**, m. **JOHN CHUDLEIGH** (217-36), lord of Cliston (or Broadclyst), co. Devon. (Pole, *op. cit.*).

Line 246C   Prepared for an earlier edition by Douglas Richardson

27. AVELINE DE CLARE (246B-27), liv. 1220, dead 4 June 1225; m. (1) William de Munchanesy of Swanscombe, Kent, and Winfarthing & Gooderstone, Norfolk, d. sh. bef. 7 May 1204; m. (2) by 29 May 1205, as 2nd wife, Geoffrey Fitz Piers, adult 1184, d. 14 Oct. 1213, bur. Shouldham Priory, Earl of Essex (right of 1st wife), Justiciar of England, 1198-1213, s. Piers de Lutegareshale by wife Maud de Mandeville (see *MC* 159-2). (*CP* V: 122-125).

28. SIR JOHN FITZ GEOFFREY, adult 1227, Justiciar of Ireland, 1245-1256, of Fambridge, Essex, d. 23 Nov. 1258; m. aft. 1230 **ISABEL BIGOD** (70-29), wid. **GILBERT DE LACY** (177A-8) of Ewyas Lacy, dau. Hugh Bigod, Earl of Norfolk. (*CP* V: 433-434, 437).

24.   ADELAIDE (or **ADELIZA**) **DE CLERMONT-EN-BEAUVAISIS** (246-24); m. (1) **GILBERT FITZ RICHARD** (184-3), b. bef. 1066, d. 1114/7, Lord of Clare, Tonbridge and Cardigan, founder of Priory of Clare, 1090. (*CP* III: 241-243).

25.   ADELIZA (or **ALICE**) **DE CLARE**, d. abt. 1163; m. Aubrey II de Vere, b. prob. bef. 1090, slain in London, 15 May 1141, of Great Addington & Drayton, sheriff of London and Middlesex, Justice and Master Chamberlain of England, 1133, s. Aubrey I de Vere by wife, Beatrice. (*CP* X: 193-199, Append. J, 110-112).

26.   ADELICIA (or **ALICE**) **DE VERE**, b. bef. 1141, liv. 1185; m. (1) as 2nd wife, Robert de Essex, Lord of Rayleigh; m. (2) Roger Fitz Richard, adult 1157, d. by end 1177, 1st Lord of Warkworth, co. Northumberland, son of Richard by Jane Bigod, dau.of Roger Bigod. (Sanders, 150; *CP* IX, Append. J, 113-116-, Sir Charles Clay, *Archaeologia Aelieana* (4th ser.) vol. 32).

27.   ROBERT FITZ ROGER b. bef. 1177, adult 1199, d. 1214, 2nd Lord of Warkworth, lord of Clavering, Essex, sheriff of Northumberland; m., as 2nd husb., Margaret (or Margery) de Chesney, wid. of Hugh de Cressi, dau. & h. of William de Chesney (styled de Norwich) of Horsford, Norfolk, sheriff of Norfolk & Suffolk. (Sanders, 150; *CP* X, Append. J, 117; Sir Charles Clay, *Archaeologia Aelieana* (4th ser.) vol. 32; Landon, *Norfolk & Norwich Arch. Soc.* XXIII: 156-159).

28.   ALICE FITZ ROBERT, de Warkworth, d. by 1225; m., as 1st wife, by settlement dtd. 28 Nov. 1203, **PIERS FITZ HERBERT** (262-29), adult 1204, d. abt. May 1235, son of **HERBERT FITZ HERBERT** (269-29), by wife, **LUCY OF HEREFERD** (237-5), Lady of Blaen Llyfni, co. Brecknock, dau. of Miles of Gloucester, Earl of Hereford. (*CP* V: 265; Sanders, 8-9; Clay, *Antiquities of Shropshire* VII: 148,150-154).

31.   SIR JOHN BEAUCHAMP, KNT., (246B-31), b. say 1285, liv. 1337, and pres. dead 1346, lord of Ryme, Dorset, & of Oburnford, Oulescombe, Teignhervy & Buckerell, co. Devon; m. (1) by 1311/2 to Joan, surname unknown; m. (2) by 1344 Alice de Nonant, dau. & coh. of Sir Roger de Nonant, lord of Cliston (or Broadclyst), co. Devon. (Refs as cited in 246B-31). See: Note at 246B-31.

32.   SIR JOHN BEAUCHAMP. KNT., s. & h., perh. by (1), b. say 1315, d. 8 Apr. 1349, lord of Ryme, Dorset, & of Oburnford, Oulescombe, Teignhervy & Buckerell, co. Devon; m. say 1340 Margaret Whalesburgh, dau. John Whalesburgh. She m. (2) by 23 Oct. 1353, Richard de Branscombe, sheriff of Devon 1358, 1366 & 1374. (Hutchins, *History & Antiquities of the County of Dorset*, p. 491; Coker, *Survey of Dorsetshire*, pp.125-126; Cal. Inq.p.m. IX: 262-263, 387, X: 228; *List of Sheriffs for England and Wales* (*Lists and Indexes*), IX: 35; Cal. Close Rolls, Edward III, X 1354-1360, pp. 242-243; Cal. Fine Rolls, Edward III, VI: 381; Harleian Add. MS 28649, fo. 518).

33.   ELIZABETH BEAUCHAMP, dau. & event. coh., b. by 1349, liv. 1410, Whympston in psh. of Modbury, co. Devon; m. (1) Richard de Branscombe, son of Adam de Branscombe; m. (2) by 1394, prob. much earlier, William Fortescue, lord of Whympston, co. Devon, b. say 1345, liv. 1410, son of William Fortescue, lord of Whympston, co. Devon, by Alice Strechlegh, dau. Walter de Strechlegh. In 1401, William and Elizabeth sued her sister Joan's husband, Sir Robert Challons, re. tenements in Oulescombe and Buckerell, co. Devon, which had been possessed by Elizabeth's brother, Sir Thomas Beauchamp. In 1410, license for an oratory was granted by Bishop Stafford to William

Fortescue, senior, and Elizabeth, his wife, and also to William Fortescue, junior, and Matilda, alias Mabilla, his wife, for the mansion of the said William (senior) at Whympston. (*Cal. Close Rolls*, Henry IV, I: 480; Vivian, *Visit. of Devon*, p. 352; Thomas (Fortescue), Lord Clermont, *A History of the Family of Fortescue*, pp. 1-9, 484; *Devon & Cornwall N & Q*, XXI, pt. VI, pp. 249-255; Sir Egerton Brydges, *Collins' Peerage of England*, V: 335-343; The Register of Bishop of Edmund Stafford, p. 275.)

34. WILLIAM FORTESCUE, s. & h., b. say 1385; m. by 1410, Matilda, alias Mabilla, Falwell, dau. and h. of John Falwell or Fawell; both were mentioned in the license for an oratory granted in 1410 by Bishop Stafford to William's father mentioned above. (Refs. as cited in Gen. 33; also Harleian MS 1567, fo. 46; Harleian MS 1091, fo. 58; Harleian MS 889, fo. 10v, all of which show Fortescue quartering the Falwell arms).

35. JOHN FORTESCUE, s. & h., b. say 1420, d. 11 Mar. 1480/1, Inq.p.m. 4 Nov. 1481, lord of Whympston, co. Devon; m. by 1450, Joan Prutteston, dau. & h. John Prutteston of Prutteston (or Preston) in the psh. of Ermington, co. Devon. Joan mentioned Inq.p.m. on her father's lands dtd. 1468. She d. 23 May 1501, Inq.p.m. 26 Oct. 1501. No. 35 not to be confused with his 1st cousin, Sir John Fortescue, lawyer who became Lord Chief Justice in England (Biography, *DNB* 7: 482-485). (Refs as cited; also Harleian MS 1567, fo. 40 and 57v, Harleian 5871, fo. 15v, both of which show Fortescue quartering the Prutteston arms; Abstracts of Inq.p.m. for John Fortescue (Year:1481) and for John Prutteston (Year:1468), Devon Record Office, Exeter, co. Devon; Cal. Inq.p.m., Henry VII, II: 264-265).

36. JOANE FORTESCUE, b. say 1450, liv. 1524, dead 1525, Staverton, co. Devon; m. say 1470-5, Thomas Hext, gent., of Kingston in the psh. of Staverton, co. Devon, d. sh. bef. 8 May 1497, writ for Inq.p.m. on estate issued to escheator of Devon. He is referred to as deceased in the Inq.p.m. on the estates of his mother-in-law, Joan Fortescue, 1501. (Vivian, *Visit. of Devon*, p. 484; Harleian MS 1091, fo. 58; Harleian MS 1194, fo. 108v; Harleian MS 1562, fol. 23v; Harleian MS 5871, fo. 7v, all name Thomas Hext's wife, Joane Fortescue, as dau. John & Joan (Prutteston) Fortescue of Whympston; Cal. Fine Rolls, Henry VII, XXII: 244; *Devon Lay* Subsidy Rolls 1524-7, ed. T.L. Stoate, pp. 212-213, where Joan Hext, wid., named on 1524 list deleted from 1525 list.)

37. THOMAS HEXT, yngr. s., b. say 1475-80, of Pickwell in psh. of Georgeham at death, escheator of Devon 1525, bur. 1 Dec. 1555, Georgeham, co. Devon; m. say 1510 as 2nd husb., Wilmot Poyntz, b. by 1487, d. 15 Apr. 1558, dau. & coh. of William Poyntz, liv. 1486, dead 1515, son of **HUMPHREY POYNTZ** (234A-36), d. 1487, of Iron Acton, Gloucester & Womberlegh, East Ansty & Langley, co. Devon, escheator of Devon 1460, by Elizabeth Pollard, dau. & h. of Richard Pollard. (Vivian, *Visit. of Devon*, p. 484; Cal. Fine Rolls, Henry VII, XXII:69, 84; Abstract of Inq.p.m. for Wilmot (Poyntz) Hyllinge Hext (Year:1560 and 1561/2) on file Devon Record Office, Exeter, Devon; Psh. Recs. of Georgeham, co. Devon; Chancery Proceedings, C3/91/77, Edward Hext, Pl. vs. Hugh Hext, Def. reg. lands held by Thomas and Wilmot Hext; *Early Chancery Procs.* III (Lists & Indexes XX, Pub. Rec. Off., London), p. 256, suit involving Wilmot Poyntz inheritance; F.T. Colby, ed., *Visit. of Somerset (1623)*, (*Harl. Soc. Publ.* XI) 49-50; *List of Escheators for England and Wales* (*List and Index Society*), 72: 36, 38; Cal. Patent Rolls, Elizabeth I, III: 302).

38. MARGERY HEXT, b. say 1510, bur. 22 Aug. 1551, Braunton, co. Devon; m. say 1532, John Collamore, b. say 1500, bur. 17 Apr. 1555, of Luscott, psh. of Braunton, co. Devon, son of Peter Collamore and Isabel Cushe. (Vivian, *Visit. of Devon*, pp. 216-217 re: Collamore, p. 484 for Hext (Vivian errors in Hext pedigree placing Margery Hext in wrong generation); Harleian MS 1163, fol. 190 identifies John Collamore's wife as dau. of ... Hext of Pickwell in the parish of Georgeham, Devon; Parish Records of Braunton, Devon).

39. HENRY COLLAMORE, 2nd s., event. h., chr. 12 Jan. 1541/2, Braunton, co. Devon, bur. 15 June 1625, Bishop's Tawton, co. Devon; m. by 1563, Margaret Blight, b. say 1545, bur. 27 Nov. 1626, Bishop's Tawton, co. Devon. (Parish Records of Braunton, Devon and of Bishop's Tawton, Devon; Vivian, *Visit. of Devon*, pp. 216-217).

40. ELIZABETH COLLAMORE, chr. 2 Sept. 1566, Bishop's Tawton, Co. Devon, bur. 7 Dec. 1647, Barnstaple, co. Devon; m. 18 Jan. 1586/7, Braunton, co. Devon, Bartholomew Harris, yeo., mayor of Barnstaple, co. Devon, 1602, b. say 1560, bur. 10 Oct. 1615, Barnstaple, co. Devon. Bartholomew's parentage not established but prob. related to John Harris, mayor of Barnstaple 1578 and 1596, will dtd. 1600, pro. 1602 (PCC 2 Montague) names Bartholomew Harris as a co-exec. of John Harris' estate. (Parish Records of Bishop's Tawton, co. Devon, of Braunton, co. Devon, and of Barnstaple, co. Devon; Abstract of probate (administration) of Bartholomew Harris, dtd. 1615, file with the Oswyn Murray Coll., the Devon Record Office, Exeter, co. Devon; Will of Elizabeth (Collamore) Harris, dtd. 1647, prob. 1649, PCC 9 Fairfax).

41. AGNES HARRIS, chr. 6 Apr. 1604, Barnstaple, co. Devon, liv. 1680, Hartford, Conn.; m. (1) say 1634, prob. Cambridge, Mass., William Spencer, chr. 11 Oct. 1601, Stotfold, Bedford, d. 1640, Hartford, Conn., deputy to Mass. General Court, 1634 through 1637, rep. to Conn. General Court, 1639-1640, s. Gerard Spencer and Alice Whitbred; m. (2) 11 Dec. 1645, Hartford, Conn., William Edwards, chr. 1 Nov. 1618, St. Botolph without Aldgate, Middlesex, England, liv. 1680, Hartford, Conn., son of Rev. Richard Edwards, BA., by wife, Anne, dau. of Mrs. Julian Munter. Agnes' identity proven by wills of mother Elizabeth Harris, 1649 (PCC 9 Fairfax), sister Priscilla Harris 1651 (PCC 173 Grey), and brother Richard Harris 1665 (PCC 50 Hyde), all of which mention her. (Parish Records of Barnstaple, Devon; Jacobus and Waterman, *Hale, House and Related Families*, pp. 524-529; *TAG* 42: 65-76; Lucius R. Paige, *History of Cambridge, Mass.*, p. 659).

Line 246F   Prepared for an earlier edition by Douglas Richardson

35. JOHN FORTESCUE (246E-35), b. say 1420, d. 11 Mar. 1460/1, lord of Whympston, co. Devon; m. by 1450, Joan Prutteston, dau. & h. of John Prutteston of Prutteston (or Preston) in psh. of Ermington, co. Devon, ment. in Inq.p.m. on father's lands dtd. 1468, d. 23 May 1501. (Refs. as cited for 246C-35).

36. WILLIAM FORTESCUE, 2nd s. & h. to part of mother's lands, b. say 1460, d. 1 Feb. 1519/20, Inq.p.m. 21 Apr. 1520, of Preston in psh. of Ermington, co. Devon; m. Elizabeth Champernowne, b. abt. 1465, d. bef. 1518, dau. & coh. of Richard Champernowne of Inworthy, Cornwall, by wife Mary Hamley, dau. & coh. Sir John Hamley. (Cal. Inq.p.m. Henry VII, II: 264-265; Vivian, *Visit. of Devon*, p. 162 for Champernowne and p. 353 for Fortescue; Thomas (Fortescue), Lord Clermont, *A History of the Family of Fortescue*, pp. 1-10; Harleian MS 1567, fol. 46; Harleian MS 1091, fo. 58; Harleian MS 889, fol. l0v; Abstract of Inq.p.m. for William Fortescue (Year:1520), Devon Record Office, Exeter, co. Devon).

37. JANE FORTESCUE, b. say 1485, dead 12 May 1527; m. abt. 1501, as 1st wife, **JOHN COBLEIGH** (25-35), b. abt. 1479, d. 24 Oct. 1540, Inq.p.m. 4 Oct. 1541, lord of Brightley, Stowford Carder, Bremridge, Wollacombe Tracy, Snape, Stowford, & Nymet St. George, co. Devon, s. John Cobleigh by wife, Alice Cockworthy, dau. John Cockworthy of Yarnscombe, co. Devon, escheator of co. Devon in 1430 and 1440. (Thomas (Fortescue), Lord Clermont, *A History of the Family of Fortescue*, pp. 1-10; Vivian, *Visit. of Devon*, pp. 353 and 357; Abstract of Inq.p.m. for John Cobleigh (Year:1541), Devon Record Office,

Exeter, co. Devon; *Devon N & Q* I: 210-214; *Devonshire Association*, 34: 689-695; List *of Escheators for England and Wales, List and Index Society*, 72: 35).

Line 246G   Contributed by Charles Fitch-Northen, who provided corrections for 8th Edition

31. ELEANOR BEAUCHAMP, (dau. of **SIR HUMPHREY DE BEAUCHAMP, KNT.** (246B-30), by Sibyl Oliver. He first served overseas 1274, and by military Summons against the Scots, as holding £40 Som. & Dorset lands. Knight of the Shire in parliament for Devon 1312, Devon & Dorset 1313), b. prob. abt. 1275; m. John Bamfield. Eleanor as seen mar. in 1292, in deed 395 of Sir Wm. Pole's collection, when her husband, John Bamfield of psh. of Weston, Somerset, permanently moved the family seat, by purchase, to the manor of Poltimore, Devon. (Principal evidence here and following derived from contributor's two articles: *TAG* 57 (1981): 32; and *The Genealogist* 9 (1988): 9-10).

32. JOHN II BAMFIELD, of Poltimore, suc. by 1329, when Babcary, Somerset lands were conveyed to him by Fine, naming his 1st wife Isabel Cobham, dau. of Lord Henry Cobham's yr. bro. Sir John Cobham of Blackborough, by Amicia Bolhay, dau. of Sir James Bolhay of Poltimore manor, Devon; m. (2) by 1337 Joan Huxham, dau. William Huxham, of that Devon Manor, who d.s.p. as Bamfield's widow. He also paid homage to his cousin John, Lord Beauchamp of Hatch, for lands held of him. (*The Gen., cit.,* p. 10).

33. JOHN III BAMFIELD , of Poltimore and, later, Huxham, seen 1361 on presenting the priest, but d. by 1362. He m. Joan Gilbert, dau. of Geoffrey Gilbert,and sister of William Gilbert, ancestors of the Elizabethan colonial explorers to N. America, Sir Humphrey and Raleigh Gilbert. Geoffrey founded Compton Castle, Marldon, Devon (The National Trust). He was M.P. Totnes 1626, Commissioner, and tax gatherer for Edward II. John and Joan received from her father's feoffees 60 acres of Huxham land with reversion to their s. & h. John, and yr. son Thomas. (Pole Coll. No. 328; *The Gen., cit.*).

34. THOMAS BAMFIELD, b. by 1345, liv. 1392/3, (became the "domicellus" of Huxham manor, with his mother Joan presenting the priest, by license of elder brother John, who d.s.p.); m. by 1376 Agnes Coplestone, dau. of Adam Coplestone, by Alice Ferrers of Churston Ferrers, Devon, dau. of Sir John Ferrers, s. & h. of Sir Hugh Ferrers. (*The Gen., cit.,* pp. 10-11).

35. AGNES BAMFIELD, (one of Thomas' five children) was prob. b. bet. 1377 and 1386; m. abt. 1406, to John Prowse of Chagford, Devon, b. abt. 1377, liv. 1447, s. & h. of John Prowse and Maud Cruwys, who all the authorities agree was a dau. & heiress of the cadet Prowse family of East Anstey, Devon. She and her husband received from trustees Chagford lands 1435. (*The Gen., cit.,* p. 11).

36. RICHARD PROWSE s. & h., of Chagford, b. abt. 1407; m. abt. 1435 to Margaret Norton, dau. of William Norton, by Elizabeth Cruwys of the Morchard, Devon, branch. William was King's Esquire and Usher to the Council Chamber under Henry IV and V with property near Exeter, Devon, and elsewhere. (*The Gen., cit.*).

37. JOHN PROWSE, s. & h., b. abt. 1436, d. 1526, lord of Chagford; m. abt. 1467, Joan Orchard, dau. of John Orchard, d. 1480, "custos rotularum" for Devon under Edward IV. Three published Inq.p.m.'s cover his heritage, and that of his wife Joan Calwoodley, and son William, who d.s.p. The ultimate heir to N. Devon holdings in Northam, Bydeford, Abbottesham, and Dodescomb in Bampton was John Prowse's s. & h. Lawrence Prowse. (*The Gen., cit.,* pp. 11-12).

38. ROBERT PROWSE, b. abt. 1475, dead 6 Aug. 1529, founder of the Tiverton, Devon, branch was named as yngr. son of John & Joan in Pole's "Description." His

Prowse shield of arms, with 4th son's martlet for difference, hung in St. Peter's. Church, Tiverton, where he and his unnamed wife are buried, according to will of his yngr. son Robert. Henry VIII's general pardon, at his accession, named Robert Sr. as of Chevythorn Manor. The lord of this until 1545 was Philip Champernoun, whose dau. mothered Sir Raleigh Gilbert and Sir Humphrey Gilbert. The overlord was the Earl of Westmorland. Robert was feoffee of a Tiverton charitable trust, which revealed his death ante 1529. He paid tax on "goods" totalling £70 in Chagford, Tiverton, and Kenton 1524. Robert's granddaughter was Richarda Prowse Gifford, Lady of Tiverton Castle. A deed to a Chevythorn parcel of land, 1589, revealed that her grandfather was "Robert, son of John Prowse of Chagford." Richarda's bro. George Prowse of Wellington, Somerset, signed the Visitation pedigree with Prowse quarterings down to Orchard, inclusive, (Cal. Pat. R. 8 Hen. 8.; *The Gen.*, *cit.*, p. 12).

39. JOHN PROWSE, clothier, s. & h. inherited copyhold land in the manor of Chevythorn, Tiverton, from his father, which he granted to Robert, his bro., of age 1524 when taxed on £2 worth of goods; by 1546, paid tax in Tiverton on over 140. At his death he left 5 manors in Devon & Cornwall with much other property, by fine, entailed for his 5 sons. His wife, Alice White, given as an heiress in Tiverton, perhaps dau. of Christopher Whyte, taxed on £10 goods 1546. His memorial slab in St. Peter's Church, Tiverton, reads: "Here lyeth John Prowse, Merchante, who departed the third daye of September 1585. And Alice his wyfe which he had in marriage 47 years, who departed the 13 daye of August ano dni 1583" (*The Gen.*, *cit.*, pp. 12-13).

40. JOHN II PROWSE, gent. of Tiverton, who, according to his father's Inq.p.m., was 39 at his death, received from feoffees the large Plymouth manor of Western Peverel, worth by the year £18.7.2., with Chevythorn and Tiverton property worth a further £5.10. But at John II's own death, 11 Sept. 1598, his Inq.p.m., taken in 1601 showed that, by then, all the property was tied by entail upon descendants and relatives with tenure for life. John m. 1 June 1567, Elizabeth Colwick, h. to Robert Colwick, her father, merchant taylor and clothier, lord of the manor of West Mere, Tiverton, whose wife, and mother of Elizabeth, his heir, was Richarda Gover, a widow, whose 1st husb. and parentage has not been established. He was bur. St. Peters 8 Aug. 1564. His long PCC will revealed property in Devon & London. (*The Gen.*, *cit.*, pp. 13, 25).

41. AGNES (or **ANNIS**) **PROWSE**, bapt. Tiverton 15 April 1576; m. John Trowbridge, bapt. St. Mary Magdalen Church 25 Mar. 1570, son of Thomas (Sr.) Trowbridge. The marriage was preceded by a settlement made by Thomas which granted to Agnes an annuity of £30 for life issuing from all his lands at Rowbarton, occupied by his mother-in-law, Alice Hutchings, for her life. On the same day, John was admitted to a life interest in his father's properties at Obridge and Staplegrove and Pyrland, partly occupied by Thomas' wife Johane (nee Hutchings). Agnes' marriage took place at St. Peter's, Tiverton, 31 July 1597, 13½ months before her father's death. Agnes herself was bur. Taunton 6 June 1622. The above Thomas Trowbridge Sr. was a leading citizen and charitable founder, a mercer, with a Tudor mansion, extant, in the high street, and had served as constable and portreve of the castle manor. Agnes' husband John Trowbridge was sole son and h. at his father's death 1620, and served Taunton as Mayor & Magistrate 1629 & 1637, and also as warden of St. Mary Magdalen, constable & portreve of Taunton castle manor. He m. (2) 11 Mar. 1623/4, Alice Reed of Tiverton. (*The Gen.*, *cit.*, pp. 1-2, 13, 15, 25).

42. THOMAS TROWBRIDGE, b. abt. 1600, and named in his father John's nuncupative will 1 July 1649 as "eldest son" (PCC pro. 25 Feb. 1649/50) when he moved from Taunton to Exeter, where he was fined for freeman £12. On 20 Dec. 1624, according to registers of St. Mary Arches, he m. Elizabeth Marshall. In his own parish of

St. Petrocks were b. to him: 6 Mar. 1627, Elizabeth; 5 Nov. 1629, John; 11 Dec. 1631, Thomas; and Sept. 1633, William. The child Eliz. d.y. & John, the s. & h., remained in England, d. 1653: local will, naming John Manning of New England, merchant, William Davis of Muskeeta, Newfoundland, implied that he had sailed the sea with father (vide *Trowbridge Family*). Sons Thomas (Jr.) and William emigrated with parents to Dorchester, Mass., where James Trowbridge was bom; they moved to New Haven, where Elizabeth the mother died. Three children remained to have large families. Thomas Sr. (No. 42) returned to Exeter to remarry, by license, widow Frances Shattuck 10 Feb. 1640 in St. David's church. She, his cousin, was dau. of Dorothy Trowbridge, dau. of Thos. Trowbridge (Sr.) (see Gen. 41) of Taunton. Thomas. Jr. paid £4 subsidy at West Muncton, nr. Taunton. By 1643 they were back in New Haven, a family of 5, rated at £500. When Taunton, under colonel, later admiral Robert Blake, was besieged by the royalists, Thomas (No. 42) served as captain in Cromwell's army, 1645. Later, he supported a wounded soldier's pension claim at Taunton Court of Sessions. He gave his New England sons power of attorney for property there 14 Jan. 1664. He and they traded to the Azores from both sides of the Atlantic. He was buried at St. Mary Magdalen Church, Taunton, Somerset, 7 Feb. 1672. (*Trowbridge Family* (1872); *The Gen.*, *cit.*).

Elizabeth, first wife of Thomas Trowbridge, and mother of his children, was bapt. at St. Mary Arches Church, Exeter, 24 Mar. 1602 of a family at the centre of commercial and civic power in the cathedral city. This was amply set forth in 1905 in an article by Emory McClintock, "Thomas Trowbridge and Elizabeth Marshall," *NEHGR* 59 (1905): 291-297. Elizabeth's father, the Alderman John Marshall, Mayor in 1615, was d. by the dau.'s marriage. Her mother Alice was the second dau. of the name, bapt. at St. Kerrians Church, Exeter, 7 June 1572, and Marshall's bride 30 Aug. 1695 at St. Mary Arches. Alice, bur. there 13 Jan. 1630/1, left to her favourite dau. Mrs Elizabeth Trowbridge, £50 and a £10 piece of plate (PCC 23 St. John). Alice's father was Richard Beavis, who d. in office as Mayor of Exeter 26 Aug. 1603. He had m. (1) Elizabeth Price, from the Welsh "Ap Rhys," mother of Alice Marshall, and (2) Jane Huish, dau. of Henry Huish of Sands. Dr. McClintock misread Price for Prowse in the register, a possible dau. to Lawrence Prowse of Chagford. This, in turn, led to more error in the Mormon records. By 1909 The Rev. J.T.G. Donaldson, whose own family had inherited the Beavis pedigree and papers, published the true names in *Trans. of The Devonshire Association*; 41: 215-240 (in article as "Bevys"). He also showed that the Beavis pedigree was not proven beyond Richard's own parents John and Christina. Donaldson also published therein his main muniment: the 21 ft. parchment roll of Richard Beavis' "Inventory of his estate." (*The Gen.*, *cit.*).

Line 247

20. MALDRED (172-20), slain in battle 1045, Lord of Carlisle and Allerdale; m. abt. 1030-1040, **EALDGYTH** (34-21), b. abt. 1010-1015, dau. of Uchtred, Earl of Northumberland, and granddau. of **ÆTHELRED II**, the Redeless (1-18), King of England.

21. MALDRED, b. abt. 1045, held the Manor of Winlaton 1084., undoubtedly son of Maldred and Ealdgyth, and certainly father of Uchtred. (*NEHGR* 106 (1952): 186-190; G. Andrews Moriarty: *Origin of Nevill of Raby*; Sir William G. Gibson, *The Manor of Winlaton*).

22. UCHTRED FITZ MALDRED, b. abt. 1075-1080, d. 1128/9, Lord of Raby, co. Durham. (*CP* IX: 494; *NEHGR* 106: 190).

23. DOLFIN FITZ UCHTRED, Lord of Raby, "a turbulent baron," b. abt. 1100-1110, noted 1128/9, 1131, d. abt. 1136, held lands in England and Scotland, granted

Staindrop and Staindropshire 1131; m. Alice, dau. of Walcher, Bishop of Durham. (*CP* IX: 494; *NEHGR* 106: 190).

24. MALDRED FITZ DOLFIN, Lord of Raby, b. abt. 1135, witness, abt. 1140, d. abt. 1183; m. abt. 1170/3, a **Daughter DE STUTEVILLE** (270A-27), of **JOHN DE STUTEVILLE** (270A-26), of Long Lawford, Newbold-on-Avon and Cosford, co. Warwick. (*CP* IX: 494; *NEHGR* 106: 190; *ES* XIII/103).

25. ROBERT FITZ MALDRED, Lord of Raby and Brancepeth, co. Durham, 1194/5-1242/8, b. abt. 1070/4, d. bet. 25 June. 1242 and 26 May 1248; went overseas in the King's service 1230, commissioner in Northumberland 1235, in Durham 1238, on an expedition against Wales Aug. 1242; m. Isabel de Neville, d. May 1254, dau. of Geoffrey de Neville, d. abt. 1193, of Ashby, co. Lincoln, and Emma de Bulmer, d. abt. 1208, wid. of Geoffrey de Valoignes, d. 1169, dau. and h. of Bertram de Bulmer. (*CP* IX: 485, 494-495; Sanders, p. 3. Gens. 20-25: ; *NEHGR* 106 (1952): 186-190).

26. GEOFFREY DE NEVILLE, (also called Geoffrey Fitz Robert or Geoffrey Fitz Robert Fitz Maldred) of Raby Castle, Sheriff of Northumberland 1258, Justice of the King's Forests; m. Joan of Monmouth?, liv. 1247, perhaps a coheir of John of Monmouth, d. 1257, lord of Monmouth, co. Monmouth. (*CP* IX: 494 note *b*, 495; Sanders, 3, 65, 96-97, shows the heirs of John of Monmouth to be his aunts, Albreda and Joan Walerand).

27. GEOFFREY DE NEVILLE, of Hornby Castle, d. sh. bef. 26 Mar. 1285, summoned to Shrewsbury 1285, Chief Justice of the King's Forest; m., in or bef. 1267, Margaret de Lungvilliers, d. Feb. 1318/9, dau. of John de Lungvilliers, and a descendant of Aleric, Lord of Hornby, 1066. (*CP* IX: 487-488, 495 note *c*; *VCH Lanc.* VIII: 192-193).

28. ROBERT DE NEVILLE, of Hornby Castle, liv. 1313, was with the King of Scots 1296; m. Isabel de Byron, dau. of Robert de Byron of Melling Manor, Melling Parish, 1280. (*CP* IX: 489; *VCH Lanc.* III: 210).

29. SIR ROBERT DE NEVILLE, KNT., of Hornby Castle, d. aft. July 1373, knighted 1344, was at the siege of Amiens, fought at Crécy, 26 Aug. 1346, commissioner for Lancashire 1344, 1346, J.P. for Yorkshire 1353, summoned to Council at Westminster 25 Feb. 1341/2; m. (1) Joan de Atherton, liv. 1348, dau. of Henry de Atherton of Atherton and Emma de Aintree, and a descendant of William de Atherton of Atherton, 1212. He m. (2) Elizabeth de St. Laurence, wid. of Sir Roger de Kirkeby, of Horton Kirby, co. Kent, d. by 1338, dau. of Thomas de St. Laurence. (*CP* IX: 489; *VCH Lanc.* III: 436-437; IV: 146; VIII: 192-193).

30. SIR ROBERT DE NEVILLE, of Hornby Castle, b. abt. 1321, d. 4 Apr. 1413, served in Gascony, M.P. for Yorkshire 1358, 1377, Sheriff of Yorkshire 1378-1379; m. abt. 1344, Margaret de la Pole, d. 1366, sis. of Michael de la Pole, Earl of Suffolk, dau. of Sir William de la Pole, Knt., d. 1366, Earl of Suffolk, by Katherine de Norwich. (*CP* IX: 490-491 esp. notes *g* and *j*; VCH Lanc. VIII: 192-193).

31. MARGARET DE NEVILLE, d. bef. 1387; m. **SIR WILLIAM HARINGTON, K.G.** (35-34), of Farleton and Chorley, co. Lancaster. (*CP* V: 204 note *b*, IX: 490-491; *VCH Lanc.* VIII: 194-202. Mr. Moriarty has revealed the one missing link in the Neville ancestry for which many have long been searching. The proof is partly circumstantial, partly factual. The holding of lands both in Scotland and England; extensive land holdings for many centuries by the same family, unusual repetition of names, especially that of Maldred; and a sound chronological succession, taken together, are conclusive).

34. WILLIAM DE FERRERS (11-34), bapt. Luton, co. Bedford, 25 Apr. 1372, d. 18 May 1445, 5th Lord Ferrers of Groby; m. (1) aft. 10 Oct. 1388, Philippa de Clifford, liv. 4 July 1405, dau. of **ROGER DE CLIFFORD** (26-32), Lord Clifford, and Maud de Beauchamp; m. (2) Margaret de Montagu, dau. of John de Montagu, Earl of Salisbury, by Maud Franceys, dau. Sir Adam Franceys; m. (3) Elizabeth de Standisshe, wid. of John de Wrottesley and of Sir William Botiller, dau. of Sir Robert de Standisshe. (*CP* V: 354-356).

35. ELIZABETH FERRERS, apptly. eldest dau. by (1); m. Sir William Colpepper (Culpepper), d. 20 July 1457, will 17 May 1445, lord of Preston Hall in Aylesford, co. Kent. (Walter G. Davis, *Ancestry of Abel Lunt*, 238-239).

36. SIR RICHARD COLPEPPER (CULPEPPER), b. abt. 1430, d. 4 Oct. 1484, lord of Oxenheath, Kent; m. (1) Sybil; m. (2) abt. 1480, as 1st husb., Isabel Worsley, b. 1460, d. 1527, dau. of Otewell Worsley. Isabel m. (2) Sir John Leigh, son of Ralph Leigh, of Stockwell, psh. of Lambeth, co. Surrey. (Davis, *Ancestry of Mary Isaac*, 343-348).

37. JOYCE COLPEPPER (CULPEPPER), by (1), b. abt. 1480, d. aft. 1527; m. (1) by 1492 (age 12+), Ralph Leigh of Stockwell, yngr. bro. of her stepfather, Sir John Leigh, (above), will dated 9 Sept. 1509, prov. 1 Feb. 1509/10; m. (2) aft. 1509, Lord Edmund Howard, d. 19 Mar. 1537, yngr. son of Thomas Howard, 2nd Duke of Norfolk. (*Mary Isaac*, *op. cit.*, 348-350).

38. ISABEL LEIGH, b. Surrey, bef. 1509, d. 1573; m. (1) abt. 18 Jan. 1531/2, as 2nd wife, Sir Edward Baynton, d. in France, 27 Nov. 1544, son of John Baynton, b. abt. 1480, Knt, of Bromham, co. Wilts. by 1st wife, Elizabeth Suliard, dau. of Sir John Suliard. After his death, Isabel m. (2) Sir James Stumpe of Malmesbury, co. Wilts., d. 1563; m. (3) Thomas Stafford. (*Mary Isaac*, *op. cit.*, 352-353; Davis, *Ancestry of Abel Lunt*, 229-237).

39. HENRY BAYNTON of Chelsea, Middlesex, b. abt. 1536, d. abt. 1570; m. Anne Cavendish, d. 1570, dau. of Sir William Cavendish and Margaret Bostock, dau. of Edmund (or Edward) Bostock.. (*Lunt*, *op. cit.*, 244-246).

40. FERDINANDO BAYNTON, bapt. Bromham, 28 May 1566, liv. 4 Nov. 1616; m. abt. 1598, as 2nd husb., Jane Weare alias Browne, wid. of John Hinckley of Salisbury, dau. of John Weare alias Browne, of Calne. (*Lunt*, *op. cit.*, 246-247).

41. ANN BAYNTON, b. Salisbury, co. Wilts., 23 Sept. 1602, will (Boston, Mass.) 14 Mar. 1678/9, pro. 21 May 1679; m. by lic. 12 Oct. 1629, **CHRISTOPHER BATT** (248A-41), bapt. 6 July 1601, d. 10 Aug. 1661. (*Lunt*, *op. cit.*, 247, 183-185).

Line 248A   New to 8th Edition. Line Contributed by Brandon Fradd

28. HENRY DE FURNEAUX, d. 1216; m. Joan FitzWilliam, sis. of Reginald FitzWilliam, d.s.p. 1201/2, dau. of Robert FitzWilliam, d. 1185/6, seised of the manor of Ashington, co. Somerset. (Davis, *Massachusetts amd Maine Families*, III: 371).

29. HENRY DE FURNEAUX. (*Visit. of Somerset*, (1531 & 1573), 108; *Mis. Gen. Her.* (3rd ser.) III (1898-1899): 272-274, n. 3).

30. MATTHEW DE FURNEAUX, liv. 1251, sheriff of Devon, 1276. (Davis, *ibid*, III: 371; ; *Mis. Gen. Her.* (3rd ser.) III (1898-1899): 272-274, n. 4; *Vis. of Somerset, cit.*).

31. SIR MATTHEW DE FURNEAUX, d. 1317/18, Lord of Ashington and Kilve, 1294; m. Maude (Matilda) de Ralegh, dau. of Warin de Ralegh of Nettlecombe by Joanna Boteler, dau. of Lord Boteler of Wales. (Joan poss. dau. of William le Botiler of Wem, b. 1274, d. 1334) Davis, *ibid*, III: 371; *Mis. Gen. Her.* (3rd ser.) III (1898-1899): 272-274, n. 5; *CP* II: 232).

32. MARGARET DE FURNEAUX; m. (2) Sir Humphrey de Langland. (Davis, *ibid*, III: 371).

33. MARY DE LANGLAND, sis. and h. of Hugh de Langland, d.s.p.; m. John St. Barbe. (For St. Barbe ancestry see: Davis, *ibid*, III: 369-376; William Berry, *County Genealogies...Hants* (1833), p. 4).

34. RICHARD ST. BARBE, heir of the Furneaux Manor of Ashington; m. NN. Richard had two sisters, Isabel de St. Barbe wife of Sir William Stradling (see 234-32) and Joan de St. Barbe wife of Ralph Durborough (or Berborow). (Davis, *ibid*, III: 371; William Berry, *County Genealogies...Hants* (1833), p. 4).

35. THOMAS ST. BARBE; m. Jane Harcourt, dau. of Sir Richard Harcourt, Lord of Wytham, co. Bucks, Ranton, co. Staffs., Shottswell, co. Warwick, d. 1486, son of Sir Thomas Harcourt of Stanton Harcourt by Joan Francis, dau. of Sir Richard Francis, of Fromark, co. Derby. (Davis, *Ibid*, III: 371; William Harcourt-Bath, *History of the Family of Harcourt*, Pt. II, pp 19, 21-22).

36. JOHN ST BARBE, Sheriff of Somerset, 1458, Sheriff of Dorset, 1460; m. Jane Sydenham, dau. of Joan Sydenham of Brampton d'Euercy, co. Somerset. (Davis, ibid. III: 371; William Berry, *County Genealogies...Hants* (1833), p. 4).

37. RICHARD ST. BARBE, Lord of Ashington, co. Somerset; said to have m. Margert Grey, dau. of Humphrey Grey, Esq. of Whittington, co. Staffs, by Anne Fielding, the grandson of **REYNOLD (REGINALD) DE GREY** (93A-32), Lord Grey of Ruthin (3ʳᵈ Baron de Ruthyn). (Davis, *ibid*, III: 372; Visit. of Warwick, 1619, pp 42-43; CP VI: 155-158).

38. THOMAS ST. BARBE, b. abt. 1518, d. 1572/3; m. Joan, par. unknown. (Davis, *ibid*, III: 273-274).

39. ALICE ST. BARBE; m. St. Martins, Salisbury, 1568, Christopher Batt, b. 1545, d. 1581, son of John Batt of Salisbury, co. Wilts, d. 1557 and Margaret Thistlethwaite, wid. of William Holmes, dau. of Alexander Thistlethwaite. (Davis, *ibid*, I: 73-78).

40. THOMAS BATT, bapt. 1571, d. 1632; m. 1600, Joan Byley, d. 1623, wid. of Robert Blytheway, dau. of Henry Byley, and Alice Holmes. (Davis, *ibid*, I: 78-80).

41. CHRISTOPHER BATT, bapt. St. Edmund's, Salisbury, 6 Jul. 1601, d. Boston, Mass., 10 Aug. 1661; m., by lic., 12 Oct. 1629, **ANN BAYNTON** (248-41), b. 1602, d. 1678/9. (Davis, *ibid*, I: 81-82).

Line 249   Revised for 8ᵗʰ Edition

30. NICHOLE D'AUBIGNY (126-30); m. **ROGER DE SOMERY** (55-29), d. 26 Aug. 1273. (*CP* XII (1): 113).

31. JOAN DE SOMERY, d. 1282; m. **JOHN IV LE STRANGE** (255-30) of Knokyn, d. bef. 26 Feb. 1275/6. (*CP* XII (1): 351; H. LeStrange, *LeStrange Records* 154-176, esp. 154-155 & chart, 159).

32. JOHN V LE STRANGE, of Knokyn, 22+ at father's death, dead 8 Aug. 1309; m. (2) Maud de Walton, wid. of John de Stradling, d. abt. Feb. 1282/3, dau. of John de Walton of Little Wellesbourne and Walton Deyville, co. Warwick. (*CP* XII (1): 352-354, XIV: 596; C. L'Estrange Ewen, *Observations on the LeStranges* (1946), chart opp. p. 1; *LeStrange Records*, 184-254).

33. ELIZABETH LE STRANGE, b. 1298; m. 8 July 1304, Gruffydd ap Madog, b. 23 Nov. 1298, of Rhuddallt (son of Madog ap Gruffydd, d. 12 Nov. 1304, son of Gruffydd Fychan ap Madog, liv. 1283, son of Madog ap Gruffydd, d. 1278, son of Gruffydd, of Bromfield, d. 1269). (Bridgeman, *Princes of South Wales* 252; *LeStrange Records* 215-216).

34. GRUFFYDD FYCHAN AP GRUFFYDD, of Rhuddallt, Baron of of Glyndyfrdwy Lord of Cynllaith Owain, m. **ELEN FERCH THOMAS AP LLEWELYN** (254-34). (Bridgeman, *op. cit.*) (To this point, see *TAG* 32: 72, generations 7-11). (*Burke's Guide to the Royal Family* (1973), "the Kings and Princes of Wales," pp 325-326; *Journal of Royal and Noble Genealogy* I (1): Robert C. Curfman, "The Triple Descent of John Lloyd of London from King John of England with an Additional Descent from Henry I," Appendix p. 18 note 11).

35. LOWRI FERCH GRUFFYDD FYCHAN, (sis. of Owen Glyndwr); m. Robert Puleston, Esq., of Emral, b. abt. 1358, d. 1399, son of Richard Puleston, Esq., of Emral by Lleiky ferch Madog Foel ap Iefan. (J. E. Lloyd, *Owen Glendower* 24; Dwyn, *Visit. of Wales* II: 150; Bryan Cooke, *Seize Quarters of the Family of Brian Cooke, Esq.* (London, G. Barclay (1857), Puleston chart). (Proceedings at Scrope-Grosvenor trial show Puleston was Owen Glendower's brother-in-law).

36. ANGHARAD PULESTON; m. Edwart (Iorwerth) Trevor ap Daffyd ap Ednyfed Gam, d. 1448. (Lloyd, *Powis-Fadog* IV: 84; Grazebrook & Rylands, *Visit. of Shropshire* (1633) II: 465; Walter Davis, *Ancestry of Mary Isaac*, chart opp. p. 334,, which chart shows Lowri with a different father, but otherwise as shown. See also Walter Davis, footnote on the Trevor ancestry).

37. ROSE TREVOR FERCH EDWART AP DAFFYD; m. abt. 1435, Otewell Worsley of Calais, b. abt. 1410, d. 24 Mar. 1470. (Mary Isaac, *op. cit.*, 331-335).

38. MARGARET WORSLEY, d. 1505; m. abt. 1460, Adrian Whetehill, Comptroller of Calais, b. abt. 1435, d. 1503. (Mary Isaac, *op. cit*, 275-278; *NEHGR* 102 (1948): 249-253).

39. SIR RICHARD WHETEHILL, of Calais, b. abt. 1465, d. 1536/7; m. abt. 1491, Elizabeth Muston, d. 1542/3. (Mary Isaac, *op. cit.*, 280-292; *NEHGR* 103 (1949): 5-19).

40. MARGERY WHETEHILL, m. by 24 June 1544, Edward Isaac, Esq., of Well Court, Kent, b. abt. 1510, d. 4 Mar. 1573, son of William Isaac and Margery Haute. (Mary Isaac, *op. cit.*, 30-38, 298).

41. MARY ISAAC, b. abt. 1549, d. Feb. 1612; m. abt. 1568, Thomas Appleton, Esq., of Waldingfield Parva, Suffolk, b. abt. 1538, d. London, 1603, son of William Appleton and Rose Sexton. (Mary Isaac, *op. cit.*, 40-41; Davis, *Ancestry of Phoebe Tilton*, 70-72).

42. SAMUEL APPLETON, Gent., bapt. 13 Aug. 1586, d. Rowley, Mass., June 1670; m. 24 Jan. 1615/6, Judith Everard, dau. of John Everard and Judith Bourne. (Mary Isaac, *op. cit*, 41; *Ancestry of Phoebe Tilton*, 75-77).

Line 250   Revised for 8th Edition

15. GISÈLE (146-15), b. 820, d. 874; m. bef. 840, **EBERHARD** (191A-16), Margrave of Friuli, d. 864/6.

16. HELWISE OF FRIULI, d. aft. 895; m. Hucbald, Count d'Ostrevant, d. by 895. (Seversmith, 2,471).

17. RAOUL (DE GOUY), b. abt. 895, Count d'Ostrevant, and Count of Amiens, Valois and the Vexin, d. 926; m. Eldegarde, perh. dau. or niece of Ermenfroi, Count of Amiens. (Seversmith, 2,468).

18. GAUTIER (WALTER) I, b. abt. 925, d. 992/8, Count of Valois, the Vexin, and Amiens; m. Adele, prob. dau. of Fulk II "the Good," Count of Anjou, d. 11 Nov. 958 and Gerberga, d. 952. (K.S.B. Keats-Rohan, Ed., *Family Trees and the Roots of Politics*, Chapt. 11, Christian Settipani, "Les comtes d'Anjou et leurs alliances aux Xe et XIe Siècles," pp 247-248; Le Moyen Age 10 (1939): 95-97; Seversmith, 2,466-2,467. *ES* III.4/657, shows this Walter I to be the son of his brother Raoul I "de Cambrai," b. abt. 920, d. 943;

however, see Dr. Seversmith's notes, pp 2,466-2,470, for detailed analysis regarding descrepancies).

19. GAUTIER (WALTER) II, the White, b. abt. 944, d. perh. 1017/1024, Count of Amiens, Valois, and the Vexin; m. Adele. (Gens. 16-19: Moriarity, 228).

20. DREUX (DROGO), Count of the Vexin, d. 1035; m. **GODGIFU** (235-20), d. 1055, dau. of **ÆTHELRED II**, (1-18) King of England, by Emma of Normandy, dau. of **RICHARD I** (121E-20). (Moriarity, 135; Seversmith, 2,465).

21. RALPH (235-21), "Comes" of Hereford, d. 1057; m. Getha, par. unknown. (*CP* XII (1): 411-412. See also Round, *Peerage and Family History*; Bannister, *History of Ewias-Harold*).

Line 251

34. GRUFFYDD FYCHAN (249-34); m. **ELEN FERCH THOMAS AP LLEWELYN AP OWAIN GLYNDWR** (254-34) (They were also the parents of Owen Glendower.) (*TAG* 32: 72).

35. TUDOR (or TWDR) AP GRUFFYDD FYCHAN; m. Maud, dau. of Ienaf ap Adda. (*TAG, cit.*) He was ae. 24+ at Scrope-Grosvenor trial, seen 1400, killed in battle, May 1405, at Pwll Melyn. (*Cit*, 76).

36. LOWRI FERCH TWDR, only dau. and h.; m. (2) Gruffyd ap Einion (of Gwyddelwern) ap Gruffyd ap Llewellyn ap Cynrig ap Osbern Wyddel, of Cors y Gedol. (*TAG, cit*; Nicholas, *County Families of Wales*, I: 419).

37. ELISAU AP GRUFFYDD, m. Margaret, dau. and coh. of Jenkyn (of Allt Llwyn Dragon in Ardudwy) ap Ieuan Llewellyn ap Gruffyd Lloyd, of Bodidris and Gell, Gynan. (*TAG* 32: 73).

38. DAVID LLOYD, of Allt Llwyn Dragonm; m. Gwenhwyfar, dau. of Richard Lloyd ap Robert Lloyd of Llwyn y Maen. (*TAG* 32: 73. Gens. 37-38: Arch. Cambrensis (4th Ser.) 6: 41-42.

39. JOHN WYNN or Ial, of Plas-yn-Yale, Denbighshire; m. Elizabeth Mostyn, dau. of Thomas Mostyn of Mostyn. The mother of his illeg. son David Yale (Gen. 40) was Agnes Lloyd, dau. of John Lloyd who is unidentified. (*TAG, cit., TAG* 50: 246).

40. REV. DAVID YALE, L.L.D. Cambridge, of Plas Grono, Denbrighshire N. Wales, d. 1626; m. Frances Lloyd, dau. of John Lloyd ap Davis Lloyd, by Elizabeth Pigott, d. 1590, dau. of Thomas Pigott. (*TAG, cit.; TAG* 56 (1980): 101-102; (*Journal of Royal and Noble Genealogy* I (1): Robert C. Curfman, "The Triple Descent of John Lloyd of London from King John of England with an Additional Descent from Henry I," p. 14; *Dict. Welsh Biog.*, 1110).

41. THOMAS YALE, d. 1619, of Plas Grono and Chester; m. Ann Lloyd, dau. of the Rt. Rev. George Lloyd, d. 1615, Bishop of Chester. She m. (2) Theophilus Eaton, Gov. New Haven Colony, 1639-1658. (*TAG, cit.; Dict. Welsh Biog.* 579, 1110). Theophilus came to New Haven 1638, with Ann, and her children by (1), incl. David Yale, father of Elihu (for whom Yale University is named) and Thomas, ancestor of the family of Yale in America.

Line 252   Revised for 8th Edition

26. DAVID OF SCOTLAND (styled **DAVID OF HUNTINGDON**) (93-26). 9th Earl of Huntingdon, b. 1144, d. Yardley, 17 June 1219; m. 26 Aug. 1190, **MAUD OF CHESTER** (131-29), b. 1171, d. 1233, dau. of **HUGH DE KEVELIOC** (125-28), 3rd Earl of Chester.

(For a chart of their ancestry, see Geo. F. Farnham, *Leicester Medieval Pedigrees*, 11). They had, with others, **MARGARET OF HUNTINGDON** (94-27) who m. 1209, **ALAN** (38-26), Lord of Galloway, d. 1234, whose dau. **DEVORGUILLA OF GALLOWAY** (94-28) m. 1236, John Baliol of Barnard Castle and had with others: John Baliol, King of Scots; **CECILY DE BALIOL** (94-29) m. John de Burgh; **ELEANOR DE BALIOL** (95-29) m. **JOHN COMYN** (121A-29) of Badenoch; and

    27. ISABELLA OF HUNTINGDON; m. Robert Brus (or Bruce), Lord of Annandale, d. 1245 (for his ancestry, see *SP* I: 4, II: 429-432; Farrer, *Early Yorkshire Charters* II: 430-432).

    28. ROBERT BRUCE, Lord of Annandale, d. by 3 May 1294; m. (1) in or bef. 1240, Isabel de Clare, b. 1226, age 13 at mar., liv. 1264, 2nd dau. of **GILBERT DE CLARE** (63-28), 3rd Earl of Gloucester and Hereford, by his wife Isabel Marshal. (*SP* II: 430-431, IX: 55).

    29. ROBERT BRUCE, eldest s. and h., Earl of Carrick, *j.u.*, b. Writtle July 1243, d. Mar. 1304; m., as 2nd husb., **MARJORIE** (121C-30) Countess of Carrick, d. 1292, bef. 27 Oct., wid. of Adam de Kilconquhar, d.s.p. 1270, eldest dau. and h. of **NEIL** (121C-29), Earl of Carrick; m. (2) Eleanor NN, d. 1330, who m. 2nd, 1306, Richard de Waleys. (*SP* II: 426-427, 432-433; *CP* II: 360, III: 55-56, IX: 167 note c; G.W.S. Barron, *Robert Bruce*, see refs. gen. 37).

    30. ROBERT BRUCE, Lord of Annandale, b. Writtle, 11 July 1274; succeeded as Earl of Carrick 9 Nov. 1292; crowned Robert I, King of Scots, at Scone, 25 Mar. 1306, d. at Cardross, near Dumbarton, 7 June 1329; m. (1) abt. 1295, Isabel (also called Matilda) of Mar, d. bef. 1302, dau. of Donald, 6th Earl of Mar; m. (2) 1302, Elizabeth de Burgh, d. 26 Oct. 1327, dau. of **RICHARD DE BURGH** (75-31), 3rd Earl of Ulster. (*SP* V: 577-578).

    31. MARJORIE BRUCE, by (1), b. bef. 1297, d. 2 Mar. 1316; m. 1315, **WALTER STEWART** (75A-32), b. 1292, d. 9 Apr. 1326, 6th High Steward of Scotland. (*SP* I: 14-15, V: 577-578).

    32. ROBERT II, Earl of Athol, King of Scots 1371-1390, succeeded his uncle, King David II, 22 Feb. 1370/1 (1st king of the House of Stewart), b. 2 Mar. 1315/6, d. at Dundonald, Ayrshire, 19 Apr. 1390; m. (1) 1348/9 (disp. Pope Clement VI 22 Nov. 1347) Elizabeth Mure, dau. of Sir Adam Mure, of Rowallan; m. (2) Euphemia of Ross, wid. of John Randolph, Earl of Moray (disp. 2 May 1355), dau. of Hugh, Earl of Ross. (*SP* I: 15-16; *CP* I: 310-311, XII (1): 389; *The Genealogist* 13 (1999): 92).

    33. ROBERT III, by (1), (named John, but took name of Robert), Earl of Carrick, King of Scots 1390-1406; b. abt. 1337 (legitimated through his parents' marriage, disp. 22 Nov. 1347), d. at Dundonald 4 Apr. 1406; m. abt. 1367, Annabella Drummond (d. 1401), dau. of Sir John Drummond, d. 1372, of Stobhall, by wife, prob., Mary Montifex, dau. & h. of Sir William de Montifex. (*SP* I: 17; *CP* I: 154-155, III: 58; *The Genealogist* 14 (2000): 208 and note *126*).

    34. JAMES I, King of Scots 1406-1437, b. at Dunfermline, July. 1394, murdered at Perth, 21 Feb. 1436/7; m., as 1st husb., 2 Feb. 1423/4 (post nuptial dispensation 21 Sept. 1439), Joan Beaufort, d. at Dunbar, 15 July 1445, dau. of **JOHN BEAUFORT** (1-31), 1st Earl of Somerset and his wife **MARGARET DE HOLAND** (47-33). Joan; m. (2) 1439, Sir James Stewart, "The Black Knight of Lorn" (*The Genealogist* 4 (1983): 149, 157).

    35. JAMES II, King of Scots 1437-1460, b. at Holyrood, 16 Oct. 1430, killed at the siege of Roxburgh Castle, 3 Aug. 1460; m. 3 July 1449, Marie (d. 1 Dec. 1463 at Edinburgh), dau. of Arnulf (Arnould), d. 1473, Duke of Geldern, by his wife, Catherine, d. 1479, dau. of Adolf I, Duke of Cleves. (*SP* I: 19-20).

    36. JAMES III, King of Scots 1460-1488, b. at Stirling, 10 July 1452, assassinated 11 June 1488; m. 13 July 1469, **MARGARET** (**MARGARETA**), of Oldenburg (252E-36), b.

1456, d. 1486, dau. of **CHRISTIAN XIV (1)** (252E-35), King of Denmark, by his wife **DOROTHEA OF BRANDENBURG (HOHENZOLLERN)**. (252A-36) (*SP* I: 20-21; *The Genealogist* 3 (1982): 33, 42 note *4*).

37. JAMES IV, King of Scots 1488-1513, b. 17 Mar. 1472/3, killed Flodden Field, 9 Sept. 1513; m., as 1st husb., 8 Aug. 1503 (disp. granted by Pope Alexander VI, Rome, 28 July 1500), Margaret Tudor, d. 18 Oct. 1542, eldest dau. of Henry VII, King of England, by whom he had his successor, James V, ancestor of the later Kings of Scotland and England. After his death, Margaret m. (2) Aug. 1514, Archibald Douglas, Earl of Angus, div. 1526; m. (3) 1526, Henry Stewart, Lord Methven. (*SP* I: 20-23. Gens. 30-37: G.W.S. Barrow, *Robert Bruce and the Community of The Realm of Scotland* (1965), pp. 37-38, 92-93, 199, 212-213, 397, 444-445, 455-464). By a mistress, Margaret (said to have died of poison, Apr. 1502), dau. of John, 1st Lord of Drummond, and his wife Elizabeth Lindsay, dau. of Alexander, 4th Earl of Crawford, King James IV had

38. MARGARET STEWART, b. 1497; m. (1) Nov. 1512, John Gordon, Lord Gordon, Master of Huntly, d. 5 Dec. 1517, s. and h. of Alexander Gordon, d. 1524, 3rd Earl of Huntly, by his 1st wife, Janet Stewart, d. 1510, dau. of Sir John Stewart, d. 1512, Earl of Atholl. (*Registrum Magni Sigilli Regum Scotorum: The Register of the Great Seal of Scotland 1424-1513*, p. 740, no. 3452; *SP* i: 22, IV: 532-533).

39. ALEXANDER GORDON, b. abt. 1516, d. 11 Nov. 1575, Bishop of the Isles 1553; Bishop of Galloway 1558, titular Archbishop of Athens, the only Scottish prelate to join the Reformers; m. Barbara Logie, of Ennis. (*DNB* 22: 159-161; *SP* IV: 533).

40. JOHN GORDON, D.D., b. 1544, d. 3 Sept. 1619, Bishop-Elect of Galloway; Dean of Salisbury 1604-19; legitimated by his cousin, Mary, Queen of Scots, 16 Sept. 1553; m. Genevieve Petau, dau. of Gideon Petau, Sieur de Maule, in France. (*DNB* 22: 212-214; *Reg. Mag. Sig. Reg. Scot., 1546-80*, p. 190, no. 848, *ibid*, 1590-93, pp. 289-290, no. 900; *SP*: IX: 110).

41. LOUISA (or **LUCY**) **GORDON**, b. 1597, d. Sept. 1680; m. London, 16 Feb. 1613, Sir Robert Gordon, 1st Bart. (created 29 May 1625 -- the premier Baronet of Scotland and Nova Scotia), of Gordonstoun, co. Moray, b. 14 May 1580, d. Mar. 1656, son of Alexander, 11th Earl of Sutherland, by his 2nd wife, Lady Jane (or Jean) Gordon, dau. of George Gordon, 4th Earl of Huntly. (Will of Dr. John Gordon, 16 Sept. 1618, quoted by Capt. Edward Dunbar-Dunbar, *Social Life in Former Days* (1865), pp. 284-285; Sir Robert Gordon, 1st Bart., of Gordonstoun, *A Genealogical History of the Earldom of Sutherland from its Origin to the Year 1630*, p. 289 (continued to 1651 by Gilbert Gordon of Sallah, but not published until 1813); *SP*: VIII: 343-345; *DNB* 22: 224-225; Francis W. Pixley, *A History of the Baronetage* (1900), pp. 59-89 (the Latin text of Sir Robert Gordon's patent creating him a baronet) and p. 154).

42. KATHERINE GORDON, b. 11 Jan. 1620/1, d. abt. 1663; m. 26 Jan. 1647/8, Col. David Barclay, 1st Laird of Urie, co. Kincardine, b. abt. 1610, d. 12 Oct. 1686. (Lt. Col. Hubert F. Barclay and Alice Wilson-Fox, *A History of the Barclay Family*, part III, 1934, pp. 3, 35-36; Alexander Gordon, "The Great Laird of Urie," *Theological Review*, Oct. 1874, p. 537 (marriage contract of Col. David Barclay and Katherine Gordon)).

43. ROBERT BARCLAY, 2nd Laird of Urie, b. 23 Dec. 1648, d. at Urie, 3 Oct. 1690, the eminent Quaker "Apologist," Governor of East New Jersey, Sept. 1682-Oct. 1690; m. Christian Mollison, d. 14 Dec. 1722. They were ancestors of the later Lairds of Urie.

43. JOHN BARCLAY, b. abt. 1650, d. at Perth Amboy, New Jersey, Apr. 1731; settled in East Jersey abt. 1684, Member of the General Assemblies of the Province of East Jersey and of the later Province of New Jersey, Deputy Surveyor of East Jersey, Town Clerk of Perth Amboy, Receiver General and Ranger General of New Jersey, Clerk of the

Governor's Council, J.P. for Middlesex and Somerset Cos., N. J., Surrogate of the Eastern Division of New Jersey; m. Katherine (Rescarrick?), bur. 6 Jan. 1702/3, by whom he had two children: John Barclay (1702-1786), of Cranberry, New Jersey (whose descendants are traced in R. Burnham Moffat's *The Barclays of New York* (1904), pp. 57-65); and Agnes Barclay. (Proofs of John Barclay's parentage and relationship to Gov. Robert Barclay: Documents abstracted in the *New Jersey Archives*, 1st ser., vol. XXI, Calendar of Records, pp. 66, 76, 182, 201, and vol. XI, Newspaper Abstracts, vol. I, p. 243 (his obituary); King James II's confirmation in 1685 of the Barclay's possession of the Barony of Urie, naming Col. David Barclay, "Catharine Gordon his spouse," and all of their children, in *The Acts of the Parliaments of Scotland*, vol. VIII, 1821, p. 531. See also Milton Rubincam: "John Barclay of Perth Amboy: The Scion of an Illustrious House," *Proceedings of the New Jersey Historical Society*, July and Oct. 1940, containing heavy footnote documentation).

Line 252A   New to 8th Edition

28.   FRIEDRICH III (I), (parentage uncertain), Count of Zollern, Burgrave of Nuremberg, d. aft. 1 Oct. 1200; m. Sophia of Raabs, d. 1204, dau. of Konrad II, of Riedfeld, Count of Raabs, Burgrave of Nuremberg. (*ES* I.1/116B, XVI/24).

29.   KONRAD I, Count of Zollern, Burgrave of Nuremberg, d. 1260/1; m. NN, poss. dau. of Friedrich II, Count of Saarbrücken and Leiningen. (*ES* I.1/116B, XVI/24)

30.   FRIEDRICH III, Burgrave of Nuremberg and Abenberg, d. 14 Aug. 1297; m. (2) bef. 10 Apr. 1280, Helene of Saxony, d. 1309, dau. of Albrecht I, Duke of Saxony and Bernburg (252B-30). ((*ES* I.1/128, I.2/196).

31.   FRIEDRICH IV, Burgrave of Nuremberg, d. 19 May 1332; m. by. 2 Aug. 1307, Margareta of Gorz (Kärnten), d. 1348, dau. of Albert of Gorz, son of Meinhard IV (II), Count of Gorz, Duke of Kärnten. (*ES* I.1/128, III.1/43).

32.   JOHAN (HANS) II, Burgrave of Nuremberg, d. 7 Oct. 1357; m. bef. 3 Mar. 1333, Elisabeth of Henneberg, b.by 1318, d. 1377-1391, dau. of Berthold VI, Count of Henneberg in Schleusingen. (*ES* I.1/128, XVI/146).

33.   FRIEDRICH V, Burgrave of Nuremburg, d. 21 Jan. 1398; m. 7 Sept. 1350, **ELIZABETH** (252D-33) of Meissen, b. 1329, d. 1375, dau. of **FRIEDRICH II** (252D-32), Margrave of Meissen. (*ES* I.1/128, 129, 105).

34.   FRIEDRICH VI (I), Burgrave of Nuremberg, Margrave and Elector of Brandenburg, b. 1371, d. 20 Sept. 1440; m. 18 Sept. 1401, **ELIZABETH** (252C-34) of Bavaria-Landshut, b. 1383, d. 1442, dau. of **FRIEDRICH** (252C-33), Duke of Bavaria in Landshut. (*ES* I.1/128, 153).

35.   JOHANN THE ALCHEMIST, Margrave of Brandenburg, b. 1406, d. 16 Nov. 1464; m. abt. 25 Aug. 1411, **BARBARA** (252B-35) of Saxony, dau. of **RUDOLF III** (252B-34), Duke and Elector of Saxony. ((*ES* I.1/129, I.2/196).

36. DOROTHEA OF BRANDENBURG (HOHENZOLLERN), b. 1430, d. 1495; m. (2) 28 Oct. 1449, **CHRISTIAN XIV (I)** (252E-35). (*ES* I.1/129, I.3/277, 279).

Line 252B   New to 8th Edition

24.   ADALBERT OF BALLENSTEDT; m. poss. Hidda, dau. of Udo I, Margrave of Nordmark, Count in Northern Thuringia.

25.   ESIKO, Count of Ballenstedt and Swabia, d. 1059/60; m. **MATHILDE OF SWABIA** (167-21), d. 1031/2, dau. Herman II, Duke of Swabia.

26. ADALBERT, Count of Ballenstedt and Northern Thuringia, d. bet. 1076 and 1080; m. bef. 29 Oct. 1074, Adelheid of Weimer, heiress of Orlamünde, d. 28 Mar. 1100, dau. of Otto, Count of Orlamünde, Margrave of Meissen.

27. OTTO, Count of Ballenstedt, Duke of Saxony, d. 9 Feb. 1123; m. Eilika, d. 12 Jan. 1142, dau. of Magnus, Duke of Saxony.

28. ALBRECHT I, Count of Ballenstedt, Margrave and Duke of Saxony, Margrave of Brandenburg, b. 1096/1100, d. 1170; m. 1124, Sofia of Winzenburg, d. 1160, dau. of Hermann I, Count of Winzenburg. (Gens. 24-28: *ES* I.2/182).

29. BERNHARD I, Count of Anhalt, Duke of Westphalia, Duke of Saxony, d. 9 Feb. 1212; m. bef. 1178, Judith of Poland, d. aft. 2 Dec. 1201, dau. of Mieszko III, Prince of Greater Poland, half bro. of **WLADISLAS II** (147-26) (see 252C-31) King of Poland. (*ES* I.2/182, 196).

30. ALBRECHT I, Duke of Saxony and Bernburg, d. 1261; m. (3) 1247/8, Helene of Brunswick, b. 18 Mar. 1223, d. 6 Sept. 1273, dau. of Otto I, Duke of Brunswick and Lüneburg.

31. ALBRECHT II, Duke of Saxony, d. in battle 25 Aug. 1298; m. Oct. 1273, Agnes of Habsburg, b. abt. 1257, d. 1322, dau. of Rudolf I, Holy Roman Emperor (uncrowned), Count of Habsburg.

32. RUDOLF I, Duke of Saxony in Wittenberg and Brehna, d. Mar. 1356; m. (3) sh. aft. 9 Apr. 1331, Agnes of Lindow, d. 9 May 1343, dau. of Ulrich I, Count of Lindow-Ruppin. (*ES* XII/36).

33. WENZEL, Duke and Elector of Saxony, d. in battle 15 May 1388; m. bef. 11 May 1371, Cecilia de Carrara, d. 1427, dau. of Francesco de Carrara.

34. RUDOLF III, Duke and Elector of Saxony, d. 9 June 1419; m. (2) 6 Mar. 1396, Barbara of Legnica (in Poland), b. 1372/84, d. 9 May 1436, dau. of Ruprecht, Duke of Legnica, gr. grand nephew of Bolko I, Duke of Jawar and Swidnica (Poland) (see 252C-31).

35. BARBARA, of Saxony, b. abt. 1405, d. Oct. 1465; m. 1412, **JOHANN THE ALCHEMIST** (252A-35), Margrave of Brandenburg. (Gens. 30-35: *ES* I.2/196).

Line 252C   New to 8th Edition

23. OTTO I, Count of Scheyern, d. bef. July 1072; m. (2) Hazziga (Hadagund) of Scheyern, d. bef. 1104, dau. of Hartwig II, Count Palatine of Bavaria. (*ES* I.1/90).

24. EKKEHART, Count of Scheyern, d. by 1087/8; m. Richgard of Krain, d. bef. 1128, dau. of Ulrich I, Margrave of Krain (Neimar-Orlamünde) and Sophie of Hungary, first cousin of Otto, Count of Orlamünde (see 252B-26). (*ES* I.1/90. 144).

25. OTTO I (III), Count Palatine of Bavaria, Count of Wittelsbach and Scheyern, d. 4 Mar. prob. 1123; m. NN dau. of Eberhard of Ratzenhofen. (*ES* I.1/90, XVI/74).

26. OTTO II, Count Palatine of Wittelsbach, d. 1156; m. Heilika of Lengenfeld-Hopfenohe-Pettendorf, d. 1170, dau. of Friedrich III, Baron of Lengenfeld-Hopfenohe-Pettendorf by Hedwig of Staufen. (*ES* I/1/90, XVI/95A).

27. OTTO I (III), Duke of Bavaria, Count Palatine of Wittelsbach, d. 11 Jul. 1183; m. Agnes of Looz, d. 26 Mar. 1191, dau. of Louis I, Count of Looz and Rieneck (see 155-25). (*ES* I.1/90, XVIII/56).

28. LUDWIG I, Duke of Bavaria, Count Palatine of the Rhine, b. 1173/4, d. 15 Sept. 1231; m. Oct. 1204, Ludmilla of Bohemia, d. 5 Aug. 1240, dau. of Friedrich, Duke of Bohemia. (*ES* I.1/90. 91. I.2/177).

29. OTTO II, Duke of Bavaria, b. 1206, d. 1253; m. at Worms, May 1222, Agnes of Saxony, b. abt. 1201, d. 1267, dau. of Heinrich of Saxony, Count Palatine of the Rhine. (*ES* I.1/91, 18).

30. LUDWIG II, Duke of Bavaria, b. 13 Apr. 1229, d. 1294; m. (3) 24 Oct. 1273, Mechtild of Habsburg, b. abt. 1253, d. 1304, dau. of Rudolf I, Holy Roman Emperor, (IV), Count of Habsburg. (*ES* I.1/91, 41).

31. LUDWIG IV, Duke of Bavaria in Upper Bavaria, Count Palatine of the Rhine, King of Italy, Holy Roman Emperor, b. 1282, d 11 Oct. 1347; m. (1) 1308/11, Beatrix of Swidnica (Poland), d. 1322, dau. of Bolko I, Duke of Jawar and Swidnica (Poland), b. 1252/6, d. 1301 (the son of Boleslas II, Duke of Legnica, d. 1278; son of Heinrich II, d. 1241, Duke of Silesia, Krakow and Greater Poland; son of Heinrich I, d. 1238, Duke of Silesia, Krakow and Greater Poland; son of Boleslas I, Duke of Silesia, d, 1201; son of **WLADISLAS II**, King of Poland (147-26)). (*ES* I.1/91, 104, III.1/9, 12).

32. STEPHEN II, Duke of Bavaria in Lower Bavaria, Landshut, and Upper Bavaria, b. 1319, d. 1375; m. (1) 1328, Isabella (Isolde) of Sicily, d. 1349, dau. of Frederick II, King of Sicily, Prince of Aragon, son of Pedro III, King of Aragon. (*ES* I.1/104, 105, II/71, 73).

33. FRIEDRICH, Duke of Bavaria in Landshut, b. abt. 1339, d. 1393; m. (2) 1381, Magdalena Visconti, b. 1361, d. 1404, dau. of Barbanò Visconti. (*ES* I.1; Isenburg II/131).

34. ELISABETH, of Bavaria-Landshut, b. 1383, d. 13 Nov. 1442; m. 18 Sept. 1401, **FRIEDRICH (VI) I** (252A-34), Burgrave of Nuremburg. (*ES* I.1/105, 128, 129).

Line 252D   New to 8th Edition

23. DEDO I, Count of Merseburg, son of Dietrich (Theodericus) of Wettin, liv. 976, d. 1009; m. bef. 985, Thietburga of Haldensleben, dau. of Dietrich, Count of Haldensleben, Margrave of Nordmark. (*ES* I.1/150).

24. DIETRICH I, Count of Eilenburg, Hassegau, and Siusli, murd. 19 Nov. 1034; m. Mathilde of Meissen, dau. Ekkhard I, Margrave of Meissen. (*ES* I.1/150, 87B).

25. THIEMO, Count of Brehna, d. aft. 1099/1101; m. Ida of Northeim, dau. of Otto I, Count of Northeim, Duke of Bavaria. (*ES* I.1/150, VIII/132).

26. KONRAD I "the Great," Count of Wettin in Brehna and Camburg, d. 5 Feb. 1157; m. bef. 1119, Liutgard of Elchingen, d. 1145, dau. of Adelbert, Count of Elchingen-Ravenstein. (*ES* I.1/150-151, XII/66).

27. OTTO "the Rich," Margrave of Meissen, d. 18 Feb. 1190; m. 1144/7, Hedwig of Ballenstedt, d. Mar. 1203, dau. of **ALBRECHT I** (252B-28), Count of Ballenstedt. (*ES* I.1/151-152, I.2/182).

28. DIETRICH, of Weissenfels, Margrave of Meissen, d. 17 Feb. 1221; m. 1194, Jutta of Thuringia, d. 1235, dau. of Herman I, Count Palatine of Saxony, Landgrave of Thuringia. (*ES* I.1/152, 145).

29. HEINRICH, "the Illustrious," Margrave of Meissen, b. 1218, d. 1288; m. (1) 1 May 1234, Konstanze of Austria, d. 1243, dau. of Leopold VI, Duke of Steyr, Duke of Austria. (*ES* I.1/152, 85).

30. ALBRECHT, "the Degenerate," Landgrave of Thuringia, Count Palatine of Saxony, b. 1240, d. 1315; m. (1) 1254/5, Margareta of Staufen, b. 1237, d. 1270, dau. of Frederick II, Holy Roman Emperor. (*ES* I.1/152, 15).

31. FRIEDRICH I, Count Palatine of Saxony, Margrave of Meissen, Landgrave of Thuringia, b. 1257, d. 1323; m. (2) Elisabeth of Lobdeburg, b. 1286, d. 1359, dau. of Hartmann of Arnshaugk, Baron of Lobdeburg. (*ES* I.1/152, XVI/111).

32. **FRIEDRICH II**, Margrave of Meissen, Landgrave of Thuringia, Count Palatine of Saxony, b. 1310, d. 1349; m. 1323, Mechtild of Bavaria, b. 1313, d. 1346, dau. of Ludwig IV, Duke of Bavaria, Holy Roman Emperor. (*ES* I.1/152-153, 104).

33. **ELISABETH**, of Meissen, b. 22 Nov. 1329, d. 21 Apr. 1375; m. **FRIEDRICH V** (252A-33), d. 1398. (*ES* I.1/153, 128).

Line 252E   New to 8th Edition

24. **EGILMAR I**, Count on the border of Saxony and Frisia, liv. 1091-1108; m. Richeza, d. aft. 1108. (*ES* I.3/276).

25. **EGILMAR II**, Count, Administrator of Rastede, d. bef. 1145; m. Eilika of Rietberg, dau. of Heinrich I, Count of Rietberg. (*ES* I.3/276, VIII/98B).

26. **CHRISTIAN I**, Count of Oldenburg, liv. 1148-1167; m. Kunigunde of Versfleth, liv. 1198, dau. of Gerbert, Count of Versfleth.

27. **MORITZ I**, Count of Oldenburg, d. bef. 1209; m. Salome of Wickrath, d. aft. 1211, dau. of Otto I, Baron of Wickrath. (*ES* I.3/276, VII/142).

28. **CHRISTIAN III**, Count of Oldenburg, liv. 1209-1233; m. Agnes. (*ES* I.3/276).

29. **JOHAN I**, Count of Oldenburg, liv. 1262; m. Richza of Hoya, d. aft. 19 Jun. 1264, dau. of Heinrich II, Count of Hoya at Steyerberg. (*ES* I.3/276, 277, XVII/132).

30. **CHRISTIAN IV**, Count of Oldenburg, d. 1285/7; m. (1) Hedwig, d. 1270. (*ES* I.3/277; *TAG* 47 (1971): 149-156, 54 (1978): 231-232).

31. **JOHAN II**, Count of Oldenburg, d. 1314/6; m. (2) 1298, Hedwig of Diepholz, dau. of Konrad V, Baron of Diepholz. (*ES* I.3/277, XVII/130).

32. **KONRAD I**, Count of Oldenburg, d. 8 Jul. 1350; m. bef. 13 May 1339, Ingeborg of Holstein-Schauenburg, d. aft. 1343, dau. of Gerhard III, Count of Holstein-Schauenburg in Segeberg. (*ES* I.3/277, 299).

33. **CHRISTIAN XI**, Count of Oldenburg, d. 1399/1403, m. bef. 29 Aug. 1377, Agnes of Honstein, d. aft. 1394, dau. of Dietrich V, Count of Honstein. (*ES* I.3/277, XVII/92).

34. **DIETRICH**, Count of Oldenberg in Delmenhorst, d. 14 Feb. 1440; m. (2) abt. 23 Nov. 1323, Heilwig of Holstein-Schauenburg, b. 1389, d. 1436, dau. of Gerhard V, Count of Holstein-Schauenburg in Rendsburg, Duke of Schleswig. (*ES* I.3/277, 301).

35. **CHRISTIAN XIV (I)**, Count of Oldenburg, King of Denmark, Norway and Sweden, b. 1426, d. 21 May 1481; m. 28 Oct. 1449, **DOROTHEA OF BRANDENBURG (HOHENZOLLERN)** (252A-36). (*ES* I.3/279).

36. **MARGARET (MARGARETA)** of Oldenburg, b. 23 Jun. 1456, d. 14 Jul. 1486; m. 1469, **JAMES III** (252-36), King of Scots. (*ES* I.3/279).

Line 253   Revised for 8th Edition

29. **EUDO LA ZOUCHE** (39-29, 39A-29), seen 1251, d. bet. 28 Apr.and 25 June 1279; m. by 13 Dec. 1273, **MILICENT DE CANTELOU** (66-30), granddau. of **WILLIAM DE BRAOSE** (177-8). (*CP* I: 22-23, XII (2): 937-938, X: 674).

30. **ELIZABETH LA ZOUCHE**, liv. 1297; m. by 20 Jan. 1287/8, as a child, **SIR NICHOLAS POYNTZ, KNT.** (234A-32), 2nd Lord Poyntz, b. abt. 1278, d. sh. bef. 12 July 1311. Sir Nicholas m. (2) by 9 Feb. 1308/9, Maud de Acton, d. 1361, dau. of John II de Acton (d. 1312). (*CP* X: 674-675).

31. HUGH DE POYNTZ, eldest son and h. by (1), b. at Hoo, Kent, proved age 12 Feb. 1316/7, d. shortly bef. 2 May 1337; m. by 1 June 1330, Margaret Pavole, dau. of Walter Pavole, co. Wilts. (*Coll. Topo. et Gen.* VII: 149; *CP* X: 675-676; XIV: 536).

32. NICHOLAS DE POYNTZ, s. and h., b. North Okenden, Essex, age 17+ in 1337, d. by Michaelmas 1376; m. (1) by 13 Oct. 1333, Eleanor Erleigh, said to be dau. of Sir John Erleigh; m. (2) by 30 Jan. 1367/8 Eve de Stokes. (Dugdale, *Baronage* II: 2; *CP* X: 676).

33. MARGARET POYNTZ, dau. and coh. by (1); m. abt. 1370, John de Newburgh, b. abt. 1340, bur. Bindon Abbey, 4 June 1381, of Lulworth, Dorset. (*CP* X: 676 note *k*; J. Gardner Bartlett, *Newberry Genealogy* (Boston, 1914), p. 10).

34. JOHN NEWBURGH, of co. Dorset, s. and h., b. abt. 1370, d. sh. aft. Feb. 1438/9; m. by 1400, Joan De la Mere, dau. of Sir John De la Mere, Knt. (Bartlett, *cit.*, p. 11).

35. JOHN NEWBURGH, s. and h., b. abt. 1400, d. in Dorset, 1 Apr. 1484; m. (1) 1422, Edith Attemore, dau. of Robert and Joan Attemore, no issue; m. (2) abt. 1435, Alice Carent, wid. of John Westbury, dau. of William Carent of Toomer, co. Somerset, who brought him the manor of Berkley, Somerset. (Bartlett, *cit.*, 10, 11).

36. THOMAS NEWBURGH, b. abt. 1445, 3rd and yngst. s., rec'd. manor of Berkley from his mother, d. 15 Mar. 1512/3; m. by 1484, Alice NN, who m. (2) Thomas Kyrton, and d. 1525. (Bartlett, *cit.*, pp. 14-16).

37. WALTER NEWBURGH (or **NEWBOROUGH**), 2nd son, b. abt. 1487, d. 12 Aug. 1517; m. abt. 1512, Elizabeth Birport, who m. (2) abt. 1520, George Strangeways, and d. 1570/1 leaving a will, and chn. by both husbands. (Bartlett, *cit.*, pp. 16-17; Gens. 33-37: *Search for the Passengers of the Mary and John 1630*, v. 17: 104).

38. RICHARD NEWBOROUGH (or **NEWBURGH**), only s. and h., b. abt. July 1517, held manors in Dorset, d. at Othe Frauncis, Dorset, by 30 Jan. 1568/9, will dated 3 Dec. 1568; m. abt. 1552, Elizabeth Horsey, dau. of William Horsey of Binghams., Elizabeth m. (2) NN Woodshaw. (Bartlett, *cit.*, pp. 17-19; *Search for the Passengers of the Mary and John 1630*, v. 17: 104-105).

39. RICHARD NEWBERRY (or **NEWBURGH**), 2nd son, b. abt. 1557, present at Netherbury, co. Dorset, d. abt. 1629 at Yarcombe, co. Devon.; m. 15 Jan. 1580, Grace Matthew, bur. Yarcombe, 18 Dec. 1632, dau. of John Matthew. (Their children were b. and rec. in Yarcombe). (Bartlett, *cit.*, 23-24; *Search for the Passengers of the Mary and John 1630*, v. 17: 105-106).

40. THOMAS NEWBERRY, 4th son (6th ch.), bapt. Yarcombe, co. Devon, 11 Nov. 1594, to America on the 'Recovery of London' Apr. 1634, d. Dorchester, Mass. Dec. 1635; m. (1) abt. 1619, Jane Dabinot, b. abt. 1600, d. Eng. abt. 1629, dau. of Christopher Dabinot of Yarcombe, co. Devon and Chardstock, co. Dorset; m. (2) Joan Dabinot, d. Norwalk, Conn., 3 Apr. 1655 (believed to have been a cousin of his 1st wife), dau. of John Dabinot. Joan m. (2) 1637, as his 2nd wife, Rev. John Warham of Norwalk, Conn. (Bartlett, *cit.*, 35-44; *Search for the Passengers of the Mary and John 1630*, v. 17: 106-107, 109-110, v. 26: 5).

Line 254

28. JOAN (27-27, 29A-27), (nat. dau. of King **JOHN** (1-25)) Princess of North Wales; m. by 1206, **LLYWELYN AP IORWERTH** (176B-27), Prince of Wales.

29. ANGHARAD, m. Maelgwn Fychan ap Maelgwn ap Rhys, lord of Cardigan Is Ayron, d. 1257. (*TAG* 38:180; Bridgeman, *Princes of South Wales*, pp. 203-204, 209; *Gen.* 5 (1881): 166).

30. ELEN FERCH MAELGWN; m. Maredudd ap Owain ap Gruffudd, d. 1265, lord of Cardigan Uch Ayron. (Bridgeman, *cit*, 209, 249; J.E. Lloyd, *History of Wales* (1954), II: 768).

31. OWAIN AP MAREDUDD, of Cardigan, d. 1275; m. Angharad ferch Owain ap Maredudd, lord of Cardigan Is Ayron. (Bridgeman, *cit.*, 249; Lloyd, *cit.*, 768).

32. LLEWELLYN AP OWAIN, lord of a moiety of Gwynnionith and of Caerwedros, d. 1309; m. a dau. of Sir Robert de Vale, Lord of Trefgarn. (Bridgeman, *cit.*, 249; Lloyd, *cit.*, 768).

33. THOMAS AP LLEWELLYN, of Iscoed Uch Hirwen, Cardiganshire, b. bef. 14 Aug. 1343; m. **ELEANOR** (260-33) ferch Philip ap Ifor, lord of Iscoed. (Bridgeman, *cit.*, 247, 249).

34. ELEN FERCH THOMAS AP LLEWELLYN, m. **GRUFFYDD FYCHAN** (249-34), lord of Glyndyfrdwy. (Gen. Mag. 16 (1969): 6-7 and chart; Bridgeman, *cit.*, 249; J.Y.W. Lloyd, *Hist. of Powys Fadog* I 198). (*Burke's Guide to the Royal Family* (1973), "the Kings and Princes of Wales," pp 325-326; *Journal of Royal and Noble Genealogy* I (1): Robert C. Curfman, "The Triple Descent of John Lloyd of London from King John of England with an Additional Descent from Henry I," Appendix, p. 18 note 11).

Line 255   Revised for 8th Edition

25. HAROLD (DE EWYAS) (235-22) of Ewyas Harold, co. Hereford, liv. 1115; m. NN. (Sanders, 43).

26. ROBERT I DE EWYAS (EWIAS), d. post 1147, Lord of Ewyas Harold; m. Sibil. (Keats-Rohan, *Domesday Descendants* II: 453.)

27. ROBERT II DE EWYAS, d. 1198, of Ewyas Harold; m. Pernel (Petronilla), liv. 1204. (Keats-Rohan, *op. cit.*; Sanders, *op. cit*; *CP* XII (2): 18).

28. SIBYL DE EWYAS, d. bef. 1 July 1236; m. (1) poss. in 1198, Robert I de Tregoz, d. bef. 29 Apr. 1215; m. (2) Roger de Clifford, d. 1231, of Tenbury, co, Worcester, son of Walter de Clifford. (*CP* XII (2): 16 note *d*).

29. LUCY DE TREGOZ, by (1); m. John III le Strange, d. by 1269, Lord Strange of Knokyn. (*Topo. et Geneal.* II: 130; *CP* XII (1): 350-351; Eyton, *Antiquities of Shropshire* X: 262; Ewen, *Observations on the Lestranges*, chart, p. 1).

30. JOHN IV LE STRANGE, d. 1275, Lord Strange of Knokyn; m. bef. 1254, **JOAN DE SOMERY** (249-31), dau. of Roger de Somery and **NICHOLE D'AUBIGNY** (126-30). (*CP* XII (1): 351; Eyton, *op. cit.*, 263; Ewen, *op. cit.*; *LeStrange Rec.*, 153-155.).

Line 255A   Prepared for an earlier edition by Douglas Richardson. (Editorial additions to 8th Edition)

28. ROBERT I DE TREGOS, d. bef. 29 Apr. 1215; m. abt. 1198, **SIBYL DE EWYAS** (255-28), d. bef. 1 July 1236.

29. ROBERT II DE TREGOZ, d. Evesham, 1265, held barony of Ewyas Harold, co. Hereford; m. 1 Aug. 1245, Juliane de Cantelou, liv. 6 Aug. 1285, (sister of Thomas, Bishop of Hereford, d. 1282, canonized 1320 as St. Thomas of Hereford), dau. of William II de Cantelou (d. 1251) by his wife Millicent de Gournay (d. 1260), dau. of Hugh V de Gournay and **JULIANE DE DAMMARTIN** (152-27). (*CP* I: 350-351, XII (2): 18-19; *Sussex Arch. Colls.* xciii: 34-56; Sanders, 43; *Beds. Hist. Rec. Soc.* V: 213-214, chart p. 215).

30. SIR JOHN DE TREGOZ, adult by 1271, d. shortly bef. 6 Sept. 1300, Lord Tregoz, lord of barony of Ewyas Harold, co. Hereford; m. (1) Mabel Fitz Warin, d. 1297, wid. of

William de Crevequer, d. 1263, and dau. of Sir Fulk Fitz Warin of Whittington, co. Salop. (*CP* XII (2): 20-22).

31. CLARICE DE TREGOZ, elder dau. and coh., inherited half the barony of Ewyas Harold, liv. April 1289, dead by 28 Aug. 1300; m. in or bef. 12 Sept. 1276, Sir Roger la Warre, 1st Baron la Warre, adult by 1279, d. 20 June 1320, of Wickwar, co. Gloucester, Brislington, Somerset, etc., son of Sir John la Warre, by Olympia de Fokinton, dau. of Sir Hugh de Fokinton. (*CP* IV: 139-141).

32. JOHN LA WARRE, b. abt. 1276/7 (age 23 or 24 in 1300), d. 9 May 1347, 2nd Baron la Warre; m. soon after 19 Nov. 1294, **JOAN DE GRELLE** (99-31), d. 20/21 Mar. 1352/3. (*CP* IV: 141-143).

Line 256

33. ROBERT III, King of Scots (252-33), b. abt. 1337 (legitimated through his parents' marriage), d. 4 Apr. 1406; m. abt. 1367, Annabella Drummond, d. 1401, dau. of Sir John Drummond of Stobhall. (*SP* I: 17-18).

34. MARY STEWART, d. in 1458; m. (1) George Douglas, Earl of Angus (marriage contract dated 24 May 1397). He was captured by the English at the battle of Homildon Hill, 14 Sept. 1402, and d. of the plague shortly thereafter. (*SP* I: 18, 173).

35. ELIZABETH DOUGLAS; m. (charter, 1423) Sir Alexander Forbes, 1st Lord Forbes, b. abt. 1380, d. 1448, son of Sir John Forbes and Margaret (or Elizabeth) Kennedy. (*SP* IV: 47-48; *CP* V: 544).

36. JAMES FORBES, 2nd Lord Forbes, d. bet. 20 Sept. 1460 and 30 July 1462; m. Egidia (or Gille) Keith, liv. 14 Aug. 1473, dau. of William Keith. (*SP* IV: 50-51; *CP* V: 544-545. XIV: 329).

37. WILLIAM FORBES, 3rd Lord Forbes, d. bet. 9 July 1477 and 5 July 1483; m. (charter 8 July 1468), Christian Gordon, dau. of Alexander Gordon, 1st Earl of Huntly, by his 3rd wife, Elizabeth Crichton, dau. of William Crichton, Lord Crichton. (*SP* IV: 51-52; *CP* V: 545). (The 3rd Lord Forbes' immediate successors were his sons, Alexander, 4th Lord, and Arthur, 5th Lord, both of whom d.s.p.).

38. JOHN FORBES, 6th Lord Forbes (succeeding his brother Arthur, 1493), d. 1547; m. (2) bef. 26 Feb. 1509/10, Christian Lundin, d. by 1515, dau. of Sir John Lundin of Lundin. (*SP* IV: 53-55; *CP* V: 545).

39. WILLIAM FORBES, 7th Lord Forbes, d. 1593; m. 19 Dec. 1538, in the Abbey of Lindores, Elizabeth Keith, d. bef. 13 Nov. 1604, dau. and coh. of Sir William Keith, of Innerugie, co. Banff. (*SP* IV: 55-57; *CP* V: 546).

40. ISABEL FORBES, b. 16 Oct. 1548, bur. at Aberdeen 22 Mar. 1622; m. 1567, Sir John Gordon, 3rd Laird of Pitlurg, co. Banff, who d. 16 Sept. 1600. He was son of John Gordon and Janet Ogilvie, and grandson of John Gordon, 1st Laird of Pitlurg, by 1st wife, Jane Stewart, dau. of Sir John Stewart, 1st Earl of Atholl, and granddau. of Sir James Stewart, the Black Knight of Lorn, by Joan Beaufort, wid. of **JAMES I** (252-34) King of Scots, and great-granddau. of **EDWARD III** (1-29). (*SP* IV: 57).

41. ROBERT GORDON, 5th Laird of Pitlurg (succeeding his bro., John, the 4th Laird, 1619), and 1st Laird of Straloch (by which title he is generally known), b. at Kinmundy, Aberdeenshire, 14 Sept. 1580, d. 18 Aug. 1661 (the distinguished Scottish geographer, mathematician, and antiquary); m. (1) 1608, Katherine Irvine, d. 3 Aug. 1662, dau. of Alexander Irvine, Laird of Lynturk. (*DNB* 8: 226-227; Balbithan Ms., p. 31, written abt. 1730 and published in *The House of Gordon*, edited by James Malcolm Bulloch, M.A., Vol. I, 1903).

42. ROBERT GORDON, 6th Laird of Pitlurg, b. 1609, d. 18 Apr. 1681; m. 1638, Catherine Burnett, dau. of Sir Thomas Burnett, 1st Baronet of Leys, by (1) Margaret Douglas, dau. of Sir Robert Douglas of Glenbervie. (George Burnett, L.L.D., *The Family of Burnett of Leys* (1901), pp. 59, 62; Balbithan Ms., p. 31, in Bulloch, *op. cit.*, Vol. I).

43. THOMAS GORDON, b. prob. at Pitlurg, co. Banff, abt. 1652; settled in the Province of East New Jersey 1684, held numerous offices: Deputy Secretary and Register for the East Jersey Proprietors, Clerk of the Court of Common Right, Register of the Court of Chancery, Judge of the Probate Court, Attorney-General of the Province of East New Jersey, Member of the General Assembly of the Province of New Jersey, Speaker of the General Assembly, Chief Justice of New Jersey, Member of the Royal Council of New Jersey, Attorney-General of New Jersey, d. at Perth Amboy, New Jersey, 28 Apr. 1722; m. (1) Helen NN, who d. Dec. 1687; m. (2) 1695, Janet Mudie, dau. of David Mudie of Perth Amboy. He had issue by both wives, but only his children by Janet seem to have survived childhood and to have left issue. (Testimony by Rev. Alexander Innes, of Monmouth Co., N.J., 12 Mar. 1712/13: "I can certify with a good Conscience that he is descended from an honorable Orthodox, and Loyal Family, being Grand child of the Eldest Son to the memorable Robert Gordon of Pitlurg and Straloch," *New Jersey Archives* (1st ser.) Vol. IV: 177-178; Letter from Thomas Gordon, brother of the Laird of Straloch, to George Alexander, advocate in Edinburgh, dated "From the Cedar Brook of East New Jersey," 16 Feb. 1685, quoted in George Scot's *The Model of the Government of the Province of East-New-Jersey in America, 1685* (published in Whitehead's *East Jersey under the Proprietary Governmemts*, 1848, pp. 326-327); and Milton Rubincam, "The Honorable Thomas Gordon: Attorney General and Chief Justice," *Proceedings of the New Jersey Historical Society*, Vol. 57, July 1939, pp. 148-150, and documentary evidence cited in the footnotes therein).

Line 257   Revised for 8th Edition

27. HENRY FITZ AILWIN FITZ LEFSTAN, liv. 1165, d. 1212, (son of Ailwin, son of Lefstan, son of Ongar), first mayor of the Commune of London 1187-1212; m. Margaret, parentage unknown. (J.H. Round, *The Commune of London*, 105; Farrer, *Honours and Knight's Fees*, III: 347-350; Keats-Rohan, *Domesday Desc.* II: 860; DNB VII: 85-86).

28. PETER FITZ HENRY, of London, d. 1207; m. Isabel de Chesney, d. by 1203, dau. of Bartholomew de Chesney, and received with her a moiety of the manor of Addington, Surrey, held by "pantry service" (Farrer, *cit.* (Honor of Warenne); J.H. Round, *The King's Sergeants*, 246-249). The reader will be interested in the meaning of "pantry service." The holder of Addington was required as a condition of tenure to provide a special dish to the monarch at coronations. This dish was called "dillegrout" and was provided at the coronation of Richard II in 1377 by **WILLLAM BARDOLF** (257-34). The following is quoted from Round's *The King's Sergeants*, pp. 248-249, under the title, ""The Maupygernoun Serjeanty" "It has been ingeniously suggested that this mess of potage (as it is subsequently described) may be represented by the recipe for "Bardolf" in an Arundel MS., said to be of early-15th cent. date, It runs thus:

"Take almonde mylk, and draw hit up thik with vernage, and let hit boyle, and braune of capons braied and put therto; and cast therto sugre, claves (cloves), maces, pynes, and ginger, mynced; and take chekyns parboyled and chopped, and pul of the skyn, and boyle al ensemble, and, in the settynge doune from the fire, put thereto a lytel vynegur alaied with

247

pouder of giner, and a lytel water of everose, and make the potage hanginge, and serve hit forth" (Household Ordinances (Society of Antiquaries), p. 466)."

After the Reign of Richard II this "mess" was presented at coronations, from the reign of Charles II onwards, by the Leigh family, but the "merry monarch,"" we are told, carefully abstained from eating it. It was still presented by the lord of the manor at the coronation of George III, and even at the last banquet, that of George IV, the right was claimed and obtained by the Archbishop of Canterbury (The Archbishops held Addington from 1807 to 1897). Accordingly, the Deputy appointed by his Grace the Archbishop of Canterbury, as Lord of the Manor of Bardolf, otherwise Addington, presented the mess of Dillegrout, prepared by the King's Master Cook (Sir George Nayler's narrative reprinted by Mr. Legg, p. 358).

29. JOAN, yngr. dau. and coh.; m. (1) Ralph de Parminter; m. (2) 1212, William Aguillon (perh. son of William Aguillon, who 1200 covenanted to deliver his son William to King John as hostage) obtained Addington with his wife. (Farrer, *cit.*; Round, *cit.*). He withdrew from allegiance to King John, but returned, lands restored 17 Sept. 1217. He d. 1244.

30. ROBERT AGUILLON, s. and h. 1244, held lands in Addington, Surrey, Walton, co. Hertford, Greatham, co. Hants., liv. 1260-1267, sheriff of Surrey and Sussex, constable of Guilford Castle 1264, lic. to crenellate manor house of Perching and to ditch 1268, d. 15 Feb. 1285/6; m. (1) in or bef. Aug. 1256, Joan de Ferrers, d. Oct. 1267, wid. of Sir John de Mohun, d. by 1254, dau. of **WILLLAM DE FERRERS**, Earl of Derby (127-30), by (1) Sibyl Marshal, dau. and coh. of William Marshal, 3rd Earl of Pembroke; m. (2) Margaret, "Countess of the Isle," d. 1292, dower assigned in manors of Addington, Surrey, Bures Taney, Essex, Greatham, co. Hants., etc. (Farrer, *cit.*; CP I: 416, IV: 199, IX: 21).

31. ISABEL AGUILLON, by (1), b. 25 Mar. 1257/8 (age 28 in 1286), lady of Perching 1316, d. by 28 May 1325; m. bef. 1282, Sir Hugh Bardolf, b. abt. 29 Sept. 1259, d. Sept. 1304, 1st Lord Bardolf of Wormegay, Norfolk, son of William Bardolf, d. 1289, of Wormegay, by his wife, Juliane de Gournay, d. 1295, dau. & h. of Hugh V de Gournay, d. 1238, by his wife, **JULIANE DE DAMMARTIN** (152-27). (CP I: 417-418).

32. THOMAS BARDOLF, 2nd Lord Bardolf, s. and h., b. 4 Oct. 1282, d. 15 Dec. 1329; m. Agnes de Grandison, d. 11 Dec. 1357. (CP I: 418, XIV: 64).

33. JOHN BARDOLF, 3rd Lord Bardolf, s. and h., b. 13 Jan. 1312/13, d. Assisi, Italy, July or Aug. 1363; m. 1326, Elizabeth Damory b. 1318, liv. 5 Feb. 1360, only dau. and h. of Roger Damory, 1st Lord Damory, d. abt. Mar. 1321/2, by **ELIZABETH DE CLARE** (11-30). (CP I: 418-419, IV: 42-46, V: 715 note d).

34. WILLIAM BARDOLF, 4th Lord Bardolf, of Wormegay, b. 21 Oct. 1349, d. 29 Jan. 1385/6, age 36, will dated 12 Sept. 1384; m. aft. 10 Feb. 1365, Agnes Poynings, d. 12 June 1403, dau. of Michael Poynings, Lord Poynings, to whom William Bardolf had been in ward. Agnes m. (2) sh. aft. 10 Apr. 1386, Sir Thomas Mortimer, dead 9 Jan. 1402/3. She d. 12 June 1403, will dated 9 Jan. 1402/3, pr. 13 June 1403. (CP I: 419, XIV: 65).

35. CECILY BARDOLF, d. 29 Sept. 1432, bur. Ingham Priory; m. bef. 1408, Sir Brian Stapleton of Ingham and Bedale (son of Sir Miles Stapleton by Ela Ufford, dau. Sir Edmund Ufford, Lord Ufford (*Topo. et Gen.* II 274)), age 40+ in 1419, d. 7 Aug. 1438, bur.

Ingham Priory, will dated 5 Apr. and 4 May 1438, pr. 6 Aug. 1438. (*CP* V: 397; *Norfolk Arch.* VIII: 222-223).

36. SIR MILES STAPLETON, KNT., b. abt. 1408, d. 30 Sept. or 1 Oct. 1466, bur. Ingham Priory, will 4 Aug. 1442, pr. 17 Nov. 1466; m (1) NN; m. (2) abt. 1436, as 1st husb., Katharine de la Pole, d. 13/14 Oct. 1488, dau. and, in 1430, h. of Sir Thomas de la Pole of Grafton Regis, co. Northampton, and Marsh, co. Bucks., by Anne Cheyney, dau. of Nicholas Cheyney. Katharine m. (2) as his 3rd wife, **SIR RICHARD HARCOURT** (143-35), d. 1 Oct. 1486. (*ES* X/139; Rosemary Horrow, *The De La Poles of Hull*, pub. 1983 by the East Yorkshire Local Hist. Soc., Local Hist. Set., no. 38, esp. chart p. 23; *VCH Buckingham* 4: 206-207).

37. ELIZABETH STAPLETON, dau. & coh. by (2), b. abt. 1440, d. 18 Feb. 1504/5; m. (1) abt. 1458 as 2nd wife, Sir William Calthorpe, b. 1409, sheriff of Norfolk 1442-58, 1464-76, d. Nov. 1494, age 85, leaving a will (he had m. 1st Elizabeth Grey, d. 1437, dau. of Reginald Grey, Lord Grey of Ruthyn); m. (2) Sir John Fortescue, d. 28 July 1500; m. (3) Sir Edward Howard, K.G., Lord High Admiral, slain 25 Apr. 1513. (*Gen. Mag.* 17: 552; *Norfolk Arch.*, IX: fac. p. 1; *CP* VI: 397; *VA Gen.* 40 (1996): 69).

38. ANNE CALTHORPE, will 1494; m., as 1st wife, Sir Robert Drury of Hawstead, M.P. Suffolk, Speaker of the House of Commons 1495, Privy Council 1526, etc., d. 2 Mar. 1535/6, bur. St. Mary's Church, Bury St. Edmunds. Sir Robert m. (2) Anne Jernegan, wid. of Edward Gray, Lord Gray, by whom no issue, and dau. of Edward Jernegan (or Jerningham) of Somerley (*Gen. Mag.* 17: 551-552; *DNB*; *Norfolk Arch.*, cit.)

39. ANNE DRURY, d. 7 June 1672; m. (1) **GEORGE WALDEGRAVE, ESQ.** (200-38), b. 1483, d. 1528, son of William Waldgrave by **MARGERY WENTWORTH** (200-37); m. (2) Sir Thomas Jermyn. Monumental brass for Anne Drury and her two husbands in parish church of Depden, Suffolk. (Muskett II: 313, 354; *Gen. Mag.* 17: 550-552; Mill Stephenson, *A List of Monumental Brasses in the British Isles* (1926), p. 454; *Visit. of Essex* (1558): 120).

Line 258   Revised for 8th Edition

27. RICHARD, Earl of Cornwall, King of the Romans, 2nd son of **JOHN** (1-25), King of England, and **ISABELLA OF ANGOULÊME** (117-27, 153A-28), b. 5 Jan. 1209, d. 2 Apr. 1272, had, by Joan de Valletort, wid. of Alexander Okeston, dau. of Sir Reginald de Valletort (or Vautort), at least one illeg. child,

28. SIR RICHARD DE CORNWALL, d. 1272, lord of Thunnock, co. Lincoln; m. Joan, liv. 1319, par. uncertain. (*NEHGR* 119 (1965): 98. *Gen.* 3 (1897) 226 calls her dau. of John, Lord St. Owen).

29. SIR EDMUND DE CORNWALL of Kinlet, eldest son, d. 22 Mar. 1354, knt. of the shire for London 1324; m. 1313/4, Elizabeth de Brampton, bapt. 12 Dec. 1295, d. aft. Mar. 1354, dau. & h. of Sir Brian de Brampton, d. 1294, lord of Kinlet, co. Salop, and Brompton Brian, co. Hereford.

30. BRIAN DE CORNWALL, b. abt. 1326, of Kinlet, co. Salop. M.P. for Shropshire six times, 1369-1383, sheriff of Shropshire & Stafford, 1377, d. 1397; m. **MAUD LE STRANGE** (259-30), dau. of Fulk le Strange, b. abt. 1267, d. 1324. (Cecil G. Saville, The House of Cornwall (1908), pp. 65-68).

31. ISABEL DE CORNWALL, dau. & h. of Kinlet, co. Salop; m., as 2nd wife, Sir John Blount, of Sodington, co. Worcester, d. 1423/4, son of Sir John Blount, d. 1357, by Isolda Montjoy, dau. of Sir Thomas Montjoy.

32. SIR JOHN BLOUNT of Balterley, co. Staffs, dead 26 Oct. 1443, wid. surviving; m. Alice Delabere, dce 28 Oct. 1445, dau. of Kynard Delabere, d. abt. 1412, of Chilstone, co. Hereford, M.P., sheriff of Hereford, 1387, 1396, 1401, by his wife, Katherine, widow of Sir John Pecche. (Gen. 29-32: *Gen.* 3 (1879): 225-230).

33. HUMPHREY BLOUNT, of Kinlet, b. 1423, sheriff of Shropshire 1460-74, writ. dce 12 Oct. 1477; m. Elizabeth Winnington, dau. of Sir Robert Winnington of Cheshire. (Gens. 31-33: *Gen. Mag.* 19 (1979): 354-355).

34. JOHN BLOUNT of Yeo, co. Salop, and co. Hereford, proof of age of his elder brother 1478; m. Elizabeth Yeo, dau. of John Yeo of Yeo, co. Hereford.

35. KATHARINE BLOUNT, bur. Alveley 20 Aug. 1591; m. Humphrey Lee of Coton Hall, Nordley Regis, co. Salop, b. 1506, d. 6 Dec. 1588, Inq.p.m. 12 Mar. 1589. (Visit. Shropshire (1623): 51-52).

Note: Gen. 36 through 38, in previous editions, has been proven to be in error. See Neil Thompson, "Lees of Northumberland and Worcester," *NGSQ* 90 (2002): 213-217.

Line 259

29. ELEANOR GIFFORD (29A-30), dead 1324/5; m. Fulk le Strange, b. abt. 1267, dead 23 Jan. 1324/5, 1st Lord Strange of Blackmere, Seneschal of Aquitaine.

30. MAUD LE STRANGE, m. **BRIAN DE CORNWALL** of Kinlet (258-30), b. abt. 1326.

Line 260 Revised for 8th Edition

29. JOHN (1-25), King of England, b. 1167, d. 1216; m. 1200, **ISABELLA OF ANGOULÊME** (117-27). (*DNB*).

30. ELEANOR, b. 1215, d. 13 Apr. 1275; m. (1) 23 Apr. 1224, William Marshal, Earl of Pembroke, d.s.p. 15 Apr. 1231, son of William Marshall, 3rd Earl of Pembroke by **ISABEL DE CLARE** (66-27); m. (2) 7 Jan. 1238/9, Simon de Montfort, Earl of Leicester, b. Normandy abt. 1208, killed at Evesham 4 Aug. 1265, son of Simon IV de Montfort l'Aumary. (*DNB* 38: 284; *CP* VII: 520, 543-547).

31. ELEANOR DE MONTFORT, b. abt. Michaelmas 1252, d. 1282; m. 13 Oct. 1278, Llywelyn ap Gruffydd, son of Gruffydd ap Llywelyn, d. 1 Mar. 1244, the son of **LLYWELYN AP IORWERTH** (176B-27), by Senena, perh. of Man.

Line 261 Revised for 8th Edition

30. WILLIAM DE FERRERS (127-30), Earl of Derby, b. abt. 1193, d. Evington, near Leicester, 24 or 28 Mar. 1254, bur. 31 Mar. 1254; m. (1) bef. 14 May 1219, Sibyl Marshal, d. bef. 1238, 3rd dau. and eventual coh. of Sir William Marshal, 3rd Earl of Pembroke, by **ISABEL DE CLARE** (66-27), dau. and sole h. of **RICHARD DE CLARE** (66-26) Earl of Pembroke, by **AOIFFE** (or **EVA**) **OF LEINSTER** (175-7). (*CP* IV: 196-198; Sanders, 62-64, 148-149).

31. MAUD (or **MATILDA**) **DE FERRERS**, Vicomtesse de Rochechouart, b. abt. 1230, d. 12 Mar. 1298/9; m. (1) Simon de Kyme of Kyme, d.s.p. sh. bef. 30 July 1248; m. (2) abt. 30 July 1248, William de Fortibus (de Fort) (de Forz) de Vivonia in Poitou (also styled le Fort), d. sh. bef. 22 May 1259, lord of Chewton, Somerset, son of Hugh de Vivonia, sheriff of Somerset and Dorset, by his wife, Mabel, dau. and coh. of **WILLIAM MALET** (234A-28), Magna Charta Surety, 1215; m. (3) by 4 Feb. 1267, Aymeric de Rochechouart,

Vicomte de Rochechouart in Poitou, liv. Apr. 1284. (*CP* IV: 199, chart; Sanders, 9, 38-39, 62-64; *Knights of Edward I*, II: 80, IV: 156; Cal. Inq.p.m. 1: 298, 3: 400-401; Cal. Pat. Rolls (Henry III, A.D. 1247-1258), p. 23; *List of Ancient Correspondence of the Chancery and Exchequer, Lists & Indexes*, no XV, p. 355).

    32. JOAN DE VIVONIA eldest dau. and coh., lady of Chewton, Somerset, through her father, heir (Inq.p.m. on her lands from William Marshal) to a 1/8 interest in the barony of Curry Malet, Somerset, through her mother, inherited an interest in the barony of Long Crendon, co. Buckingham, b. 1251 (age 8 in 1259), d. 1 June 1314; m. (1) abt. 10 May 1262, Ingram de Percy, d.s.p. sh. bef. 10 Oct. 1262; m. (2) as 2nd wife (his 1st named Alice), **SIR REYNOLD** (or **REGINALD**) **FITZ PIERS, KNT.**, (262-30), lord of Blaen Llyfni, co. Brecknock, Sheriff of Hampshire and Constable of Winchester Castle, 1261, d. 4/5 May 1286, h. of elder bro. Herbert and son of Piers Fitz Herbert, lord of Blaen Llyfni, co. Brecknock, by his 1st wife, **ALICE FITZ ROBERT**, de Warkworth (246D-28). (*CP* IV: 199, chart, V: 465, notes c and d; Cal. Inq.p.m., 2: 364-366, 5: 274-275; Sanders, 38-39, 63, 89; *Knights of Edward I*, II: 52-53, 80; *VCH Beds.* II: 351-352; *Sussex* IV: 158-159).

    33. SIR PIERS (or **PETER**) **FITZ REYNOLD** (or **FITZ REGINALD**), **KNT.**, eldest surv. son by (2) to whom mother gave Chewton 1299, lord of Chewton, Somerset, conservator of array, Surrey and Sussex, 1321, b. abt. 1274 (age 40 in 1314), d. 18 Nov. 1322; m. (1) Ela Martel, age 7 in 1280, liv. 1306/7, dead by 1309, elder dau. and coh. of Sir Roger Martel, d. 1280, lord of Hinton Martel and Broadmayne, co. Dorset, Glen Magna, co. Leicester, and Merston, co. Sussex, by his wife, Joan. (Her sister Joan, then age 4, m. Reynold fitz Reynold, yngr. bro. of Piers). (*VCH Sussex* IV: 158-159; *VCH Leics.* V: 77, 104-109 *CP* IV, *cit.*; Public Record Office, L. & I. 17: 51; Sanders, 38-39; *Knights of Edward I*, II: 56-57, III: 123; Cal. Inq.p.m., 2: 201, 5: 274-275, 6: 242-243, 459-460; Cal. Pat. Rolls (Edward II, A.D. 1313-1317), p. 403, (Edward II, A.D. 1317-1321), p. 459; E.A. Fry and G.S. Fry, ed., *Dorset Records* V: 240 (being Dorset Feet of Fines from Richard I)).

    34. ROGER FITZ PIERS (PETER) (or **ROGER MARTEL**), eldest son and h. app., b. abt. 1295, d.v.p. by 6 Dec, 1322, of Chewton; m. by 30 Nov. 1318 to an unknown wife, who was prob. dau. of Sir Henry de Urtiaco (or otherwise del Ortiay or de Lorty), d. 1321, Lord Urtiaco of Curry Rivell, Somerset, by his wife Sibyl, also d. by 1322. (*VCH Sussex* IV: 158-159; *VCH Leics.* V: 104; Sanders, 38-39, 84; *CP* IV: 199, chart, X: 183-184).

    35. SIR HENRY FITZ ROGER, KNT., eldest son and h., b. Curry Rivell, co. Somerset 30 Nov 1318, d. 29 Jan. or 18 Feb. 1352, bur. Chewton Mendip, Somerset, held manors of Chewton, Somerset, West Kington, co. Wilts, Sturminster Marshall, co. Dorset, Merston, co. Sussex (which he held jointly with his wife Elizabeth), Glen Magna, co. Leicester, Selling, co. Kent, Hinton Martel and Broadmayne (Mayne Martell), co. Dorset; m. by 23 May 1340 Elizabeth de Holand, d. 13 July 1387, dau. of Sir Robert de Holand, 1st Lord Holand of Upholland, co. Lancaster, by his wife, **MAUD LA ZOUCHE** (32-30). (*CP* IV: 528-531; Sanders, 38-39; Cal. Inq.p.m., 6: 242-243, 8: 154, 10: 10-11, 16: 209-210; *VCH Sussex* IV: 158-159; *VCH Leics.* V: 77, 104; Cal. Inq.p.m. II: 272, 14: 73, in which the lady of the manor of Glen Magna, co. Leicester, is specifically called Elizabeth de Holand, dau. of Robert de Holand).

    36. JOHN FITZ ROGER, lord of Chewton, b. bet. 1345-1352, dead by 1372 (when his wid. was m. to 2nd husb.), 3rd son, but in issue in 1382, h. to his older bros., 2nd of whom, Thomas, b. bet. 1345-52, was godson of Thomas de Holand and Maud de Holand; m. by 26 Apr. 1369, Alice (a minor) parentage uncertain, d. 27 Mar. 1426; who m. (2) 1371/2 as 2nd wife, Sir Edmund de Clyvedon, d. 16 Jan. 1375/6; m. (3) as 2nd wife, Sir Ralph Carminow, d. aft. Jan. 1387; m. (4) as 2nd wife, Sir John Rodeney, d. 19 Dec. 1400; m. (5) as 2nd wife, **SIR WILLIAM BONVILLE** (124A-35) of Shute (father-in-law of her dau.), d. 1408. She had surviving issue only by John Fitz Roger. (*VCH Sussex, cit.; VCH Leics.,* cit.; *Devon & Cornwall N. & Q.* XXIV: 56-59, XXV: 141; Cal. Pat. Rolls, 14 (A.D. 1362-1370), p. 239; Cal. Inq.p.m. 15: 203, 16:92-93, 209-210).

37. ELIZABETH FITZ ROGER, dau. and sole h. in 1382 to Chewton, etc., b. 15 Aug 1370, d. 15 Apr 1414, held the manors of Chewton, co. Somerset, Glen Magna, co. Leicester, Merston, co. Sussex, ¼ of Sturminster Marshall, co. Dorset; m. (1) by 18 Oct 1377, age 8 or 9, Sir John Bonville, b. abt. 1371, d. 21 Oct 1396 (see his Inq.p.m. 20 Rich II no. 11), son and h. app. of **SIR WILLIAM BONVILLE** (124A-35), of Shute, co. Devon, by his first wife, Margaret de Albemarle (or Daumarle); m. (2) sh. aft. 1396 but bef. 2 Dec 1398, Richard Stucle (or Stukeley), of Trent, co. Somerset, gent., King's Esquire, escheator of Somerset and Dorset, 1412-1413, d. sh. aft. 1420. (He was likely son of Geoffrey de Stucle, King's Esquire, of co. Bucks, liv. 1349-1380). They made settlement (1410) of the manors of Great Glen, co. Leicester, and Merston, co. Sussex, on themselves and heirs. (*CP* II: 218; *VCH Sussex* & *VCH Leics.*, cit.; *Feudal Aids*, III: 123; Cal. Close Rolls (Henry VI), I: 194, (Richard II), VI: 364, 368, 1346-1349, p. 551, 1377-1391, p. 287; Cal. Pat. Rolls (1364-1367), p. 391, (1367-1370) p. 379, (1391-1396) pp. 700, 719, (1441-1446) pp. 26-27·, Vivian, *Visit. of Devon*, pp. 101, 721; Cal. Inq.p.m. 15: 203, 16: 92-93, 209-210); Inq.p.m. for John Bonville 20 Richard II (Year: 1396); *List & Index Society*, 72: *List of Escheators for England and Wales.* Gens. 30-37: *NGSQ* 59: 254-262, 60: 25-35).

38. HUGH STUKELEY (or **STUCKLEY**), a yngr. son, b. aft. 1398, estate admin. 13 Dec 1457, sheriff of Devon 1448-9, held manors of Affeton, East and West Wolrington, Bradford Tracy, Bridgerule, Meshaw and Thelbridge, co. Devon, in right of his wife; m. by 1451, as her 1st husb., Katherine Affeton, d. 26 Mar. 1467, dau. and sole h. of John Affeton of Affeton, co. Devon. She m. (2) 9 Jan 1458/9, as 2nd wife, Sir William Bourchier (or Bourghchier) (who had m. (1) bef. 3 Aug. 1437 Thomasine Hankford), b. bef. 12 Dec. 1469, bur. Church of the Austin Friars, London, 3rd Lord FitzWarin of Bampton, co. Devon, son of Sir William Bourchier, Count of Eu, by his 3rd wife **ANNE** (4-32), Countess of Buckingham, Hereford and Northampton, dau. of **THOMAS OF WOODSTOCK, K.G.** (4-31). (*CP* V: 507-508 and notes e and f; Vivian, *Visit. of Devon*, pp. 106, 721; *Lists & Indexes* no. IX: *List of Sheriffs for England and Wales*, p. 35; *Devon & Cornwall N & Q* XXVII: 120).

39. NICHOLAS STUKELEY (or **STUCKLEY**), b. abt. 1451 (age 16 in 1467), d. 27 May 1488, held manors of Affeton, East and West Wolrington, Bradford Tracy, Huntshaw, and Meshaw, co. Devon, Trent and Chilton Cantelowe, co. Somerset, and Preston, Halfhyde, and St. Mary Blanford, co. Dorset; m. (1) Thomasine Cockworthy, d. 29 Nov 1477, wid. of Robert Chudleigh, dau. of John Cockworthy of Yarnscombe, co. Devon, escheator of Devon, by his wife, Thomasine Chichester, dau. of Sir John Chichester of Raleigh, co. Devon; m. (2) abt. 1479, as her 2nd husb., Anne Pomeroy, wid. of Robert Budockshide and dau. of Henry Pomeroy of Berry Pomeroy, co. Devon, by his wife, Alice Raleigh. (*CP*, cit., esp. note f; Vivian, cit.; Cal. Inq.p.m., Henry VII, 1: 172-173, 178-179, 181, 558-560; Thomasine Stukeley, Inq.p.m. 17 Edward IV (Year: 1477/8), Chancery File 63 (49); *Devon and Cornwall N. & Q.*, April 1959, pp. 60-61).

40. SIR THOMAS STUKELEY (or **STUCKLEY**), **KNT.**, son and h., b. Affeton, parish of West Wolrington, co. Devon, 24 June 1475 (age 4 at mother's Inq.p.m.), d. there 30 Jan 1541/2, held manors of Affeton, East and West Wolrington (both with advowsons), Mewshaw (with advowson), Bridgerule, Drayford, Huntshaw, Thelbridge (with advowson), Studlegh, Bradford Tracy, and Pyllaven, all in co. Devon, Sheriff of Devon 1520-1521; m. Anne Wood (misidentified by Colby as Elizabeth), dau. and h. of Sir Thomas Wood (or Wode), Chief Justice of the Common Pleas, of Childrey, co. Berks, by his wife, Margaret de la Mare, wid. of NN Lenham, dau. of Sir Thomas de la Mare, Sheriff of Berkshire,

1473-1490. (Vivian, *cit.*; Cal. Inq.p.m. (Henry VII), 1: 558-560; *Devon & Cornwall N. & Q.* XXVII: 52, 61, 120; Inq.p.m. for Thomas Stuckley, Knt., 34 Henry VIII (Year: 1542)).

    41. MARGERY STUKELEY (or **STUCKLEY**); m. Charles Farrington or Farringdon. (Vivian, *cit.*, 340, 721).

    42. ANN FARRINGDON; m. Thomas Dowrish of Dowrish House, b. abt. 1532, d. 1590. (Vivian, *cit.*, 290, 292, 339, 340; *NEHGR* 115: 248-253).

    43. GRACE DOWRISH; m. Robert Gye (or Guy), d. prob. 1604-1608, age 5 yrs. at Inq.p.m. of his father John Gye 29-30 Hen. VIII. (*NEHGR, cit.*).

    44. MARY GYE, b. abt. 1580, liv. 1666; m. Ilsington, 28 Oct. 1600, Rev. John Maverick, bp 27 Oct. 1578 at Awliscombe, co. Devon, son of Rev. Peter Maverick and Dorothy Tucke, to Mass. on the 'Mary and John', May 1630, lived in Dorchester, Mass., d. Boston, 3 Feb. 1635/6, age 60. (*NEHGR, cit.*; Weis, *Colonial Clergy of New England*, p. 137. See also: *Search for the Passengers of the Mary and John 1630*, v. 13 (1990): 13, v. 17 (1992): 100).

Line 261A   Prepared for an earlier edition by Douglas Richardson

    37. ELIZABETH FITZ ROGER (261-37); m. (1) **SIR JOHN BONVILLE** (124A-36).

    38. SIR WILLIAM BONVILLE, K.G., b. 13 Aug. 1393, beheaded 18 Feb. 1460/1, Lord Bonville, sheriff of Devon, seneschal of Aquitaine; m. (1) abt. 12 Dec. 1414, **MARGARET GREY** (93A-33); m. (2) abt. 9 Oct. 1427, Elizabeth Courtenay, d. 1471, wid. John Harington, Lord Harington, dau. Edward Courtenay, Earl of Devon, by Maud Camoys, dau. of Thomas Camoys. (*CP* II: 218-219; ident. of William Bonville's first wife, Margaret Grey, made by Robert Behra based on Cal. Close Rolls, 1413-1419, p. 199).

    39. ELIZABETH BONVILLE, by (1), d. 14 Feb. 1490/1; m. **SIR WILLIAM TAILBOYS** (224-36), b. abt. 1415, beheaded 26 May 1464, Lord Kyme, of Kyme, co. Lincoln. (*CP* VII: 359-361).

Line 262

    26. EMMA OF BLOIS, illegitimate dau. of **STEPHEN OF BLOIS** (137-23), Count of Blois, a leader of the First Crusade and Crusade of 1101, slain on crusade 1101, (Emma was half-sister to **STEPHEN** (169-25), King of England); m. Herbert of Winchester (also styled Herbert the Chamberlain) of unproven ancestry, d. in or sh. bef. 1130, Chamberlain and Treasurer under William II and Henry I, held lands in Hampshire in 1086, and afterwards held other lands in Bedfordshire, Hampshire, Gloucester and Yorkshire. (*Eng. Hist. Rev.* XLV: 273-81; *N. & Q.* CLXII (1932): 439-441, 453-455; Eyton, *Antiqu. of Shrop.* VII: 146-147; *NSGQ* 59: 256-7, 60: 33-35; T.F. Tout, *Chapters in the Administrative History of Medieval England*, I: 76-77; W. Farrer, *Yorkshire Charters*, II: 27, 127).

    27. HERBERT FITZ HERBERT, s. and h., adult by 1127, succeeded to his father's lands in 1130, dead by 1155, brother of St. William (Fitz Herbert), d. 1154, Archbishop of York; m. Sibyl (or Adela or Lucia) Corbet, liv. 1157, dau. and coh. of Robert Corbet, sometime mistress of **HENRY I** (121-25), lady of Alcester, co. Warwick and of Pontesbury and Woodcote, co. Salop (by Henry I she was mother of **REGINALD FITZ ROY** (121-26), Earl of Cornwall. (See also 195-26). (*Eng. Hist. Rev., cit.*; A.E. Corbet, *Family of Corbet* I: 34; Eyton, *cit.* 149; *CP* V: 465 note *d*; *NGSQ, cit.*).

28. HERBERT FITZ HERBERT, s. and event. h., adult by 1165, d. sh. bef. June 1204; m. **LUCY OF HEREFORD** (237-5), liv. 1219/20, bur. Chapter House of Lanthony, near Gloucester, lady of Blaen Llyfni and Bwlch y Dinas, co. Brecknock, dau. and coh. of Miles of Gloucester, Earl of Hereford, by **SIBYL DE NEUFMARCHE** (177-4, 193-4, 237-4). (Eyton, *cit.*; *CP*, *cit.*, VI: 457 note c; *NGSQ*, *cit.*; Sanders, 8-9).

29. PIERS FITZ HERBERT (237-6), s. and event. h., seen 1204, d. sh. bef. 6 June 1235, bur. at Reading, through mother, heir to a 1/3 interest in the barony of Miles of Gloucester, Earl of Hereford; m. (1) settlement dated 28 Nov. 1203,`ALICE FITZ ROBERT (246D-28) of Warkworth, dau. of Robert Fitz Roger, 2nd Baron of Warkworth (father of **JOHN FITZ ROBERT** (186-1)); m. (2) in or bef. 1225, Isabel de Ferrieres, d. sh. bef. 29 Apr. 1252, widow of **ROGER DE MORTIMER** (132C-28), dau. of Walkelin de Ferrieres, seigneur of Ferrieres-Saint-Hilaire and lord of Oakham, co. Rutland. (Eyton, *cit.*; *CP* V: 442 note c, 465 note d; Sanders, 9; *NGSQ*, *cit*; *The Notebook of Tristram Risdon*, pp. 75-77; *The Gen.*, n.s., 10: 29; *Devonshire Association*, 50: 433-434).

30. SIR REGINALD (or **REYNOLD**) **FITZ PIERS**, son by (1), and eventual h., adult by 1248, d. 4 or 5 May 1286, succeeded to his brother Herbert Fitz Piers in 1249, lord of Blaen Llyfni, co. Brecknock, etc., sheriff of Hampshire and Constable of Winchester Castle, 1261; m. (1) by Sept. 1249 Alice (or Amice), liv. 1264, dau. & h. of William de Stanford, liv. 1224-5, lord of Stanford Dingley, co. Berks; m. (2) by 1274 **JOAN DE VIVONIA** (261-32), b. 1251, d. 1 June 1314, wid. of Ingram de Percy, dau. and h. of William de Fortibus (also styled le Fort) & Maud de Ferrers. Through her father, Joan inherited a 1/8th interest in the barony of Curry Malet, Somerset. (Eyton, *cit.*; *CP*, *cit.*; Sanders, *cit.*; *CP* XI: 324; *NGSQ*, *cit.*; Cal. Inq.p.m. 2: 364-365, 5: 275; *Knights of Edward I*, II: 52-53, 80; *VCH Berkshire* 4: 110-111).

31. ALICE, dau. by (1), liv. 1305; m. by 29 June 1256, Sir John de St. John, d. 20 or 29 Sept. 1302, of Basing, Hampshire, Constable of Porcestre Castle, Seneschal of Gascony, Seneschal of Aquitaine, s. & h. of Sir Robert de St. John, d. 1266/7, of Basing, Hampshire, Constable of Porchester Castle, & Agnes de Cauntelou, dau.of William II de Cauntelou, d. 1251, of Calne, co. Wilts, and Eaton Bray, co. Bedford, & Millicent de Gournay, dau. of Hugh V de Gournay and **JULIANE DE DAMMARTIN** (152-27). (*CP* XI: 323-324).

32. AGNES DE ST. JOHN, d. 1340; m. **HUGH DE COURTENAY**, Earl of Devon (51-31). (*CP* XI: 325 note e).

Line 263   New to 8th Edition

24. CONON, of Grandison, named **FALCON** DE LA SARRAZ, d. aft. 1114, son of Adalbert; m. Adelaide de Rameru, dau. of , **HILDUIN III** (or **IV**) **DE RAMERU** (151A-22), d. 1063, and **ADELE DE ROUCY** (151-22), d. 1062, heiress of Roucy. (*ES* XI/ 153, III.4/677).

25. EBEL I DE GRANDISON, d. 4 May 1130/1135; m. Adelaide.

26. BARTHELEMY DE GRANDISON, Sire de Belmont, d. Jerusalem, 1158.

27. EBEL III DE GRANDISON, Sire de Belmont 1154/1177; m. Jordane. (*ES* XI/158; Clifford, Esther Rowland, *A Knight of Great Renown. The Life and Times of Othon de Grandison* (1951), pp 11-13; *Gen. Mag.* 19: 56-57, chart).

28. EBEL IV DE GRANDISON, d. 16 Jan aft. 1235; m. Beatrice of Geneva, dau. of **AMADEUS I OF GENEVA** (133-24), d. 26 June 1178, and 2nd wife, NN of Domene. (West Winter, XIII.1212, XII.802; *ES* XI/153, 158).

29. PIERRE (PETER) DE GRANDISON, d. 29 Dec. 1257/15 July 1259; m. Agnes of Neuenberg (Neuchâtel), dau. of Ulrich III, Count of Neuenberg, d. 1 Aug. 1225 (son of Ulrich II, son of Rudolf I of Neuenburg and Emma de Glane, d. 27 Oct. 1196, dau. of Pierre de Glane), by (1) Gertend. (*ES* XI/153-154; XV/6-7, 19A).

30. WILLIAM DE GRANDISON, 1st Lord Grandison, of Ashperton, co. Hereford, d. 27 June 1335; m. (1) bef. 1287, Sibyl de Tregoz, d. 27 Oct. 1334, dau. and coh. of **SIR JOHN TREGOZ** (255A-30), Lord Tregoz, of Ewyas Harold, by Mabel Fitzwarin, dau. of Sir Fulk Fitzwarin. (*CP* VI: 60-62; *ES* XI/154). [William had bros. Otes de Grandison, and Jacques de Grandison who m. Blanche, dau. of Richard, Seigneur de Belmont. Sibyl had sist. Clarice who m. Roger la Warre, Lord La Warre].

31. PETER DE GRANDISON, d. 10 Aug.1358; m. bef. 10 June 1330, Blanche de Mortimer, d. 1347, dau. of **ROGER DE MORTIMER** (120-33) of Wigmore (Lord Mortimer), cr. Earl of March, and **JOAN DE GENEVILLE** (71-32), *suo jure*, Baronness Geneville. (*CP* VI: 62-63; *ES* XI/154).

31. MABEL DE GRANDISON (dau. of Gen. 30); m. **SIR JOHN DE PATESHULL** (184A-12). (*CP* VI: 67-68; *ES* XI/154)

32. SIBYL DE PATESHULL (184A-13), liv. 26 Oct. 1331; m. **ROGER DE BEAUCHAMP** (85-31).

31. KATHERINE DE GRANDISON (dau. of Gen. 30), m. abt. 1327, William de Montagu, d. 1344, Lord Montagu, 1st Earl of Salisbury, d. 1344. (*CP* VI: 68; *ES* XI/154)

32. JOHN DE MONTAGU, d. 1390, Lord Montagu; m., bef. 1340, **MARGARET DE MONTHERMER** (8A-31), b. 1329, d. 1395.

Line 264   New to 8th Edition

25. GAUTIER, de Moëlan, d. 1080.

26. THIBAUD, Seigneur de Dampierre, de St. Just, de St. Dizier en Champagne d. 1107; m. Isabel (Elizabeth) de Montlhéry, Viscomtessa de Troyes, dau. of Milon I "le Grand," Seigneur Montlhéry and de Bray, by Lithuaise, sis. of **STEPHEN OF BLOIS** (169-25), King of England. (ES III.1/51, II/46; Evergates, p. 177).

27. GUY I, Vicomte de Troyes, Signeur de Dampierre, de St. Dizier, de Moëlan, and de St. Just, d. 1151; m. 1120/5, Helvide de Baudement, dau. of Andre de Baudement. (ES III.1/51; Anselme, III: 154).

28. HELVIS (HELVIDE) DE DAMPIERRRE; m. **GEOFFROI IV DE JOINVILLE** (71A-28).

Line 265   New to 8th Edition

23. ULF, of Grimthorpe.

24. WILLIAM FITZ ULF, of Grimthorpe, temp. Henry I. (*CP* V 750 note c; Clay, 95).

25. RALPH FITZ WILLIAM, of Grimthorpe, liv. 1131 [Pipe Roll, 31 Hen. I]; m. Emma de Teisa, dau. & coh. of Waltheof, son of Ailsi, of Domesday Lincolnshire Claims (*CP* V: 750 note c; Clay, 95, Keats-Rohan, *Domesday Desc.* II: 731, 69).

26. RALPH FITZ RALPH, of Grimthorpe, liv 1 Dec. 1189; m. Emma. (CP V: 750 note c; Clay, 95, Keats-Rohan, *Domesday Desc.* II: 731).

27. WILLIAM FITZ RALPH, of Grimthorpe and Hotham,.d. bef. 26 Aug. 1218; m. Joan, dau. of Stephen de Meisnill (Meinell). (*CP* V: 750 note c; Clay, 96).

28. RALPH FITZ WILLIAM, of Grimthorpe and Hotham, liv. 9 Feb. 1226/1227. (*CP* V: 750 note c; Clay, 96).

29. SIR WILLIAM FITZ RALPH, Lord of Grimthorpe and Hildreskelf, liv. July 1269 [Fine Rolls, 53 Hen. III]; m. **JOAN DE GREYSTOKE** (265A-29). (*CP* V: 750 note c; Clay, 96).

30. SIR RALPH FITZ WILLIAM, of Grimthorpe and Hildreskelf, co. York, 1st Lord Greystoke, of age July 1277, d. 11 Feb. 1316/7; m. (by royal lic.) as her 2nd husb., **MARGERY DE BOLEBEC** (267A-29), 2nd dau. and coh. of **SIR HUGH IV DE BOLEBEC** (267A-28) Baron of Angerton, by Tiphaine (Theophania) de Baliol (Balliol). (*CP* V: 750-751; *The Ancestor* No. 6 (1903): chart fol. 132; Clay, 96; *ES*: III.4/696).

31. ROBERT FITZ RALPH, age 40+ in 1316/7, d. sh. bef. 15 Apr. 1317; m. Elizabeth Neville, d. 17 Nov. 1346, dau. of Ralph Nevill(e) of Scotton. (*CP* V: 516-517; *The Ancestor* No. 6, (1903) chart fol. 132; Clay, 96).

32. RALPH DE GREYSTOKE, feudal Lord of Greystoke, b. 15 Aug. 1299, d. by poison 14 July 1323; m., as 1st husb., aft. 25 Nov. 1317, **ALICE DE AUDLEY** (207-32), dau. of Hugh de Audley, Lord of Audley, by **ISOLDE (ISEUDE) DE MORTIMER** (207-31), dau. of **SIR EDMUND DE MORTIMER** (207-30). Alice m. 2nd 1326/7, **RALPH DE NEVILLE** (186-5), Baron Neville of Raby. (*CP* VI: 190-191).

33. WILLIAM (DE GREYSTOKE), Lord Greystoke and Lord FitzWilliam, b. 6 January 1320/I, d. 10 July 1359, aged 38; m. (2) abt. 1351 **JOAN** (266-33), dau. of **SIR HENRY FITZ HENRY** (266-32) "of Ravensworth," by Joan de Fourneux, d. 1 Sept. 1403, dau. of Sir Richard de Fourneux, and sis. and coh. of William de Fourneux. (*CP* VI: 192-194).

34. RALPH (DE GREYSTOKE), Lord Greystoke and Lord FitzWilliam, b. 18 Oct. 1353, d. 6 Apr. 1418; m. **KATHARINE CLIFFORD** (202-33), d. 23 Apr. 1413, dau. of **ROGER DE CLIFFORD** (26-32), Lord Clifford, by Maud Beauchamp, dau. of **THOMAS BEAUCHAMP** (87-31), Earl of Warwick. (*CP* VI: 195-196).

35. JOHN (DE GREYSTOKE), Lord Greystoke, and Lord FitzWilliam, age 28+ in 1418, d. 8 Aug. 1436; m. (contr. 28 Oct. 1407) **ELIZABETH DE FERRERS** (62-35), elder dau. and coh. of **SIR ROBERT FERRERS** (62-34) by **JOAN BEAUFORT** (2-32) dau of **JOHN OF GAUNT** (1-30) Duke of Lancaster, by 3rd wife, Catherine Swynford. (*CP* VI: 196).

Line 265A   New to 8th Edition

22. SIGULF, prob. the son Forne, the King's Thegn. (Clay, 94, *NEHGR* 97 (1943): 240-241, *The Ancestor*, No.6 (1903): 121-123, & chart fol. 132).

23. FORN, Lord of Greystock (Greystoke), d. 1129/30; m. NN. His dau. Edith was a mistress of **HENRY I** (121-25), King of England and the mother of Robert Fitz Edith, one of the King's illeg. sons, and afterwards married Robert II d'Oilli, royal Constable of Oxford Castle. (Clay, 94; Sanders, 50, 54; Keats-Rohan, *Domesday People* I: 199; *CP* XI: Append. D, 108-109; *NEHGR* 97 (1943): 240-241; *The Ancestor*, No. 6 (1903): 122-123; Horace Round, *Geoffrey de Mandeville*, 94, 434).

24. IVO (IVES or YVES) FITZ FORNE, Lord of Greystoke, d. bef. 1156; m. Agnes, dau. of Walter, parentage unknown. (Clay, 94, Sanders, 50, *NEHGR* 97 (1943): 243; *The Ancestor*, No. 6 (1903): 124 & chart fol. 132). (Note: Ivo had three other sons, Robert, Adam and William, and a dau., Alice, who m. **EDGAR OF DUNBAR** (41-24)).

25. WALTER FITZ IVO (IVES or YVES), Lord of Greystoke, d. 1162; m. Beatrice de Folkinton. (Clay, 94, Sanders, 50, *NEHGR*, 97 (1943): 242, *The Ancestor*, No. 6 (1903): 125 & chart fol.132).

26. RANULF (or RANULPH) FITZ WALTER, Lord of Greystoke, d. abt. 1190; m. Amabel. (Clay, 94; Sanders, 50, *NEHGR*, 97 (1943): 243; *The Ancestor*, No. 6 (1903): 125 & chart fol. 132).

27. WILLIAM FITZ RANULF, Lord of Greystoke, of age 1194, d. 1209; m., as 3rd husb., **HELEWISE DE STUTEVILLE** (270C-27), wid. of **WILLIAM DE LANCASTER II** (40-26), Baron of Kendal, d. 1184, and of Hugh de Morville (see 40-26), d. 1202, dau. of **ROBERT III (IV) DE STUTEVILLE** (270-26),. (Clay, 94, Sanders, 50, *NEHGR*, 97 (1943): 243; *The Ancestor*, No. 6 (1903): 126 & chart fol. 132).

28. SIR THOMAS FITZ WILLIAM, Lord of Greystoke, minor in 1212,, died 1246/7; m. Christian de Vipont, dau. of Robert de Vipont of Appleby (see 82-30) (Clay, 94-95; Sanders, 50, *NEHGR* 97 (1943): 243; *The Ancestor*, No. 6 (1903): 126 & chart fol. 132, which calls her Mary).

29. JOAN DE GREYSTOKE, dau. of Sir Thomas Fitz William of Greystoke, liv. July 1269 [Fine Rolls, 53 Hen. III]; m. **SIR WILLIAM FITZ RALPH**, (265-29) Lord of Grimthorpe & Hildreskelf, liv. July 1269. (*CP* V: 750 note c; Clay, 95 & 96).

Line 266 New to 8th Edition

24. BARDOLF, brother of Bodin, who held Ravensworth at Domesday.

25. AKARIS FITZ BARDOLF, held Ravensworth. (*CP* V: 654 [417]).

26. HERVEY FITZ AKARIS, forester of the New Forest and Arkengarthdale, co. York , by the grant of Conan, Duke of Brittany. (*CP* V: 653 [416]).

27. HENRY FITZ HERVEY, "of Ravensworth," liv. 16 May 1212; m. Alice, dau. of Ranulf Fitz Walter (or Randolf Fitz Wauter), of Greystock (*CP* V: 653 [416]).

28. RANULF FITZ HENRY, d. bef. 13 Jan. 1242/3; m. Alice, dau. and h. of Adam de Staveley, of Staveley, by Alice, d. bef. 11 Nov. 1253, dau. of William de Percy, of Kildale. (*CP* V: 653 [416]).

29. SIR HENRY FITZ RANULF, "of Ravensworth," liv. 17 Jan. 1257/8, d. 1262. (*CP* V: 653-654 [416-417]).

30. SIR HUGH FITZ HENRY, "of Ravensworth," liv. 1276-1294, d. 12 Mar. 1304/5; m. Aubrey, d. bef. 25 Jan. 1302/3, wid. of sir William de Steyngrave, of Stonegrave, co. York, d.s.p. sh. bef. 26 Sept. 1264. (*CP* V: 653-654 [416-417]).

31. SIR HENRY FITZ HUGH, "of Ravensworth," Lord FitzHugh, d. 1356; m. (1) Eve de Bulmer, d. prob. bef. 1337, dau. of Sir John de Bulmer, by Tiphaine, dau. and coh. of Sir Hugh de Morewike. (CP V: 654-656 [417-419], II: 414).

32. SIR HENRY FITZ HENRY "of Ravensworth," d.v.p. 24 Sept. 1352; m. Joan de Fourneux, dau. of sir Richard de Fourneux, and sis. and coh. of William de Fourneux, d.s.p. 17 or 21 Aug. 1349. (*CP* V: 656 [419]).

33. JOAN, d. 1 Sept. 1403; m. abt. 1351, **WILLIAM (DE GREYSTOKE)** (265-33), b. 1320/1, d. 1359. (*CP* VI: 192-194).

Line 267   New to 8th Edition

    25. **WALTER I DE BOLEBEC**, liv. 1133, d. abt. 1142, Baron of Styford, co. Northhants, perh. son of Hugh de Bolebec, liv. 1180; m. Helewise (*ES* III.4/696).
    26. **HUGH II DE BOLEBEC**, d. abt. 1165. (*ES* III.4/696).
    27. **ISABELLA DE BOLEBEC**, d. 3 Feb. 1245; m. (1) Henry de Novaunt (Nonant); m. (2) **ROBERT DE VERE**, (246-27) 3rd Earl of Oxford, d. bef. 25 Oct. 1221 (50-29, 60-28, 246-27). (*ES* III.4/696, *CP* X: 210-213).

Line 267A   New to 8th Edition

    25. WALTER I DE BOLEBEC (267-25), d. abt. 1142.
    26. WALTER II DE BOLEBEC, Baron of Styford, d. abt. 1187; m. **SIBIL DE VESCY** (269-26). (*ES* III.4/696, Keats-Rohan, *Domesday Desc.* II: 769; *CP* XII (2): 274-275).
    27. SIR HUGH DE BOLEBEC III, d. abt. 1240, Baron of Styford; m. **MARGARET DE MONTFICHET** (184B-7). (*ES* III.4/696).
    28. SIR HUGH IV DE BOLEBEC, Baron of Angerton, etc., d. 1262 m. Tiphaine (Theophania) de Baliol. (*ES* III.4/696).
    29. MARGERY DE BOLEBEC, b. aft. 1241, d. bef. 1303; m.(1) Sir Nicholas Corbet, of Stanton;   m. (2) **SIR RALPH FITZ WILLIAM** (265-30) of Grimthorpe, 1st Lord Greystock, d. 1316/7. (*ES* III.4/696; *CP* V: 750-751 and note c; *The Ancestor*, No.6 (1903): chart fol. 132; Clay, 96).

Line 268   New to 8th Edition

    24. ROBERT DE MEINELL, "the first member of this family in England of whom there is record," liv. 1100-1109, d. bef. 1135; m. Gertrude, prob. dau. of Nele Fossard, and sister of Robert Fossard. She m. (2) Jordan Paynel. (*CP* VIII: 619-620).
    25. STEPHEN DE MEINELL, liv. 1119-1145; m. Sibil, prob. dau. of Ansketil de Bulmer, Sheriff of Yorkshire, 1115-1129. (*CP* VIII: 620, *Eng. Gen.* No.10 (1978): 226).
    26. ROBERT II DE MEINELL, liv. 1166. (*CP* VIII: 621).
    27. STEPHEN II DE MEINELL, liv. 1176, d. by 1188; m. Joan de Ros, prob. niece of Walter de Ros, bro. of Piers de Ros. (*CP* VIII: 621, XI: 90-91).
    28. ROBERT III DE MEINELL, liv. 1201/1203, d. bef. 30 Jan. 1206/7; m. Emma, dau. of Richard Malebisse. (*CP* VIII: 621-622).
    29. STEPHEN III DE MEINELL, of age bet. Oct. 1224 and Feb. 1225/6, liv.1268, d. bef. 16 July 1269. (*CP* VIII: 623-624).
    30. NICHOLAS DE MEINELL, 2nd but 1st surv. son, by unknown mother, liv. 1257-1295, cr. Lord Meinell 24 June 1295, d. bef. 27 May 1299; m. Christine. (*CP* VIII: 625-627).
    31. NICHOLAS DE MEINELL, Lord Meinill, born 6 Dec. 1274, d. 26 Apr. 1322, unm. (*CP* VIII: 627-630).
    32. NICHOLAS DE MEINELL, (88-32) (natural son of Nicholas de Meinill by **LUCY DE THWENGE** (88-31)); m. **ALICE DE ROS** (54-35), d. 4 July 1344. (*CP* VIII: 632-634).
    33. ELIZABETH DE MEINELL (88-33), Baroness Meinill of Whorlton, b. 15 Oct. 1331, d. 9 July 1368; m. (1) abt. 1344/5, as 2nd wife, John Darcy, 2nd Baron Darcy, d. 5

Mar. 1355; m. (2) bef. 18 Nov. 1356, **SIR PIERS VI DE MAULEY** (156-31), Lord Mauley of Mulgrave Castle, d. 19 or 20 Mar. 1382/3. (*CP* VIII: 634 & 568).

Line 269   New to 8th Edition

21. **RANULF THE MONEYER**, whose antecedents are unknown, liv. 1035, d. by 1061. (*CP* XII (2): 268-269).

22. **RICHARD (FITZ RANULF)**, 2nd but 1st surv. son & heir, d. 1061. (*CP* XII (2): 269).

23. **JOHN (FITZ RICHARD)**, prob. b. bef. 1056, of age 1076, liv. 1107. (*CP* XII (2): 269-270).

24. **EUSTACE FITZ JOHN**, 2nd son, (bro. & h. of Payn Fitz John), b. bef. 1100, d. 1157, Lord of Alnwick and Malton; m., as 1st wife, Beatrice de Vescy, only dau. & h. of Yves de Vescy, Lord of Alnwick and Malton, poss. by Alda Tyson, dau. of William Tyson, also Lord of Alnwick and Malton. (*CP* XII (2): 272-274).

25. **WILLIAM DE VESCY**, son & h., adopted his mother's name of Vescy, by which he and his successors were known, Lord of Alnwick, Sheriff of Northumberland & Yorkshire, liv. 1157-1174, d. 1183; m. (I) Agnes, liv. 1165, parentage unknwn; m. (2) **BURGA DE STUTEVILLE** (270B-27), liv. 1185, dau. of **ROBERT III (IV) DE STUTEVILLE** (270-26), by his wife, Helewise. (*CP* XII (2): 274-275, Keats-Rohan, *Domesday Desc.* II: 769).

26. **SIBIL DE VESCY**, by (1); m. **WALTER II DE BOLEBEC** (267A-26), Baron of Styford. (Keats-Rohan, *ibid*).

Line 269A   New to 8th Edition

25. **WILLIAM DE VESCY** (269-25), d. 1183; m.(2) **BURGA DE STUTEVILLE** (270B-27). (*CP* XII (2): 275, Keats-Rohan, *Domesday Desc.* II: 769).

26. **EUSTACE DE VESCY**, 1st son & h., b. 1169/71, age 14 in 1185, d. Aug. 1216; m. 1193, Margaret, liv. 1226, illeg. dau. of **WILLIAM THE LION** (170-26), King of Scots. (*CP* XII (2): 275-276).

27. **WILLIAM DE VESCY**, minor at his father's death in 1216, d. sh. bef. 7 Oct. 1253; m. (2) bef. 1244, Agnes de Ferrers, d. 11 May 1290, dau. of **WILLIAM DE FERRERS** (127-30), 5th Earl of Derby, by his 1st wife, Sibyl Marshal, dau. of William Marshal, 3rd Earl of Pembroke and **ISABEL DE CLARE** (66-27) (*CP* XII (2): 276-278).

28. **JULIANA DE VESCY**, (see 63A-33); m., as 2nd wife, Sir Richard de Vernon (Burke's Peerage (1953), p. 2134).

Line 270   New to 8th Edition

24. **ROBERT I (II) D'ESTOUTEVILLE**, liv. 1066-1106, Crusader, taken prisoner at the battle of Tinchebrai, 1107; prob. son of Robert d'Estouteville (aka Robert Fronte-boef) in Battle of Hastings 1066, d. abt. 1090, said to have m. Jeanne de Tallebot, dau. of Hue, Lord of Cleuville; m. Beatrix, parentage unknown. (*ES* XIII/103; Keats-Rohan, *Domesday Desc.* II: 723-724; *NEHGR* 79 (1925) 377-378; Planche, *Conqueror and His Companions*, II: 253-258).

25. **ROBERT II (III) DE STUTEVILLE**, liv. 1124-1135, in Battle of the Standard 1138, d. bef. 1140, Sheriff of Yorkshire; m. Erneburga (Eremburga) (Emberga), perh. dau. of

Hugh Fitz Baldric, Domesday tenant in Yorkshire. (Keats-Rohan, *Domesday Desc.* II: 723-724).

26. ROBERT III (IV) DE STUTEVILLE, liv. 1138-1179, d. abt. 1183, of Cottingham, co. Yorks., Sheriff of Yorkshire; m. Helewise, liv. 1183, whose parentage is unknown, but poss. a niece of Geoffrey Murdac.

27. NICHOLAS I DE STUTEVILLE, liv. 1174-1214, d. bef. 30 Mar. 1218, of Liddell, co. Cumb.; m. (2) by 25 Apr. 1197, Gunnor d'Aubigny, wid. of **ROBERT DE GAUNT** **(GANT)** (156-25), sis. of Raoul d'Aubigny, dau. of Ralph D'Aubigny.

28. NICHOLAS II DE STUTEVILLE, d. bet. 8 Sept. and 19 Òct. 1233; m., as 1st husb., Devorguilla of Galloway, dau. of **ROLAND** (38-25), Lord of Galloway. (*CP* IX: 593).

29. JOAN DE STUTEVILLE, d. sh. bef. 6 Apr. 1276; m. (1) by by 29 May 1229, **HUGH WAKE** (184A-8, see at 236-9), d. 1241; m. (2) bef. 5 Feb. 1243/5, **HUGH BIGOD** (69-29), d. 1266, Chief Justiciar of England. (Gens. 24-29: *NEHGR* 79 (1925): 373-378; *ES* XIII/103, 104).

Line 270A New to 8th Edition

25. ROBERT II (III) DE STUTEVILLE (270-25), d. bef. 1140; m. Erneburga.

26. JOHN DE STUTEVILLE, d. abt. 1184, Lord of Lawford, Newbold-in-Avon, and Cosford, co. Warwick; m. Agnes, liv. 1200, family unknown. They had

27. Daughter DE STUTEVILLE (given name unkn.); m. abt. 1170/3, **MALDRED FITZ DOLFIN** (247-24), Lord of Raby, b. abt. 1135, d. abt. 1183. (*CP* IX: 494; *TAG* 46 (1970): 166, *NEHGR* 106 (1952): 186-190. Gens. 25-27: *ES* XIII/103).

Line 270B New to 8th Edition

26. ROBERT III (IV) DE STUTEVILLE (270-26), liv. 1138-1179, d. abt. 1183; m. Helewise, liv. 1183. (*NEHGR* 79 (1925): 373-378).

27. OSMOND DE STUTEVILLE, b. abt. 1140/5, held lands in Cowesby, etc., co. Yorks. 1166, d. abt. 1192; m. Isabel, d. 1207, dau. of William Fitz Roger of Gressinghall, co. Norfolk. Isabel m. (2) **SIR WILLIAM DE HUNTINGFIELD** (187-2). (*ES* XIII/104; Keats-Rohan, *Domesday Desc.* II: 723).

27. BURGA DE STUTEVILLE, (dau. of Gen. 26), liv. 1185; m. bef. 1169/1171, **WILLIAM DE VESCY** (269-25, 269A-25), d. 1183. *CP* XII (2): 275; Keats-Rohan, *Domesday Desc.* II: 769. Gens. 26-27: *ES* XIII/103-104).

Line 270C New to 8th Edition

26. ROBERT III (IV) DE STUTEVILLE (270-26), liv. 1138-1179, d. abt. 1183; m. Helewise, liv. 1183. (*NEHGR* 79 (1925): 373-378).

27. HELEWISE DE STUTEVILLE, d. aft. 1226/8; m. (1) **WILLIAM II DE LANCASTER** (88-26), d. 1184; m (2) Hugh de Morville (see 40-26), d. 1202; m. (3) **WILLIAM FITZ RANULF**, Lord of Greystoke (265A-27), of Alnwick, d. 1183. *CP* XII (2): 274-275; *ES* XIII/103-104; Keats-Rohan, *Domesday Desc.* II: 769).

25.   ROBERT II (III) DE STUTEVILLE (270-25), liv. 1124-1135; m. Erneburga (Eremburga) (Emberga). (Keats-Rohan, *Domesday Desc.* II: 723-724). They were prob. parents of

26.   OSMUND DE STUTEVILLE. (*NEHGR* 79 (1925): 375-376; *ES* XIII/103).

27.   ROGER DE STUTEVILLE, of Burton Agnes, Sheriff of Northumberland 1169-1183, d. by Sept. 1202; m. NN. (*NEHGR* 79 (1925): 375-378; *ES* XIII/103).

28.   ALICE DE STUTEVILLE, d. 1219; m. **ROGER DE MERLAY** (42-25), d. 1188. (*NEHGR* 79 (1925): 377-378; *ES* XIII/103; *Visit. of Yorkshire,* 1563-1564, p. 361).

Line 271   New to 8th Edition

17.   GEOFFROY DE THOUARS, Viscount of Thouars, liv. 876.

18.   AIMERY I DE THOUARS, Viscount of Thouars, d. 936; m. Aremburge, liv. 930-935.

19.   AIMERY II DE THOUARS, Viscount of Thouars, liv. 935/955; m. Aliénor (or Hardouine). (*ES* III.4/810).

20.   HERBERT (ARBERT) I DE THOUARS, liv. 951/975, d. bef. Jan. 987; m. Aldéarde d'Aunay, dau. of Cadelon III, Viscount d'Aunay and Sénégundis de Marcillac. (*ES* III.4/814; West-Winter VII.47b).

21.   SAVARY III, Viscount of Thouars, liv. 980/1004, bro. of Raoul I, Viscount of Thouars (see 275-21).

22.   GEOFFROY II DE THOUARS, Viscount of Thouars, 1010-1055; m. Aénor.

23.   AIMERY IV DE THOUARS (183-1), Viscount of Thouars, liv. 1048, d. 1093; m. (1) Aurengarde de Mauléon, sis. of Raoul and of Geoffroy de Mauléon. (*ES* XIV/101).

24.   GEOFFROY III DE THOUARS, Viscount of Thouars, Crusader, liv. 1088-1123; m. Ameline, liv. 1106-1123.

25.   AIMERY VI DE THOUARS, Viscount of Thouars, d in battle 1127; m. by 11 Apr. 1106, **AGNES OF POITOU AND AQUITAINE** (111-25), dau. of **WILLIAM VII DE POITOU** (110-24), Count of Poitou.

26.   GEOFFROY V DE THOUARS, Viscount of Thouars, 1139-1173, d. aft. 1173; m. Aimée de Lusignan, dau. of **HUGH VII DE LUSIGNAN** (275-23) "le Brun" Sire de Lusignan and Sarasine. (West-Winter XII.416; *ES* III.3/564).

27.   GUI DE THOUARS, 3rd son, Count of Brittany, d. 13 Apr. 1213; m. (1) **CONSTANCE,** *suo jure,* Countess of Brittany (96-27). (*CP* X: 794-795).

28.   ALIX DE THOUARS, (96-28), Countess of Brittany, b. 1201, d. 4 Sept. 1221; m. Mar. 1213, **PIERRE DE DREUX** (135-29). (*CP* X: 796. Gens. 17-28: *ES* III.4/810).

Line 272   New to 8th Edition

22.   LAMBERT I, Burgrave of Gent (Ghent), Admin. of St. Peter of Gent, liv. 1010-1031/4. (*ES* VII/81).

23.   FORLKARD I, Burgrave of Gent (Ghent), liv. 1031/4-1073. (*ES* VII/81).

24.   LAMBERT II, Burgrave of Gent (Ghent), liv. 1031/34-1073; m. Geyla, liv. 1071. (*ES* VII/81).

25. WENEMAR I, Burgrave of Gent (Ghent), liv. 1074/88-1126; m. Gisela of Guines, dau. of Baudoin I, Count of Guines, d. 1091. (*ES* VII/81; Warlop 4: 821-822, 828; Stokvis II: 56).

26. ARNOULD OF GHENT, Count of Guines, 1142, b. abt. 1129, d. 1169; m. Mathilda (Mahaut) de St. Omer, dau. of William de St. Omer II (son of William I de St. Omer by Agnitrude von Brugge) and Millesende de Picquigny, dau. of Arnould de Picquigny. (West-Winter XIV.111; *ES* III.4/623, VII/81; Warlop 4: 192; Stokvis II: 56).

27. BALDWIN (BAUDOIN) II, Count of Guines, d. 2 Jan. 1205; m. Christine d'Ardres, d. 2 July 1177, dau. of Arnould IV de Marco, Seigneur d'Ardres and Adelaide d'Ardres. (West-Winter XIII.313; XIV.1111). [Baldwin's sister, Margaret, m. (1) Eustache de Fiennes, son of **EUSTACHE II** (158B-25) Seigneur de Fiennes m. (2) Roger I, Burgrave of Kortrijk and Gent].

28. ARNOULD II, in Ardes, Count of Guines, d. 1220; m. bef. Mar. 1200, Beatrix de Bourbourg, d. 1214, heiress of the Chatelain Bourbourg, dau. of Walter de Bourbourg, d. abt. 1190 (the son of Henry I, b. 1115, d. 1186, Castellan of Bourboug by (2) Beatrix of Aalst, dau. of Balduin III of Gent and Aalst), and Mathilde de Bethune, dau. of Robert IV de Bethune and Adelisa de St. Pol. (Warlop 4: 703-4, 699, 3: 668; West-Winter XIII.1159; *ES*/81, VIII/22A).

29. BALDWIN (BAUDOIN) III, Count of Guines, Chatelain de Bourbourg, Signeur d'Ardes, d. 1244; m. **MAHAUD (MATHILDA) DE FIENNES** (158B-28), dau. of **GUILLAUME (WILLIAM) DE FIENNES** (158B-27, 158C-27), Seigneur de Fiennes and de Tingry by **AGNES DE DAMMARTIN** (152-27), dau. of Albri de Luzarches and **MATHILDA (MABLE), OF CLERMONT, PONTHIEU & DAMMARTIN** (144-26). (*ES* III.4/649. Warlop 4: 704; West-Winter XIV.1607; LaChesnaye, *Dict. de la Noblesse*, VIII/40).

30. ARNOULD III, Count of Guines, Chatelain de Bourbourg, Signeur d'Ardres, d.aft. Feb. 1282; m. **ALIX DE COUCY** (273-30), dau. of **ENGUERRAND III** (273-29) Seigneur de Coucy, Count of Perche, d. 1243 by Marie de Montmirail, dau. of Jean (John) I de Montmirail and Helvise (Helvide) de Dampierre-sur-Aube. Arnould III and Alix were prob. parents of Margaret who m. **RICHARD DE BURGH** (75-31, 94A-31). (*ES* VII/80-81. XIII/139, III.4/683. *Gen. Mag.* 20: 335-340; CP XIV: 619).

Line 273   New to 8th Edition

24. DREUX (DROGO), Seigneur de Boves, liv. 1042-1069.

25. ENGUERRAND I, Seigneur de Coucy and de Boves, Count d'Amiens; m. (1) Ada (Adele) de Roucy, dau. of Lietard de Marle and Mathilde. (*ES* VII/80, III.4/675A; West-Winter XI.207).

26. THOMAS DE COUCY, Seigneur de Coucy and de Marle, Count d'Amiens d. bef. 1131; m. (3) Milisende, whose parentage is in doubt (see: Moriarty, 196 and 163). (West-Winter XI.207; *ES* VII/80).

27. ENGUERRAND II DE COUCY, Seigneur de Coucy and de Marle, d. aft. 1147; m. 1132, Agnes de Baugency dau. of Raoul, Sire de Baugency by Mahaut de Vermandois, b. abt. 1080, (niece of **PHILIP I** (101-23), King of France), dau. of **HUGH MAGNUS** (53-23). (*ES* XIII/45, III.1/55; West-Winter XII.821, XII.347, XI/506, XII.20, X.300).

28. RAOUL I DE COUCY, d. in battle 1191; m. (2) aft. 1173, Alex de Dreux, d. aft. 1217, dau. of **ROBERT I** (135-27), Count of Dreux by (3) Agnes de Baudemont (*ES* III.1/63, XIV/51; West-Winter XIII.593).

29. ENGUERRAND III DE COUCY (see 120-30), Seigneur de Coucy; m. (3) Marie de Montmirail, d. abt. 1267, dau. of Jean I de Montmirail, Seigneur d'Oisy and Helvise

Helvide) de Dampierre, dau. of William I, Sire of Dampierre-sur-Aube and Ermengarde de Mouchy, poss. dau. of Dreux IV of Mouchy. (Moriarty, 151; *ES* VII/80, XIII/139, III.1/51; West-Winter XV.136, XVI.190, XV.136, XVI.190).

    30. ALIX DE COUCY (see 94A-31), sis. of Mary (Marie), wife of Alexander II, King of the Scots; m. **ARNOULD III** (272-30), Count de Guines, d. 1282. (LaChesnaye, Dict. de la Noblesse, VI: 302-303).

Line 274   New to 8th Edition

    21. HUMBERT I "The White Handed," Count of Savoy and Maurienne, d. 1 July 1047/51; m. bef. 1020, Ancilie (Auxilia).

    22. EUDES (ODO) Count of Maurienne and Savoy, Margrave of Susa, Count of Chablis, d. 1 Mar. 1060; m. as 3rd husb., abt. 1046, Alix (Adelaide), Duchess of Turin, Margravine of Susa, b. abt. 1015, d. 27 Dec. 1091, wid. of Herman IV, Duke of Swabia, dau. of Olderich Manfred II. (West Winter, X.285 note, XI.491a; *ES* III.3/593).

    23. BERTHA, of Turin, b. abt. 21 Sept. 1051, d. 27 Dec. 1087; m. 13 July 1066, **HENRY IV** (45-23) King of Germany. (Gens. 21-23: *ES* II/190).

Line 274A   New to 8th Edition

    22. EUDES (ODO) (274-22), Count of Maurienne and Savoy; m. abt. 1046, Alix (Adelaide), Duchess of Turin. (West Winter, X.285 note, XI.491a).

    23. AMADEUS II (I) Count of Maurienne and Savoy, Margrave of Susa, d. 26 Jan. 1080; m. abt. 1065/70, Jeanne of Geneva, dau. of **GÉROLD** (133-22) of Geneva, by 1st wife, Gisele. (West Winter, XI.491a, X.285 note).

    24. HUMBERT II "Le Renforcé," Count of Maurienne, Savoy and Turin, d. 14 Oct. 1103; m. abt. 1090, Gisele of Burgundy, b. abt. 1070, d. aft. 1133, dau. of **WILLIAM I** (132-24), Count Palatine of Burgundy. (West Winter, XII.800a).

    25. ADELAIDE, of Savoy, b. abt. 1092, d. 18 Nov. 1154; m. (1) Apr/May 1115, as his 2nd wife, **LOUIS VI** (101-24, 117-24, 135-26), King of France. (West Winter, XII.285, *Dict. de la Noblesse*, XVII: 349. Gens. 22-25: *ES* II/190).

Line 274B   New to 8th Edition

    24. HUMBERT II "Le Renforcé," (274A-24) Count of Maurienne, Savoy and Turin, d. 14 Oct. 1103; m. abt. 1090, Gisele of Burgundy. (West Winter, XII.800a).

    25. AMADEUS III, Count of Savoy, Maurienne and Turin, b. abt. 1095, d. Cyprus 30 Aug. 1148; m. 1123, Mahaud (Mathilde) d'Albon, d. aft. 1145, dau. of Guigues VIII, Count d'Albon. (West Winter, XII.286).

    26. MAUD (or **MATHILDA**) of Savoy, d. 4 Nov. 1157; m. 1146 **ALFONSO I** (112-25), King of Portugal.

    26. AGNES, of Savoy (dau. of Gen. 25), d. abt. 1172; m., as 1st wife, **WILLIAM I OF GENEVA** (133-25), Count of Geneva. (Gens. 24-26: *ES* II/190).

Line 274C   New to 8th Edition

25.   AMADEUS III, (274B-25) Count of Savoy, Maurienne and Turin; m. 1123, Mahaud (Mathilde) d'Albon, d. aft. 1145. (West Winter, XII.286).

26.   HUMBERT III, Count of Savoy, Maurienne and Turin, b. abt. 4 Aug. 1136, d. 4 Mar. 1189; m. (1) Feydive of Toulouse, dau. of Alphonse I Jourdain, Count of Toulouse, first cousin of **PHILIPPA (MATHILDA) OF TOULOUSE** (185-3); m. (2) abt. 1155 (div. by 1162), Gertrude of Flanders, d. bef. 1162, dau. of **THIERRY I (DIETRICH) OF LORRAINE** (164-25), Count of Flanders by **SIBYL OF ANJOU** (129-25); m. (3) Clementia von Zähringen, d. 1173/6, dau. of Konrad I, Duke of Zähringen by Clementia of Namur; m. (4) abt. 1175, Beatrix of Mâcon (see 133-26), d. 1230 (bef. 8 Apr.), dau. of Gerard I of Burgundy, Count of Mâcon. (West Winter, XIII.447; *ES* I.2/265).

27.   THOMAS I, by (4), Count of Savoy and Maurienne, b. 20 May 1178, d. 1 Mar. 1233; m. May 1195, **MARGARET (BEATRIX) OF GENEVA** (133-26), dau. of **WILLIAM I OF GENEVA** (133-25), Count of Geneva. (West Winter, XIV.665a).

28.   BEATRIX OF SAVOY, (133-27), d. Dec. 1266; m. Dec. 1220, **RAYMOND V BERENGER** (111-29), Count of Provence and Forcalquier. (West Winter, XV.932. Gens. 25-28: *ES* II/190).

Line 274D   New to 8th Edition

27.   THOMAS I, (274C-27) Count of Savoy and Maurienne, b. 20 May 1178, d. 1 Mar. 1233; m. May 1195, **MARGARET (BEATRIX) OF GENEVA** (133-26). (West Winter, XIV.665a).

28.   AMADEUS IV, Count of Savoy and Maurienne, b. 1197, d. 13 July 1253; m. (1) 1222, Anna of Burgundy, d. 1243, dau. of Hugh III, Duke of Burgundy; m. (2) 1244, Cecile of Baux, d. 1275. (West-Winter, XV.920).

29.   BEATRIX (see Line 28-31), by (1), d. 10 May bef. 1259; m. (1) 1233, Manfredo III di Saluzzo (see 28-31), Marquis of Saluzzo, d. 29 Oct. 1244; m. (2) 21 Apr. 1247, Manfred, King of Sicily. (Gens. 27-29: *ES* II/190).

Line 274E   New to 8th Edition

27.   THOMAS I, (274C-27) Count of Savoy and Maurienne; m. May 1195, **MARGARET (BEATRIX) OF GENEVA** (133-26). (West Winter, XIV.665a).

28.   THOMAS II, Count of Savoy and Maurienne, b. 1199, d. 7 Feb. 1259; m. (1) as 2nd husb., Apr. 1237, Jeanne of Flanders, b. 1200, *suo jure* Countess of Hainaut and Flanders, dau. of **BALDWIN VI** (168-28), Count of Hainaut and Flanders by **MARIE OF CHAMPAGNE** (102-27); m. (2) Beatrice Fieschi, dau. of Teodoro Fieschi, Count of Lavagna. (West Winter XV.922; Gens. 27-28: *ES* II/190).

21. **HUGH V DE LUSIGNAN**, "The Pious," Sire de Lusignan, d. in Battle 8 Oct. 1060, son of Hugh IV, d. 1025/32 and Auliarde de Thouars, dau. of Raoul I, Viscount of Thouars; m. Almodis of La Marche, dau. of Bernard I, Count of La Marche and Pérogord. (*ES* III.4/815).

22. **HUGH VI, DE LUSIGNAN**, "The Devil," Sire de Lusignan, d. 1106/10; m. bef. 1060, Hildegarde (Aldéarde) de Thouars, sis. of **ALÍENOR DE THOUARS** (183-2), dau. of **AIMERY IV DE THOUARS** (271-23). (*ES* III.4/815, 810).

23. **HUGH VII DE LUSIGNAN**, "The Dark," Sire de Lusignan, d. bef. 1151; m. Sarazine, d. bef. 1144. (*ES* III.4/815).

24. **HUGH VIII DE LUSIGNAN**, "The Old," Sire de Lusignan, d. in the Holy Land abt. 1173; m. bef. 1147, Bourgogne de Rancon, d. aft. 11 Apr. 1169, dau. of Geoffrey III de Rancon, Sire de Taillebourg. (*ES* III.4/815, XIV/157).

25. **HUGH DE LUSIGNAN**, d.v.p. bef. 11 Mar. 1169 (see also 123-28); m. Orengarde. (*ES* III.4/815-816; III.3/564).

26. **HUGH IX DE LUSIGNAN**, Sire de Lusignan, Count of La Marche, on Crusades from 1190, d. Damietta, Egypt, 5 Nov. 1219; m. (1) Agatha de Preuilly, dau. of Peter (Pierre) II, Sire de Preuilly; m. (2) aft. 1194, Mahaut de Angoulême, d. aft. 1233,), and dau. of Wulgrin III, Count of Angoulême, bro. of **AYMER (ADHÉMAR) "TAILLIFER" DE VALENCE** (153-27). (*ES* III.4/816, 725, 818).

27. **HUGH X DE LUSIGNAN**, by (1), Sire de Lusignan, Count of la Marche and of Angoulême, d. 1249 aft. 15 Jan.; m. Mar./Apr. 1220, **ISABELLA OF ANGOULÊME** (117-27), d. Apr. 1246, wid. of **JOHN I** (1-25) King of England. (*ES* III.4/816).

28. **HUGH XI DE LUSIGNAN** (117-28), b. 1221, d. Damiette 1250, Count of La Marche and Angoulême, Count of Ponthieu; m. 1238, **YOLANDE DE DREUX** (135-30), of Brittany. (*ES* III.4/816).

29. **HUGH XII DE LUSIGNAN** (135-31), Count of La Marche and Angoulême, Sire of Lusignan, d. sh. aft. 25 Aug. 1270; m. 29 Jan. 1254, **JEANNE DE FOUGÈRES**, (214A-30) Dame of Fougères, d. aft. 1273, dau. and h. of **RAOUL III DE FOUGÈRES** (214A-29), Sire of Fougères and Isabel de Craon. (*ES* III.4/816; *CP* V: 632, 634).

NAME INDEX

All references are to the Ancestral Line and Generation Number -- not to page numbers

A

Aalst
Balduin III of, 272–28
Beatrix of, 272–28
Rudolph I, L. of, 143–21

Abbott
Agnes, w. of John, 246A–35
Alice, 7–35, 246A–35
John, 246A–35

Abell
George, 56A–43
Joanna, w. of Robert, 56A–44
Robert, 56A–44

Abergavenny
Lords of. see Cantelou

Abington
Mary, 230A–40
Richard, 230A–39

Abney
Bathusa, w. of George, 81A–42
Dannett, 81A–43
Edmund, 81A–40
George, 81A–39, 81A–42
Paul, 81A–41

Achym
Thomas, 209–39

Acre
Joan of, 8–29, 8A–29, 9–29, 11–29, 63–30, 94A–32, 110–31

Acton
Helen, w. of John II de, 234A–32
John de, 234A–33
John II de, 234A–32, 253–30
Joyce, 230A–40
Maud de, 234A–32, 253–30
Walter, 230A–40

Adams
John Quincy, 199–40

Adelhelm, Ct., 48–13

Affeton
John, 261–38
Katherine, 261–38

Aguillon
Isabel, 257–31
Robert, 257–30
William, 257–29

Aigle
Gilbert de l', 113A–25
Hugh, de l', 18A–23
Lucie de l', 98–26
Margaret de l', 113A–25
Maud de l', 18A–23
Richard II de l', 98–26
Richer de l', 18A–23

Aintree
Emma de, 247–29

Albemarle
Margaret de. see Daumarle

Albon
Guigues VIII, Ct. d', 274B–25
Mahaud d', 274B–25, 274C–25

Albret
Bernard Ézy I, Sire d', 71A–31

Alcock
John, 15–40

Alderwich
Joanne, 86–34

Alemania
Emma of, 184–4
Godfried, D. of, 182–1
Houching, Ct. in, 182–2
Nebi, Ct. in, 182–3

Alençon
Counts of. see Talvas

Allen
Jane, 31–40, 85–40
Thomas, 31–40

Allin
John, 84–40

Allington
Hugh, 15A–36

Allyn
Matthew, 52–45
Richard, 52–45

Alost. see Aalst

Alpin. see Scotland

Alsace
see also Boulogne; Flanders; Lorraine; Tours
Adalric, D. of, 181–1
Adelaide (Aelis) of, 181–6
Adelaide of, 45–20
Adelbert, D. of, 181–2
Bava, w. of Hugh III, Ct. of, 181–5

Gerald IV, Ct. of, 164–24
Gerard, 45–20
Gerberga of, 100B–22
Hugh III, Ct. of, 48–17, 181–5
Luitfride I, D. of, 181–3
Luitfride II, Ct. of, 181–4
Matthew of. see Boulogne
Thierry I, Ct. of. see Flanders

Amancier
Jean d', 1A–34

Amcotts
Frances, 1–39

Amiens
see also the Vexin; Valois
Ermenfroi, Ct. of, 250–17
Thomas de Coucy, Ct. d', 273–26

Andrew
Anne, 57–43

Andrewe. see Andrews

Andrews
Elizabeth, 12–35, 12A–35, 59–39
John, 12–34, 59–39

Angell
Mary, 15A–39
William, 15A–39

Angelus
Alexius III, 103–29
Andronicus, 45–27
Anna, 103–29
Irene (Maria), 45–27
Isaac II, 45–27

Anglo-Saxons
see Wessex; Mercia; Kent; West Saxons; Wiltshire

Angoulême
see also Valence
Amelia d', 185A–4
Aymer (Adhémar) "Taillifer" de Valence, Ct. of. see Valence
Isabella of, 1–25, 80–29, 117–27, 153A–28, 154–28, 258–27, 260–29, 275–27
Mathilde de, 275–26
William IV "Taillifer", Ct. of, 153A–25
Wulgrin II, Ct. of, 153A–25
Wulgrin III, Ct. of, 275–26

Angus
Earls of. see Douglas; Umfraville
Malcolm, E. of, 224–30
Maud of, 224–30

Anjou
Adelaide of, 53–21, 101–21, 136–21, 137–21, 141A–20
Adele of, 250–18

Amaury I d', K. of Jerusalem, 114–28
Baldwin III, K. of Jerusalem, 118–24
Ermengarde of, 108–22, 110–22, 118–22, 119–24, 119A–21, 119A–25, 121–21, 214–21
Fulk II, Ct. of, 53–21, 101–21, 118–20, 141A–20, 250–18
Fulk III, Ct. of, 110–22, 118–21
Fulk IV, Ct. of, 118–23, 119–23, 119A–25
Fulk V, Ct. of, 103A–25, 118–24, 129–24, 169–26
Geoffrey V (Plantagenet), Ct. of, 1–23, 83–26, 118–25, 123–25, 225–35
Geoffroy I "Grisgonelle", Ct. of, 118–20, 121–20
Gerberga, w. of Fulk II, Ct. of, 118–20, 250–18
Hildegarde of, 110–23
Hildegarde, w. of Fulk II, Ct. of, 110–22
Hildegarde, w. of Fulk III, Ct. of, 118–21
Isabella of, 114–28
Sibyl of, 274C–26
Sybil of, 129–25, 164–25, 165–25

Annabel
Joan, 208–41

Annandale
Lords of. see Bruce

Antioch
Bohémond I, Pr. of, 103–24
Bohémond II, Pr. of, 103–25, 103A–26
Constance of, 103–26
Renaud de Châtillon-sur-Loing, Pr. of, 103–26
Robert Guiscard in, 103–24

Antwerp
Lionel of. see Clarence

Appleton
Samuel, 249–42
Thomas, 249–41
William, 249–41

Aquitaine
Agnes of, 111–25
Eleanor of, 1–24, 101–25, 102–25, 110–26
Ranulf I, D. of, 144A–16
William III of (I of Poitou). see Poitou
William IX, D. of, 110–24, 111–24, 183–4, 185–3
William X, D. of, 110–25

Aragon
Alfonso II, K. of, 105A–28, 111–27, 116–26

Isabella of, 101–29, 103–32, 105–30, 168–32
James I, K. of, 105–29, 105A–29
Pedro II, K. of, 105–29, 105A–28
Pedro III, K. of, 252C–32
Petronilla of, 111–26
Ramiro II, 111–25
Sancho I (IV) Ramirez, K. of, 111–25
Sancho Ramiros, K. of, 185–3

Arcedekne
Philippa, 6–32
Warin, L., 6–32

Arches
Joan, 6–35, 214–35
Richard, 6–35, 214–35

Arcis
Jean d', 17–29, 71A–31

Arcis-sur-Aube
Helpuin d', 151A–19

Ardennes
Cunegonde, w. of Wigeric, Ct. in the, 100B–20, 143–18, 149–21, 155–21
Wigeric, Ct. in the, 100B–20, 143–18, 149–21

Arderne
Agnes, 150–31
Alice, 230–35
Hugh de, 230–34
John de, 230–32
Margery, w. of Peter de, 150–30
Peter de, 150–30, 230–33
Walkelin de, 150–29

Ardres
Adelaide d', 272–27
Christine d', 272–27

Arles
see also Provence
Boso of, 49–17, 145–18
Boson II, Ct. of, 141A–19, 185–2
Rotbald I of, 141A–19
Theobald, Ct. of, 145–17
Willa of, 145–19, 146–18

Arlon
Walrun II, Ct. of, 168A–27

Armenia
see also Melitene
Leo II, K. of, 114–28
Stephanie of, 114–28

Arnold
Alicia, 81C–45
Benedict, 1–40
Elizabeth, 224A–42
Freelove, 1–40
John, 224A–42

Michael, 81C–44
Arnulf, House of. see France
Artois
Blanche of, 17–28, 45–30
Robert, Ct. of, 45–29, 113–29

Arundel
see also Fitz Alan
Alice d', 28–35
Earls of. see Aubigny; Fitz Alan
Joan d', 59–35
John d', L., 9–33, 21–31, 59–34
John of Lanherne, 214–37
Margaret, 214–37
Margaret d', 9–33, 21–32

Arundell
see also Arundel
Alice d', 16B–29

Ashaw
Anne, 233–43
Leonard, 233–43

Ashe. see Esshe
Assheton
Douce (Dulcia), 233B–37
Mary, 9–39, 170A–39
Richard, 9–39, 170A–39
Thomas, 233B–37

Asteley
Joan, 93A–32
William, L., 93A–32

Astley
Alice, 51–34
Elizabeth, 1A–37, 13A–39
Richard, 1A–37
Thomas, 13A–39
Thomas, L., 51–34

Aston
Edward, 7–38
Frances, 7–38

Atherton
Henry de, 247–29
Joan de, 247–29
William de, 247–29

Athol
Earls. see also Stewart
Isabel de, 204–35
Malcolm, E. of, 121A–25

Aton
Catherine de, 204–35, 206–35
Gilbert de, 206–34
William de, L., 206–34

Attemore
Edith, 253–35
Joan, w. of Robert, 253–35

Robert, 253–35
Aubigny
Alice d', 139–26
Amice, w. of Roger, 18A–21
Cecily d', 150–27
Gunnor d', 156–25, 270–27
Isabel d', 89–29, 149–28, 208–29, 215–29
Maud d', 16C–27
Nele d', 18A–23
Nichole d, 210–30
Nichole d', 55–29, 81–29, 126–30, 249–30, 255–30
Ralph d', 156–25, 270–27
Raoul d', 270–27
Roger d', 18A–21
William d', 18A–21, 18A–22
William d', E. of Arundel, 1–22, 16C–26, 18A–23, 126–29, 139–26, 149–25, 149–26, 149–27
William d', L. of Belvoir, 89–29
William de, 215–29
Aubrey
John, 8A–32
Audley
see also Tuchet
Alice de, 186–5, 207–32, 265–32
Anne de, 9–35, 32–35
Anne de (Tuchet), 176B–37
Hugh de, L., 9–30, 186–5, 207–31, 265–32
Hugh de, L., E. of Gloucester, 9–30
James de, 122–30, 207–31
James de, L., 71–33, 122–33, 176B–32
Joan de, 176B–33, 176C–33
Lords of. see Tuchet
Margaret de, 9–31, 10–31, 55–32, 61–33, 81–33
Nicholas, L., 71–33, 122–31, 122–32
Aumale
Agnes de, 136–25
Bertha of, 130–24
Counts of. see also Dammartin
Stephen, Ct. of, 136–24
Aunay
Aldéarde d', 271–20
Cadelon III d', 271–20
Austrasia
Gainfroi, Ct., son of Mainier, Ct. of Sens, D. of, 240–14
Mainier, Ct. of Sens, D. of, 240–14
Pepin I of Landen, Mayor of the Palace, 190–9

Pepin II of Heristal, Mayor of the Palace, 190–10
St. Begga of, 190–9
Austria
Konstanze of, 252D–29
Leopold II, Mrg. of, 147–26
Leopold III, Mrg. of, 45–24, 147–26
Leopold VI, D. of, 252D–29
Auvergne
Ermengarde of, 119A–23, 136–21, 137–21
Gerard, Ct. of, 144A–15
Robert I, Ct. of, 136–21, 137–21
Auxerre
Adèle of France, Cts. of, 107–21
Conrad I, Ct. of, 48–17, 181–6
Auxonne
Béatrix d', 71A–29
Counts of. see Bourgogne
Avalgau
Ermentrud of, 100B–22, 143–20
Megingoz, Ct. in, 100B–22, 143–20
Avenal
Cecily, 189–3
NN dau. of Richard, 89–27, 170–25
William, 189–3
Avesnes
see also Hainaut, Holland
Ade d', 168A–24
Bouchard d', 168–29, 168A–29
James d', sn. d', 168A–28
John I d', Ct. of Hainaut & Holland, 100–29, 168–30, 168A–30
Nicholas d'Oisy, sn. d', 168A–27
Wauter (Walter) d'Oisy, sn. d', 168A–26
Wédric II d', 168A–24
Avignon. see Arles
Avranches
Hugh d', E. of Chester, 132A–26
Margaret d', 132A–25, 132B–25
Maud d', 138–26
Richard le Goz d', 132A–25, 132B–25
Robert d', 138–26
Aylesbury
Eleanor, 55–36, 187–11
John, 187–9
Thomas, 55–36, 136–31, 187–10
Thomas de, 187–8
Ayscough
Elizabeth (Margaret), 224A–38
John, 224A–37
William, 224A–37

B

Babenberg
  see also Austria
  Agnes de, 147–26
Badlesmere
  Bartholomew de, 79–31
  Bartholomew de, L., 18A–30, 54–32, 65–33, 65A–33
  Elizabeth de, 15–30, 29–32, 65–34, 97–32
  Guncelin de, 54–32, 70–33
  Margery de, 54–33, 89–31, 212–33
  Maud de, 17–31, 18A–30, 65A–34, 70–33, 79–31
Bagot
  William, 58–30
Baldock
  Cecily de, 216A–31
  Thomas de, 216A–31
Baldwin
  John, 33–42
Baliol
  Ada de, 186–1
  Cecily de, 94–29, 99–29, 130–31, 252–26
  Eleanor de, 95–29, 121A–29, 252–26
  Ellen de, 161–26
  Ingram (Enguerrand) de, 161–26
  John de, 94–28, 95–28, 121A–29, 186–1, 252–26
  Margery, 94–29
  Tiphaine (Theophania) de, 265–30, 267A–28
Ballenstedt
  Adalbert, Ct. of, 252B–26
  Adalbert of, 252B–24
  Albrecht I, Ct. of, 252B–28, 252D–27
  Esiko, Ct. of, 252B–25
  Hedwig of, 252D–27
  Otto, Ct. of, 252B–27
Balliol. *see* Baliol
Balsareny
  Ermengarde de, 108–23
Balun
  Walter de, 207–31
Balzo. *see* Baux
Bamfield
  Agnes, 246G–35
  Joan, 246G–31
  John, 246G–31
  John II, 246G–32
  John III, 246G–33
  Richard, 6–40

  Thomas, 246G–34
  Ursula, 6–40, 209–39
Banastre
  Adam, 34–32
  Katherine, 34–32
Banester. *see* Banestre
Banestre
  Christopher, 9A–36
  Elizabeth, 9A–37, 170A–36
  Ellen, 9A–36, 170A–35
  Richard, 170A–35
  Thurstone, 9A–37, 170A–36
Banister
  Thomas, 170A–38
Bar
  Ermengarde of, 140–20
  Henry II, Ct. of, 168–31, 234B–26
  Margareta of, 168–31, 234B–26
  Reinald of, 140–20
Bar-le-Duc
  see also Montbéliard
  Clémemce de, 144–25
  Reinald I, Ct. of, 144–24
  Sophie, Cts. of, 144–23, 167–22
  Thierry (Dietrich) I, Ct. of, 144–23
Bar-sur-Aube
  Alice de, 71C–24
  Hildegarde de, 71C–25
Bar-sur-Seine
  Ermengarde of, 50–20
  Eustace of, 151A–24
  Reinald, Ct. of, 50–20
Barcelona
  Berenger Ramon I of, 71B–24, 108–23, 112–23
  Berenguela of, 113–25, 114–25
  Ramon Borrell I, Ct. of, 108–23
  Raymond II, Ct. of, 144–22
  Raymond III Berenger, Ct. of, 111–26, 113–25
  Raymond IV Berenger, Mrq. of, 111–26
  Sibylle of, 71B–24, 108–23, 112–23
Barclay
  Agnes, 252–43
  David, 252–42
  John, 252–43
  Katherine, w. of John, 252–43
  Robert, 252–43
Bardolf
  Beatrice (or Cecily), 184A–10
  bro. of Bodin, of Ravensworth, 266–24
  Cecily, 257–35
  Edmund, 211–39
  Hamelin, 132D–28

held Ravensworth, etc in Domesday
    Book, 226–24
Hugh, 132D–28, 152–27, 184A–10,
    234A–29
Hugh, L., 257–31
John, L., 257–33
Juliana, 132D–29, 234A–29
Maud, 211–39
Robert, 234A–30
Rohesia, 195–27
Thomas, 132D–28
Thomas, L., 257–32
William, 152–27, 257–28, 257–31
William, L., 257–34
Barley
John, 211–39
Margaret, 209–39
Barnaby
Richard, 230A–40
Thomas, 230A–40
Winifred, 230A–41
Basset
see also Bassett
Alan, 215–27
Alice, 189–1, 234A–28
Aline, 50–30, 51–30, 58–30, 72–31,
    148A–31
Edward, 84–38
Eleanor, 188–8, 238–8
Eustache, 30–27, 122–29
Gilbert, 30–27, 122–29, 143–28
Hawise, w. of Ralph, L., 55–30
Isabel, 84–27
Jane, 84–39, 143–41
Joan, 187–8
Joan, w. of Ralph, 188–7
Katherine, 215–27
Margaret, 9–31, 55–31
Philip, 51–30, 58–30, 72–31, 148A–31
Ralph, 187–7, 188–7
Ralph, Bar., 55–30, 210–31
Ralph, L., 16A–32, 55–30, 238–7
Richard, L., 187–6, 188–6, 238–6
Thomas, 189–1, 234A–28
Bassett
see also Basset
Margery, 12A–28
Miles, 12A–28
Bassingbourne
Warin de, 25–27
Batt
Christopher, 248–41, 248A–39, 248A–
    41
John, 248A–39

Thomas, 248A–40
Baudemont
Agnes de, 135–27, 273–28
André de, 264–27
Gui de, 135–27
Helvis (Helvide) de, 71A–28, 264–27
Baugency
Agnes de, 273–27
Alberge, w. of Lancelin II, 119–23
Hildegarde of, 119–23
Lancelin II, Sn. of, 119–23
Raoul de, 273–27
Baux
Cecile of, 274D–28
Francesco de, 234B–32
Marguerite de, 234B–32
Bavaria
see also Scheyern; Wittelsbach
Friedrich, D. of, 252A–34, 252C–33
Hartwig II, Ct. Palatine of, 252C–23
Henry I, D. of, 166–24, 243–7
Judith of, 45–25, 140–14, 146–14, 148–
    14, 166–25, 191A–16
Ludwig I, D. of, 252C–28
Ludwig II, D. of, 252C–30
Ludwig IV, D. of, 252C–31, 252D–32
Mechtild of, 252D–32
Otto I, D. of, 252D–25
Otto I (III) Ct. Palatine of Wittelsbach, D.
    of, 155–25, 252C–27
Otto I of Wittelsbach, Ct. Palatine of,
    252C–25
Otto II, D. of, 252C–29
Stephen II, D. of, 252C–32
Swanhilde of, 191–11
Welf I, D. of, 140–14
Welf IV, D. of, 166–23
Bavaria-Landshut
Elizabeth of, 252A–34, 252C–34
Bayeux
Berenger of, 121E–18
Poppa of, 121E–18
Ranulph II, Vct. of, 132A–25, 132B–25
Bayley
John, 170A–31
Richard de, 170A–31
Baynard
Richard, 246–34
Baynton
Ann, 248–41, 248A–41
Edward, 248–38
Ferdinando, 248–40
Henry, 248–39
John, 248–38

Bealknap
Elizabeth, 56B–36
Hamon, 56B–36
Beauchamp
Anne, 225–36
Anne de, 84–35
Beatrice de, 122A–30, 216–29
Eleanor, 1–32, 87–34, 246G–31
Elizabeth, 246E–33
Elizabeth, w. of John de, 84–31
Emma de, 222–28
Eustache, w. of Richard de, 197–30
Giles de, 84–30, 85–30, 189–6
Guy de, E. of Warwick, 86–30, 87–30, 98–31
Humphrey de, of Ryme, 246B–30, 246G–31
Isabel de, 72–31, 74–31, 74A–31, 93A–29, 94A–33
Jane, 217–36, 246B–32
Joan, 120–36, 234B–33, 246E–33
Joan de, 7–33
Joan, w. of John of Ryme, 246B–31, 246E–31
John, 81B–42, 197–31, 234B–33
John de, 84–31, 197–29
John de, of Bletsoe, 225–37
John de, of Bletsoe, Bar., 85–34
John de, of Powyk, Bar., 84–33
John, L., of Hatch, 246G–32
John, L., of Kidderminster, 197–32
John of Ryme, 217–36, 246B–31, 246E–31, 246E–32
Margaret, 197–33
Margaret de, 85–35, 202–35, 212–36, 225–37
Mary, 81B–42
Mary, w. of Roger de, of Bletsoe, Bar., 85–33
Maud, 265–34
Maud de, 11–34, 18A–27, 26–32, 86–31, 202–32, 248–34
NN, w. of Roger de, 85–32
Philippe, 10–32
Richard, D. of Warwick, 225–36
Richard de, 197–30
Richard de, Bar., 55–37
Richard de, of Powyk, Bar., 84–34
Richard, E. of Warwick, 1–32, 39–34, 87–33
Richard, E. of Worcester, 87–33
Robert IV de, L. of Hatch, 246B–29
Robert V de, L. of Hatch, 246B–29
Roger de, 34–25, 85–32

Roger de, of Bletsoe, Bar., 85–31, 85–33, 263–32
Roger de, of Bletsoe, L., 184A–13
Sarah, 84A–29
Simon de, 18A–27, 122A–29
Thomas, 246E–33
Thomas de, E. of Warwick, 10–32, 26–32, 120–34
Thomas, E. of Warwick, 11–34, 87–31, 87–32, 202–32, 265–34
Walter de, 84–29
William, Bar., 86–28
William, Bar. of Abergavenny, 120–35
William de, 84–32, 197–28
William de, Bar., 84A–28, 84–28
William de, Bar. of, 216–29
William de, Bar. of Bedford, 18A–27, 122A–29, 184A–9
William de, E. of Warwick, 72–30, 74–30
William, E. of Warwick, 86–29
William I de, 222–28
Beaufitz. *see* Byaufiz
Beaufort
Edmund, D. of Somerset, 1–32, 87–34
Eleanor, 1–33
Henry, 199A–33, 234–31
Joan, 2–32, 3–32, 10–34, 78–35, 207–34, 252–34, 256–40, 62–34
Joan (Jane), 199A–33, 234–32
John, E. of Somerset, 1–31, 47–33, 252–34
Beaumont
Agnes de, 114–29
Alice de, 84–27
Catherine de, 12–32
Constance, 17–36, 98–37
Constance de, 98–27, 98A–27
Elizabeth, 51A–35
Elizabeth de, 121B–26
Hawise de, 63–26, 124–27
Henry, 17–34, 17–35, 221–37
Henry de, 81A–37
Henry de, E. of Warwick, 84–25, 151–24
Henry de, L., 17–30, 72–33, 79–32, 114A–29
Henry de, L., E. of Buchan, 114–30
Henry, E. of Warwick, 84–26
Henry, L., 17–31, 17–33
Isabel de, 66–25, 72–33, 184–4
John, 12–32, 18B–33
John de, L., 17–30, 114–31
John, L., 17–32, 51A–35
Margaret de, 53–27, 54–28, 56–27, 60–27, 98A–26

Maud de, 50–27, 215–25
Raoul VIII de, 114–29
Richard I de, 98–26, 114–29
Robert de, Ct. of Meulan, 50–26
Robert de, E. of Leicester, 53–26, 63–25, 66–24, 98A–26, 141–24, 151–24
Robert de, L., E. of Leicester, 50–24, 53–24, 140–24, 215–24
Robert I de, 121B–26
Robert II, E. of Leicester, 53–25
Roger de, 50–24, 151–24
Roger de, E. of Warwick, 84–25, 88–25, 151–25
Waleran de, Ct. of Meulan, 50–25
Waleran de, E. of Warwick, 84–26
Beaumont-au-Maine. *see* Beaumont
Beauvoir
Jeanne de, 234B–27
Beauvoir-en-Arrouaise
Mathieu II, 234B–27
Beavis
Alice, 246G–42
Christina, w. of John, 246G–42
John, 246G–42
Richard, 246G–42
Bedford
Barons of. *see* Beauchamp
John of Lancaster, D. of, 234B–33
Beethom
Mabel de, 41–32
Beke
Elizabeth, 32–'32
John, L. of Eresby, 93–29
Margaret, 93–29
Nicholas, 32–'32
Walter, L. of Eresby, 93–29
Belesby
Thomas, 74A–36
Bell
Anne, 209–39
Edward, 209–39
Margaret, 246A–41
Bellême
Robert II de, E. of Shrewsbury, 108–25
Bellers
Anice (Amice) de, 210–34
Roger de, 210–34
Bellesme
Adeline de, 151–23
Warin, 151–23
Bellingham
Margaret, 37–36
Richard, 1–39
Roger, 37–36

William, 1–39
Belmeis
Alice de, 39–27, 136B–28
Philip de, 39–27, 132C–27, 136B–27
Walter de, 136B–27
William de, 39–28
Belmont
Blanche de, 263–30
Richard, sn. de, 263–30
Bennett
Jane, 12–39
John, 12–39
Bensted
Edward, 218–33
Bentheim
Otto von Salm, Ct. of, 100B–25
Bentworth. *see* Sale
Berborrow
Ralph, 248A–34
Bere
Clement, 211–42
Bereford
Baldwin de, 42–32
Joan de, 42–32
John de, 79–32
Margaret de, 79–32
Berenger
see also Provence
Judicael, 214–21
Berkeley
Anne, 197–35, 209–37
Edward, 120–37
Elizabeth, 1–32, 81–36, 81A–36, 84–37, 187–16, 221–36
Elizabeth de, 39–34, 87–33
Isabel, 26–31
James, L., 18A–33
John, 81–36, 81A–36, 84–37, 187–15
Lora, 120–37
Maurice, 209–37
Maurice de, L., 26–28, 26–30, 39–30, 39–32, 59–31
Milicent de, 59–32
Richard, 187–14
Roger IV de, 55–27
Thomas, Bar., 1–32
Thomas de, 26–29, 59–30
Thomas de, L., 26–28, 39–31, 39–33, 81–36, 81A–36, 87–33
Walter de, 161–26
William, 187–13
Bermingham
Eve de, 178–4
Robert de, 178–4

Bernake
John, 210–35, 218–31
Maud, 210–35, 218–32
William, 218–31
Berners
Barons. *see* Bourchier
Lords of. *see* Bourchier
Margery, 4–33
Richard, 4–33
Berney
Elizabeth, 232–36
Bernicia
Aelfled of, 98A–23, 130–25
Aldred of, 98A–23, 130–25
Berry
Anne, 179–14
Nicholas, 179–14
Bessiles
Elizabeth, 143–37
William, 143–36
Bessin
Anschitil, Vct. of the, 132A–24
Ranulph, Vct. of the, 132A–24
Bethune
Mathilde de, 272–28
Robert IV de, 272–28
Betteshorne
Elizabeth, 81–36, 81A–36
John, 81–36, 81A–36
Betuwe
Adelheid (Adela), dau. of Eberhard,
155–22, 160–22
Eberhard, Ct. in the, 155–22, 160–22
Bibar
Christina (Elvira) de, 113A–24
Diego Lainez, sn. de, 113A–22
Rodrigo Diaz, Sn. de, 113A–23
Bidgau
see also Ardennes
Cunigonde in, 100B–20, 143–18
Wigeric, Ct. in, 100B–20, 143–18
Bigod
Gunnor, 246–26
Hugh, 69–29, 83–27, 121D–31, 224–31,
270–29
Hugh, E. of Norfolk, 69–28, 70–28,
177A–8, 232–28, 246C–28
Isabel, 70–29, 71–29, 72–29, 73–29,
75–29, 82–29, 177A–8, 177B–9,
246C–28
Jane, 246D–26
Joan, 69–32, 121D–31, 224–31
John, 69–30, 156–33
Margaret, 93–27

Maud, 18A–22
Ralph le, 148A–29
Roger, 69–31, 72–31, 93–27, 156–33,
246D–26
Roger, E. of Norfolk, 69–28, 69–29
Roger le, Bar., 18A–22
Roger. *see also* Felbrigge
Simon, 232–29
Bigorre
Garsinde de, 144–22
Bigot
John, 246–31
Billing
John, 42–33
Thomas, 42–33
Bingham
Richard, 230A–35
Birmingham
Joan de, 40–32
Thomas, 56B–35
Walter de, 40–31, 40–32
Birport
Elizabeth, 253–37
Bisby
Mary (Smith), 69A–42
Bisset
Ela, 234A–28
Isabel, 234A–28
John, 234A–28
Margaret, 234A–28
Bittlesgate
Joan, 234B–33
Thomas, 234B–33
Blackburn
John, 34–32
Blayney
Edward, 18–39
Margaret, 18–39
Blennerhasset
Elizabeth, 208–40
John, 208–40
Blessing
Alice, 224A–43
Blewett
Edmond, 224A–41
Margaret, 224A–41
Bliesgau
Folmar, Ct. in the, 167–21
Richilde (von Blieskastel), 167–21
Blight
Margaret, 246E–39
Blois
Adela, mother of Aubri I, Ct. of, 240–11
Aubri I, Ct. of, 240–12

Aubri II, Ct. of, 240–13
Bertha of, 119–24, 119A–23
Emma of, 262–26
Eudes I, Ct. of, 101–21, 119–24, 136–20, 159–20
Eudes II, Ct. de, 136–21
Eudes II, Ct. of, 119A–23, 137–21
Henry, Ct. of, 102–26
Lithuaise, sis. of Stephen of, K. of England, 264–26
Mary of, 165–26, 169–26
Stephen of, 137–23, 139–23, 169–24, 262–26
Stephen of, K. of England. see England
Theidlindis, dau. of Aubrii II, Ct. of, 240–14
Theobald I, Ct. of, 49–19, 136–19
Theobald III, Ct. of, 137–22
Theobald IV, 102–26
Theobald IV, Ct. of, 137–24
Theobald (Tetbald), Ct. of, 49–18
William of, 83–26
Blount
Constance, 81–35
Elizabeth, 12–36, 59–39, 201–39
Humphrey, 258–33
John, 258–31, 258–32, 258–34
Katharine, 258–35
Thomas, 230A–39
Walter, 81–35
Walter, L. Mountjoy, 58–38
William, 58–38, 70–32
Blunt
Emma, 230–38
John, 230–38
Blythe
Margaret, 81B–39
William, L. of Norton, 81B–39
Blytheway
Robert, 248A–40
Bodrugan
Henry, 124A–33
Joan, 124A–33
Bohemia
Anne of, 232–33
Boleslaw I "the Cruel", 244–7
Friedrich, D. of, 252C–28
Judith, Pss. of, 147–24, 244–8
Ludmilla of, 252C–28
Venceslav, D. of ("Good King Wenceslas"), 244–7
Vratislav II, K. of, 147–24, 244–7

Bohun
Alianore de, 57–30, 69–30, 97–34, 130–31
Alice de, 84–29, 98–29
Eleanor de, 4–31, 7–30, 13–30, 73–32
Elizabeth de, 15–31, 18A–32, 20–31, 47D–33, 60–33, 120–35
Henry de, 97–27
Humphrey de, 1A–32, 84–26, 84–29
Humphrey de, E. of Northampton, 97–33
Humphrey III, B. de, L. of Hereford, 193–5
Humphrey IV de, 97–26, 193–6
Humphrey V de, 97–28, 98–29, 123–29
Humphrey VI de, 68–29, 97–29
Humphrey VII de, 97–30, 158C–29
Humphrey VIII de, 6–29, 7–29, 15–29, 97–31
Margaret de, 6–30, 12–30, 51–32
Mary de, 1A–32
Maud de, 84–26, 130–28, 148A–26
William de, E. of Northampton, 15–30, 65–34, 97–32
Bois
Arnold du, 215–29
Isabel du, 212–31, 215–29
Bold
Henry, 34–38, 170–34
Sibyl de, 34–38, 170–34
Bolebec
Helewise, w. of Walter I de, 267–25
Hugh de, 267–25
Hugh II de, 267–26
Hugh III de, 184B–7, 267A–27
Hugh IV de, 265–30, 267A–28
Isabel de, 50–29
Isabella de, 60–28, 246–27, 267–26
Margery de, 265–30, 267A–29
Osbern de, 184–1
Walter I de, 267–25, 267A–25
Walter II de, 267A–26, 269–26
Boleyn
Anne, 120–39, 158A–23
Anne, Q. consort of England, 22–37
Mary, 1–35, 22–37
Thomas, E. of Wiltshire, 22–36, 120–39
William, 120–38
Bolhay
Amicia de, 246G–32
James, 246G–32

Bolles
Benjamin, 202–40
Joseph, 202–42
Thomas, 202–41
Bonner
Anthony, 57–40
Mary, 57–41
Thomas, 57–40
Bonville
Alice, w. of William, 124A–35
Elizabeth, 28–36, 224–36, 261A–39
John, 124A–36, 261–37, 261A–37
Nicholas de, 124A–34
William, 28–36, 124A–35, 261–36, 261–37
William, L., 93A–33, 224–36, 261A–38
Booth
Alice, 36–38
Elizabeth, 34–36
Elizabeth (Eleanor), 224A–40
Ellen, 233–38
George, 33–36, 86–37
Henry, 224A–38
Jane, 33–38
John, 36–38, 74A–39, 224A–39
Robert, 233–38
Thomas, 34–36
William, 33–35, 33–37, 224A–38
Boroughdon
Eleanor de, 74A–35, 224–33
Gilbert de, 224–32
Bostock
Edmund (Edward), 248–39
Margaret, 248–39
Bosum
Elizabeth, 6–36
John, 6–36
Bosvile
Elizabeth, 1–39, 69A–41
Geoffrey, 69A–41
Boteler
see also Butler
Alice, 170–31, 233B–35
Joanna, 248A–31
John, 20–34
John, Bar. of, 46–36
John, Bar. of Warrington, 46–35, 199–34
John (Robert), Bar. of Warrington, 170–30
Margaret, 20–35
Margery, 9–38, 46–38
Maud le, 70A–29, 149–29
Thomas, 9–38

Thomas, Bar. of Warrington, 46–37
Thomas (Theobald) le, 70A–29, 149–29
William le, L. of Warrington, 34–26
William le, of Bewsey, 170–30
Botetourte
Joan, 188–9, 238–9
Joan de, 216A–32
John, 238–9
John de, 30–32, 143–33, 216A–31
John de, L., 98–32, 122A–31, 216–29, 216–31, 216A–29
Joyce de, 98–33, 216–32, 230A–33
Otto (Otes) de, 216A–30
Sibyl, w. of Otto (Otes), 216A–30
Thomas de, 216–30
Botiller. see Butler
Botillier. see Butler
Botreaux
Margaret, 18–34, 51A–35
William, L., 18–34, 51A–35
Boulogne
Baldwin de, 158A–23
Eustace de, 158A–23
Eustace I, Ct. of, 148–21, 158–21
Eustace II, Ct. of, 158–22, 158A–22, 235–20
Eustace III, Ct. of, 158–23, 169–25
Eustace IV, Ct. of, 169A–26
Faramus, son of William de, 158A–23
Farramus de, sn. de Tingry, 158A–25
Godfrey (or Geoffrey) Ct. of, 158A–23
Lambert of, Ct. of Lens, 130–24, 148–22
Mathilde of, 100–28
Matilda of, 158–24, 165–26, 169–25, 169A–25
Matthew of Alsace, Ct. of, 100–28, 155–26, 165–26, 169–26
Maud (Matilda), w. of Farramus de, 158A–25
Sybil, dau. of Faramus, w. of Enguerrand de Fiennes, 158A–23
William de, 158A–23, 158A–24
Bourbourg
Beatrix de, 272–28
Henry I de, 272–28
Walter de, 272–28
Bourchier
Eleanor, 18B–34
Henry, 18B–34
Humphrey, 4–34, 22–35, 136–34
Jane, 4–36, 188–14
John, L. Berners, 4–33, 4–35, 16–35, 136–34

Robert, L., 155A–31
William, Ct. of Eu, 4–32, 261–38
William de, 155A–31
William, E. of Eu, 18B–34
William, L. FitzWarin, 261–38

Bourges
Eldeburge, 139–24

Bourgogne
see also Burgundy
Étienne III de, Ct. of d'Auxonne, 71A–29

Bourne
Emma Fitz Baldwin of, 184A–5
Judith, 249–42

Bournonville
Alix de, 158B–24
Louis, sn. de, 158B–24
Silvie, w. of Louis, 158B–24

Bourtetourt
John de, 13A–32
Maud, 13A–32

Boves
Dreux (Drogo), sn. de, 273–24
Enguerrand I, sn. de Coucy & de, 273–25

Bowden
Elizabeth, 179–14
John, 179–14

Bowen
Francis, 179–16
Griffith, 179–17
Gruffudd, 179–14
Philip, 179–15

Boyce
Alice, 69–35, 69A–35
Thomas, 69–35

Boynton
Joan, 204–38

Boys
John, 223–40
Margaret, 223–40

Brabant
Godfrey I of Brabant. see Louvain
Henry I, D. of, 100–28, 155–26, 165–27
Henry II, D. of, 45–28, 155–27
Henry II of Brabant. see Louvain
Henry III, D. of, 155–28
Marie of, 16–28, 101–29, 155–29
Matilda of, 45–29, 113–29
Mechtild of, 100–28

Bracebridge
Maud, 86–32
Ralph, 86–32

Bradbury
Matthew, 246A–40

Philippa, 211–39
Robert, 211–38
Thomas, 246A–42
William, 211–38, 246A–40, 246A–42
Wymond, 246A–41

Bradeston
Thomas de, 213–32

Bradford
William, 9–41

Bradshagh
Alice, 85–36
Elizabeth, 34–35
Hugh de, 34–35
Thomas, 85–36
William, 34–35

Bradshaw. see Bradshagh

Bradstreet
Simon, 143–42

Braine. see Dreux

Brampton
Amy, 4–39
Brian de, 258–29
Elizabeth de, 258–29

Brandenburg
Dorothea of, 252–36, 252A–36, 252E–35
Friedrich (VI) I, Elector of, 252A–34
Johann the Alchemist, Mrg. of, 252A–35, 252B–35

Brandon
Charles, 15–35
Eleanor, 15–35
William, 15–34

Branscombe
Adam de, 246E–33
Richard, 246E–33
Richard de, 246E–32

Braose
Aline de, 18A–29
Bertha de, 222–28
Eleanor de, 68–29, 68–29, 97–29
Eva de, 93A–28
Eve de, 39–29, 66–29
John de, 29A–28, 246–30
Laurette de, 63A–29
Margaret de, 70–29, 98–28, 177A–7, 177B–7
Margery de, 246–30
Maud de, 28–29, 63A–29, 67–29, 77–29, 176B–29
Philip de, 177–5
Reynold de, 132C–29, 176B–28, 177–7
Richard de, 246–30
Sibyl de, 194–6

William de, Bar., 66–28, 67–28, 68–28,
70–29, 98–28, 177–8, 253–29
William de, Bar. of Gwentland, 177–5,
194–5, 222–28
William de, L., 18A–29, 29A–28, 63A–
28, 177–6, 177A–6
Bray
Lords of. *see* Ridelisford
Bredbury
Adam de, 230–33
Cicely, 230–33
Brehna
Thiemo, Ct. of, 252D–25
Breos. *see* Braose
Brereton
Eleanor, 57–37
Elizabeth, 36–37, 56A–41
Sybil, 233–41
Urian, 233–41
William, 36–37
Bréteuil
William de, 215–25
Brett
Joan, 52–42
Robert, 52–42
Brewes
see also Braose
Giles de, 99–32
Robert de, 99–32
Brewster
Francis, 12–40
Lucy, w. of Francis, 12–40
Nathaniel, 12–40
Brian
Guy de, 63A–30
Maud de, 63A–31
Brien
William de, 59–35
Brienne
Blanche de, L. of Loupeland, 120–31
Engelbert de, 71A–24, 151A–24
Englebert I of, 50–20
Erard I, Ct. of, 71A–27, 151A–24
Erard II, Ct. of, 114–28
Félicité de, 71A–27
Gautier I of, 151A–24
Jean de, 114–28, 120–29
Jean de, of Acre, 120–30
Louis, Ct. of, 234B–31
Louis de, 114–29
NN, dau. of Engelbert de, 71A–24
Yolande de, 114–28
Brightley
Isabel de, 25–33

John de, 25–32
Brionne
Gilbert, Ct. of, 130–27
Brito
Cecily de, 148A–27
Brittany
see also Dinan; Rennes
Agnora of, 214–25
Alan I, K. of, 119A–21
Alan III, D. of, 119–24, 119A–23
Alan IV, D. of, 119–24, 119A–25
Bardolf of, 226–24
Bertha of, 119–26, 227–25
Conan, D. of, 266–26
Conan I, D. of, 119A–21, 121–21, 214–
21
Conan III, D. of, 119–25
Conan IV, D. of, 96–26, 119–27
Constance, Cts. of, 96–27, 271–27
Eudes I, Co-Regeant of, 214–23, 226–23
Geoffrey, D. of, 119A–22, 214–22
Hawise of, 119–24, 119A–24
Hawise, w. of Stephen I, Ct. of, 214A–
24, 227–24
Hoel, D. of, 119–24, 119A–24
Jubel Berenger, 119A–21
Judicael Berenger of, 214–21
Judith of, 121–22, 121E–21, 132–22,
132A–22, 166–22
Maud of, 18A–24, 143–23, 156–24
Olive of, 214A–25
Oreguen, w. of Alan I, K. of, 119A–21
Orguen, w. of Eudes I, Co-Regeant of,
214–23
Stephen I, Ct. of, 18A–24, 119–26, 143–
23, 156–24, 214–24, 214A–24, 227–
24
Briwere
Alice, 143–27, 246B–28
Grace de, 177–7
Isabel, 26–27, 218–27, 184A–7
William de, 143–27, 177–7, 184A–7,
218–27, 246B–28
Brocton
Edward, 81B–41, 81C–41
Helen, 81B–41, 81C–41
Brokesby
George, 81A–41
Mary, 81A–41
Bromley
John, 233B–38
Margaret, 233B–38
Brooke
Anne, 81B–44

279

Elizabeth, 246–36
Reginald, 246–36
Roger, 81B–43
Brotherton
Thomas of, E. of Norfolk. *see* Norfolk
Broughton
John, 213–33
Browne
Anne, 232–40
Nathaniel, 230B–41
Nicholas, 230B–38
Percy, 230B–40
Thomas, 230B–38
William, 230B–39
Broyes
Simon de, 71A–27
Bruce
see also Brus; Scotland
Marjorie, 75A–32, 252–31
Robert de, of Annandale, 121C–30
Robert, L. of Annandale, 252–27, 252–28, 252–30
Bruen
John, 33–39, 33–40
Mary, 33–42
Obadiah, 33–41
Sarah, w. of Obadiah, 33–41
Brugge
Agnitrude von, 272–26
Brun
Elyn de, 37–31
Robert de, 37–31
Brunswick
Helene of, 252B–30
Otto I, D. of, 252B–30
Brus
see also Bruce
Adam de, 136–25
Adam II de, 161–25
Agnes de, 136–27, 184B–8, 208–30
Isabel de, 161–25
Lucy de, 88–29
Piers I de, L. of Skelton, 88–28, 136–25, 161–25
Piers II de, L. of Skelton, 88–28, 136–26, 184B–8
Piers III de, 136–27
Buchan
Counts, Earls of. *see also* Beaumont
Counts, Earls of. *see also* Comyn
Fergus, E. of, 114A–26, 121A–26
Margaret, Cts. of, 114A–26, 121A–26, 224–29

Buckingham
Anne, Cts. of, 4–32, 155A–32, 261–38
Budockshide
Robert, 261–39
Builly
Beatrice de, 139–25
Roger de, 139–25
Bulgaria
see also West Bulgars
Ivan Vladislav of, 45–27
Maria of, 45–27
Trojan of, 45–27
Bulkeley
Dorcas, 31E–40, 203–40
Edward, 31–39, 31A–39, 31B–39, 31C–39, 31D–39, 85–40, 203–39, 245–39
Elizabeth, 31C–40
Frances, 31B–40, 223–42
Gershom, 69–40
Margaret, 231–34
Martha, 31A–40
Peter, 7–40, 31–40, 69–40, 85–40
Richard, 231–34
Sarah, 31D–40, 31E–39, 85–40, 245–40
Thomas, 31–38
Bull
Mathilda, 57–41
Bullen
Charles, 158A–23
Bulmer
Ansketil de, 268–25
Bertram de, 247–25
Emma de, 247–25
Eve de, 266–31
John de, 266–31
Sibil de, 268–25
Bulmere
Eve, 208–31
Ralph, 208–31
Burdet
Elizabeth, 55–35
John, 55–35
Buren
Frederick of, 45–24
Bures
Catherine de, 84–30, 189–6
John de, 84–30, 189–5
Burgh
Devorguilla de, 94–29, 130–31
Egidia de, 75A–31
Eleanor de, 40–30, 75–32
Elizabeth de, 5–31, 94A–34, 252–30
Hawise de, 94–29, 99–30
Hubert de, E. of Kent, 94–29

Joan de, 7–31
John de, 11–30, 94–29, 94A–32, 99–29, 130–31, 252–26
John de, Bar. Lanvallei, 94–29
Margery de, 73–30
Richard de, 73–30
Richard de, E. of Ulster, 7–31, 75–31, 94A–31, 252–30, 272–30
Richard de, L. of Connaught, 75A–30, 177B–8
Walter de, E. of Ulster, 75–30, 75A–30, 177B–9
William de, E. of Ulster, 5–31, 94A–33
William de, L. of Connsught, 177B–8
Burghersh
Bartholomew de, L., 70–33, 70–34
Elizabeth de, 70–35, 74–34
Robert de, L., 70–33
Burgundy
see also Bourgogne
Adelaide of, 118–19, 147–19
Adelgunde of, 147A–17
Alix of, 155–28
Anna of, 274D–28
Beatrice of, 71A–26, 71B–25, 71C–26
Beatrix of, 45–26
Bertha of, 133–21, 136–20, 159–20
Boso, K. of, 141B–17
Chilperic, K. of, 240A–3
Clemence of, 155–23, 161–23
Conrad I, K. of, 133–19. see France, Conrad I, K. of
Constance of, 113–23
Ermengarde of, 118–19
Ermentrude of, 144–23, 167–23
Eudes I, D. of, 105A–27, 108–24
Gerard I of, Ct. of Mâcon, 274C–26
Gerberga of, 157–20, 167–20
Giselbert, Ct. of, 118–19
Gisele of, 101–24, 274A–24, 274B–24
Hélie of, 108–25, 109–25
Henry I, D. of Lower, 108–22
Henry I of, 71B–24, 108–23, 112–23
Hugh II, D. of, 105A–27
Hugh III, D. of, 274D–28
Hugh IV, D. of, 155–28
Konrad II, Mrg. of, 147A–17
Matilda of, 105A–27, 133–20
Raymond of, 113–24, 132–25
Renaude I, Ct. of, 132–23
Renaude III, Ct. of, 45–26
Robert the Old, D. of, 108–22, 110–22, 113–22
Rudolf I, K. of, 145–18

Rudolph II, K. of, 147–19, 157–19
St. Clothilde, 240A–3
Stephanie, w. of William I, Ct. of, 101–24, 135–26, 144–22
William I, Ct. of, 101–24, 108–24, 117–24, 132–24, 135–26, 144–22, 161–23, 274A–24
Burgundy-Ivrea
Sibylle of, 105A–27, 108–24
Burnel
Philip, 81–31
Burnell
Isabel de, 222–34
Maud, 215–30
Philip, 215–30
Burnett
Catherine, 256–42
Thomas, 256–42
Burrough
George, 200–41, 200–43
Nathaniel, 200–42
Thomas, 200–40
Bury
Alicia de, 34–35
Bute
James, E. of, 75A–31
Jean of, 75A–31
Butler
see also Boteler
Anne, 84A–30, 84B–30
Beatrice, w. of William, of Oversley, 77–32
Edmond, 25–30
Edmund, 7–30, 73–31, 178A–8
Elizabeth, 7–34, 8–35
Elizabeth, of Wem, 62–33, 77–34
Emoine, 40–29
James, E. of Ormond, 1–33, 7–30, 7–31, 7–32, 7–33, 13–30, 73–32, 95–32, 120–36
John, 7–36, 40–29
Margaret, 7–36, 120–38
Petronilla, 13–31, 13A–32, 14–31, 73–32, 95–32
Philip, 136–32
Theobald, 73–30
Thomas, E. of Ormond, 120–37
Thomas, L. Sudeley, 222–35
William, 11–34, 248–34
William, L. of Wem, 248A–31
William, L., of Wem, 77–33
William, of Oversley, 77–32
William, of Wem, 77–32, 84A–30, 222–35

Button
Robert, 224A–43
Buxhall
Alan, 8A–32
Byaufiz
Alice, 170–29, 170A–30
Henry, 170–29
Byley
Henry, 248A–40
Joan, 248A–40
Byron
Elizabeth, 233B–37
Ellen, 58–38
Isabel de, 247–28
John, 58–38, 233B–37
Robert de, 247–28
Byzantine Empire
Alexius Comnenus, 105A–26
Alexius I Comnenus, Emp., 45–27, 103–29, 105A–23
Alexius III Angelus, 103–29
Andronicus Angelus, 45–27
Andronicus Comnenus, 105A–25
Andronicus Ducas, 45–27, 105A–23
Anna Angelus, 103–29
Anna of, 141A–17, 141B–18
Anne Dalassene, 105A–22
Basil I, Emp., 141A–15
Constantine Monomachos, Emp. of, 45–23, 242–6
Eudocia Ingerina, 141A–15
Eudoxia Comnenus, 105A–27
Euphrosyne Castamonitia, w. of Andronicus Angelus, 45–27
Irene Ducas, 45–27, 105A–23
Irene (Maria), dau. of Isaac II Angelus, 45–27
Irene, w. of Andronicus Comnenus, 105A–25
Isaac II Angelus, 45–27
John I Comnenus, 105A–22
John I Tsimices, 147–20
John II Comnenus, Emp., 105A–24, 244A–8
Leo VI, Emp., 141A–16, 141B–18
Manuel Comnenus, 105A–21
Maria Ducas, 105A–26
Maria Lascaris, 103–29
Maria Monomacha, 242–6, 45–23
Michael III, Emp., 141A–15
Romanus II, 147–20
Theodora Comnena, 45–27
Theodore I (Comnenus) Lascaris, 103–29

Theophana, 147–20
Zoe Tzautzina, 141A–16

C

Caen. see Gloucester
Calthorpe
Anne, 257–38
William, 257–37
Calverley
Joan, 9A–36, 170A–35
Walter, 9A–34
William, 9A–35, 170A–34
Calvert
Mary (Wolseley), 81B–43
Calwoodley
Joan, 246G–37
Camberlain. see Chamberlayne
Cambernon. see Chambernon
Cambridge
Richard of Conisburgh, E. of, 225–34
Cammock
Margaret, wid. of Thomas, 211–43
Thomas, 211–43
Camoys
Maud, 261A–38
Thomas, 261A–38
Campernon. see Chambernon
Campo Ernulfi. see Champernon
Camville
see also Canville
Idonea de, 30–27, 122–29
Isabel, 84–26
Richard de, 30–27, 84–26, 122–29, 246A–25
Candavaine
Anselme, Ct. of St. Pol, 109–27, 169A–27
Beatrice, of St. Pol, 109–27, 169A–28
Hugh III, 169A–27
Cansfield
Agnes, 34–30
Richard, 34–29
Cantelo
Nicholas de, 170–27
Cantelou
Agnes de, 262–31
George de, L. of Abergavenny, 39–29
Joan de, 93A–28, 99–32
John de, 56–29
Juliane de, 255A–29
Milicent de, 39–29, 39A–29, 66–30, 200–30, 212–30, 234A–32, 253–29
Thomas, Bishop of Hereford, 255A–29

William de, Bar. Abergavenny, 39–29, 39A–29, 66–29, 93A–28, 234A–32
William II de, 255A–29, 262–31
Canville
see also Camville
Geoffrey de, L., 63A–31
Maud de, 63A–33
William de, 63A–31
William de, L., 63A–32
Capell
Dorothy, 214–37
William, 214–37
Capetians. see France
Carcassonne
Roger I de, 144–22
Carent
Alice, 253–35
William, 253–35
Carew
Edmund, 6–36
John, 28–35
Katherine, 6–37
Leonard, 28–35
Mary, 13A–38
Nicholas, 13A–38
Nicholas, Bar., 6–33, 6–35, 28–37
Thomas, 28–36
Thomas, Bar., 6–34
Carinthia
Bruno of (Pope Gregory V), 45–20
Engelbert, D. of, 137–24
Matilda of, 137–24
Otto, D. of, 45–19
Carleton
Edward, 2–42, 121D–41
John, 2–40
Thomas, 2–40
Walter, 2–41
Carlisle
Maldred of Scotland, L. of, 34–21
Carminow
Joan, 6–34
Ralph, 124A–35, 261–36
Thomas, 6–34
Carolingians. see France
Carpenter
Alexander, 9–41
Alice, 9–41
Carrara
Cecilia de, 252B–33
Francesco de, 252B–33
Carrick
Duncan, E. of, 121C–28

Earls of (& Kings of Scotland). see Scotland
Isabella (or Margaret) w. of Neil, 121C–29
Marjorie (Margaret) Cts. of, 121C–30, 252–29
Neil, E. of, 121C–29, 252–29
Robert Bruce. see Scotland
Carter
John, 12–40
Robert, 12–40
Cary
Emma (NN), 12A–32
Katherine, 1–36, 18–38
Thomas, 1–34
William, 1–34, 1–35, 22–37
Castile
see also Leon
Alfonso VI, K. of, 112–24, 113–23
Alfonso VII, K. of, 101–25, 113–25, 114–25, 116–25, 147–27
Alfonso VIII, K. of, 110–27, 113–27
Alvaro, noble of, 113A–22
Berengaria of, 110–28, 114–27, 120–28
Blanche of, 101–27, 104–27, 113–28
Constance of, 1–30, 101–25
Diego Lainez, sn. de Bibar in, 113A–22
Eleanor of, 1–27, 6–28, 7–29, 8–28, 9–29, 11–29, 12–30, 14–31, 15–29, 22–33, 63–30, 120–31
Eleanor of, Cts. of Ponthieu, 110–30
Fernando I, K. of, 113–23
Fernando III, K. of, 109–30, 110–29
Isabella of, 225–34
Lain Nuñez, noble of, 113A–21
Pedro I, K. of, 1–30, 225–34
Sancha of, 111–27, 116–26
Sancho III, K. of, 113–26, 113A–26
Theresa of Leon &, 112–24
Urraca I, Q. of. see Leon
Castile & Leon. see Castile
Cauntelou. see Cantelou
Cave
Anthony, 11–40
Mary, 11–40
Cavendish
Anne, 248–39
William, 248–39
Cecil
David, 15A–36
Elizabeth, 15A–36
Richard, 15A–36
William, 15A–36
Ceoche. see Zouche

Ceva
George di, Mrq. of, 28–31
Luisa di, 28–31
Chadderton
dau. of Dr., 225–42
Challons
Robert, 246E–33
Châlon
Lambert, Ct. of, 108–22
Mathilda de, 108–22
Chalon-sur-Saône
Hugh II, Ct. de, 113–23
Châlon-sur-Saône. *see* Thiers
Chamberlain
Ann, 99–34
Herbert the, 262–26
Richard, 99–34
Chamberlayne
Anne, 14–37, 238–13
Richard, 14–37, 238–11, 238–12
Chambernon. *see* Champernon
Chambers
Hester, 57–42
Champagne
see also Aumale; Blois; Joinville
Adela, w. of Stephen II, Ct. of, 136–22
Adelaide de, 137–25
Alix of, 101–25, 109–28
Eudes, Ct. of, 130–24, 136–23
Eustachie of, 109–27, 169A–27
Margaret of, 139–25
Marie of, 102–27, 168–28, 168A–29,
274E–28
Stephen II, Ct. of, 136–22
William of, 139–24
Champernon
Henry de, 124A–28, 124A–29, 124A–31,
124A–33
Isabel, w. of Henry de, 124A–28
Joan de, 124A–34
Jordon de, 124A–27
Oliver de, 124A–30
William de, 124A–32
Wymarca, w. of Oliver de, 124A–30
Champernoun
Alexander, 51–34, 217–37
Arthur, 6–38, 6–40, 209–39
Elizabeth, 25–35
Francis, 6–41
Gawine, 6–39
Joan, 51–34, 217–37
John, 51–37
Philip, 6–37, 246G–38
Richard, 25–35, 51–34

William, 51–37
Champernowne
Elizabeth, 246F–36
Richard, 246F–36
Chandos. *see* Chaundos
Charibert, in Neustria, 48–8
Charleton
Edward, L. of Powys, 225–34
Charlton
Alan de, 31–30, 31–'31
Ann Phoebe Penn Dagworthy, 81C–47
Anna de, 31–33
Anne, 31–37
Richard, 31–36
Robert, 29B–34, 31–35
Thomas de, 31–32
Thomas de Knightley, 31–34
Charnells
Cecily, 224A–35
Maud, 150–34
Robert, 224A–35
Thomas. L. of Elmesthorpe, 150–34
Charon
Alexius, Präfect in Italy, 105A–22
Chartley
Lords of. *see* Ferrer
Chartres
Counts of. *see* Blois
Chateau-Porcien
Roger, Ct. of, 246A–23
Sibylle, dau. of Roger, Ct. of, 246A–23
Châteaudun
Geoffrey VI of, 120–30
Jeanne of, 120–30
Chatellerault
Aimery I, Vcte de, 110–25, 183–3
Boso II, Vcte de, 183–2
Eleanor de, 110–25, 183–4
Hugh de, 183–2
Châtillon
Agnes de, 103–27, 242–10
Geoffroy de, 103–26
Jean de, Ct. of St. Pol, 234B–30
Mahaud de, 234B–30
Châtillon-sur-Loing
Renaud de, Pr. of Antioch, 103–26
Chaucer
Alice, 8A–33
Geoffrey, 8A–33
Thomas, 8A–33
Chaucombe
Amabil de, 16B–26, 81–29, 126–30
Robert de, 16B–26, 81–29, 126–30
Chauncey. *see* Chauncy

Chauncy
Barnabas, 69–40
Charles, 69–39
Elizabeth, 69A–38
George, 69–38
Henry, 69–37, 69A–37
Isaac, 69–40
Israel, 69–40
John, 69–33, 69–34, 69–35, 69–36, 69A–35
Katherine, w. of John, 69–36
Lucy. w. of Henry, 69–37
Nathaniel, 69–40
Sarah, 69–40
Thomas de, 69–32
William, 69–32, 69A–36
Chaundos
Alice, w. of Robert de, 234A–32
Robert, 234A–32
Roger de, L., 234A–32
Chaworth
Elizabeth, 13A–35
Maud de, 17–29, 18–29, 19–29, 72–32, 94A–33
Patrick, 72–31
Patrick de, 108–26
Patrick de, L. of Kidwelly, 72–31, 94A–33
Sibyl de, 108–26
Thomas, 13A–35
Cheney
Elizabeth, 22–35, 136–33
Laurence, 22–35, 136–32
Cherleton
Edward, L., 47D–33, 81–36, 81A–36
Isabel de, 81–32
Joan, 47D–34
John de, L. of Powis, 81–32
John, L., 47D–33, 234–31
Chesney
Adelaide de, 132D–27
Bartholomew de, 257–28
Isabel de, 257–28
Margaret de, 246D–27
William de, 132D–27, 246D–27
Chester
see also Avranches; Meschin
Adeliz (Alice) of, 132D–27
Agnes of, 82–30, 127–29, 194–7
Gerbod the Fleming, E. of, 50–24
Gundred, sis. of Gerbod the Fleming, 50–24, 83–24
Hawise of, Cts. of Lincoln, 54–28, 125–29

Hugh, E. of, 18A–23
Hugh of Kevelioc, E. of, 93–26, 125–28, 126–28, 127–28, 131–28, 252–26
Judith of, 18A–23
Lucy, w. of Ranulph III, E. of, 132A–26, 132D–26
Mabel of, 16C–26, 126–29, 149–27
Maud of, 93–26, 94–26, 131–29, 252–26
Ranulf III, E. of, 54–29
Ranulph III, E. of, 132A–26, 132D–26
Chetham
Margaret, 230B–38
Chetwode
Elizabeth, 150–36
Grace, 7–40, 31–40
John, 16–34, 150–36
Margaret, 4–35, 16–34
Richard, 7–39, 150–41, 150–42
Roger, 150–41
Chetwynd
Philip, 56B–35
Cheyne
see also Cheney
John, 65A–35, 136–31, 200–33
William, 136–31
Cheyney
see also Cheyne
Anne, 257–36
Edmund, 224–35
Henry, 224–35
Nicholas, 257–36
Chichester
Amyas, 25–37, 52–43
Frances, 52–44
John, 25–34, 52–39, 52–42, 261–39
Nicholas, 52–41
Richard, 52–40
Thomasine, 25–34, 261–39
Chidderley
Elizabeth, 51–37
John, 51–37
Chideoke
Katherine, 214–37
Chilham
Lords of. see Douvres, Fitz Roy
Chiny
Arnold II, Ct. of, 149–23
Otto II, Ct. of, 149–23
Chiny & Namur
Ida of, 149–24, 155–23
Chrodobertus, in Neustria, 48–11, 48–9
Chudleigh
James, 51–34, 217–37

John, 217–35, 217–36, 246B–32
Robert, 261–39
Clanvowe
Elizabeth de, 84B–32, 234A–33
Philip de, 84B–31, 234A–33
Clapham
Gresham, 170A–39
Clare
Adeliza de, 246–25, 246D–25
Adeliza de (alias Tonebridge), 161–24
Avelina de, 143–28
Aveline de, 72–29, 246B–27, 246C–27
Baldwin Fitz Gilbert de Clare, 184A–4
Eleanor de, 8–30, 39–32, 74–32
Elizabeth de, 11–30, 70–32, 94A–32, 257–33
Gilbert de, E. of Gloucester, 8–29, 8A–29, 9–29, 11–29, 11–30, 18A–28, 63–28, 63–30, 94A–32, 110–31, 117–29, 252–28
Gilbert de, E. of Pembroke, 66–25, 184–4
Isabel de, 66–27, 69–27, 76–27, 80–27, 127–30, 252–28, 260–30, 261–30, 269A–27
Margaret de, 9–30, 16A–30, 18A–30, 54–32, 65–33, 65A–33, 79–31, 185B–4, 223–39
Maud de, 29A–28, 54–29, 63A–28, 64–32, 82–32, 205–32
Richard de, 54–32
Richard de, E. of, 54–30, 63–27, 63–29, 63A–27
Richard de, E. of Gloucester, 18A–28, 63A–29
Richard de, E. of Pembroke, 66–26, 175–7, 261–30
Richard Fitz Gilbert, L. of, 132D–27, 246B–25
Roese de, 18A–28
Roger de, E. of Hertford, 63–27, 149–26, 149–26, 246B–26
Thomas de, 54–31, 54–32, 64–31, 178–7, 216–30
Clarence
George, D. of, 225–36
Lionel of Antwerp, D. of, 5–31, 29–34, 94A–34
Thomas, D. of, 1–31
Clarke
see also Clerke
James, 11–42
Jeremy, 11–41, 220–41
Mary, 11–42, 220–42

Walter, 11–42
Weston, 11–42
Clavering
Eupheme de, 186–4
Robert Fitz Roger, Bar. of, 186–3
Claypole
see also Claypoole
Adam, 15A–37
James, 15A–37
John, 15A–38
Claypoole
see also Claypole
James, 15A–39
Norton, 15A–39
Rachel, w. of Norton, 15A–39
Claythorpe
Elizabeth, 224A–37
Clayton
Ellen, 170A–37
John, 170A–37
Clerke
see also Clarke
George, 11–38
James, 11–37, 11–39
John, 11–37
William, 11–40
Clermont
see also Dammartin; Ponthieu
Beatrix de, 234B–28
Reinald, Ct. of, 50–23
Clermont-en-Beauvaisis
Adelaide de, 66–25, 177A–7, 184–3, 184A–3, 184B–3, 246–24, 246B–24, 246D–24
Hugh de, 246–23
Hugh de Creil, Ct. of, 144–25
Renaud II, Ct. of, 144–25
Cleuville
Hue, L., 270–24
Cleves
Adolf, D. of, 252–35
Catherine of, 252–35
Clifford
Alice, 197–36
Idoine (Idonea) de, 161–29, 205–33, 206–33
Isabella de, 143–31
James, 197–34, 197–36
John, 143–31
John de, L., 5–34, 26–34
Katharine, 62–35, 197–34, 202–33, 265–34
Margaret de, 64–33, 156–30
Matilda, 5–36, 81–37, 198–36

Maud de, 29A–29, 122–31
Philippa de, 11–34, 248–34
Robert de, L., 26–31, 64–32, 82–32,
    156–30, 161–29, 205–32
Roger de, 82–31, 255–28
Roger de, L., 11–34, 26–32, 202–32,
    248–34, 265–34
Thomas de, L., 5–35, 26–33, 89–33
Walter de, 29A–28, 122–31, 255–28
Clifton
Constantine, 218–33
Constantine, L., 188–10, 218–34, 238–
    10
Cuthbert, 23–36
Elizabeth, 23–36, 188–10, 218–35,
    238–10
John, 232–33
John, L., 218–33
Katherine, 232–33
Clinton
see also Fiennes
Edward, L., E. of Lincoln, 225–40
Geoffrey I de, 70A–26
Henry, L., E. of Lincoln, 225–40
Ida, 230A–33
Joan, 81–33, 86–33
John, 81–33, 86–33, 230A–33
John de, L., 86–32
Lescelina de, 70A–26
Margaret de, 86–33
Thomas de, 86–32
Thomas, L., E. of Lincoln, 225–41
William de, the younger, 246B–29
Clivedon
John de, 39–31
Katherine de, 39–31
Clopton
Elizabeth, 211–40
Joan, 85–32
Walter, 85–32
William, 211–40
Clovis the Riparian
Frankish K. of Cologne, 190–1
Clun
Lords of. *see* Mortimer
Clyvedon
Edmund de, 124A–35, 261–36
Katherine, 81–36, 81A–36
Cobham
Eleanor, 1A–33
Henry, 246G–32
Isabel, 246G–32
Joan de, 74A–33
John, 246G–32

John de, 74A–33
Ralph, 155–31
Reginald, 1A–33
Reynold de, L., 61–33
Cobleigh
John, 25–33, 25–34, 25–35, 246F–37
Margaret, 25–36
Cock
Alice, 234B–35
John, 234B–35
Cockworthy
Alice, 25–34, 246F–37
John, 25–34, 246F–37, 261–39
Thomasine, 261–39
Cogan
Mary, 12–39
Philobert, 12–39
Thomas, 12–39
William, 40–33
Cokayne
Elizabeth, 22–35, 136–32
John, 136–32
Cokefield
Agnes, 224A–35
Roger, 224A–35
Cokesey
Thomas, 207–37
Coles
Richard, 43A–38, 246A–41
Ursula, 43A–38
Coleville
see also Colville
Alice, wid., 246B–29
Juliana, 246B–29
Collamore
Elizabeth, 246E–40
Henry, 246E–39
John, 246E–38
Peter, 246E–38
Collier
Elizabeth, 9–42
William, 9–42
Cologne
Childebert, Frankish K. of, 190–2
Cloderic the Parricide, Frankish K. of,
    190–4
Clovis the Riparian, Frankish K. of, 190–
    1
Sigebert the Lame, Frankish K. of, 190–
    3
Colpepper
Joyce, 248–37
Richard, 248–36
Sybil, w. of Richard, 248–36

William, 248–35
Colville
see also Coleville
Alice de, 246–30
Isabel de, 208–34
John, 208–33
Roger de, 246–30
William, 208–32
Colwick
Elizabeth, 246G–40
Robert, 246G–40
Combe
Thomas, 57–41
Comminges
Arsenda de, 141A–20
Comnena
Theodora, 45–27
Comnenus
Alexius, 105A–26
Alexius I, 45·27, 105A–23
Andronicus, 105A–25
Eudoxia, 105A–27
John I, 105A–22, 105A–22
John II, 105A–24
Manuel, 105A–21, 105A–21
Comyn
Alexander, 114–30, 114A–28
Alexander, E. of Buchan, 114A–27,
121D–30, 224–29
Alice, 17–30, 72–33, 114–30, 114A–29
Amabilia, w. of John "the Red", 121A–28
Elizabeth, 84A–31, 95–31, 121D–30,
224–30
John, 121A–25, 252–26
John, L. of Badenoch, 84A–31, 95–29,
95–30, 154–30
John of Badenoch, 155–31, 236–11
John "the Black", 121A–29
John "the Red", 121A–28
Richard, 121A–25
Richard, L. Badenoch, 121A–27
Robert, 121A–25
William, 114A–26, 121A–25, 224–29
William, E. of Buchan, 121A–26
Conan of Grandison
son of Adalbert, 263–24
Conches
de. *see* Toeni
Conde
Isabel de, 152–28, 158C–28
Jacques de, 158C–28
Nicholas de, 158C–28
Nicholas I, sn. de, 152–28

Condet
Isabel de, 132D–28, 184A–10
Osbert de, 132D–27
Robert de, 132D–27
Coningsby
Amphillis, 232–37
Humphrey, 232–37
Conisburgh
Richard of, E. of Cambridge, 225–34
Conningsby
Elizabeth, 187–14
Humphrey, 187–14
Conrad the Wise
in Wormsgau, D. of Lorraine, 45–18
Constable
Ann, 223–39
Isabel, 121D–36
John, 121D–34, 121D–35
Constantinople
Emp. of. *see* Courtenay, Peter de
Conversano
Louis, Ct. of, 234B–31
Marguerite d'Engheim, Cts. of, 234B–31
Conyers
Jane, 3–37
Cooke
Edmund, 211–42
Lawrence, 246A–37
Maud, 246A–37
Theodora, 211–42
Cope
Elizabeth, 14–39
John, 14–38
William, 14–38
Coplestone
Adam, 246G–34
Agnes, 246G–34
Copley
Eleanor, 18–35
Roger, 18–35
Corbet
Alice, wid. of Peter, 246B–30
Dorothy, 56A–40
Joan, 29A–32
Margaret, 86–32, 98–35
Mary, 29B–34, 31–35
Peter, 246B–30
Richard, 56B–38
Robert, 16A–34, 29A–31, 29B–31, 29B–
33, 56A–39, 56B–38, 56B–39, 121–
26, 262–27
Roger, 29B–32, 56B–38
Sibyl, 124A–29, 195–26, 237–5, 262–27
Sybil, 121–26

Thomas, 98–35
William, 86–32
Cornhill
Ralph de, 155A–26
Cornu
Robert, 25–33
Walter, 25–33
Cornwall
Brian de, 258–30, 259–30
Earl of. *see* Fitz Roy
Earls of. *see also* Gaveston
Earls of. *see also* Mortain
Edmund de, 258–29
Eleanor, 18–35
Isabel de, 258–31
Jane, 69–38
Joan, w. of Richard de, L. of Thunnock, 258–28
John, 18–35, 69–38
John, L. Fanhope, 47C–32
Reginald Fitz Roy, E. of. *see* Fitz Roy
Richard de, L. of Thunnock, 258–28
Richard, E. of, 63–28, 258–27
Cornwallis
Elizabeth, 208–40
Coryton
Anne, 25–36
John, 25–36
Cosynton
William de, 18A–30
Cotesford
Idony, 14–35
Thomas, 14–35
Cotton
Audrey, 7–35
Catherine, 233–40, 246A–36
Frances, 56A–43
John, 224A–43, 246A–34
Margaret, w. of John, 246A–34
Mary, 12–39
Richard, 56A–42, 233–40
Walter, 246A–34
William, 7–35, 246A–35
Coucy
Alix de, 272–30, 273–30
Enguerrand I, sn. de, 273–25
Enguerrand II de, 273–27
Enguerrand III de, 120–30, 272–30, 273–29
Mary de, 120–30, 273–30
Milisende, w. of Thomas de, 273–26
Raoul de, 135–28
Raoul I de, 273–28
Thomas de, 273–26

Yolande de, 135–28
Courcelles
Family, 234A–25
Courcy
Hawise de, 138–26
Richard de, 156–25
William de, 138–26
Courtenay
Alice de, 117–26, 153A–27
Edeline de, 222–34
Edward, 6–31
Edward, E. of Devon, 261A–38
Eleanor de, 143–30
Elizabeth, 261A–38
Elizabeth de, 12–31, 107–26, 117–25
Gervase de, 25–27
Hugh, 6–32, 25–27
Hugh de, 18A–30
Hugh de, Bar. of Oakhampton, 50–30, 51–30, 222–34
Hugh de, E. of Devon, 6–30, 12–30, 50–31, 51–31, 51–32, 51A–31, 143–30, 214–33, 262–32
Joan, 6–33, 28–37
Jocelin de, 107–24, 138–24
John, 51–34, 217–37
John de, Bar. of Oakhampton, 50–29, 214–30
Margaret, 51–37
Margaret de, 51–35
Milo (Miles) de, 107–24, 138–24
Muriel de, 214–33
Peter de, Ct. of, 105–28, 107–27, 163A–28
Peter of France, Sn. of. *see* France
Philip, 51–33, 51–35, 51–36
Reginald de, 25–27
Renaud de, 107–25, 138–25, 138–26
Robert de, 50–28, 138–27
Thomas de, 51A–32, 214–33
Yolande de, 105–28, 163A–29
Coventre
Emma de, 150–28
Walter de, 150–28
Coytemore
Elizabeth, 199–40
Rowland, 199–39
William, 199–38
Cradock
Jenkin ap Ieuan, 179–12
Mabel, 179–11
Wilcock, 179–11

Cranage
Dorothy, 198–40
Laurence, 198–40
Cranston
James, 220–42
John, 11–42, 220–42
Samuel, 220–43
Craon
Amaury de, 214A–29
Isabel de, 135–31, 214A–29, 275–29
Creil
Hugh de, Ct. of Clermont-en-Beauvaisis, 144–25
Crepi
Alix (Adela) de, 137–22
Thibaut III, sn. de, 144–25
Cressi
Hugh de, 246D–27
Crevequer
William de, 255A–30
Crichton
Elizabeth, 256–37
William, L., 256–37
Crispin
Joan, 12A–30
William, 12A–30
Croatia
Almos, K. of, 242–9
Croft
Douce, 41–33
John, 37–31
Margaret, 37–31
Nicholas de, 41–33
Cromwell
Elizabeth, 218–33
Maud, 210–36
Ralph de, 55–30, 210–31, 210–32, 210–33, 210–34
Ralph, L., 210–35, 218–32
Crosse
Elizabeth, 212–35
William, 212–35
Crowne
Henry, 198–41
William, 198–41
Cruse
Robert, 234A–36
Thomasin, 234A–36
Cruwys
see also Cruse
Elizabeth, 246G–36
Maud, 246G–35
Cuiseau
Hugh, Sn. of, 133–24

Matilda of, 133–24
Culpepper. see Colpepper
Culwen
see also Curwen
Edith, w. of Gilbert I de, 37–27
Gilbert I (of Workington), 37–27
Gilbert II (of Workington), 37–28
Gilbert III (of Workington), 37–29
Gilbert IV (of Workington), 37–30
Patric de (of Workington), 37–26
Cumans
Elizabeth of the, 103–30
Kuthen (Zahan), Pr. of the, 103–30
Cumbrai
Pernel de, 176C–27
Roger de, 176C–27
Cundy. see Condet
Curwen
see also Culwen
Christopher, 37–32, 37–36
Christopher II, 37–34
Henry, 37–38
Margaret, 37–35
Thomas, 37–33, 37–35, 37–'37
William, 37–31, 37–35
Curzon
Catherine, 99–36
Richard, 99–36
Cushe
Isabel, 246E–38
Cutleer
Margaret, 224A–40

D

d' Audley. see Audley
Dabinot
Christopher, 253–40
Jane, 253–40
Joan, 253–40
John, 253–40
Dacre
Joan, 5–35, 34–31
Thomas, L., 5–35
Dagsburg-Egisheim
Gerald III, Ct. of, 133–21
Dalassene
Anne, 105A–22
Dallison
George, 85–38
Jane (Anne), 85–38
Dalriada
Kings of. see Scotland

Dalton
Alice, 199–35
Richard, 199–35
Dalyngridge
Edward, 4–33
Philippe, 4–33
Dammartin
Agnes de, 152–27, 158B–27, 158C–27, 272–29
Jeanne de, Cts. of Ponthieu, 109–30, 110–29
Juliane de, 152–27, 255A–29, 257–31, 262–31
Lancelin I, Ct. of, 144–25
Mathilda of Clermont, Ponthieu &, 109–29, 144–26, 152–26, 272–29
Simon de, Ct. of Aumale, 109–29, 144–27
Damory
Elizabeth, 257–33
Roger, L., 11–30, 94A–32, 257–33
Dampierre
see also Flanders
Alix (Alice) of Flanders, 234B–29
Guy I de Moëlan, sn. de, 71A–28, 264–27
Guy of, Ct. of Flanders, 234B–30
Guy V of, sn. de Richebourg, 234B–29
Helvis de, 71A–28, 264–28
Thibaud, sn., 264–26
Dampierre-sur-Aube
Helvise (Helvide) de, 272–29, 273–29
William I, Sire of, 273–29
Danvers
Amy, 43A–35
Jane, 238–12
John, 43A–35
Danyell
Thomas, 233B–37
Darcy
Alice, 208–33
Arthur, 13A–38
Edward, 13A–39
Elizabeth, 7–31
Isabella, 13A–40
John, 7–31, 13A–34
John, L., 208–33
John, L., of Knyath, 13A–33, 62–36, 88–33, 88–35, 268–33
Philip, L., of Knyath, 88–34
Richard, 13A–35
Thomas, L., 13A–37
William, 13A–36
d'Ardres. see Selvesse

Darnau
Giselbert, Ct. of, 140–16, 240–16
d'Arundel. see Arundel
d'Aubigny. see Aubigny
Daumarle
Margaret, 28–36, 124A–35, 261–37
William, 124A–35 `
Daunteseye
Roger de, 97–27
Davenport
Christopher, 230–35, 230–38
Edward, 230A–41
Henry, 230A–41
John, 230–36, 230–37, 231–35
Margaret, 230–37, 231–36
Nicholas, 230–35, 230–37, 231–36
d'Avesnes. see Avesnes
Davis
William, 246G–42
d'Avranches. see Avranches
Davye
Jane, 18–39
Dawkins
James, 81B–44
Dawney
Emeline, 6–31
John, 6–31
de Albemarle. see Daumarle
de Audley. see Audley
de Ewyas. see Ewyas
De la Mere. see Mere
De la Warr. see West
de la Warre. see Warre
de Riviers. see Riviers
de Vernon. see Riviers
Dean
William, 232–39
Deighton
Frances, 84–40
Jane, 84–40
John, 84–39, 143–41
Katherine, 84–40, 143–41
Deincourt
John, 200–32
Margaret, 65A–35, 200–33
William, L., 65A–35, 200–32
Delabere
Alice, 258–32
Kynard, 258–32
Delaware. see West
Delves
John, 46–37
Margaret, 46–37

Dene
  John de, 56A–31
Denebaud
  Elizabeth, 52–41
  John, 52–41
Denmark
  Arques of, 121E–20
  Astrid (Margaret) of, 121E–21
  Avelina (Duvelina) of, sis. of Gunnora, 184–1
  Christian XIV (I), K. of, 252–36, 252A–36, 252E–35
  Gorm the Old, K. of, 1B–22
  Gunnora of, 1–18, 121E–20, 184–1, 235–19
  Harald "Bluetooth", 1B–22, 243A–20
  Klak-Harald, K. of Jutland, 243A–16
  Margaret of Oldenburg, 252–36, 253E–36
  Sigeferth of, 1–19
  Swen I, K. of, 121E–21
  Thyra, 1B–22
  Thyri, dau. of Klak-Harald, K. of Jutland, 243A–16
Dennis
  Eleanor, 84C–37, 209–37
  Frances, 84C–38
  Hugh, 84C–38
  Isabel, 187–15
  William, 84C–37, 187–15, 209–37
Dennys
  Philippa, 234A–40
  Robert, 234A–40
Denton
  Alice, 143–38
d'Envermeu. *see* Envermeu
Derby
  Earls of. *see* Ferrers; Stanley
Desmond
  Earls of. *see* Fitz Maurice
Despencer. *see* Despenser
Despenser
  Anne le, 58–30
  Edward, 74–33, 212–34, 70–35, 74–34
  Eleanor le, 50–30, 51–30, 222–34
  Elizabeth, 21–32, 39–32, 74–35, 212–34
  Hawise le, 74A–34
  Hugh le, 16B–25, 50–30, 51–30, 58–30, 148A–31
  Hugh le, Bar., 8–30, 39–32, 74–32
  Hugh le, E. of Winchester, 72–31, 74–31, 74A–31, 93A–29
  Hugh le, L., 72–31

  Isabel, 8–31, 28–33
  Isabel le, 87–33, 93A–29
  Joan le, 148A–31
  Margaret le, 56B–34, 70–36
  Margery, 200–35
  Philip le, 74A–32, 74A–33, 200–34
  Richard le, 207–35
  Rohese, 16B–25
  Thomas, 16B–25
  Thomas le, E. of Gloucester, 87–33
d'Estouteville. *see* Stuteville
d'Eu. *see* Eu
Devereux
  Elizabeth, 56B–38
  John, L., 17–31, 79–32
  Walter, 56B–37
  Walter, L. Ferrers, 56B–37
Devon
  Ælfthryth of, 1–17
  Earls of. *see* Courtenay
  Ordgar, E. of, 1–17
d'Eyncourt. *see* Eyncourt
Diaz
  Rodrigo, Sn. de Bibar, 113A–23
Diepholz
  Hedwig of, 252E–31
  Konrad V, Bar. of, 252E–31
Digby
  Elizabeth, 99–41
  Everard, 99–37, 99–40
  John, 99–37
  Simon, 99–39
  William, 99–38
Dinan
  Alan de, L. of, 108–27
  Emma de, 108–27
  Geoffrey de, 108–27, 214–26, 214–27
  Geoffrey de, of Brittany, 214–25
  Oliver II, Sire de, 214–25
  Oliver III de, 214–26
  Orieldis, w. of Oliver II, 214–25
Dinan(t)
  Oliver de, 214–28
Dinham
  Geoffrey de, 214–29
  John de, 214–32, 214–33, 214–34, 215–34
  Josce de, 214–31
  Margaret, 6–35
  Margaret, w. of John de, 214–32
  Oliver de, 214–30
d'Oilly. *see* Oilly
d'Oisy. *see* Oisy

Dol
Geldouin I, sn. of, 214A–26
Jeanne de, 214A–26
Domene
NN of, 263–28
Donjon & Corbeil
Frederick (Guy) du, 107–25
Helvis, sis. of Frederick du, 107–25,
138–25
Douglas
Archibald, E. of Angus, 252–37
Elizabeth, 256–35
George, E. of Angus, 256–34
Margaret, 256–42
Robert, 256–42
Douglass
William de, 58–30
Douvres
Foubert de, L. of Chilham, 26–27, 218–
27
Lorette de, 218–28
Rohese de, 26–27, 218–27
Dover
see also Douvres
Fulbert de, 184A–7
Dowrish
Grace, 261–43
Thomas, 261–42
d'Oyly. see Oyly
Drake
John, 234A–39
Robert, 234A–39
William, 234A–40
Dreux
Alex de, 273–28
Philippa de, 168–31, 234B–26
Pierre (de Braine) de, 135–29, 271–28
Pierre de (or Pierre de Braine), 96–28
Robert I, Ct. of, 135–27, 273–28
Robert II, Ct. of, 135–28, 168–31,
234B–26
Robert III, 155–28
Yolande de, 63–30, 117–28, 135–30,
155–28, 275–28
Drew
Alice, 12A–32
Lawrence, 12A–33
Thomas, 12A–32
Drewe. see Drew
Driby
Alice, 218–31
Alice de, 16A–32, 16C–32
John de, 16A–31, 16C–30, 16C–31
Robert, 16A–31, 218–31

Robert de, 16C–29
Drokensford
Clarice, 12A–29
John de, 12A–27
Margaret de, 12A–27
Drummond
Annabella, 252–33, 256–33
John, 252–33
Drury
Anne, 200–38, 257–39
Robert, 200–38, 257–38
Dryden
Bridget, 14–40
John, 14–39
du Plessis. see Plessis
Dublin
Kings of. see Ireland
Ducas
Andronicus, 45–27, 105A–23
Irene, 45–27, 105A–23
Maria, 105A–26
Dudley
Anne, 143–42
Barons. see Somery
Deborah, 84–40
Edmund, 225–40
Elizabeth, 225–40
John, D. of Northumberland, 224–40
Joseph, 84–41
Lord. see Somery
Lords. see Sutton
Mary, 143–39
Mercy, 143–42
Paul, 84–40
Roger, 143–40
Samuel, 143–42
Susan, 143–39
Thomas, 84–40, 143–39, 143–41
Duglas. see Douglass
Dunbar
Agnes of, 41–25
Athelreda of, 40–23, 171–22
Edgar of, 41–24
Edward of, 41–23
Gospatric I, E. of, 34–22, 38–22, 40–22,
41–22
Gospatric II, E. of, 41–23, 42–23, 121B–
27
Gunnild of, 38–24, 121B–27
Gunnilda of, 88–24, 34–23
Juliana of, 42–24
Sigrid, w. of Waldeve, 38–23
Waldeve of, L. of Allerdale, 38–23,
121B–27

Dungan
Thomas, 220–41
William, 11–41
Dunkeld
Crinan the Thane, Abbot of, 34–21,
170–19, 172–19
Dunster. *see* Mohun
Durborough
Ralph, 248A–34
Durham
Alice, dau. of Walcher, Bishop of, 247–
23
Walcher, Bishop of, 247–23
Durvassal
Joyce, 56A–37
William, 56A–37
Dutton
Anne, 23–35, 176B–38
Hugh, 33–38
Isabel, 9–36
John, 9–35, 32–34, 33–34
Maud, 33–35
Piers, 32–34
Thomas, 9–35, 23–35, 32–35, 176B–37
Dyall
Elizabeth, 234A–30
Timothy, 234A–30
Dymoke
Anne, 202–38
Englesia, 52–38
Lionel, 202–37
Philip, 202–36
Thomas, 202–36
Walter, 52–38
Dynham
Joan, 212–38, 214–36
John, L., 6–35, 214–35, 214–36

E

Easton
Mary, 11–42
Rebecca (Thurston), 11–42
Eaton
Samuel, 69A–41
Theophilus, 251–41
Echyngham
Margaret de, 58–38
Thomas de, 59–36, 59–37
William de, 59–35
Eddowes
Martha, 12–41
Eden
Richard, 246–38
Thomas, 246–38

Edessa
Baldwin, Ct. of. *see* Jerusalem
Edon
Ann, 246A–40
Henry, 246A–39
Joan, w. of Thomas, 246A–39
Thomas, 246A–39
Edwards
Edward, 43A–38
John, 15–40
Margaret, 43A–39
Peter, 43A–37
Richard, 246E–41
William, 246E–41
Egerton
Anna, 232–39
Thomas, 232–39
Egisheim
Bruno of, 163–23
Edith (Helvide) of, 144–24
Gerard, Ct. of, 144–24
Hildegarde of, 167–22
Hugo VI, Ct. of, 167–22
Richarde, w. of Gerard of, 144–24
Egwina
Mistress of Edward I, 1–15
Eland
Dyonis, 121D–36
William, 121D–36
Elchingen
Liutgard of, 252D–26
Elchingen-Ravenstein
Adelbert, Ct. of, 252D–26
Eldred the Thane
L. of Workington, 34–23, 34–24, 88–23
Ellis
Jacquette, 99–37
John, 99–37
William, 202–35
Elrington
John, 58–38
Emildon
Richard de, 170–29
Emperors of the East
see Byzantine Empire
Emperors of the West
see Holy Roman Emperors
Engaine
Egeline, 34–24
Elizabeth, 136–30, 187–10
John, 136–28, 187–5
John, L., 136–29, 187–10
Joice, 187–5
Nicholas, 136–28

Ranulf, 34–24
Engheim
Marguerite d', Cts. of Conversano,
  234B–31
England
Ælfgifu, Q. consort, 1–16
Æthelred II, K. of, 1–18, 34–19, 172–20,
  235–19, 243A–21, 247–20, 250–20
Alfred the Great, K. of, 1–14, 44–15,
  147–19, 162–17, 170–21
Anne Boleyn, Q. consort, 22–37
Canute, K. of, 1–18, 243A–21
Constance of, 98–25
Ealdgith (Edith) Swansneck, w. of
  Harold II, 1B–23
Ealhswith, w. of Alfred the Great, 44–15
Edgar, K. of, 1–17
Edith of, 45–17, 147–19, 192–20
Edmund "Crouchback", E. Lancaster,
  17–28. see Lancaster
Edmund II, K. of, 1–19
Edmund, K. of, 1–16
Edmund of Langley, D. of York, 225–34
Edmund of Woodstock. see Kent
Edward I, K. of, 1–27, 6–28, 7–29, 8–28,
  8A–29, 9–29, 11–29, 12–30, 14–31,
  15–29, 16–28, 22–33, 47–31, 63–30,
  97–31, 110–30, 155–30, 216–29
Edward II, K. of, 1–28, 101–31
Edward III, K. of, 1–29, 2–31, 3–32, 4–
  30, 5–30, 16A–31, 29–34, 97–34,
  103–34, 207–34, 225–32, 225–34,
  256–40
Edward IV, K. of, 18B–36, 225–35
Edward, the Atheling, 1–20, 158–23,
  169–25, 170–21, 241–6
Edward, the Black Prince, 236–12
Edward, the Elder, K. of, 1–15, 45–16,
  50–20, 148–17
Egbert, K. of, 1–12
Eldgyth, Q. consort, 1–19
Eleanor of, 21–30, 110–27, 113–27,
  260–30
Elizabeth (or Isabel) of, 38–24, 121B–
  26, 121C–26
Elizabeth, Pss. of, 6–29, 7–29, 15–29,
  97–31
Godgifu (Godiva), 176A–2
Godgifu of, 235–20, 250–20
Harold II, K. of, 1B–23, 103–27, 176–2,
  176A–4, 242–7
Harold, s. of Harold II, K. of, 176A–4
Hengist, anc. of royal line, 170–21

Henry I, K. of, 1–22, 33A–23, 50–26,
  98–25, 118–25, 119–25, 121–25,
  121B–26, 124–25, 124A–29, 138–
  25, 149–25, 153–24, 195–25, 222–
  25, 262–27, 265A–23
Henry II, K. of, 1–24, 30–25, 33–34, 53–
  30, 101–25, 110–26, 122–28, 122A–
  28, 130–27
Henry III, K. of, 1–26, 16–31, 17–27,
  20–30, 21–30, 93A–29, 111–30, 22–
  33
Henry IV, K. of, 1A–32
Henry VII, K. of, 252–37
Henry VIII, K. of, 22–37
Joan of Acre. see Acre
Joan of Lancaster. see Lancaster
John I, K. of, 275–27
John, K. of, 1–25, 26–27, 26–26, 29A–
  26, 67–29, 80–29, 117–27, 153A–28,
  176B–27, 218–27, 254–28, 258–27,
  260–29
Margaret of, 1–21, 158–23, 169–25,
  170–21
Margaret Tudor, 252–37
Matilda of, 1–23, 118–25, 153–24
Maud of, 119–25
Ogiva of, 50–20, 148–17
Rædburga, Q. consort, 1–12
Ralph "Comes" of Hereford. see Hereford
Richard Fitz Roy. see Fitz Roy
Richard II, K. of, 236–12
Richard III, K. of, 225–35
Richard of Conisburgh, E. of Cambridge,
  225–34
Richard (Plantagenet), D. of York, 225–
  35
Rohese of, 124A–29, 195–26
Stephen of Blois, K. of, 83–26, 137–24,
  139–24, 158–24, 165–26, 169–25,
  169A–25, 262–26, 264–26, 137–24
Thomas of Brotherton. see Norfolk
Thomas of Woodstock. see Gloucester
Thorold, sheriff of Lincs., 176A–2
Ulf, s. of Harold II, K. of, 176A–4
William I the Conqueror, K. of, 49–19,
  98A–23, 121–24, 121E–19, 130–24,
  132A–25, 136–23, 137–23, 139–23,
  148–22, 162–23, 169–23, 185–1
English
Dionisia, 124A–31
Isabel, 34–33, 35–33
Robert, 124A–31
William, 34–33, 35–33

Enham
Herman von, Ct. in Eifelgau &
Westphalia, 106–22
Envermeu
Godiva d', 184A–4
Hugh d', 184A–4
Erdington
Giles, 16A–33
Giles de, 29B–32
Margaret, 29B–32
Eresby
Lords of. see Beke
Erleigh
Eleanor, 253–32
John, 253–32
Essex
Agnes of, 246–26
Cicely, w. of Henry of, 246–26
Earls of. see Bohun; Mandeville
Geoffrey Fitz Piers, E. of, 72–29, 246B–
27, 246C–27
Henry of, L. of Rayleigh, 246–26
Robert de, L. of Rayleigh, 246D–26
Esshe
Henry, 217A–42
Prudence, 217A–42
Ethiconides
House of. see Alsace
Eton
Cicely de, 231–31
Nicholas de, 231–31
Etwell
Henry, 150–37
Joan, 150–37
Eu
Alice d', 123–28
Counts or Earls of. see Bourchier
Henry d', Ct. of, L. of Hastings, 123–27,
139–25, 139–27
John d', Ct. of, L. of Hastings, 139–26
Maud d', 97–28, 98–29, 123–29
William d', L. of Hastings, 139–25
Eure
Catherine, 204–36
Elizabeth, 121D–38
Ralph de, 204–35, 206–35
Everard
John, 249–42
Judith, 249–42
Everingham
Alice de, 202–35
Catherine, 17–32
Thomas, 17–32
William de, 202–35

Evreux
Agnes of, 118–23
Counts of. see also Montfort
Richard, Ct. of, 118–23
Ewyas
see also Hereford
Harold de, 235–22, 255–25
Pernel, w. of Robert II de, 255–27
Robert I de, L. of Ewyas Harold, 255–26
Robert II de, of Ewyas Harold, 255–27
Sibyl de, 255–28, 255A–28
Sibyl, w. of Robert I de, 255–26
Exeter
Dukes of. see Holand
Eyncourt
Alice, w. Ralph d', 41–27
Elizabeth d', 41–28
Gervase d', 41–26
Ralph d', 41–26, 41–27
Eyre
Catherine, 69–39
Robert, 69–39
Eyton
Joan de, 98–33
Ézy
Bernard I, Sire d'Albret, 71A–31, 135–
32

F

Fabian
Joan, 143–37
Fairfax
Mary, 37–38
Nicholas, 37–38
Falais
Fulbert of, 121–23, 121E–22, 130–23
Herleve of. see Normandy
Falcon de la Sarraz, 263–24
Falwell
John, 246E–34
Matilda (Mabilla), 246E–34
Fanhope
Lord of. see Cornwall, John
Farrand
Rebecca, 208–42
Farringdon
Ann, 261–42
Charles, 261–41
Farwell
Henry, 31B–41, 223–43
Faucigny
Aimon I of, 133–25
Aymon de, 71A–29

Beatrix de, 133–25
Clementia, w. of Aimon I, 133–25
Fauconberge
Agnes de, 136–28
Joan de, 208–32
John de, L., 208–31
Peter de, 136–27, 184B–7
Walter de, L., 136–27, 184B–7, 184B–8, 208–30
Faulkner
Christian, 12A–33
Richard, 12A–33
Felbrigge
Cecilia, w. of Roger Bigod de, 232–30
Helena (Alana), 232–34
Margaret, w. of Simon, 232–33
Maud de, 232–29
Richard de, 232–29
Roger, 232–32
Roger Bigod de, 232–30
Roger de, 232–29
Simon, 232–31, 232–33
Fenlis
Margaret de, 70–32, 120–32, 176B–30
William de, 120–31
Fenne
Hugh, 225–38
Margaret, 225–38
Fennes
Jeanne (Joan), 236–10
Fermor
Anne, 232–38
Henry, 232–38
Ferrers
Agnes de, 189–4, 269A–27
Alianore de, 130–31
Alice, 246G–34
Alice de, 52–32, 217–32
Anne, 56B–37
Anne de, 74–33
Edmund, L., of Chartley, 56B–35
Eleanor de, 57–32
Elizabeth, 11–37, 248–35
Elizabeth de, Lady of Wem, 62–35, 265–35
Fulk de, 52–32, 217–32
Gilbert de, 52–32, 217–32
Henry, 11–33, 11–36, 18A–33
Henry, L., of Groby, 11–31, 58–32
Henry, of Groby, 70–32
Hugh, 246G–34
Isabel, 197–32
Isabel de, 143–28
Joan, 51–34, 217–37

Joan de, 26–29, 59–30, 124A–32, 257–30
Joan, wife of Henry, Bar., 11–33
John, 246G–34
John de, L. of Chartley, 189–5
John de, L., of Chartley, 57–31, 61–31
John de, of Chartley, 61–33
Margaret, 84–33
Margaret de, 87–32
Margaret, w. of Robert de, of Chartley, 61–32
Martin, 51–34, 217–37
Mary, 10–34
Mary de, 2–33
Maud de, 70A–27, 261–31, 262–30
NN dau. of Robert de, E. of Derby, 55–26
Philippa de, of Chartley, 14–34
Richard, 84–33
Robert de, 2–32, 10–34, 62–33, 62–34, 77–34, 265–35
Robert de, E. of Derby, 55–26, 57–30, 69–30, 130–31
Robert de, of Chartley, 56B–34, 61–32, 61–34, 62–32, 70–36
Robert I de, 70A–27
Sibyl de, 82–30
Thomas, of Groby, 11–35, 216–34
Walter Devereux, L.. see Devereux
William de, 124A–32
William de, E. of Derby, 57–29, 58–29, 59–29, 82–30, 127–29, 127–30, 143–28, 189–4, 194–6, 194–7, 257–30, 261–30
William de, E. of Pembroke, 269A–27
William, L., of Groby, 11–32, 11–34, 58–30, 58–31, 87–32, 248–34
William, of Chartley, 56B–36
William, of Groby, 18A–33, 74–33, 155A–28
Ferrieres
Henry de, 132C–28
Isabel de, 132C–28, 262–29
Walkelin de, 132C–28, 262–29
Fettiplace
Anne, 143–38
Beatrice, w. of Thomas, 143–37
John, 143–37
Richard, 143–37
Thomas, 143–37
Fielding
Anne, 248A–37
Fiennes
see also Clinton

Arbella, 225–42
Conan, sn. & Bar. de, 158B–24
Enguerrand de, 158A–23
Enguerrand I de, 158A–26, 158B–26
Enguerrand II de, 97–30, 152–28, 158C–28
Eustache II, sn. & Bar. de, 158B–25, 272–27
Eustache, sn. & Bar. de, 158B–23, 272–27
Guillaume (William) de, 152–27, 158B–27, 158C–27, 272–29
Jean de, 234B–30
Jeanne de, 234B–30
Mahaud de, 97–30
Mahaud (Mathilda) de, 158B–28, 272–29
Mahaud (Maud) de, 158C–29
Susan, 225–42, 228–40
Sybil, w. of Enguerrand de, 158A–23
Thomas, L. Clinton, E. of Lincoln, 225–41

Fieschi
Beatrice, 274E–28
Teodoro, Ct. of Lavagna, 274E–28

Firmage
Abigail, 224A–43
Alice (Blessing), 224A–43

Fisher
Elizabeth, 11–39, 12–39

Fitz Aer
Margery, 31–'31

Fitz Akaris
Hervey, 266–26
Hervey, of Ravensworth, 226–26

Fitz Alan
Alice, 47–32, 47D–32, 47D–33, 78–33, 199A–33, 234–31
Brian, L., 30–31
Catherine, 30–31
Edmund d' Arundel, 28–34
Edmund, E. of Arundel, 28–32, 60–31, 83–30
Elizabeth, 15–32, 16–32, 18A–32, 18B–32, 20–32
Isabel, 8–32
Joan, 97–33, 120–35
John, L. of Clun & Oswestry, 28–30, 70A–29, 77–30, 149–29, 149–29, 215–30
John, of Arundel, 21–32, 74–35, 212–34
John, of Clun & Oswestry, 149–28
Margaret, 77–32
Maud, 215–30

Richard, E. of Arundel, 8–31, 15–31, 17–30, 18A–32, 20–30, 20–31, 21–30, 28–31, 28–33, 47D–33, 60–32, 60–33, 77–31, 78–32, 97–33, 120–35, 215–30, 234–31
Thomas, 234–31

Fitz Ansculf
Beatrice, 55–25
William, 55–25

Fitz Baldric
Erneburga, dau. of Hugh, 270–25

Fitz Baldwin
Emma, 184A–5

Fitz Bardolf
Akaris, of Ravensworth, 226–25, 266–25

Fitz Dolfin
Maldred, L. of Raby, 247–24, 270A–27

Fitz Duncan
William, 40–24

Fitz Edith
Robert, 138–25, 265A–23

Fitz Edward
Walter, 108–26

Fitz Forn
Ellen, 265A–23

Fitz Forn(e)
see also Greystoke

Fitz Forne
Ivo, L. Greystoke, 265A–24

Fitz Geoffrey
Hawise, 246B–28
Hawise, dau. of Geoffrey Fitz Piers, 143–28
John, 72–29, 73–29, 75–29, 82–29, 177B–9, 246C–28
Maud, dau. of Geoffrey Fitz Piers, 97–27

Fitz-Geoffrey
William, 158A–23

Fitz Gerald
David, 187–3
Joan, 7–30, 73–31, 178A–8
John Fitz Thomas, E. of Kildare, 7–30, 73–31, 178A–7
Juliane, w. of Maurice, Bar. of Offaly, 178–5, 178A–5
Maurice, 54–31, 187–3
Maurice, Bar. of Offaly, 178–5, 178A–5
Maurice Fitz Maurice, L. of Offaly, 54–31, 178–6
Thomas Fitz John, E. of Kildare, 7–31
Thomas Fitz Maurice, 178A–6

Fitz Gerold
Roger, 132A–26

Fitz Gilbert
Ada, dau. of Richard, 177–3
John (styled John the Marshal). *see*
Marshal
Richard, 130–27, 177–3, 184–2
Richard, L. of, 246B–25
Richard, L. of Clare, 132D–27, 161–24
Fitz Hamon
Maud, dau. of Robert, 63–26, 124A–26,
125–26
Robert, 63–26, 124A–26, 125–26
Fitz Henry
see also Fitz Roy
Amabilis, 33A–25
Henry, 33A–24
Henry, of Ravensworth, 265–33, 266–32
Hugh, of Ravensworth, 266–30
Joan, 265–33, 266–32
Joan Fitz Peter, 257–29
Meiler, 33A–24
Peter, 257–28
Ranulf, of Ravensworth, 34–27, 226–28,
266–28
Fitz Herbert
Alice, 18–32
Herbert, 124A–29, 237–5, 246D–28,
262–27, 262–28
Piers, 89–28, 237–6, 246D–28, 261–32,
262–29
Reynold, 18–32
St. William, 262–27
Fitz Hervey
Henry, L. of Ravensworth, 226–27
Henry, L. Ravensworth, 34–27
Henry, of Ravensworth, 266–27
Fitz Hugh
Elizabeth, 78–37, 201–37
Henry, 219–33
Henry, L., 78–36, 219–33, 219–35,
266–31
Lora, dau. of William, L., 121D–35
Lords, of Ravensworth, 226–24
Ralph, 170–27
Robert, 121A–26
Sarah, dau. of Robert, 121A–26
William, 78–36
William, L., 121D–35, 219–34
Fitz Ivo
Adam, 265A–24
Robert, 265A–24
Walter, L. of Greystoke, 265A–25
William, 265A–24

Fitz John
Avelina, dau. of John Fitz Geoffrey, 75–
30, 75A–30, 177B–9
Eustace, 269–24
Isabel, dau. of John Fitz Geoffrey, 82–30
Isabel, w. of Roger, 186–2
Joan, dau. of John Fitz Geoffrey, 73–30
Maud, 86–29
Maud, dau. of John Fitz Geoffrey, 72–
30, 74–30
Payn, 269–24
Richard, 82–30
Roger, 186–2
Fitz Lefstan
Ailwin, 257–27
Henry Fitz Ailwin, 257–27
Margaret, w. of Henry Fitz Ailwin, 257–
27
Fitz Maldred
Robert, L. of Raby, 247–25
Uchtred, L. of Raby, 247–22
Fitz Martin
Nicholas, 63A–31
Fitz Maurice
Gerald, Bar. of Offaly, 178–4
Juliana, 54–31, 64–31, 178–7
Maurice, 178A–6
Maurice, E. of Desmond, 9–32, 89–32
Maurice, L. of Offaly, 54–31
Fitz Neel
Leucha, d. of William, 150–27
William, 150–27
Fitz Nichol
Katherine, dau. of Thomas, 234A–34
Margery, w. of Thomas, 234A–34
Thomas, 234A–34
Fitz Osbern
Emma, dau. of William, 53–25
William, 53–25, 215–25
William, E. of Hereford, 163–23
Fitz Otes. *see* Fitz Otto
Fitz Other
Walter, 12A–21, 187–2
Fitz Otho. *see* Fitz Otto
Fitz Otto
Maud Fitz Thomas, 122A–31, 216–29
Thomas, 122A–30, 216–29
Fitz Patrick
William, E. of Salisbury, 108–27
Fitz Payn
Joan, 143–31
Robert, 18A–30, 79–31, 143–31
Fitz Piers
Alice, dau. of Reginald, 262–31

Eleanor, dau. of Reginald, 71–33, 122–32
Geoffrey, E. of Essex, 72–29, 97–27, 143–28, 246B–27, 246C–27
Herbert, 261–32, 262–30
Lucy, dau. of Piers Fitz Herbert, 89–28, 170–26, 237–7
Reginald (or Reynold), 71–33, 122–32, 261–32, 262–30
Roger, 261–34
Fitz Ponz
Richard, 29A–28
Fitz Ralph
Emma, w. of Ralph Fitz Ralph, 265–26
Eustache, dau. of Ralph Fitz Hugh, 170–27
Hugh, 170–27
Ralph, of Grimthorpe, 265–26
Robert, 265–31
William, L. Grimthorpe, 265–29, 265A–29, 265A–29
William, of Grimthorpe, 265–27
Fitz Ranulf
Alice, 266–27
Henry, of Ravensworth, 266–29
Richard, 269–22
William, L. of Greystoke, 265A–27, 270C–27
Fitz Reinfrid
Gilbert Fitz Roger, L. of Kendal, 88–27
Roger, 88–27
Fitz Reynold
Piers, 261–33
Reynold, 261–33
Fitz Richard
Gilbert, E. of, 246B–24
Gilbert, E. of Clare, 66–25, 177A–7, 184–3, 184A–3, 184B–3, 246–24, 246D–24
John, 269–23
Mabel, dau. of William, 50–26, 121–26
Nesta, dau. of Osborn, 177–3
Osborn, 176–3, 177–2
Robert, 130–27
Roger, 246D–26
William, 121–26
William, L. of Cardinand, 50–26
Fitz Robert
Alice, 237–6, 246D–28, 261–32, 262–29
Geoffrey, Bar. of Kells, 178–4
John, 186–1, 237–6, 262–29
Walter, 30–28, 86–32, 130–28, 130–30, 148A–26

William, E. of Gloucester, 63–26, 124–27
Fitz Roger
Alice, w. of John, 261–36
Elizabeth, 124A–36, 261–37, 261A–37
Gilbert, 88–27
Henry, 77–33, 261–35
Isabel, 187–2
Isabel, dau. of William, 270B–27
John, 124A–35, 261–36
Robert, 246D–27, 262–29
Robert, Bar. of Clavering, 186–3
Robert, Bar. of Warkworth, 237–6
Thomas, 261–36
William, 187–2, 270B–27
Fitz Rogus. see Roges
Fitz Roy
Isabel, 26–28
Maud, dau. of Reginald, 50–26
Reginald, E. of Cornwall, 50–26, 121–26, 124A–29, 262–27
Richard, 26–27, 218–27
Fitz Scrob
Richard, 177–2
Fitz Simon
Agnes, 184B–7
Pons, 132D–29
Robert, L. of Hatch (Robert IV de Beauchamp), 246B–29
Simon, 184B–7
Fitz Suein
Robert, of Essex, 246–26
Fitz Thomas
John. see Fitz Gerald
Maud, 122A–31, 216–29, 216A–29
Fitz Uchtred
Dolfin, L. of Raby, 247–23
Fitz Ulf
William, of Grimthorpe, 265–24
Fitz Walter
Agnes, 265A–24
Alan, 121C–28
Alice, 226–27
Avelina, dau. of Alan, 121C–28
Ela, 30–29, 86–32
Isabel, 176B–32
Isabel, dau. of Robert, L., 71–33
Maud, 148A–27
Ranulf, 226–27
Ranulf, L. of Greystoke, 265A–26, 266–27
Robert, 30–28, 94–29, 130–29, 176B–32
Robert, L., 71–33, 130–31

Rohese, w. of Robert, 130–29
Fitz Warin
    Fulk, 74A–32, 255A–30, 263–30
    Hawise, dau. of Fulk, 74A–32
    John, 25–32
    Mabel, 99–31, 255A–30, 263–30
    William, 25–31
Fitz William
    Amabel, 40–25
    Isabel, 270B–27
    Joan, 248A–28
    John, 210–37
    John de Greystoke, L., 265–35
    Ness, L. of Leuchars, 53–27
    Orabel, dau. of Ness, 53–27
    Ralph de Greystoke, L., 265–34
    Ralph, L. Greystoke, 265–30, 267A–29
    Ralph, of Grimthorpe, 265–25, 265–28
    Reginald, 248A–28
    Robert, 248A–28
    Thomas, L. of Greystoke, 265A–28
    William de Greystoke, L., 265–33, 266–32
    William, L. of Emley, 210–36
Fitzwarin. see Fitz Warin
FitzWilliam. see Fitz William
Fitzwith
    Joan, 197–31
    Robert, 197–31
Flaitel
    Agnes, 184–1
    Gerald, 184–1
Flamstead
    Lords of. see Toeni
Flamville
    Maud de, 155A–26
Flanders
    see also Dampierre; Hainaut; Lorraine
    Alix (Alice) of, 234B–29
    Arnold I, Ct. of, 48–20, 162–18
    Arnold II, Ct. of, 146–19, 162–20
    Arnulf, Ct. of, 100A–19
    Baldwin I, Ct. of, 162–16
    Baldwin II, Ct. of, 44–16, 162–17
    Baldwin III, Ct. of, 106–22, 162–19
    Baldwin IV, Ct. of, 162–21
    Baldwin V, Ct. of, 128–22, 162–22, 163–22, 164–22
    Baldwin VI (I) de Mons, Ct. of, 163–23
    Baldwin IX, Ct. of, 168A–29
    Counts. see also Hainaut
    Dietrich I. see Thierry I
    Gertrude of, 164–24, 274C–26
    Guy of Dampierre, Ct. of, 234B–30

    Guy V, sn. de Richebourg, 234B–29
    Hildegarde of, 100A–19
    Isabella of, 234B–30
    Jeanne of, 274E–28
    Margarite of Lorraine, heiress of. see Lorraine
    Mathilde of, 155–26, 165–27
    Maud of, 121–24, 162–23, 169–23
    Robert I, Ct. of, 100A–22, 164–23
    Robert II, Ct. of, 161–23
    Thierry I of Lorraine, Ct. of, 129–25, 163A–27, 164–25, 165–25, 274C–26
    Yolande of, 107–27, 163A–28
Flêche
    Helie de la. see Maine
Fleming
    Aline (Alicia) le, 34–29
    Anselm le, 41–25
    Eleanor le, 41–26
    Gerbod the. see Chester
    Henry, 179–17
    Margaret, 179–17
    Michael II le, 34–26, 41–25
    Michael III le, 34–27, 226–29
    William le, 34–26, 34–28
Flete
    Richard de, 40–27
    Sarah de, 40–27
Flower
    Anne, 3–39
    John, 3–39
Flowerdew
    Temperance, 18–39
Foix
    Bernard I Roger de, 144–22
    Clemence de, 144–22
Fokinton
    Hugh de, 255A–31
    Olympia de, 255A–31
Foliot
    Beatrice, 184A–10
    Joan, 79–30
    Jordon, 184A–10
    Richard, 79–30, 184A–10
Folkinton
    Beatrice de, 265A–25
Forbes
    Alexander, L., 256–35
    Arthur, L., 256–38
    Isabel, 256–40
    James, L., 256–36
    John, 256–35
    John, L., 256–38
    William, L., 256–37, 256–39

Forcalquier
Rainou, Ct. of, 111–28
Forez
Counts of. *see* Lyon
Forn
the King's Thegn, 265A–22
Fort
William de. *see* Fortibus
Fortescue
Jane, 25–35, 246F–37
Joane, 246E–36
John, 25–34, 246E–35, 246F–35, 257–37
William, 25–35, 246E–33, 246E–34, 246F–36
Fortibus
William de, of Vivonia, 261–31, 262–30
Fossard
Gertrude, 268–24
Nele, 268–24
Robert, 268–24
Fougères
Geoffrey de, 214A–28
Henry de, 214A–25
Jeanne de, 71A–31, 135–31, 214A–30, 275–29
Raoul de, 214A–26
Raoul III de, 71A–31, 135–31, 214A–29, 275–29
William de, 214A–27
Foulshurst
Cecily, 233B–37
Robert, 233B–37
Fourneux
Joan de, 265–33, 266–32
Richard de, 265–33, 266–32
Robert de, 187–7
William de, 265–33
Fowler
Richard, 14–37, 238–12
Sybil, 14–37, 238–12
Fox
Anne, 33–40
William, 33–40
France
Adelaide of Paris, 143–16, 148–16
Adele (Aelis) of, 128–22, 162–22, 163–22, 164–22, 166–22
Adèle of, Cts. of Auxerre, 107–21
Adelhard of Paris, 148–16
Aelis, w. of Robert I, K. of, 48–18, 50–18, 136–18
Agnes, w. of Robert the Strong, 48–17
Alice (Alix) of, 109–28

Alpais, w. of Begue (Bogo), 191–14
Ansegisel (Duke), Mayor of the Palace, 190–9
Arnégonde, w. of Cloitaire I, 240A–4
Aupais, concubine of Pippin II Heristal, 190–10
Bathilde, w. of Clovis II, 240A–8
Bego, Ct. of Paris, 143–16
Begue (Bogo), Ct. of Paris, 191–14
Bernard, D., 50–14
Berthe, Merovingian Pss., 240A–10
Bertrade, w. of Clotaire II, 240A–6
Bodegeisel I, 190–6
Bodegeisel II, 190–7
Carloman, Mayor of the Palace, 191–12
Charlemagne, K. of, 50–13, 140–13, 146–13, 148–13, 182–5, 190–13
Charles II, K. of, 1–13, 49–17, 148–15, 162–16
Charles III, K. of, 50–20, 121E–18, 148–17
Charles Martel, Mayor of the Palace, 50–11, 190–11, 191–11
Childebert, Frankish K. of Cologne, 190–2
Childebert, K. of Cologne, 190–2
Chilpéric I, K. of the Franks, 240A–5
Cloderic the Parricide, K. of Cologne, 190–4
Cloitaire I, K. of the Franks, 240A–4
Clotaire II, K. of the Franks, 240A–6
Clotilde, w. of Thierry III, 240A–9
Clovis I, K. of the Franks, 170–21, 190–1, 240A–3
Clovis II, K. of the Franks, 240A–8
Clovis the Riparian, Frankish K. of Cologne, 190–1
Conrad I, K. of, 101–21, 133–19, 157–19, 159–19
Constance of, 103–24, 169A–26
Dagobert, 190–9
Dagobert I, K. of the Franks, 240A–7
Emma of, 121E–20
Ermentrude of, 143–17
Eudes (odo), K. of, 48–17
Frédégonde, w. of Chilpéric I, 240A–5
Girard, Ct. of Paris, 143–17, 191–13
Gisèle of, 146–15, 191A–16, 250–15
Haduich of, 141–17
Hedwig of, 106–21, 144A–21
Henrich, Mrq. of, 141–17
Henry I, K. of, 53–22, 101–22, 141–22, 241–6
Hildegarde, w. of Charlemagne, 140–13
Hugh Capet, K, of, 53–20

Hugh Capet, K. of, 101–20, 106–20, 107–19, 121E–20, 141–20, 144A–20
Hugh Magnus, D. of, 48–17, 53–19, 53–23, 101–19, 141–19, 273–27
Hugh Magnus (II), D. of, 50–23, 140–23, 141–23
Ingonde, w. of Cloitaire I, 240A–4
Isabella of, 1–28, 101–31
Judith of, 1–13, 162–16
Landry (Landegisel), 240A–7
Liegarde of, 48–19, 50–18, 118–18, 136–18
Lothair I, s. of Louis I, K. of. see Italy
Louis I, K. of, 140–14, 144A–14, 146–14, 148–14, 191A–16, 182–5
Louis II, the Stammerer, K. of, 100B–20, 143–16, 148–16
Louis IV, d'Outre-Mer, K. of, 133–19, 140–18, 142–18, 148–18, 157–18
Louis IX, K. of, 101–28
Louis VI, K. of, 96–28, 101–24, 117–24, 135–26, 169A–26, 274A–25
Louis VII, K. of, 1–24, 101–25, 102–25, 109–28, 110–26, 137–25
Louis VIII, K. of, 45–29, 101–27, 104–27, 113–28
Margaret of, 1–27
Marguerite of, 16–28, 47–31, 155–30
Marie of, 102–26, 165–27
Mathilda of, 101–21, 133–19, 157–19, 159–19
Munderic, of Vitry-en-Perthois, 190–5
Nanthilde, w. of Dagobert I, 240A–7
Pepin I of Landen, Mayor of the Palace in Austrasia, 190–9
Pepin II of Heristal, Mayor of the Palace in Austrasia, 190–10
Pepin III, the Short, K. of the Franks, 50–12, 50–14, 190–12, 240A–12
Pepin, K. of Italy, 50–14
Peter of, 107–26, 117–25
Philip I, K. of, 101–23, 103–23, 273–27
Philip II, K. of, 101–26, 163–28, 165–27
Philip III, K. of, 16–28, 101–29, 103–32, 105–30, 155–29, 168–32
Philip IV, K. of, 45–31, 101–30
Robert I, K. of, 48–18, 50–18, 53–18, 101–18, 136–18
Robert II, K. of, 53–21, 101–21, 107–20, 108–21, 128–21, 141–21, 141A–21, 146–19, 162–20
Robert the Strong, 48–17, 181–6
Rothilde of, 49–17
Rotrou, w. of Charles Martel, 50–11, 190–11, 191–11
Rotrude of, 144A–15, 191–13
Siegbert, 190–9
Sigebert the Lame, Frankish K. of Cologne, 190–3, 190–3
St. Arnulf, Mayor of the Palace, Bishop of Metz, 180–8, 190–8
St. Begga, w. of Duke Angegisel, 190–9
St. Gondolfus, Bishop of Tongres, 190–6
Thierry III of Merovia, K. of the Franks, 240A–9
Wido, bro. of Rotrou, w. of Charles Martel, 190–11

Franceys
Adam, 8A–32, 11–34, 248–34
Elizabeth, 31–34
Jane, 143–34
Maud, 8A–32, 11–34, 248–34
Robert, 31–34, 143–34
Francis
see also Franceys
Hugh, 246–35
Joan, 248A–35
Margaret, 246–35
Richard, 248A–35
Franklyn
Ellen, 179–16
Thomas, 179–16
Franks, the. see France
Fray
Catherine, 187–12
Elizabeth, 200–37
John, 187–12
Freeman
Alice, 43A–40
Henry, 43A–39
Freville
Baldwin II, 230A–33
Baldwin III, 98–33, 216–32, 230A–33
Baldwin IV, 11–35, 216–33, 230A–34
Baldwin V, 230A–35
Elizabeth, 11–35, 216–34
Margaret, 230A–35
Maud, w. of Baldwin IV, 216–33, 230A–34
Friuli
Eberhard, Mrg. of, 146–15, 191A–16, 250–15
Engeltron, w. of Hunroch, 191A–15
Gisèle of, 146–17
Helwise of, 250–16
Hunroch (Unroc), Mrg. of, 191A–15
Fronte-boef
Robert. see Stuteville

Fulford
Alice, 1–34
Baldwin, 1–34, 6–36
Bridget, 6–40, 209–39
Mary, 209–39
Thomas, 6–40, 209–39
Fulshurst
Ralph, 14–37
Furneaux
Henry de, 248A–28, 248A–29
Margaret de, 248A–32
Matthew de, 248A–30
Matthew de, L. of Ashington, 248A–31
Furnes
Erard de, 158B–23
Furnival
Bertha, w. of Thomas de, 148A–29
Eleanor de, 156–29
Gerard de, 72–30, 148A–28
Maud de, 148A–32, 218–30, 219–30
Thomas, 70–32
Thomas de, 148A–29, 148A–30
Thomas de, L., 148A–31, 156–29
Furnivalle
Eleanor de, 34–36
Joan de, 8–34
Lords of. see Neville
Maude, Bar., 8–34
Thomas de, 34–36
William de, L., 8–34

G

Gabaston
see also Gaveston
Arnaud de, Bar. of Béarn, 16A–29
Garsie-Arnaud, L., 16A–28
Garsie de, 16A–28
Raimond-Garsie de, 16A–28
Gael. see Montfort
Gaini
Æthelred Mucill, E. of, 1–14
Ealhswith of, 1–14
Edburga of, 1–14
Gallo-Roman
Ansbertus, Senator, 180–6
Ansbertus, the Senator, 190–9
Avitus, Emp., 180–3
Bilichilde, w. of Ansbertus, 180–6
dau. of Syagrius, 180–2
Dode, abbess of St. Pierre de Rheims, 180–5
Ferreolus, 180–2
Ferreolus, senator in Narbonne region, 180–5
Flavius Afranius Syagrius, Senator, 180–1
Industria, w. of Tonantius Ferreolus, senator, 180–4
Papianilla, 180–3
Ruricius, Bishop of Uzes, 180–4
Sidonius Apollinaris, 180–3
Tonantius Ferreolus, Praet. Prefect of Gaul, 180–3
Tonantius Ferreolus, senator of Narbonne, 180–4
Galloway
Alan, L. of, 38–26, 53–28, 94–27, 114A–27, 252–26
Devorguilla of, 69–29, 94–28, 95–28, 121A–29, 184A–8, 186–1, 236–9, 252–26, 270–28
Fergus, L. of, 38–24, 121B–26, 121C–26
Gilbert of, 121B–27, 121C–27
Helen of, 38–27, 53–28, 57–28, 114A–27, 224–28
Malcolm of, 121B–27
Roland, L., 69–29
Roland, L. of, 38–25, 184A–8, 236–9, 270–28
Uchtred of, 38–24, 121B–27
Gant. see Gaunt, Ghent
Gardinis
Alexandra de, 42–30
Thomas de, 42–30
Garland
NN, w. of William Chauncy, 69A–36
Garlande
Agnes de, 50–25
Anseau (Ansel) de, 50–25
Garneys
Thomas, 246–35
Gascaryk
Elizabeth, 224A–38
William, 224A–38
Gascoigne
Dorothy, 3–36
Margaret, 2–36
William, 2–35, 2–35, 2–36, 3–35
Gater
Judith, 246A–42
Gates
Dorothy, 211–40
Jeffrey, 211–40
Gâtinais
Aubri Geoffrey (Geoffroy Ferréol), Ct. of the, 110–22, 118–22
Geoffrey III, Ct. of the, 118–22

Gaunt
Agnes de, 143–24
Alice de, 18A–24
Gilbert de, 143–22, 156–27
Gilbert de, E. of Lincoln, 156–26
John of. *see* Lancaster
Nichole de, 156–28
Robert de, 156–25, 270–27
Walter de, 18A–24, 143–23, 156–24
Gaveston
see also Gabaston
Amy de, 16A–31, 16C–31
Piers de, 16A–30
Piers de, E. of Cornwall, 9–30
Gay(t)
family, NN dau., 124–26
Geldern
Adelaide of, 100–27
Agnes of, 234B–25
Arnulf (Arnould), D. of, 252–35
Gerald de Wassenberg, Ct. of, 163–25
Henry I, Ct. of, 234B–25
Marie of, 252–35
Otto I, Ct. of, 100–27
Yolande of, 98A–25, 163–25
Geneva
Aimon I, Ct. of, 133–23
Amadeus I, Ct. of, 133–24, 263–28
Beatrice of, 263–28
Gérold, Ct. of, 133–22, 274A–23
Gisele, w. of Gérold, Ct. of, 133–22, 274A–23
Humbert of, 71A–30
Ita, w. of Aimon I, Ct. of, 133–23
Jeanne of, 274A–23
Margaret (Beatrix), 28–31
Margaret of, 133–26, 274C–27, 274D–27, 274E–27
Peter of, 71A–30
Robert, Ct. of, 133–20
Tetberge, w. of Gérold, Ct. of, 133–22
William I, Ct. of, 133–25, 274B–25, 274C–27
Geneville
see also Joinville
Alix de, 17–29, 71A–31
Geoffrey de, 71–30, 71A–30
Jean (John) de, 71A–30
Joan de, 10–32, 29–32, 39–31, 71–32, 71A–32, 120–33, 176B–31, 263–31
John de, 17–29
Piers de, 71–31, 71A–31, 135–32
Gent. *see* Ghent

Geoffrey
Aubri. *see* Gâtinais
Gerard
Catherine, 217A–40
Constance, 170–32
Isabel, 9–37
Isabel, w. of John, 233A–42
Isabel, w. of Thomas, 233B–34
Jane (Jaine) w. of Thomas, 233A–41
John, 170–31, 233A–42, 233B–35
Peter, 233B–34, 233B–36, 233B–38
Thomas, 217A–38, 217A–39, 233A–39, 233A–41, 233A–43, 233B–34, 233B–37, 233B–39
William, 233A–40
Germany
see also Bavaria, Swabia
Adalhard of Ripuaria, 147A–17
Adelheid, w. of Adalhard, 147A–17
Agnes of, 45–24, 147–26
Conrad II, K. of, 45–21, 157–21
Eberhard I, 147A–18
Erenfried I of the Ezzonen fam. in Ripuaria, 147A–17
Erenfried II, 147A–19
Frederick I, Emp. of, 45–26
Friederich II, K. of, 252D–30
Helwig, w. of Herman Pusillus, 147A–20
Henry III, K. of, 45–22
Henry IV, K. of, 45–23, 274–23
Henry V, Emp. of, 1–23
Herman Pusillus, 147A–20
Luitgarde of, 45–18, 192–20
Otto I the Great, K. of, 45–17, 147–19, 192–20
Otto II, K. of, 147–20
Philip II, Emp. of, 45–27
Richwara, w. of Erenfried II, 147A–19
Ulrich, Bishop of Augsburg, 147A–20
Gernon
Alice, wid. of John Bigot, w. of John, 246–31
Joan, w. of, 246–31
John, 246–30, 246–31
Margaret, 246–32
Ralph de, 246–28
Ranulph de, E. of Chester, 125–27, 132A–27
William, 246–29
William de, 246–28
Gevauden
Dulce de, 111–26, 113–25
Gilbert, Ct. of, 111–26

Ghant
Gwrgi, 179–4
Ghent
see also Gaunt
Arnould of, 272–26
Balduin III of, 272–28
Forlkard I of, 272–23
Geyla, w. of Lambert II of, 272–24
Lambert I of, 272–22
Lambert II of, 272–24
Ralph of, 143–21
Roger I of, 272–27
Wenemar I of, 272–25
Gibbon
Jane, 2–41
Gibbons
James, 17–41
Gibson
Richard, 17–41
Gibthorpe
Katharine, 224A–36
William, 224A–36
Giffard
see also Gifford
Amy, 43A–36
Ann, 84–35
Elizabeth, w. of Roger, 42–32
Jane, 25–37, 52–43
John, 42–30, 43–34, 43A–34, 69–33
Katharine, 42–33
Margaret, 43–37, 69–33
Margery, w. of Thomas, 42–31
Nicholas, 43–36, 84–35
Roger, 25–36, 42–32, 43–32, 43–35, 52–43
Rohese, 130–27, 184–2
Sybil, w. of Thomas, 42–31
Thomas, 25–36, 43–33, 43A–35, 42–31
Walter I, 184–1
Walter II, E. of Buckingham, 184–1
William, 69–33
Gifford
see also Giffard
Alice, 234A–37
Cassandra, 81B–40
Catherine, 122–31
Eleanor, 8–32, 29A–30, 259–29
John, L., 29A–29, 122–31
Richarda (Prowse), 246G–38
Stephen, 234A–37
Thomas, 81B–40
Gilbert
Geoffrey, 246G–33
Humphrey, 246G–33, 246G–38

Joan, 246G–33
Raleigh, 246G–33, 246G–38
William, 246G–33
Gill
Francis, 246A–41
Glane
Emma de, 263–29
Pierre de, 263–29
Glanville
Emma de, 187–4
Geoffrey de, 187–4
Gleiberg
Ermentrude of, 100B–22, 143–20, 162–21
Heribert, Ct. of, 100B–22, 143–20
Glemham
Anne, 15–36
John, 15–35
Gloucester
Amice, Cts. of, 63–27, 63A–27
Antigone of, 1A–34, 47D–35
Earls of. see Audley; Despenser; Fitz Robert
Humphrey, D. of, 1A–33, 47D–35
Mabira de Caen, of, 124A–27
Maud de Caen, of, 125–27, 132A–27
Miles of, E. of Hereford, 177–4, 193–4, 237–4, 246D–28
NN (Mabel?) of, 179–1
Robert de Caen, E. of, 63–26, 124–26, 124A–26, 125–26, 179–1
Thomas of Woodstock, D. of, 4–31, 97–34, 155A–32, 155A–32, 261–38
Walter of, 177–4, 237–4
William Fitz Robert, E. of, 124–27, 179–1
Glover
Elizabeth, 232–41
Sarah, 232–41
Gobaud
Guy, 246–30
Gobion
Joan, 42–28
Matilda, w. of Hugh, 42–27
Richard, 42–26
Goditha
Dau. of Eldred the Thane, 34–24, 88–24
Goel
Ascelin, 215–25
Goldington
Eleanor de, 41–29
William de, 41–29
Gometz
Hodierne de, 103A–24

Goodrick
Ann, 202–40
John, 202–38
Lionel, 202–39
Gordon
Alexander, 252–39
Alexander, E. of Huntly, 252–38, 256–37
Alexander, E. of Sutherland, 252–41
Christian, 256–37
George, E. of Huntly, 252–41
Helen, w. of Thomas, 256–43
Jane, 252–41
John, 252–40, 256–40, 256–41
John, L., 252–38
Katherine, 252–42
Louisa, 252–41
Robert, 252–41, 256–41, 256–42
Thomas, 256–43
Gorges
Edmund, 209–38
Edward, 209–38
Eleanor, 59–32
Ferdinando, 209–39, 211–42, 246A–42
Ralph de, 59–32
Gorz
see also Kärnten
Albert of, 252A–31
Margareta of, 252A–31
Meinhard IV (II), Ct. of, 252A–31
Gournay
Gerard de, 18A–23
Gundred de, 18A–23
Hugh de, 18A–23
Hugh V de, 152–27, 255A–29, 257–31, 262–31
Juliane de, 152–27, 257–31
Millicent de, 255A–29, 262–31
Goushall
Joan, 233–36
Goushill
Elizabeth, 15–33, 15A–33
Joan, 20–33, 23–33, 57–36
Margaret de, 74A–32
Ralph de, 74A–32
Robert, 15–32, 20–32, 57–36
Gover
Richarda, 246G–40
Grammaire
Joan le, 136–25
Richard le, 136–25
Grandison
Adele, w. of Ebel I, 263–25
Agnes de, 257–32
Bartholomey de, 263–26

Conon of, (son of Adalbert), 263–24
Ebel I de, 263–25
Ebel III de, 263–27
Ebel IV de, 263–28
Jacques de, 263–30
Jordane, w. of Ebel III, 263–27
Katherine de, 8A–31, 28–34, 29–33, 263–31
Mabel de, 85–31, 184A–12, 263–31
Otes de, 263–30
Peter de, 263–31
Peter (Pierre) de, 263–29
William de, 8A–31, 28–34, 29–33, 184A–12, 263–30
Grandmesnil
Hugh de, 53–26
Petronilla de, 53–26
Grandpre
Alix de, 71A–30
Grapinel
Margery, 212–32
Gray
see also Grey
Elizabeth, 88–34
Thomas, 88–34, 199–39
Green
Agnes, 212–34
Eleanor, 210–37
Henry, 210–37, 212–34
Greene
Deborah, 197–41
Elizabeth, 14–35
Joan, 216–33, 230A–34
Joane, 12A–34
John, 197–41
Margaret, 224A–40
Thomas, 14–33, 14–34, 216–33, 230A–34
Greenman
Content, 11–42
John, 11–42
Greinville
see also Grenville
Gilbert de, 187–5
Joan de, 136–28, 187–5
Grelle
Joan de, 18–31, 47B–31, 99–31, 255A–32
Robert de, 94–29, 99–30
Thomas de, 18–31, 99–30
Grene
Ralph, 232–33
Grenville
Amy, 234A–39

Gresley
Agnes de, 170–27
NN, dau. of Thomas, 81B–41, 81C–41
Ralph de, 170–27
Thomas, 81B–41, 81C–41
Greville
Edward, 69A–41
Frances, 18–39
Margaret, 57–39, 69A–41, 84–36, 84C–
36, 209–36
William, 84–36
Grey
see also Gray
Agnes, 121D–33
Alice, 93B–34, 188–12
Aline, 215–27
Anne, 99–39, 207–37
Anselme, 197–36
Arthur, L., of Wilton, 214–39
Edmund, L., of Wilton, 207–38
Edmund of Ruthin, E. of Kent, 207–36,
207–37
Edward, L., 257–38
Elizabeth, 1A–35, 257–37
Elizabeth de, 219–33
Emma, 187–4
Eve, 93–29
Henry, 1A–34
Henry de, L. of Wilton, 13A–32
Henry de, of Codnor, L., 143–30
Henry, E. of Tankerville, 47D–35
Henry, L., of Codnor, 212–37
Humphrey, of Whittington, 248A–37
Jane de, 39A–31, 143–32
Joan, w. of Thomas, 47D–34
John, 18A–33, 47C–33, 93B–33
John de, L., of Rotherfield, 30–31, 219–
31
John de, L., of Wilton, 93A–30
John de, of Codnor, 143–29
John de, of Codnor, L., 143–32
John de, of Rotherfield, 30–'30, 143–33
John de, of Shirland, 187–4
John, E. of Tankerville, 47D–34
John, L., of Wilton, 207–37
John, of Ruthin, 207–36
Lord, of Codnor, 20–34
Lucy, 212–37
Margaret, 93A–33, 224–36, 248A–37,
261A–38
Margaret de, 13A–33, 62–36, 88–35
Maud, 223–35
Maud de, 30–32, 143–33, 219–31
NN, L., mar. Margaret Stanley, 199–34

Philip, L., of Wooton Basset, 215–27
Reginald, 99–39
Reginald, L., of Ruthyn, 257–37
Reynold de, 13A–32
Reynold de, L., of Ruthin, 89–33, 93A–
31
Reynold, L. of Ruthin, 47C–33, 248A–37
Reynold, L., of Ruthin, 93A–32, 93B–32
Richard de, 143–29
Richard de, of Codnor, 143–31
Richard, L., 212–37
Richard, of Codnor, 187–7
Robert de, L. of Wilcote, 219–32
Robert de of Rotherfield, 30–'30
Roger de, L., of Ruthin, 93A–30
Sedzilia, w. of Philip, L., of Wooton
Basset, 215–27
Tacy (Tasy), 197–36, 207–37, 207–39
Thomas, 47D–34, 121D–33
Thomas, of Wark, 223–34
Walter de, 93–29
Greystock. *see* Greystoke
Greystoke
Alice de, 41–24
Amabel, w. of Ranulf Fitz Walter, L. of,
265A–26
Edith of, 265A–23
Forn, L. of, 265A–23
Ivo Fitz Forne, L. of, 41–24, 265A–24
Joan, 13A–34, 62–36
Joan de, 265–29, 265A–29, 265A–29
John de, L., 62–35, 265–35
Maud, 202–34
Ralph de, 186–5
Ralph de, L., 202–33, 207–32, 265–34,
265–32
Ralph Fitz William, L., 265–30, 267A–29
Ranulf Fitz Walter, L. of, 265A–26
Thomas Fitz William, L. of, 265A–28
Walter Fitz Ivo, L, of, 265A–25
William de, L., 265–33, 266–32
William Fitz Ranulf, L. of, 88–26, 265A–
27, 270C–27
Griffin
Catherine, 99–37
Nicholas, 99–35
Nicholas, L. Latimer, 99–36
Richard, 99–34
Thomas, 99–33
Griffith
Dorothy, 199–37
Joan, 202–37
Joan ferch Rhys ap, 56A–35
Rhys ap, 56A–35

NDEX

Richard, 202–37
William, of Penrhyn, 199–35, 199–36, 199A–36
Grimstom
John, 121D–38
Margaret, 121D–38
Grimthorpe
Ralph Fitz Ralph of, 265–26
Ralph Fitz William of, 265–25, 265–28
Ulf of, 265–23
William Fitz Ralph, L., 265–29, 265A–29, 265A–29
William Fitz Ralph of, 265–27
William Fitz Ulf, of, 265–24
Grosvenor
Elizabeth, 31–38
Mary, 233–40
Randall, 31–37
Richard, 233–40
Guines
Arnould II, Ct. of, 272–28
Arnould III, Ct. of, 75–31, 94A–31, 272–30, 273–30
Baldwin (Baudoin) II, Ct. of, 272–27
Baldwin (Baudoin) III, Ct. of, 158B–28, 272–29
Baudoin I, Ct. of, 272–25
Gisela of, 272–25
Margaret of, 75–31, 94A–31, 272–27, 272–30
Guise
see also Gyse
Alix (Adeline) de, 168A–28
Alix, w. of Bouchard, 168A–28
Bouchard, sn. de, 168A–28
Gunton
Alice, 15–37
Robert, 15–37
Gurdon
Brampton, 3–41, 4–39
John, 4–39
Muriel, 3–41, 4–40
Guzman
Ximena Nuncia de, 112–24
Gye
John, 261–43
Mary, 59–35, 261–44
Robert, 261–43

Gyse
Elizabeth, 197–39
John, 197–34, 197–35, 197–36, 197–38, 207–37, 207–39
Reynold, 197–34

William, 197–37

H

Habington. *see* Abington
Habsburg
Agnes of, 252B–31
Mechtild of, 252C–30
Rudolf I, Ct. of, 252B–31, 252C–30
Hackburne
Samuel, 84–40, 143–41
Hainaut
Adela, w. of Reginar III, Ct. of, 155–19
Agnes de, 135–28
Alberade, of Mons, Dame of, 140–17
Baldwin I, Ct. of, 163–23
Baldwin II, Ct. of, 160–23, 163–24
Baldwin III, Ct. of, 98A–25, 143–25, 163–25, 168A–26
Baldwin IV, Ct. of, 135–28, 163–26
Baldwin V, Ct. of, 163–27, 163A–27, 164–26, 168–27
Baldwin VI, Ct. of, 102–27, 168–28, 168A–29, 274E–28
Beatrix of, 106–22, 144A–22, 151–21
Herman, Ct. of, 163–23
Ida of, 98A–25, 143–25
Isabella of, 101–26, 163–28
John, Ct. of Holland &, 168–31
Margaret de, 168–29, 168A–29
Philippa of, 1–29, 4–30, 5–30, 16A–31, 97–34, 103–34, 207–34, 225–34
Reginar I, Ct. of, 140–17, 155–17, 240–17
Reginar II, Ct. of, 155–18, 240–18
Reginar III, Ct. of, 155–19
Regnier III, Ct. of, 106–21
Regnier IV, Ct. of, 106–21, 144A–21
Regnier V, Ct. of, 106–22
Richilde of, 168A–26
William, Ct. of Holland &, 1–29
William III, Ct. of Holland &, 103–33, 168–32
Haldensleben
Dietrich, Ct. of, 252D–23
Thietburga of, 252D–23
Hales
Alice, 16–29, 155–31
Roger, 155–31, 16–29
Hall
Henry, 52–41
Hamby
Edward, 224A–40
George, 224A–40
Katherine, 224A–43

309

Robert, 224A–42
William, 224A–41
Hamley
John, 246F–36
Mary, 246F–36
Hammerton
Agnes, 2–39
Hankeford
Anne, 120–37
Richard, 120–37
Hankford
Thomasine, 261–38
Hanmer
Joseph, 12–41
Sarah, 12–41
Harby
Katherine, 201–41
Thomas, 201–40
William, 201–40
Harcourt
Agnes, 4–37
Alice, 143–36
Alice de, 84–26
Arabella de, 56–29, 56–30
Aubreye de, 89–27
Jane, 248A–35
John, 4–37
John de, 39A–30, 93–30
Margery de, 56–29
Richard, 79–35, 143–35, 257–36
Richard de, 56–28, 56–29, 93–28, 93–29
Richard, L. of Wytham, 248A–35
Robert de, 84–26
Thomas, 248A–35
Thomas de, 30–32, 143–33, 219–31
Thomas II de, 143–34
William de, 39A–31, 56–28, 56–29, 93–28, 143–32
Hardres
Elizabeth, 69A–40
Harford
John, 230A–41
Margery, 230A–41
Harington
see also Haverington
Agnes, 35–'35, 36–35
Alice, 34–38, 170–35
Edith, 37–28
Isabel, 40–33, 46–35, 57–35
James, 34–'34, 35–36, 170–35
James, L. Verdon, 34–37
John, 34–32
John, L., 40–32, 261A–38

Margaret, 34–36
Nicholas, 34–33, 35–33
Richard, 34–35
Robert, 34–32, 40–31
Robert, L., 40–33
William, 35–34, 46–34, 247–31
William, L. Verdon, 34–36
Harlakenden
Mabel, 69A–41
Richard, 69A–40
Roger, 1–39, 69A–40, 69A–41
Harleston
William, 12–33
Harley
Robert I de, 29A–32
Harlyngrugge
Cecily, 246A–33
William of Checkenden, 246A–32
Harmar
Charles, 1A–41
Harpersfield
Edward, 17–38
John, 17–37
Harrgat
Agnes, 43–38
Harris
Agnes, 246E–41
Bartholomew, 246E–40
Dorothy, 199–39
John, 246E–40
Mary, 84C–39
Priscilla, 246E–41
Richard, 246E–41
Thomas, 84C–39
Hart
Mary, 220–43
Haselden
Alice, 85–40
Hastang
Eve, w. of John, 55–32
John de, 55–32, 55–34
Katherine de, 32–'32, 55–32
Maud de, 55–34
Hastings
see also Eu
Alice de, 88–33, 155A–26
Ann, w. of Ralph, 207–38
Catherine, 225–40
Elizabeth de, 93A–30
Florence, 207–38
Francis, E. of Huntingdon, 225–39
George, E. of Huntingdon, 225–39
Henry de, 16B–25, 93–27, 93A–27, 93A–27, 99–32

Hillary de, 56–29, 93–28
Ida, 16B–25
John, L., 93A–29
Lora de, 99–32
Nicholas de, 88–33
Ralph, 207–38
Robert de, 155A–26
William de, 93–27
Hatch
Edith, 234A–38
William, 234A–38
Haugh
Atherton, 31C–40
Samuel, 31C–41
Haute
Margery, 249–40
Havering
Elizabeth de, 170–30
Nicholas de, 170–30
Haverington
see also Harington
John, L. Harington, 34–31, 40–31
Robert de, 34–30
Haviland
Jane, 197–40
Matthew, 197–39
Robert, 197–39
Haynes
Christiana, 199–39
John, 69A–41
Ruth, 69A–42
Heckington
Jane, 15A–36
William, 15A–36
Heckstall
Margaret, 11–36
William, 11–36
Heigham
Clement, 246A–37, 246A–38
Elizabeth, 246A–39
Thomas V, 246A–36
Helion
Alice de, 52–32
Hervey de, 52–32
Margaret de, 217–33
William de, 217–33
Henneberg
Berthold VI, Ct. of, 252A–32
Elizabeth of, 252A–32
Herbert
Elizabeth, 199A–34
Walter, 225–39
William ap Thomas, 199A–34
William, E. of Pembroke, 199A–34

Hereford
Bertha of, 177–5, 194–5, 222–28
Earls of. see Bohun
Getha, w. of Ralph "Comes" of, 235–21,
    250–21
Harold (de Ewyas) of Ewyas Harold,
    235–22, 255–25
Lucy of, 237–5, 246D–28, 262–28
Margaret of, 193–5
Miles of Gloucester, E. of, 177–4, 193–
    4, 237–4, 246D–28, 262–28
Ralph "Comes" of, 235–21, 250–21
St. Thomas of, 255A–29
Heron
Elizabeth, 223–37, 223–38, 224–37
Emmeline, 88–33
John, 223–37, 224–37
Walter, 88–33
William, 223–36, 223–37
William I, 223–37
Heronville
Henry, 17–34
Joan, 17–34
Herring
Mary, 17–40
Hertford
Earls of. see Clare
Hesbaye
Ermengarde of the, 140–14, 144A–14
Ingerman of the, 140–14
sis. of Echard, Ct. of, 240–15
Hesden
Ernulf de, 108–26
Maude de, 108–26
Hevyn
Anne, 230A–37
John, 230A–37
Hext
Margery, 246E–38
Thomas, 246E–36, 246E–37
Higham
Bridget, 200–40
John, 200–39
Thomas, 200–39
Hill
Jane, 6–34
Mary, 208–41
William, 208–41
Hillary
Joan, 86–33
Hilton
Elizabeth, 74A–38, 224A–39
Godfrey, 74A–36, 74A–37, 74A–38
Margery, w. of Godfrey, 74A–37

Hinckley
John, 248–40
Hingston
Elizabeth, 51–36
Robert, 51–36
Hobrugg
Joan de, 187–3
William de, 187–3
Hohenstauffen. see Swabia
Hohenzollern. see Brandenburg
Holand
Alianore, 88–33
Constance de, 18A–33, 47C–33, 93B–33, 207–36
Eleanor de, 47D–33, 78–34, 225–33, 8A–33
Elizabeth, 77–33
Elizabeth, w. of Robert de, L., 47A–31
Henry, 261–35
Joan (Alice), w. of Robert de, 47A–32
John, 85–34
John de, 207–36
John de, E. of Huntingdon, 47C–32, 93B–33
Margaret, 85–34
Margaret de, 1–31, 18–31, 34–32, 47–33, 47B–31, 252–34
Maud de, 32–31, 47A–33, 215–32, 261–36
Robert de, 34–32, 47A–32, 88–33, 215–32
Robert de, L., 18–31, 32–30, 47–30, 47A–30, 47A–31, 47B–30, 215–32
Robert, L., 77–33, 261–35
Thomas de, 261–36
Thomas de, E. of Kent, 8A–33, 47–31, 47–32, 47C–31, 47D–32, 78–33, 207–36, 225–33, 236–12
Holderness
Earls of. see also Aumale
Theobald, E. of, 130–24
Holford
Dorothy, 33–39
Thomas, 33–38
Holland
Adelaide of, 100–29, 168–30, 168A–30
Arnulf, Ct. of, 100A–20
Bertha of, 101–23, 103–23
Dietrich II, Ct. of, 100A–19
Dietrich III, Ct. of, 100A–21
Dietrich V, Ct. of, 100A–23
Dietrich VI of, 100A–25
Dietrich VI, of, 100B–26

Florent I, Ct. of, 100A–22, 101–23, 103–23, 164–23
Florent II, Ct. of, 100A–24
Florent III, Ct. of, 100–26, 100A–26
Florent IV, Ct. of, 100–28
Jacqueline, Cts. of, 1A–33
John, Ct. of, 6–29, 7–29
Othehilde, w. of Dietrich V, Ct. of, 100A–23
William, Ct. of, 1A–33
William I, Ct. of, 100–27
Holmes
Alice, 248A–40
William, 248A–39
Holstein-Schauenburg
Gerhard III, Ct. of, 252E–32
Gerhard V, Ct. of, 252E–34
Heilwig of, 252E–34
Ingeborg of, 252E–32
Holt
Christian, 120–37
Richard, 120–37
Holy Roman Emperors
Charlemagne, K. of France, 50–13, 140–13, 146–13, 148–13, 182–5, 190–13
Charles II, K. of France, 1–13, 49–17, 148–15, 162–16
Conrad II, K. of Germany, 45–21
Frederick I (III Barbarossa), K. of Germany, 45–26
Frederick II, K. of Germany, 252D–30
Henry I, K. of Saxony, 50–19, 53–19, 101–19, 141–18, 142–17, 147–18, 240–18
Henry III, K. of Germany, 45–22
Henry IV, K. of Germany, 45–23, 274–23
Henry V, K. of Germany, 1–23
Lothair I, K. of Italy, 140–15, 141B–15, 145–15, 240–16
Louis I, K. of France, 140–14, 144A–14, 146–14, 148–14, 182–5, 191A–16
Louis II, K. of Italy, 141B–16
Ludwig IV, K. of Italy, 252C–31
Ludwig IV of Bavaria, 252D–32
Otto I the Great, K. of Germany, 45–17, 147–19, 192–20
Otto II, K. of Germany, 147–20
Rudolf I, Ct. of Habsburg (uncrowned), 252B–31, 252C–30
Hommet
Agnes du, 184A–6
Lucy, w. of William du, 184A–6
William du, 184A–6

Honstein
 Agnes of, 252E–33
 Dietrich V, Ct. of, 252E–33
Hoo
 Anne, 18–35
 Margaret, 79–34
 Thomas, 11–33
 Thomas, L., 18–35
 William, 79–34
Hopton
 Elizabeth, 56B–38
Hornby
 Aleric, L. of, 247–27
Horne
 Alice, 69–36
 John, 69–36
 Robert, 143–37
Horsey
 Elizabeth, 253–38
 William, 253–38
Horton
 Margaret, 234A–38
 Thomas, 234A–38
Hosier
 Elizabeth, 198–39
Howard
 Edmund, L., 248–37
 Edward, 257–37
 Elizabeth, 22–36, 120–39, 200–36
 Henry, 200–36
 John, 188–10, 200–36, 218–34
 John, D. of Norfolk, 4–35, 18A–34, 136–34
 John, L., D. of Norfolk, 16–34, 22–34
 Katherine, 4–35, 16–35
 Margaret, 188–10, 218–34
 Robert, 16–33, 18A–33, 22–33
 Thomas, D. of Norfolk, 16–35, 22–35, 120–39, 136–34, 248–37
Howell
 Mary, 202–42
 Morgan, 202–42
Hoya
 Heinrich II, Ct. of, 252E–29
 Richza of, 252E–29
Hubbard
 Martha, 31C–41
Huberd
 Edward, 69A–39
 Eleanor, w, of Edward, 69A–39
 Margaret, 69A–40
 Richard, 69A–38
Huddlesfield
 Katherine, 6–36

William, 6–36
Hudleston
 Anne, 37–35
 Elizabeth, 37–32
 John, 37–32, 37–35
Hudson
 John, 69–40
 Sarah, 69–40
Huish
 Henry, 246G–42
 Jane, 246G–42
Hulse
 Margaret, 199–34
Humberston
 Edward, 69–38
Humez
 Lucy de, 143–29
Hummet
 Agatha, 214A–27
 Lucy, w. of William, 214A–27
 William du, sn. of Le Hommet, 214A–27
Humphrey
 Anne, 228–41
 John, 225–42, 228–40
Hungary
 Adelaide of, 147–24
 Adelaide, w. of St. Ladislav, K. of, 244A–7
 Almos, Pr. on, 243–1
 Andrew I, K. of, 243–5, 244–6
 Andrew II, K. of, 103–28, 105–28, 105A–29, 163A–29
 Arpád, Pr. in, 243–1
 Béla I, K. of, 166–24, 243–5, 243–6, 243A–23, 244A–6
 Béla II, K. of, 242–9
 Béla III, K. of, 103–27, 242–10
 Béla IV, K. of, 103–29
 Géza I, K. of, 242–9
 Géza II, K. of, 103–27, 242–9
 Géza, Pr. of, 243–4
 Marie of, 103–31, 104–29
 Michael (Mihaly), D., 243–4
 NN, w. of Zoltán, dau. of Marót, Khagan of Jewis Khazars, 243–2
 Prisca (Irene) of, 105A–24, 244A–8
 Sophia of, 166–24, 242–9, 243–7, 243A–23
 Sophie of, 252C–24
 St. Elizabeth of, 103–28
 St. Ladislav, K. of, 244A–7
 Stephen V, K. of, 103–30
 Taksóny, Pr. of, 243–3
 Vasul, Magyar Pr., 243–5, 244–5

Yolande of, 105–29, 105A–29
Zoltán, Pr. in, 243–2
Hungerford
Eleanor, 51A–36
Elizabeth, 51–35
Katherine, 18–34, 51A–36
Robert, 18–34
Robert, L., 51A–35
Thomas, 51A–34
Walter, L., 51–35, 51A–34
Huntingdon
Ada of, 93–27, 93A–27, 100–26, 100A–26
David of Scotland, E. of, 93–26, 94–26, 131–29, 252–26
Earls of. see Hastings; Holand; St. Liz
Henry of Scotland, E. of, 89–25, 93–25, 96–25, 100–25, 119–27, 170–23
Isabella of, 252–27
John (le Scot), E. of, 236–8
Margaret of, 38–26, 94–27, 96–26, 97–26, 119–27, 193–6, 252–26
Maud of, 89–25, 130–26, 170–22
Huntingfield
Joan de, 187–6, 188–6, 238–6
Roger de, 187–1, 187–3, 187–5
William de, 187–2, 187–4, 270B–27
Huntley
Earls of. see Gordon
Hussey
Edmund, 51A–34
Elizabeth, 234A–35
Henry, 234A–35
Joan, 51A–34
Hutchings
Alice, 246G–41
Johane, 246G–41
Hutchinson
Edward, 14–41, 224A–43
William, 14–41, 224A–43
Huxham
Joan, 246G–32
William, 246G–32
Hyde
Cicely de, 230–34
Ralph de, 230–34
Hydon
Margaret de, 214–31
Richard de, 214–31
Hywel
William ap, 84B–31

I
Inge
Joan, 212–32
William, 212–32
Ingoldsby
Anthony, 31E–40, 203–40
Olive, 31E–41, 203–41
Irby
John, 31–39, 31A–39, 31B–39
Olive, 31–39, 31A–39, 31B–39, 31C–39, 31D–39, 31E–39, 85–40, 203–39
Ireland
Anlaf (Olaf) K. of Dublin, 175–1
Aoiffe (Eve) of Leinster, 66–26, 175–7, 261–30
Brian (Borama, Boru) of the Tribes, 175–1, 239–1
Brion, 170–3
Darbforgaill, 239–1, 175–3
Diarmait MacMael nam Bo, K. of Hy Kinsale, 175–3
Diarmait MacMurchada, K. of Leinster, 66–26, 175–6
Domnall Ua Briain, 175–5
Donnchad, K. of Munster, 175–2, 239–1
Donnchad MacMurchada, K. of Dublin, 175–5
Dunlang, K. of Leinster, 239–3
Eochaid Mugmedon, 170–3
Eochaid Muinremur, K. of Dalriada, 170–1
Ercc, K. of Dalriada, 170–1
Feldelm Foltchain, 170–3
Fergus, K. of Dalriada in Argyle, 170–2
Fergus, K. of Dalriada. see also Scotland
Gormflaith of Naas, 175–1, 239–1, 239–2
Loarn, K of Dalriada, 170–1
Mael-Secnaill, K. of, 175–1
Maelcorcre of Leinster, 239–3
Mor, w. of Diarmait MacMurchada, 175–6
Muirchertach Ua Tuathail (O'Toole), 175–6
Murchad, 175–4
Murchad, K. of Leinster, 175–1, 239–2
Niall of the Nine Hostages, 170–3
Olaf Kvaaran, K, of York & Dublin, 239–2
Olaf, of Dublin, 239–3
Orlaith, w. of Donnchad MacMurchada, 175–5
Ragnaillt, 239–4
Sihtric, K. of Dublin, 239–2

Slani, 239–2
St. Patrick, 170–3
Irvine
Alexander, 256–41
Katherine, 256–41
Isaac
Edward, 249–40
Mary, 249–41
William, 249–40
Isingard
W. of Rutpert II, 48–15
Isle-Bouchard
Bartholomew, sn. de l', 183–3
Dangerose (Dangereuse) l', 183–3
Gerberga, w. of Bartholomew, 183–3
Isles
NN dau. of Reginald, L. of the, w. of
Alan, L. of Galloway, 38–26
Reginald, L. of the, 38–26
Italy
see also Friuli; Spoleto
Alexius Charon, Präfect in Italy, 105A–
22
Berengarius I, K. of, 146–16
Berengarius II, K. of, 145–19, 146–18
Bernard, K. of, 50–15
Cunigunde, w. of Bernard, K. of, 50–15
Ermengarde of, dau. of Louis II, 141B–
17
Lothair I, K. of, 140–15, 141B–15, 145–
15, 240–16
Lothair of, 147–19
Louis II, K. of Italy, 141B–16
Louis III the Blind, K. of, 141A–17,
141B–18
Ludwig IV, K. of, 252C–31
Pepin, K. of, 50–14, 182–5
Ivrea
see also Burgundy
Rosela (Susanna) of, 101–21, 146–19,
162–20
Ivry
William d', 215–26

J

James
Thomas, 31E–41, 203–41, 203–42
Jenkyns
Morgan ap, 85–37
Sybil ferch Morgan ap, 85–37
Jermyn
Thomas, 200–38, 257–39
Jernegan
Anne, 257–38

Edward, 257–38
Jerusalem
Amaury I d'Anjou, K. of, 114–28
Amaury I of Rethel, K. of Jerusalem,
118–24
Baldwin I, Ct. of Edessa, K. of, 158A–23
Baldwin II, Ct. of Rethel, K. of, 103–25,
103A–25, 118–24
Baldwin III of Anjou, K. of, 118–24
Fulk V, K. of, 103A–25, 118–24, 129–24
Jean de Brienne, K. of, 114–28, 120–29
Kings. see also Rethel
Johnson
Abraham, 225–42
Isaac, 225–42
Joigny
Adelaide de, Cts. of, 71A–24
Fromond I, 71A–24
Garnie de, 71A–24
Renaud I de, 71A–24
Joinville
see also Geneville
Geoffroi de, 71A–25
Geoffroi III de, 71A–27
Geoffroi IV de, 71A–28, 264–28
Pierre, 71A–31
Roger I de, 71A–26, 71B–26
Simon de, 17–29, 71–30, 71A–29
Jones
Philip, 11–42, 220–42
Ruth, 203–42
Josselyn
George, 211–39
Henry, 211–41, 211–43
John, 211–39, 211–43
Thomas, 211–40, 211–42, 211–43

K

Kärnten
see also Gorz
Meinhard IV (II), D. of, 252A–31
Kaye
Grace, 3–40
John, 3–38
Robert, 3–39
Keith
Egidia (Gille), 256–36
Elizabeth, 256–39
William, 256–36, 256–39
Kemp
Anne, 18–39
Thomas, 18–39
Kempe
Robert, 246A–39

Kendal
see also Tailbois
Avice de Lancaster, 38–25
Christiana of, 34–24, 88–24
Gilbert, Bar., 34–24, 88–24
Gilbert Fitz Roger Fitz Reinfrid, L. of, 88–27
Hawise (Helewise) de Lancaster, 88–27
Ketel, Bar., 34–23, 34–24, 88–24
NN, w. of William I de Lancaster, 88–25
Orm, s. of Ketel, 34–23, 88–24
William I de Lancaster, Bar., 34–24, 38–25, 88–25
William II de Lancaster, Bar., 34–26, 88–26, 265A–27, 270C–27, 41–25
Kennedy
Margaret (Elizabeth), 256–35
Kent
Druella of, 239–1
Eadgifu of, 1–15
Ealhmund, K. of, 1–11
Earls of. see also Burgh; Holand
Edmund of Woodstock, E. of, 236–11, 155–31
Godwin, E. of, 239–1
Joan, Fair Maid of, 47–31, 47C–31, 155–31, 207–36, 236–12
NN dau. of Æthelberht II, 1–11
Sigehelm, E. of, 1–15
Kevelioc
Hugh of. see Chester
Key
Ann, 81C–47
Francis, 81C–46
Francis Scott, 81C–47
John Ross, 81C–47
Keynes
Margaret, 52–40
Nicholas, 52–40
Khazars
Marót, Khagan of Jewis, 243–2
NN, w. of Zoltán, Pr. in Hungary, 243–2
Kidwelly
see also Beauchamp, Beaumont, London,
Hawise de, 72–31
Kiev
Adelaide of, 244–7
Agatha of, 1–20, 158–23, 241–6
Anastasia (Agmunda), dau. of Iaroslav I, 244–6
Anne of, 53–22, 101–22, 141–22, 241–6
Dobronega of, 147–23, 241–5
Euphrosyne of, 242–9

Eupraksiya of, 45–23
Helga (St. Ol'ga) Regent, 241–2
Iaroslav I, Pr. of, 1–20, 53–22, 241–5, 241A–5, 242–5, 244–6
Igor', Pr. of, 241–2
Isialav I, Pr. of, 241A–6
Malusha, w. of Sviatoslav I, Pr. of, 241–3
Mstislav II, Pr. of, 242–8
NN, w. of St. Vladimir I, & dau. of Kuno, Ct. of Ohningen, 241–4
St. Vladimir I, Pr. of, 147–23, 241–4
Sviatopolk II, Pr. of, 147–25
Sviatopolk (Michael), Pr. of, 241A–7
Sviatoslav I, Pr. of, 241–3
Vladimir II Monomakh, Pr. of, 1B–24, 242–7
Vsevolod I, Pr. of, 45–23, 242–6
Zbyslava of, 147–25, 241A–8
Kilconquhar
Adam de, 121C–30
Kildare
Earls of. see Fitz Gerald
Kinnemerland
Dietrich I, Ct. in, 100A–18
Geva, w. of Dietrich I, 100A–18
Kirkeby
Roger de, 247–29
Knightley
Richard de, 31–33
Thomas de, 31–34
William de, 31–33
Knipe
Anne, 81C–44
Thomas, 81C–43
Knollys
Anne, 1–37, 18–38, 228–38
Francis, 1–36, 18–38
Knovill
Bewes de, L., 34–36
Bogo de, 29A–30
Margaret de, 34–36
Knowsley
Katherine, 57–32
Knyvet
Abigail, 4–38
Edmund, 4–36, 188–13, 188–14
Elizabeth, 225–41
Henry, 225–41
John, 4–37, 59–36, 93B–34, 188–10, 188–11, 188–8, 188–9, 216A–32, 218–35, 238–10, 238–8, 238–9
Margaret, 59–36, 238–11
William, 93B–34, 188–12

Krain
Ulrich I, Mrg. of, 252C–24
Kumans
NN dau. of Tugor Khan, 241A–7
Tugor Khan, 241A–7
Kyme
Lords. *see* Tailboys
Lucy, 121D–31, 224–31
Philip de, L., 121D–31, 224–31
Simon de, 261–31
Kynaston
Jane, 1A–36
Roger, 1A–35
Kyrton
Thomas, 253–36
Kytchin
Mary, 197–39
Robert, 197–39

L

la Coche. *see* Zouche
La Marche. *see* Marche
la Marche
see also Lusignan
La Roche
Henry I, Ct. of, 168A–27
Matilda (Maud) de, 168A–27
la Rochefoucauld. *see* Rochefoucauld
la Warre. *see* Warre
La Warre
Lord. *see* West
Lacy
Egidia de, 75A–30, 177B–8
Gilbert de, 70–29, 71–29, 71A–30, 72–29, 177A–8, 246C–28
Henry de, E. of Lincoln, 71–33
Hugh de, 31–27, 177A–7, 177B–7
Hugh de, E. of Ulster, 33A–27
Ilbert de, L. of Pontefract, 18A–24
John de, E. of Lincoln, 18A–28, 54–29
Margaret de, 70–30, 70A–30
Maud de, 18A–28, 54–30, 63–29, 71–30, 71A–30, 148A–26
NN dau. of Hugh de, E. of Ulster, 38–26
Pernel de, 98–28
Roger de, 38–26, 54–29
Walter de, L. of Meath, 70–29, 75A–30, 98–28, 177A–7
Walter, L. of Meath, 177B–7
l'Aigle. *see* Aigle
Laigle. *see* Aigle
Lamporte
Margaret, 150–38

Thomas, 150–38
Lancaster
see also Kendal; Stainton
Blanche of, 1–30, 1A–31, 47C–32
Earls of. *see* Leicester
Edmund "Crouchback", E. of, 17–28, 18–29, 45–30
Eleanor of, 17–30, 20–30, 23–33, 28–33, 78–32, 97–33, 114–31
Elizabeth of, 47C–32, 93B–33, 207–36
Hawise (Helewise) de, 88–28, 136–26, 184B–8
Henry, D. of, 1–30, 47C–32
Henry, E. of, 5–31, 17–29, 18–29, 18A–30, 19–29, 71A–31, 72–32, 94A–33, 161–30
Henry "the Wryneck", E. of, 72–33
Joan of, 16–31, 18–30, 18A–30, 22–33, 47B–32
John of, D. of Bedford, 234B–33
John of Gaunt, D. of, 1–30, 1A–31, 2–31, 8A–33, 47C–32, 62–34, 93B–33, 207–36, 265–35, 234–30
Mary of, 19–30, 161–30
Maud de, 5–31
Langland
Hugh de, 248A–33
Mary de, 234–32, 248A–33
Langley
Grace, 246–34
Langrich
Elizabeth, 12–38
Langston
Jane, 43A–35
John, 43A–35
Langton
Eupheme, 13A–36
Helen de, 9–37
John, 13A–36
Richard de, 9–37
Lantbertus, Ct. in Neustria, 48–12
Lantbertus, in Neustria, 48–10
Lanvallei
Hawise de, 94–29
William de, 94–29
Laon
Berthe of, 50–12, 190–12, 240A–12
Charibert (Herbert), Ct. of, 50–12, 190–12, 240A–11
Gisele, w. of Charibert (Herbert), Ct. of, 240A–11
Larke
Joan, 233–39
Peter, 233–39

Lascaris
Maria, 103–29
Theodore I (Comnenus), 103–29
Lascelles
Agnes, 12A–28
John, 12A–28
Latham
Frances, 11–41, 220–41
Lewis, 11–41, 220–41
Lathom
Isabel de, 57–34, 81A–37
Margaret de, 41–31
Robert de, 57–32
Thomas de, 57–32, 57–33
Latimer
Elizabeth, 99–33
Joan, 114A–28
Lords. see Griffin
Thomas, L., 99–32
William, 114A–28
William, L., 88–31
Launce
John, 13A–40
Mary, 13A–41
Robert, 13A–40
le Boteler. see Boteler
le Botiller. see Butler
le Despenser. see Despenser
le Meschin. see Meschin
le Strange. see Strange
Lee
Dorothy, 198–39
Humphrey, 258–35
Joseph, 81A–42, 81A–43
Mary, 2–42, 81A–43, 121D–40
Richard, 197–38
Lefstan
son of Ongar, 257–27
Legenfeld-Hopfenohe-Pettendorf
Friedrich III, Ct. of, 252C–26
Heilika of, 252C–26
Legh
George, 233–39
Jane, 217A–39
Lucy, 233–43
Peter, 217A–39
Robert de, 233–38
Thomas, 233–38, 233–40, 233–41
Urian, 233–42
Legnica. see Poland
Leicester
Earls of. see also Beaumont
Earls of. see also Lancaster
Robert, E. of, 63A–29

Leigh
Isabel, 248–38
John, 248–36, 248–37
Ralph, 248–36, 248–37
Leinster
Aoiffe (Eve) of, 66–26, 261–30, 175–7
Kings of. see Ireland
Lenham
NN, 261–40
Lens
see also Boulogne
Judith of, 98A–23, 130–25
Lenthall
Katharine, 212–37
Rowland, 212–37
Lenton
Agnes, 14–40
John, 14–40
Leon
see also Castile
Alfonso IX, K. of, 110–28, 114–27, 120–28
Alfonso V, K. of, 113–23, 113A–23
Berengaria of, 114–28, 120–29
Fernando II, K. of, 112–26, 114–26
Fernando III, K. of, 109–30
Sancha of, 113–23
Urraca I, Q. of, 113–24, 132–25
Ximina of, 113A–23
Leon & Castile. see Leon
Lescrope
Henry, 219–33
Joan, 219–33
Leventhorp
Anne, 69–34
John, 69–34
Leventhorpe
Alice, 211–41
Thomas, 85–38
Leverett
Mary, 84–40
Lewis
Andrew, 17–40
Judith, 17–41
Mary, 17–41
Thomas, 17–40
Leyburn
Thomas de, 98–31
Ligon. see Lygon
Lille
Guyotte, Chatelaine de, 234B–28
Jean IV, Chatelaine de, 234B–28
Limbourg
Heinrich III, D. of, 234B–25

Henry II, Ct. of, 155–25
Margaret of, 155–25, 234B–25
Walram IV, D. of, 234B–25
Limburg
Mathilde von, 168A–27
Udo, Ct. of, 168A–27
Limburg-Arlon
Heinrich von, 168A–27
Limesy
John de, L. of Cavendish, 84–26
Limoges
Aisceline de, 185A–3
Geraud, Vcte. de, 185A–3
Lincoln
Earls of. *see* Chester; Lacy
Lindau-Ruppin
Ulrich I, Ct. of, 252B–32
Lindow
Agnes of, 252B–32
Lingen
Isabel, 150–35
Lisle
Gerald de, 18–33
Margaret de, 39–33, 87–33
Warin de, 130–31
Warin de, L., 39–33, 87–33
l'Isle-Bouchard. *see* Isle-Bouchard
Lister
Christopher, 9A–36, 170A–35, 170A–37
John, 9A–36
Lawrence, 9A–36, 170A–35
Rosamond, 9–40, 170A–39
William, 9–40, 9A–37, 170A–36, 170A–38
Littleton
Edward, 1A–40
John, 1A–39
Nathaniel, 1A–41
Lloyd
Agnes, 251–39
David, 251–38
Davis, 251–40
Frances, 251–40
Gruffyd, 251–37
Gwenhwyfar, 251–38
John, 251–39
John ap Davis, 251–40
Richard ap Robert, 251–38
Robert, 251–38
Lluca
Gisla de, 108–23
Sunifredo II de, 108–23
Lobdeburg
Elizabeth of, 252D–31

Hartmann, Bar. of, 252D–31
Lodington
William, 121D–34
Logie
Barbara, 252–39
Lolle
Amee, 230B–37
William, 230B–37
Lomme
Robert I, Ct. of, 149–20
London
Thomas, L. of Kidwelly, 72–31
Longespee
Ela, 31–28, 53–30, 122–30, 207–31
Emmeline, 178–6
Ida, 30–28, 122A–29, 130–30, 184A–9
Stephen, 31–27, 33A–27, 178–6
William, E. of Salisbury, 30–26, 31–26, 33A–27, 108–28, 122–28, 122A–28
William II, E. of Salisbury, 30–27, 122–29
William III, E. of Salisbury, 29A–29, 122–31
Longwy
Albert de, D. of Lorraine, 144–22
Stephanie de, 108–24
Looz
Agnes of, 155–25
Imaine of, 155–25, 155A–25
Louis I, Ct. of, 155–25, 155A–25
Loring
Isabel, 40–33
Margaret, 213–33
Nele, 40–33, 213–33
Lorraine
see also Flanders; Wormsgau
Adelheid, w. of Charles of, 148–19, 149–19
Agatha of, 45–26
Alberade of, 151–19
Bertha of, 145–17
Charles of, 148–19, 149–19
Conrad the Wise, D. of, 45–18, 192–20
Dada (Ida), w. of Godfrey, D. of, 158–22, 158A–22
Dietrich (Thierry) II, D. of, 100A–24
Ermengarde of, 149–20, 164–24
Ezzo, Ct. of, 147–21, 147A–21
Frederick II, D. of, 167–21
Gerald IV, Ct. of Alsace, D. of, 164–24
Gerard of, Ct. of Vaudemont, 144–24
Gerberga of, 50–19, 140–19, 142–19, 148–20, 155–20
Gertrude of, 100A–24

Giselbert, D. of, 50–19, 140–18, 142–
18, 148–18, 151–18, 240–18
Godfrey, D. of, 158–22, 158A–22
Godfrey (or Geoffrey) D. of, 158A–23
Gozelon, D. of, 149–21, 155–21
Helletrude (Ermengarde) of, 240–16
Ida of, 158–22, 158A–22
Lothair II the Saxon, K. of, 145–16
Margarite of (heiress of Flanders), 163–
27, 163A–27, 164–26, 168–27
NN (perh. Ermengarde), 140–16
Oda of, 155–21
Regilinde of, 149–21
Simon I, D. of, 45–26
Thierry I, D. of, 167–21
Thierry I of. see also Flanders
Thierry II, D. of, 164–24
Waldrada, w. of Lothair II the Saxon, K.
of, 145–16
Louthe
Anne, 208–39
Edmund, 208–38
Thomas, 208–37
Louvain
Adeliza of, 1–22, 139–26, 149–25
Godfrey, Ct. of, 161–23
Godfrey I, Ct. of, 149–24, 155–23
Godfrey II, Ct. of, 155–24
Godfrey III, Ct. of, 155–25, 155A–25,
234B–25
Henry II of Brabant, Ct. of, 149–24,
155–22, 160–22
Ida of, 160–23, 163–24
Jocelin of, 161–24
Lambert I, Ct. of, 148–20, 155–20
Lambert II, Ct. of, 155–21
Maud of, 148–21, 158–21
Lovaine
Alice de, 155A–28
Eleanor de, 58–30, 155A–28, 155A–31
Godfrey de, 155A–26
Hawise de, 72–31, 148A–31
Helisent, w. of Matthew de, 155A–28
Joan, w. of John de, 155A–30
Joan, w. of Thomas de, 155A–29
John de, 155A–30
Margaret de, 79–33
Matthew de, 58–30, 72–31, 148A–31,
155A–27, 155A–27, 155A–28
Muriel, w. of Matthew de, 155A–27
Nicholas de, 17–31, 79–32
Thomas de, 155A–29
Lovel
Isabel, w. of John, L., 215–31

Isabel, w. of William, 215–26
James, 213–31
Joan, 51A–32
John, 215–27, 215–28
John, L., 47A–33, 200–31, 212–31,
214–34, 215–29, 215–30, 215–31,
215–32, 215–33
Maud, 200–31, 212–31
Muriel, 213–31
Philippe, 214–34, 215–34
Richard, L., 51A–33, 213–31
William, 215–26
William de, sn. d'Ivry, 215–25
Lowe
Isabel, 81C–42
Patrick, 81C–42
Lowthe. see Louthe
Lowther
Anne, 37–33
Robert, 37–33
Lucelles
Beatrice de, 42–26
Hugh, 42–27
Lucy
Amabel de, 40–27
Aveline de, 184B–5
Maud, 130–28
Reginald de, 40–25
Richard de, 40–26, 130–28, 184B–5
Rohese, w. of Richard de, 130–28,
184B–5
Ludlam
Catherine, 81A–40
William, 81A–40
Ludlow
Benedicta, 56A–36
Gabriel, 12–39, 12–40, 12–41
George, 12–37
John, 56A–36, 150–35
Margery, 150–35
Martha, w. of Gabriel, 12–40
Phyllis, w. of Gabriel, 12–39
Roger, 12–39
Sarah, 12–40, 12–40
Thomas, 12–38, 12–39
William, 12–37
Lugg
John, 84–40
Lundin
Christian, 256–38
John, 256–38
Lungvilliers
John de, 247–27
Margaret de, 247–27

Lusignan
Aiméee de, 271–26
Alice de, 63–30, 83–28, 117–29, 153A–29
Hugh de, 123–28, 275–25
Hugh IV de, 275–21
Hugh V de, 275–21
Hugh VI de, 275–22
Hugh VII de, 183–2, 271–26, 275–23
Hugh VIII de, 123–28, 275–24
Hugh IX de, 275–26
Hugh X de, 80–29, 83–28, 95–30, 117–27, 153A–28, 154–28, 275–27
Hugh XI de, 63–30, 117–28, 135–30, 275–28
Hugh XII de, 135–31, 214A–30, 275–29
Jeanne de, 71–31, 71A–31, 135–32
Maud de. *see* Eu
Orengarde, w. of Hugh de, 275–25
Raoul I de, 123–28
Sarazine, w. of Hugh VII de, 275–23
Lutegareshale
Piers de, 246B–27, 246C–27
Luttrell
Andrew, 12–31, 74A–35
Andrew, L., 74A–34
Elizabeth, 12–33
Geoffrey, 74A–34
Hawise, 74A–36
Hugh, 12–32
Luvetot
Maud de, 148A–28
Richard de, 148A–27
William de, 148A–27
Luxembourg
Conrad I, Ct. of, 163–26
Ermesinde of, 163–26, 234B–25
Frederick I, Ct. of, 100B–22, 143–20, 162–21
Frederick of, D. of Lorraine, 246A–22
Giselbert, Ct. of, 100B–23, 168A–27
Gisele of, 143–21
Guy of, 234B–30
Heinrich, Ct. of, 234B–25
Heinrich II, Ct. of, 168–31, 234B–26, 234B–30
Herman I of, 100B–24
Jacquetta of, 18B–33, 225–39, 234B–33
Jean I of, 234B–29
Jean (John) II of, 234B–31
Judith of, 168A–27
Liutgard of, 100A–20
Ogive (Otgiva) of, 162–21
Philippine of, 168–31
Pierre of, Ct. of St. Pol, 234B–32
Siegfried, Ct. of, 100B–21, 143–19, 100A–20
Valéran II of, 234B–28
Walram I of, 234B–27
Luzarches
Albri de, 109–29, 144–26, 152–26, 272–29
Lygon
Anne, 57–39
Cicely, 209–38
Elizabeth, 84–38
Henry, 84–37, 187–16
Richard, 57–39, 84–36, 84C–36, 209–36
Thomas, 84–35, 84C–38, 84C–39
William, 84C–37, 209–37
Lynde
Enoch, 99–41
Nathan, 99–42
Simon, 99–42
Lynne
Alice, 93B–34, 188–11
William, 188–11
Lyon
Artald (II) III, Ct. of, 107–23
Ida of, 107–23
Lyster. *see* Lister

M

Maasgau
Giselbert, Ct. on the, 240–15
Machell
Ann, 230B–40
Mackall
James, 81B–44
Mackworth
Agnes, 198–41
Humphrey, 198–41
John, 198–39
Richard, 198–40
Thomas, 198–39
MacMurchada
Diarmait. *see* Ireland
MacMurrough
Dermot. *see* Macmurchada
Mâcon
Beatrix of, 118–22, 133–26, 274C–26
Gerard I of Burgundy, Ct. of, 274C–26
William I, Ct. of. *see* Burgundy
Maelog
Ann, 179–4
Ralph, 179–3

Maghull
Eleanor, 23–37
Robert, 23–37
Magnaville
Ernulf de, 148A–27
Magyar. *see* Hungary
Maine
Blichilde of, 144A–16
Erembourg, Cts. of, 118–24, 129–24
Helie de la Flêche, Ct. of, 118–24, 129–24
Richilde of, 49–17
Roger, Ct. of, 49–17
Rorick, Ct. of, 144A–16
Roscelin (Raoul), Vcte of, 98–25
Mainwaring
Agnes, 7–37
Anne, 31–36
Arthur, 56A–41
Margaret, 56A–41
Mary, 56A–42
Maud, 150–32
Oliver, 217A–41, 217A–42, 217A–43
Randall, 56A–41
Richard, 56A–40
Warin, 150–31
William, 31–36
Maister
Agnes, 43–36
John, 43–36
Makerness
Ellen, 43–38
William, 43–38
Malbank
Philippa, 234A–28
Malebisse
Emma, 268–28
Richard, 268–28
Malet
Gilbert, 234A–27
Hawise, 132D–30, 189–2, 234A–29
Mabel, 261–31
Robert, 234A–25
William, 189–1, 234A–25, 261–31
William I, 234A–26
William II, 234A–28
William, L. of Curry Malet, 132D–30
Mallory
Anketil, 16A–32, 16C–32
Margaret, 16A–34, 29B–33, 56B–38
Margaret, w. of William, 16A–33
William, 16A–33, 29B–33
Malpas
Beatrice de, 81–31

Mandeville
Beatrice de, 158A–23
Geoffrey de, 158A–23
Geoffrey de, E. of Essex, 169A–27
Maud de, 246B–27, 246C–27
Maud Fitz Geoffrey de, 97–27
William de, E. of Essex, 143–28, 246B–28
Manfield
Richard, 69–36
Manning
John, 246G–42
Manny
Walter, L., 16–30
Mar
Donald, E. of, 75A–32, 252–30
Isabel of, 75A–32, 252–30
Marbury
Anne, 14–41, 224A–43
Catherine, 14–41
Francis, 14–40
William, 14–40
March
Earls of. *see* Mortimer
Marche
Adalbert I, Ct. of La, 185A–3
Almode of La, 185–2, 185A–5
Almodis La, 275–21
Amelia, w. of Bernard I of La, 185–2
Bernard I, Ct. of La, 185–2, 185A–4, 275–21
Boso I, the Old of La, 185A–2
Hugue XII "le Brun", Ct. de La, 71A–31
Marcillac
Sénégundis de, 271–20
Marco
Arnould IV de, sn. d'Ardres, 272–27
Mare
Joan de la, 210–33
Margaret de la, 261–40
Thomas de la, 261–40
Marisco
Geoffrey de, 178–4
Herbert de, 25–30
Markenfield
Alice, 3–37
Elizabeth, 9A–34
Ninian, 3–36
Thomas, 9A–34
Marle
Lietard de, 273–25
Thomas de Coucy, sn. de, 273–26
Marmion
Agnes, w. of Thomas, 246A–31

Alice, 246A–32
Avice, 30–31, 219–31
Geoffrey, of Checkenden, 246A–28
Isabel, w. of John, 218–29
Joan, 210–35, 218–31
John, L., 30–31, 148A–32, 218–29,
    218–30, 219–30
John, of Checkenden, 246A–30
Maud, w. of William, of Checkenden,
    246A–29
Robert, 246A–25, 246A–26
Robert, the Younger, 218–28
Roger, 246A–25
Rosamund, w. of Geoffrey, 246A–28
Thomas, 246A–31
William, 218–28
William, of Checkenden, 246A–27,
    246A–29
Marrow
Catherine, 201–38
William, 201–38
Marsan
Arnaud-Guillaume de, 16A–29
Claramonde de, 16A–29
Marsh. *see* Marisco
Marshal
Eve, 66–28, 67–28, 68–28, 177–8
Gilbert, 66–27
Isabel, 63–28, 252–28
Joan, 80–28
John (Fitz Gilbert), the, 55–28, 66–27,
    81–28
Margaret, 55–28, 81–28, 122A–29
Maud, 69–28, 70–28, 76–28, 83–27,
    177A–8, 232–28
Sibyl, 127–30, 143–28, 257–30, 261–
    30, 269A–27
Walter, E. of Pembroke, 54–29
William, E. of Pembroke, 55–28, 63–28,
    66–27, 69–27, 76–27, 80–27, 81–28,
    127–30, 143–28, 257–30, 260–30,
    261–30, 269A–27
Marshall
Anne, 12–39
Elizabeth, 17–40, 246G–42
John, 246G–42
Roger, 17–39
Thomas, 12–39
Martel
Ela, 261–33
Joan, 261–33
Joan, w. of Roger, 261–33
Roger, 261–33, 261–34

Martin
Joan, 71–33, 122–32
Nicholas, 63A–31
William, L., 71–33, 122–32
Massey
Alice, 57–34
Edward, 230–35
Ellen, wid. of Edward, 230–35
Hugh, 57–34
Master. *see* Maister
Masterson
Ellen, 150–41
Thomas, 150–41
Mathew
Janet, 199A–35
Thomas, 199A–35
Mathews
Samuel, 18–39
Matthew
Grace, 253–39
John, 253–39
Mauduit
Isabel, 84–28, 84A–28, 86–28, 197–28
Robert, L. of Hanslope, 84–27
Roger, 161–25
Roger de, 121D–31
William, L. of Hanslope, 84–27
Mauléon
Aurengarde de, 183–1, 271–23
Geoffroy de, 271–23
Raoul de, 271–23
Mauleverer
Dorothy, 3–38
Robert, 3–37
William, 3–37
Mauley
Constance de, 156–33
Piers IV de, L., 156–29
Piers V de, L., 64–33, 156–30
Piers VI de, L., 88–33, 156–31, 268–33
Piers VII de, L., 156–32
Maurienne. *see* Savoy
Mautravers
Eleanor, 21–31, 59–34
Gwenthlin, w. of John, 59–33
John, 59–32, 59–33
John, L., 59–32
Maverick
John, 59–35, 261–44
Peter, 261–44
Mayenne
Mathilda of, 105A–27
Meath
Lords of. *see* Lacy

Mechyll
Gwenthlian, 84A–29
Rhys, 84A–29
Meinell
Christine, w. of Nicholas de, L., 268–30
Elizabeth de, 88–33, 156–31, 268–33
Joan de, 265–27
Nicholas de, 268–31
Nicholas de, Bar., 54–34, 88–32, 268–32
Nicholas de, L., 88–31, 268–30
Robert de, 268–24
Robert II de, 268–26
Robert III de, 268–28
Stephen de, 265–27, 268–25
Stephen II de, 268–27
Stephen III de, 268–29
Meisnill. see Meinell
Meissen
Dietrich, Mrg. of, 252D–28
Ekkhard I, Mrg. of, 252D–24
Elizabeth of, 252A–33, 252D–33
Friedrich I, Mrg. of, 252D–31
Friedrich II, Mrg. of, 252A–33, 252D–32
Heinrich, Mrg. of, 252D–29
Mathilde of, 252D–24
Otto II, Mrg. of, 252D–27
Melitene
Gabriel, Armenian gov. of, 103A–25
Morfia (Malfia) of, 103A–25
Mellowes
Abraham, 31A–40
Meopham
Elfreda of, 1–15, 45–16
Ethelhelm, L. of, 1–15, 45–16
Meran
Berthold VI, D. of, 103–28
Gertrude of, 103–28
Merbery
Elizabeth, 56B–37
John, 56B–37
Mercer
Helen, 15A–39
Mercia
Aelfgar, E. of, 176–2, 176A–3
Aelfgifu, w. of Aelfgar, 176A–3
Æthelfrith, E. of, 1B–17
Aethelgifu, w. of Eadric, 1B–18
Burchard, s. of Aelfgar, 176A–3
Eadric, E., 1B–18
Eadwine, s. of Aelfgar, 176A–3
Edith of, 1B–23, 176–2, 176A–4, 177–1
Godgifu (Godiva), w. of Leofric, 176A–2
Leofric, E. of, 176A–2

Leofwine, E. of, 176A–1
Morkere, s. of Aelfgar, 176A–3
Mere
Joan, 253–34
John de la, 253–34
Meriet
Agnes, 124A–35
Merlay
Agnes de, 42–26
Ralph de, L. of Morpeth, 42–24
Roger de, 42–25, 270D–28
William de, 42–24
Merovingians. see France
Merseburg
Dedo I, Ct. of, 252D–23
Merston
Constance de, 42–28
Merton
Agnes de, 25–32
Richard de, 25–32
Meschin
see also Chester
Adeliz (Alice) le, 246B–25
Lucy, w. of Ranulph le, E. of Chester, 125–27, 246B–25
Maud la, 39–27, 132C–27, 136B–27
Ranulph le, E. of Chester, 125–27, 246B–25
William le, 39–27, 40–24, 132B–26
Metz
Arnoaldus, Bishop of, 180–7, 190–9
Bouvin, Ct. of, 49–17
Dode (Clothilde), w. of St. Arnulf, Bishop of, 180–8, 190–8
Hildegarde of, 108–22
Itta of, 190–9
Richaut of, 49–17
St. Arnulf, Bishop of, 180–8, 190–8
St. Clodulf, Bishop of, 190–8
Meulan
Adeline of, 50–24, 151–24
Counts of. see also Beaumont
Waleran, Ct. of, 50–24, 151–24
Middlemoore
Joan, 98–36
Middleton
John, 223–36
Midhope
Anne, 170A–38
Roger, 170A–38
Mildmay
Jane (Joanne), 246–37
Thomas, 246–37

Miles
Katherine, 199–39
Robert, 199–39
Mill
Elizabeth, 234A–35
Thomas, 234A–35
Missenden
Elizabeth de, 42–31
Mitton
see also Mytton
John, 17–36
Joyce, 17–37
Katherine, 17–39
Moëlan
Gautier I de, 264–25
Guy I de, 71A–28
Moels
Joan de, 52–35
John de, L., 51A–32, 214–33
Muriel, 51A–32, 214–33
Nicholas de, 52–34
Roger de, 52–34
Mohaut
John de, 39–29, 39A–29
Leuca de, 150–28
Leucha, w. of Robert de, 150–27
Robert de, 150–27
Roger de, 150–27
Mohun
Adeliz, w. of William de, L. of Dunster, 143–24
Alice de, 246B–29
John de, 257–30
Lucy de, 143–29
Lucy, w. of William de, Bar. of Dunster, 143–26
Margaret de, 28–35
Reynold de, 143–27, 246B–28
Reynold de, L. of Dunster, 143–28, 246B–28
William de, Bar. of Dunster, 143–25, 143–26
William de, E. of Somerset, 143–24
William de, L. of Dunster, 143–24
Moleyns
Catherine, 16–34, 22–34, 136–34
James, 12A–29
Johanna, 12A–29
William, 16–34, 22–34, 136–34
Mollison
Christian, 252–43
Molyneux
Alice, 23–38, 34–41
Richard, 23–34, 23–37, 36–39

Thomas, 23–35, 176B–38
William, 23–36
Moncler
Ermengarde de Walcourt, 71A–29
Jean de, 71A–29
Monçon
Ramiro, Ct. of, 113A–24
Mondeford
Mary, 232–36
Osbert, 232–36
Moneyer
Ranulf the, 269–21
Monmouth
Badeion de, 177A–7
Joan of, 247–26
John of, L. of, 247–26
Rohese de, 177A–7, 177B–7
Monomacha
Maria, 45–23
Mons
Alberade of, 140–17, 155–17, 240–17
Renier V, Ct. of, 163–23
Richilde of, 163–23
Montacute. see Montagu
Montagu
Alice de, 78–35
Anne, 120–37
John de, E. of Salisbury, 11–34, 248–34
John de, L., 8A–31, 263–32
John de, L., E. of Salisbury, 8A–32
Margaret de, 11–34, 135–29, 248–34
Sibyl de, 28–34
Thomas de, E. of Salisbury, 8A–33, 78–34
William de, 15–32
William de, L., E. of Salisbury, 8A–31, 28–34, 29–33, 263–31
Montbéliard
Louis, Ct. of, 144–23, 167–22
Richard II de, Sn. de Montfaucon, 114–28
Sophie de, 114–28
Thierry I, Ct. of, 144–23, 167–23
Montchensy
William de, 122A–30
Montdidier
Beatrix de, 113A–25, 151–23, 153–23, 153A–23
Counts. see Rameru
Montfaucon
Agnes de, 114–28
Richard II de Montbéliard, Sn. de, 114–28

Montferrat
Conrad de, 114–28
Mary de, 114–28
Montfichet
Gilbert de, 184B–5
Margaret de, 136–27, 184B–7, 267A–27
Millicent, w. of Richard de, 184B–6
Richard de, 136–27, 184B–6
William de, 185B–4
Montford. *see* Montfort
Montfort
Agnes de, 50–25
Alice de, 130–31, 143–22
Amauri de, Ct. of Evreux, 50–25
Amaury V de, Ct. of Evreux, 179–1
Amice de Gael de, 53–25, 63–25
Amice de Gaul de, 98A–26
Baldwin de, 86–33, 86–35
Bertrade de, 118–23, 125–28, 126–28, 127–28, 131–28
Eleanor de, 260–31
Hugh, L., 143–22
Isabel (Elizabeth) de, 98A–24
John, 81–33
John de, 86–33
Katharine, 33–36, 86–37
Maud de, 222–33
Peter de, 86–33
Piers de, 130–31, 222–33
Ralph de Gael de, 53–25, 63–35
Ralph de Gael de, E. of Norfolk, 53–25
Robert, 86–36
Simon de, 98A–24, 125–28
Simon de, E. of Leicester, 260–30
Simon I de, 118–23
Simon IV de, 260–30
William de, 86–34
Montfort-sur-Risle. *see* Montfort
Montgomert
Sybil, 63–26
Montgomery
Alice de, 187–3
Arnulph de, 187–3
Ellen, 33–37
Gabriel, Ct. de, 6–39
John, 33–37
Mathilda de, 185–1
Roberte de, 6–39
Roger de, 187–3
Roger de, E. of Shrewsbury, 185–1
Monthermer
Margaret de, 8A–31, 263–32
Ralph de, L., 8A–29, 63–30
Thomas de, L., 8A–30

Montifex
Mary, 252–33
William de, 252–33
Montjoy
Isolda, 258–31
Thomas, 258–31
Montlhéry
Guy de, 107–24, 138–24
Guy I de, Sn., 103A–24
Isabel de, 107–24, 138–24, 264–26
Mélisende de, 103A–24, 246A–24
Milon I, sn. de, 264–26
Montmirail
Jean (John) I de, 272–30, 273–29
Marie de, 272–30, 273–29
Montmorency
Mathieu de, 109–29, 144–27
Montpellier
Maria of, 105A–28
William VII, Sn. de, 105A–27
William VIII, Sn. de, 105A–27
Moore
Jane, 12–37
Nicholas, 12–37
Moray
Earl of. *see* Randolph
Morel
Arkil, 41–23
Sybil, 41–23
Morewike
Hugh de, 266–31
Tiphaine de, 266–31
Morialmé
Elizabeth de, Dame de Fraire, 158C–28
Morpeth
Lords of. *see* Merlay
Mortagne
Everard, sn. de, 168A–26
Ida de, 168A–26
Routrou II, Ct. of, 151–23
Mortain
Agnes de, 108–27
Agnes of, 55–26
Emma of, 110–24, 185–2
Reginald Fitz Roy de. *see* Fitz Roy
Robert, Ct. of, 55–26, 108–27
Robert de, E. of Cornwall, 121–26, 185–1
Morteyn
Edmund de, 42–30
John de, 42–28, 42–29
Lucy de, 42–30

Mortimer
Anne de, 225–34
Blanche de, 263–31
Catherine de, 10–32, 11–34, 87–31, 120–34
Edmund de, 29–32, 65–34
Edmund de, Bar., 9–30, 70–32, 120–32, 176B–30, 207–30, 265–32
Edmund de, E. of March, 5–32, 29–34, 47D–33, 225–32
Elizabeth, 5–33, 18–35, 19–32
formerly de Mortimer. see Zouche
Hawise de, 136–24
Hugh, 18–35
Hugh de, L., 132C–27, 136B–27
Isabella, 77–30
Isabella de, 28–30, 149–29
Isolde de, 9–30, 186–5, 207–31, 265–32
Joan de, 71–33, 122–33, 176B–32
John, 18–35
Katherine de, 26–32
Margaret, 176B–34
Margaret de, 39–31
Maud de, 70–32
Millicent, w. of Ralph de, L. of Wigmore, 136–24
Ralph de, L., 132C–29, 176B–28
Ralph de, L. of Wigmore, 136–24
Roger, 176B–34
Roger de, Bar., 28–29, 67–29, 77–29, 176B–29
Roger de, E. of March, 10–32, 29–32, 29–33, 39–31, 47D–33, 71–32, 71A–32, 120–33, 176B–31, 225–33, 263–31
Roger de, L., 132C–28
Thomas, 257–34
William de, 189–5
Morton
Elizabeth, 18–36
Robert, 18–36
Morville
Ada de, 40–26
Elena de, 38–25
Hugh de, 40–26, 88–26, 265A–27, 270C–27
Richard de, 38–25
William de, 38–25
Morvois
Bertha de, 50–17, 53–18
Bertha of, 118–17
Guerri I, Ct. of, 50–17, 118–17

Moseley
Anne, 81B–41, 81C–41
Humphrey, 81B–41, 81C–41
Mostyn
Elizabeth, 251–39
Thomas, 251–39
Mote
Edmund de la, 62–32
Joan de la, 2–32, 62–32
Mouchy
Dreux IV of, 273–29
Ermengarde of, 273–29
Mountjoy
see also Montjoy
Lord. see Blount
Mowbray
Ann de, 18B–36
Avice (agnes) of, w. of William, 18A–26
Christianna, 170–29
Eleanor, 18–31, 47B–32, 202–34
Isabel de, 18A–33
Joan de, 223–34
John de, L., 16–31, 18–30, 18A–29, 18A–30, 18A–31, 18B–33, 18B–34, 18B–35, 47B–32, 202–34, 223–33
Mabel, w. of Nele, 18A–25
Margaret, 22–33
Margaret de, 16–33, 18A–33
Nele de, 18A–25
Robert, E. of Northumberland, 18A–23
Roger de, 18A–24, 18A–27
Roger, L., 18A–28
Thomas de, 18A–32, 18A–33
Thomas de, D. of Norfolk, 15–32, 16–32
Thomas de, L., 18B–32, 47C–33
William de, 18A–26
Moyle
Loveday, 217A–42
Richard, 217A–42
Mudie
David, 256–43
Janet, 256–43
Mullett
Winifred (Wolseley), 81B–43
Mulso
Anne, 208–37
William, 208–36
Multon
Elizabeth de, 40–31
Ida, w. of Thomas de, 40–28
Lambert de, 40–27
Thomas de, 40–26, 40–27, 40–28, 40–29
Thomas de, L., 40–30, 75–32

Munchanesy
William de, 246B–27, 246C–27
Munchensi
Joan de, 80–29, 93A–29, 154–29
Warin de, 80–28
Munnings
Anne, 246A–38
Margaret, w. of Thomas, 246A–38
Thomas, 246A–38
Munster
Kings of. see Ireland
Munter
Anne, 246E–41
Mrs. Julian, 246E–41
Murdac
Geoffrey, 270–26
Geoffrey de, 88–26
Mure
Adam, 252–32
Elizabeth, 252–32
Muscegros
Hawise de, 57–31, 61–31, 189–5
John de, 189–3
Robert de, 189–2, 189–4, 234A–29
Muschey
Joan, 136–31
Musters
Elizabeth, 208–34
Muston
Elizabeth, 249–39
Myles
Ann, w. of Samuel, 228–42
John, 228–41
Samuel, 228–42
Mytton
see also Mitton
John, 17–36, 98–36, 98–37
Richard, 98–34
William, 98–35

N

Namur
Adelaide (Alix) of, 163–26
Adelaide of, 149–23
Albert I, Ct. of, 149–20, 164–24
Albert II, Ct. of, 149–21
Albert III, Ct. of, 149–22, 163–26,
168A–27, 246A–22
Alice of, 135–28
Elizabeth of, 246A–24
Godfrey, Ct. of, 163–26
Godfrey of, 246A–23
Hadwide of, 164–24
Henry I, Ct. of, 168A–27

Nanseglos
Mary, 43–35
William, 43–35
Nansicles. see Nanseglos
Naples
Charles I, K. of, 104–28
Charles II, K. of, 103–31, 104–29
Margaret of, 103–32
Narbonne
Ferreolus, senator in the region of, 180–
5
Tonantius Ferreolus, senator of, 180–4
Navarre
see also Aragon
Blanche of, 113–26, 113A–26
Garcia VII, K. of, 113A–25
Henry III (1), K. of, 45–30, 101–30
Jeanne of, 45–31, 101–30
Ramiro, Ct. of Monçon, 113A–24
Neale
Jane, 85–39, 245–40
John, 85–39
Needham
Dorothy, 7–39, 150–42
Robert, 7–37, 7–38
Thomas, 7–37
Negus
Jonathan, 84–40
Nerford
Maud, 231–31
Neuchâtel. see Neuenberg
Neuenberg
Agnes of, 263–29
Rudolf I of, 263–29
Ulrich II of, 263–29
Ulrich III, Ct. of, 263–29
Neufmarche
Bernard de, L. of Brecon, 177–3
Geoffrey, 177–3
Sibyl de, 177–4, 193–4, 237–4, 262–28
Thurcytel, 177–3
Nevers
Aremburge of, 108–22
Ermengarde de, 107–24, 138–24
Henry I, Ct. of, 108–22
Renaud I, Ct. of, 107–21
Renaud II, Ct. of, 107–23
William I, Ct. of, 107–22
Nevill. see Nevill
Neville
Alexander, 204–36
Alice de, 78–36, 219–35
Alice, w. of William, 204–38
Catherine, 18B–33

Cecily de, 225–35
Edward, 201–39
Eleanor, 3–33, 19–33, 207–35
Elizabeth, 265–31
Geoffrey de, 247–25
Geoffrey de, of Hornby, 247–27
Geoffrey de, of Raby, 247–26
George, 201–39
George, L. Abergavenny, 225–38
Isabel, 225–36
Isabel de, 247–25
Jane, 2–35, 3–35
John, 2–34
John de, L., of Raby, 2–32, 205–34,
    207–33
Katherine, 2–38, 41–36, 201–39
Margaret de, 19–31, 35–34, 46–34,
    186–6, 247–31
Phillippe, 5–35
Ralph, 2–33, 2–37, 10–34, 204–39
Ralph de, E. of Westmorland, 2–32, 2–
    33, 3–32, 5–35, 10–33, 18B–33, 78–
    35, 207–34, 225–35
Ralph de, of Raby, 186–5, 207–32, 265–
    32
Ralph of Scotton, 265–31
Ranulph de, L., of Raby, 186–4
Richard de, 78–35
Richard de, E. of Warwick & Salisbury,
    78–36, 225–36
Robert de, 186–4
Robert de, of Hornby, 247–28, 247–29,
    247–30
Thomas, L. Furnivalle, 8–34
William, 204–37, 204–38
Newberry
    see also Newburgh
    Richard, 253–39
    Thomas, 253–40
Newborough. see Newburgh
Newburgh
    see also Newberry
    Alice, w. of Thomas, 253–36
    John, 253–34, 253–35
    John de, 253–33
    Richard, 253–38
    Thomas, 253–36
    Walter, 253–37
Newenham
    Anne, 150–38
    William, 150–38
Newgate
    Hannah, 99–42

Newmarch
    Elizabeth, 2–34
    Hawise de, 52–34
    James de, 52–34
    Robert, 2–34
Newton
    Ellen, 2–42, 121D–41
    John, 121D–37, 121D–38, 121D–39
    Lancelot, 2–42, 121D–40
    Marie, w. of John, 121D–39
Nichols
    Elizabeth, 211–42
    Isaac, 69–40
    John, 211–42
    Mary, 69–40
Noel
    Alice, 56–28
    Charles, 17–34
    Thomas, 56–28
Nola
    Niccoló Orsini, Ct. of, 234B–32
Nonant
    Alice, 217–36, 246B–31, 246E–31
    Roger, 217–36, 246E–31, 246B–31
Nordgau
    Eberhard, Ct. in the, 100B–21, 143–19
    Hedwig, dau. of Eberhard, Ct. in the,
        100B–21, 143–19
Nordmark
    Bernard I, Mrg. of, 100A–21
    Dietrich, Mrg. of, 252D–23
    Hidda of, 252B–24
    Othelendis, 100A–21
    Udo I, Mrg. of, 252B–24
Norfolk
    see also England, Thomas of Brotherton
    dau. of Gilbert de, L. of Beeston, 232–
        29
    Dukes of. see Howard; Mowbray
    Earls of. see Bigod
    Joan of, 59–36
    Margaret, Dss. of, 16–30, 16B–30, 155–
        31
    Thomas of Brotherton, E. of, 16–29,
        155–31
Normandy
    Adela of, 137–23, 139–23, 169–24
    Adelaide (Judith) of, 132–23
    Adelaide of, Cts. of Aumale, 130–24,
        136–23, 148–22
    Adele (Gerloc) of, 121E–18, 144A–19
    Agatha du Hummet. see Hummet
    Alice of, 132A–24

Emma of, 1–18, 132A–25, 235–19, 250–20
Ganger Rolf "the Viking", 121E–18, 243A–17
Ganger Rolf "the Viking". *see also* Rollo
Geoffrey V, D. of. *see* Anjou
Hawise of, 119A–22, 214–22
Herleve, mistress of Robert I, D. of, 121–23, 121E–22, 130–23
Judith of, 166–23
Papia of, 177–3
Poppa, w. of Richard II, D. of, 121E–21
Ranulph the Rich, in, 130–26
Richard I, D. of, 1–18, 118–23, 119–24, 119A–22, 121E–20, 177–3, 184–1, 214–22, 235–19, 250–20
Richard II, D. of, 121–22, 121E–21, 132–22, 132A–22, 166–22
Richard III, D. of, 128–22, 132A–23, 162–22, 166–22
Robert I, D. of, 121–23, 121E–22, 130–23
Rollo, D. of, 121E–18, 243A–17
Sprota, w. of William I, 121E–19
William I the Conqueror. *see* England
William II, D. of. *see* England
Norreys
John, 16–34
Norris
Henry, 6–38
Katherine, 6–38
Lord, 6–38
North Wales
see also Wales; South Wales
Angharad ferch Llywelyn ap Iorwerth, Pr. of, 254–29
Angharad ferch Maredudd ap Owain, 176A–1
Angharat of Tegaingl, dau. of Owain ap Edwin, 239–5
Christina ferch Gronw ap Owen ap Edwin, 176B–25
Cynan ap Iago, Pr. of, 239–4
Dyddgu, of Builth, 176B–24
Edwart Trevor ap David ap Ednyfed Gam, 249–36
Ellen of, 236–8
Fychan ap Gwilym of, 199–35
Gladys Dhu of, 132C–29, 176B–28, 177–7
Gladys, w. of Owain I Gwynedd, 176B–25, 239–6
Griffith, son of Ragnaillt, 239–5
Gruffydd ap Llywellyn, 260–31

Gruffydd I ap Llywelyn, Pr. of, 1B–23, 66–28, 176–2, 176A–4, 177–1, 237–4
Gryffydd ap Cynan, 176B–26
Helen, dau. of Llywelyn ap Iorwerth, 184A–9
Iorwerth Drwyndwn, Pr. of, 176B–26
Joan, Pss. of, 27–'27, 29A–27, 176B–27, 236–7, 254–28
Llywarch ap Trahaern, 176B–24
Llywelyn ap Gruffydd, 260–31
Llywelyn ap Iorwerth, Pr. of, 27–'27, 29A–27, 132C–29, 176B–27, 177–7, 236–7, 246–30, 254–28, 260–31, 184A–9
Llywelyn ap Seisyll, Pr. of, 176A–1
Maredudd ap Owain ap Hywel Dda, 176A–1
Margaret ferch Llywelyn ap Iorwerth, 29A–28, 246–30
Nesta of, 176–3, 176A–4, 177–2
Owain ap Edwin, 239–5
Owain I Gwynedd, Pr. of, 176B–25, 239–6
Susanna, w. Iorwerth Drwyndwn, 176B–26
Tangwystl, mistress of Llywelyn ap Iorwerth, 176B–27, 177–7
Northampton
Earls of. *see* Bohun
Northcote
John de, 52–35
Northeim
Gertrude von, 100B–25
Heinrich, Ct. of, 100B–25
Ida of, 252D–25
Otto, Ct. of, 252D–25
Northumberland
Alice of, 98A–24, 143–25
Ealdgyth of, 34–21, 172–20, 247–20
Earls of. *see* Dunbar; Huntingdon; Mowbray; Percy
Sigurd, E. of, 98A–23, 130–25
Uchtred, E. of, 34–20, 170–18, 247–20
Waltheof II, E. of, 98A–23, 130–25
Northumbria
Ælfgifu, of, 1–18, 34–19, 34–20
dau. of Siward, Danish E. of, 170–20
Thored, E. of, 1–18, 34–19
Tostig, E. of, 166–23
Waltheof, E. of, 34–20, 170–18
Norton
Margaret, 246G–36
William, 246G–36

Norway
Alfhilde, w. of Gudröd, 243A–15
Alfrim, 243A–15
Asa, w. of Gudröd, 243A–15
Asta, w. of Harold "Grenski", 243A–20
Björn, 243A–18
Cacilie, w. of Gudröd, 243A–19
Eric "Bloodaxe", 243A–18
Eystein Glumra, E. of Upplands, 121E–
16, 243A–17
Ganger Rolf, the Viking (aka Rollo, D. of
Normandy), 121E–18, 243A–17
Gudbrand Kula, 243A–20
Gudröd, 243A–15, 243A–19
Halfdan, the Black, 243A–16
Halfdan, the Old, 121E–14
Halfdan "White-Leg", 243A–15
Harald "Goldbeard", 243A–16
Harald "Grenski", 243A–20
Harald I, K. of, 121E–16, 243A–17
Harold, K. of Agdar, 243A–15
Hiltrude (Raginhilde), dau. of Hrolf
Nefia, 121E–17
Hrolf Nefia, 121E–17
Ivar Oplaendinge, 121E–15
Ragnhild, w. of Halfdan, the Black,
243A–16
Ragnvald I, 121E–17
Sigurd Hiort, 243A–16
St. Olaf II, K. of, 243A–21
Swanhild of, 121E–16, 243A–17
Thora, w. of Halfdan, the Black, 243A–
16
Ulfhilde (Wulfhilde), 243A–22
Norwich
Katherine de, 247–30
Margaret de, 11–32
Walter de, 11–32
Nottingham
Henry de, 246A–30
Margery de, 246A–30
Novgorod
dau. of Dmitrii?? I, Pr. of, 242–8
Riurik, Pr. of, 241–1
Nuremberg
Friederich V, Brg. of, 252D–33
Friedrich III, Brg. of, 252A–28, 252A–30
Friedrich IV, Brg. of, 252A–31
Friedrich V, Brg. of, 252A–33
Friedrich (VI) I, Brg. of, 252A–34, 252C–
34
Johan (Hans) II, Brg. of, 252A–32
Konrad I, Brg. of, 252A–29

O
O'Brien
dau. of Donnell, 177B–8
Donnell, 177B–8
Odingsells
Ida d', 86–32
Margaret de, 30–'30
William de, 30–29, 86–32
Ogilvie
Janet, 256–40
Ogle
Anne, 223–36
Robert, 223–35
Oilli
Robert II d', 265A–23
Oilly
Henry d', 84–26
Margery d', 84–26
Oisy
Fastré II d', in Tournay, 168A–25
Nicholas d', sn. d'Avesnes, 168A–27
Wauter (Walter) I d', sn. d'Avesnes,
168A–26
Oldenburg
Agnes, w. of Christian III, Ct. of, 252E–
28
Christian I, Ct. of, 252E–26
Christian III, Ct. of, 252E–28
Christian IV, Ct. of, 252E–30
Christian XI, Ct. of, 252E–33
Christian XIV (I), K. of Denmark, Ct. of,
252E–35
Dietrich, Ct. of, 252E–34
Hedwig, w. of Christian IV, Ct, of, 252E–
30
Johan I, Ct. of, 252E–29
Johan II, Ct. of, 252E–31
Konrad I, Ct. of, 252E–32
Margaret of, 252–36, 253E–36
Moritz I, Ct. of, 252E–27
Oliver
Sibyl, 246B–30, 246G–31
Walter, 246B–30
Orchard
Joan, 246G–37
John, 246G–37
William, 246G–37
Orlamünde
Adelheid of Weimer, heiress of, 252B–
26
Otto, Ct. of, 252B–26, 252C–24
Orléans
Engeltrude, w. of Eudes, Ct. of, 148–15

Ermentrude of, 1–13, 148–15, 162–16
Eudes, Ct. of, 1–13, 148–15
Hadrian, Ct. of, 48–16
Waldrat, w. of Hadrian, Ct. of, 48–16
Wiltrud (Waldrada), 48–16
Ormond
Earls of. *see* Boleyn; Butler
Orreby
Agnes de, 150–27, 150–29
Philip de, 150–28
Orsini
Niccoló, Ct. of Nola, 234B–32
Sueva, 234B–32
Oslac
Fa. of Osburga, 1–13
Ostrevant
Eldegarde, w. of Raoul de Gouy, Ct. d',
250–17
Hucbald, Ct. d', 250–16
Raoul de Gouy, Ct. d', 250–17
Oswestry
Lords of. *see* Mortimer
Other
Fa. of Walter, 12A–21
O'Toole
Muirchertach, 175–6
St. Laurence, 175–6
Overton
Cutler, 31A–39, 31B–39
Rose, 31A–39, 31B–39
Owpye
Elizabeth, 25–35
Oxenbridge
Daniel, 201–41
John, 201–41, 201–42
Theodora, 201–43
Oxford
Earls of. *see* Vere
Oyly
see also Oilly
Geoffrey d', 40–27
Ida, wid. of Geoffrey d', 40–27

P

Pabenham
Alice, w. of Thomas, 136–30
Katherine, 136–31, 187–10
Lawrence, 136–30, 187–10
Thomas, 136–30
Paganel. *see* Paynel
Pagrave. *see* Palgrave
Palgrave
Anna, w. of Richard, 15–39

Edward, 15–38
Elizabeth, 15–40
Henry, 15–36
John, 15–36
Mary, 15–40
Richard, 15–39
Sarah, 15–40
Thomas, 15–37
Palmes
William, 228–41
Pantuff
Iseult, 16C–27
William, 16C–27
Papworth
NN, 16A–33
Paris
Counts of. *see* France
Hugh Magnus, Ct. of. *see* France
Parke
Robert, 43A–40
Parminter
Ralph de, 257–29
Parr
Agnes, 41–34
Elizabeth, 78–39, 150–39
Katherine, 150–39
Thomas, 41–34
William, 78–37, 150–39
William, Bar., 78–38
Passau
Ulrich the Rich, Ct. of, 137–24
Uta of, 137–24
Pateshull
Hawise, w. of John, 184A–11
John de, 85–31, 184A–11, 184A–12,
263–31
Sibyl de, 85–31, 184A–13, 263–32
Simon de, 184A–11
Patrick
Isabel, 81–31
William, 81–31
Paty
Joan, 52–44
Paulet
Christina, 52–41
George, 233–39
William, 52–41
Pauncefort
Jane, 197–38
Richard, 197–38
Paveley
Margaret, 234A–31
William, 234A–31

Pavely
Alice de, 213–32
John de, 213–32
Pavole
Margaret, 253–31
Walter, 253–31
Paynel
Alice, 156–25
Fulk, 55–25
Gervase, 55–27, 81–27
Hawise, 55–27, 81–27
Jordan, 268–24
Ralph, 55–26, 81–27
William, 143–27, 156–25
Pecche
Katherine, wid. of John, 258–32
Peche
Hugh de, 16B–25
Peele
Margaret, 86–34
Peirsey
Abraham, 18–39
Pelham
Edward, 1–40
Elizabeth, 228–40
Herbert II, 1–38
Herbert III, 1–39, 69A–41
Herbert, the elder, 18–39, 228–39
Herbert, the younger, 18–39, 228–39
Penelope, 1–39, 1–40
Pell
Thomas, 12–40
Pembroke
Earls of. see Marshal; Valence
Pembrugge
Fulke de, 56–30, 56A–31, 56A–32, 56A–34
Isabel, w. of Fulke de, 56A–31
Juliana de, 56A–34, 63A–35
Maud, w. of Fulke de, 56A–32
Robert de, 56A–33, 63A–35
Pennington
Anne, 37–34
Elizabeth, 41–35
John, 37–34, 41–35
Penthièvre
Eudes I, Co-Regeant of, 226–23
Eudes I, Ct. of, 214–23
Orguen, w. of Eudes I, Ct. of, 214–23
Perche
Enguerrand II de Coucy, Ct. of. see Coucy
Geoffrey IV, Ct. of, 113A–25, 151–23, 153–23, 153A–23

Juliana of, 113A–25
Margaret de, 151–24
Maud de, 153A–24
Routrou III, Ct. of, 153–24
Percy
Agnes de, 161–24
de, 266–28
Elizabeth, 5–34, 26–34
Henry, 5–33
Henry de, 153A–30, 161–25, 161–27
Henry de, L., 11–32, 19–30, 19–31, 161–28, 161–29, 161–30, 186–6, 205–33, 206–33
Henry, E. of Northumberland, 3–33, 3–34, 19–33, 207–35
Henry "Hotspur", 19–32
Ingram de, 261–32
Isabel de, 206–34
Katherine, 207–36
Margaret, 2–36, 3–35, 11–32
Maud, 205–34, 207–33
Maud de, 2–32
William de, 161–24, 161–26
William de, of Kildale, 266–28
Périgord
Counts of. see Marche
Emma of, 185A–2
Perkins
Elizabeth, 202–41
John, 246A–42
Mary, 246A–42
Thomas, 202–41
Peshale
Adam de, 98–33, 216–32
Margaret de, 98–34
Robert de, 18A–29
Petau
Genevieve, 252–40
Gideon, 252–40
Peverel
Joan, 136–29
Robert, 136–29
Peverell
Catherine, 51–35, 51A–34
Thomas, 51–35, 51A–33
Peyton
Christopher, 246–37
Francis, 246–36
John, 246–32, 246–33, 246–34
Margaret, 246–38
Robert, 246–35
Thomas, 246–35
Peyvre
Mary, 213–33

Thomas, 213–33
Philip
    Jenkyns ap, 85–37
    John, 8A–33
Picot
    Agnes, 187–3
    Alice, 234A–27
    Ralph, 234A–27
    William, 187–3
Picquigny
    Arnould de, 272–26
    Millesende de, 272–26
Picts
    Kings of the. *see* Scotland
Pigot
    Bartholomew, 170A–38
    Bridget, 9–40, 170A–38
Pigott
    Elizabeth, 251–40
    Thomas, 251–40
Pilkington
    Edmund, 34–36
    Elizabeth, 34–36
    John, 34–35, 34–36, 99–35
    Lora, 170–32
    Margaret, 99–35
    Roger, 34–35
    Thomas, 34–36
Pipard
    Margaret, 39–33
    William, 39–33
Pitres
    Roger de, 177–4, 237–4
Plaiz
    John, L., 218–34
    Margaret, 218–34
(Plantagenet)
    Geoffrey V, Ct. of Anjou. *see* Anjou
    Richard, D. of York, 225–35
Plantagenet. *see* Anjou, England, Surrey
Plescy
    see also Plessis
    Christine, 58–31
    Hugh de, 58–31
Plessis
    see also Plescy
    Christian du, 16B–28
    Grimald du, 18A–21
    Hugh du, 16B–28
Pleurs
    Hugue de, 151A–23

Plumpton
    Alice de, 170–30, 170A–30
    Katharine, 212–37
    Robert, 170–28
    William, 212–37
    William de, 170–29, 170A–30
Poitou
    Ada, w. od Ranulf II, Ct. of, 144A–17
    Adelaide of, 53–20, 101–20, 106–20,
        107–19, 141–20, 144A–20
    Agnes of, 45–22, 111–25, 271–25
    Aremburge, w. of Ebles Mancer, 144A–
        18
    Ebles Mancer, Ct. of, 144A–18
    Emiliane, w. of Ebles Mancer, 144A–18
    Ermengarde, mother of Ebles Mancer,
        144A–18
    Geoffrey (William), Ct. of, 110–23
    Ranulf II, Ct. of, 144A–17
    William I, Ct. of, 110–23, 121E–18,
        144A–19
    William II, Ct. of, 110–23
    William III, Ct. of, 45–22
    William VII, Ct. of, 110–24, 111–24,
        183–4, 185–3, 271–25
    William VIII, Ct. of, 110–25
Poland
    Adeljda of, 243–4
    Barbara of Legnica, 252B–34
    Beatrix of Swidneca, 252C–31
    Boleslas I, D. of Silesia, 252C–31
    Boleslas II, D. of Legnica, 252C–31
    Boleslaw III, K. of, 147–25, 241A–8
    Bolko I, D. of Jawar & Swidnica, 252B–
        34, 252C–31
    Casimir (Kazimierz) I, K. of, 241–5
    Gertrude of, 241A–6
    Heinrich I, D. of Silesia, Krakow &,
        252C–31
    Heinrich II, D. of Silesia, Krakow &,
        252C–31
    Judith of, 252B–29
    Kazimierz (Casimir) I, K. of, 147–23
    Mieszislav I of, 243–4
    Mieszislav II, K. of, 147–22, 243–6
    Mieszko II, K. of, 241A–6
    Mieszko III, Pr. of, 252B–29
    Richenza (Rixa) of, 113–25, 116–25,
        147–22, 147–27, 243–6, 244A–6
    Rogneda of, 241–4
    Rogvolod, Pr. of, 241–4
    Ruprecht, D. of Legnica, 252B–34
    Wladislas I, K. of, 147–24

Wladislas II, K. of, 147–26, 252B–29, 252C–31
Pole
Anne de la, 18–33
Cardinal Reginald, 225–38
Catherine de la, 218–33
Geoffrey de la, 225–37
Henry, L. Montagu, 225–38
Katharine de la, 257–36
Katherine, 225–39
Margaret de la, 247–30
Michael de la, 18–33
Michael de la, E. of Suffolk, 247–30
Richard de la, 225–37
Thomas de la, 257–36
William de la, 218–33
William de la, E. of Suffolk, 247–30
Pollard
Elizabeth, 234A–36, 246E–37
Richard, 25–33, 234A–36, 246E–37
Pomerai
Henry I de la, 195–26
Henry II de la, 195–27
Jocelyn de la, 195–26
Rohese de, 124A–29
Pomeroy
Anne, 261–39
Henry, 261–39
Henry de, 124A–29
Henry III de la, 195–28
Henry IV de la, 195–29
Pontefract
Lords of. *see* Lacy
Ponthieu
see also Dammartin, Clermont; Talvas
Agnes of, 108–25
Enguerrand II, Ct. of, 130–24, 148–22
Guy I, Ct. of, 108–25
Guy II, Ct. of, 109–26
Hugh II, Ct. of, 130–24
Ida, w. of Guy II, Ct. of, 109–26
John I, Ct. of, 109–27, 169A–28
Marie, Cts. of, 109–29, 144–27
Matilda, w. of John I, Ct. of, 109–27
William II Talvas, Ct. of, 109–28
Popes
Gregory V, 45–20
Leo IX, 163–23, 167–22
Porhoët
Eudo, Ct. of, 214A–28
Eudon I, Vct. of, 39–25
Geoffrey, Vct. of, 39–26, 136B–28
Guethenoc, Vct. of Chateautro·en, 39–23

Hawise, w. of Geoffrey, Vct. of, 39–26
Margaret, w. of Eudo, 214A–28
Maud of, 214A–28
Port
John, 233A–39
Portugal
Alfonso I, K. of, 112–25, 274B–25
Henry I, Ct. of, 112–24
Urraca of, 112–26, 114–26
Poultney
Thomas, 99–38
Power
Hopestill, 11–42
Powys
Gwladus of, w. of Rhys ap Tudor Mawr, Pr. of N. Wales, 178–1
Madog ap Maredudd of, 176B–26
Marared of, w. of Iorwerth Drwyndwn, Pr. of N. Wales, 176B–26
Rhiwallon ap Cynfyn, 178–1
Poynings
Agnes, 257–34
Eleanor de, 3–34
Luke, 11–33
Michael, L., 257–34
Richard de, 3–34
Robert, L., 3–34
Poyntz
Anne, w. of Robert, 234A–34
Hugh, 132D–30, 189–2, 234A–29
Hugh de, 253–31
Hugh, L., 234A–31
Humphrey, 234A–36, 246E–37
John, 84B–32, 234A–33, 234B–35
Katherine, 234A–37
Margaret, 253–33
Maud, 155A–28
Nicholas, 132D–29, 234A–29, 234A–30, 234A–35, 234B–35
Nicholas de, 253–32
Nicholas, L., 234A–32, 253–30
Robert, 234A–34, 234B–35
William, 246E–37
Wilmot, 246E–37
Prayers
Thomas, 155A–31
Preaux
Peter de, 50–28
Prescott
Alice, w. of William, 34–40
James, 23–38, 34–40, 34–41
William, 34–40

Presfen
 Margaret, 88–34
 William, 88–34
Prestwich
 Rose, 99–38
 William, 99–38
Prestwick
 Alice, 230–36
 Ralph, 230–36
Preuilly
 Agatha de, 275–26
 Peter II de, 275–26
Price
 Elizabeth, 246G–42
Prideaux
 Elizabeth, 234A–39
 Fulk, 234A–37
 Humphrey, 234A–38
 William, 234A–37
Prior
 Matthew, 11–42
 Sarah, 11–42
Profitt
 Elizabeth, 69–36
 John, 69–36
Prouz
 Alice, 52–34
 Julian le, 52–36
 Margaret, w. of Richard, 217–34
 Richard, 217–33, 217–34
 Thomasine, 217–35
 William le, 52–32, 52–33, 52–36, 217–
  32
Provence
 see also Arles; Italy
 Alfonso, Ct. of, 111–28
 Beatrix of, 104–28
 Constance of, 53–21, 101–21, 107–20,
  108–21, 128–21, 141–21, 141A–19,
  141A–21, 185–2
 Counts of see also
 Eleanor of, 1–26, 17–27, 111–30
 Emma of, 185–2
 Ermengarde of, 136–21, 137–21
 Gerberga of, 111–26
 Raymond V Berenger, Ct. of, 101–28,
  104–28, 111–29, 133–27, 147–27,
  274C–28
 William II, 53–21
 William II, Ct. of, 101–21, 141A–20
 William II, Mrq. of, 136–21, 137–21
Prowse
 Agnes, 246G–41
 George, 246G–38

 John, 246G–35, 246G–37, 246G–39
 John II, 246G–40
 Lawrence, 246G–37, 246G–42
 Richard, 246G–36
 Richarda, 246G–38
 Robert, 246G–38, 246G–39
Prutteston
 Joan, 246E–35, 246F–35
 John, 246E–35, 246F–35
Puleston
 Angharad, 249–36
 Jane, 199–36
 Richard, 249–35
 Robert, 249–35
Pulteney
 John de, 79–32
Purefoy
 Edward, 143–38
 John, 143–39
 Mary, 143–39
 Nicholas, 143–38
Pyle
 Jane, 12–38
 Thomas, 12–38
Pynchon
 John, 57–43
 William, 57–43
Pyne
 Joanna, 25–33
 Thomas de, 124A–34
Pype
 Robert, 56A–37

Q

Quarles
 John, 15A–35
 Margery, 15A–35
Quincy
 Arabella de, 56–28
 Elena (Ellen) de, 53–29
 Elizabeth de, 114A–27, 121D–30, 224–
  29
 Hawise de, 50–29, 60–28, 184A–9, 214–
  30, 236–9
 Helen de, 38–28
 Margaret de, 54–29, 57–29, 58–29, 59–
  29, 127–30, 189–4
 Robert de, 184A–9
 Robert de, E. of Winchester, 189–4
 Robert de, L. of Buckley, 53–27
 Robert II de, 54–28, 125–29, 236–8
 Roger de, E. of Winchester, 38–27, 53–
  28, 57–28, 114A–27, 121D–30, 224–
  28, 236–8

Saher I de, L. of Daventry, 53–27, 130–27

Saher IV de, E. of Winchester, 53–27, 54–28, 56–27, 60–27, 236–8

R

Raabs
Konrad II, Ct. of, 252A–28
Sophia of, 252A–28

Raby
Dolfin Fitz Uchtred, L. of, 247–23
Maldred Fitz Dolfin, L. of, 247–24
Robert Fitz Maldred, L. of, 247–25
Uchtred Fitz Maldred, L. of, 247–22

Radcliffe
Alexander, 23–37, 34–37, 35–'35, 36–35, 36–38
Eleanor, 23–37, 36–39
Isabel, 34–37, 35–36
John, 35–'35, 36–37, 170–33
Margaret, 170–33
Richard, 170–33
William, 36–'36

Rainsborough
Judith, 232–41

Ralegh
Maude de, 248A–31
Warin de, 248A–31

Raleigh
Alice, 261–39
Bridget, 14–38
Edward, 14–36, 14–37, 150–39, 238–13
John, 14–35, 52–39
Mary, 150–39
Thomasine, 52–39
William, 14–35

Rameru
Adela de, 149–23
Adelaide de, 263–24
Adele, w. of Andre I de, 151A–23
Alix de, 71A–27, 151A–24
Andre I de, 71A–27, 151A–23
Guisemode, w. of Andre I de, 151A–23
Hersende, Cts. of, 151A–19
Hilduin I (II) de, 151A–20
Hilduin II de, 144A–22
Hilduin II (III) de, 151A–21
Hilduin III (IV) de, 111–25, 149–23, 151–22, 151A–22, 246–22, 263–24
Manasses Calva Asina de, 144A–22
Margaret de, 246–23

Rancon
Bourgogne de, 275–24

Geoffrey III de, Sire de Taillebourg, 275–24

Randolph
John, E. of Moray, 252–32

Ranulf the Moneyer, 269–21

Rastede
Egilmar II of, 252E–25

Ratzenhofen
NN dau. of Eberhard of, 252C–25

Ravensworth
Agatha of, 34–27, 226–29
Akaris Fitz Bardolf of, 226–25
Bodin in, 226–24
Henry Fitz Hervey, L. of, 226–27
Hervey Fitz Akaris of, 226–26
Ranulf Fitz Henry of, 226–28

Rayleigh
Lord of. *see* Essex

Raymond
Hannah, 217A–43

Raynor
Elizabeth, 9–42
John, 9–42

Rede
Joan, 246A–34
John, 246A–33

Reed
Alice, 246G–41
Elizabeth, 12A–30
Walter, 12A–30

Reigney
John de, 52–33
NN dau. of John de, 52–33

Reigny
William de, 52–33

Rennes
see also Brittany; Porhoët
Conan, Ct. of, 121E–21
Josselin of, Vct. of Brittany &, 39–24
Jubel Berenger of, 119A–21
Pascwitann, Ct. of, 119A–21

Rescarrick
Katherine, 252–43

Retdam. *see* Roddam

Retelberg
Ita of, 147–26

Rethel
Alix of, 103–25, 103A–26
Baldwin II, Ct. of, 103–25, 103A–25, 118–24
Gervais, Ct. of, 246A–24
Hugh I, Ct. of, 103A–24, 246A–24
Manassas III, Ct. of, 103A–23
Melisende de, 103A–25, 118–24

Milicent de, 246A–25
Reviers
  Adelise, w. of Baldwin de, 50–27
  Baldwin de, E. of Devon, 50–27
  Mary de, 50–28, 138–27
  William de, E. of Devon, 50–27
Reynel
  Alix de, 71A–30
  Arnoul, Ct. of, 71A–25
  Blanche of, 71A–25
  Gautier de, 71A–30
  Hélisende, w. of Gautier de, 71A–30
Reyner. *see* Raynor
Rheims
  Dode, abbess of St. Pierre de, 180–5
Rheims & Roucy
  Ebles I, Ct. of, 106–22, 144A–22, 151–21
Rhys ap Griffith
  Joan ferch, 56A–35
Ribemont
  Agnes, 184–1
  Anselm, L. of Longueville, 184–1
Rich
  Anne, 230B–40
  Nicholas, 230B–40
  Richard, Bar., 230B–40
Richards
  Alice, 197–40
Richmond
  see also Brittany
  Alan II, E. of, 119–26, 227–25
  Conan IV, E. of, 119–27
  Stephen I, L. of, 18A–24, 119–26, 214–24, 214A–24, 227–24
Ridelisford
  Annora, w. of Walter, L. Bray, 33A–26
  Emeline de, 31–27, 33A–27, 178–6
  Walter de, 33A–25
  Walter de, L. of Bray, 33A–26
Rietberg
  Eilika of, 252E–25
  Heinrich I, Ct. of, 252E–25
Rigby
  Alexander, 233–43, 233–44
  Edward, 233–44
Ringelheim
  Dietrich, Ct. of, 141–18, 142–17
  Mechtilde of, 141–18, 142–17
Rivers
  Earls. *see* Wydvill
Roche
  Blanche, 73–31, 178A–7
  Ellen, 56B–35

  John, 73–31, 178A–7
  Thomas, 56B–35
Rochechouart
  Aymeric de, 261–31
Rochefoucauld
  Gerberga de la, 183–2
Roches
  Clemence des, 120–30
  Jeanne des, 214A–29
  William des, 120–30
Roddam
  Adam de, 121D–32
  Joan de, 121D–32
Rodeney
  John, 124A–35, 261–36
Rodolfus
  barbatus, Normanne, 71C–22
Roet
  Katharine, 234–30
  Payn (Paon), 1–30, 2–31
Roges
  Simon de, 25–30
Rokell
  Margaret, 211–38
  Thomas, 211–38
Rokes
  Elizabeth, 15A–34
  Robert, 15A–34
  Thomas, 15A–34
Rokesley
  Walter, 1–32, 87–34
Rollos
  Adeline de, 184A–4
  Richard de, 184A–4
Ros
  Agnes de, 65A–34
  Alice de, 54–34, 88–32, 246–30, 268–32
  Elizabeth de, 26–33, 89–33, 212–33
  Everard de, 89–27
  Isabel de, 208–30
  Joan de, 215–29, 268–27
  Lucy (Lucia) de, 170–28
  Margaret de, 9–34, 89–33, 93A–32, 93B–32, 176B–36
  Mary de, 155–31
  Maud, 7–32
  Piers de, 268–27
  Robert de, 89–27, 89–29, 170–25, 208–29, 215–29
  Thomas de, B., 9–32
  Thomas de, L., 89–32, 93A–32
  Thomas, L., 1–32
  Thomas. L., 87–34

Walter de, 268–27
William de, 7–32, 19–31, 89–28, 170–
26, 170–27, 186–6, 237–7
William de, Bar., 9–33, 21–32
William de, L., , 54–33, 65A–34, 89–30,
89–31, 155–31, 212–33
Rosoy
Clarembald de, 246A–24
Ross
Anne Arnold, 81C–46
Euphemia of, 252–32
Hugh, E. of, 252–32
John, 81C–45
Rothwell
Joan de, 42–29
Richard de, 42–29
Rotsy
John, 197–37
Mary, 197–37
Roucy
Ada (Adele) de, 273–25
Adele de, 111–25, 149–23, 151–22,
151A–22, 246–22, 263–24
Counts of. *see also* Rheims
Felicie de, 111–25
Giselbert, Ct. of, 103A–23, 151–20
Margaret de, 144–25
Reinald (Ragenold) comes de, 151–19
Yvette de, 103A–23
Roumare
Agnes de, 88–28
William de, 136–25
Rous
Juliana le, 234A–35
Thomas le, 234A–35
Roussillon
Eve of, 50–17, 118–17
Rowse
Margaret, 246A–40
Rowson
Constance, 233A–40
Rugge
Jane, 23–36
Richard, 23–36
Rumilly
Alice de, 40–24
Cecily de, 40–24, 132B–26
Robert de, 40–24, 132B–26, 136B–27
Russia. *see* Kiev; Novgorod
Rutbert II, Ct. in Wormsgau, 48–15
Rutbert III, Ct. in Wormsgau, 48–16
Rutpert I, Ct. in Wormsgau, 48–13
Rydge. *see* Rugge

S
Saarbrücken
Friedrich II, Ct. of, 252A–29
Sablé
Marguerite de, 120–30
Sabran
Gersenda of, 111–28
Sackville
Thomas, L. Buckhurst, 224A–41
Saffenberg
Adolph, Ct. of, 155–25
Matilda of, 155–25
Sale
Margaret de la, 12A–29
Salisbury
Earls of. *see* Longespee; Montagu;
Neville
Ela, Cts. of, 30–26, 31–26, 108–28,
122–28, 122A–28
Jane, 69–37
Leonia of, 123–27
Margaret (Plantagenet), Cts. of, 225–37
Mary, 78–38
Patrick, E. of, 108–26
Sibyl of, 66–27, 81–28
Walter of, 66–27, 81–28, 108–26
William, 78–38
William Fitz Patrick, E. of, 108–27
Salm
Herman I, Ct. of, 100B–24
Otto von, Ct. of Bentheim, 100B–25
Sophie von, 100A–25, 100B–26
Saltonstall
Richard, 3–40, 3–41, 4–40
Salusbury
Henry, 199–37
Lowry, 199–37
Saluzzo
Alasia di, 28–31, 77–31
Manfredo III di, Mrq. of, 28–31, 274D–
29
Thomas I di, Mrq.of, 28–31
Samlesbury
Elizabeth, 32–30
Lords of. *see* Southworth
William, 32–30
Samwell
John, 43A–36
Richard, 43A–36
Susanna, 43A–37
Sanford
Alice de, 60–29, 79–29

Gilbert de, 60–29
Sapcott
Henry, 202–39
Winifred, 202–39
Sargent
Hugh, 43–37
Roger, 43–38
William, 43–39
Sarraz
Falcon de la, 263–24
Savage
Bridget, 57–40
Christopher, 57–38, 57–39
John, 32–33, 57–37, 233–37, 233A–37
Katherine, 233–38
Margaret, 9–35, 32–34, 33–34, 230–37, 233A–38
Mary, 230B–39
Saville, 99–35
Savoy
Adelaide of, 101–24, 117–24, 135–26, 274A–25
Agnes of, 133–25, 274B–25
Amadeus II (1), Ct. of, 274A–23
Amadeus III, Ct. of, 112–25, 133–25, 274B–25, 274C–25
Amadeus IV, Ct. of, 28–31, 274D–28
Ancilie (Auxilia) w. of Humbert I, Ct. of, 274–21
Beatrix of, 28–31, 104–28, 111–29, 133–27, 274C–28, 274D–29
Eudes (Odo), Ct. of Maurienne &, 45–23, 274–22, 274A–22
Humbert I, Ct. of, 274–21
Humbert II, Ct. of, 101–24, 135–26, 274A–24, 274B–24
Humbert III, Ct. of, 133–26, 274C–26
Maud of, 112–25, 274B–25
Thomas I, Ct. of, 28–31, 133–26, 274C–27, 274D–27, 274E–27
Thomas II, Ct. of, 274E–28
Saxby
Edward, 11–39
Mary, 11–39
Saxons. see West Saxons
Saxony
Agnes of, 252C–29
Albrecht, Ct. Palatine of, 252D–30
Albrecht I, D. of, 252A–30, 252B–30
Albrecht II, D. of, 252B–31
Barbara of, 252A–35, 252B–35
Bernard I, D. of, 243A–22
Bernard II, D. in, 100A–22, 101–23, 149–22

Bernard II, D. of, 164–23, 246A–22
Bernhard I, D. of, 252B–29
dau. of Magnus, D. of, 252B–27
Egilmar I, Ct. in Frisia &, 252E–24
Gerberga of, 50–19, 133–19, 140–18, 142–18, 148–18, 151–18, 157–18, 240–18
Gertrude of, 100A–22, 101–23, 164–23
Hedwig of, 53–19, 101–19, 141–19
Heinrich of, Ct. Palatine of the Rhine, 252C–29
Helene of, 252A–30
Henry I, K. of, 50–19, 53–19, 101–19, 141–18, 142–17, 147–18, 148–18, 157–18, 240–18
Herman Billung, D. of, 106–22, 162–19
Herman I, Ct. Palatine of, 252D–28
Ida of, 149–22, 246A–22
Ludolph, D. of, 141–16
Magnus, D. of, 166–24, 243–7, 243A–23
Mathilde of, 106–22, 162–19
Matilda of, 147–21, 147A–21
Oda, w. of Ludolph, D. of, 141–16
Ordulf, D. of, 243A–22
Otto, D. of, 141–17
Richeza, w, of Egilmar I, 252E–24
Rudolf I, D. of, 252B–32
Rudolf II, D. & Elector of, 252A–35
Rudolf III, D. & Elector of, 252B–34
Wenzel, D. & Elector of, 252B–33
Wulfhilda of, 166–24, 243–7
Say
Beatrice de, 97–27
Geoffrey IV de, 86–31
Idonea de, 86–32
William de, 97–27
Scales
Eleanor (Isabelle), 222–34
Elizabeth de, 232–32
Robert de, L., 222–34, 232–32
Scandinavia. see Denmark, Norway, Sweden
Scarpone
Richwin, Ct. of, 167–22
Scheyern
see also Bavaria
Ekkehart, Ct. of, 252C–24
Hazziga (hadagund) of, 252C–23
Otto I, Ct. of, 252C–23
Schweinfurt
Elica of, 100A–22, 149–22, 243A–22, 246A–22
Henrich, Mrg. of, 100A–22, 149–22, 246A–22

Scot. *see* Calverley
Scotland
see also Athol, Buchan; Carrick; Dunbar;
  Galloway
Aed Find "the White", K. of Dalriada,
  170–10
Aedan, K. of Dalriada, 170–5
Alexander II, K. of, 120–30, 273–30
Alpin of, 170–12
Amabel Fitz William of, 40–25
Bethoc (Beatrix) of, 34–21, 170–19,
  171–22
Bethoc of, 121A–24
Causantin (Constantine), K. of, 170–14
Cinaed (Kenneth). k. of, 170–17
Cinaed (Kenneth MacAlpin), K. of, 170–
  13
David I, K. of, 89–25, 130–26, 170–22
David II, K. of, 252–32
David of, E. of Huntingdon, 93–26, 94–
  26, 131–29, 252–26
de Bruce (as surname). *see* Bruce
Domnall Brecc, K. of Dalriada, 170–7
Domnall, K. of, 170–15
Domongart, K. of Dalriada, 170–3
Domongart of, 170–8
Donald Bane, K. of, 121A–23
Duncan I Mac Crinan, K. of, 34–21,
  121A–23, 170–20
Duncan II, K. of, 40–23, 171–22
Eochaid II, K. of Dalriada, 170–9
Eochaid III, K. of Dalriada, 170–9A
Eochaid "the Poisonous", K. of Dalriada,
  170–11
Eochu (Eochaid) Buide, K. of Dalriada,
  K. of the Picts, 170–6
Ercc, son of Loarn's dau., 170–2
Fergus, K. of Dalriada in Argyle, 170–2
Gabran. *see* Wales
Henry of, E. of Huntingdon, 100–25
Henry of Huntingdon. *see* Huntingdon
Isabel of, 89–27, 170–25
James I, K. of, 252–34, 256–40
James II, K. of, 252–35
James III, K. of, 252–36
James IV, K. of, 252–37
James V, K. of, 252–37
John Baliol, K. of, 252–26
Kenneth MacAlpin (Cinaed), K. of, 170–
  13
Loarn, K. of Dalriada in Scotland, 170–2
Mael·Coluim (Malcolm) II, K. of, 170–18
Mael·Coluim (Malcolm), K. of, 170–16

Malcolm III Canmore, K. of, 1–21, 158–
  23, 169–25, 170–21, 171–21
Malcom II, K. of, 34–21
Maldred of, L. of Carlisle, 34–21, 172–
  20, 247–20
Maldred, s. of Maldred, 247–21
Margaret "Cts. of the Isle", 257–30
Margaret of, 269A–26
Mary of, 158–23, 169–25
Mary, Q. of, 252–40
Matilda (Maud) of, 1–22, 121–25
Robert de Bruce of Annandale, 121C–
  30, 252–29
Robert I, K. of, 75A–32, 121C–30, 252–
  30
Robert II, K. of, 252–32
Robert III, K. of, 252–33, 256–33
St. Margaret of. *see* England, Margaret
  of
Thorfill Sigurdson, E. of Orkney, 170–21
William Fitz Duncan of, 40–24
William the Lion, K. of, 89–26, 170–24,
  269A–26
Scots. *see* Scotland
Scott
Hannah, 11–42
Isabel, 223–36, 223–37
Richard, 11–42, 14–41, 223–36, 223–
  37
Scrope
Eleanor, 13A–35
John, L., 13A–35
Sechevill
Robert de, 124A–29
Sedley
Martin, 4–38
Muriel, 4–39
Segrave
Eleanor de, 31–29, 32–29
Elizabeth de, 16–31, 18A–31, 202–34,
  223–33
Ellen, 58–31
Gilbert de, 16B–24, 16B–26, 81–29,
  126–30
Hereward de, 16B–24
John de, L., 16–30, 16B–28, 16B–30,
  58–31
Maud (de Lucy?) w. of Nicholas, 16B–27
Nicholas de, L., 16B–27, 31–29
Stephen de, 16B–25
Stephen de, L., 16B–29
Selvesse
Adèle de, 158B–23
Adèle de, Dame d'Ardres, 158B–23

Semur-en-Brionnais
Dalmas I of, 108–22
Dalmas I, of, 113–22
Hélie (Eleanor) of, 108–22, 113–22
Senlis
see also St. Liz
Alice de, 187–1
Pepin, Ct. of, 50–16
Senliz. see St. Liz
Sens
Gainfroi, Ct. son of Mainier, 240–14
Mainier, Ct. of, 240–14
Sexton
Rose, 249–41
Seymour
see also St. Maur
Alice, 212–36, 213–34
Richard, L. St. Maur & Lovel, 213–33
Richard. L. St. Maur & Lovel, 213–32
Seyntclere. see St. Clair
Shattuck
Frances, 246G–42
Sherburne
Alice, 9A–35, 170A–33
John, 170–30, 170A–30
Margaret, 170A–31
Richard, 170–30, 170A–30, 170A–32
Sherman
John, 13A–41
Roger, 15–40
Shireburne. see Sherburne
Shirley
Cecily, 18–39
Eleanor, 230B–38
Hugh, 230A–37
John, 230A–36, 230A–38, 230B–35
Joyce, 230A–39
Ralph, 230A–36, 230B–35, 230B–37
Robert, 230B–36
Thomas, 18–39, 230A–38
Shrewsbury
Earls of. see Montgomery; Talbot
Shute
Hawise, 124A–34
Sicily
Frederick II, K. of, 252C–32
Isabella (Isolde) of, 252C–32
Manfred, K. of, 274D–29
Sigulf
prob. son of Forne, the King's Thegn, 265A–22
Sigurdson
Thorfill. see Scotland

Siusli
Dietrich I, Ct. of Eilenburg, Hassegau &, 252D–24
Skelton
Lords of. see Brus
Skinner
Joan, 57–40
Skipsey
William, 121D–39
Skrimshire
Anne, 17–38
Smith
Anne, 150–40
John, 150–40
Snow
Eydreth (Judith), w. of John, 233A–43
John, 233A–43
Susanna, 233A–43
Somerset
Earls of. see Beaufort; Mohun
Somery
Agnes, w. of Roger de, Bar. Dudley, 81–30
Joan de, 26–28, 216–30, 249–31, 255–30
John de, 55–27, 81–27
John de, L., 216–30
Margaret de, 55–30, 81–31, 210–31
Ralph de, 122A–29
Ralph de, Bar. Dudley, 26–28, 55–28, 81–28, 122A–29
Roger de, Bar. Dudley, 81–30, 126–30, 216–30
Roger de, L. Dudley, 16B–26, 55–29, 81–29, 210–30, 249–30, 255–30
South Wales
see also Wales; North Wales
Nest ferch Rhys ap Tudor Mawr, 33A–23
Nest of, 187–2
Rhys ap Tudor Mawr, 33A–23
Rhys ap Tudor Mawr, Pr. of, 178–1
Southall
Jane, 69A–39
John, 69A–39
Southworth
Bridget, 170A–38
Christopher, L. of Samlesbury, 9–36
Constant, 9–42
Edward, 9–41
John, 9–39, 170A–39
John, L. of Samlesbury, 9–37
Rosamond, 170A–38
Thomas, 9–38, 9–40, 9–42, 46–38, 170A–38, 170A–39

Southy
Ann, 1A–41
Spain
see also Aragon; Castile; Leon; Navarre;
Spanish Lines
El Cid, 113A–23
Rodrigo Diaz, Sn. de Bibar, 113A–23
Spanish Lines
see also Aragon; Castile; Leon; Navarre;
Spain
Alvaro, noble of Castile, 113A–22
Christina, dau. of Fernando
Gundemariz, 113A–23
Christina (Elvira), 113A–24
Diego, Ct. of Orviedo, 113A–23
Diego Lainez, sn. de Bibar in, 113A–22
Eilone, dau. of Ferán Ruiz, 113A–20
El Cid, 113A–23
Ferán Ruiz, 113A–20
Fernán Lainez, 113A–18
Fernando Gundemariz, 113A–23
Lain Calvo, Judge in Castile, 113A–17
Lain Fernandez, 113A–19
Lain Nuñez, of Castile, 113A–21
Nuño Lainez, 113A–20
Rodrigo Alvarez, Ct. in the Asturias,
113A–22
Rodrigo Diaz, Sn. de Bibar, 113A–23
Teresa, dau. of Rodrigo Alvarez, Ct. in
the Asturias, 113A–22
Ximina, dau. of Diego, Ct. of Orviedo,
113A–23
Sparrow
Frances, 200–41
Nicholas, 200–41
Speccot
John, 25–33
Spencer
Gerard, 246E–41
Jane, 14–38
Margaret, 1–34
Robert, 1–33
William, 246E–41
Spinney
Eleanor, 43–34
Guy, 43–34
Spoleto
Bertila of, 146–16
dau. of Alard, bro. of Garnier, anc. of the
Mrg. of, 191–12
Engelberge of, 141B–16
Gui I, D. of, 141B–16
Suppo of, 146–16

St. Barbe
Alice, 248A–39
Isabel, 199A–33, 234–32, 248A–34
Joan, 248A–34
Joan, w. of Thomas, 248A–38
John, 234–32, 248A–33, 248A–36
Richard, 248A–34
Richard, L. of Ashington, 248A–37
Thomas, 248A–35, 248A–38
St. Clair
Edith, 79–35, 143–35
John, 79–34
Philip de, 79–33
Thomas, 79–34, 143–35
St. Hilary
Aveline, w. of James de, 149–26, 246B–
26
James de, 63–27, 149–26, 246B–26
Maud de, 63–27, 149–26, 246B–26
St. John
Agnes, 214–33
Agnes de, 50–31, 51–31, 51A–31, 262–
32
Alexander, 85–38
Edith, 225–37
Elizabeth, 85–41, 212–36, 245–41
Henry, 85–39, 245–40
John, 85–36, 85–37
John de, 262–31
Oliver, 31D–40, 85–35, 85–40, 212–36,
225–37, 245–40
Robert de, 262–31
William de, 214A–25
St. Laurence
Elizabeth, 247–29
Thomas, 247–29
St. Liz
Maud de, 53–27, 130–27
Simon de, E. of Huntingdon, 84–27,
130–26
St. Lo
Ela de, 213–32
John de, 213–32
St. Maur
see also Seymour
Lawrence de, 213–30
Nicholas de, L., 213–30, 213–31
St. Omer
Alice, 79–34
Mathilda (Mahaut) de, 272–26
William I de, 272–26
William II de, 272–26
St. Owen
Joan?, 258–28

John, 258–28
St. Paul
John, 223–41
St. Pol. see Candavaine; Châtillon
St. Pol
see also Luxembourg
Adelisa de, 272–28
St. Quintin
Herbert de, 219–32
Lora de, 219–32
St. Valerie. see St. Valery
St. Valery
Aenor de, 155–28
Bernard III of, 109–27
Gilbert de, 177–3
Laurie of, 109–27
Maud de, of Haie, 63A–28, 70–29, 177–6, 177A–6
Stackpole
Richard, 56A–35
Stafford
Alice, 224–35
Anne, 187–13, 225–39
Beatrice, 9–32, 89–32
Beatrice de, 93A–32
Edmund de, 9–31
Edmund de, Bar., 55–31
Edmund de, E. of, 4–32, 155A–32
Elizabeth, 55–37, 84–34
Elizabeth de, 61–33
Henry, D. of Buckingham, 225–39
Hugh, E., 10–32
Humphrey, 55–35, 55–36, 84–34, 187–11, 187–12, 224–35
Isabel, dau. of Maud de, 222–29
Jane de, 32–'32
John, 55–33, 150–33, 231–32
Katharine, 81–33
Margaret, 5–35, 10–33, 55–33, 207–34, 231–32
Maud de, 222–29
Nicholas de, 55–31
NN dau. of John, 150–33
Ralph de, 55–34
Ralph de, E. of, 9–31, 10–31, 32–'32, 55–32, 61–33, 81–33, 32–'32
Thomas, 248–38
Thomas de, E. of, 155A–32
William, 55–33
Stainton
Christian de, 34–26, 41–25
Gilbert de Lancaster, L., 41–25, 34–26
Standish
Alexander, 34–38, 170–32, 170–34

Alice, 23–38, 34–40
Clemency, 35–'35
Hugh, 35–'35
Lawrence, 170–32
Ralph, 34–38, 170–33, 170–35
Roger, 34–39
Standisshe
Elizabeth, 11–34, 248–34
Robert, 248–34
Robert de, 11–34
Stanford
Alice de, 262–30
William de, 262–30
Stanley
Agnes, 170A–32
Anne, 57–38, 81A–38, 81B–38
Elizabeth, 23–34
George, 81A–37
John, 40–33, 57–34, 57–35, 57–38, 81A–37
Katherine, 57–37, 233–37, 233A–37
Margaret, 20–34, 46–36, 199–34
Margaret (Margery), 233B–38
Thomas, 81A–37
Thomas, E. of Derby, 23–34
Thomas, L., 20–33, 23–33, 57–36, 233–36
William, 56B–38, 57–34, 170A–32, 233B–38
Stanton
John, 11–42
Stapleton
Brian, 212–37, 257–35
Elizabeth, 212–37, 257–37
Johanna (Joan), 12A–28
Leonard, 86–36
Mary, 86–36
Miles, 257–35, 257–36
Nicholas, 12A–28
Staufen
Hedwig of, 252C–26
Margareta of, 252D–30
Staundon
Margaret, 12A–31
Staunton
Margaret, 230B–35
Staveley
Adam de, 226–28, 266–28
Alice de, 226–28, 266–28
Stewart
Alexander, 75A–31
Henry, L. Methven, 252–37
James, 75A–31, 252–34, 256–40
Jane, 256–40

Janet, 252–38
John, E. of Athol, 252–38, 256–40
Margaret, 252–38
Mary, 256–34
Walter, 75A–32, 252–31
Steyngrave
see also Stonegrave
Aubrey de, 266–30
William de, 266–30
Stiles
John, 200–42
Rebecca, 200–42
Still
Anne, 69–39
John, 69–39
Stockport
Margaret de, 63A–34
Robert de, 63A–34
Stokes
Eve de, 253–32
John, 42–32
Stonegrave
Isabella de, 184A–11
John de, 184A–10
Simon de, 184A–10
Stourton
Esther, 85–34
John, 85–34
Ursula, 225–40
William, Bar., 225–40
Stouteville
see also Stuteville
Henry de, 123–27
Robert de, 123–27
Stowford
Joan, 25–31
John, 25–30
Stradling
Edward, 199A–33, 234–32
Henry, 199A–34
Jane, 199–36, 199A–36
John de, 249–32
Thomas, 199–36, 199A–35
William, 199A–33, 234–32, 248A–34
Strange
Alianore (Eleanor) le, 93A–31
Ankaret le (of Blackmere), 8–33, 14–32
Elizabeth, 18–37, 18A–32
Elizabeth le, 29A–31, 29B–31, 249–33
Eubolo le (of Knokyn), 187–9
Fulk le (of Blackmere), 8–32, 29A–30, 258–30, 259–29
Isabel le, 187–9
John III le (of Knokyn), 29A–30, 255–29

John IV le, (of Knokyn), 249–31, 255–30
John, L. (of Blackmere), 93A–31
John le, 230A–33
John le, Bar. (of Blackmere), 8–32
John le, L. (of Blackmere), 18A–32
John V le, (of Knokyn), 249–32
Lucy, 17–33, 219–34
Maud le, 258–30; 259–30
Robert le, 29A–30
Roger, L. (of Knokyn), 17–33, 219–34
Roger le, 18A–27
Thomas, 18–37
Strangeways
George, 253–37
Isabel, 233B–36
Thomas, 18B–33, 233B–36
Stratton
Elizabeth, 12–34
John, 12–33
Streche
Elizabeth, 12A–30
John, 12–32, 12A–30
Strechlegh
Alice, 246E–33
Walter de, 246E–33
Stretele
Isabel, 42–32, 43–32
Strickland
Agnes, 37–'37
Ellen, 2–40
Mabel, 13A–37
Robert de, 41–28
Thomas de, 41–30, 41–32, 41–34
Walter, 2–38, 2–39, 13A–'37, 41–33, 41–35, 41–36
Walter de, 41–29, 41–31
William de, 41–28
Strong
Abigail, 69–40
John, 69–40
Stuckley. see Stukeley
Stucle
see also Stukeley
Geoffrey, 124A–36, 261–37
Richard, 124A–36, 261–37
Stukeley
see also Stucle
Edith, 208–38
Hugh, 261–38
John, 208–38
Margery, 261–41
Nicholas, 261–39
Thomas, 261–40

Stumpe
Elizabeth, 225–41
James, 225–41, 248–38
Sturdon
Joan, 187–7, 238–7
Stuteville
see also Stouteville
Agnes, w. of John, 270A–26
Alice de, 42–25, 270D–28
Beatrix, w. of Robert I (II) de, 270–24
Burga de, 269–25, 269A–25, 270B–27
dau. of John de, 247–24
Erneburga (Eremburga), w. of Robert II (III) de, 270–25, 270A–25, 270D–25
Helewise de, 40–26, 88–26, 265A–27, 270C–27
Helewise, w. of Robert III (IV) de, 88–26, 270B–26, 270C–26
Helewise, w. of Robert III (IV) of, 270–26
Joan de, 69–29, 184A–8, 236–9, 270–29
John de, 270A–26
Nicholas de, 184A–8, 236–9
Nicholas I de, 156–25, 270–27
Nicholas II de, 69–29, 270–28
NN daughter of John de, 270A–27
Osmond de, 187–2, 270B–27
Osmund de, 270D–26
Robert de, 270–24
Robert I (II) de, 270–24
Robert II (III) de, 270–25, 270A–25, 270D–25
Robert III (IV) de, 88–26, 265A–27, 269–25, 270–26, 270B–26, 270C–26
Roger de, 42–25, 270D–27
Styford
Barons of. see Bolebec
Sudeley
Bartholomew de, 222–31, 222–33
Imenia, w. of Ralph de, 222–30
Joan de, 77–32, 222–35
Joan, w. of Bartholomew de, 222–31
John de, 222–27, 222–35, 235–23
John, L., 222–32, 222–34
Ralph de, 222–28, 222–29, 222–30
Suliard
Elizabeth, 248–38
John, 248–38
Sully
Agnes de, 139–24
Gilles de, 139–24
Sulzbach
Berenger I, Ct. of, 155–24
Luitgarde of, 155–24

Surrey
Earls of. see Fitz Alan; Howard; Warenne
Hamelin (Plantagenet), E. of, 83–26, 123–26, 218–27
NN dau. of Hamelin, 218–27
Susa
Eudes I, Mrg. see Savoy
Sutherland
Alexander, E. of, 252–41
Sutton
Agnes de, 74A–34
Constance, 156–31
Dorothy, 198–37
Edmund, 5–36, 81–37, 198–36. see Dudley, Edmund
Eleanor, 17–35, 81A–37, 221–37
Hamon, 246–33
Jane, w. of John IV de, 81–34
Joan, 246–33
John I de, 81–31
John II de, 81–32
John III de, 81–33
John IV de, 81–34
John V, Bar. of, 81–35
John VI, L. Dudley, 81–36, 81A–36, 221–36
John, L. Dudley, 5–36
Margery, 156–32
Richard de, 74A–34, 81–31
Thomas, 156–31, 156–32
Swabia
see also Germany
Frederick I, D. of, 45–24
Frederick II, D. of, 45–25, 166–25
Frederick III, D. of, 45–26
Gerold of, 50–13, 184–4, 190–13
Gisele of, 45–21, 157–21
Herman II, D. of, 45–21, 157–20, 167–20, 252B–25
Herman IV, D. of, 274–22
Hildegarde of, 50–13, 148–13, 182–5, 190–13
Konrad, D. of, 167–20
Konrad II of, 114–27
Marie of, 45–28, 155–27
Mathilde of, 167–21, 252B–25
Oda of, 190–7
Philip II, D. of, 45–27
Sweden
Astrid of, 243A–21
Erik Segersäll, 241–5
Finn Arnason, E. of Halland, 170–21
Githa of, 1B–22
Ingibiorg of, 170–21, 171–21

Ingigerd of, 1–20, 53–22, 241–5, 241A–5, 242–5, 244–6
Olaf Bjornson, K. of, 1B–22
Olov II Skötkonung, K. of, 53–22, 241–5, 243A–21
Sigrid Storråda, 241–5, 243A–20
Skoglar-Tosti, 241–5, 243A–20
Styr-Bjorn, 1B–22
Thorkill Sprakalaeg, Jarl, 1B–22

Swinfen
Margaret, 56A–37
William, 56A–37

Swinnerton
Anne, 17–36, 98–36
Thomas, 98–36

Swynford
Catherine (Roet), 1–30, 2–31, 234–30, 265–35
Hugh, 1–30
Hugh, Sir, 2–31

Swynnerton
Matilda, w. of Roger, 32–31
Maud de, 32–33, 233–37
Robert de, 32–'32
Roger de, 32–31
Thomas de, 32–31

Sydenham
Jane, 248A–36
Joan, 248A–36
Maud de, 215–28
William de, 215–28

Symmes
Sarah, 31C–41

T

Tailbois
Christiana de, 34–24, 88–24
Ivo de, 132A–26
Ivo de, Bar. of Kendal, 34–24, 88–24

Tailboys
see also Talboys
Henry, 74A–35, 224–33
Joan, 74A–35
Margaret, w. of Walter, 224–34, 224A–34
Maud, 223–38
Robert, L. Kyme, 223–38, 224–37
Walter, 224–34, 224–35, 224A–34
William, 224–33, 224–36, 261A–39

Taillebourg
Geoffrey III de Rancon, Sire de, 275–24

Talbot
Anne, 7–37, 56A–38
Elizabeth, 6–32, 13A–32, 18B–35

Gilbert, 7–35
Gilbert, L., 13–31, 13A–32, 14–31, 73–32, 95–32
Gilbert, of Eccleswall, 84A–29
Gilbert, of Eccleswall, L., 84A–30, 84B–30
John, 6–32, 7–36, 20–36
John, E. of Shrewsbury, 7–34, 8–34, 8–35, 18B–35, 56A–38
Mary, 14–33
Philippa, 84B–31, 234A–33
Richard, Bar., 8–33
Richard, L., 14–32, 84A–31, 95–31
Richard, L. of Eccleswall, 84A–29

Talboys
see also Tailboys
John, 224A–35
John "the Younger", 224A–36
Margaret, 224A–37

Tallebot
Jeanne de, 270–24

Talvas
Ela, 83–25
Ela, of of Alençon & Ponthieu, 108–26
Mabel, 185–1
William I (III), Ct. of Alençon & Ponthieu, 108–25, 109–25
William II, Ct. of Ponthieu, 109–28
William, L. of Belleme, sn. of Alençon, 185–1

Taney
Roger Brooke, 81C–47

Tanfield
Avice de, 218–28
Gernegan de, 218–28

Tankerville
Earl of. see Grey

Tarbock. see Torbock

Tateshal
Joan de, 16C–29, 218–31
Nichole, w. of Robert de, 16C–28
Robert de, 16C–27, 16C–28, 210–35, 218–31
Walter de, 16C–27

Tateshale. see Tateshal

Teisa
Emma de, 265–24

Tempest
Agnes, 9A–35, 170A–34
Dowsabel, 13A–37
John, 9A–35, 170A–33
Peter, 170A–33
Richard, 13A–37

Tenderyng
Joan, 69A–37
Robert, 69A–37
Teyes
Henry, L., 8A–30
Margaret, 8A–30
Thacher
Oxenbridge, 201–43
Peter, 201–43
Thane
Crinan the. see Dunkeld
Thatcher
Catherine, 18–39
Theoderata
W. of Rutpert II, 48–15
Therouanne
Francois, Bishop of, 158B–23
Theuber
Katherine, 99–40
Stockbridge de Vanderschaff, 99–40
Thiers
Béatrix de, 71A–29
Thimbleby
Anne, 74A–39, 224A–39
Elizabeth, 31B–40, 223–41
John, 223–40
Richard, 31B–40, 74A–38, 223–40, 224A–39
Thistlethwaite
Alexander, 248A–39
Margaret, 248A–39
Thoars. see Thouars
Thomas
Rhys ap, 199A–35
Thorley
Margaret, 18–33, 51A–36
Robert, 18–33
Thorne
Susan, 143–39, 143–40
Thomas, 143–39
Thornes
Alice, 1A–39
John, 1A–37
Margaret, wife of, 1A–38
Richard, 1A–38
Roger, 1A–36
Thorpe
Alice de, 232–31
Edmund, L., 136–33
George de, 232–31
Isabel, 136–33
Margaret, 121D–37
Stephen de, 121D–36

Thouars
Aimery I de, 271–18
Aimery II de, 271–19
Aimery IV de, 183–1, 271–23, 275–22
Aimery VI de, 111–25, 271–25
Aliénor de, 183–2, 275–22
Aliénor (or Hardouine), w. of Aimery II de, 271–19
Alix de, Cts. of Brittany, 96–28, 135–29, 271–28
Ameline, w. of Geoffroy III de, 271–24
Aremburge, w, of Aimery I de, 271–18
Auliarde de, 275–21
Geoffroy de, 183–1, 271–17
Geoffroy II de, 271–22
Geoffroy III de, 271–24
Geoffroy V de, 271–26
Gui de, Ct. of Brittany, 96–27, 271–27
Herbert I de, 271–20
Hildegarde (Aldéarde) de, 183–2, 275–22
Raoul I de, 271–21
Raoul I of, 275–21
Savary III de, 271–21
Throckmorton
Agnes, 43–34
Bassingbourne, 208–41
Clement, 201–39
George, 201–38
John, 43–34, 208–42
Katherine, 201–40
Lionel, 208–40
Robert, 201–38
Simon, 208–39
Thuringia
Albrecht, Lndgrv. of, 252D–30
Herman I, Ct. Palatine of Saxony, Lndgrv. of, 252D–28
Jutta of, 252D–28
Thurston
Rebecca, 11–42
Thwenge
Lucy de, 88–31, 268–32
Marmaduke de, 88–29
Robert de, 88–30
Tingry
see also Fiennes
Sibylle de, 158A–26, 158B–26
Tiptoft
John, E. of Worcester, 56B–38
Toeni
Alice de, 84–29, 86–30, 87–30, 98–31
Godeheut de, 143–25
Isabel, w. of Roger V de, 98–29

Mary, w. of Ralph VII de, 98–30
Ralph III de, 98A–24
Ralph IV de, 98A–24, 143–25
Ralph V de, 98A–26
Ralph VI de, 98–28
Ralph VII de, 86–30, 98–30
Robert, L. Tony, 86–30
Roger III de, 98A–25, 143–25
Roger IV de, 98–27, 98A–27
Roger V de, 84–29, 98–29
Tomes
Alice. *see note*, 98–37
Tompson
John, 43A–40
Tonnerre
Ermengarde of, 107–22
Ingeltrudis, w. of Milon, Ct. of, 50–20
Milo I, Ct. of, 151A–24
Milon II of, 50–20
Renaud, Ct. of, 107–22
Tony
Lord. *see* Toeni
Torbock
Margaret, 217A–41
William, 217A–40
Torrell
Anne, 211–41
Humphrey, 211–41
Torrey
Haviland, 197–41
Philip, 197–40
William, 197–40, 197–41
Toteneis
Aenor de, 177–5
Juhel (Judhael) de, 177–5
Totnes
Alved, L. of, 177–5
Touche
Isabel de la, 6–39
Toulouse
Alphonse I Jourdain, Ct. of, 274C–26
Bertrand, Ct. of, 108–25
Feydive of, 274C–26
Philippa of, 110–24, 111–24, 185–3, 274C–26
Pons, Ct. of, 185–2, 185A–5
William, Ct. of, 48–16
William III, Ct. of, 185–2
William IV, Ct. of, 110–24, 185–2
Tournay
Fastré I of, 168A–24
Fastré II d'Oisy, noble in, 168A–25
Tours
see also Alsace

Adelaide of, 48–17
Ermengarde of, 140–15, 145–15
Hugh II, Ct. of, 140–15
Hugh III, Ct. of, 48–17
Tracy
Eva de, 25–27
Eve de, 63A–30
Grace de, 222–27, 235–23
Henry de, 25–29, 63A–29
Isabella de, 25–30
NN de, 25–27
Oliver de, 25–28, 63A–29
Rose (Rohese) de, 124A–29
William de, 25–26, 25–27, 124A–29, 222–26
William de, of Toddington, 222–28
Trafford
Edmund, 36–'36, 233–42, 233A–38
Jane, 36–'36
Margaret, 217A–38, 233–42
Margaret (Margery), 233A–39, 233B–39
Tregoz
Clarice de, 99–31, 255A–31, 263–30
Hawise de, 246–28
John de, L., 8A–31, 29–33, 99–31, 184A–12, 255A–30
John, L., 263–30
Lucy de, 29A–30, 255–29
Nicholas de, 246–28
Robert I de, 255–28, 255A–28
Robert II de, 255A–29
Sibyl de, 8A–31, 28–34, 29–33, 184A–12, 263–30
Treverbin
Sybil, 6–31
Treves
Dode (Clothilde), nun at, w. of St. Arnulf, Bishop of, 180–8, 190–8
St. Lievin, Bishop of, 190–11
Trevor
Edwart (Iorwerth) ap Daffyd ap Ednyfed Gam, 249–36
Rose (ferch Edwart ap Daffyd), 249–37
Troutbeck
Adam, 7–36, 20–35
Joan, 199–35
John, 199–34
Margaret, 7–36, 20–36
William, 20–34, 199–34
Trowbridge
Dorothy, 246G–42
Elizabeth, 246G–42
James, 246G–42
John, 246G–41, 246G–42

Thomas, 246G–41, 246G–42
Thomas, Jr., 246G–42
William, 246G–42
Troyes
Garnier de, 141A–18
Isabel de Montlhéry, Vcts. of, 264–26
Robert, Ct. of, 118–19
Teurberg de, 141A–18
Trussebut
Robert, 89–27
Roesse, 89–27
William, 89–27
Trussell
Isabel, 150–36
Lawrence, 150–34
Warin, 150–33
William, 150–32, 150–35
Tsimices
John I, 147–20
Tubb
George, 13A–40
Susan, 13A–40
Tuberville
Margaret, 56A–35
Richard, 56A–35
Tuchet
Agnes, w. of Robert, 176C–31
Alice, w. of Robert, 176C–29
Anne de Audley, 9–35, 32–35
Elizabeth, w. of Thomas, 176C–28
Henry, 176C–25, 176C–26, 176C–29
Isabel (Elizabeth), w. of John, 176B–35
James, 9–34
James (styled L. Audley), 176B–36
Joan, w. of Thomas, 176C–32
John, 176B–33, 176B–34, 176B–35, 176C–33
Joscelin, 176C–24
Margery, w. of Thomas, 176C–30
Maud, w. of Henry, 176C–26
Robert, 16A–32, 176C–29, 176C–31
Simon, 176C–27
Thomas, 176C–28, 176C–30, 176C–32
Tucke
Dorothy, 261–44
Tucker
Rose, wid., 233A–43
Tudor
Margaret, 252–37
Tudor Mawr
Nest ferch Rhys ap, 33A–23
Rhys ap, 33A–23
Tunstall
Alice, 41–34

Thomas, 41–34
Turenne
Boson I, Vct. de, 153A–24
Marquerite de, 153A–25
Turin
see also Savoy
Alix (Adelaide) of, 45–23, 274–22, 274A–22
Berta of, 45–23
Bertha of, 45–23, 274–23
Olderich Manfred II, Mrg. of, 45–23, 274–22
Udalrich Manfred, 45–23
Turincbertus, 48–14
Tuscany
Willa of, 145–18
Tybotot
Elizabeth, 200–34
John, L., 65A–34
Payn, L., 65A–34
Robert de, L., 65A–35, 200–33
Tye
Robert de, 59–36
Tyldesley
Margaret, 217A–39
Nicholas, 217A–39
Tylney
Elizabeth, 4–34, 22–35, 136–34
Frederick, 4–34, 22–35, 136–33
Philip, 136–33
Tyndal
John, 232–37, 232–39
Margaret, 232–40
Thomas, 232–38
William, 232–36
Tyndale
Hextilda of, 121A–25
Huctred, son of Waldef, 121A–24
John, 232–34
Thomas, 232–35
William, 232–34
Tyng
Edward, 84–41, 199–40
Rebecca, 84–41
William, 199–40
Tyrrel
Eleanor, 188–13
William, 188–13
Tyrrell
William, 51A–36
Tyrwhit
Katharine, 223–40
Robert, 223–39
William, 223–39

Tyson
  Alda, 269–24
  William, 269–24
Tzautzina
  Zoe, 141A–16

U
Ufflete
  Catharine, 84–32
  Gerard de, 84–32
Ufford
  Catherine d', 232–32
  Edmund, L., 257–35
  Ela, 257–35
  Margaret d', 11–32
  Ralph d', 94A–33
  Robert d', E. of Suffolk, 11–32, 232–32
Ulf
  of Grimthorpe, 265–23
Ulster. see Lacy
Ulster
  Earls of. see Burgh
  Philippa, Cts. of, 5–32, 29–34, 47D–33, 225–32
Umfraville
  Eleanore, w. of Robert d', E. of Angus, 121D–31
  Elizabeth d', 224–32
  Gilbert d', Bar. of Prudhoe, 121D–30
  Gilbert d', E. of Angus, 54–32, 121D–30, 224–30
  Margaret, 121D–34
  Robert d', 11–32
  Robert d', E. of Angus, 121D–31, 224–31
  Thomas d', 121D–32, 121D–33
Umfreville. see Umfraville
Upplands. see Norway
Urswick
  Ellen, 34–'34
  Thomas, 34–'34
Urtiaco
  dau. of Henry de, 261–34
  Sibyl, w. of Henry, 261–34
Usflete
  Gerard, 15–32
Uzes
  Ruricius, Bishop of, 180–4

V
Vale
  dau. of Robert de, 254–32
  Robert de, 254–32

Valence
  Aymer (Adhémar) "Taillifer" de, Ct. of Angoulême, 117–26, 153A–27, 275–26
  Isabel de, 93A–29
  Joan de, 84A–31, 95–30, 154–30
  William de, L., 154–29
  William de, L. of, 80–29, 93A–29, 95–30
Valencia
  Christina (Elvira) de Bibar, of, 113A–24
  Rodrigo Diaz, Sn. de Bibar, Ct. of, 113A–23
Valle. see Vaux
Valletort
  see also Vautort
  Joan de, 258–27
  Reginald de, 258–27
Valognes
  Joan de, 30–'30
  Sibyl de, 89–27, 170–25
  Thomas de, 30–'30
Valoignes
  Geoffrey de, 247–25
Valois
  see also Amiens; Vexin
  Adela de, 140–22
  Adele, w. of Gautier (Walter) II, Ct. of, 250–19
  Charles of France, Ct. of, 1–29, 103–32
  Eldegarde, w. of Raoul de Gouy, Ct. d', 250–17
  Gautier (Walter) I, 250–18
  Gautier (Walter) II, Ct. of, 250–19
  Jeanne of, 103–33, 168–32
  Joan of, 1–29
  Raoul de Gouy, Ct. of, 250–17
  Raoul III, Ct. of, 50–22, 140–22
Valois & Vexin. see Valois
Vaudemont
  see also Baudement
  Gerard of Lorraine, Ct. of, 144–24
  Gisele of, 144–24
Vaughan
  Elsbeth, 179–15
  Hopkin John, 179–15
  William, 11–41
Vaughn
  Elizabeth, 207–37
  Thomas, 207–37
Vautort
  see also Valletort
  Joan de, 195–29

Vaux
Beatrice de, 143–27, 177–7, 184A–7, 246B–28
Eleanor, 43–33
Étienne (Stephen) de, 71A–24
John de, 89–30
Katharine, 201–38
Maud de, 65A–34, 89–30
Nicholas, L. Harrowdon, 201–37
Oliver de, 89–30
William, 43–33
Veel
Piers, 39–31
Venables
Alice, 36–'36
Alice de, 230–32
Hugh, 57–33
Hugh de, Bar. of Kinderton, 230–32
Johanna, 57–33
William, 36–'36
Verdon
Edmund de, 34–35
John de, 34–35, 34–36
Lords of. *see* Harington
Margaret de, 34–35
Thomas de, 34–36
Verdun
Bertran de, 38–26
Bertran I de, 70A–25
Bertran II de, 70A–27
Clemencia, w. of Nicholas de, 70A–28
Elizabeth de, 70–33
Gottfried, Ct. of, 106–22
Henry, Ct. of, 45–19
Isabel de, 11–31, 58–32
Isabella, 70–32
Joan de, 70–32
John de, 70–30, 70A–30
Judith of, 45–19
Lesceline de, 38–26
Margaret de, 70–32
Margery, w. of Theobald de, 70–31
Mathilde of, 106–22
Nicholas de, 70A–28, 149–29
Norman de, 70A–26
Richwin, Ct. of, 143–18
Rohese de, 149–29
Rohesia de, 70A–29
Rohesia, w. of Bertran II de, 70A–27
Theobald de, 11–30
Theobald de, L., 70–31, 94A–32, 70–32
Vere
Adelicia de, 246D–26
Alfonso de, 79–30

Aubrey de, E. of Oxford, 246–26
Aubrey I de, 246–25, 246D–25
Aubrey II de, 246–25, 246D–25
Beatrice, w. of Aubrey I de, 246D–25
Eleanor de, 246–28
Elizabeth de, 18A–30
Hugh de, E. of Oxford, 50–29, 60–28, 214–30
Isabel de, 50–29, 214–30
Joan de, 60–30, 83–29, 231–29
John de, E. of Oxford, 17–31, 18A–30, 79–31
Margaret de, 17–31, 79–32
Robert de, E. of Oxford, 50–29, 60–28, 60–29, 79–29, 214–30, 246–27, 267–26
Vermandois
Adelaide de, 118–20, 121–20
Adelaide de, Cts. of, 50–23, 53–23, 140–23, 141–23
Albert I, Ct. of, 50–19, 140–19, 142–19
Alix de, 48–20, 162–18
Beatrix of, 48–18, 53–18, 101–18
Herbert I, Ct. de, 48–18, 50–17, 53–18, 101–18, 118–17, 143–20
Herbert II, Ct. de, 48–19, 49–19, 50–18, 118–18, 121E–19, 136–18
Herbert III, Ct. of, 50–20, 140–20
Herbert IV, Ct. de, 50–22
Herbert IV, Ct. of, 140–22
Isabel, 140–24
Isabel de, 50–24, 53–24, 66–24, 83–24, 84–24, 89–24, 93–24, 141–24, 151–24, 197–28, 215–24
Luitgarde de, 49–19, 121E–19, 136–19
Mahaut de, 273–27
NN dau. of Herbert I, Ct. de, 143–20
Otho, Ct. of, 140–21
Otho (Eudes), Ct. of, 50–21
Parvie, w. of Otho, Ct. of, 50–21, 140–21
Rudolph II, Ct. of, 164–26
Verney
Margaret, 14–36
Ralph, 14–36
Vernon
see also Reviers
Alice, 195–28
Elizabeth, 56A–39, 56B–39
Henry, 56A–38
Joan, 86–35
Richard, 56A–35, 56A–36, 86–35
Richard de, 56A–34, 63A–33, 63A–35, 269A–28

Thomas, 230B–38
William, 56A–37
William de, 63A–34
Versfleth
Gerbert, Ct. of, 252E–26
Kunigunde of, 252E–26
Vescy
Agnes, w. of William de, L.
of Alnwick,
269–25
Beatrice de, 269–24
Eustace de, 269A–26
Juliana de, 63A–33, 269A–28
Sibil de, 267A–26, 269–26
William de, 269A–27
William de, L. of Alnwick, 269–25,
269A–25, 270B–27
Yves de, 269–24
Vestfold. see Norway
Vexin
see also Amiens; Valois
Adela of, 50–22
Dreux (Drogo), Ct. of the, 235–20, 250–
20
Veysey
Charles, 224A–42
Vienne
Charles Constantine, 141A–18
Vieuxpont. see Vipont
Vignory
Aldéarde de, 71A–26, 71B–26
Guy I de, 71C–23
Guy II de, 71C–25
Guy III de, 71A–26, 71B–25, 71C–26
Mathilde, w. of Roger I de, 71C–24
Roger I de, 71C–24
Vipont
Christian de, 265A–28
Isabel de, 82–31
John de, L. of Appleby, 82–30
Robert de, L. of Appleby, 82–30, 265A–
28
Visconti
Barbanò, 252C–33
Magdalena, 252C–33
Vitré
Andre de, 55–26, 108–27
Eleanor de, 108–27
Emma, w. of Robert II de, 108–27
Hawise de, 55–26
Maud de, 195–27
Robert I de, 108–27
Robert II de, 108–27
Robert III de, 108–27

Vivonia
Hugh de, 261–31
Joan de, 122–32, 261–32, 262–30
William de Fort, 262–30, 261–31
Vychan
Evan Lloyd, 1A–38
Joan, 1A–38
W
Wac
Geoffrey, 184A–5
Wade
Jonathan, 84–40
Wahull
Agnes de, 7–39
Wake
Anne, 51–33
Baldwin, 184A–6, 184A–7, 184A–9,
236–9
Hugh, 184A–5, 184A–8, 236–9, 270–29
Ida, 184A–10
John, L., 155–31, 236–10
Margaret, 155–31, 236–11
Thomas, 51–33
Walcot
Walter, 85–32
Walcourt
Ermengarde de, 71A–29
Jean de, 71A–29
Thierry I de, 168A–27
Waldegrave
Edward, 246–38
George, 200–38, 257–39
Grisella, 246–38
Jemima, 1–39
Phillis, 200–39
Thomas, 1–39, 200–37
William, 200–37, 200–39, 257–39
Walerand
Albreda, 247–26
Joan, 247–26
Wales
see also North Wales; Powys; South
Wales
Alice ferch John of Swansea, 179–13
Angharad ferch Owain ap Maredudd,
254–31
Ann Maelog, 179–4
Ann, w. of Hywel ap Gruffudd, 179–7
Brychan, 170–4
Catherine, w. of Hywel Melyn ap Gwilym
Gam, 179–10
Catrin, w. of Hywel Fychan ap Hywel,
179–8

Cynrig ap Osbern Wyddel, 251–36
Dyfnwal Hen, 170–4
Einon ap Gruffyd, 251–36
Eleanor ferch Philip ap Ifor, 254–33
Elen ferch Maelgwn, 254–30
Elen ferch Thomas ap Llewelyn, 249–34, 251–34, 254–34
Elisau ap Gruffydd, 251–37
Gabran "the Treacherous", 170–4
Griffith Llewelyn Voythys, 179–10
Gruffudd ap Ifor Bach, 179–1
Gruffyd ap Einon ap Gruffyd ap Llewellyn ap Cynrig ap Osbern Wyddel, 251–36
Gruffyd ap Llewellyn ap Cynrig, 251–36
Gruffyd Lloyd, 251–37
Gruffydd ap Madog of Rhuddallt, 249–33
Gruffydd Fychan ap Gruffydd, 249–34, 251–34, 254–34
Gruffydd Fychan ap Madog, 249–33
Gruffydd, of Bromfield, 249–33
Gwenllian, w. of Gwilym Gam ap Hywel Fychan, 179–9
Gwilym ap Ieuan, 179–9
Gwilym ap Jenkin, 179–6
Gwilym Gam ap Hywel Fychan, 179–9
Gwrgi Ghant, 179–4
Hywel ap Gruffudd, 179–7
Hywel Fychan ap Hywel, 179–8
Hywel Melyn ap Gwilym Gam, 179–10
Ieuan Gwyn ap Hywel Melyn, 179–11
Ieuan Llewellyn ap Gruffyd Lloyd, 251–37
Ieuan Llwyd, 179–8
Jenkin ap Gwrgi, 179–5
Jenkyn ap Iuean Llewellyn, 251–37
Joan, dau. of Thomas ap Gwilim Vachan, 179–12
Joan ferch Rhys, 179–3
Joan, Prs. of, 176B–27
John of Swansea, 179–13
Jonet, w. of Jenkin ap Ieuan, 179–12
Lleian, dau. of Brychan, 170–4
Lleiky ferch Madog Foel ap Iefan, 249–35
Llewellyn ap Owain, 254–32
Lowri ferch Gruffydd Fychan, 249–35
Lowri ferch Twdr, 251–36
Mabel ferch Gruffudd, 179–10
Madog ap Gruffydd, 249–33
Maelgwn ap Rhys, 254–29
Maelgwn Fychan ap Maelgyn, 254–29
Maredudd ap Owain, 254–30

Margaret, dau. of Jenkyn ap Ieuan Llewellyn ap Gruffyd Lloyd, 251–37
Maud, dau. of Ienaf ap Adda, 251–35
Osbern Wyddel, of Cors y Gedol, 251–36
Owain ap Gruffydd, 254–30
Owain ap Maredudd, 254–31
Owain (Owen) ap Jenkin, 179–13
Owen Glyndwr, 249–35
Philip ap Ifor, 254–33
Ralph Maelog, 179–3
Rhys ap Gruffudd, 179–2
Rhys ap Thomas, 199A–35
Thomas ap Gwilim Vachan, 179–12
Thomas ap Llewellyn, 254–33
Tudor (or Twdr) ap Gruffydd Fychan, 251–35
Walron
William, 74A–37
Walsh
Anne, 209–38
John, 197–37
Margaret, 197–37
Walter
Edmund, 1A–40
Mary, 1A–40
Waltheof
son of Ailsi, 265–24
Walton
John, 249–32
Maud de, 249–32
Wandesford
Alice, 208–36
Idonea, w. of Thomas, 208–35
John, 208–34
Thomas, 208–35
Ward
Anne, 2–37, 204–38
Christopher, 2–36
Warenne
see also Arundel and Fitz Alan
Ada de, 89–25, 93–25, 96–25, 100–25, 170–23
Alice de, 28–32, 60–31, 83–30
Beatrice de, 94–29
Cicely de, 231–35
Edith de, 18A–23
Edward de, 231–31
Eleanor de, 153A–30, 161–27
Gundred de, 84–25, 88–25, 151–25
Isabel de, Cts. of, 83–26, 123–26
John de, 231–32
John de, E. of Surrey, 83–28, 153A–29, 231–30, 231–31
Lawrence de, 231–34

Maud de, 123–27, 139–27
Nicholas de, 231–33
William de, 18A–23, 50–24, 197–28
William de, E. of Surrey, 50–24, 60–30,
   69–28, 76–28, 83–24, 83–25, 83–27,
   83–29, 84–24, 89–24, 93–24, 108–
   26, 140–24, 141–24, 231–29
William de, of Wormgay, 94–29
Warham
   John, 253–40
Warin
   Fitz. *see* Fitz Warin
Warkworth
   Alice Fitz Robert de, 237–6, 246D–26,
      261–32, 262–29
Warre
   Catharine la, 99–32
   Joan la, 18–32
   John la, 47B–31, 255A–31
   John la, Bar., 18–31, 47B–31, 99–31,
      255A–32
   Roger la, Bar., 18–31, 47B–32, 99–31,
      255A–31, 263–30
Warrington
   Barons of. *see* Boteler
   Lords of. *see* Boteler
Warwick
   Earls of. *see* Beauchamp; Beaumont;
      Neville
Washburn
   Margaret, 69–40
Washington
   George, 223–38
Wassenberg
   Gerald I Flaminius de, Ct. of Geldern,
      163–25
Waterton
   Joan (Cecily) de, 202–35
   Robert de, 202–35
Watts
   Eleanor, 230B–41
   Elizabeth, w. of Richard, 230B–41
   Richard, 198–41, 230B–41
Wauton
   William de, 155A–30
Weare alias Browne
   Jane, 248–40
   John, 248–40
Welby
   Olive, 31B–41, 223–43
   Richard, 31B–40, 223–42
   Thomas, 31B–40, 223–41
Welles
   Anne, 7–32

Cecily de, 41–30
Eleanor de, 18–35
Eudo de, 202–34
John de, 7–32
John, L., 202–34
Lionel de, L., 18–35, 202–35
Margaret de, 202–36
Robert de, 41–30
Robert de, L., 64–32
Wellington
   Roger, 15–40
Welsh
   Anne, 69–38
   Edward, 69–38
Wentworth
   Henry, 200–36
   John, 200–35
   Margery, 200–37, 257–39
   Roger, 200–35, 223–39
Werner
   Count in Wrmsgau, 45–18
Wessex
   Æthelmaer Cild, E. in Devonshire, 1B–
      20
   Æthelred I, K. of, 1B–15
   Æthelwerd, E. in, 1B–19
   Æthelwulf, K. of, 1–13, 1B–14
   Alfthryth (Ethelswith) of, 44–16, 162–17
   Ceawlin, K. of, 1–3
   Cenred of, 1–7
   Ceolwald of, 1–6
   Cutha of, 1–5
   Cuthwine of, 1–4
   Eafa of, 1–10
   Eoppa of, 1–9
   Godwin, E. of, 1B–22, 166–23
   Gytha of, 1B–24, 242–7
   Ina, K. of, 1–7
   Ingild of, 1–8
   Osburga, Q. consort, 1–13, 1B–14
   Wulfnoth Cild, Thegn of Sussex, 1B–21
West
   Ann, w. of Gov. John West, 18–39
   Elizabeth, 18–39, 228–39
   Francis, 18–39
   George, 18–36
   John, 18–39
   Margaret, 59–37
   Nathaniel, 18–39
   Penelope, 1–38, 1–39, 18–39, 228–39
   Reynold de, 59–37
   Reynold, L. de la Warre, 18–33
   Reynold, L., L. La Warre, 51A–36
   Richard, L. de la Warre, 18–34

Richard, L., L. La Warre, 51A–36
Thomas, 1–37
Thomas, L., 18–32
Thomas, L. de la Warre, 18–35, 18–38,
  18–39, 228–38
William, L. de la Warre, 18–37
West Bulgars
Mary, dau. of Trajan, Khan of the, 105A–
  23
Trajan, Khan (Tzar) of the, 105A–23
West Franks. *see* France
West Saxons
Cerdic, K. of, 1–'1, 170–21
Cynric, K. of, 1–2
Westbury
John, 253–35
Westmorland
Earls of. *see* Neville
Weston
Jerome, 11–40
Margaret de, 155A–30
Mary, 11–40
Thomas de, 155A–30
Westphalia
Bernhard I, D. of, 252B–29
Wetterau
Udo I, Ct. in, 143–20
Wettin
Dietrich of, 252D–23
Konrad I, Ct. of, 252D–26
Weyland
Alice, 12–34
Cicely de, 70–34
Katherine, 216A–31
Richard de, 70–34
Robert, 216A–31
Whalesburgh
John, 246E–32
Margaret, 246E–32
Wheelwright
John, 246A–42
Rebecca, 246A–42
Whetehill
Adrian, 249–38
Margery, 249–40
Richard, 249–39
Whitbred
Alice, 246E–41
Whitchurch
Eleanor de, 29A–30
White
Alice, 246G–39
Christopher, 246G–39

WhiteJohn
Eleanor, 51A–36
Whitgift
Elizabeth, 246A–41
John, 246A–41
William, 246A–41
Whiting
John, 85–41
Joseph, 85–42, 245–42
Samuel, 85–41, 85–42, 245–41, 245–42
Whittingham
John, 31C–41
Richard, 31C–40
Whyte. *see* White
Wickrath
Otto I, Bar. of, 252E–27
Salome of, 252E–27
Widworthy
Alice de, 52–32
Hugh, 52–32
William de, 52–32
Wiham
Christina de, 12A–23
Willesford
William, 25–33
Williams
Freeborn, 11–42
Jane, 199–38
Richard, 84–40
Roger, 11–42, 220–43
William, 199–37
Williswint
Heiress of Ct. Adelhelm, 48–13
Willoughby
Eleanor, 230A–36, 230B–35
Elizabeth, 17–33
Hugh, 230A–35
Margery, 219–34, 78–36
William, L., 17–33, 219–34
Wilsford
Elizabeth, 11–38
Thomas, 11–38
Wilson
Jennet, 2–40
Wiltshire
Æthelhelm, E. of, 1B–16
Earls of. *see* Boleyn; Butler
Richard of, 54–29
Winchester
Earls of. *see* Quincy
Herbert of, 262–26
Windsor
Andrews, Bar., 12–36, 59–39, 201–39
Edith, 12–37

Eleanor, 201–39
Gerald of, 187–2
Miles, 12–35, 12A–34
Thomas, 12–35, 12A–35, 59–39
Wingfield
Dorothy, 15A–37
Elizabeth, 15–34
Henry, 15A–34
Robert, 15–33, 15A–33, 15A–35, 15A–36
Winnington
Elizabeth, 258–33
Robert, 258–33
Winslow
Josiah, 1–40
Winslowe. see Wynslow
Winthrop
Adam, 232–40, 232–41
Deane, 232–41
Elizabeth, w. of Samuel, 232–41
John, 232–40
Samuel, 232–41
Stephen, 232–41
Winzenburg
Herman I, Ct. of, 252B–28
Sofia of, 252B–28
Wittelsbach
see also Bavaria
Otto II, Ct. Palatine of, 45–27, 252C–26
Otto IV of, 45–27
Otto V of, 45–27
Wodhull
Agnes, 150–41
Anthony, 150–40
Fulk, 150–38
John, 150–37
Nicholas, 78–39, 150–39
Thomas, 150–36
Wolseley
Anne, 81C–43
Anthony, L., 81B–39
Devereux, 81C–42
Ellen, 81A–39
Erasmus, L., 81B–40
John, L., 81A–38, 81B–38
Mary, 81B–43, 81B–43
Ralph, 81A–38
Robert, 81B–41
Robert Warren St. John, 81C–47
Thomas, L., 81B–41, 81C–41
Walter, 81B–42
Winifred, 81B–43
Wood
Anne, 261–40

Thomas, 261–40
Woodbridge
John, 143–42
Woodliff
William, 11–39
Woodshaw
NN, 253–38
Woodville
see also Wydvill
Anthony, E. Rivers, Bar. Scales, 234B–34
Catherine, 225–39
John, 18B–33
Margaret, 234B–35
Woodward
Frances, 201–42
Hezekiah, 201–42
Worcester
Earls of. see Beauchamp; Tiptoft
Workington
see also Culwen
Ada of, 34–26
Eldred the Thane, L. of, 34–23, 34–24
Gospatric, L. of, 34–24
Grace, w. of Thomas, 34–25, 37–25
Thomas of, 34–25, 37–25
Wormsgau
see also Lorraine
Conrad the Wise, Ct. in, 45–18, 192–20
Henry, Ct. in, 45–20
Otto of, D. of Carinthia, 45–19
Rutpert I, Ct. in Wormsgau, 48–13
Rutbert II, Ct. in Wormsgau, 48–15
Rutbert III, Ct. in Wormsgau, 48–16
Rutpert IV, Ct. of (Robert the Strong of France). see France
Werner, Ct. in, 45–18, 192–19
Worsley
Isabel, 248–36
Margaret, 249–38
Otewell, 248–36, 249–37
Wotton
Alice, 52–39
John, 52–38
John de, 52–35
Richard, 52–36
William, 52–37
Wroth
John, 230A–38
Margaret, 230A–38
Wrottesley
Eleanor, 197–38
John de, 11–34, 248–34
Richard, 198–37

Wyatt
John, 52–44
Margaret, 52–45, 52–45
Philip, 52–44
Wydvill
see also Woodville
Anthony, E. Rivers, Bar. Scales, 234B–34
Richard, 234B–33
Richard, E. Rivers, 18B–33, 225–39, 234B–33
Wydworthy
Alice de, 52–33
William de, 52–33
Wyfolf
Nicholas, 16–34
Wyger
Christian, w. of Thomas, 52–37
Gundred, 52–37
Thomas, 52–37
Wylde
Elizabeth, 78–38
Thomas, 78–38
Wyllys
Amy, 57–43
George, 57–42, 69A–42
Richard, 57–42
Samuel, 69A–42
Wymondham
Adam de, 12A–31
Alice de, 12A–31
Wyndesore
see also Wyndsore; Windsor
Bryan, 12A–32
Hawisia, w, of William III, 12A–24
James, 12A–30
Miles, 12A–31
Richard de, 12A–28, 12A–29
William Fitz Walter de, 12A–22
William II de, 12A–23
William III de, 12A–24
William IV de, 12A–25
William V de, 12A–26
William VI de, 12A–27
Wyndsore
Miles, 12A–33
Richard, 12A–33
Wynn
John, 251–39
Wynnington
Agnes, 231–33
Richard de, 231–33
Wynslow
Agnes, 43–34, 43A–34

Thomas, 43–34
Wysham
Alice, 197–34
John de, 197–33

Y
Yale
Ann, 251–41
David, 251–39, 251–40, 251–41
Elihu, 251–41
George, 251–41
Thomas, 251–41, 251–41
Yeardley
George, 18–39
Yelverton
Margaret, 15–36, 232–35
William, 15–36, 232–35
Yeo
Elizabeth, 258–34
John, 258–34
Yonge
Bridget, 57–42
John, 57–41
William, 57–41
York
Edmund of Langley, D. of, 225–34
Richard, D. of, 18B–36
Richard (Plantagenet), D. of, 225–35
Yorke
Dorothy, 143–41
Edmund, 143–41

Z
Zähringen
Clementia of, 274C–26
Konrad I, D. of, 274C–26
Zollern. see Nuremberg
Zouche
Alan la, 39–27, 136B–28
Alan la, Bar., 31–29, 32–29, 38–28, 39–29, 39A–29, 53–29, 88–33, 186–3
Alianore la, 214–34, 215–33
Alice la, 56–29
Dorothy la, 214–39
Eleanor la, 39A–30, 93–30
Elena la, 31–30, 213–30
Elizabeth, 81C–42
Elizabeth la, 234A–32, 253–30
Eon, 26–30
Eudo la, 39–29, 39A–29, 66–30, 200–30, 212–30, 212–32, 234A–32, 253–29
Eva la, 39–30, 59–31

Eve la, 26–30
John, 81C–42
John la, L., 212–38, 214–36, 214–37
Joyce la, of Mortimer, 98–32, 216–31
Juliana la, 56A–33
Loretta (Lora) la, 60–29
Margaret, w. of Roger la, 39–28, 56–29
Margery la, 186–3
Maud la, 32–30, 47–30, 47A–30, 47B–
   30, 88–33, 261–35
Milicent la, 200–32
Richard la, L., 214–38
Roger la, 39–28, 56–29, 60–29, 98–31
Roger la, Bar., 31–28, 38–28, 53–30
William la, 8–30, 26–30
William la, L., 200–31, 212–31, 212–33,
   212–34, 212–35, 212–36, 212–37,
   213–34, 214–34, 215–33
William la, of Mortimer, L., 86–30, 98–
   31, 216–31